Chinese Thought

Marcel Granet

Chinese Thought

Marcel Granet

CHINESE THOUGHT
© and translation 2022 by Daniel Bernardo

ANTIQUA SAPIENTIA

Translated from:
La Pensée Chinoise

All rights reserved under International
and Pan-American Copyright Conventions

ISBN: 978-1-989586-78-5

Table of Contents

Introduction.   1

Book I
THE EXPRESSION OF THOUGHT..   17

Chapter I
LANGUAGE AND WRITING..   19
   I. Vowel Symbols   19
   II. The Graphic Symbols.   25

Chapter II
STYLE   33
   I. Sentences   34
   II Rhythms..   43

Book II
THE GUIDING IDEAS   49

Chapter I
TIME AND SPACE.   51

Chapter II
YIN AND YANG 69

Chapter III
NUMBERS 89
    I. Numbers, Cyclical Signs, Elements 90
    II. Numbers, Places, Divinatory Symbols 103
    III. Numbers and Musical Relations 127
    IV. Numbers and Architectural Proportions 152
    V. Classificatory and Protocolar Functions of Numbers ... 168

Chapter IV
THE TAO 183

Book III
THE SYSTEM OF THE WORLD 207

Chapter I
THE MACROCOSM 209

Chapter II
THE MICROCOSM 221

Chapter III
ETIQUETTE 239

Book IV
SECTS AND SCHOOLS 257

Chapter I
THE PRESCRIPTIONS OF GOVERNMENT 261
    I. The Art Of Success 262
    II. The Art of Persuasion 265
    III. The Art of Qualifying 274
    IV. The Art of Legislating 282

Chapter II
THE PRESCRIPTIONS OF THE PUBLIC GOOD 291
    I. Confucius and the Humanistic Spirit 292
    II. Mö Tseu and Social Duty 302

Chapter III
The Prescriptions of Sanctity 311
    I. The Art of Long Life 315
    II. The Mystique of Autonomy 322

Chapter IV
Confucian Orthodoxy 343
    I. Mencius: Government by Charity 344
    II. Siun tseu: Government by Ritual 349
    III. Tong Chong-Chou: Rule by History 356

Conclusion 363

Bibliography 369
    Periodicals 369
    Books and Miscellaneous Works 370

Concordance Tables 375

Introduction

In analyzing the system of attitudes and behavior which governs the public and private life of the Chinese, I have already attempted to give an idea of their civilization. I shall now attempt, in order to clarify the outline, to describe the system of prejudices, conceptions and symbols which govern the life of thought in China. In this way this book serves as a complement to *La Civilisation chinoise*.[1]

When I published the latter work, I indicated that at the time I did not see the possibility of writing a Handbook of Chinese Antiquity. This opinion dictated the plan of my first volume. A similar sentiment inspired the second; I would not have accepted the task of writing a Handbook of Chinese Literature or Philosophy.

Many works have been published which can claim that title. I refer immediately to these excellent books[2] for those who wish to inquire into the classification of works or the affiliation of Chinese doctrines. Even if the inventory of docu-

---

1 *La Civilisation chinoise*, published in 1929, is one of the most famous sinological works of the 20th century. The second volume, like the first, covers only the ancient period ending with the Han dynasty. The reign of orthodoxy and scholasticism begins with the Empire; the main features of the Chinese mentality are already fixed. I shall retain for this second volume the bibliography of the first. Some recent or special works have been added.

2 Giles, *History of Chinese literature*; Grube, *Geschichte der chinesischen Literatur*; Mayers, *Chinese reader's manual*; (Leang K'i-tch'ao) Liang Chi-chao, *History of Chinese political thought*, trans. by L. T. Chen; Fr. Wieger, *Histoire des croyances religieuses et des opinions philosophiques en Chine, depuis l'origine jusqu'à nos jours*; Tucci, *Storia della filosofia cinese antica*; Forke, *Geschichte der alten chinesischen Philosophie*; Suzuki, *A brief history of early chinese philosophy*; Hackmann, *Chinesische Philosophie*; Hu Shih, *The development of logical method in ancient China*; Maspero, *La Chine antique* (Book V, pp. 543-621).

ments had not shown me that attempting to reconstruct in detail the history of "philosophical theories" was a premature undertaking to say the least, I would have proposed to give a glimpse of the essential rules to which Chinese thought as a whole obeys. It should be noted that in order to discover what constitutes, so to speak, the institutional basis of Chinese thought, we have fairly good information at our disposal, but which could hardly authorize the composition of a History of Philosophy comparable to those that could have been written for countries other than China.

* * *

Ancient China, more than a Philosophy, possessed a Wisdom. This was embodied in works of very diverse character, which were rarely expressed in the form of dogmatic statements.

Only a small number of works attributed to antiquity have come down to us. Their history is obscure, their text uncertain, their language little known, and their interpretation is vitiated by late and tendentious scholastic glosses.

Moreover, we know almost nothing positive about ancient Chinese history.

Whether it is Confucius, Mö tseu, Tchouang tseu, etc., we hardly get a glimpse of the personalities of the most illustrious thinkers. Most of the time, we have little or no useful or concrete information about their lives. In general, we only know dates, sometimes disputed; moreover, they refer to epochs for which history is particularly devoid of facts. Some "authors," such as Tchouang tseu or Lie tseu, do not even have a legend.

About the teachings, we rarely have direct testimonies. The orthodox tradition attributes to Confucius the writing of a large number of works, almost all classics. Insofar as they escape apologetic or scholastic concerns, critics admit that the most that remains of the Master is a collection of talks (the *Louen yu*). It is not certain that this collection, in its original form, was the work of the early disciples; in any case, we do not possess this compilation, which is undoubtedly late; all that has come down to us is a re-worked edition, dating from some five hundred years after the Sage's death.[3] The Sage's writings, however, have not been published.

All interpreters agree in recognizing certain interpolated chapters in the more authentic and better edited works. The agreement ceases at the moment when it comes to resolving them. Tchouang tseu[4] is a vigorous thinker and the most original of Chinese writers; one critic will recognize Tchouang tseu's manner and style in the chapter on the swordsmen, but not in the chapter on the bandit Che, while another scholar will eliminate *the swordsmen* in order to preserve *the bandit*. The *Han Fei tseu* is the work of one of the authors whose life is best known; it was written shortly before the formation of the Empire, and its early transmission has been fluid. However, one of the best contemporary critics, of the 55 sections of the work, wants to retain only 7. This, moreover, does not prevent him, in analyzing the doctrine, from referring to the condemned sections.

---

3   Sseu-ma Ts'ien, *Mémoires historiques* (*SMT*), V, pp. 441 ff.
4   For simplicity, I write (for example) Tchouang tseu when I speak of the author (real or supposed) of the work I designate, for convenience, writing: the *Tchouang tseu*.

After endeavoring to assign a date to the works and establish their original appearance, we often comes to such vague and disappointing conclusions as these: "*On the whole*, the work *appears* to date from the second half of the third century (BC), but it is not entirely from the hand of Han Fei; as in the case of Tchouang tseu, Mö tseu and most of the philosophers of *this period, an important part* is due *to the disciples* of the Master... It is only on *quite* rare occasions that it is possible to distinguish between those parts which can be traced back to the Master and those which must be attributed to his school."

Since at least the fourth century BC, the role played by the schools (*Kia*) or rather the importance given to polemics between schools has been considerable. The fiercest of these polemics were those which confronted the disciples of the same patron; such was the case, according to the Tchouang tseu,[5] of the disciples of Mö tseu; such seems to have been also the case of the disciples of Confucius.[6] But (and this is a significant fact) up to the Han period, when thinking of doctrines, all the followers of Mö tseu (*mö*) and the followers of Confucius (*jou*) are always confused under a common designation (*jou-mö*); this expression is very rarely duplicated. The polemics between schools reflect conflicts of prestige. They are not evidence of a strictly doctrinal opposition.

Moreover, if the custom is to translate the word *Kia* by School, it is important to note that the Chinese give it a very wide acceptance. They use it in connection with the various Arts (the bodies of prescriptions possessed by masters in mathematics, astronomy, divination, medicine, etc.),[7] as well as with the various Methods of conduct (the prescriptions for living sponsored by this or that master of Wisdom). These methods, whose aim is to regulate behavior, are taught with the help of attitudes. Each of them certainly presupposes a certain conception of life and of the world, but none of them has as its main objective to translate itself into a dogmatic system.

The idea of the separation of schools, as if their main purpose were to provide theoretical instruction, is relatively late. It was born of practical concerns, if not of mnemonic inspiration. The division of works and authors into schools, which is at the origin of all the proposed classifications, is taken from the *Treatise on Literature* found in the *History of the Early Han*. However, this treatise is a librarian's work, and the classification it has succeeded in imposing is a mere catalog classification. After classifying the preserved works, it was accepted that each lot corresponded to the teaching of a related School or Schools whose dogmatic originality was then considered.

---

5   P. Wieger, *Les Pères du système taoïste*, p. 501.
6   *Li ki*, C., I, pp. 133, 153, 164, 175, 212, 216.
7   The following diagram (see next page) will serve to illustrate this fact: I borrow it (simplifying it slightly) from one of the most ingenious essays (Hsu Ti-shan, Dec. 1927, p. 259, from *Yenching Journal*, in Chinese) that has recently been made in China to show the relations between schools or doctrines (philosophical or technical). The author wishes above all to show the origins of Taoist doctrine; he does not pretend to be complete and neglects, for example, the School of Laws and the School of Denominations.

Even if we could assume that the *Schools* or Authors with whom we are concerned are mainly interested in their theoretical conceptions, the project of setting forth the details and relations of the theories would have to be considered extraordinarily adventurous, for the study of the "philosophical vocabulary" presents singular difficulties in China.

Later I will show that the Chinese language does not seem to be organized to express concepts. Instead of abstract signs that can help to specify ideas, it favors symbols rich in practical suggestions, which, instead of a definite meaning, have an indeterminate efficacy; this tends to procure – instead of an acquiescence to simple judgments intended to allow precise identifications, after analysis – a global adherence to thought, a sort of total conversion of behavior. It is therefore necessary to break with the tendency, which still prevails, to express these symbols, full of value judgments in which an original civilization expresses itself, with terms borrowed (after a rapid assimilation that does not take into account the divergence of mentalities) from the vocabulary – also conventional, but expressly aiming at an impersonal and objective precision – of Western philosophers. Otherwise, we would expose ourselves to the worst anachronisms, as happens, for example, when we translate the term *jen* (characteristic of the Confucian position) as "altruism"[8] or the expression *kien ngai*[9] (significant of Mö tseu's attitude) as "universal love." Another serious consequence would be to betray, so to speak, in its own spirit (this it is the case, for example, when we attribute to the Chinese a distinction between "substance" and "force"), a philosophical mentality that departs from definite conceptions, because it is commanded by an ideal of efficiency.

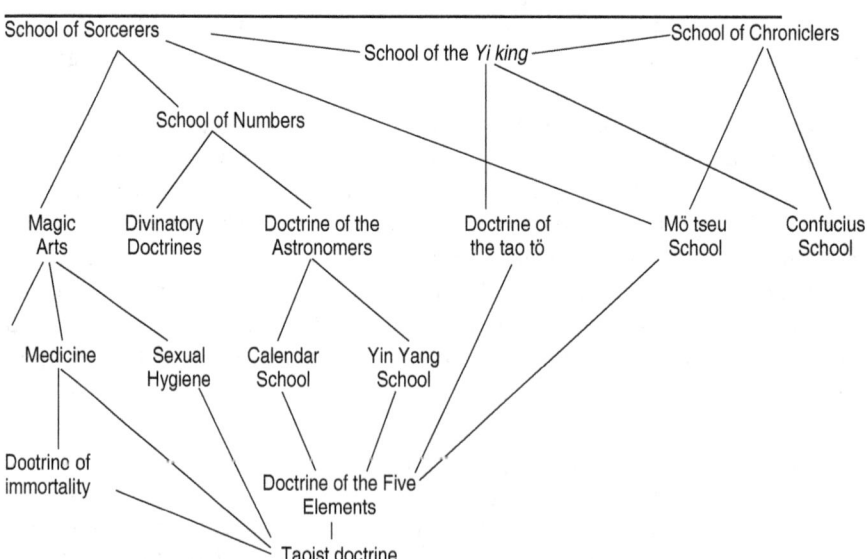

[8] P. Wieger, *Histoire des croyances religieuses et des opinions philosophiques en Chine, depuis l'origine jusqu'à nos jours*, pp. 133, 134 and, following him, Maspero, *La Chine antique*, p. 464.

[9] Maspero *op. cit.* p. 473.

INTRODUCTION   5

On the other hand, even if we could suppose that the Chinese Sages constructed a vocabulary intended to allow the conceptual expression of the "theories," any attempt to reconstruct a history of the Doctrines would encounter (for the moment) another difficulty. We depend, for the reading of the ancient texts, on the commentaries with which all the works were endowed. The oldest commentaries date from the Christian era. They do not predate the movement of thought which, at the time of the Han, definitively oriented China towards the paths of orthodoxy. They give the "*correct* interpretation," that is, the one that was required of candidates in the examinations that gave access to honors and official careers. No reader (Chinese even less so) reads a text freely. He is influenced by the glosses, even if he knows that they are inspired by a system of interpretation impregnated with academic, moral and political concerns. In fact, no one has access to the text, written in an archaic language, except through the commentaries. The work of going beyond the commentary must be done without (for the moment) any help from a manual of stylistics or at least of Chinese philology. This task, moreover, is dominated by the gravest uncertainty; the orthodox spirit, which inspires all the details of the glosses, oscillates between two passions: a passion for polemics, which inclines one to attribute an irreducible value to opposing interpretations, and a passion for conciliation, which always prevents a rigorous definition. It is not easy, in the detail of the cases, to distinguish in the orthodox formulas the original aspect of the ideas. It would take a constant delight in divination to restore to the "theories" their purity and thus to be able to define their relations ideologically. What possibility is there of reconstructing, moreover, the history of their real relations?

At present, there is no agreement among scholars on the general lines of ancient Chinese history.

Before the awareness of the dogmatic character of Chinese traditions, and especially those relating to literary history, it was possible to venture to tell the story of the "Doctrines." It was accepted that the preserved works, though few in number, were nevertheless the most important; they were not thought to have become classics because they were the only ones preserved. As tradition spread them over several good centuries (from Yu the Great to Confucius, passing through the Duke of Tcheou), there was no difficulty in tracing the evolution of Chinese conceptions, or rather in speaking of the greatness and decadence of the Doctrines, while believing that a historical work was being done.

Can we maintain the same illusion today, when critics attribute to a brief period (5th-3rd centuries BC) almost all the works they still consider ancient? To justify a negative answer, it is enough to point out that, of all the periods of Chinese history (so little known as a whole), this is one of the least known and for which the least historical information is available. Moreover, all the facts are doubtful, and the whole is reduced to an abstract chronology, often uncertain.

However, those who see in the period between the 5th-3rd centuries BC the epoch of "historical novels" and literary supercheries continue to imagine that the first or only positive work is to establish a chronological classification of the "Theories." This follows from the classification they accept for the works. They do not resist the temptation to determine the date of appearance of a given conception; they do not consent to ignore those who "invented" it. They know, for example, that the invention of the "philosophical theory" of Yin and Yang (developed, they say, during the fifth century BC and "generally adopted by all philosophers" at the end of that century) is due to a "School of Metaphysicians," whose "work is contained in a pamphlet (the *Hi ts'eu*)."[10] It need only be said that the *Hi ts'eu* is the philosophical fragment they consider the oldest of those naming Yin and Yang. No doubt philosophy is prone to confuse the history of facts with the history of documents, but should not a historian who sets out to date something other than references constantly remember that proof by absence is forbidden to him? He can only ascertain the absence of testimony. If it were a matter of writing the philosophical history of a known epoch by sincere and verifiable testimonies, and if, moreover, these documents formed a *supposedly intact* whole, no one would believe that the supposedly complete revision of the *recorded facts* alone would authorize him to attribute a kind of absolute beginning to this or that conception. Are we to take advantage of the proclaimed mediocrity of the attestations to speak of invention and first origin, as soon as we believe we have dated the attestation which, in an almost total vacuum of attestations, appears to be the oldest?

If, in this case, literary criticism is so presumptuous, it is because it starts from postulates that it forgets to make explicit. It is all too easy to admit that a conception (say, for example, that of Yin and Yang) common to all thinkers of the late fifth century (hardly any earlier ones are known) was developed in the course of the fifth century because it is postulated that before Confucius and the beginning of the fifth century BC Chinese philosophy had not "come out of infancy."[11] This judgment on the facts is no more than the transposition of an opinion on the documents; no "metaphysical" work is believed to have been written before the time of Confucius. Let us grant, if so required, that *no one*, indeed, wrote any before that date… Shall we go so far as to assert that there was no oral teaching before that date either? The Works of the period from the 5th to the 3rd centuries BC were (no one denies this for most of them) transmitted orally at first. Before the small number of writings that have not been lost were produced, did oral teaching not "invent" any ideas or "theories"? If one writes a history in which one is at pains to attribute to the author of a given preserved document the invention of a given Doctrine, one is (implicitly) giving a negative answer to this question; and, if one answers in the negative, one is obeying, with a semblance of critical freedom, an orthodox conception of Chinese history. One starts (with the traditionalists) from the assumption that the fifth to the third centuries BC were a time of anarchy; one then postulates (by virtue of a prefabricated idea) that this anarchy "favored the flowering" of philosophical reflection; one finally induces that before the agitated period of the Warring Kingdoms the Chinese had not "philosophized," because they possessed a stable political regime and lived in passive obedience to perfect conformism. This

---

10   *Ibid.*, p. 480.
11   *Ibid.*, p. 468.

is simply admitting that the traditions of official history are correct and that China once had a homogeneous state with a firmly established civilization.

I, for one, do not accept this theoretical view of Chinese history. However, I will not oppose any other view. For the moment, it will suffice to note that, even ignoring any hypothesis about its origins, the analysis of the opinions formulated by thinkers known to us through the written word runs the risk of being singularly inaccurate and, above all, misguided, if it is not supplemented by an inventory of ideas belonging to an anonymous tradition.

The above remarks indicate the reasons why I have refrained from giving this essay on Chinese thought the form of a continuous history of doctrines. I have decidedly rejected any chronological order and have not attempted to give information on everything, that is, on any details of the traditional debates. I see, for example, no way of determining whether Confucius considered the "nature" of man to be good or bad, and I would not find, by entering into the debate, any of the advantages which such and such patrons of wisdom, missionaries imported into China or native politicians, think they gain thereby; to play the role of arbiter in a melee of adventurous opinions is to gain, at best, a reputation for finesse or even erudition. I will simply propose to analyze a certain number of Chinese conceptions and attitudes as objectively as possible. Moreover, in order to examine them closely, I have only considered the most significant ones.

* * *

The Book IV of this work is entitled *Sects and Schools*. The first three Books aim to make known Chinese conceptions that it was neither possible, nor advantageous for that matter, to present otherwise than as *common notions*, that denote certain habits of mind to which the Chinese seem to attribute imperative power. I have reserved for the last Book the conceptions that I felt it was possible, I will not say to refer to an Author or a "School," but to study *comfortably* in relation to certain Works that testify to certain trends in Chinese thought; these conceptions point to less constant or less profound tendencies and are remarkable, precisely, for their varying fortune; their chief interest is that they may contribute to give an idea of the orientation which Chinese thought as a whole has acquired.

Under the heading *Sects and Schools*, I shall give the few data which do not seem too uncertain about the men and the works. On the other hand, I will not extract from the works, to lend them to the authors, any kind of dogmatic statement.

All the masters of ancient China added to the "vast knowledge" the science of "some specialty."[12] All of them could talk about everything, and very few were concerned to give a systematic turn to their teaching as a whole. Each of them was concerned to emphasize the efficacy of the recipe of wisdom that constituted the secret of their "School."

I will not attempt to define the teachings by enumerating the ideas embraced by each of the Schools. Such inventories would not even allow me to conclude anything about the connections of the various "doctrines." All the works abound

---

12   *SMT*, V, p. 414.

in purely parasitic developments; the writers found it profitable to flaunt their information or convenient to argue *ad hominem*. No one takes as much pleasure as a Chinese in juxtaposing themes borrowed (without conviction) from the most divergent conceptions, or in employing, by sheer stratagem and without accepting their legitimacy in their own right, reasonings that will appeal to others. Therefore, I will beware of asserting, for example, that a writer of the School of the Legists who sometimes argues as a "Taoist" is somehow an adept of Taoism. The ornamental or dialectical use of ideas borrowed from a competing teaching is, in itself, a significant fact; it deserves to be noted, not because it can be taken immediately as an indication of a doctrinal connection, but because it reveals a feature of the Chinese mentality. It is a testimony both to the strength of the sectarian spirit and to the attractiveness of syncretism. This general indication must be retained once and for all. On the other hand, if we want to get at the essence of a Chinese "doctrine," it would be unwise to focus on ideas which its followers seem to have accepted and yet have not attempted to adjust to their conceptions.

In order not to run the risk of betraying the facts too much, we must never forget that a Chinese "doctrine" must be defined, not by trying to determine the articulations of a dogmatic system, but by trying to identify a sort of master formula or central recipe. Confucius is reported to have said, "No doubt you think that I am a man who has learned many things and remembers them. Not so, one *single* (one principle is enough for me) *to embrace* (everything)."[13] These words allow us to perceive a new characteristic of the Chinese mind: no recipe is worthwhile if it does not seem to possess both a singular essence and a virtue that works as a panacea. It must present itself as something specific, which at the same time claims to be omnivalent. Every Master of Wisdom claims, then, to dispense a Knowledge of a very particular quality (it is the Knowledge of this or that Sage) and of an indefinite efficacy (it implies a total understanding of life). To make known the conceptions or, rather, the attitudes proper to a School or, rather, to a Sect, is equivalent to trying to discover the secret or the master word that was once revealed to the adepts by means of the procedures proper to esoteric teachings.

These secrets, of course – master words or concepts – were acquired by the disciples, not in a discursive way, but by way of initiation, after a long training. Thus, we cannot presume to reach the essence of a teaching as long as we don't know the system of practices that (much more than a doctrinal body) made it possible to apprehend or, to put it better, to realize that essence. Some famous books, such as the *Tao Tö King* or the *Yi king*, are composed of a series of adages; taken in their literal sense, they seem empty, extravagant or insipid; it is a fact, however, that for many centuries and even today, these books have inspired meditation exercises or even a *discipline* of life. They may, not without reason, seem hermetic. Other books do

---

13   *Louen yu*, L., p. 159, (Legge translates: *I seek an all-pervading unity*). SMT, V, p. 367. (Chavannes translates: I have only the one principle that makes everything comprehensible). The characters used suggest that Confucius (?) wanted to express his thought by means of a metaphor; a single (rod or rope) is sufficient to thread (to unite, bind, hold a whole set of objects).

not seem so, just because they seem to lend themselves to a discursive analysis of ideas, we tend to assume that we understand them. The doctrine they may advocate remains impenetrable until we can determine the attitudes it commands and which actually express it.

To restore the meaning of the various bodies of practice and divine the magisterial formula of the "doctrines," we must first try to recognize the kind of efficacy that the old masters attributed to their prescriptions. It has long been observed that all Chinese wisdom has political purposes. Let us specify by saying that the Sects or Schools have all set out to realize an *ordering* of human life and activities taken in their *totality*, that is to say, in the totality of their extensions, not only social, but cosmic. Each Master professes a Wisdom that goes beyond the moral order and even the political order; it corresponds to a certain attitude towards civilization or, if you will, to a certain *recipe of civilizing action*. It follows that it is not impossible to find the precise meaning of a given attitude or a specific prescription if we first try to clarify the position occupied by the various sectarian groupings in the history of Chinese society, in the development of Chinese civilization.

The first consequence is that critical work must be dominated, not by philological research, not even by pure history (which, given the state of documents and studies, is, after all, very fortunate), but by the study of social facts. No one knows better than I do how novel the research on Chinese society is, and how little the results can be taken for granted. However, one hint can be drawn sufficiently sure to serve as a guide; the period when the Sects whose "doctrine" we may try to understand appeared was the period when the feudal order was collapsing and imperial unity was being prepared. This simple observation, as we shall see later, provides a starting point from which we can advance, for example, towards a precise interpretation of the attitude of Mö tseu or that of the Taoist masters.

A second consequence is that we will have to establish the position of the various sectarian groupings in the late feudal world, rather than determine (assuming it were possible) the chronological order of the "doctrines." I will therefore describe the most significant attitudes expressed in the conceptions of the Chinese "Schools," without thinking of presenting them in a historical order. I will group them in such a way as to show that these attitudes correspond to a certain number of technical concerns. They betray various types of *corporate mentalities*. They indicate the importance of the impulses that Chinese thought can receive when society is preparing for a new conformism; these favorable circumstances then make it possible to welcome the influence of specialists whose esprit de corps is momentarily animated by an increase in consciousness or creative imagination.

Two "doctrines" – because of their continuity and popularity through time – deserve special attention: that which is called Taoist and that which claims the patronage of Confucius. I will study the "Taoist school" more closely than any other, and devote an entire chapter to Confucian orthodoxy.

Both "doctrines" stand out for the strength of their sectarian spirit and, at the same time, for the strength of their syncretic appetites. Both, in fact, have the ambition to constitute an orthodoxy. In both cases, this orthodoxy is characterized by a claim to Wisdom that is both universal and exclusive, without any dogma being professed or the articles of teaching being in the least ordered in a system. They form a sort of encroaching confederacy whose mass is constantly swelled by a bias of annexation or conciliation. Such gatherings of ideas lack (like the Chinese Empire) organization and articulation, but (like the Empire they are founded on a unity of civilization) Taoism and Orthodoxy derive their power from a particular animating force. If their opposition seems to be that of two biases (one in favor of a kind of naturism with a magical-mystical background, the other in favor of a kind of socio-centrism of positive intentions), both Taoism and Confucian orthodoxy are inspired (in an unequal but equally profound way) by a double tendency, at once "universalist"[14] and humanist. It is this dual and common tendency that explains their double fate and their opposition in history, as well as their reconciliation in minds.

* * *

The views professed by these various sects or schools indicate certain secondary orientations of Chinese thought. To glimpse, as well as by contrast, their deeper orientation, it is necessary to consider the data furnished by the myths and folklore as carefully as the evidence taken from the "philosophical works." The first three Books of this work deal with common notions which it was not advantageous to consider at first under the aspect given to them by one or another technical work of reflection or corporate mentality. If I began with them, it is because it seemed to me that they made it possible to get at a kind of institutional background – very resistant – of the Chinese mentality.

This resistance certainly invites the assumption that this background is very old. I do not intend, however, by the place I assign them, to give the impression that these "common notions" represent a kind of Wisdom pre-existing the activity of any School or Sect. If the activity of sects and schools is only partly known from a relatively late period (5th century BC), the documents that inform about the institutional background of thought are, for their part and by nature, timeless. I do not mean to suggest, by this qualification, that this background has remained unchanged, nor that nothing can be known of its evolution; I will tell in a moment how I thought I could give an idea of the progress of Chinese ideas. For the moment, I would like to point out that it is not a view of history, but reasons of convenience and, moreover, the state and nature of the documents, which have led me not to begin by speaking of the Schools and Sects. I think it would be difficult to understand the attitudes of the various Schools if we don't first become acquainted with a set of mental attitudes which – more directly and better than the conceptions of the Schools – shed light on the fundamental rules of thought adopted by the Chinese. But the reader is warned: I am not presenting the conceptions with which I am concerned in the first place as a system of notions which would be, globally and in all its aspects, prior to the theoretical work of the first known Schools.

---

14   J.-J.-M. de Groot, *Universismus*.

First of all, I have given some information on language and style. It would not be useless, to begin with, to insist on the characteristics of the *expression* (oral or written) of thought in China (Book I). Any attempt at criticism or interpretation of works and ideas must take this into account. In particular, all that is said about the differences between the spoken and written language leads us to suppose that the literary language has been a kind of dead or learned language since ancient times. However, Chinese, as it is written, seeks above all the effects of action that seem to be reserved for the living word. This fact makes it possible to appreciate the long-standing importance of oral teaching. It even seems to indicate that at the time when the works in which many generations have sought models of style were conceived, writing was hardly used outside of official events. On the pretext that the invention of writing dates back to at least the second millennium BC, we are tempted to attribute ancient origins to Chinese literature, while the relatively early date attributed to the preserved writings often leads us to declare the awakening of philosophical or scholarly thought to be late. This set of contradictory postulates leads to anarchic attempts to date "theories" that distort a positive history of ideas. These postulates and errors will be discarded in favor of a better oriented research, as soon as we have ascertained that the language of Chinese "philosophers," far from being bookish, comes from a tradition of oral and pragmatic teaching.

The observations I present on language and style have not been inspired by purely linguistic or literary criticism concerns, nor by the intention of offering, as a preliminary, a detailed description of language or an outline of the history of styles. If I have grouped these initial chapters under the heading of *The Expression of Thought*, it is because I have considered *symbolic* language as the most convenient starting point for pointing out certain dispositions of the Chinese mentality. Examination of the elements of language and style leads to two essential observations. On the one hand, the Chinese seem to avoid all artifices which tend to use the verbal expression of ideas in such a way as to economize mental operations; they disdain analytical forms; they use no sign to which they lend the simple value of a sign; they intend that all the elements of language, words and spellings, rhythms and phrases, should display the efficacy proper to *symbols*. They want written or spoken expression to *represent* thought and this concrete representation to impose the feeling that to express or rather to represent is not simply to evoke, but to arouse or to realize. If the Chinese, on the contrary, demand such perfect efficacy from language, it is because they do not separate it from a vast system of attitudes destined to enable men to represent in its various aspects the civilizing action they intend to exercise on all human filiations, including the Universe.

The same idea of the universe is found in all Chinese authors. The scholastic overload may weigh it down to a greater or lesser extent, but it comes directly from mythical conceptions. Sages do not borrow from scholars; this is probably the reason why we know almost nothing about the development of scientific thought in China. On the basis of this lack of information, it has been argued that it was only after the conquests of Darius, or even those of Alexander, that "foreigners" revealed to the Chinese "the properties of the circle and the square";[15] it would also be foreigners who would have introduced to them the compass, the set square and the gnomon[16]... I would find it hard to believe that the progress of indigenous techniques (let us recall Biot's admiration for Chinese chariots and arches) was not accompanied, *in certain circles*, by an effort of properly scientific reflection.[17] But the fact is that no definite trace of this remains. And it is also a fact that, when arguing on any subject, Chinese thinkers think only of crediting their opinions with the help of venerable stories, legends and mythical themes. The history of thought is remarkable in China for the independence that philosophical knowledge claims to maintain with respect to what we call science. To record this fact is more important for our subject than to draw up an inventory of knowledge in which an attempt is made (without much hope of achieving any accuracy) to mark the progress of the scientific spirit: whatever this progress may have been, it has exerted no notable influence on Chinese thought in the past.

I have not, therefore, dealt with *The System of the World* (Book III) conceived by the Chinese in order to make known the results they had obtained in various sciences and to determine to what classification of the sciences these results had led them. I have only tried to discover what spirit animated certain techniques which were cultivated neither by pure knowledge nor even by acquiring it; I have pointed out the system of all the practical ends which these arts tended to attain, and I have tried to determine the principles of this system. As it was not my intention to enumerate positive knowledge whose order of acquisition it would have been important to fix, and as I had only to give examples, taking care (as far as possible) to distinguish between mythical or scholastic formulas from a homogeneous fund of *knowledge*, to go deeper (when I have been able to), I have borrowed my examples preferably from mythical thought, but I have by no means neglected the pedantic or comparatively late formulations proclaiming the *enduring* authority of this ancient knowledge, which entirely inspires the scholasticism to which the thought effort of the *Sects and Schools* (Book IV) finally led. I have therefore reserved for Book III the examination of the *System of the World* imagined by the Chinese. Moreover, the main idea of the system cannot be conveniently identified until the analysis of the *Guiding Ideas of Chinese Thought* (Book II) reveals its foundation. The Chinese representation of the universe is based on a theory of the microcosm. This theory is linked to the earliest attempts at classification in Chinese thought. It arises from the tenacious belief that man and nature do not form two separate realms, but a single society. This is the principle on which the various techniques regulating human attitudes are based. It is through the active participation of human beings and the effect of a kind of *civilizing discipline* that universal order is achieved. Instead of a Science whose object is the knowledge of the World,

---

15 Maspero *op. cit.* p. 620.
16 *Ibid.*, pp. 616-620.
17 On this point, one may consult the remarks of A. Rey, *La Science orientale*, pp. 351, 352. But I must say that, as to the possibilities of knowing the scientific ideas of the ancient Chinese, I do not have Rey's optimism.

the Chinese have conceived a *Protocol* of life which they suppose to be effective in establishing a total Order.

The category of Order or Totality is the supreme category of Chinese thought; its symbol is the Tao, an essentially concrete symbol. I began the study of the concrete categories of the mind as soon as I demonstrated, by examining the elements of language, that the Chinese lent to their symbols a figurative power which they did not distinguish from a realizing efficacy. Some symbols, remarkable for being the most synthetic of all, seem to be endowed with a power of animation and organization that can only be described as total. The sovereign function attributed to them highlights the fact that Chinese thought has refused to distinguish between logic and reality. It has disdained the resources of clarity that a logic of extension and a physics of quantity bring to the mind. It has not wanted to consider numbers, space and time as abstractions. Nor did it consider it useful to constitute abstract categories such as our categories of Genus, Substance and Force. The notion of Tao goes beyond the notions of force and substance, and Yin and Yang, valid interchangeably as forces, substances and kinds, are something else, for the function of these symbols is to classify and animate together the antithetical aspects of the universal Order; Tao, Yin and Yang evoke synthetically, give rise globally to the rhythmic order that presides over the life of the world and the activity of the spirit. Chinese thought seems to be totally driven by the combined ideas of order, totality and rhythm.

The close relationship between these notions and, moreover, the sovereign efficacy attributed to them, would suffice to reveal the social origin of the Chinese categories. This origin is confirmed as soon as we analyze the content of the *guiding ideas*. Whether it is the Chinese notion of Space or those of Time, Number, Elements, Tao, Yin and Yang, this content cannot be explained solely by the conceptions of the thinkers or technicians who used them. To interpret them, it is certainly not useless to consider the use they received in this or that specialty of the knowledge that teaches to order occasions and places; the geographical or calendrical art, music or architecture, the art of the diviners, the technique of mutations… But we can only get to the heart of the matter, and the interpretation has any chance of being correct and complete, when we consider the guiding concepts and attempts to determine their relation to the structure of Chinese society. Accordingly, while I have refused to date these ideas by the (supposed) date of the "philosophical" fragment in which the terms pointing to them are first mentioned, I have tried to fix the time and order of their formation by taking advantage of the fact that they are linked to social circumstances. The notions to which the Chinese attribute a function of categories depend, for the most part, on the principles on which the organization of society rests; they represent a kind of institutional background to Chinese thought, and their analysis is confused (as we shall see, for example, with the ideas of Time, Space and even Number) with a study of social morphology. But not all these key ideas were made explicit at the same moment in history; they are also marked by certain features that situate or date them. If Yin and Yang form a pair and seem to preside jointly over the rhythm that founds the universal Order, it is because their conception comes from a time in history when a principle of rotation was sufficient to regulate social activity distributed between two complementary groups. The conception of the Tao goes back to a less archaic time; it could only be made explicit at a time when the structure of society was more complicated and in circles in which the authority of leaders who justified themselves by presenting themselves as the sole authors of order in the world was venerated; then and only then could the idea of a *unique* and *central* animating power be imagined.

To classify notions by relating them to circles whose place and role in the history of Chinese society are known, is to sketch the history of ideas, and even to indicate dates. If these dates cannot be expressed with figures, they are certainly not at all precise in concrete terms. However, I know that some people will read with distaste "essays" in which, in the absence of abstract dates and proper names, the ideas will seem to come directly from the crowd. What can I do about this? I have refrained from using even such (obviously convenient but fictitiously accurate) appellations as "the School of the Diviners." I have avoided them out of sheer prudence and not out of forgetfulness of the fact that, to produce ideas, individuals are needed. I have been able to show that the content of the guiding ideas is explained by the structure of Chinese society and that the evolution of these ideas depends very strictly on social evolution. Of course, it is unfortunate that we do not have the means to cite the names and dates of the people who actively witnessed these parallel developments. However, the main thing is that we can see the parallelism. Whatever the genius of the sages who knew the guiding principles of Chinese thought and organization, the explanation of these principles lies not so much in this genius as in the history of the social system.

In China, this history is remarkable for a continuity that is unparalleled anywhere. Chinese philosophers of all schools have never ceased to think that the national system of symbols, the fruit of a long tradition of wisdom, could not, on the whole, fail to be adequate and effective; in other words, they profess the same confidence in it that we in the West have in Reason.

We are of the opinion that this corresponds to a set of guiding notions from which Chinese notions seem to differ profoundly. As we shall see, the latter are linked to a system of classification very close to "primitive classifications." It would be quite easy to attribute to the Chinese a "mystical" or "prelogical" mentality if we were to interpret literally the symbols they venerate.

But, if I were to consider these products of human thought as strange and singular inventions, I would be ignoring the spirit of humanism, as well as the principle of all positive research. Moreover, the injustice that an unfavorable prejudice would entail is demonstrated by an analysis of the guiding ideas; these permanent frameworks of thought are modeled on the frameworks of a social organization whose duration is sufficient to demonstrate their value; it is necessary, then, that these rules of action and thought respond in some way to the nature of things.[18]

---

18   Cf. Durkheim, *Les formes élémentaires de la vie religieuse*, pp. 633 ff.

Chinese wisdom has probably not been able to avoid drifting into pure scholasticism; since the foundation of the Empire, orthodoxy imposed its reign, and the main preoccupation of scholarly thought has been the mnemonic classification of ancient knowledge; since then, the experimental sense has been absent. But this scholastic knowledge had been built up from experiments from which emerged, along with the very notion of classification, the idea that any organization derives its value from an observed efficiency. Arbitrary to a certain extent, like all human creations, the social arrangements that served as a model for the arrangement of the mind are nevertheless based on a persevering effort of experimental adaptation. The origin of the Chinese categories is an ancient attempt to *organize experience*; it would be imprudent to prejudge that they are in any way ill-founded. They seem to oppose the ideas that guide us and may surprise us by their hostile bias toward abstraction. But the Chinese have been able to develop a logic of hierarchy or efficiency that fits perfectly with their taste for concrete symbols. And if, by refusing to give an aspect of abstract entities to Time, Space and Numbers, they turned away from a quantitative physics and limited themselves (not without profitable results) to the search for the furtive or the *singular*, nothing prevented them – no theological prejudice led them to imagine that Man alone formed a mysterious kingdom in nature – from building all their wisdom on a psychology of the positive spirit. Perhaps a more equitable appreciation of Chinese thought will be achieved when it is realized that the merit of the notions which serve as its guiding principles does not lie in the fashion of this or that teaching, but in the long-proven efficacy of a system of social discipline.[19]

* * *

I had to make known the system of thought which, together with its social system, defines the civilization of the Chinese; it was necessary to make slow analyses, which I had to present in the form of separate essays, since I had only incomplete and rough information at my disposal. I have tried to group them in such a way as to indicate the structure and movement that characterize the set of "doctrines" or rules of action that I have had to interpret. The idea that seems to animate them is

---

19   It may be (and this would not be news) that, from various quarters, and, I imagine, as a compliment, these pages seem to indicate that I have tried to elucidate Chinese facts by means of "sociological theories" or (equally) that I have tried to illustrate "sociological theory" by means of Chinese facts. Am I to claim that I know nothing of what is called sociological theory or theories? For as long as sociologists have existed, has it not been their first aim, when they work, to discover facts? Perhaps I have pointed out some that have not attracted attention. The beginning of their discovery is to be found in Durkheim's and Mauss's memoir of "*primitive classifications*"; I am pleased to say – and perhaps it is not without interest – that although few scholars have cited them (see, however, Forke, Lun-Heng, *Selected Essays of the philosopher Wang Ch'ung*, (*MSOS*, 1911) t. II, p. 442), the few pages of this dissertation dealing with China should be a landmark in the history of Sinological studies. I will also add that, although I have undertaken the analysis of Chinese categories with the sole concern of extracting a correct interpretation of Chinese facts exclusively, the best reason I have for believing that this analysis is accurate is that it brings out the preeminence of the category of totality on which, after vast research, Durkheim (*Formes élémentaires*, p. 630), had insisted so much.

that the function of human thought is not pure knowledge, but civilizing action; its role is to give rise to an active and total order. There is no concept that is not an attitude, no doctrine that is not a recipe for life. To define, in essence, the Chinese system of thought is to characterize all Chinese attitudes. So the conclusion I have given to this volume is also valid for the previous volume. If this title did not imply an inappropriate ambition, I might say that its purpose is to give an insight into the "spirit of Chinese manners." I have set out to point out the most notable of the biases from which the civilization of China draws its originality. This summary, of course, is only a summary of my experience. It will no doubt be recognized that if a systematic spirit appears in these tentative conclusions, it is because I have had to define the spirit of a system.[20]

---

20 References are (as far as possible) to translations or publications in Western languages; they will help to find the context. – In most cases I had to propose a new translation.

Book I
THE EXPRESSION OF THOUGHT

The purpose of these first chapters is to provide information on the Chinese language, writing, stylistics and rhythm. We are accustomed to regard language as symbolism specially organized to communicate ideas. The Chinese do not separate the art of language from the other processes of signaling and action. It seems to them to be linked to a whole set of techniques that serve to situate individuals in the system of civilization formed by society and the universe. These various attitudinal techniques are primarily directed to action. When they speak and when they write, the Chinese, by means of stylized gestures (vocal or otherwise), try to represent and suggest behaviors. Their thinkers have no different pretensions. They are perfectly content with a traditional system of symbols that is more powerful for guiding action than for formulating concepts, theories or dogmas.

Chapter I
Language and Writing

Chinese is a great language of civilization that has managed to become and remain the instrument of culture of the entire Far East. It has also been the organ of one of the most varied and richest literatures. Chinese language belongs to the monosyllabic type and its writing is figurative.

I. Vowel Symbols

As far as we know, the phonetic and morphological evolution of Chinese can only be traced from the 6th century AD to modern times.[1] For the earlier period, documents do not provide sufficient information on pronunciation and spoken language.

Scholars admit that Chinese is a language of the so-called *Sino-Tibetan* group. All languages of this group are characterized by a tendency to monosyllabic speech. Was "common Sino-Tibetan" a monosyllabic language? Some think that "it would be inaccurate" to so define it "if we refer to a language in which all words originally had only one syllable."[2] It does not seem possible, for the time being, to isolate the primitive roots. However, it is considered probable that in antiquity "many words were longer than at present and included, in addition to the root, one or more affixes and perhaps even a desinence." Over the centuries, these aggregates have been progressively reduced. Karlgren has even attempted to show that the Chinese

---

1 Przyluski, *Le sino-tibétain* (in *Langues du monde*), 1924, p. 374; Karlgren, Études sur la phonologie chinoise, and *Sound and symbol in China*; Maspero, *Le dialecte de Tch'ang-ngan sous les T'ang*, BEFEO, 1920.
2 Przyluski, *op. cit*, p. 363.

formerly used different personal pronouns in the case of subject and complement.[3] The documents he studied are certainly not earlier than the 8th-5th centuries BC. The Chinese of feudal times would therefore have spoken a language in which there were traces of inflection (declension, if not conjugation).

It seems, on the other hand, that archaic Chinese was phonetically less poor than modern Chinese. There were more consonants, both initial and final. The voice series included a fairly large number of diphthongs and triphthongs. Each word had a tone, which varied according to whether the initial was mute or voiced, while the inflection seemed to depend on the final. There were eight such tones; four in the lower series, four in the upper series, which could help to differentiate homophones.[4] If, in pronouncing a word, the tone was changed from the lower to the upper series or vice versa, the value of the word was modified. Again, there is (apparently) evidence of an ancient process of derivation.

It is impossible to say whether the various derivational processes which are thought to have been restored, and the significance of which can hardly be determined, are evidence of an archaic state of Chinese, or whether they are to be regarded as the beginning of a development of the language, which otherwise came to a rapid halt.

In any case, the language spoken in the earliest period of Chinese history[5] seems to have been a language with a very poor phonetics and an extremely reduced morphology.

Even if it is postulated that the words of the Chinese language were not originally monosyllabic, it must be recognized that nowhere was the tendency to monosyllabism stronger. If it is true that the Chinese used affixes, the function of these was, in any case, so restricted that the speaker had little means of knowing any derivation. He had to use words which, reduced to monosyllables, devoid of any flexibility, of any fluidity, were presented to him, practically, as so many independent roots.

We are also unaware of the importance of the dialectal varieties that could distinguish the languages of the different countries of ancient China.

The fact that the same language is found in all the local songs (*Kouo fong*: Songs of the country) which form the first part of the *Che king* shows little. It is not impossible that these songs were reworked at the time they were added to an anthology. However, it may be assumed that all subjects of the ancient Chinese Confederacy were aware that they spoke the same language.

It is likely that the custom of inter-feudal meetings favored the development of a common language among the nobles of the various lordships, who considered this common language to be the only one worthy of them. A prince of Wei (Honan manor), who returned to his country after a period of captivity, liked to imitate

---

3   Karlgren, *Protochinese, an inflectional language*, JA, p. 1920. Karlgren's demonstration suffers from a dubious classification of ancient texts. On the other hand, the analogies that can be found in Burmese seem to postulate in favor of the advancing theory.

4   Maspero, *La Chine antique*, pp. 18-19.

5   8th to 5th century BC.

the way of speaking of his conquerors, the people of Wou (Ngan-houei). They immediately exclaimed, "The prince of Wei will not avoid Fate! Must he not die with the barbarians? He has been their prisoner. He is pleased to speak their language. He is bound to them for ever!"[6]

It must be admitted that, since feudal times, Chinese has been the language of civilization.[7]

It deserves to be so because it is the organ of an original culture and because it has certain qualities. These qualities, in fact, are very different from those we would be tempted to ask of a language chosen to guarantee the correct transmission of thought.

The words, which were excessively short and whose poor phonetics often made it difficult to distinguish them, could, for the most part, be used interchangeably as nouns, verbs or adjectives, without their form being appreciably modified.[8] A few particles, each of which served several functions and were used mainly as an oral punctuation mark, helped to convey the meaning of the sentence. But only a rigid construction could bring some clarity to the expression of ideas. When people wrote, they used to make strict use of the position rule that fixed the syntactic role of each word. But when speaking, the order of words was determined by the succession of emotions. This order merely underlined the degree of emotional and practical importance attributed to the various elements of an emotional set.

This language offered few facilities for the abstract expression of ideas. Yet its fortunes as the language of civilization have been prodigious.

Chinese, it is true, has an admirable power to communicate a sentimental shock, to invite one to take sides. A language at once rough and fine, concrete and powerful in action, it is clear that it was formed in discussions where astute wills clashed.

It was not important to express ideas clearly. One wanted, above all, to be able to make one's wishes heard (discreetly and imperatively). – A warrior, before beginning a battle, turns to a friend he has on the other side. He wants to give him prudent advice, to urge him to flee across the mud of the flooded plain, to make him see that in this case he could help him? However, he merely says to him, "Have you any leaven of wheat?" – "No," replies the other (who may not understand). – "Do you have yeast (from plants) from the mountains?" – "No," again replies the other. (Despite the insistence on the word *yeast* – yeast was considered an excellent preventive against the pernicious influence of *dampness* – he still does not under-

---

6   *Tso tchouan*, C., III, p. 682. The same bad fate is predicted (*Ibid.*, II, p. 565) for a prince who has had a house of foreign architecture built for him. (Comp. *Civ. Chin.*, p. 270). One defines his personality, fixes his destiny by the language he adopts, the architecture (rites, music, dances, etc.) he prefers. Language and all other symbol systems have the same virtue: they are indicative of a certain order of civilization.

7   The later success of Chinese as a language of civilization is largely due to its unified and fixed figurative transcription. In the feudal period, Chinese writing can no longer be considered absolutely uniform. Chinese, as a spoken language, was, in the first place, a civilizing language.

8   We have seen that the tone can vary.

stand – or pretends not to understand; no doubt he wants to receive, with more explicit advice, the commitment that he will be helped.) The friend continues (again avoiding the essential word, but strongly suggesting it), "The fish in the river will have a bellyache. What remedy will you give them?" And the other (who finally makes up his mind), "Look at the wells *without water*. You'll draw it out." So, after the battle, he hides in a muddy swamp and, when the danger has passed, his friend found him there. The one giving the advice has focused attention on a word that he has been careful not to pronounce, while at the same time he has managed to give it all the value of a complex imperative ("Think of the water! Watch out for the water! – Use the water! = *Save yourself*, using, with caution, the flood!").

The language is, above all, one of action. It is not so much intended to inform with clarity as to direct behavior. "The art of expression (*wen*) makes speech powerful."[9] This art, as it appears in ancient accounts of transactions or conversations, is not concerned with explicit notions or formal reasoning. To gain control over an adversary, to influence the behavior of a friend or a client, it is enough to accumulate formulas to impose on the mind a word, a verb, that possesses it completely.

The word, in Chinese, is much more than a sign used to indicate a concept. It does not correspond to a notion whose degree of abstraction and generality we wish to fix in the most definite way possible. It evokes an indefinite complex of particular images, making the most active of them appear first.

There is no word that simply means "old." Instead, there are a large number of terms representing different aspects of old age: the aspect of those who already need a richer diet (*k'i*), the aspect of those whose breathing is labored (*k'ao*), etc. These concrete evocations lead to a series of visions, all equally concrete; all the details, for example, of the way of life proper to those whose decrepitude demands a meat diet – they are the ones who must be exempt from military service – those who can no longer be obliged to go to school, those for whom, in anticipation of their death, all the funeral goods must be ready, the preparation of which requires a year of work, those who are entitled to carry a cane in the middle of the city, at least when it is not a capital city, etc. Such are the images aroused, among others, by the word *k'i*, which, as a whole, corresponds to an almost singular notion, that of an old man of sixty to seventy years of age. At seventy, one becomes specifically old. One then deserves to be called *lao*. This word evokes a characteristic moment of life which is the arrival at old age. It is not equivalent to the concept "old." It brings up a series of images that do not merge into an abstract idea. If this current of evocations is not stopped, the representation will encompass all the aspects that distinguish the different categories of people for whom the active period of life has ended. When it has reached its maximum extent, this representation will continue to be dominated by a characteristic vision, that of the entry into retirement or, more precisely, that of the ritual gesture by which one bids farewell to one's chief. Thus, the word *lao*, like most Chinese words, retains a kind of living value even

---

9   *Tso tchouan*, C., II, pp. 437-439.

when used nominally. It does not cease to evoke an action and remains basically a verb (to declare oneself old; to be declared old; to retire).

The word, just as it does not correspond to a concept, is not a simple sign either. It is not an abstract sign that is only given life by grammatical or syntactic devices. In its immutable monosyllabic form, in its neutral aspect, it retains all the imperative energy of the act of which it is the vocal correspondent, of which it is the symbol.

This power of words and their character of being considered not as mere signs, but as vocal symbols, is shown in certain terms, which are often used twice and form descriptive aids.

The importance of these descriptive aids is one of the characteristics of ancient poetry. They also play a considerable role in Chinese poetry of all times, and prose itself does not ignore them. When a poet describes the games of two kinds of grasshoppers with the help of the auxiliaries *yao yao* and *t'i-t'i*, he does not intend (his interpreters tell us) merely to describe them in words. He wants to advise – he intends to *command* – his listeners to obey a set of rules of which the gestures of the grasshoppers are the *natural symbol*, of which the auxiliaries describing them are the *vocal symbol*. These rules are very particular, and yet they guide behavior to a large extent. It is not conceivable (it cannot be) that, by a kind of direct effect, the vocal symbols *yao-yao* and *t'i-t'i* do not, by their force alone, impose respect for obligations (marriage outside the family and residence, entry into the home after the season of agricultural work, etc.) involving a whole discipline of life (separation of the sexes, rites of domestic life, etc.).[10] The auxiliary *siu* describes the particular noise made by pairs of wild geese with their wings; the auxiliary *yong* describes the cry of these same geese when the female responds to the call of the male. Even today, it is enough to evoke these vocal paintings (one can simply inscribe the corresponding characters on a sign, the *scriptural symbol* taking the place of the *vowel symbol*, which is itself the equivalent of the *natural symbol*), to be assured (at least if this sign is carried, in the appropriate place, at the head of a wedding procession) that the bride will immediately be imbued with the virtue of a female goose; she will follow, without ever reaching him, the head of the house, and, henceforth, subject to all his commands, she will answer him in the tone of a unison harmony.[11] Would the abstract concepts of modesty, submission and modesty have more powerful effects if used by the most skillful rhetoric?

Some of the descriptive aids resemble onomatopoeias. Most are word paintings, but not in the realistic sense of the word. *K'i-k'i*, which paints the crowing of the cock as well as that of the oriole, still evokes the gusts of the north wind.[12] Homophonous monosyllables abound in Chinese, which is very poor in sounds and very rich in words; two homophones, each with the same suggestive force, both singular and indefinite, may awaken the most dissimilar series of images. There is nothing in their vocabulary or grammar to suggest that the Chinese felt the need

---

10 Granet, *Fêtes et chansons...*, pp. 117 ff.
11 *Id*, Some peculiarities of the language..., p. 118.
12 *Ibid.*, p. 119; *Id., Fêtes et chansons...*, p. 41, and *Che king*, C., p. 189.

to give words a clearly individualized aspect to indicate their meaning or function. One can sometimes think of finding in certain words a kind of imitative music. It is not from there that they derive such evocative power that their utterance alone is convincing. If in each of them there remains, with a kind of efficacy, a latent value of imperative, this is due to an overall attitude towards the word. It does not seem that the Chinese were concerned with creating a material of clear expressions that would be valid only as signs, but which, in themselves, would be indifferent. They seem to want every word in their language to invite them to feel that speech is an act.

The Chinese term for life and destiny (*ming*) is not unlike the term (*ming*) for speech symbols (or graphics). It does not matter that the names of two beings are so similar that there is a possibility of confusing them, each of these names fully expresses an individual essence. It is an understatement to say that it expresses it: it calls it, brings it into reality. To know the name, to say the word, is to possess the being or to create the thing. Every beast is tamed by those who know how to name it. I know how to pronounce the name of this young couple: they immediately assume, male and female pheasant, the form that fits their essence and gives me a hold. I have tigers for soldiers if I call them "tigers." I don't want to become ungodly, so I stop the car and turn back, because I just learned that the name of the next town is "the oppressed mother." When I make a sacrifice, I use the right word, and the gods immediately accept my offering: it is perfect. I know the correct formula for asking for a bride: the girl is mine. The curse I exhale is a concrete force: it assaults my adversary, who suffers its effects and recognizes its reality. I come from princely blood, but I will become a stable boy, for I have been called a stable boy. My name is Yu, I have the right to the fief of Yu, the sovereign's will cannot take it away from me, I cannot be dispossessed of the thing, for I possess the symbol of it. I have killed a lord: no crime has been committed if no one has dared to say "it is murder!" For my domain to perish, it is enough for me to designate myself by violating the protocol rules of language, with an expression that is not convenient: it disqualifies, along with me, my country.[13]

It is in the art of the word that the magic of *breath* and the virtue of *etiquette* are exalted and culminate. To assign a name is to assign a rank, a spell, a symbol. When we speak, we name, we designate, we do not limit ourselves to describe or ideally classify. The term qualifies and contaminates, provokes destiny, gives rise to reality. As emblematic reality, the word orders phenomena.

The ancient vocabulary includes a certain number of these worn-out terms that modern grammarians call "empty words" or "dead words." The others, the "living words," are infinitely more numerous; they are those in which there is a force capable of resisting wear and tear. Whether they express an action, a state (any kind of phenomenal appearance), all these words give rise, so to speak, to an individual essence. They all partake of the nature of proper names. They are valid as *denominations*, as singular denominations. Hence this proliferation of words which

---

13 See *Civ. Chin*: pp. 276-277, 287, 322, 376.

Book I - Chapter I - Language and Writing

contrasts so strangely with the poverty of phonetism. There are many terms, of very different meanings, which are pronounced *peng, hong, sseu, tsou*; on the other hand, there is no expression which, phonetically well individualized and clear to the ear, expresses the general, abstract and neutral idea of "to die." One cannot express the idea of "dying" without qualifying and judging the deceased, without evoking (by means of a single monosyllable) a whole set of ritual practices, a whole order of society. Depending on whether *peng, hong, sseu* or *tsou* has been said, the deceased will have died (i.e., it will have been appropriate, as far as mourning is concerned, to treat him) as a Son of Heaven, as a proud lord, as a great official, or as a common man. By the effect of a single word, you will have disposed of the fate of the deceased, fixed his destiny in the next life, ranked his family, unless, unable to make a valid judgment, you have disqualified yourself – for the force of a symbol turns against those who do not know how to assign it well. Chinese life is dominated by etiquette. The vocabulary has expanded immeasurably, so that for every situation there is a protocol term that is correct and therefore effective. This immense vocabulary does not correspond to an inventory that aims at clarity; it forms a repertoire of value judgments, singular and effective judgments. It constitutes a system of symbols whose use, as active symbols, should make it possible to achieve an order regulated by Etiquette.

Ancient Chinese, with its abundant vocabulary, does not have a large number of easily recognizable signs pointing to different notions, but a rich repertoire of vocal symbols. It matters little to give them a sensible individuality, a concrete exterior, an appearance that appears or is distinguished. Each one, depending on the circumstances – and on the mimicry – that will direct the concerns of the interlocutors in a certain direction, can find, as a whole, a particular power of suggestion. The Chinese language has not been more concerned with preserving or increasing its phonetic richness than with developing its morphology. It has not sought to perfect itself in the sense of clarity. It has not been molded to appear to be made to express ideas. It has sought to remain rich in concrete values and, above all, not to allow the emotional and practical power of each word to diminish to the extent that it feels like a symbol.

II. The Graphic Symbols

The Chinese, when expressing themselves, seem more concerned with efficiency, rather than obeying needs of a strictly intellectual nature.

This mental orientation undoubtedly explains the fact that writing has never ceased to be an emblematic form in China.

This writing is often described as ideographic, because a special character is assigned to each word. The characters are more or less complicated, and are resolved into a series of graphic elements, devoid of meaning, which simply correspond to a certain movement of the tool used by the writer. These lines, grouped in greater or lesser numbers, form small figures. Figures that can be broken down into elementary strokes are called symbols or images. Some represent a thing (a tree); others seem to evoke an idea (expressed). These so-called simple characters are relatively few. The so-called complex characters are much more numerous. If we consider that a complex character is only made up of components (images or symbols), which in their totality contribute to indicate the meaning (dress + knife = beginning), we admit that we are still in the presence of an ideogram. Most of the time, graphic analysis leads to the isolation of two parts. The first part (simple) is then qualified as *radical*; it is supposed to give an indication of its meaning. The second part (considered more or less complex) is called *phonetic* and is supposed to give an indication of pronunciation. Characters of this type, known as phonetic complexes, are not presented as ideograms. They evoke a word, making one think first (through their radical) of a category of objects, and then specifying (through phonetics) this object; it will be the category indicated, to which (or one of which) corresponds (approximately) to that pronunciation {lining (*li*) = garment (radical) + *li* (phonetic; the sign having to this pronunciation means village)}.

Mou: wood (tree shape); writing known as seal script.	Mou: wood; writing known as clerical script.	Tch'ou: go out; seal script.	Tch'ou: go out; clerical script.
Yi: clothing.	Yi: clothing (in composition, as a key).	Tao: knife.	(Clothing + knife =) beginning.
Li: village.	Clothing + li, (village), =] lining (*li*).	Stop (shape of a foot).	Shape (without strokes) representing a spear.	Stop (the) spears = warrior.
Dog: seal script.	Dog: clerical script.	Right hand: seal script.	(Two right hands=) friendship; seal script.	Friendship: clerical script.
Cold: seal script.	Cold: clerical script.	Horse: clerical script.	Long, chief (= man with horse head or long hair fastened by a clip).	(Hair fastened by a clip=) long, chief; seal script.

Leibniz wrote[14]: "If there were (in Chinese writing)... a certain number of fundamental characters of which the others were only combinations," this writing "would have a certain analogy with the analysis of thoughts." It is enough to know that most of the characters are considered phonetic complexes, to understand how false is the idea that the Chinese would have proceeded to the invention of their writing as if it were an algebra, combining signs chosen to represent essential notions.

The merits of Chinese writing are of another order; practical, not intellectual. It can be used by people who speak different dialects – or even idioms – and the reader reads what the writer has written in his or her own way, thinking of words that have the same meaning, but which he or she might pronounce very differently. Regardless of the changes in pronunciation over time, this writing is an admirable organ of traditional culture. Regardless of local pronunciations, which it tolerates, its main advantage is that it is what we might call a civilizing script.

It has served powerfully to spread Chinese civilization. Partly for this reason, it has not yet been replaced by a phonetic script. On the other hand, it could be preserved because the tendency of the language to monosyllabism did not diminish appreciably, and to write it, it was only necessary to represent the roots. It was not necessary to write down the inflections. Moreover, we can think that the habit of figurative writing was an obstacle to any development of the language that would have led to the use of the various possible derivation processes.

In languages that admit these procedures, awareness of derivations can predispose and assist in the analysis of ideas. Contrary to what Leibniz imagined, the Chinese script is not designed to render an analogous service. The combinations of strokes, properly called radicals, are not at all characters symbolizing fundamental notions. It will suffice to point out that one of these so-called radicals is intended to represent the canine teeth and another the incisors, but that there are none corresponding to the "general" idea of teeth. In fact, these radicals correspond to rubrics intended to facilitate, not a classification with a claim to objectivity, but a practical search in the lexicons and, no doubt, an easier learning of writing.

Ts'in Che Houang-ti,[15] in order to impose throughout the Empire the official script used in the country of T'sin, had his minister Li Sseu publish a collection containing, it is said, three thousand characters, the use of which was made obligatory for all scribes. The proscription of the manuscripts of the "Hundred Schools" was, perhaps, among other reasons, enacted to prevent the preservation of the modes of writing peculiar to the Six Kingdoms destroyed by Ts'in. On the other hand, the development of the imperial bureaucracy favored the use of a cursive script (known as court script) which scholars considered a modern script, derived *by simple deformation* from the correct script, the only one in use, it was claimed, in antiquity.[16] Favored by the need to interpret in *modern* characters the manu-

---

14 Leibniz, ed. Dutens, V, p. 488.
15 *Civ. Chin.*, pp. 119, 120.
16 Mestre, *Quelques résultats d'une comparaison entre les caractères chinois modernes et les siao-tchouan*; Laloy, *La musique chinoise*; Grube, *Die Religion der alten Chinesen*; Karlgren,

scripts with archaic or archaizing scripts that Han scholars were able to find or restore, they reconstituted the classical works;[17] lexicographical work continued and resulted (around 100 AD) in the composition of a large collection known as *Chouo wen*. Its author attempted to isolate in each character the component elements it presented to indicate meaning or pronunciation. Among the significant elements, he determined 540 graphic signs that served as epigraphs to classify all the characters studied, which number about 10,000. From these headings, reduced in number, he extracted the radicals which, in modern dictionaries, allow us to look up a word, in the manner of the initials of our phonetic dictionaries. They should be called keys, and should not be confused with *graphical roots*. However, the idea that the development of writing was unilinear, and that the *Chouo wen* analysis was valid for the different types of graphic symbolization, gave this analysis the credence of an etymological explanation. *From then on, an attempt was made to explain the characters from a set of primitive forms from which they were derived by way of combination.* And it was accepted, without discussion, that since the primitive characters were originally realistic drawings, the complex characters must be understood as a hieroglyph.

The idea that the characters have the value of a hieroglyph seems to be ancient. A victorious chief, when urged to erect a triumphal monument, replies that his first duty is to put the weapons back in their scabbards, for "the character *wou* (warrior) is made up of the elements: *stop* (image of a foot) *the spears* (image of a spear)."[18] This anecdote hints at the practical value of the explanation of the hieroglyph. In order to justify the conduct or the judgments that motivate it, recourse is had to a kind of experience, recorded in writing.

This experience is considered perfectly adequate to the reality of things. By this is meant that it is full of efficacy, or, if we prefer, full of divine wisdom. According to tradition, writing was invented by a minister of Houang-ti, the first of the sovereigns, after examining the tracks left by birds on the ground. The origin of the divinatory figures is also explained from the omens. The latter are also explained from the use of knotted strings, and precisely the most ancient writing system (to which is attributed the value of a system of government) consisted in the use of knots or carvings (*fou*). The carvings were used as talismans (their name is still used to designate them). Graphic signs (as these traditions demonstrate) are not easily distinguishable from symbols with magical properties. Moreover, their use by their men proved their perfect efficacy. As soon as graphic symbols were invented, the demons fled with a groan;[19] the humans had them under control.

Sound and symbol in China; Karlgren, *Philology and ancient China*.

17   *Civ. Chin.*, pp. 61-63.

18   *Tso tchouan*, C., III, p. 635. It is to this text that the use of divination with the aid of personages is usually attributed. It provides a first indication of the relationship between graphic symbols and divinatory figures.

19   *Lu che tch'ouen ts'ieou*, 17, § 2. *Chouo wen*, pref. Knots and notches serve to grasp realities; likewise vocal or figurative signs.

The first duty of the Chief is to provide men with the symbols that will enable them to tame Nature, because they point out, for each being, his personality, as well as his place and rank in the World. In the early days of Chinese civilization, Houang-ti acquired the glory of a founding hero, for he took care to give to all things a correct designation (*ming*) (*tcheng*), "in order to enlighten the people as to the resources they could use." "To make the designations correct (*tcheng ming*)" is, in fact, the first of governmental duties. The task of the Prince is to set things and actions in order; he adjusts actions to things. He achieves this from the outset by fixing the names (*ming*: the pronunciation of words) and the writing signs (*ming*: the characters).[20]

Houang-ti, the first ruler, began by founding the social order; he assigned to the different families a name intended to distinguish their virtue. It is said that he achieved this by playing the flute. It is known that the specific virtue of a lordly race was expressed by means of a sung dance (with an animal or vegetable motif). There is no doubt that it is appropriate to recognize the value of ancient family names as a kind of musical motto, which is graphically translated into a kind of coat of arms, all the efficacy of the dance and songs remaining in the graphic as well as in the vocal symbol. But men do not form a separate kingdom in nature, and the same rules that apply to those who wish to define human families also apply when it comes to adapting a sign to each thing. The essential duty of all government is to obtain a harmonious distribution of all beings. To this end, it distributes symbols, oral and graphic slogans. Its main function is to supervise the system of designations. Any vicious designation in language or writing would reveal an insufficiency of the sovereign Virtue. Therefore, every nine years[21] the sovereign must convene a commission to check whether the visual or auditory symbols do not fail to constitute a symbolism in keeping with the genius of the dynasty. This commission is concerned with words as well as characters; it is therefore composed of scribes and blind musicians.[22]

The equally powerful symbols, writing signs and vocal signs, which are referred to by the same term (*ming*), are considered strictly interdependent. This conception makes it possible to understand why signs in which we recognize "*phonetic complexes*" are no less *representative of reality* than characters, called *ideographic*, in which we only want to see drawings. Surprisingly, the so-called *phonetic* part of these complexes most of the time is the stable element. The *radical*, on the other hand, is unstable and is usually eliminated. It is the least significant element. At

---

20   *Li ki*, C., II, p. 269. Later on we shall study the philosophical aspects of the doctrine of correct designations. Let us say beforehand that, for the advocates of this doctrine, to name is to classify and to judge; it is to endow with a certain virtue, beneficial or maleficent.

21   It is also said that every nine years the distribution of offices (and, undoubtedly, of lands) was to be made. It is also said that officials were examined every nine years.

22   *Tcheou li*, Biot, The "*Tcheou li*" or the *Rites of the Tcheou* (Classic of the Rites), II, p. 120. It is known (*Civ. Chin.*) that at birth the personal name is chosen after the quality of the newborn's voice has been determined with the aid of a brass tube by a musician: sometimes it is recognized as that of an animal whose nature the child possesses.

most, it plays the role of a specifier. Normally, its only practical use is to facilitate a (technical) classification of signs (and not a classification of concepts). These so-called radicals appear as superfluous elements. On the other hand, each of the groupings of strokes, which are usually called "phonetic," forms a complete symbol in itself and usually corresponds, much better than the radical, to what we might be tempted to call a root. In conjunction with a vowel sign in which one wants to see an emblematic value, the graphic sign is itself regarded as a suitable figuration, or rather, so to speak, as an effective appellation.

With these attitudes in mind, writing need not be ideographic in the strict sense of the word. On the other hand, it cannot do without figuration. Consequently, discourse is linked, for the same purpose, to writing. Hence the importance of the latter in the development of the Chinese language and the fact that (like an amulet that is reinforced by a talisman) the virtue of words is sustained by the virtue of writing. The spoken word and the written sign are – united or separate, but always tending to support each other – symbolic correspondents that are considered exactly adequate to the realities they note or evoke; in them lies the same efficacy, at least as long as a certain order of civilization remains in force.

This order does not differ from the general system of symbolization. There is, therefore, a complete identity (or, rather, one would like to think that it really exists) between the sense of the correctness of language (written or spoken), the feeling of civilization, and the consciousness of the *etymological value* of signs.

These conceptions and doctrines, which give a glimpse of the Chinese attitude towards expressive processes, do not imply that vocal symbolization was a realistic art of singing and graphic symbolization a realistic art of drawing.

Confucius is said to have declared that the sign of the dog was the perfect drawing of the dog.[23] From this sign it is clear that, for the Sage, a representation can be adequate without trying to reproduce all the characteristics of the object. It is adequate when, in stylized form, it shows an attitude considered characteristic or significant of a certain type of action or relationship. The same is true of figurative ideas. The idea of a friend or friendship is suggested by the schematic representation of two joined hands (a character called simple). The various contracts (engagement, military companionship, affiliation) that created extra-familial bonds were linked by the hand. The handwriting sign brings into play a type of *idea with general value* by evoking a *consecrated gesture rich in diverse consequences*. Also suggestive is the character (known as complex) that triggers the series of representations leading to the idea of cold. We find several elementary signs that make us think of the man, the straw and the house. All of these evoke the *initial gesture* of winter. When Chinese peasants returned to their village (abandoned during the season of work in the fields and heavy rains), they began by filling the adobe walls and thatched roofs of their huts with straw.

The graphic symbol registers (or pretends to register) a stylized gesture. It has a proper evocative power, because the gesture it represents (or pretends to represent)

---

23 P. Wieger, *Caractères* (Rudiments, V, 12), p. 364.

is a gesture with *ritual* value (or, at least, felt as such). It provokes the appearance of a flow of images that allows a sort of *etymological reconstruction* of notions.

This reconstruction, from which notions, like signs, derive a kind of authority, has nothing in common (is it superfluous to say so?) with what a scholar would call an etymological investigation. The diversity of opinions formulated by paleographers is proof of this. Each one, or rather each school, isolates, defines and groups in his own way the elements whose combination has formed, it is claimed, the character; each one, according to the orientation of his thought or according to the needs of the moment, finds the meaning of the hieroglyph. In the character pronounced *tchang* (to grow, to enlarge) or *tch'ang* (long, chief), some see hair long enough to fasten with a pin; in the same character, others effortlessly distinguish a man with a horse's head.[24] In fact, these two etymological explanations are easily and suggestively related. The double meaning and the double etymology are explained by the relationship of two ancient dances. One is the dance of the chief (and his wives), which is done whirling and with hair outstretched. The other is a horse dance; the riders ride in circles, with hair and *crines* spread out. A significant account shows that it was thought that a vegetation genie could be caught by having him surrounded by riders with their hair spread out and, also (for the graphic symbol is no less powerful than the ritual dance), that the genie could be reduced to piety by the mere representation of a head with hair spread out.[25] When, in dancing, the chief has to show his power over nature and when, in full action, he lets a divine force escape from the long hair which he then spreads, the *chief* qualifies himself as such and, at the same time, makes vegetation and herds *grow* and *develop*. Figurative writing tends to retain some of the etymological value. But it does not matter whether it actually preserves the original meaning; it does not matter whether the etymological reconstruction is imaginary or accurate; the main thing is that the spellings provide the sense that the concepts are still attached to real symbols.

The main merit of figurative writing lies in the fact that it allows the graphic signs and, through them, the words, to give the impression of being valid as acting forces, as real forces.

Since the Chinese language was as little concerned with phonetic richness as with the enrichment provided by the use of derivations, writing was resorted to in order to increase the vocabulary. As soon as the idea that signs were formed by combination was accepted, and as soon as it was learned to break them down into meaningful elements, the resources for creating characters became unlimited. To obtain a new term with a definite pronunciation, it was enough to combine one of the old graphic sets with one or another similar pronunciation with a certain radical. From then on, graphic invention could function in the manner of a derivation process, but by multiplying homophones, which often masked the real relationship of the concepts. Each new character (as well as any *phonetic complex*) could

---

24 *Ibid.*, p. 322; Mestre, *op. cit.*, p. 8.
25 Granet, *Danses et légendes…*, pp. 364-365.

represent a concrete reality. The taste for the concrete, coupled with a passion for etiquette, led to an extraordinary proliferation of graphic signs.

In AD 485, the lexicons were augmented by imperial decree with a thousand new terms.[26] The concept that the head of state is the master of the national system of symbols remains intact. At the same time, the idea that the graphic signs as a whole are linked to a certain order of civilization and that each of them possesses the power of realization peculiar to symbols remains valid.

There is no record of such massive enrichments in antiquity. But the proliferation of characters is certainly an ancient fact. From very early on, the art of writers, and especially that of poets, seemed to depend on the abundance of graphic signs used in their manuscripts. This fact indicates the dominant action that the writing system has exerted on the development of language. It must be assumed that the poems, in the course of their recitation, spoke to the eyes, so to speak, thanks to the setting in motion of a graphic memory that duplicates the verbal memory. It is difficult to imagine the process, but it is clear that it had a decisive effect: words never became mere signs.

Figurative writing helped most words to retain, with a kind of freshness and the character of *living words*, all the power of concrete expression. Preserved, if not chosen, by virtue of a disposition of the Chinese mind that seems profound, it has prevented the vocabulary from forming abstract material. It seems adapted to a way of thinking that does not propose to economize on mental operations.

---

26   *SMT*, V, p. 380.

Chapter II
Style

We know little about Chinese stylistics, even less than about language. The art of writing has hardly been the subject of precise "studies" in China. When Western sinologists deal with questions of style, if they do not confine themselves to formulating assessments, they devote themselves almost exclusively to dating or locating works.[1] Moreover, they pretend to achieve this by the ordinary means of simple philology and hardly go as far as stylistic research. Moreover, the literary history of China has not yet been completely remade; it is still dominated, even in our country, by the tenets of native orthodoxy. For example, the idea is often expressed that Chinese prose derives, on the one hand, from the art of the scribes and, on the other, from the art of the soothsayers;[2] the former are said to have established the principles of the historical or documentary style, and the latter to have created the philosophical or scientific style. We limit ourselves to characterizing these two styles by stating that the first is concise to the point of obscurity, the second simple, arid, precise and dry. These generalities dispense with the need to demonstrate that scribes and soothsayers formed distinct schools, opposing corporations. The facts seem to impose the contrary opinion, but it does not matter if one intends to continue to believe that the thought of Confucius, the great patron of the historical school, was only remotely influenced by the technicians of magic and divination; in the face of dogma, what do the facts matter? If, on the basis of these facts, we were to free ourselves from the dogmatic prejudices that still govern the classification of works and characters, an observation might posi-

---

1   This is the first object of Karlgren's attempt, which is new and interesting, on the authenticity and nature of *Tso chuan*.
2   E.g., Maspero's *La Chine antique*, pp. 432 ff.

tively orient the investigation of Chinese stylistics. The ancient works (whatever school we choose to ascribe them to)[3] contain numerous passages in verse, so little separated from the context that critics have often only very late discerned their poetic character. There is therefore some reason to suppose that the forms of speech in Chinese literary prose do not differ much from those used in ancient poetry. In suggesting that archaic prose (a model of cultured prose whose prestige lies in the use of a written language so different from the vulgar that it seems almost sacred or passes for a dead language) is not a creation entirely of the learned or the learned, we certainly run the risk of putting forward an opinion that will be received as heretical;[4] the attack will be aggravated if we add that the poetry from which archaic or archaizing prose derives its procedures appears, not as learned poetry, but simply as poetry of a religious order. However, these hypotheses explain, as we shall see, the most notable characteristics of the Chinese style.

The Chinese, when they speak and when they write, express themselves uniformly using time-honored formulas. They compose their speeches with the help of phrases that they link rhythmically. Rhythms and phrases contribute to the authority of developments and sentences. The latter (just as words are worth their weight in gold) aim above all at an effect of action.

I. Sentences

Chinese literature is a literature of combinations. When they want to demonstrate or explain, when it occurs to them to tell or describe, the most original authors use stereotyped stories and consensual expressions, drawn from a common background. This collection is not very abundant and, moreover, there are few attempts to renew it. Many of the themes that have enjoyed permanent favor are to be found in the older and more spontaneous productions of Chinese poetry.

An important body of ancient poems has been preserved in the *Che King*.[5] We have no authentic Chinese work that is significantly older. This classic probably contains only pieces prior to the 5th century BC. The choice of poems, if we are to believe tradition, is due to Confucius. The Master would only have admitted in his anthology poems inspired by the purest wisdom. In his collection they are grouped into four sections. All belong to the genre of so-called regular poetry (*che*); the verses, which are usually of four characters (four syllables), are divided into couplets offering little varied rhyme schemes. The last three sections contain sometimes very short, but sometimes quite long pieces; those in the first part (*Kouo fong*) have mostly only three couplets (usually twelve lines in all). In general, nei-

---

[3] There are passages in verse in both the *Chou king* and the *Yi King* (the one considered the work of scribes, the other the work of diviners), in the *Lao tseu* as well as in the *Tso tchuan* or Historical Memoirs.

[4] Modern Chinese critics who, out of democratic feeling, defend the use of the spoken language (*pai houa*) try to substantiate their opinions by showing the importance of this language in ancient literature.

[5] Granet, *Fêtes et chansons anciennes de la Chine*, Introd.

ther the composition nor the rhythmic procedures differ much from one section to another. The orthodox tradition, on the other hand, affirms the unity of inspiration. All the poems of the *Kouo fong* were composed and sung on the occasion of specific and well-known historical circumstances. They are all said to have both a political interest and a ritual value, since their purpose is to dictate to the princes their conduct and to make it conform to good manners.[6] This traditional doctrine has the merit of emphasizing the religious character common to all these poems. This character is essential; it alone explains the preservation of these poems and the use which has been made of them in the course of Chinese history, for the *Che king* is the classic which commands the most respect; in it are to be found, better than in the rituals themselves, principles of conduct. Even today, the views common in Western criticism are much more simplistic. Westerners usually recognize only a religious sense in some "odes" of the last sections; they immediately assert that, being extremely banal, their poetic value "is not very high,"[7] and give more interest to the poems, which they readily call "elegies" or "satires," because they intuit in them a wholly profane inspiration. As for the poems of the *Kouo fong*, they see them, like the Chinese, as works of circumstance, but they do not understand that they could, equally, have had a ritual interest. That is why they call them *lieder* or "poems of popular imitation" and thus believe that they are happily freed from the autochthonous tradition.[8] Unless the latter inspires blind faith, we must give up the pretension of determining, one by one, the meaning of poems which are mostly reworked, even if they are composed of ancient elements. On the other hand, if we focus our attention on these elements and consider these themes as a whole[9] some important facts clearly emerge, and first of all this: ancient Chinese poetry belongs to the gnomic type. It likes to adorn itself with all the wisdom and prestige of proverbs.

It cares little for new expressions, new combinations or original metaphors. The same images appear again and again. They all have a very similar inspiration and, moreover, are based on a very small number of models. "Here come the plums! – Behold how the oriole sings! – The seagulls scream in unison! –"Answering each other, the deer bray! These images were not invented for the sake of a new expression, destined to fade with time; they are calendar sayings. A good many of them are found in the rustic calendars that the Chinese have preserved.[10] They refer mainly to the spring and autumn periods. We know that at that time great festivals were celebrated, the tradition of which has been preserved in some parts of Asia. The purpose of these festivals is to renew a good agreement between men and nature, on which the destiny of all beings seems to depend. All beings, in the same way, contribute to the festival. The festival takes place between songs and dances. While the spring dew glistens on the flowers or ripe fruits and the withered

---

6 *Ibid.*, pp. 18 ff, 78 ff.
7 Maspero, *La Chine antique*, p. 429.
8 Grube *Geschichte der chinesischen Literatur*, p. 46; Maspero, *op. cit.*, p. 430.
9 Granet, *op. cit.* pp. 27 ff, 31.
10 *Ibid.*, pp. 53 ff.

leaves fall on the frozen earth with the autumn wind, mingling their voices and gestures with the calls of male and female grasshoppers, of deer and gulls as they chase each other, the boys and girls of the fields form dancing choruses that respond to each other in alternating verses. Men and things, plants and beasts merge their activities as if conspiring toward the same goal. It seems that, united by the desire to obey in concert a command valid for all, they send each other signals or respond to commands.[11] It is these signals and commands that, collected in verse, are valid as poetic themes and as calendar sayings. In each festival, as their ancestors did, all the actors strive to collaborate with Nature. The same ritual landscape imperiously proposes the same images to all of them and always has. Each one reinvents them and believes he is improvising. They all think they are collaborating effectively in the common work, as they have rediscovered, through free effort, the formulas whose power was proven by their ancestors. Fresh as restored centons,[12] the themes that can inspire the games of this traditional improvisation[13] remain, in the form of proverbs, but, freely recreated, they are chosen for their perfect appropriateness. They are valid as appropriate signs because they correspond exactly to the signs that nature repeats and invents in celebration, while in their sung jousts, men compete with traditional knowledge and inventive spirit. Preserving in them all the creative genius that had to be expended over time to perfect them, rich in efficacy, they are worth as symbols.[14]

Composed of calendrical sayings, the poems of the *Kouo fong* have been able to preserve, at the same time as the gnomic power affirmed by the Chinese tradition, an air of freshness and free grace which may invite us to call them "lieder." In these sayings remains, along with an essence of necessity which is the primary virtue of all rites, the spontaneity which is the driving force of all games. They possess the full efficacy and ever-increasing youthfulness of games and rites. They will never take on the aspect of worn-out metaphors to which a definite and abstract meaning can be given. They are living symbols, overflowing with affinities, brimming with evocative power and, as it were, symbolic omnivalence. They cannot fail to dictate to men, with a first gesture, all the appropriate acts to help nature and, to which they always know how to remind, with a single sign, all their traditional duties. In

---

11   *Civ. Chin.*, p.187.
12   The French word "centons" is the plural of "cento": In music and literature, a composition made up of selections from the works of various authors or composers; a pasticcio; a medley. The equivalent word in English is the same: "cento", but when using the plural "centons", it tends to be confused with a similar word, with a slightly different meaning (a patched coat), hence this clarification.
13   This mixture of traditional inspiration and free invention can still be observed today. In February 1922, during an Annamite festival in Tonkin, the protagonists sang verses borrowed from *Che king* and then improvised in alternate songs.
14   See (*Civ. Chin.*, pp. 191, 204, 212) for examples of emblematic dances with animal motifs. Dances with floral symbols must have been no less important. One of the best preserved dances of the courtly tradition reproduces the movements of flowers and branches. The *Houainan tseu* (ch. XIX) says of a dancer: "Her body is an autumnal iris in the wind."

the spring festivities, the young people who pass by the river, dancing and with their clothes raised, sing these verses:

> *It is the flood at the ford where the water rises!*
> *It's the call of the partridges crying!*[15]

The theme of the spring flood is echoed in this song in the theme of the search for love. But in the reality of the feast, these signs of solidarity originate mutually, and both are mutually awakened as soon as the dance and song of the young couples symbolically realize one or the other; it is this dance and song that, by bringing about the mating of the partridges and the season's flooding, will succeed in making *all* the signs of spring appear. The doe that is killed to offer its skin as a wedding gift, the white bed of grass on which this gift is to be presented when the time comes for marriage in autumn, the petitions of boys moved by the influence of *Yin* (the feminine principle) as winter approaches, and, in the case of young girls, the memory of the spring days when they had the opportunity to marry, the memory of the spring days when they were to obey the call of *Yang* (the male principle), all these themes which raise each other, but which also evoke a host of corresponding themes, can, in a single verse, suggest all the emotions and invite all the acts which the rites and games of the seasonal festivals present as a linked whole. But, instead of singing:

> *On the plain lies the dead hind!*
> *Wrap her in white grass!*
> *A little girl dreams of spring!*
> *Good young man, ask for her!*[16]

it will suffice, *in two words*, to recall the theme "dreaming of spring," for games and rites, human gestures and natural correspondences to appear in their necessary and intended connection. And if a poet uses even the word "spring" alone, he will not only suggest, with its ritual procession of images, all the alternatives of amorous anguish, but he will think to compel the hearer to feel, in full accord with the wills of nature and the customs of heaven, a feeling so active that it must have the value of a vow and a command. We can see why the word, like the formula itself, is, in Chinese, not a mere sign, but a symbol, why the right word is not a term with a clear and distinct meaning, but an expression in which bursts forth the force of requesting and compelling. The word, isolated, continues to appear as the most active verb of a phrase that evokes in its omnipotence of sign and symbol. It retains, condensed in it, all the virtues (the realizing energy of the imperative, the ingenious piety of the optative, the inspired charm of the play, the adequate power of the rite) possessed by the poetic subject in the first place, rite, prayer, command, play.

Some of the poems of the *Kouo fong* remain, in the form in which they have been handed down to us, quite close to the impromptu songs of the old rustic fes-

---

15 Granet, *Fêtes et chansons anciennes de la Chine*, p. 102.
16 *Ibid.*, p. 123.

tivals. But most of them, whether reworked folk songs or compositions based on borrowings, stand as more or less well-known works. There is no reason to reject the tradition that presents them as court poetry. Nothing is more instructive than the detailed explanation based on this tradition. The Chinese take it for granted that poetic themes, calendar sayings, put into couplets by wise poets or faithful vassals (all is one), had the power to instruct and correct.[17] Allegorical sentence, every consecrated comparison reveals the order of nature and, consequently, reveals and provokes Fate. The partridge that sings, calling the male at the time of the spring floods, can – without naming her, and yet giving her advice, hurling an invective at her – evoke the princess Yi Kiang. This lady, who married Duke Siuan of Wei (718-699 BC) after having been her father's wife, was destined to end badly. She committed suicide as soon as the duke replaced her in his favor with the supposed wife of his own son. The theme of the search for love is linked to a whole set of natural customs and human observances. In this case (and by effect of an intention that need not even be expressed), the singing partridges indicate to Yi Kiang that she will have to pay for her irregular union with Duke Siuan with the unfortunate fate that befits those who contravene the order of things.[18] A time-honored metaphor gives the poet the power to accurately curse and link a given culprit to his fate. The occasional use of a poetic theme does not, as we see, detract from its convening power. This remains true even if the theme deviates completely from its original meaning. Princess Siuan Kiang, initially destined for the eldest son of Duke Siuan of Wei, married the duke himself and then, like a true stepmother, had her first fiancé killed. She would later marry a younger brother of her unfortunate suitor and finally regularize her situation. To invite her to marry properly, a poet is said to have sung to her:

> *The quails go in pairs*
> *And magpies come in pairs!*

Now, the same verses were used (in 545 BC) in a singing tournament given on the occasion of a diplomatic banquet. The diplomats at these gatherings did not invent anything, neither verses nor themes. They contented themselves with giving an indirect meaning to the proverbial verses by means of an insinuation made evident by the circumstances. In this way, they think they are seducing wills and forcing decisions. When, for the benefit of a foreign minister, an ambitious man sang:

> *The quails go in pairs*
> *and magpies go in pairs!*

the theme of the pursuit of love was used, by virtue of a latent transposition, to induce a statesman not to marry, but to be secretly linked with a conspirator.[19] By the mere fact of speaking with authority, the poetic theme can say anything. If the authors speak by means of proverbs, it is not that they think in a common way, but

---

17   Ibid., pp. 78 ff; 140 ff; 235 ff.
18   Ibid., pp. 101 ff; Id., Civ. Chin.
19   Granet, *Fêtes et chansons anciennes de la Chine*, p. 36; Id., Civ. Chin.

BOOK I - CHAPTER II - STYLE   39

that the most suitable and refined way of making their thought clear is to slip it into a tried formula from which it will take credit. The centons have a kind of neutral and concrete force that can be latently particularized to infinity, retaining in the most singular applications a real power of invitation to action.

Conventional expressions, powerful for suggesting action, can also be used to describe, even with singular vigor. There is a "narrative passage" in the *Che King* where European taste has been able to discover a small "vivid image." It is, it is said, a drinking scene in which we see "the drunken courtiers quarrelling."[20] In fact, it is a question of the vassals getting drunk as a duty during a feast offered to the Ancestors; it is not these who have least to drink, or at least the concourse, whose souls the spirits have possessed. They all become agitated, inspired by a traditionally regulated frenzy, *"overturning vases and pots"* (after having used them in a sanctifying orgy, the sacred dishes must be broken),[21] *"dancing restlessly, staggering"* (thus must act those who work to enter into a trance and pretend to carry the weight of a holy spirit),[22] *"rising and taking turns"* (the relay dance is necessary in ceremonies in which the circulation of souls is sought),[23] *"the caps tilted about to fall off"* (of course, the expression may be quaint; in reality, it has a ritual value; an essential rite of the orgiastic feasts obliged the actors to tear off each other's headdresses, for the liberated hair was to unfurl "like stiff banners" in the whirlwind that preceded the final prostration) *"dancing endlessly in a whirlwind"* (this whirling dance, which was to be performed with the body bowed, the head inverted and the dancer seeming to take off as if sucked by the wind, is here represented by a descriptive auxiliary which forms a repeated theme, in prose and verse, as soon as the ecstatic dance is evoked). If Western critics find that this "picturesque" description offers a sharp contrast to the passages of the "strictly religious" odes, which they consider "extremely banal," it is because they forget that nothing, apart from the dance, has more ritual value than drunkenness – that no act involves so much piety as dancing in a state of intoxication – and, finally, that the ballets preparing for ecstasy are the most meticulously regulated of all. Thus, in describing an orgiastic dance, the author has not indulged in fancy any more than if he had undertaken to evoke a more sympathetic-looking ceremonial. At solemn receptions, a master of ceremonies supervises every detail of the greetings, while a chronicler hastens to record the smallest faults in dress. But at sacred drinking parties there is also a chronicler and an officer of ceremonies who are obliged to call to order and to point out with infamy those who, by becoming inappropriately drunk or staggering about inappropriately, shirk the slightest duties of ecstatic drunkenness.[24] While the actors, by correct gesticulation, perfect the ceremony, the poet who evokes the scene, not to paint a "picture" but *to provide a model*, applies himself, *if he is sincere* (if he puts *all*

---

20   Maspero, *La Chine antique*, p. 430.
21   On the destruction of ritual instruments, see *Li ki*, C., II, p. 218.
22   De Groot has given an excellent description of the characteristic movements of spirit-bearers (*Fêtes d'Emouy*, p. 289).
23   *Tch'ou tseu*, 2 (*Li houen*).
24   *Che king*, L., p. 395 and notes on p. 399.

his heart into obeying the custom), by using the traditional formulas which alone are appropriate. His description may be thought to be picturesque, but it is only intended to be effective.

The effectiveness of the formulas is also the main objective of the poems sung during sacred ceremonies. To declare the "odes" of the *Che king* (whose themes have been taken up indefinitely by religious poetry) banal is to misunderstand them; they are no less rich than any other piece in descriptive vigor and nuance of feeling. To confer the coming of age, using the power of realization possessed by the agreed formulas, the young nobleman is wished (made capable) of reaching the great age at which "the eyebrows lengthen," at which "the hair turns yellow."[25] These are very concrete wishes, the repercussions of which are infinite. Each time they are formulated, they arouse a singular emotion. A poet who, for example, wants to bring luck to the prince of Song[26] will use the same centons. In addition to the beneficent power that it retains in its entirety and an air of impersonal grandeur from which the poem takes its lyrical flight, the theme of the yellowish hair and long eyebrows can serve perfectly well (the glosses affirm it) to express a desire impregnated with a very intimate effusion and particularized by the most determined intention. It is not convenient that the prayer, the vow, the commandment seem too particularized. They would lose in efficacy what they seem to gain in precision. On the contrary, stereotyped formulas, whose power of concrete suggestion is indefinite, have the power to indicate, by some secret extension, the finer nuances of desire; those same nuances which, in analytical terms, would be inexpressible. The sentences of *Che king* which are written in the most proverbial language are certainly those (public opinion attests) where the subtlest thoughts are indicated. The same rule applies to works of all times, of all genres. The odes richest in consecrated expressions are the most admired. In none of them are conventional formulas so crowded as in that type of mystical meditations[27] where Chinese lyricism gives its highest note. Density in centons does not only measure the poet's traditional knowledge; the greater density is the mark of deeper thought.

The ancient forms of lyrical improvisation make us understand the value of poetic sayings as symbols, their power of suggestion, their descriptive vigor. The essential fact to bear in mind is that the role of the centons is no less important in prose than in poetry, in the cultured style than in the vulgar language. The historian's task seems to be to record singular facts. It is true that by means of names and dates he places the events. But for locating, dating and naming, there are agreed forms; they alone imply a kind of judgment; the historian has already passed judgment when he seems to begin a narrative. This narrative, moreover, will be no more than a series of judgments, rendered by means of time-honored and, consequently, decisive formulas. Confucius was a master in the skillful use of these formulas; he also succeeded in showing "what rites and equity are"; such is the ideal

---

25   *Yi li*, Steele, *I Li, or the Book of Etiquette and Ceremonial*, vol. II, pp. 14 and 15. The translator has lost all concreteness of these expressions.

26   *Che king*, C., p. 461.

27   They belong to the genus called *fou*, which will be discussed later.

of the historian, according to Sseu-ma Ts'ien, well versed in this field.[28] However, Sseu-ma Ts'ien himself composed narratives which give Westerners the impression of a "wonderfully clear picture," such as the passage in the *Historical Memoirs* where he shows how the Empress Lu took revenge on a rival.[29] It would be easy to show that, being composed of folkloric elements, this narrative is written entirely in stereotyped expressions. The case is so unexceptional that an attentive reader of the Chinese Annals constantly doubts: do they intend to present him with particular and singularized facts, or to teach him what he should or should not do? Is the writing in ritualistic terms merely a stylistic bias, or is the story simply a succession of ritual incidents? It is not necessary to decide; in fact, the taste for prefabricated formulas is only one aspect of the general adherence to a conformist morality. Proverbial expressions can serve to draw the physical and moral portrait of characters whose constant ideal was to mark their resemblance to this or that typical hero. They may also serve to relate events adequately if men's actions always seek to conform to ceremonial forms. The biographies are *rightly* considered the most vivid and informative parts of the Chinese Annals. It is most likely that most of them are derived from *panegyrics*.[30] It is true, in any case, that they seem all the more successful the richer they are in centons. One of the most praised pieces of history, Sseu-ma Ts'ien's biography of Kouan tseu, is nothing more than a "Chinese discourse," a mosaic of proverbs. In it we find, surprisingly, the main merit of historical accounts: it teaches attitudes. – I suppose we can already guess that, of all authors, those who must possess the genius of the proverb to the greatest degree are philosophers. But (and this is a remarkable fact), the genius of the proverb is indispensable not only for adherents of the orthodox tradition, but also, and above all, for masters of mystical thought, for those whose object is to express the inexpressible. With the help of sayings they record the most fleeting feelings of an ecstatic experience which they present as strictly individual. In Lao tseu or Tchouang tseu, the mystical outpouring is expressed by means of traditional locutions, quite analogous to the descriptive aids whose proverbial character I have previously pointed out, while noting their indefinite power of suggestion.

Like the writers of annals, Chinese philosophers are narrators. In works of all kinds, the same anecdotes are used over and over again, so that the Western reader reading a Chinese work for the first time almost always feels that he has read it before. Sometimes the anecdotes differ in some detail of arrangement or style; sometimes the themes are retained, varying in landscape, time and place, and characters; more often they are repeated verbatim, and their form seems stereotyped. In this case, critics do not hesitate to speak of borrowings. They claim, for example, that a certain number of anecdotes common to the *Tchouang tseu* and *Lie tseu* come from a contamination of the two works. In reality, it is not even certain that the use of the same material of expressions demonstrates a community

---

28 *SMT, Introd.*, p. LIX. The book of Confucius (the *Tch'ouen ts'ieou*) is said to be the code of the true ruler.
29 *SMT, Ibid*, p. CLXIV, and t. II, p. 410; *Civ. Chin.*
30 On the latter, see *Civ. Chin.*

of doctrine or thought. The same anecdote, told in the same terms, can serve to defend very different opinions. When he speaks of the monkeys who, condemned by an impoverished breeder to a less abundant diet, indignantly refused a dinner of four taro beans[31] and a lunch of three, and then contentedly ate four taro beans in the morning and three in the evening, Lie tseu's aim is to belittle human pride and to emphasize the deep analogies between man and animal. The same fable, without the slightest change, defends, in Tchouang tseu, the thesis that all judgment is subjective; this is a fortunate fact: if one knows how to take advantage of the variability of judgments, which can, fortunately, reach the absurd, one has the means to train monkeys and govern men.[32] Each author, in order to compose his mind, borrows from tradition, but it is enough that the spirit of the developments in which it is inserted differs for the traditional account to serve to provoke the most diverse movements of thought. The stereotyped anecdotes form a background from which the most original authors drink. The success of these fables lies in the neutral power that comes from them; it is, as in the case of simple formulas and also of words, all the more active because, from the outside, these fables are more common in appearance. It is not so much a matter of making them express ideas, *one by one*, as of using their prestige to endow *the whole* development with authority. Their virtue is not to define the thought in its elements, but to accredit it as a whole. They dispose the mind to accept a suggestion. They do not make the mind penetrate, in a logical order, with ideas determined from the beginning. They set the imagination in motion and make it docile, while the general movement of development invites it to move in a definite direction. Thought is propagated (rather than transmitted) from author to reader (let us say from master to disciple; let us say better: from the leader to the faithful) without the latter being spared the least effort, without, moreover, being allowed the slightest facility of escape. They are not asked to accept the ideas, in their detail and their system, after having been allowed to control them analytically. Dominated by a global suggestion, they find themselves immediately apprehended by a whole system of notions.

The set of anecdotes that gave authority to the ideas, far from diversifying, tended to be reduced, while each anecdote was expressed more attractively in invariable terms. It is easy to understand that the choice to arouse thought rather than inform it had great advantages both in the life of the court and in the teaching of the sects. In these circles, the main thing is to get along with others, increase intellectual ingenuity and develop intuition. Moreover, in relations between people, thanks to the mimicry that accompanies formulas and the art that can be used to free words, the most precise suggestions can be insinuated in the most neutral of formulas. But the significant fact is that written literature has settled for a limited fund of schematized stories, which has tended to reduce them in number and

---

31   Common name for several tropical food tubers (*colocasia, alocasia amorphophophallus, xanthosoma*) (TN).

32   P. Wieger, *Les Pères du système taoïste*, pp. 103 and 219.

likewise to reduce each of them to a simple saying of invariable form.³³ Instead of recounting, with anecdotal details, that K'ouei, a *one-legged* (*yi tsiu*) dancer, was sufficient by himself (*yi tsiu*) to animate with irresistible movement the sacred feasts of the royal court, it was preferred, in one development or another, to limit oneself to writing *K'ouei yi tsiu* or even to evoke K'ouei's name. Thus, it was pointed out that a well-chosen minister was sufficient to direct the affairs of the State effectively, or that a uniped was not surpassed in the art of moving by the legless beings or the millipedes. And one or the other sense was imposed depending on whether the overall development was intended to awaken the idea, at times, that by virtue of the equivalence of the various states of nature efficiency results from the simple conservation of natural characters, and on the contrary that a strict adaptation to function is the true principle of efficiency.³⁴ The idea, in both cases, takes its force from the same mystical theme linked to a ritual practice. Dancing on one foot is one of the great duties of the chief; charged with fertilizing nature, he causes the sap to rise by dancing.³⁵ As we see, the authority of a mythical complex linked to a system of ritual practices remains intact and multiple in the centon where this complex tends to crystallize.

Thus, the mythical scheme, the literary theme, the word itself, have been able to preserve, in their freshness, the omnivalent plasticity of symbols, even when, without the direct aid of mimicry, they are employed by written literature. Varied, powerful, refined, this literature cares little for discursive forms. The most cultured prose preserves the same ideal as the most archaic poetry. It prefers symbols that speak with more authority. It does not matter that they can hardly evoke clear and definite concepts; the main thing is that they suggest strongly and provoke adherence. The written word (with the help of emblematic writing) seeks first of all to preserve all the efficacy of the living word; it strives to preserve the force of the chants that are accompanied by ritual mimicry.

II. Rhythms

Mime and rhythm, together with the use of descriptive aids, are the principal means of action available to a speaker of Chinese. Even in written prose, rhythm is no less essential than in poetry. Rhythm is what binds speech together and makes it comprehensible.

Just as words, root-like words, which appear in locutions, are simply juxtaposed, none of them being appreciably modified in form by the use made of them

---

33   Chinese sculptors and draftsmen (who also intend to teach) do not need a large number of motifs, any more than do poets and philosophers. Those they use may often have as their legend a stereotyped anecdote, a concretization of a mythical theme (cf. Granet, *Danses et légendes...*, p. 598; *Id., Fêtes et chansons anciennes...*, note 2 on p. 236, and *Civ. Chin.*).

34   Granet, *Danses et légendes...*, pp. 505 and 509.

35   The tradition of kings on one foot was maintained in Siam and Cambodia until the nineteenth century. After plowing a furrow (desecration of the soil by the chief at the beginning of an agricultural campaign), they had to lean against a tree and stand on one foot (the right foot placed on the left knee) (cf. Leclère, *Le Cambodge*, p. 297). Cf. *infra*, Book II, Ch. IV.

or by their contact with neighboring words, so stories, which are voluntarily kept in their traditional form, follow one another in a work without the need to mark their connections; similarly, the stereotyped formulas which line up to form a sentence follow one another without influencing each other and are arranged on the same plane. All the elements of the discourse seem, intangible in their form and isolated in the composition, preserving a kind of jealous independence. The formulas, elements of the sentence, comprise only a small number of words. Nothing, except their position, determines the role and relations of these words; even so, the rule of position is not valid in all cases; the syntactic value of words is only perceived when the overall sense of the formula has first been grasped; this sense is apprehended at once, but on condition that the formula is brief. On the other hand, short phrases are sometimes found in quite a large number in the same sentence. They are simply placed end to end, separated, in some cases, by words that deserve the name of oral punctuation. They indicate different kinds of pause of the thought rather than point to different modes of connection and relationship. Isolated by them, rather than connected, fixed-form formulas follow one another; they seem much less like propositions than adverbial locutions. In written Chinese (if we were to read simply with the eyes) there is often nothing to distinguish, as dominant, one locution among the others; nor would we see, clearly, the various subordinations of these. To understand, the voice must punctuate and find the movement of the sentence.

This is the reason why, since ancient times, teaching has consisted of a recitation sung by the teacher, taken over by the pupils, who were trained to "divide the sentences of the authors according to their meaning."[36] This learning process was repeated almost for each author, and always by the sole process of sung recitation, without any exercise comparable to grammatical or logical analysis. To find the meaning, the essential thing, therefore, is to know the punctuation. It seems (one imagines) that, in order to facilitate reading, the Chinese must have thought of publishing punctuated books very early on. In fact, it took them longer to come to this conclusion than people writing a language in which there is little difficulty in discerning the end of sentences. And even a few years ago, they still reserved their typographical genius for the invention of signs (sometimes multicolored, in deluxe editions) used to mark important passages and notable words in texts without punctuation.

These practices are significant. They show that, in that exercise of the mind which is reading, the important thing is not to spare the reader's efforts, and, perhaps even, to get him, not having spared his effort, to bestow his admiration or assent with more abandon. In esoteric lectures, or even in simple verbiage, the primary object of the speaker is to slip into an accumulation of formulas rich in neutral and urgent solicitations a locution or an acting verb, whose precise force and background the vulgar does not deserve to guess, but which will perhaps be perceived by awakened minds by some agreed gesture or delivery. In the same way, the writer, his exegetes and his editors, if they agree to mark the active words and

---

36 *Li ki*, C., II, pp. 30 and 34.

the dominant locutions, will refrain from indicating the movements of detail and the secret articulations of the thought. This thought, in all its richness, will only be communicated to the reader, who, if his mind awakens to the powerful and furtive signal that a formula or a verb will have made him hear, will be able, by an effort comparable to that of an adept seeking initiation, to penetrate the rhythmic essence of the phrase.

To compose in Chinese, there is no other way (since this language has refused to ask for any support to a varied and precise syntax) than to resort to the magic of rhythms. We only succeed in expressing ourselves after having trained ourselves to use, in all their effectiveness, not only the proverbial formulas, but also the consecrated rhythms.

Chinese works are divided into genres, which native critics consider to be clearly defined. The classification is determined by the type of inspiration (which seems to be linked to a certain moral attitude) and, at the same time, by the rhythmic system; the latter seems to be imposed as a general attitude and corresponds to a certain way of looking at the world and life. For example, all the ancient *fou*, which present themselves as elegiac meditations show a propensity for a certain quality of mystical effusion; this type of inspiration is rhythmically translated by a sort of sigh which is necessarily placed at the end of each verse. The particular rhythm of the *fou* could, of course, be characterized by many other rules. No one has ever felt the need to define them; one learns to compose a *fou*, not because one is taught the details of the rules, but because one trains oneself to grasp the rhythmic essence of the genre. This essence is considered significant of a particular mode of spiritual activity. It cannot be transmitted dialectically. Neither the understanding of a particular language, nor the sense of language, nor the understanding of particular rhythms, nor the sense of rhythm can be taught in chapters by a course in rhetoric. The genius of phrases and the genius of rhythms are not intended to decorate and diversify discourse. Both always merge with a power of inspiration that is indistinguishable from traditional knowledge.

These characteristics of literary learning are understandable, as well as the importance of rhythm and the success of certain rhythms, as soon as we know the ancient conditions of lyrical invention. Some of the songs of the *Kouo fong*, despite their reworking, give a good idea of these conditions. The invention of the poetic phrases that compose them is due to a traditional improvisation; it corresponds to a real test of knowledge imposed on young people at the time of their initiation. The initiation takes place during seasonal festivals. Forming choirs that compete in singing, the boys and girls face each other and answer each other in turn. Each of the verses exchanged forms a verse or rather a couplet; a couplet is made as soon as two verses are exchanged. The following couplets contain hardly more than variants of the two themes opposed in the first couplet.[37] Generally, one of these themes records a signal given by nature, the other gives the formula of the gestures with which humans respond to this signal. This exchange of lines highlights the

---

37 Granet, *Fêtes et chansons...*, p. 224 ff.

solidarity established by the festival between all the actors delegated by society and nature. The themes (human theme, natural theme) are paired by their symmetry and acquire the value of symbols; they call each other, provoke each other, provoke each other. Rhythm is inherent to the phrases and is one of the elements of their effectiveness, because the symbolic equivalence of the realities evoked by the twin couplets is made sensible by their rhythmic analogy.

But the rhythmic analogy also increases the power of the symbols; it multiplies their affinities and their power of evocation. When the end of the equinoctial assemblies comes, and Yang and Yin, the masculine and feminine principles of the alternation of the seasons, oppose each other and call each other to play face to face, the poignant signs that prelude their marriage multiply in the World. These multiple signs are taken up in alternating verses by opposing choruses. They serve to compose twin litanies, coupled incantations linking wills and matching desires.[38] The antithetical forces whose union gives life to the universe will celebrate with discipline their equinoctial nuptials, as soon as, to the sound of clay tambourines, the dancing choirs, evoking the rolling of the Thunder and the roar of the Waters, have, in a stomping procession, slowly traversed the ritual landscape, or leapt, without tiring, over the sacred mound. Sometimes, in the songs, the themes follow one another in a stumbling progression, and sometimes, like a leaping refrain, the same theme is taken up again without a break, barely nuanced by a few variations. Whether the phrases are repeated or accumulated, the same hammering effect is added to discipline the refrains to their original effectiveness.[39] In all genres, even in the genre of the choruses, the same effect of hammering is added.

In all genres, even in prose, where, seeking nobility and strength, they want to act by first communicating the feeling of orderly and powerful balance (such are the characteristics of the *kou-wen* style, the ideal of cultured prose), Chinese authors compose using strictly balanced short sentences linked together by rhythmic analogy. They accumulate them without fear of redundancy, sometimes repeating, like a refrain, a dominant formula which acquires the value of a central motif (and which we would translate in the form of a main proposition); or, thanks to subtle processes of parallelism, they replace a main theme with related formulas; the idea then increases in strength, sustained rather than diversified by the development of these thematic variations.

Rhythm in Chinese prose has the same function as syntax elsewhere. The preferred rhythms of this prose derive from choral poetry. However, it sometimes uses more abrupt, if not freer, rhythms that were also created for poetry. The jerky verses and breathless stanzas of *fou* contrast with the regular verses (*che*) and couplets of the *Che king*. While the latter have the slow majesty of the ensemble dances and the quiet symmetry of the choral songs, the others bear the mark of a very different dance and music. Some of the older *fou* accompanied ceremonies of a magical

---

38 We have a lament of this kind; tradition attributes to it the value of a procedural incantation. It was fought in court by rhythmically linking proverbs. Granet, *op. cit.* pp. 261 ff.

39 *Ibid.*, pp. 235, 266, 267.

rather than religious character.[40] The object was to evoke souls (*tchao houen*), not as in the regular ceremonies of ancestral worship, to come and take possession of their descendants, as is right and proper, but to come into contact with a world of spiritual energy through their intermediary; the object was to acquire an increase of life, personal power, and magical prestige. The essential rite of these ceremonies was a dance performed by the women, the chief's wives, or witches. Naked and perfumed, they attracted and captured the seduced souls, turning in turn a flower in their hands and passing the soul and the flower to each other when, with swollen eyes, tired of carrying the god, exhaustion threw them to the ground. However, squeezed into an enclosed room where light drums hummed accompanied by zithers and sharp flutes, the attendants, feeling the "wind that terrifies" blowing over them, heard supernatural voices rising. These graceful sabbaths are no less finely tuned ballets than the others, but the breathless evocation of spirits, punctuated by dying sighs, frenzied calls, forms a tumultuous chant where consecrated formulas clash over the spasmodic rhythm characteristic of mystical ejaculations.

This rhythm has remained particular to the *fou*. However, it is to be thought that, well known to the writers of the mystical school, it has not ceased to influence their more varied and nervous prose. In this prose, rhythmic nuances abound, which take the place in Chinese of what we call syntactic nuances. They serve to organize the discourse. They also serve to give sentences a particular vibration; this, by situating them in a certain world of mental activity, qualifies their inspiration and gives them a specific efficacy.

We can hardly understand a Chinese author until we have penetrated the rhythmic secrets by means of which he signals and emits the last word of his thought. On the other hand, no author could make himself heard if he did not know how to use the virtue of rhythms. On this point, no one has possessed the mastery of Tchouang tseu. However, Tchouang Tseu seems to us to be the least inscrutable of the Chinese thinkers. At the same time, he gives the impression of being also the most profound and the most refined. His power and rhythmic fluency seem to correspond to the free play of a very concrete intelligence. Should we not deduce that, in its expression, Chinese thought, as soon as it rises a little, is of a strictly poetic and musical nature? In order to transmit itself, it does not seek to rely on a material of clear and distinct signs. It communicates itself, plastically and, so to speak, surreptitiously – not discursively, detail after detail, by means of the tricks of language – but en bloc and as if by coincident movements, induced, mind to mind, by the magic of rhythms and symbols. Also, in schools where the most profound thought has flourished, it has been possible to propose as an ideal of true and concrete teaching a teaching without words.[41]

* * *

---

40 The most characteristic pieces are (in the *Tch'ou tseu*) the *Yuan yeou* and the *Tchao houen*.

41 Let us note here the link between the doctrine of mute teaching and the practice of confirming the convert by smiling. It is also by smiling that a father recognizes a child as his own, at the very moment he gives him a name, i.e., a personality and a soul. We can see the

The Chinese language has been able to become a powerful language of civilization and a great literary language despite its limitations in terms of phonetic richness and graphic comfort, without claiming to create an abstract material of expression or possessing syntactic tools. It managed to preserve a totally concrete symbolic value for words and phrases. It knew how to organize the expression of thought through rhythm. As if it wanted, above all, to save the mind from the fear that ideas would become sterile if expressed mechanically and economically, it refused to offer them those convenient instruments of specification and apparent coordination which are abstract signs and grammatical devices. It stubbornly resisted formal precision, for the sake of adequate, concrete and synthetic expression. The imperious power of the verb understood as complete gesture, order, vow, prayer and rite, that is what this language has tried to retain, effortlessly abandoning everything else. The Chinese language does not seem to be organized to record concepts, analyze ideas or expound doctrines discursively. It is entirely configured to communicate sentimental attitudes, to suggest behavior, to convince, to convert.

These features will not seem uninteresting, if we do not forget that Chinese is the language of civilization or, if you will, the instrument of culture that has most easily withstood the longest test.

---

relationship between the techniques and doctrines of expression and the magic of the breaths. Words, formulas and rhythms are both symbols and things.

Book II
THE GUIDING IDEAS

A Chinese, especially if he is a philosopher and intends to teach, would never resort to other formulas to detail his opinions, except those whose efficacy was guaranteed by their antiquity. As for the notions which seem intended to order thought, they are indicated in all authors by symbols which, more than others, seem to be endowed with an indeterminate efficacy. Rejecting by this very fact any abstraction, these symbols denote guiding ideas whose principal merit lies in their character of synthetic notions. They play the role of categories, but they are concrete categories.

Nothing suggests that any sage of ancient China felt the need to appeal to notions comparable to our abstract ideas of number, time, space and causality… It is, on the other hand, with the help of a pair of concrete symbols (the Yin and Yang) that the Sages of all the "Schools" try to translate a feeling of *Rhythm* which allows them to conceive the relations of Time, Space and Numbers by conceiving them as a set of concerted games. The Tao is the emblem of a still more synthetic notion, totally different from our idea of cause and much broader; I cannot say that by it is evoked the unique Principle of a universal order; rather I must say that by it is evoked, in its totality and its unity, an Order at once ideal and acting. Tao, the supreme category, and Yin and Yang, the second categories, are active Symbols. They order both the order of the World and the order of the Spirit. No one thinks of defining them. On the other hand, everyone gives them a quality of efficacy, which does not seem to be distinguished from a rational value.

These cardinal notions inspire unanimous confidence in the Chinese. Most Western interpreters, however, see them as products of one or another doctrinal thought. They treat them as learned conceptions and therefore susceptible to abstract definition or qualification. They usually begin by looking for equivalents in the conceptual language of our philosophers. They usually end, as soon as they present them as scholastic entities, with statements as curious as they are useless. They seem to testify that Chinese thought belongs to a mentality that can be qualified as "prelogical" or "mythical"[1] (to use fashionable expressions).

To analyze these notions, I have had to use mythical or ritual themes; this is because I wanted to respect what makes them original, that is, their quality as synthetic and effective notions. Without attempting to define or qualify them, I have tried to recognize their content and to show their multiple uses. The analysis required a certain meticulousness. So much the worse if it may seem slow... So much the worse if it requires some detours... We can hardly indicate the role of the notions of Yin and Yang without first saying how Time and Space are imagined. It was also necessary to provide information on the Chinese conception of Numbers, to which they attribute mainly classificatory and protocol functions, before addressing the notion of Tao, supreme category of thought, and the analysis of the Chinese attitudes towards physics and logic. The subject imposes this process of successive approaches. Only in this way can it be made clear that the guiding ideas of Chinese thought, although concrete, have the value of categories; their quality as concrete notions in no way prevents them from introducing into the life of the mind, or pointing out in it, a principle of organization and intelligibility.

---

1 Hackmann, *Chinesische Philosophie*, p. 35.

Chapter I
TIME AND SPACE

In China, thought, whether scholarly or vulgar, obeys a representation of Space and Time which is not purely empirical. It is distinct from the impressions of duration and extension that make up individual experience. It is impersonal. It imposes itself with the authority of a category. But Time and Space do not appear as neutral places to the Chinese; they have no need to harbor abstract concepts in them.

It has not occurred to any philosopher to conceive of Time as a monotonous duration consisting of the succession, according to a uniform motion, of qualitatively similar moments. No philosopher has found it interesting to consider Space as a simple extension resulting from the juxtaposition of homogeneous elements, as an extension of which all parts would be superimposable. All prefer to see Time as a set of *eras*, seasons and epochs, Space as a complex of *domains*, climates and directions. In each direction, extension is singularized and acquires the particular attributes of a climate or a domain. At the same time, duration is diversified into periods of a different nature, each with the characteristics of a season or an epoch. But, while two parts of Space may differ radically from each other, and, likewise, two portions of Time, each period is linked to a climate, each direction to a season. To each individualized part of duration corresponds a singular portion of extension. The same nature belongs to them in common, indicated, for both, by an *indivisible* set of attributes.

An era, a world, both new, were constituted, as soon as, manifesting the virtue of the *Tcheou*, a red raven appeared. Red (among other symbols) characterizes the *Tcheou* Era, the *Tcheou* Empire, and continues to characterize both the Summer and the South.¹ The virtue of sociability (*jen*) is an attribute of the East. An ethnographer engaged in describing the customs of Eastern countries finds, to begin with, that there is exemplary goodness. He then tells the story of the end of the most famous hero of these regions. He was a being without stiffness, without bones, all muscle, and he perished for the very reason that he was too good. Muscles belong to the East, like the liver and the color green, which is the color of spring; it is the season in which nature manifests her goodness, the virtue of the East.² Humps, like mountains, abound in the West, which they qualify, just as the harvest basket evokes the Autumn. A hump is an excrescence of the skin; the skin depends on the lung, the lung of Autumn, and equally on the color white. But the skin signifies leather and armor, which signifies war and punishment. Thus the barbarians of the West are said to be in the mood for fighting, while executions, whether criminal or military, are reserved for the autumn, and the genius of punishment, notable for its white hair, resides in the West. Hair is like skin and white is the significant emblem of the West and of Autumn, as it is of the Yin era. This was inaugurated by the reign of T'ang the Victorious, a hero famous for the punishments he inflicted and for the way he walked with his body hunched over.³

These examples will suffice to show that, having to locate in Time and Space, not definite and distinct concepts, but symbols rich in affinities, the Chinese had no disposition to conceive, as two independent and neutral spheres, an abstract Time and Space. On the contrary, in order to accommodate their symbolic games, it was in their interest to preserve a solidarity favorable to the interaction of symbols between linked representations of Space and Time, with a maximum of concrete attributes.

As long as we do not see in Space and Time two independent concepts or two autonomous entities, they can constitute a medium of action which is also a receptive medium. Discontinuous and supportive, they assume qualities together, while receiving determinations. Any location, spatial or temporal, is therefore sufficient to particularize, and in the same way to impose on Time as on Space one or the other concrete characteristics. We can act on Space by means of temporal symbols; on Time, by means of spatial symbols; on both at the same time, by means of the multiple and linked symbols that point out the particular aspects of the Universe. Does a guitarist want to recover summer in the middle of winter? If he knows his art well, he has only to make the note of the scale resonate which is the emblem of Summer, of Red, of the South.⁴ To grasp the masculine energy of Yang in its strength, we must face the South; a wise general (whatever route he gives his army) always knows how to grasp this energy; he only needs to unfurl the banner of the Red Bird⁵ in the vanguard.

---

1   *Civ. chin*, p. 222.

2   *Heou Han chou*, p. 115; *Houai-nan tseu*, p. 4.

3   *Houai-nan tseu*, p. 4; *Song chou*, p. 27; *Kouo yu*, p. 8; Granet, *Danses et légendes...*, p. 258.

4   *Lie tseu*, P. Wieger, *Les Pères du système taoïste*, p. 141.

5   *Civ. Chin*, p. 292.

Book II - Chapter I - Time and Space

Time and space are never conceived independently of the concrete actions they exercise as complexes of solidary symbols, independently of the actions that can be exercised upon them by means of symbols called to singularize them. The words *che* and *fang* apply, the former to all portions of duration, the latter to all parts of extension, but each time considered, like the others, under a singular aspect. These terms evoke neither Space *per se*, nor Time *per se*. *Che* appeals to the idea of circumstance, the idea of opportunity (favorable or not for a given action); *fang*, to the idea of orientation, of site (favorable or not for a particular case). Forming a complex of symbolic conditions at once determining and determined, Time and Space are always imagined as a set of groupings, concrete and diverse, of rites and occasions.

These groupings are the object of a knowledge which, by the matter on which it is exercised, as well as by its practical purposes, is distinguished from the sciences of extension and those of duration. The ancient Chinese were long admired for their astronomical chronology. Today, it is said that they received belatedly from abroad their first geometrical notions and all the precision of their astronomy.[6] It is not necessary to enter here into a debate in which the lack of information makes itself cruelly felt. It will suffice to point out, on the one hand, that Chinese techniques would hardly have attained the perfection they have if they had not been based on elementary geometrical knowledge; on the other hand, philosophical speculation has always been based, if not limited, on *knowledge* whose purpose is *to classify, from the point of view of action and by their particular efficacy, places and occasions*. The sages hoped to discover the principles of a supreme art. The object of this art, which takes the place of physics as well as morality, is to order the Universe at the same time as Society. These last concerns of the philosophers give a glimpse of the fundamental character of Chinese ideas concerning Space and Time. The collective representations from which they derive are nothing more than the translation of the principles that presided over the distribution of human groupings; the study of these representations merges with a study of social morphology.

* * *

The proper virtue of Time is to proceed by revolution. This cyclic character likens it to the round and contrasts it with Space, whose first character is to be square. Such are, so to speak, the pure forms of duration and extension. Each of the intermediate forms, combinations of the round and the square – as, for example, the oval[7] – are only the symbol of a particular interaction of Space and Time. We have seen that the convexity of mountains and arched backs is the emblem of an extension of an autumnal character; the whole of Space is formed by its connection with a kind of Time. But Space, in principle, is square; any surface, therefore, is, in itself, square (so that to give the dimension of the area illuminated by the light produced, for example, by a large lantern, it will suffice to indicate the dimension

---

6   See on this subject Biot, *Astronomie chinoise*; D'Oldenberg, *Nakshatra und Sieou*; De Saussure, *Les Origines de l'astronomie chinoise*; Maspero, *La Chine antique*, pp. 607 ff; Rey, *La Science orientale*, pp. 333 ff.
7   *Tch'ouen ts'ieou fan lou*, p. 7.

of one of its four sides).⁸ The Earth, which is square, is divided into squares. The outer walls of the principalities must form a square, as well as the walls of the cities they enclose, the fields and camps also being square.⁹ Each side of the earth corresponds to a direction. Fields, buildings and cities, likewise, must be oriented. The determination of the orientations, as well as that of the locations (the word *fang*,¹⁰ to orient, to place, still has the meaning of square and square) corresponds to the Chief, since he presides over the religious assemblies.¹¹ The techniques of division and planning of space (surveying, urban planning, architecture and political geography) and the geometrical speculations that they imply are apparently related to the practices of public worship.

The faithful, in effect, were formed into squares. The Altar of the Earth, around which the great gatherings were usually held, was a square mound; its top was covered with yellow earth (the color of the Center); its sides (facing the four directions), lined with green, red, white or black earth. *This sacred square represents the whole Empire.* A property was obtained at the moment of receiving a clod of earth taken from the Altar of the Earth. This clod would be white and taken from the Western side if the fief granted belonged to the West, green if it was in the East.¹² But when an eclipse occurs, for example, which men see as a threat of destruction, then the vassals rush to the center of the country, to save it, to reconstitute, in its integrity, the unhinged Space (and Time like it), they group together and form the square. They succeed in warding off danger if each of them presents himself with the insignia that express, if we may say so, his spatial nature and that of his fiefdom. For those of the East, who line up in the East, it will be a crossbow, green clothes and a pennant.¹³ Space is restored in all its dimensions (and even in the realm of the stars), by the sheer force of the symbols correctly arranged in the sacred place of the federal meetings.

We can see that the idea of a square Earth, of a square Space seems to be linked to a set of social rules. One of these rules, the order of the assemblies, must have played a decisive role in sensitizing and imposing on all the details of the symbols that make up the representation of Space. This explains the square shape, significant of the extension. It also explains the heterogeneous character of the latter; the symbols of the different types of space merge with the active symbols of the different social groups belonging to these spaces. But they are not only distinguished by the particularities corresponding to the attributes of the human groups that share the world. In addition to these specific differences, there is a difference in value.

The expansion does not continue indefinitely. Beyond the four sides of Space, there are, forming a kind of fringe, four vague regions called the Four Seas. In these various seas live four species of barbarians. These, related to different ani-

---

8   *Chan hai king*, p. 12; Granet, *Danses et légendes...*, note 1357.
9   *Civ. chin*, p. 272.
10 This word is used in the expression *fang che* = magician, sorcerer.
11 *Civ. Chin.*, p. 265.
12 Chavannes, *Le T'ai chan*, pp. 451 ff.
13 Granet, *La religion des Chinois*, p. 55; Id, *Danses et légendes...* p. 233.

mals, share the nature of the Beasts. The Chinese – the humans – cannot reside in the Frontiers of the World without immediately losing their status as men. The banished, whom we wish to disqualify, adopt, as soon as we expel them, the partially animal appearance that marks the beings of these deserted confines.[14] The uncultivated space admits only imperfect beings. It is only a diluted space, a vanishing extension.

The Full Space only exists when the extension is socialized. When a chief in charge of ordering the world promulgates his orders, beyond the square formed by the faithful who crowd around him; a larger square is drawn by the savage chiefs summoned to the ceremony to represent the barbarism and the distant waves where the Universe vanishes. But the barbarians of the Four Seas must line up outside the ritual enclosure that is only filled by the faithful, who are the only ones who are part of the constituted society.[15]

Thus the hierarchy of extensions is manifested and established. The extension is entirely itself, it possesses, so to speak, its integral density only in the enclosure where all its attributes are federated. The sacred place of the federal meetings is a closed world that is equivalent to the total Space and to the whole of Space. It is the place where, bringing together the symbols of its different parts, the social group knows its diversity, its hierarchy, its order, and where it becomes aware of its unique and complex force.

Only there the federated group experiences its union, the extension, compact and full, concentrated, coherent, can appear as one. The Capital, where it gathers, must be chosen (after an inspection of the extension) at a site which proves to be near the "celestial residence," at a site which, by the convergence of the rivers and the confluence of the climates, proves to be the center of the world.[16] Only in its vicinity do the measures of distance remain constant there, "to bring tribute from the four sides of the world, the *li* of the road are uniform."[17] The Chief lives in a medium of pure Space where the extension is, in a certain sense, *homogeneous,* but not because it is *empty of attributes*; at this point of convergence and union, Space is constituted in its totality, for there it receives the *set of its attributes.*

Space is sometimes imagined as composed of sectors, *singularized spaces* each corresponding to a station and which, touching at the points, unite at the center of a square; sometimes as formed of nested squares, *hierarchical spaces* which are distinguished, so to speak, a difference of tension rather than of content.[18] These squares are five; in the center is the real domain; at the edges, the barbarian frontiers. In the three central squares live the vassals, called to court more or less frequently because of the distance of their domains. Their dignity, like that of the space in which they rule, is expressed by the frequency of their communions with

---

14   Granet, *Danses et légendes…*, pp. 245 ff; 257 ff.
15   Ibid., p. 249; Id, *La religion des Chinois*, p. 52; *Li ki*, C., I, p. 726.
16   *SMT*, I, pp. 242, 243; *Tcheou li*, Biot, *Le* Tcheou li, *ou les Rites des Tcheou*, I, p. 201 and notes.
17   *SMT*, I, p. 247; *Civ. Chin.*, p. 281.
18   Granet, *Danses et légendes…*, pp. 231 ff.

the chief; they go every month, every season, or every year to the intact center of the space which is the capital; there, the sovereign delegates to them a certain power of animation from which proceeds the particular *quality of cohesion* of his domain.[19] This power of spatial animation, if it is to be exercised in a more central and noble portion of the area, must be restored more frequently at the source of all cohabitation. The dignity of spaces results from a kind of *rhythmic creation*, the capacity for coexistence that underlies, so to speak, every extension, as a function of a capacity to make it last; Space cannot be conceived independently of Time.

The need for a periodic renewal of Space is no less necessary when it is a matter of imprinting a singular character on its different portions. The King spends four years receiving visits from his vassals; then he returns the visits and travels through the fiefdoms. He cannot fail to make a tour of the Empire every five years. He regulates his journey to be in the East at the spring equinox, in the South at the summer solstice, in the West in the middle of autumn, in the North in the middle of winter. At each of these cardinal seasons, the sovereign gives audience to the feudatories of one of the four Directions. Gathering around him a quadrant of the Empire, he holds first an all-green court, then an all-red one, then a white one, then a black one, for he must, at consequent times and places, verify the insignia which proclaim and establish the proper nature of each of the quarters of the Universe.[20]

The Chief strives to order the Space by adapting the extensions to the durations, but the reason for his sovereign circulation lies first of all in the need for a rhythmic reconstitution of the Extension. The five-year reconstitution revives the cohesion he inaugurated when he came to power. At each accession, the five interlocking squares that make up the Empire return to the Capital, where all of Space must recreate itself for a time. The King then opens the gates of his square city and, expelling the wicked from the four frontiers of the world, welcomes guests from the four directions. Even in the confines of the Universe, he qualifies the different spaces. Just as it singles them out by distributing symbols according to the different places, so it hierarchizes them by conferring the insignia that reveal unequal dignities.[21] It is by means of the classification and distribution of the different spaces that it classifies them.

It is through the classification and distribution of the groups that make up human society at particular times that the Chief succeeds in *instituting and maintaining* a certain order of Space. This order may be described as feudal; indeed, it was conceived by a feudal society, and it is doubtless because this society has remained feudal in essence that Space has not ceased to be imagined as a hierarchical federation of heterogeneous zones. Characterized by a kind of coherent diversity, it is not the same *everywhere*. Nor is it *always* the same. There is only an empty space where extension is not socialized, and the cohesion of extension diminishes[22] like the memory of federal assemblies where, in a sacred enclosure that gathers them in

---

19   *Kouo yu*, 1, SMT, I, pp. 251 ff; 746 ff; *Tcheou li*, Biot, *op. cit.*, p. 167 and p. 276.
20   SMT, I, p. 62.
21   SMT, I, pp. 79 , 62; Granet, *Danses et légendes*.... pp. 249 ff.
22   To a decadent dynasty corresponds a disrupted space.

a rhythmic time, men manage to give the world a kind of unity, because it is then that the pride of belonging to a society that forms a whole and seems to be one is reinforced in them. Thus, the representation of a complex, closed and unstable Space is accompanied by a representation of Time that makes of duration a set of returns, a succession of closed, cyclical, discontinuous epochs, complete in themselves, each one centered, like Space, around a sort of point of temporal emanation.

* * *

No Chinese philosopher wanted to see in Time a parameter. For all of them, extension appears sometimes diluted, sometimes concentrated. Nor is duration always imagined to be equal to itself. The discontinuity attributed to it is not at all the effect of the variable course of the activity of the mind in individuals. It is neither anarchic nor total. The Chinese divide Time into periods, just as they divide Space into regions, but they define each of its component parts by a set of attributes.[23] This definition is accepted by all minds; to each type of Time corresponds an impersonal, though concrete, notion. This concrete character is manifested in the fact that each period is marked by the attributes proper to a season of the year, to an hour of the day. We should not immediately conclude that the Chinese constructed their conception of duration by not distinguishing Time (in the absolute sense) from atmospheric time (weather) or astronomical time. The seasons have only provided symbols for the Chinese conception of Time. If it is asked to provide them, it is because (Space was represented as closed) Time seems to have a cyclical nature and the year, with its seasons, offers the image of a cycle, as well as symbols capable of characterizing several cycles.

The Chinese representation of Time is confused with that of a liturgical order. The annual cycle of the seasons is not the prototype. This order covers a moment in history (dynasty, reign, part of a reign) that is distinguished by a set of rules or, if you will, a formula of life that singles out this period of civilization. This set of conventions includes, first of all, the decrees which, together with a particular arrangement of Space, give rise to a particular arrangement of Time. The promulgation of a *Calendar*, the inaugural decree of a reign, is the decisive act of a ceremony of coming to the throne. But before a new order of Time can be established, the old order must be abolished. Every stage of duration presupposes an eviction linked to a creation. This is true of the different stages of human life.[24] A woman does not pass from the state of daughter to the state of wife, a man does not leave life to enter death, a newborn child does not leave the world of the ancestors to enter the living part of the family unless gestures of farewell have preceded the festivities of welcome. Initial in appearance, the inaugural rite of birth, marriage and death has the value of a central rite. The power it gives off is like the propagation of a wave. Both forward and backward, marking, as it were, the peaks of a series of concentric undulations, the ceremonies, separated by periods of internment, work toward the same result as the central rite. This kind of rhythmic spread, which controls the or-

---

23 *Civ. Chin.*, pp. 27, 28, 48, 49.
24 On the liturgical use of time, see Granet, *Le dépôt de l'enfant sur le sol* (Rev. arch., 1922), pp. 34-46.

ganization of a liturgical whole, is indicated by the use of certain numbers. To mark the total value of any liturgy, we start from the unit, because it is the emblem of the total; but, as it must be possible to break it down, we consider it under the aspect of the ten or the hundred. 10 can be broken down into 3 + (2 + 2) + 3, 100 into 30 + (20 + 20) + 30. At the two extremes of the series, 3 or 30 indicate the duration of the periods immediately bordering the entrance or exit; 7 {= 3 + (2 + 2) or (2 + 2) + 3}, or 70, that of the liminal or terminal periods (of which 50 or 5 sometimes mark an important moment). Thus, the terms of ceremonies distributed around a central gesture are often indicated by the numbers 3 (=30), {5 (=50)} and 7 (=70), which serve to give rhythm to Time.[25] The properly liturgical durations are not the only ones that are felt to be rhythmic and total. Historical time does not seem to be constituted in any other way. Scholars, when they reconstruct the past, are convinced that they have reached the chronological truth as soon as they succeed in placing the events in the rhythmic framework of a liturgy.

Chouen, barely in his thirties, became a minister of Yao. At the age of fifty, he exercised the power that, after a new ceremony, was ceded to him by his lord. After ascending the throne, he himself was to cede the leadership of the Empire to a successor minister. The rule (preserved in domestic usage) is that a ruler relinquishes power at the age of seventy. To make the story appear correct in all respects, we should have been told that Chouen, leaving government at seventy, as Yao did, could have reserved for himself a retirement of thirty years (since the time he spent, early in his life, out of office had lasted thirty years), for (a perfect ruler and one whose virtue was to benefit a hundred generations of descendants), Chouen lived exactly *one hundred* years. The essential has been said, however, if it is not said in the case of Chouen, whose career, in all other respects, is so regular, it is at least given in the case of Yao, who has reached the true age of retirement.[26] A reign is a part of duration in itself, and historians are convinced that it should be arranged with a rhythmical organization identical with that of a liturgical ensemble.

The reign of Chouen deserved the regularity of a perfect liturgy. This ruler is known for a feat that allowed him to renew the duration. He inaugurated the new times by proceeding, to begin with, with an expulsion ceremony. He banished to the margins of the world those infested by noxious virtue: the degenerate offspring, the malignant remnants of dynasties whose time had passed. Any outdated order of duration must finish fading away in the vague distance where extension dilutes and ends.[27]. Two domains cannot remain contiguous, simply separated by an ideal frontier, they must be isolated by an abyss. Two epochs cannot succeed each other without breaking continuity, they are two cycles that cannot intertwine. However, a cycle, when it is completed, is not condemned to definitive destruction; it is enough that an outdated order of time be put out of order, so that it does not contaminate the prevailing order.

---

25   Id. in *Ibid.* p. 35.
26   Id. in *Danses et légendes…*, pp. 286 ff.
27   Id. in *Ibid.* pp. 238 ff. The margins of the Universe form a kind of outdated space corresponding to mythological times; this non-humanized world is outside historical time.

Book II - Chapter I - Time and Space

At the moment when a Chinese dynasty proclaimed its advent, promulgated the calendar destined to particularize its period of domination, it took care to separate from the Empire the fiefs destined to the descendants of the fallen dynasties. The latter were charged with preserving in these *closed domains* the significant regulations of a *past historical cycle*.[28] Likewise, the Soil Altars of the fallen dynasties were not destroyed, but simply walled up.[29] If the preservation of these "witnesses" was considered necessary, it was because a return of fortune was foreseen for the order of the civilization whose memory and – if we may say so – its seed, they preserved.

Similar conceptions are found in the rules of the ancestral cult.[30] Only ancestors belonging to the four generations immediately preceding that of the cult leader are entitled to a reserved place in the domestic temple. There they are represented by tablets preserved in chapels oriented and arranged in a square. On these tablets, which preserve their memory, their personal name must be inscribed. None of the names of the deceased family members can be taken up by the relatives as long as the tablets bearing them remain in one of these chapels. But when the head of the cult dies and a place must be given to the tombstone of this new ancestor, the tombstone on which the name of his great-great-grandfather is inscribed must be removed. Immediately this name can be given to a child of the family. With this child, one of the virtues presiding over the domestic order reappears; this virtue was preserved in the retreat of the ancestral temple, where it underwent a kind of internship that prepared it for rebirth, while *four* generations of family heads succeeded each other in the exercise of authority.

Similarly, when it comes to making history and putting the past in order, the Chinese admit that dynasties take turns in power animated by different virtues and succeed each other in a cyclical manner. While one of the five virtues that can characterize an epoch reigns, the other four, destined to reappear, are preserved by the effect of a kind of restorative quarantine. The idea of the cyclical return of the Five Sovereign Virtues is only attested, as a theory, from the 4th-13th centuries. From then on it inspired full confidence, for it was then that it served as a framework for scholars eager to reconstitute national antiquities.[31] As for the sentiments from which this idea originates, they are found at the heart of the ancient mythical data. When Chouen expelled the lapsed virtues, he sent them to the margins of the universe, not to destroy them, we are told, but to enable them to renew themselves. While he himself, a new virtue ready to dominate, took possession of a square capital in the center of humanized Space, it was on the four borders of the expanse that the temporarily exhausted virtues, which happened to be four, were lodged for a long penance.[32]

The conception of a Time that breaks down into epochs, complete in themselves, both finite and finite in number, agrees with a conception of Space that

---

28　*Civ. Chin.*
29　Chavannes, *Le T'ai chan*, p. 462.
30　*Civ. Chin.*; Granet, *Danses et légendes...*, pp. 21 ff.
31　*SMT, Introd.*, pp. CXLIII ff; *Civ. chin.* Cf. *infra*, in this same book, chap. IV.
32　Granet, *Danses et légendes...*, p. 241.

breaks down a closed world into a confederation of sectors. Both are based on a federal order of society. A sovereign, whose authority rests on a power of delegation, does not appear clothed in a Majesty that confers on him indefinite powers. He has companions, and these companions expect to have their turn of domination. The power to animate Time and Space is conferred only for an epoch whose end will come and whose return must be foreseen, for the prestige of a dynasty or a chief is subject to the regulated games of feudal fortune.

The dynastic epochs are marked by the same sets of symbols as the seasons and the directions of space. Did the seasonal rhythm directly inspire the idea of their cyclical succession? This is difficult to admit if we take into account the importance of the idea of the Center; it plays an equal role in the representations of Time and in those of Space. Considered from the point of view of extension, it corresponds to the idea of federation. On the other hand, it seems to be linked to a liturgical conception of duration; the liturgical order which characterizes an epoch and which has its source in a regulating power of finite essence seems to emanate from a sort of emitting center which is simultaneously determined by the proclamation of a calendar and the inauguration of a federal capital. The idea that all duration is not conceivable without a center has not passed without artifice from units of time of a properly social character (such as epochs) to the year, a unit of conventional duration, but linked to experiential data. It was only possible to apply it to a duration defined by the course of the stars by virtue of a pre-established link between the representations of Time and Space.

As we have seen, an ancient tradition[33] tells us that the rulers of old periodically made a tour of the Empire, starting from the East and following the course of the Sun, in order to adapt Time exactly to the Spaces. These rulers were only obliged to imitate the Sun every five years. After this five-yearly commemoration of the promulgation of the calendar, they could remain in their capital for four whole years. They then indicated the center of Space after having traced its perimeter. They also defined the cycle of the seasons, while commemorating the foundation of an era. But in the course of their circumvallation, they could not fix the center of the year.

According to another tradition,[34] a capital only deserves this name if it has a *Ming t'ang*. The *Ming t'ang* is a properly royal prerogative and the mark of a firmly established power. It is a Calendar House, which is seen as a concentration of the universe. Built on a square base, because the Earth is square, this house must be covered with a thatched roof, round like Heaven. Every year and throughout the year, the ruler circulates under this roof. By positioning himself in the proper orientation, he inaugurates the seasons and the months in succession. The stop he makes, in the second month of spring, dressed in green and situated in the center of the East, is equivalent, since he is not wrong in either the site or the symbol, to an equinoctial visit to the Levant. But the chief cannot continue indefinitely with

---

33 *SMT*, I, pp. 58 ff.
34 Granet, *op. cit.* pp. 116 ff; *Civ. Chin.*

his peripheral circulation on pain of never wearing the insignia that corresponds to the Center, which is the prerogative of the sovereign. That is why, when the third month of summer is over, he interrupts the work that allows him to singularize the different durations. Then he dresses himself in yellow and, ceasing to imitate the march of the sun, he goes to the center of the *Ming t'ang*. If he wants to animate Space, he must occupy this royal place and, as soon as he stops there, it is from where he seems to animate Time; he has given a center to the year. – In order that the sovereign may exercise his central action, it is necessary, between the sixth month, which marks the end of summer, and the seventh, which is the first of autumn, to institute a sort of period of rest, which is counted as a month, though no definite duration is attributed to it.[35] It is only of reasonable length; this takes nothing away from the twelve months or the seasons, and yet it is far from being zero; it is equivalent to the whole year, for in it seems to reside the motor of the year.

Time is constituted by the cyclical succession of epochs, all of which – dynasties, reigns, quinquennia, years proper – must be assimilated to a liturgy, and all of them, even the year, have a center. No order, indeed, whether liturgical or geographical, temporal or spatial, is received without supposing that it has, if we may say so, as guarantor, an eminent power whose place, seen in Space, appears as central. This conception reflects the progress of social organization, which is now oriented towards an ideal of hierarchy and relative stability. The notion of the center, whose importance reflects this progress, is far from being primitive; it has replaced the notion of the axis. The role played by the latter is still noticeable in the calendars of feudal times, where we see that the days surrounding the two solstices deserve particular respect.[36] This role is even more remarkable in several myths of archaic spirit. In them has been preserved the memory of a time when the conception of a hierarchical order of Space and Time tended to replace a representation of the Universe and of society based simply on the ideas of opposition and alternation.

Yao, without thinking of visiting the Empire or circulating in a *Ming t'ang*, brought order to the world by merely sending four astronomical delegates to the four poles; Chouen, in turn, succeeded in establishing a new order by merely sending four banished ones to the four polar mountains. – Yao's[37] delegates were the two brothers Hi and the two brothers Ho. Hi-ho is the Sun, or, rather, the Mother of Suns, of which there are ten (one for each of the days of the denary cycle). Hi-ho is *one*, since it is ten, but first it is *a couple*, since the Mother of Suns is married. So Hi and Ho are an astronomical couple. A complex pair, indeed: there are 3 Hi and 3 Ho. However, they form a total, not of 6, but of 4, as soon as the seasons and orientations are distributed to them. This is because Yao, by eliminating his chiefs from these opposing groups, has taken care to keep in the Capital – close emanations of his regulative power – the eldest of the 3 Hi and the eldest of the 3 Ho. With these elders he forms a triad, august and central. If we want to count it by 1, a center

---

35 *Yue ling, Li ki*, C., p. 371.
36 *Id.* in *Ibid.*, pp. 303 and 402.
37 Granet, *Danses et légendes…*, pp. 252 ff.

is formed in the middle of the square. Like a central and fixed Sun, the eminent authority of the Chief bursts forth there, while it manifests itself, distributed in the four directions, under the particular aspect that suits each of the quadrants of the world. The year is then distributed in sectors to which we can lend symbols taken from the seasons. These radiating sectors seem to emanate from a Master-Sun condemned to deviate, because he must govern the different spaces. However, it is the 6 and not the 4 (or the 5) that is the true number of a solar family, just as it is the simple confrontation by bands and not the distribution in squares that indicates the primary division of Space.

We know of other sons of the Sun besides Hi and Ho; not only were there six like these, but we also know that they came out of their mother's womb, 3 *from the left* (= East) and 3 *from the right* (= West).[38] Like the Hi and the Ho, those banished by Chouen,[39] who renew their virtues in the four directions, seem at first to count as four, and yet they also form a double band of three. One of them is called Trois-Miao. The others form a trio in which two companions flank a powerful figure. The latter, named Kouen, was to transform himself into a *three* legged turtle and go to rule in the Far East (= left), on a mountain of birds. Opposite him, and also on a Bird Mountain, but in the Far West (= right), were the Three-Miao, a *three*-bodied owl. Guilty of having disturbed Time, the Three-Miao were, in the course of a dance party, tamed by a Hero to whom this feat – he himself danced dressed in feathers – earned him the throne.[40] As for Kouen, who could only dance an impotent dance, he was sacrificed by Chouen, to whom he had disputed the Empire.[41] Now, in the ballets of old, the dancers, we are told, were grouped in threes.[42] We even know, by a significant example, that the festivities for the inauguration of a new era consisted of a ritual combat between two chiefs, each flanked by two seconds.[43] They represented two *complementary* groups, two *halfs* of society which, *by rotation*, shared authority.[44]

This principle of simple alternation explains the face-to-face opposition of the actors. Instead of forming the square, they were arranged in the ritual area on either side of an axial line separating the two camps. The representation of Time and Space, which assumes them decomposed into sectors linked to a center from which derives their power to endure and coexist, made it possible to borrow the seasons and to orient the symbols intended to particularize durations as well as extensions. This conception comes from an older representation. The elements of the latter derive entirely, not from simple individual sensations or from the observation of nature, but from purely social uses. They are borrowed from the image offered, in particularly touching circumstances, by two bands facing each other in

---

38 *Ibid.*, p. 254.
39 *Ibid.*, pp. 241 ff; pp. 250 ff; pp. 257 ff.
40 *Ibid.*, pp. 243, 244, 248.
41 *Ibid.*, pp. 245, 248, 268.
42 *Ibid.*, p. 270.
43 *Ibid.*, p. 271; *Civ. Chin.*, p. 221.
44 *Civ. Chin.*, pp. 231 ff.

a ritual joust. Before the games of feudal politics had alternated in the sovereign seat the representatives of the various virtues expressing the particular aspects of duration and extension, it was a ritual combat that brought in turn to power the representatives of two complementary groups. A two-beat rhythm, based on simple opposition and simple alternation, commanded the social organization. It also commanded the twin representations of Time and Space.

This simple rhythm is that which is imposed on the life of society by a periodic need for renewal. Space is composed of sometimes full and sometimes diluted expanses; it empties and exhausts itself where all social life seems to be lacking; it seems to reside entirely in the sacred precincts of federal meetings. The duration is made up of weak and strong times; it seems to take refuge entirely in the periods of feasts and plenary assemblies. The words *houei* and *ki* both mean time, but in the sense of occurrence; *ki* evokes above all the idea of an appointment or a term; *houei*, those of a meeting (market, fair, festival), of a congregation, of a society. Duration is only really itself, intact and dense, in those occasions enriched by life in common that make an appointment and seem to found Time.

The season which the learned rituals impose once a year on the Sovereign standing in the center of the *Ming t'ang*, as if it were the pivot of the year, seems to correspond to a period of retreat during which the ancient chiefs had to seclude themselves in the depths of their abode.[45] As to the duration of this retreat, the various mythical data do not agree; it is said to have lasted twelve days, or to have ended on the seventh day. There is reason to think that the six or twelve days of retreat were dedicated to the six domestic animals or to the twelve animals that are the symbols of the twelve months.[46] These days were used to perform rituals and observations[47] that made it possible to predict (or, to put it better, to determine with the help of omens) the prosperity of the livestock and the success of the harvest. The twelve days, for example, were considered a prefiguration of the twelve months of the year. This privileged period was considered a kind of concentrated time, equivalent to the whole year. The variable duration attributed to it is explained by the competition of two scholarly definitions of the year and the existence of a luni-solar calendar. The solar year is calculated to have 366 days; the religious year has only 360 days. The 12 lunar months first had 29 days (the fifteenth day was always considered the full moon and the center of the month), and then six of them were extended to 30 days. The total length of the 12 lunations {(348 or) 354 days} was 6 (or 12) days less than the religious year, and 12 (or 18) days less than the solar year. In practice, this led to the adoption of the system of *quinquennial cycles* and intercalary months; 354 days and 12 months were attributed to the first, second and fourth years of each cycle, and 13 months and 384 days to the third and fifth

---

45   *Civ. Chin.*, pp. 223 ff.
46   Granet, *Danses et légendes...*, pp. 305 ff.
47   *SMT*, III, p. 400.

years.[48] Religious thought did not, however, fail to grant a kind of separate existence to the first twelve days of the year.[49]

To these days of particular character seems to have been attached a feast whose name may be understood to mean the feast of *the night* (the longest one). This meaning was imposed ever since the idea of running the axis of the year through the solstices was born, and the winter solstice was regarded as the starting-point. But the beginning of the Chinese year is, in principle, variable; it is by fixing the initial hours, days and months, that the different dynasties determined their insignia and their calendar to mark the time of their domination. Surprisingly, the beginning of the year only oscillated between the different months of the cold season. The winter festival was not, from the beginning, a solstice festival; its name may mean festival of the lengthening of the nights, and it is true that it has all the characteristics of a harvest festival. Its duration, at first very long, was in fact determined by real terms, those of freezing and thawing.[50] It extended, with its opening and closing ceremonies, over the whole winter period, so that numerous ritual episodes could be distinguished; attributed to the eighth and second months,[51] they marked the two extremes of an equinoctial axis of the year. The ceremonies of the annual liturgy then tended to be distributed taking into account both this equinoctial axis and that of the solstice; thus, conforming to a division of Space into quadrants, a liturgical order, based on the division of the year into four seasons, served to give rhythm to Time. However, it should be noted that one of the ends of the cross has remained almost empty of religious value, corresponding simply to the summer vacations, a simple time of rest and abstention. The winter vacations have a different meaning. Even reduced to a period of six or twelve days, they seem to be worth as much as the whole year.

They owe this value to the fact that they have ended by absorbing within themselves all the force released by the festivals of the low season.[52] The latter, which falls between two real years, between two agricultural campaigns, contains within itself the only Time that *marks a date*. It is the period when men who are no longer dispersed by life in the fields gather in the villages and towns. A secular, selfish, monotonous and emotionless time is followed by a time filled with religious hopes and the creative activity of community exercises. A simple rhythm opposes – like a weak time to a strong time – the period of dispersed life in which only a latent social activity remains, to the period of congregation dedicated entirely to the repair of social bonds. This rhythm is not directly based on the seasonal rhythm. If it seems to depend on the set of natural conditions governing the existence of a society that lives mainly on agriculture, it is because the season during which

---

48   *SMT*, I, p. 49; *Yi king*, L., pp. 365 and 368. {5 x 366 = (384 x 2) + (354 x 3) = 768 + 1062 = 1830}.

49   And perhaps (also) the 6 days surrounding each of the two solstices. *SMT*, III, p. 320 ff; *Yue ling*, 5th and 11th months.

50   Granet, *Danses et légendes...*, pp. 330 ff; pp. 470, 476.

51   Or the ninth and third months.

52   Granet, *op. cit.* pp. 327 ff, *Civ. Chin.*

the Earth no longer accepts human labor is the time when men can most conveniently occupy themselves with interests that are not profane. Nature offers the signal and provides the opportunity. But the need to seize the opportunity and perceive the signal has its origin in social life itself. A society cannot last without recreating itself. The Chinese believed that duration could not subsist without periodic renewals, because they themselves felt compelled to meet periodically in assemblies. Since the festivals at which the human group came back to life were celebrated at every low season, they imagined that the renewal of Time must take place every year. Hence, with the very idea of an annual cycle and the desire to find its equivalent in Nature, the desire to link each of the manifestations of social life to an external sign provided by natural manifestations. But the ancient festivals of the low season expressed, in principle, only human needs, properly social needs.[53] The proof of this lies in the fact that their first and foremost aim was not to merit happy seasons or a good year, but to obtain the perpetuation of the social grouping.

To achieve this, the group used all the forces at its disposal. It spent everything and spent itself completely; living and dead, beings and things, goods and products of all kinds, humans and gods, women and men, young and old, all mixed in a fierce and invigorating orgy. The jousts that prepared this total communion sought above all to pit the dead against the living, the old against the young, all the past against all the future, in every possible way. In this way a continuity was established between the generations, from which Time itself benefited, to the point that its renewal seemed like a *rejuvenation*. It was easy to imagine that the feast was celebrated with the intention of inaugurating the new year and preparing for the success of the next agricultural campaign. However, the festivities ended with an ovation that was repeated indefinitely from near and far: "Ten thousand years! Ten thousand years!"[54] When the feast was celebrated for the benefit of the chiefs invested with the power to make endure and live together, this acclamation seemed to correspond to an acclamation of advent, to a dynastic desire, to the inauguration of an era. When it was used to designate the chief, it also served to concentrate in his person a vital power implying unlimited hopes of perpetuation.[55] At a time when the feast of the long night was still the winter assembly of a peasant community, the cry of "Ten years!" signified above all the confidence of a race in the success of its labors, a success which was constantly renewed and which guaranteed to the human group a gateway to perpetuity. Empty and as if without force in the current of the days, the duration, during the assemblies of the off-season, was suddenly filled with living reality. Rich in hopes and memories, it was imbued with that power of realization which signals desires exalted by action in common. All the past, all the future, all Time (with all Space) seemed to be condensed in the sacred occasions (attached to sacred places) in which a human group came to conceive of itself as a permanent and total unity.

---

53   Id. *Fêtes et chansons anciennes de la Chine*, pp. 178 ff.
54   Id. *La religion des Chinois; Civ. Chin.*
55   *Civ. Chin.*, pp. 45, 228. "10,000 years" is equivalent to "Son of Heaven." These two expressions designate the sovereign.

* * *

In civilizations in which social activity hardly ceases to be intense, continuity seems to be an essential character of duration. The social life of the ancient Chinese was most intense during the winter retreat, but as soon as the resumption of secular work forced men to disperse, it suddenly dwindled to nothingness. Time (and space) thus seemed fully dense only at the times (and places) reserved for assemblies and feasts. Linked to full spaces, strong times alternate with weak times linked to empty spaces. The need for a rhythmic repair of social feeling led to the idea that Space and Time had a common rhythmic constitution. This rhythmic constitution, the principle of which lies in the antithesis of periods of dispersion and concentration, was first expressed in the joint ideas of simple opposition and alternation, and the representation of Space and Time implied from the beginning the feeling of a difference in value between two qualities of extension and duration.

On the other hand, duration and extension seemed to exist fully only where they were socialized; subject to the necessity of periodic creation, they seemed to emanate from some kind of center. This allowed spatial representations to react upon the representation of Time that had shaped them in the first place. To the idea that both extensions and durations were of unequal value was added the idea that both durations and extensions were of a varied nature. This progress was made as soon as the representation of Space was ordered, no longer by the spectacle of two camps full of bands facing each other face to face, but by that of a square formation, the axial line separating the parts having been reabsorbed in a center occupied by a Chief. This last arrangement has as its principle the increase of the complication of the social structure. It is no longer based on a division into two complementary groups which dominate in turn. It is based on a federal organization. Situated at a point of convergence, the sovereign whose virtue governs the confederation seems to be engaged in unifying the diverse. During federal celebrations, this diversity appears divided into four quadrants; it also borrows its symbols from the four directions. Space is thus diversified into oriented extensions; time appears immediately broken down into durations with seasonal attributes. If the groups of a confederation no longer alternate in power according to the simple rhythm that suits two complementary groups, a principle of rotation continues to govern the feudal organization. Thus, time seems to be made up of epochs which, following one another in cyclical succession, are themselves imagined in the form of cycles. This explains the theory of the Five Sovereign Virtues, sometimes located in a central command post, sometimes relegated to quarantine at the four extremes of the Empire. But Space, having imposed a quinary rhythm on Time because of its division into quadrants, must itself borrow this rhythm. This explains the division of the extension into five interlocking squares, hierarchical spaces distinguished by their degree of cohesion; this is indicated, for each of them, by the characteristic periodicity of the rhythm of repair that is proper to them.

The Chinese did not bother to conceive Time and Space as two homogeneous environments capable of housing abstract concepts. They have broken them down into *five* main sections, which they use to distribute the symbols indicating the diversity of occasions and places. This conception provided them with the framework for a kind of total art; based on a knowledge that seems to us completely scholastic, this art tends to achieve, through the simple use of effective symbols, an ordering of the world that is inspired by the ordering of society. On the other hand, the Chinese have avoided seeing Space and Time as two independent concepts or two autonomous entities. They see in them *a* complex of *sections* identified with active sets, with concrete groupings. Far from appearing incoherent, the interplay of these sections seems to them to be ordered by a principle of order; this principle is confused with the feeling of the efficacy of rhythm. This efficacy, which is evident in the field of social organization, seems to have no less value when it is a question of organizing thought. – We shall see that this same feeling of the universal efficacy of rhythm lies at the heart of the conception of Yin and Yang.

Chapter II
YIN AND YANG

Chinese philosophy (at least in the known part of its history[1]) is dominated by the notions of Yin and Yang. All scholars recognize this. Moreover, they all regard these symbols with the tinge of respect that accompanies philosophical terms, which demands to see in them as the expression of scholarly thought. They are inclined to interpret Yin and Yang with the rigor that seems proper to doctrinal creations, and they hasten to qualify these Chinese symbols by borrowing terms from the language defined by Western philosophers. Thus, they declare at once, sometimes, that Yin and Yang are forces, sometimes, that they are substances. Those who call them forces – this is the general opinion of contemporary Chinese critics – consider it advantageous to bring these ancient symbols closer to the symbols used in modern physics.[2] The others – they are Westerners – pretend to react against this anachronistic interpretation.[3] They therefore assert (quite to the contrary) that Yin and Yang are substances, without thinking to ask whether, in the philosophy of ancient China, there is any semblance of a distinction between substances and forces. To avoid any bias, they have given the Tao

---

   1   It must be remembered that no fragment (containing a philosophical concern) has come down to us which can be estimated as significantly earlier than the fifth century BC.
   2   Hu Shih, *The development of logical method in ancient China*, and (following him) Tucci, *Storia della filosofia cinese antica*, p. 15, and Suzuki, *A brief history of early Chinese philosophy*, p. 15.
   3   Maspero, *La Chine antique* pp. 482-483. Very different ideas, which seem to be inspired by another interpretation, are expressed on pp. 273 ff. of the same book. Comp. Wieger, *Histoire des croyances religieuses et des opinions philosophiques en Chine, depuis l'origine jusqu'à nos jours*, p. 127.

the name of a supreme reality analogous to a divine principle,[4] and are ready to discover in the Tao a tendency to a substantial dualism.

To avoid any bias, it is well to review the ancient uses of the terms *yin* and *yang*, avoiding any chronological pedantry and bearing in mind the dangers of proof by absence. – Chinese tradition traces the concept of Yin and Yang to the earliest astronomers[5] and, in fact, the symbols are mentioned in a calendar whose history goes back to the third century BC.[6] It is fashionable today to attribute to divination theorists the first idea of a metaphysical conception of Yin and Yang; these terms appear, indeed, quite frequently in a pamphlet concerning the divinatory art. For a long time this treatise was thought to be the work of Confucius (early 5th century BC). Today, it is preferred to date it between the fourth and third centuries BC.[7] Music theorists have never ceased to base their speculations on the theme of a concerted action (*tiao*) attributed to the Yin and Yang. This theme is one that Tchouang tseu, a 4th century BC author whose thought is linked to the Taoist current, is particularly fond of evoking.[8] A brief and precise allusion to this concerted action is found in a passage of Mö tseu;[9] like the doctrine of Confucius, that of Mö tseu is linked to a tradition of humanist thought. His work dates from the late 5th century BC. Moreover, the terms *yin* and *yang* appear in geographical nomenclature, which, at least as far as sacred places and capitals are concerned, was undoubtedly inspired by religious principles. – From the period between the 5th and 3rd centuries BC, the symbols of yin and yang were used by theorists of very different orientations. This wide use gives the impression that these two symbols indicate notions that inspire a wide range of techniques and doctrines.

This impression is confirmed as soon as we think of checking the use of the words *yin* and *yang* in the *Che king*, something that is often overlooked. It is assumed that they can only be vulgar usages which are denied any philosophical interest. However, when it comes to a study of terms and notions, the *Che king* provides the most solid background; this poetic collection, the compilation of which cannot be later than the beginning of the fifth century BC, is, of all ancient documents, the one which has best withstood interpolations. In the language of the *Che*

---

4   Maspero, *op. cit.* p. 483, note 1, and pp. 499 ff.
5   *Ts'ien Han chou*, 30, p. 15b.
6   This treatise, the *Yue ling* (Cf. *Li ki*, C., I, pp. 330 ff.), has come down to us in three editions preserved by the *Lu che tch'ouen ts'ieou*, the *Houai-nan tseu* and the *Li ki*.
7   This treatise, the *Hi ts'eu*, is an appendix to the divinatory manual called *Yi king* (Cf. *Yi king*, L., p. 348 ff.). See Legge's *Prolegomena* (Ibid., pp. 26 ff.; pp. 36 ff.), and Maspero, *op. cit.* p. 480.
8   SMT, III, pp. 301 ff. and P. Wieger, *Les Pères du système taoïste*, p. 321.
9   Mö tseu, 7. See Forke: *Mo Ti, des Socialethikers und seiner Schiller philosophische Werke*, p. 324. Maspero professes that the authors of the *Hi ts'eu* are the inventors of the theory of Yin and Yang; he therefore admits (the *Hi ts'eu* is judged to be later than Mö tseu's work) that this passage is interpolated, although he acknowledges that it forms part of a chapter of this work considered authentic.

Book II - Chapter II - Yin and Yang

king, the word *yin* evokes the idea of cold and cloudy weather,[10] of rainy skies;[11] it is applied to that which is interior (*nei*)[12] and, for example, qualifies the dark and cold retreat where, during the summer, ice is kept. [^163] The word *yang* evokes the idea of sun[13] and heat;[14] it may also be used to represent the masculine aspect of a dancer in action;[15] it is applied to the spring days, when the heat of the sun begins to make itself felt[16] and also to the tenth month of the year, when the winter retreat begins. 168] The words *yin* and *yang* indicate antithetical and concrete aspects of Time. They also indicate antithetical and concrete aspects of Space. It is said of the shady slopes, north of the mountain, south of the river, they are *yin*; but the sunny slopes (north of the river, south of the mountain), the *sunny side*[17], are *yang*, a good location for a capital city.[18] Now, when it was a question of determining the site of the city, the Founder, in his sacred vestments, began by inspecting the sites, followed by divinatory operations; this inspection is described as an examination of the Yin and Yang (or, if one wishes to express it in another way, an examination of the dark or sunny slopes).[19] It may be useful to recall here that the tenth month of the year, described as a yang month by the *Che king*, is the month in which the rites ordained the beginning of construction; we should think that the site was then chosen. The first days of spring are those in which the constructions should be completed and, no doubt, inaugurated;[20] the epithet *yang* is also appropriate for these days. These testimonies, the oldest and surest of all we have, cannot be neglected. They point to the concrete richness of the terms *yin* and *yang*. These symbols seem to have been used in a variety of techniques, but they are all ritual techniques and are related to a total knowledge. This knowledge is one whose importance and antiquity can be intuited from the analysis of the representations of Time and Space. Its object is the religious use of places and occasions. It orders liturgy and ceremonial, topographical art and chronological art.

* * *

---

10   *Che king*, C., p. 35.
11   *Ibid.*, pp. 39, 159, 254.
12   *Ibid.*, p. 144.
13   *Ibid.*, p. 197.
14   *Ibid.*, p. 161.
15   *Ibid.*, p. 78.
16   *Che king*, C., p. 161.
17   *Che king*, C., pp. 23, 104, 143, 202, 324; Granet, *Fêtes et chansons*, p. 246, n.1.
18   *Ibid.*, pp. 349, 463.
19   *Ibid.*, p. 362. *Civ. chin.* Note that the passage in *Che king* where this inspection is mentioned establishes the antiquity of the practices from which the famous Chinese art of geomancy arose. The aim of geomancy (*fong chouei*) is to determine the value of places by taking into account flowing waters (*chouei*) and air currents (*fong*); these are always related to mountains; it is easy to see the interest that terms such as yin and yang might have, the main meaning of which seems to be north or shady side (of a valley) and sunny side (of a valley). Note also that the inspection of shadows and light is expressed in this passage by the word *king*. This same word means *gnomon* and is similar in spelling and pronunciation to the word *king*: capital.
20   *Civ. Chin.*, p. 265.

On this knowledge depends the whole of the techniques known as divinatory. It is not surprising, therefore, that it turns out (let us bear in mind the fortuitousness of the preservation of documents) that the oldest known developments on Yin and Yang are contained in the *Hi ts'eu*, a small treatise appended to the *Yi king* (the only divination manual that has not been lost). Nor is it surprising that the author of the *Hi ts'eu* speaks of Yin and Yang without thinking of giving a definition.[21] In fact, it is enough to read it without prejudice to feel that it proceeds by allusion to known notions. We shall even see that the only aphorism containing the words yin and yang in which we can guess the idea he had of these symbols appears as a ready-made formula, as a true centon; even in this fact lies the only possibility we have of interpreting this aphorism.

"*One* (time) *Yin, one* (time) *Yang* (yi Yin yi Yang), *that is the Tao!*",[22] says the *Hi ts'eu*. In this saying, everything is left to our imagination. The most literal translation runs the risk of distorting its meaning. The one I have just given is already biased, it suggests the interpretation: "a time of Yin, a time of Yang...." Undoubtedly, there is the possibility that an author concerned with divination might consider things from the point of view of Time; however, taken by itself, the formula could just as easily be read: "a (*side*) Yin, a (*side*) Yang...." What we have learned about the connection between the representations of Space and Time already enables us to reject both interpretations as partial. There is reason to suppose that the ideas of alternation and opposition are suggested, both (*lei*) together, by the connection of the symbols Yin, Yang and Tao. But that is not all; the transcription alone is already interpretative, for it implies the use of upper or lower case. It should be written:

$$\left\{ \begin{array}{l} \text{First the Yin, then the Yang,} \\ \text{Here is the Yin, there is the Yang,} \end{array} \right\} \quad \text{this is the Tao!}$$

or:

$$\left\{ \begin{array}{l} \text{Once Yin, once Yang, again Yang,} \\ \text{One side Yin, one side Yang,} \end{array} \right\} \quad \text{this is the Tao!}$$

Are they alternate or opposite Substances or Forces (or, let's say to be more prudent, Principles)? Or are they opposite and alternate aspects? It is impossible to decide anything by trying to fix the meaning of the word *tao* at once; all that the *Hi ts'eu* can teach us is that this word indicates a notion related to the ideas of *yi* (mutation), *pien* (cyclic change) and *t'ong* (mutual interpenetration). We have only

---

21 Maspero, *La Chine antique*, p. 482. This fact – puzzling to them – should have been pointed out by interpreters who attribute to the author of the *Hi ts'eu* the invention of a "metaphysical" system of which the notions of Yin and Yang would form the center. These interpreters, on the other hand, do not hesitate to suppose that these terms are the subject of two sentences in which the author of the *Hi ts'eu* does not mention them. Maspero has taken the precaution, in translating these two sentences, of putting in parentheses the words *yin* and *yang*, which the Chinese text does not contain, but which he does not hesitate, relying on the glossators, to restore.

22 *Yi king*, L. p. 355.

one path open to us. The aphorism of the *Hi tseu* is notable for its form; perhaps we may hope to clarify its meaning if we compare it with similarly constituted formulas.

The *Hi tseu* provides two such formulas. At the beginning of the treatise, there is a passage intended to make clear the exact correspondence between divinatory manipulations and the operations of Nature. The aphorism "*one* (time) *cold, one* (time) *hot*" or "*one* (time of) *cold, one* (time of) *hot*" immediately follows a formula evoking the revolutions of the Sun and the Moon. It precedes the indication that the Tao, under the aspect of *K'ien* (*K'ien tao*), constitutes the masculine and that, under the aspect of *K'ouen* (*K'ouen tao*), it constitutes the feminine. The whole tradition recognizes in *K'ien* and *K'ouen* (which are, undivided or split lines, the primordial symbols of divination) the graphic representation of Yang and Yin. The *Hi tseu*, elsewhere, equates *K'ouen*, the female symbol, with the door when closed {the female remains hidden and internally forms (*nei*) a hiding-place for the embryo} and K'ien, the male symbol, with the door when open {the male extends and produces; produces, grows and grows (*cheng*); externalizes (*wai*)}.[23] Then the author adds:"once closed, once open, this is the cycle of evolution (*pien*)! a coming and going (*wang lai*) without end, this is mutual interpenetration (*t'ong*)!"[24] The combination of these formulas suggests that the notions of Yin and Yang are part of a set of representations dominated by the idea of rhythm. We even think that this idea can have as its symbol *any image* that registers two antithetical *aspects*.

The *Kouei tsang* offers a similar formula. This is the name of a long-lost divination manual.[25] It is likely that the *Kouei tsang* was related to ancient religious traditions in a much closer way than the *Yi king*. Judging from the preserved fragments, it abounded in mythological themes.[26] We have preserved two passages in which Hi-ho is mentioned. It was to the astronomers Hi and Ho that tradition, in Han times,[27] attributed the conception of Yin and Yang. But we know that Hi-ho is the mother of the Suns or the Sun itself. The *Kouei tsang*, which tells us of him in verse, knows him as such. He describes his ascent along the hollow mulberry tree, a solar and royal abode, which is in the Valley of the Levant (*yang*).[28] It is there, he says, that Hi-ho "(by) *entering*, (by) *exiting* (makes) *darkness* (or the) *light* (*houei ming*)." The *Kouei tsang* says elsewhere, "See how he ascends to heaven – *a* (time of) *light, a* (time of) *darkness* (*yi ming yi houei*) – he is the son of Hi-ho – *coming out* of the Valley of the Rising!" These two fragments are worthy of attention. They reveal the mythical background and the close correspondence of the themes of coming and

---

23 This is the traditional interpretation taken up by the glosses. Note the sexual character of these representations. We shall return to this point.
24 *Yi king*, L., p. 372.
25 The *Kouei tsang*, according to tradition, was the divinatory book of the Yin (kept by the princes of Song, their descendants); the *Yi king*, the book of the Tcheou, successors of the Yin.
26 The *Yi king* is almost devoid of mythical themes, hence its favor among the school of moralists claiming to be Confucian, and consequently its preservation.
27 *Ts'ien Han chou*, 30, p. 15b.
28 Granet, *Danses et légendes...*, p. 253. One could translate: the valley of the Yang.

going (open and closed door, inside and outside) and of the opposition of shadow and light. They also show that these are stereotyped formulas, with refrains rich in poetry.

I have shown above that these centons stand out by a kind of symbolic equivalence that allows them to elicit each other. The saying:

"*yi ming yi houei*" { first the light, then the darkness!
here the light, there the darkness

so close in form and meaning (at least if one does not forget the original meanings of the terms *yin* and *yang*) in the *Hi ts'eu* aphorism:

"*yi yin yi yang*" { first the shadow, then the sun.
here the shady, there the sunny!

can be found, as it is, in a passage from Tchouang tseu.

It is placed there (as in the aphorism of the *Hi t'seu* "*one* (time) *cold, one* (time) *hot*") next to a formula evoking the revolutions of the Sun and the Moon. In this development, which has nothing properly Taoist about it, Tchouang tseu purports to describe explicitly the interaction of Yin and Yang.[29] He describes them at greater length in another passage,[30] which abounds with sayings of the same form: "a (time of) fullness, a (time of) decay… a (time of) refinement, a (time of) coarsening… a (time of) life, a (time of) death… a (time of) sinking; a (time of) rising…" Tchouang tseu multiplies these sayings in a very poetic page in which he tries to give a literary transposition of an ancient symphony (he may have used the libretto); this symphony was precisely related to the myth of Hi-ho: it celebrated the Sacred Pond, where, every morning, the Mother of the Suns washes the Rising Sun.[31]

One of the sayings that appear in this type of poems deserves special attention. It is the saying: "*yi ts'ing yi tchouo.*" I have translated it with the formula: "a time of refinement, a time of thickening." *Ts'ing* gives the idea of the pure, the tenuous; *tchouo*, the idea of the mixed, the heavy. These opposite terms evoke the image of *sediments* settling under the clarified part of a fermented beverage. They can be used to evoke the two antithetical aspects of what we would call matter or substance. But *tchouo* is also used to refer to muddy and dull sounds, to low and low notes; *ts'ing* to clear and pure sounds, to high and sharp notes.[32] Thus the saying should be read as meaning.

indistinctly: { here the light, there the heavy
$\updownarrow$ $\updownarrow$
first acute, then grave.

---

29 Tchouang tseu, Wieger, *Les Pères du système taoïste*, p. 383.
30 *Ibid.*, p. 321.
31 Granet, *op. cit.*, p. 435.
32 Note that, like substance (= food), rhythm is evoked by an image provided by drink.

And, indeed, when Tchouang tseu, wishing to reveal the constitution of all things, writes, with many centons, a kind of cosmic symphony, he does not seem to have the slightest idea of distinction between matter and rhythm.[33] He does not think of opposing forces or substances as independent entities; he does not suppose any reality transcendent to any principle; he simply evokes a selection of contrasted images. Now, the centon *"yi ts'ing yi tchouo"* is followed by a formula (which also seems to imply a musical metaphor) that has above all the value of a summary: "Yin and yang come into concert (*tiao*) and harmonize (*ho*)," such is the formula enunciated by Tchouang tseu after enumerating some of the significant contrasts that reveal the rhythmic constitution of the universe. The antithesis of Yin and Yang can, it seems (no doubt because it is particularly poignant),[34] serve to evoke all possible contrasts; hence the tendency to find in each of them the antithesis of Yin and Yang, which seems to sum them all up. This antithesis is not at all that of two Substances, two Forces, two Principles. It is simply that of two Symbols, richer than all others in power of suggestion. Between them, they know how to evoke, grouped in pairs, all the other symbols. They evoke them with such force that they seem to give them origin and coupling. Thus, Yin and Yang acquire the dignity and *authority* of a pair of *Section-masters*. It is by this authority that we attribute to the Yin-Yang pair this harmonious union, this concertante action (*tiao ho*) which is imagined to be grasped at the bottom of every antithesis and which seems to preside over the totality of the contrasts which constitute the Universe.[35]

By a significant coincidence (it demonstrates the credibility of the centons and that the philosophers are inspired by common wisdom), *Mö tseu* also evokes this concertante action (*tiao*) in the only passage in which he names Yin and Yang. This fragment (if it has not been interpolated) is the earliest that mentions these symbols.[36] It is interesting in other respects. Mö tseu speaks of Yin and Yang (after having also indicated the antithesis of cold and heat) in a development which deals with Heaven and the course of time and which, moreover, is notable for its use of metaphors borrowed from music. The concerted action of Yin and Yang (no less remarkable) is not given as having its beginning in Yin and Yang themselves. Its origin is the *social order*. Rhythm has, not an author, but a kind of *responsible ruler* belonging to the human world. The quality of regulator of the universal rhythm is a princely prerogative, for it is to the Head that society delegates plenary *responsibility, authority*. "A Holy King causes the four seasons to arise in due season (*tsie*);[37]

---

33 Not only are the ideas of rhythm and substance confused, but the opposition between the antithetical terms imaged in both Time and Space implies the idea of a juxtaposition as well as an alternation. I have already indicated the similarity of the ideas of *pien* (cyclic evolution) and *t'ong* (interpenetration).

34 This is the point to be explained. I will try to do so, see below.

35 Note that the expression *ho tiao* (the same words reversed) means, "To harmonize and bring into harmony (the primordial flavors that make up the food)." Rhythm and substance are the object of a global and indistinct intuition.

36 *Mö tseu*, 7.

37 The word *tsie* means "articulation, union" and evokes the image of a bamboo knot. It designates the instrument used to mark the compass (*the King makes Yin and Yang coincide by*

he causes Yin and Yang, rain and dew, to coincide (*tiao*)." We see that the two great symbols are here placed in the same rank as rain and dew.[38] This is undoubtedly the most interesting feature of this passage. It confirms what previous analyses suggested: Yin and Yang are valid as symbols, and express concrete aspects. What Mö tseu wishes to evoke, in this case, is precisely the image that, taken in its initial meaning, these two symbols evoke; when mentioned together with the opposition of dew and rain, the opposition of Yang and Yin certainly points to the antithesis of the gloomy and sunny aspects. It will be necessary to explain why this antithesis, among many others, provided the symbols called upon to play the role of the master sections. It will then be necessary to remember that the contrast of Yin and Yang composes a kind of spectacle that a musical order seems to regulate. The essential thing, for the moment, is to note that nothing invites us to see, in Yin and Yang, Substances, Forces or Principles; they are only Symbols endowed with a power of evocation truly indefinite and, to express it more appropriately: total.

The "theory" of Yin and Yang undoubtedly owes much to musicians, perhaps even more than to astronomers and soothsayers. But, certainly, soothsayers, astronomers and musicians started from a representation which, translated into myths,[39] formed part of common thought. This thought seems to be dominated by the idea that the contrast of two concrete aspects characterizes the Universe as well as each of its appearances. When (out of some technical concern) the contrast is considered from the point of view of duration (this is the case with the strictly divinatory sciences insofar as they are distinguished from the science of places and are concerned above all with the knowledge of occasions), the opposition of aspects leads to the idea of their alternation. It is therefore conceivable that the world presents no appearance which does not correspond to a *cyclic totality* (*tao, pien, t'ong*) constituted by the conjugation of *two alternate and complementary manifestations*. But this conjugation occurs no less in the domain of Space than in that of Time. The idea of alternation can be suggested both by a spatial arrangement and by a temporal arrangement. The juxtaposition of radiating sectors evokes it as well as a succession in the form of a cycle. Even, as we have seen, it is by virtue of its connec-

---

marking the compass in the four seasons) and the divisions of time which serve to give rhythm to the course of the seasons. It is also the emblem of loyalty and chastity and, ultimately, of measure. The various concrete aspects of the notion of measure seem to imply a musical image that appears to be linked to the representation of a (bamboo) instrument *measured* by the number of its *articulations*.

38   Rain and dew constitute poetic themes that serve as symbols for certain periods of the year. Rain and dew are opposites. The idea of rain is linked to representations of a feminine nature (*yin*); dew arouses the idea of princely beneficence (masculine, *yang*). It should be noted that Yang is opposed to Rain *in the list of the Five Signs provided by the* Hong Fan (SMT, IV, p. 228), which further demonstrates: 1° that "the theory" of Yin and Yang was known to the editors of the Hong Fan; 2° that, for them, (Yin and) Yang were concrete categories. Cf. *infra*, Book II, chap. IV, and Book III, chap II.

39   The most interesting is that of *Hi-ho*. According to tradition, the elder *Hi* and the elder *Ho*, chief astronomers who *assist* the sovereign, were assigned, one to Yin and the other to Yang. SMT, pp. 43 and 44, and note 1; Granet, *Danses et légendes*..., p. 253.

tion with Space and not by an abusive extension of the characteristics of concrete time that Time is broken down into cyclical units, some of which (the reign or the era) are clearly distinguished from the year. This observation leads to the supposition that Yin and Yang, as symbols used by astronomers, may have been taken for cosmogonic entities, but that they did not correspond, in principle, to simply temporal representations. Chinese thought, whether common or technical, never separates the consideration of time from that of extension. The fact that the terms adopted to express the cyclical opposition of the constitutive aspects of all reality involve spatial images gives further proof of this. The aphorism of the *Hi t'seu*: "*yi yin yi yang*"[40] may safely be translated by the formula "*a* (time) *yin*, *a* (time) *yang*," when interpreted from the point of view of the diviners. But it also implies the idea: "*one* (side) *yin*, *one* (side) *yang*."[41] The only way to avoid too partial an interpretation is thus to read: "*one* (aspect) *yin*, *one* (aspect) *yang*" – without forgetting that this opposition awakens a concrete and complex image, that of a shadow aspect combined with a light aspect – and to imply, finally, that these antithetical aspects are always perceived as alternating; they seem to alternate not only when we contemplate the succession of periods of darkness (night, winter) and periods of light (day, summer), but also when we simultaneously evoke the double spectacle of a landscape in which we can pass from a shady slope (*yin*: shady side) to a sunny slope (*yang*: sunny side).

* * *

It is difficult, as we see, to consider the terms *yin* and *yang* as terms arbitrarily assigned by astronomers or soothsayers to entities invented by them. These words evoke, in the first place, an image, and this is remarkable because it implies a linked representation of Spaces and Times. However, the idea of alternation seems to have prevailed (however slightly) over the idea of opposition. This fact should not be overlooked. It points to one of the services rendered by the symbols of Yin and Yang. The sages who organized the Calendar used them as guiding principles. The Chinese see in the Calendar a supreme law.[42] They believe that this law governs the practices of Nature because it is the rule that dominates all human habit. In the use of the calendar, Yin and Yang appear as the principles of the rhythm of the seasons. – If scholars have been able to attribute this role to them, it is because these symbols had the power to evoke the *rhythmic formula of the regime of life* formerly adopted by the Chinese.

---

40   I transcribe without using capital letters; it is not a question of the opposition of two principles, but of the contrast of two aspects.

41   One of the traditions concerning the symbols used in divinatory techniques (symbols which the *Yi king* represents graphically by lines solid and continuous or either hollow in its center) is that the diviners used tokens, one side of which remained intact and probably bulging (yang = masculine = protruding) and the other was hollow (yin = feminine = hollow). – The best translation of the formula *Hi ts'eu* in divinatory terms would thus be: "one (once *the face*) yin, one (once *the face*) yang."

42   *Civ. chin.*

Immediately after speaking of the concerted action of Yin and Yang, Tchouang tseu quotes the saying: "Animals that hibernate begin to move." Always linked (as in this passage from the *Tchouang tseu*) to the idea of a spring awakening of Thunder activity, this theme recurs in all calendars, scholarly or otherwise. According to the *Yue ling*, the Thunder begins to be heard, and the hibernating animals come out of their hiding places – they shut themselves in and the Thunder ceases to manifest itself – at two precise moments of the solar year; these are the two equinoxes, dramatic moments when, it is said, the energies of Yin and Yang are exactly balanced, preparing, one or the other, to triumph or decline. In the *Yue Ling*, an astronomically based scholarly calendar, Yin and Yang appear as two antagonistic entities: one corresponds to all destructive energies (Winter), the other to all life-giving energies (Summer).[43] Yin and Yang are not mentioned in the older calendars, which also do not indicate the need to divide Time by markers provided by the march of the sun. The times of the year which the Chinese first considered worthy of mention were only those which the centons sufficed to indicate. These peasant observations on the habits of Nature can, without the aid of any astronomical precision, perfectly indicate to men the succession of useful tasks. On the other hand, they make visible the main rules governing social activity. Thus, for example, the disappearance and reappearance of hibernating animals mark the beginning and the end of the low season, respectively. Humans spend this dramatic period hiding in their winter shelters. In fact, the time of seclusion never lasted from the autumn equinox to the spring equinox. Thus, far from thinking of relating the departure of the hibernators to a termination of the solar year, an ancient calendar makes, *on the contrary*, the year begin at the moment fixed by this natural sign.[44] It sees it as the starting point of a liturgical cycle, whose times are concretely determined by the signs (gestures of animals, habits of vegetation) that the rustic centons know how to record. If the ancient calendars were valid as laws, it was because they were formed by proverbs. The astronomical annotations were not imposed until later. The cultured art of the Calendar then had to distribute, in relation to the celestial landmarks, the peasant observations which had previously been considered sufficient to organize social activity.[45] It was also at this time that this art explicitly resorted to the symbols of Yin and Yang. Mere concepts, artificial products of a doctrinal conception, these notions would not have had the virtue of establishing a correspondence between proverbial observations and astronomical landmarks. In spite of the new faith inspired by astronomy, the technicians of the calendar did not intend to get rid of a rustic notation of time made of venerable signs. It seems that it is in the very heritage of these symbols that they found, even if only to transform them little by little into scholastic principles, the notions which, at first totally concrete, could effectively serve as classificatory principles.

Yin and Yang were called upon to organize the material of the calendar, because these Symbols evoked with special force the rhythmic conjugation of two concrete

---

43   *Li ki*, C., I, pp. 345, 348, 377, 382.
44   *Little calendar of the Hia, Ta Tai Li ki*, 47.
45   Granet, *Fêtes et Chansons anciennes de la Chine*, pp. 53 ff.

Book II - Chapter II - Yin and Yang

antithetical aspects. In fact, the most remarkable feature of the set of themes used by the calendars is that they combine in pairs, coupling in the same way as Yin and Yang. Hibernators enter or leave their shelters; wild geese fly north or south. According to the theory held by the glossators, the movements of coming and going, of entry and exit, which express these opposite sayings, are controlled by the rhythm of solar activity; they deserve as such to point out the alternating games and triumphs of Yin and Yang. The viewpoint of mythical thought was very different. We have good evidence of this. Regulating their life on the march of the sun, the swallows, according to scholars, mark exactly, with their arrivals and departures, the two equinoctial terms. However, rustic calendars tell us that swallows do not just move. In autumn they retire to their hiding places in the sea, while the hibernators (i.e., rodents, bears, and also leopards) return to their underground hiding places.[46] The information in the myths was even more precise and concrete. Swallows *stop* being swallows when it is time to overwinter; when they enter their watery shelters, they *become* shellfish. The most learned calendars have not forgotten that sparrows were imposed a life formula similar to that of quails. At the end of the good days, sparrows dive into the sea or the Houai River; during the cold season, where they hide, they are nothing but oysters. Similarly, the quail is a mouse that transforms in spring. After having sung all summer, it buries itself and remains a mouse until the new season.[47] Every change of habitat is linked, as we see, to the adoption of a new regime of existence, which implies a substantial change of appearance; I do not say a change of substance, for it is really only a mutation. This mutation is quite analogous to those concerning the divinatory art when considering the alternations obtained by substituting one for the other the graphic symbols representing Yin or Yang. Precisely because they record these mutations, calendar centons are valuable as signs. Hunting and fishing are forbidden until the hunting and fishing season opens with a sacrifice of an otter and a hawk. At the very moment the hawk is slaughtered, it undergoes a mutation; from the close of the hunt, it lives with the habits and appearance of a wood pigeon. Men, on the other hand, only become hunters again at the moment when, by means of a sacrifice that causes a mutation of symbols, the sign of the falcon replaces that of the woodpigeon in the skies. Conversely, for women to take care of silkworms, the cry of the hawk chasing its prey, and not the song of the woodpigeon, must be heard in the mulberry trees.[48] Animal mutations are the signs and symbols of the transformations of social activity. The latter, like the mutations themselves, are accompanied by habitat changes and morphological variations. We know how important the theme of coming and going has remained, and even in the *Hi ts'eu* it is linked to the ideas of *coming and going out*. It is also known that retreat and the hidden life have Yin as their emblem, while Yang symbolizes all active manifestations. Philosophical tradition has never failed to see in the one the symbol of spreading activities, in the other the emblem of folded and latent energies. Does it not seem that (long before the time when

---

46   *Ta Tai Li ki*, 47.
47   *Yue ling* and *Hia calendar*.
48   *Id.* in *Ibid.* and *Wang tche, Li ki*, C., I, pp. 283, 332, 340, 389.

scholarly thought attempted to give them the value of cosmogonic entities), the notions of Yin and Yang were included in the antithetical sayings which gave the formula of life to animals, served as signs to the activity of men, marked the times of the universal rhythm, and finally deserved to provide the symbols chosen to preside over the organization of the Calendar?

The Calendar technicians have distributed the rustic signs throughout the year. With greater or less skill, they have attached them one by one to the whole sequence of terms of the solar year. No similar distribution is found in the older calendars.[49] On the contrary, the signs abound and crowd together at periods when men changed both their way of life and their habitat. Moreover, these ancient calendars are scarcely distinguishable from songs of hope or thanksgiving, linking together, in veritable litanies, a host of rustic themes. We have preserved one of these hymns and we know that it was sung in the peasant assemblies of the low season. All the signs which Nature had lavished upon them bountifully in past years, men repeated in their turn in the hope of compelling Nature, by the efficacy of their singing, to repeat them again in the years to come.[50] These litanies of proverbs owed an additional efficacy to the disposition of the singers and the arrangement of the feast. These are details we know only from scholarly descriptions of the rituals. It is indicated that the participants had to form themselves into oriented groups. The choristers represented the alternate and opposite aspects that constitute Space and Time; they represented Heaven and Earth, Sun and Moon, South and Summer, Winter and North, Spring and East, West and Autumn. All the actors, when the joust was over, communed by eating the flesh of a dog, which had been boiled in the East (for the East is Spring), the starting point, we are told, of the activity of Yang.[51] In these late descriptions or interpretations a number of theoretical refinements have doubtless been introduced. It was certainly not an *elaborate* conception of Yin and Yang that first mandated the celebration of the festival. On the contrary, what made it possible to develop this conception was the reflective work for which this arrangement provided the material. The out-of-season gatherings, at which the men recalled in verse and probably imitated by their gestures the habits of the animals,[52] were held in a underground shelter, a sort of common house, the memory of which is preserved in the traditions relating to the *Ming t'ang* and in such myths as that of Hi-ho and the Hollow Mulberry Tree. Hibernators and migratory birds lead a slow, secluded life in a hiding place suited to their winter appearance. Men, on their part, while waiting for the coming of spring to break the ice that imprisoned the waters and the earth and shut them up in a gloomy hiding place,[53] underwent, in the shade, a retreat; they prepared, for the days of renewal, the awakening of their energies. These practices and the feelings that accompany them explain one of the ideas that dominate the scholarly conception of Yin and

---

49   Granet, *op. cit.* p. 54.
50   *Che king*, C., p. 160; Granet, *op. cit.* p. 56; *Civ. Chin.*
51   Granet, *Fêtes et Chansons*, p. 184; *Li ki*, C., pp. 652 ff. The dog is a yang animal.
52   Granet, *op. cit.* p. 181; Id., *Danses et légendes...*, pp. 305 ff.
53   *Civ. Chin.*, pp. 189 ff, 281.

Yang. The philosophers admit that, throughout the winter, the Yang, circumvented by the Yin, undergoes, at the bottom of the subterranean springs,[54] beneath the frozen earth, a sort of annual test from which it emerges invigorated. It escapes from its prison at the beginning of spring by striking the ground with its heel; it is then that the ice cracks of its own accord and the springs awaken.[55] Without the slightest metaphysics, the ancient Chinese knew how to listen for this sign of liberation. They had only to listen to the dance of the pheasants. Men had good reason not to ignore the habits and gestures of these birds. They had learned to dance the dance of the pheasants themselves by putting on their feathers. They knew, therefore, that the pheasants had prepared themselves to give the impulse to renewal, to make the sap rise, to release the waters, to release the Thunder, spending the off-season confined in subterranean or aquatic retreats, here in the form of oysters, there in the form of snakes.[56] – A (aspect of) *dragon, a* (aspect of) *serpent!*" exclaims Tchouang tseu[57] when he wishes to give the formula of a well-regulated life; no one can escape the universal law of rhythm; the Sage knows how to follow an alternative regimen of liberated activity and restorative retreat. This is the regime followed by the ancient Chinese, whose social life was controlled by a periodic need for renewal. Myths imposed the same regime on dragons as on pheasants: the pheasant could provide men with signs for action and the dragon with advice for wisdom. – But is it not striking that the precept with which Tchouang tseu sums up the whole experience of his nation is taken from the theme of rhythmic mutations and takes the exact form of the aphorism of the *Hi ts'eu*: "One (aspect) *yin,* one (aspect) *yang*"?

The notions of Yin and Yang could serve to organize the Calendar, because, like the sayings that compose it, these notions are based on *a rhythmic order of social life which is the counterpart of a double morphology*. This double morphology was translated, in the realm of myths, by the theme of the alternation of forms. The need for natural signs led to attributing to things a formula of life in which the rhythm that animated society could be found. By a parallel route, this formula of life was determined by attributing to the realities chosen to provide signs *alternating forms* intended to serve in turn as symbols of the *contrasted aspects* successively acquired by social life, both in occupations and in habitat. The universe, as this set of mythical notations made it appear, seemed to consist of a set of antithetical forms that alternated in a cyclical manner. Thereafter, the order of the world seemed to result from the *interaction of two* sets *of complementary aspects*. It was enough that Yin and Yang were regarded as the master symbols of these two opposing groupings for

---

54 These are the abodes of the dead (cf. Granet, *La vie et la mort, croyances et doctrines de l'antiquité chinoise*, pp. 15 ff.). The low season is the season of the dead (cf. Granet, *Danses et légendes...*, pp. 321 ff.). Philosophers make this season of Yin the season of death, and Yin the symbol of destructive energies.
55 Granet, *La vie et la mort...*, pp. 15 ff.; *SMT*, III, p. 305.
56 Id., *Danses et légendes*, pp. 570 ff.; *Hia Calendar*, 10th month.
57 *Tchouang tseu*, P. Wieger, *Les Pères du système taoïste*, p. 369. This precept is glossed with the formula: "One (time) of elevation, one (time) of descent." Tchouang tseu says shortly after "One (time) up, one (time) down."

scholars to attribute to them the value of two antagonistic entities. The soothsayers saw in them the principles of all mutation. Astronomers, with the same facility, made of them two cosmogonic principles held responsible for the order of the seasons and the rhythm of solar activity. Even in these technical uses, the social origin and the concrete value of these two symbols remain sensitive. The classical opposition of Yin and Yang, taken as symbols of latent or active, hidden or manifest energies, recalls exactly the ancient formula of social life, sometimes spent in sunny fields and sometimes restored in the darkness of winter retreats.

* * *

To give the formula and indicate the time of the rhythm that governs the one that governs the activity of men and seems to preside over the life of the Universe, a set of sayings was chosen that indicate alternative aspects. These sayings have the appearance of poetic formulas. Why were they borrowed from poetry and why do we usually like to express the idea of the rhythm of the seasons with the help of musical metaphors? And why do Yin and Yang deserve to be treated as the master symbols of this collection of antithetical symbols?

The terms *yin* and *yang*, even when used in academic and technical thought, do not simply designate antagonistic entities. They also serve as rubrics for two opposing classes of symbols. If we tend to see them as efficient principles, we also tend, simultaneously and to the same extent, to see them as efficient rubrics. They form both a pair of alternating activities and a bipartite grouping of alternating forms. They preside over the classification of all things. The Chinese, indeed, have managed to organize their thinking without really thinking about the constitution of species and genera. They are content with various numerical divisions and endow, so to speak, simple bipartition with a kind of sovereign power in matters of classification. In their language, however (and the contrast is noteworthy), the idea of genus (in the grammatical sense of the word) does not seem to play any role. Chinese ignores the grammatical category of gender, whereas Chinese thought is totally dominated by the category of sex. No word can be qualified as masculine or feminine. Instead, all things, all notions are divided between Yin and Yang.

The philosophical tradition agrees that all that is *yin* has a feminine nature, and all that is *yang* has a masculine nature. Thus, for example, the divinatory symbols K'ien and K'ouen are opposed as masculine and feminine, the former being considered to represent Yang and the latter Yin. This sexual representation of Yin and Yang is not peculiar to divination theorists. The *Hi tsèu*, in interpreting a passage of the *Yi king* concerning human marriage, uses the saying "the male and female mix their essences (*tsing* = sexual liquors) and the ten thousand Beings are produced."[58] The crudity of the expression is significant. It must be remembered, however, that the expressions "ten thousand beings," "male and female" refer, in this case, only to divinatory symbols. In fact, one of the main efforts of the orthodox tradition has been to eliminate any realistic meaning of the sexual opposition of Yin and Yang.

---

58   *Yi king*, L., p. 393. The expression "ten thousand beings" (more exactly: the ten thousand – the totality of – emblematic realities) indicates the 11,520 Yin or Yang realities represented by the 64 divinatory hexagrams.

Book II - Chapter II - Yin and Yang

It has succeeded to the extent that the Chinese have long been praised for never having given the slightest place to "sensuality" in their religious conceptions or practices.[59] Even today, there are exegetes who discuss Yin and Yang without pointing out that the fortune of these symbols is due to the importance of the category of sex.[60] This category, in spite of the appearances, is the one of sex.

This category, despite the appearances imposed by a growing concern for probity, has not ceased to rule philosophical thought. It owes this empire to the fact that it first ruled mythical thought; the theme of hierogamy dominates the whole of Chinese mythology. The ritualists, for their part, have always maintained that the harmony (*ho*) of all things *yin* and *yang* (Sun and Moon, Heaven and Earth, Fire and Water) depended on the sexual life of the rulers and on a regulation of morals that excluded excesses of debauchery and, moreover, of chastity. The multiplication of the animal and vegetable species was due, like the health of the world, to the practice of regular hierogamy.[61] The Chiefs, who at first bore the title of Great Entertainers, had as their first function to preside over sexual feasts. These feasts were intended to establish, at particular times, the harmony of two antagonistic groups. One represented the society of men, the other that of women, for the opposition of the sexes was the cardinal rule of Chinese organization.[62] It has never ceased to be so. Nor has the category of sex ever lost its prestige.

Only by considering the ancient forms of the opposition of the sexes can we come to understand the notions of Yin and Yang, their content, their role, their fortune and their proper names. In ancient China, men and women opposed each other in the manner of two competing corporations. A barrier of sexual and technical prohibitions separated them. Ploughmen and weavers formed groups that, because of their different lifestyles, interests, wealth and attractions, were rivals, but also supporters. These *complementary groups* divided the work among themselves, distributing the different tasks, as well as the times and *places* in which they were to be carried out. Each had a formula for life, and social life was the result of *the interaction of these two formulas*.

The weavers, who never left their village, took advantage of the winter to prepare the hemp cloth for the new season. Winter was the low season for the men. They would take a break before going to work in the fields. Yin and Yang took turns working in the same way: the former in winter, the latter in warm season. - The men and women, who were enriched in turn by their industry, met at the beginning and end of the winter season. At these gatherings, fairs (*houei*) and

---

59   See in this respect the categorical statements of J.-J.-M. de Groot (*Fêtes d'Emouy*, p. 745 of the French translation). A more recent fashion is to find phallic representations everywhere, even in writing characters (e.g., Karlgren, *Some fecundity symbols in ancient China*, in "Bulletin of the Museum of Far Eastern antiquities", no. 2, Stockholm, 1930). Sexual themes abound in Chinese literature. However, there is no reason to believe that the Chinese ever thought of deifying sex. In any case, they refrained from opposing Yin and Yang by regarding one as a feminine principle and the other as masculine.

60   Maspero, *La Chine antique*, pp. 480 ff.; pp. 270 ff.

61   Granet, *Fêtes et chansons anciennes*, p. 79; *Civ. Chin.*, pp. 196, 209 ff.

62   *Civ. Chin.*

appointments (*ki*) were held at which each corporation, the weavers in spring, the husbandmen in autumn, took turns at being the protagonists. The Yin and Yang also meet (*ki*) and reunite (*houei*), scholars say, in the equinoctial terms, before one or the other ceases or begins its reign. – Yin and Yang are known to have the gate as a symbol; the gate is also the emblem of sexual festivals.[63] In spring the gates of the hamlets were opened and the husbandmen went out to spend the summer working in the fields; Yang evokes the image of a gate opening, bringing with it the idea of generation, production, and force manifesting itself. In winter, village gates were kept closed; winter is the season of Yin, the symbol of which is a closed gate. – Scholars say that during the cold season, Yang is condemned to live in a underground shelter, surrounded on all sides by Yin. There is reason to believe that the common house where the men gathered during the low season was a sort of cellar situated in the center of the village and surrounded by all the private dwellings; these, at the beginning of village life, belonged to the women. – The men, once they had regained their energy, went to work in the sun in the open fields. The weavers, on the other hand, worked only in dark places; as soon as they began to weave festive garments, they had to flee from the sun.[64] The two sexes were subject to an antithetical discipline. Their respective domains were the inner (*nei*) and the outer (*wai*); so are also the respective domains of Yin and Yang, of shadow and light. Thus the opposition of the sexes was mythically translated into the opposition of Yin and Yang.

These symmetrical oppositions were jointly manifested in the spectacle offered in spring and autumn by the assemblies of the sexual festivals. These festivals were held in valleys where the river marked a kind of sacred border. It was when crossing it that the representatives of the two rival corporations began to mingle and to prelude the collective hierogamy that put an end to the festivities. But they began by forming antagonistic choruses. On both sides of a ritual axis, they provoked each other in verse, lined up face to face. If the female camp was then disturbed to recognize a truly masculine aspect (*yang-yang*) in the opposite camp,[65] it was apparently because the yang (sunny side) was reserved for the group dedicated to work in full sun. To the men belonged the sunny side (*yang*) and to the women the shady side (*yin*). The festive field presented a spectacle, with the shadow side touching the light side, sexual groups facing each other to unite, the ensemble of yin and yang.[66] The sunny side was reserved for the group dedicated to working in the full sun.

"Yang calls, Yin answers"; "boys call, girls answer."[67] These two formulas point to the antithetical discipline governing the relationship of the two antagonistic

---

63   *Kouan tseu*, 3; Granet, *Fêtes et chansons anciennes*..., p. 132.
64   *Civ. chin.*
65   *Che king*, C., p. 78.
66   Granet, *Fêtes et chansons anciennes*..., pp. 244 ff.
67   *Id.* in *Ibid.*, p. 43. The two formulas are interchangeable; both serve to indicate the universal rhythm and the social rhythm. The initiative attributed to Yang, as well as to boys, is an indication of the primacy which the adoption of an agnatic organization has given to males.

symbols, just as it governs the competition of the two rival corporations. The terms used are significant; they can only be explained as allusions to the rites and games of the sexual festivals. Yang is said to call and start the singing (*tch'ang*); this is what the boys actually do during the singing festival. Yin is said to respond by giving a harmonious response (*ho*); this was actually the role of the girls. The girls and boys prefer their union (*ho*) with a joust (*king*); the Yin and Yang also joust (*king*) before joining (*ho*), and do so, as the delegates of the two rival guilds, every spring and autumn. The word (*ho*), which designates these symmetrical unions, is still applied to the sung replications which mark the perfect concordance of the actors; it is also used to express the harmony (*ho*) which results from the concerted action (*tiao* or *tiao ho*) of Yin and Yang. Now we can understand why it is customary to evoke by musical metaphors the rhythmic competition of the symbols of Yin and Yang; both the conception and the name of these symbols derive from the spectacle of the assemblies in which, lined up in front of the shadow or the sun, two choruses of singers gave each other the reply. They competed in inventive talent and proverbial knowledge, participating in traditional improvisation. This is how most of the poetic centons that formed the material of the calendar were invented; these centons evoke the images offered by the ritual landscape of the festivals at the changes of seasons; hence their value as symbols and signs. Their origin also explains the link that, from the beginning, binds them to the symbols of Yin and Yang. It is by virtue of this primary connection that this pair of symbols was able to preside over the wise organization of the calendar. A theory of Time was constituted as soon as the mass of poetic centons, opposing each other in pairs like so many antithetical couples, was distributed among the stations classified under one or the other of these master columns. In this set of contrasting symbols provided in turn by the landscape of the autumn and spring assemblies, the essential opposition, the most visible, the most poignant, the only one that instantly evoked the whole drama, was the opposition of the antagonistic choruses facing each other like light and shadow. Thus, Yin and Yang deserved to be considered as symbols that summarized, evoked and provoked all the others. In this way, they constituted a pair of effective rubrics responsible for the classification of all aspects of alternation and, likewise, a pair of effective symbols responsible for universal alternation.

The conception of Yin and Yang was outlined on the occasion of dramatic performances in which two supportive and rival corporations, two complementary groups, played and communicated with each other. The audience seemed to include the whole human group, and the totality of the things of nature, present or evoked, figured in the festival. The field in which these assemblies met represented the totality of space, the whole duration sustained in the joust in which the poetic centons recalled the successive signs of the Universe. This total spectacle was an *animated* spectacle. For the duration of the combat of dance and poetry, the two rival parties had to alternate their songs.[68] While the jousting field, replete with

---

It should be noted that, in the past, the initiative in marriage belonged to girls; the classical formula of the alternating action of yin and yang evokes in the first place the "yin aspect."

68   *Id.* in *Ibid.*, pp. 92, 146 ff.; pp. 261 ff.; *Civ Chin.*.

antagonistic choruses, seemed to be composed of clashing extensions of opposite gender, the time of the joust, occupied by an alternation of antithetical songs and dances, seemed to be constituted by the interplay of two rival groupings of opposite gender. This explains, along with the diversity of extensions and durations, the *rhythmic linkage* of Space and Time under the dominance of the Yin and Yang categories. Being distributed in opposite and alternating durations or extensions, neither Space nor Time are one, nor can they be conceived separately, but together they form an indissoluble whole.[69] This same whole embraces both the natural and the human world; it is, to put it more precisely, identical with the *total society* which groups, in two opposing camps, all conceivable realities. – The opposition of the sexes appeared as the foundation of the social order and served as a principle for the seasonal distribution of human activities. Similarly, the opposition of Yin and Yang appeared as the foundation of the universal order; it was seen as the principle of a rhythmic distribution of natural works. Never could the *unity* of the Universe be perceived more perfectly, nor felt better as a whole, than in those sacred moments when, by proceeding to a coherent distribution of places, occasions, activities, works and symbols, a total order was restored by thinking of celebrating collective nuptials, while Yin and Yang also united and communicated sexually. If Time, Space, Society and the Universe owe a *bipartite order* to the category of sex, it is not at all due to a metaphysical tendency towards a substantialist dualism.[70] The idea of *couple remains associated with the idea of communion, and the notion of totality rules over the rule of bipartition.* The opposition of Yin and Yang is not conceived in principle (and has never been conceived) as an absolute opposition comparable to those of Being and Non-Being, Good and Evil.[71] It is a relative and *rhythmic* opposition, between two rival and supportive groupings, complementary in the same way as two sexual corporations, which alternate as they do in the task and pass in turn to the foreground. The basis of this alternation is to be found in the fact that, at the time when the conception of Yin and Yang was formed (and this is a decisive proof of the antiquity of this conception), the social order rested, not on an ideal of authority, but on a principle of rotation.[72] Thus Yin and Yang are imagined neither as Principles nor as Substances. If it is said that in order to re-establish universal order they must celebrate their wedding at every equinox, it is not to imply that a male Principle then unites with a female Principle. They are real weddings, but their reality is symbolic. They correspond, in the natural world, to the festivals which, each spring and autumn, revive, in human groups, the feel-

---

69   Granet, *Fêtes et chansons anciennes...*, pp. 244 ff.
70   See to the contrary Maspero, *La Chine antique*, p. 482.
71   His conception is dominated by the idea of exchange: the father is yang; but the son, yin before his father, is yang before his own children. The minister is yin, and becomes the yang when he succeeds and takes the title of ruler. If we say that Yin is a principle of death and punishment (*hing*), Yang a principle of beneficence (*tö*), it is because one expresses the virtue of the Chief, the other that of the Minister. The minister and the chief form a pair. See Granet, *Danses et légendes de la Chine ancienne*, pp. 117-421.
72   *Civ. Chin*, pp. 183, 231 ff.

ing of a *communal unity*. The weddings of Yin and Yang, like those of the peasants, are *collective weddings*. They are visible in the rainbow. The rainbow itself is but an emblem or a sign. The festival is reflected in it. It is therefore composed of bands of opposite colors, dark and light.[73] These antithetical colors do not point to two different substances; they are simply *belongings* of the female and male groups, for *shadow belongs to the women and light to the men*. Even when they confront and unite, we must see in Yin and Yang only the *rubric-masters of two sets of symbols*. They are not two antagonistic realities, but *two rival groupings*. Much more than groupings of realities or forces, they are *groupings of aspects and usages*; they are, in fact, two *classes of attributes or attributions shared between the two halves of the social body*.

* * *

Yin and yang can be defined neither as pure logical entities nor as mere cosmogonic principles. They are neither substances, nor forces, nor genders. To common thought they are all these things indistinctly, and no technician considers them under one of these aspects to the exclusion of the others. They are neither realized nor transcended nor abstracted. Completely dominated by the idea of efficacy, Chinese thought moves in a world of symbols composed of *correspondences* and *oppositions* which, when we want to act or understand, we need only bring into play. We know and we can as soon as we have the double list of symbols that attract or oppose each other. The category of sex reveals its efficacy in the ordering of human groupings. It imposes itself, then, as the principle of a global classification. From there, the totality of the contrasted aspects that make up the society formed by men and things is arranged in two opposing strips of masculine or feminine filiation. Symbols of sexual *oppositions* and *communions*, Yin and Yang seem to lead the concerted joust in which these aspects call and respond to each other like so many symbols and signs. They raise them in pairs and form themselves a pair of rubrics.

The Chinese are not given to classify by *genres* and *species*. They avoid thinking with the help of concepts which, lodged in an abstract Time and Space, define the idea without evoking reality. Instead of defined concepts, they prefer symbols rich in affinities; instead of distinguishing in Time and Space two independent entities, they house the games of their symbols in a concrete environment constituted by their interaction; they do not detach Yin and Yang from the social realities whose rhythmic order these symbols evoke. The empire they accord to the category of sex implies contempt for the category of gender.[74] One allows a neutral classification of notions that distances them from duration and extension; the other leads to classifications of symbols that are dominated by the vision of their concrete relations, that is, their *respective positions* in the active milieu of Space and Time. At first we see them opposing each other, governed by a simple law of alternation, and we group them into pairs; this is because the category of sex reigns alone, in the manner of a *category of couple*. In this sense, it is the first of the *numerical categories*.

---

73   Granet, *Fêtes et chansons anciennes de la Chine*, pp. 272 ff.
74   In the logical sense of the word.

It makes it possible to ascertain the simplest arrangement in Space and Time of a totality that cannot be conceived as *indivisible*, for what has made it possible to imagine it is the spectacle of the plenary assemblies of a human grouping; *if this grouping were entirely homogeneous, it would have no need to remake its unity.*

The sense of harmonious order which the jousts gave to the whole of beings conferred on the bipartite classification such religious prestige that no other could surpass it in authority. The Chinese did not condemn themselves to find order only where bipartition reigned; but the principle of their various classifications has not changed. They all involve the analysis of a more or less complex *total* sense, and this analysis always proceeds from an *image*; this image, at once *rhythmic* and *geometric*, shows the distribution, in Space and Time, of the elements among which the total is decomposed, so that it follows a *numerical symbol* to indicate the mode of grouping of these elements and, consequently, to detect the intimate nature of the total. Hence the importance of the related notions of *Number* and *Element*.

Chapter III
NUMBERS

The idea of quantity plays no role in Chinese philosophical speculation. Numbers, however, had an exciting interest for the sages of ancient China.[1] But whatever the arithmetical or geometrical knowledge[2] of certain guilds (surveyors, carpenters, architects, wheelwrights, musicians, etc.), no sage was inclined to use them, except insofar as this knowledge facilitated numerical games, without ever forcing them to perform operations whose results could not be controlled. Everyone pretended to manipulate the Numbers as he manipulated the Symbols; and, for the Chinese, the Numbers are, in fact, remarkable, like the Symbols, for a versatility conducive to effective manipulations.

Knowing, for example, (and wishing, in the first place, to justify this knowledge by attaching it to a global knowledge), that, for the human species, embryonic life

---

[1] According to Chavannes, "a philosophy of numbers" has shone forth, "like the Pythagorean doctrine, in China". Certainly, it is easier to boast of the brilliance of this "philosophy" than to determine its influence and grasp its principles. The observations I have collected over many years allow me, at most, to present a few remarks on the attitude of the Chinese toward numbers. I will not include any hypotheses or look for the origin of numbers – a premature question – without even pointing out any comparisons, I will stick to Chinese ideas. I have tried to interpret them by dealing with various themes (questions of places, of the Elements, of divinatory symbols, of musical pipes...) chosen for the importance that the Chinese attribute to them and which they have, indeed. I had to discover the facts and their historical order, and I also had to show how they can be discovered. I also had to interpret them in our language, which does not lend itself to expressing Chinese conceptions. I need not apologize for the thoroughness of the analysis and the length of a chapter in which I had to explain one of the fundamental features of Chinese thought, namely, an extreme respect for numerical symbols combined with an extreme indifference to any quantitative conception.

[2] On this point, see the discussion initiated by A. Rey on pp. 389 ff. of *Science orientale*.

lasts 10 months, a philosopher[3] reasoned thus: "(The) Heaven (*is worth*) 1; (the) Earth (*is worth*) 2; Man (*is worth*) 3; 3 (*times*) 3 (*make*) 9; 9 (*times*) 9 (*make*) 81 {= (eighty and) 1}; 1 rules the Sun; the number of the Sun is {1 (ten) =} 10; the Sun rules Man; that is why (every) man is born in the tenth month (of gestation)[4]." And the sage continued, teaching us {*since* 9 x 8 *make* (*seventy and*) 2} that the horse, ruled by the Moon which *is worth* 2, needs – there are {2 (+ one ten) =} 12 lunations[5] – of 12 months of gestation. Then (and simply continuing the multiplication of 9 by 7, 6, 5, etc.),[6] he still found it necessary to teach that bitches are 3 months pregnant {9 x 7 = (sixty and) 3}; sows 4 months {9 x 6 = (fifty and) 4}; monkeys 5 months {9 x 5 = (forty and) 5}; hinds 6 months {9 x 4 = (thirty and) 6}; tigresses 7 months {9 x 3 = (twenty and) 7}... It follows: on the one hand, that a *symbolic equivalence* brings 81 close to 10, but also 72 to 12, while 63 or 54 signify 3 or 4; and, on the other hand, that the 2 (interchangeable with the 12 or 72) rules the Moon and (*value*) the Earth, while the 10 (interchangeable with the 1 and 81, which in turn equals the 9 and 3) rules the Sun and (*value*) Heaven.[7]

A numerical symbol *commands* a whole quantity of realities and symbols; but, to this same set, several numbers can be attached, which are considered, *in this particular case*, as *equivalents*. In addition to a quantitative value which distinguishes them, but which tends to be neglected, Numbers possess a much more interesting symbolic value, because, offering no resistance to the operative genius, they can lend themselves to a kind of alchemy. Numbers are susceptible to mutation. They are so because of the multiple efficacy with which they seem to be endowed and which derives from their principal function; they serve and have value as *symbolic rubrics*.

Numbers make it possible to classify things, but not in the manner of simple ordinal numbers, nor by defining collections quantitatively. The Chinese are not concerned with assigning a rank that is only a rank, nor with establishing a count from the sole point of view of quantity. They use numbers to express the *qualities* of particular groupings or to indicate a *hierarchical* order. In addition to their *classificatory function* and linked to it, Numbers have a *protocolary* function.

I. Numbers, Cyclical Signs, Elements.

The distinction between a cardinal, ordinal or distributive use of Numbers is not of essential interest to the Chinese. Numbers are used to classify because they serve to situate and represent concretely. They are symbols. In the first place, a real descriptive power is attributed to them.

* * *

---

3   *Houai-nan tseu*, 4. Cf. *Ta Tai Li ki*, 81.
4   The days are counted with the help of a denary cycle. Mythically there are 10 Suns.
5   There are also 12 moons.
6   It is seen that the Numbers serve to perform a certain form of induction.
7   The equivalence: 1 (*yi*) and Heaven (*T'ien*), is so perfect that it is written: *T'ien yi*, without copula. It should also be written (*vaut*) in parentheses.

Book II - Chapter III - Numbers

To describe numerically, the Chinese have three series of signs: a) denary; b) duodenary[8] and c) decimal. In fact, the signs of these three series are called numerals (*chou*), without distinction.

The numbers of the denary and duodenary series are represented by symbols that are rarely considered without giving them an image value.

Jen (one of the terms of the series of ten) suggests to Sseu-ma Ts'ien the idea of a burden (*jen*);[9] this sign shows the ten thousand species of beings at the moment when they are carried and nourished in the depths of the World. The *Chouo wen*, for its part, recognizes in *jen* the figure of a fat woman (*jen*), carrying her burden, who nourishes an embryo. Similarly, according to the *Chouo wen*, *tch'en* (of the duodenary series) indicates the tremor (*tchen*) produced by the Thunder; it shows, says Sseu-ma Ts'ien (the females) of the ten thousand species that have just conceived (*tchen*).[10] These are complementary images, since another sign (also pronounced *tchen*) evokes the woman *shaken* by fertilization or the Earth *shaken* by Thunder.[11]

The values attributed to these images are remarkable; they reveal an intimate concordance between Nature's gestures and human behavior. We may suppose that, as such, they can be used as calendar signs. These, as is natural, include a topographical indication.

Tch'en, in fact, is the emblem of the East-South-East, as well as of the third month of spring; only after the equinox has passed should the first rumblings of the Thunder be heard. The Thunder, then, opening and shaking the earth, escapes from the subterranean refuge where winter has confined it; thenceforth men may open the earth and move it by means of the fruitful plough; but, lest, as soon as fertilized, its fruit should escape and fail to ripen, every woman must live withdrawn as soon as she hears the signal of the Thunder or the warning repeated by a wooden clapper vibrating a bell.[12] Likewise, as an emblem of the North and of the winter solstice, *jen* presides over the *birth* of yang, indicated in the duodenary cycle by the sign *tseu* (whose meaning is "*child*"), which is framed by *jen* and *kouei* in the denary cycle. While *jen* means "gestation," *kouei* represents the Waters penetrating

---

8   The signs of the denary cycle are called the ten stems (*kan*); those of the duodenary cycle, the twelve branches (*tche*). Although *kan* is opposed to *tche* as the stem to the branches, *tche*, like *kan*, designates a vertically planted pole. *Kan* or *tche*, branches or stems, are used to locate, to mark positions (geometers use denary signs to mark the angles of their figures), but stems and branches are also used to compare magnitudes; *tche* (branch) means: measure, count, number, quantity, and the expression *jo kan* (*Jo* = such, *kan* = stem) means *such a number, so much or so much*.

9   *SMT*, III, p. 305. Chavannes erroneously translated this *jen* as goodness.

10 *SMT*, III, p. 308.

11 All these images are linked to a representation of Mother Earth.

12 *Li ki*, C., I, p. 342 The *Yue ling* fixes the third day after the equinox as the time of the first peals of thunder and the proclamation by the herald with the wooden bell of the prohibitions imposed on women. I must insist on the ritual value of the images evoked by the cyclical signs according to Chinese interpreters; too many Sinologists have tried to see in these interpretations only pedantic puns. See *SMT*, III, p. 303, N. 1 and notes on the following pages.

the Earth from the four directions. The Earth opens for them toward the North Pole; thus *kouei*, while marking their locations, designates the fertile humors that enable women to conceive and nourish their charge; the times favorable for conception are both the full winter and midnight, and the full north is the favorable orientation.[13]

The signs of the denary and duodenary series give rise to groups of images (which are not arbitrary, for in their assemblage is expressed the factual link that binds this or that category of uses to its natural environment). These symbols – which we consider as numbers – thus serve as rubrics for concrete sets that seem to *specify*, by the mere fact of situating them in Time and Space.

The World is a closed universe; like it, both Space and Time are finite. Therefore, the numerical signs assigned as rubrics to the sectors of Space-Time are finite in number. Each of them corresponds to a place in Time as well as to a spatial event and are ordered, oriented, in the form of a cycle.

While the numbers of the duodenary cycle are arranged one by one, around the circumference of a circle, the numbers of the denary are grouped in five pairs, four pairs being the points of a cross and the fifth the center. As this arrangement indicates, the conception of a cycle of ten numerical rubrics is linked to a system of classification by **5**; we know the importance of this system which completes, by opposition, a system of classification by **6**. Now, the transverse arrangement presupposes a representation of the square and the set square. The square and the set square are considered significant of the Space and of the terrestrial order. On the other hand, the **2** (even) is, as we shall see shortly, the emblem of the Earth and of the square (at least when we consider the perimeter without thinking of the center); the **3** (odd) is, on the other hand, the symbol of Heaven and of the circle (or, rather, of the semicircle which, inscribed in a square of side 2, has 2 as its diameter). Indeed, Heaven (*masculine*, yang, **3**, *even*) has the number 6 (= 3 × 2), while Earth (*feminine*, yin, **2**, *even*) has the number 5 {= (2 + 2) + 1}, since, if we think of a cross, we cannot neglect the center; thus, as soon as we have assigned them a numerical symbol, Earth and Heaven (feminine and masculine) find themselves exchanging their attributes (even and odd). Symmetrically, the denary signs (*kan*), arranged in the form of a cross, qualify, however, as celestial (*t'ien kan*: celestial branches), while the duodenary signs (*tche*), arranged in a circle, qualify as terrestrial (*ti tche*: earthly branches). This important inversion demonstrates the interdependence of the two cycles. There is reason to suppose that, linked to the classification by **6**, the conception of a duodenary cycle refers to the representations of Heaven and Time, just as, integral to the classification by **5**, the conception of a denary cycle derives from the representations of Earth and Space. But, between Space and Time, Heaven and Earth, no independence is conceivable, and the connection of the two cycles is no less important than their opposition. Both are the set of places and occasions which each of them allows to be arranged in

---

13   Granet, *La vie et la mort...*, pp. 12 ff.

Book II - Chapter III - Numbers 93

such an order that it suits the Earth and imposes itself on Heaven, or, significant of Heaven, governs the Earth.

While the signs denary or duodenary preside, as rubrics, over different sets of realities which their situations in Space and Time suffice to *identify*, the cycles constituted by these signs evoke two *complementary* modes of geometrical distribution. They correspond to *two numerical analyses* that claim to reveal *together* the composition of the ordered total that forms the Universe.

It is by virtue of their descriptive power (and because, by suggesting compositions and arrangements, they can indicate distributions and situations) that the different cycles possess the characteristic efficacy of Numbers, deserve their name and, consequently, are similar to the symbols of the decimal series.

For the Universe to present itself as an *ordered* whole, it is necessary and sufficient that an enacted Calendar governs, in a renewed World, a new Era. The World is recreated anew as soon as a Chief worthy of exercising a civilizing mission has merited to be "entrusted with the *Numbers* of the Calendar of Heaven (*T'ien tche li chou*)."[14] Conversely, the Universe goes out of order when a decadent Virtue causes *the Calendar Numbers (li chou) to lose their order*.[15] The Numbers (*li chou*) to which these consecrated formula refer are symbols which happen to indicate situations (*ts'eu*)[16] distributed in Time (as well as in Space); they do not differ, at least as regards their object, from the signs of the denary and duodenary cycles. Precisely the latter of these signs has been assigned to the notation of the hours, and the former to the designation of the days.[17] But they are also used in combination. The signs of the two series are sometimes arranged so as to form a rose of 24 winds corresponding to 24 half-months of fifteen days.[18] Most often they were used by combining them in pairs to constitute a cycle of 60 binomials, **6** times the char-

---

14   *SMT*, III, p. 325.

15   *SMT*, III, p. 326.

16   *Ts'eu* means: order, series, place, station. Interpreters recognize in the "Numbers" of the Calendar the symbols of astronomical (or solar) sites or positions.

17   I have not (premature question) to deal here with the question of the origin (foreign or Chinese) of the system of the twelve double hours (conceived as framing, each one, one of the points of a rose with twelve directions). Chinese mythology admits the real existence of 12 moons and 10 suns.

18   To obtain 24 sites with 10 + 12 cyclic signs, one begins by adding 4 terms (assigned to the 4 directions of the angle), then uses the 12 duodenary signs and only 8 denary signs, the remaining 2 denary signs forming a binomial always reserved for the center. See *Houai-nan tseu*, 2 and Granet, *op. cit.* p. 13, n. 2. Note that the division into 24 orientations corresponds to an administrative division into 24 departments (divided into 4 directions) entrusted to chiefs designated by bird names (these birds, at least, appear on the calendrical signs). The head of these departments (phoenix) presides over the calendar. Cf. *Tso tchouan*, C., t. III, pp. 276 and 277, and Granet, *Danses et légendes...*, p. 236, n. 1. Note that the 24 months of 15 days each are subdivided into 3 periods of 5 days; the 72 periods of 5 days that make up the year (360 = 72 x 5) are assigned 72 calendrical sayings, concrete labels (cf. Granet, *Fêtes et chansons anciennes*, p. 54), there is another division of the days of the year into 30 (= 5 x 6) 12-day periods (cf. Granet, *op. cit.*, pp. 54 and 132, *Kouan tseu*, 14; Granet, *Danses et légendes...*, p. 270, n. 1, and note 902). In these various provisions the solidarity of the classifications by 5 and by 6 became apparent.

acters of the denary series (first terms of each binomial) and **5** times those of the duodenary series (second terms) being used.[19] These numerical pairs were used in ancient times to identify days and, more recently, years, months and hours. Thus, by means of four binomials of the sexagenary cycle, it has been possible to characterize temporal (and spatial) situations with extreme precision. It is known that the eight characters {*Pa tseu* (the four cyclic binomials)} which situate the birth of individuals, still must be examined today, before any marriage, it is also known that the principle of all the rules of choice, in matrimonial matters, is the exogamy of the *name*.[20] The practice of *Pa tseu* (remarkable for its persistence) does not go back to antiquity,[21] but recalls two practices which are among the oldest attested. On the one hand, the *Yi li* enjoins the bridegroom to ask for the personal name (*ming*) of the bride-to-be, in order, it is said, to be able to consult fortune and not risk contravening the rule of exogamy.[22] On the other hand, under the Yin dynasty,[23] the personal name was chosen from among the signs of the series of the bereaved; the emblem of the day of birth served as an individual emblem. By the very fact that they situate beings (*wou*), cyclic signs *identify* them; like names, they define individualities, essences (*wou*).

Suppose a divine apparition occurs and we have (as in the case of a birth) to determine, so that we may propitiate without sacrilegious error, the personality which has just revealed itself; the problem will seem susceptible of two solutions, basically indistinct: to discover the *name* of the genius who has manifested or to fix the place of manifestation. We have, for a case of this kind, a double account.[24] On the one hand, we are told that the chronicler in charge of the identification recognized that it was Tan-chou; such was the name of the son of Yao the Sovereign, ancestor of the Li family. It was therefore the responsibility of the Li family to provide the sacrificer {and the offerings; the latter are only agreeable if, because of the domain and cuisine from which they come, they belong to a symbolic species

---

19 Note this imbricated action of 5, multiplier of 12 (= 6x2) and 6, multiplier of 10 (= 5x2).

20 Associated with territorial exogamy, but we know (cf. *Civ. Chin.*, pp. 178, 204, and Granet, *Danses et légendes*..., end of note 341) that there must have been a consonance between domain, habitat, site and name.

21 The *Pa tseu* was in use from the time of the T'ang, if not from the time of the Han. In any case, the *Tcheou li* (Biot, *Le Tcheou li, ou les Rites des Tcheou*, t. II, p. 307) shows that in the past the year, month, day of birth, and personal name were taken into account in pairings.

22 Granet, *Danses et légendes*..., p. 159. This usage assumes that the personal name (which is asked for, because it is secret) bears a relationship to the (known) family name similar to that between an essence (*wou*) and a species (*lei*). Family names reveal a virtue (*tö*) specific (*lei*), susceptible of four particularizations which (because of ideas about reincarnation) seem to have corresponded to a set of four names (*ming*) distinguishing four successive generations. (Cf. Granet, *op. cit.*, pp. 368 ff.). The personal name (*ming*) situates (in such and such a family) the generation, it expresses a kind of rank.

23 Cf. *SMT*, I, pp. 169, 175, 176. Archaeology seems to have confirmed the tradition.

24 Cf. Granet, *op. cit.* p. 158. The two accounts come from works of similar date, inspiration and style.

Book II - Chapter III - Numbers

(*lei*) to which the recipient also belongs}.[25] In the other story in which it was considered unnecessary to give the name of the genie who appeared, the chronicler, after having stated at the beginning, "An offering must be made to him using his essence (*wou*)," specifies by adding, "On the day of his appearance, this is, in truth, his essence!" Once the cyclical sign that locates the manifestation to propitiate is determined, the nature of the offerings is fixed, which should belong to the same sector of the world {and at the same time, apparently, of the sacrificer, since both belong to the same species (*lei*)}.

As we see, there is an *equivalence* between a species (*lei*) or essence (*wou*), i.e., a name (*ming*), and a place or sector of Space-Time. But it also happens that cyclic signs evoking species and sectors, places and essences – and having the value of a name, of an appellative – suggest at the same time directly numerical representations. It is enough to say of an apparition that it refers to a site *kia yi* (the first denary binomial) for it to be immediately known that the ceremonies will have to be performed (which will determine the choice of victims, colors, etc.) under the sign of the eastern spring, the sector to which this binomial serves as a rubric.[26] But we also know that the whole order of the liturgy (dimensions of the protocol, durations, quantities, etc.) will have to be ordered by the number **8**.[27] In other words, the situations characterized by the rubric *kia yi* necessarily correspond to dispositions governed by the classifier 8; 8 and *kia yi* are contemplated together under the aspect of *numerical rubrics*. The numerical rubric (taken from the cyclic series), while indicating (by revealing a specific essence) a specific place referring to a global arrangement implying a definite composition, evokes a set of symbols characterized, on the other hand, by a definite mode of composition; this is signaled by a *master number* (taken from the decimal series). This master number has the role of *classifier* and is able to impose meaningful presentations (geometric or rhythmic) of this or that emblematic situation and essence.

Thus, as Sseu-ma Ts'ien tells us, to an S-S-E site, marked by the duodenary sign *sseu* (which expresses the perfection of Yang) corresponds the number 7 (for, *says* the historian, the Yang numbers attain their perfection in 7); so that the characteristic constellation of this site is formed of 7 (*ts'i*) stars and is called *Ts'i sing*: the Seven Stars.[28] Similarly, if the male development is marked by the number 8, and the female by the number 7, it is because, we are told, the places of the male or female births are respectively "the *Numbers*" (of the duodenary cycle) *yin* (E-N-E = 8) and *chen* (S-S-W = 7).[29]

---

25 Ibid., p. 157 ff. The ritual principle is that spirits eat nothing except what (by the nature of the offerer and the nature of the offering) is of their kind (*lei*).

26 Ibid. p. 158.

27 Cf. *Tch'ouen ts'ieou fan tou*, ch. 13. Everything, in a sacrifice made in spring (East), is ordered by 8 (by 7 in summer, by 9 in autumn, etc.), and if one wants then, for example, to make rain, it will be necessary to make 8 dancers dance, offer 8 fish, build a mound 8 feet on a side, make 8 dragons: 1 large (8 feet long) + 7 small (8/2 feet long), etc.

28 *SMT*, III, pp. 308-309.

29 Granet, *La vie et la mort...* pp. 1 ff. Seven, which is equivalent to *chen* (S-S-W) in this example, is equivalent to sseu (S-S-E) in the previous example. Attached to the same set of

The duodenary and denary signs are not used to establish counts, nor to indicate an *abstract range* like the ordinal numbers; they deserve the name numerals (as do the signs of the decimal series) because they serve as emblems for specific situations which they represent in concrete terms. Each of them can evoke – in its place in a global organization (characterized by a certain mode of division into singularized sectors) – a *local grouping* whose essence (*wou*) is expressed by an organization (of a rhythmic or geometrical character) also specified by a characteristic divisor.

* * *

The Chinese have given the name of Numbers to cyclic signs intended to designate not ranges but places and capable of evoking orderings rather than *totals*. For counting and numbering, they have another system of symbols constituting a linearly ordered decimal series (1, 2, 3... 11, 12... 101...). The numbers of this third series are considered, however, as symbols, remarkable, as much as the others, for their descriptive power. They, too, form an image, and in the representations they suggest, the ideas of *addition* and *unity* are much less important than a kind of concrete analysis intended to specify the kind of division or organization that seems appropriate for a given *grouping*.

Although they seem to be used for numbering and counting, the numbers of the decimal series are used to represent concrete modes of arrangement. A passage from the *Tso tchouan*[30] manifests this; the indifference to distinguishing between a cardinal and an ordinal function of numbers is clearly evident.

This passage, singularly instructive, tends, by the simple enumeration of a series of sorting types, to suggest the feeling of a rhythmic progression. It is inserted in a development on harmony (*ho*), where the intention is to make sensible the intimate correspondences which unite tastes and sounds, food and music; in short, what we would call substance and rhythm.[31] Everything is harmony, that is to say, dosage, and the different dosages are but one and the same harmony whose modalities, *in order of increasing complication*, are expressed by a series of numerical symbols. These symbols govern a classification by categories, while at the same time showing the *internal arrangement* which suits each of the realizations (always total and always specific) of the universal harmony.

It is expressed by nine words, each preceded by one of the first nine numbers. It cannot be translated as: "1° the breath... 9° the songs" nor as "**1** (is) the breath... **9** (are) the songs." It should be understood as: "**1** (= One and in the first place is the) Breath (*k'i*). **2** (= Two and in second place are the) Sets {(*ti*) which form, fac-

---

symbols, different numbers (72, 12, 2), may be considered equivalent; likewise, a number may, attached to two different sets, change its emblematic value; this is a simple consequence of the competition of different classification systems.

30   *Tso tchouan*, C., III, p. 327. Extract from a discourse attributed to Yen tseu, a contemporary of Confucius.

31   Comp. (264) *Yo ki*, in *Li ki*, C., II, p. 83. These correspondences are established within the framework of the various classification systems, in particular the fivefold classification system.

ing each other like Yang and Yin (antithetical pair), the civil and military dances; these dances are suitable for both Summer (South) and Winter (North) (simple opposition)}. **3** (= Three and in the third place are the) Modes {poetic (*lei*) which, distributed among the lords, the supreme king-chief and the gods, are arranged hierarchically (in a centered line); situated between the gods and the feudatories, the supreme chief occupies an intermediate and eminent situation at the same time central}. **4** (= Four and in fourth place are the) Symbols {of dance (*wou*), for the four directions (square arrangement, significant of the proper form of Space and Earth) provide, with the dancers and their insignia, the four types of dances}. **5** (= Five and in the fifth place are the) Sounds {primordial (*cheng*): essence of music, the sounds call the classifier 5 (emblem of the Center) and deserve to occupy in the progression (between 1 and 9) the central place; assigned to the four seasons-directions and to the Center, they allow to classify the whole of the things of music in the Space-Time (crossed disposition)}. **6** (= Six and in the sixth place are the) Tubes {musical (*liu*) or, rather, the six pairs of musical tubes (6 yin tubes duplicating the 6 yang tubes); between them, they recall the twelve months and realize the distribution of harmony in Time (symmetrically to the four Symbols which realize it in Space) (hexagonal – or dodecagonal – disposition evoking Time, Heaven, the round)}. **7** (= Seven and in the seventh place, are the Notes {of the scale (*yin*) figuring either the total of the Influences exerted by the Seven Astronomical Rectors, or a week of seven days. The seven (like the five) gives the idea of a centered total, namely either (6 + 1) a hexagon (= circle) planned with its center, or (4 + 3) a square (4) arranged around a perpendicular axis (3) marking the Up (Zenith), the Down (Nadir) and the Center of the world}. **8** (= Eight and in the eighth place are the) Winds {(*fong*), which correspond, together with eight instruments of different *matter* (the timbres come into consideration after the intervals), to the eight concrete regions of Space, namely the eight outer squares of the expanse (square and subdivided into nine squares)}. **9** (= Nine and in the ninth place are the) Songs {(*ko*), i.e. music and dance in their most sensitive manifestations; the dancers and musicians at work evoke the nine activities (all real activities); the set of realizations (*kong*) which makes possible an ordered, totally hierarchical activity, occupies the whole concrete space (8) plus its ideal center (1); this set is represented by three lines which, centered and hierarchized, are each worth three and which, together, compose the figure of a square subdivided into nine and presided over, so to speak, at its center, by a master square (domain of the Chief)}.

The Breath is placed at the beginning of the progression, because it is considered the unique and primary element, simple and *total*, of the rhythm, and the Nine Cantos end it, because they mark the full and supreme realization, ultimate and *complete*, of all that the rhythm contains in itself. Do we wish to show how realities (of all kinds) are constituted and how they are grouped together? Do we wish, in order to indicate concretely their rank, their essence, to reveal the typical form in which they are constituted? Suffice it to indicate that the things of music are arranged in categories under symbols taken from the series of Numbers. These numerical labels not only mark the places in the progression, but also determine the composition and figure that distinguish each category; what, for example, *occurs* and is *arranged* in the fourth place, *is* arranged in a square and *presented* in fours, constituting a grouping of realities whose essence is to be both fourth and fourfold.

Ontological order and logical order are translated together into rhythmic and geometric images. They merge so well that it seems possible to classify and characterize them by means of numerical expressions. By their descriptive power, Numbers, indexes of a concrete analysis, are called upon, as classifiers, to identify real groupings. They can be used as rubrics, because they are significant of the various types of organization imposed on things when they are realized in their place in the Universe.

The world is a closed universe. Assigned to designate places, cyclic signs evoke dispositions. Symmetrically, the numbers of the decimal series seem to be intended to specify dispositions, but they are also given the power to represent places.

Practically indefinite, the decimal series seems to be arranged linearly. In fact, when we want to communicate the feeling of a progression, we apparently use the numbers in their linear sequence. But, as we have just seen, between the beginning and the end of the progression no other distance is imagined than that which separates a total, envisaged at the beginning only in its unity, from a whole susceptible of analysis, but always considered as complete. To give the idea of a similar progression, fundamentally static, so to speak, and imagined with a view to distributing among *hierarchical categories* the significant aspects of a finite universe, there is no reason to appeal to numbers by making it appear that they can form an *unlimited* sequence; we would prefer to imagine them as composing a set of *finite* series, one of which, that of simple units, can represent entirely.

As an image of the progression of numbers, the first ten thus acquires the character of a *cycle*; hence the possibility of relating its symbols to cyclic symbols, especially those of the denary cycle. The simple cyclic signs, however, are symbols of groupings whose locations they fix without attempting (in principle) to indicate their hierarchy. By the fact of noting a progression, the first numbers, on the contrary, by serving as category headings, allow us to imagine a hierarchical order. Now, the idea of hierarchy is translated in Chinese thought by the realistic representation of a center. Placed *in the middle* of the first nine numbers, the 5 is the symbol of the center.

From the attribution of the center to the 5, the neighboring signs, escaping from their linear formation, are distributed in Space and assume in their turn spatial attributions. Consequently, if they seem at first suitable to characterize the places in the manner of cyclic symbols, the symbols of the decimal series can also, as we shall soon see, be called upon to represent, in relation to a centered set, the adjustment of the different sectors; they then compose a sort of image in which the order of the world is represented numerically.

The passage of the *Tso tchouan* just analyzed has shown that the 5 primordial sounds, the essence of rhythm, are entitled to a central place conferred or conferred upon them by the classifier 5. The same theme is found, illustrated even more significantly, in a venerable document.

The *Hong fan*,[32] a small treatise which is usually considered the oldest essay in Chinese philosophy, deals with the sum of prescriptions which a worthy ruler must know. This sum of wisdom takes the form of **9** points, each of which is numbered, or rather characterized by a number.

It has been written[33] that there is no relationship between the numbers assigned to the sections of the *Hong fan* and the ideas expressed in them. If this relationship is indeed non-existent in most cases, it is evident in the seventh section. It is devoted to things of divination. The 7 must classify them, because the 7 rules them; to practice their art, diviners handle 49 (= 7 x 7) magic wands and consider (says the *Hong fan*) 7 categories of indexes. – But the fifth section is even more interesting. It speaks of "the highest perfection of the Sovereign (*Houang ti*)."[34] The sovereign, as we know, is the fortune of the country. Therefore, we are told that he must, *in his Capital*, work to collect and then spread the totality of Happiness to all the faithful. Therefore, he and "his perfection" are entitled to the *central section*. It is the one governed by the classifier 5, and, in fact, the total happiness that the chief dispenses and possesses is divided into 5 Happinesses.

The numerical label, in this case also, is something more than a simple number, but, in addition, it seems that the conception of an order expressed by numerical classifiers entails the representation of a *spatial device*.

This was, moreover, the idea which inspired the ancient interpreters when they explained the *Hong fan* as a whole and also when they explained the first section, in which the 5 Elements are enumerated.

They saw in the *Hong fan* a kind of meditation on the structure of the Universe, from which a Sage could derive the principles governing all Politics. Because of a narrowly rationalistic prejudice, moderns refuse to confuse the science of the ancient sages with simple common sense. They wish to discover in the *Hong fan* only a series – more or less well ordered – of helpful hints, of useful information. How could they admit that the author of the treatise, *coordinating the ancient systems of classification*, could have had the idea of bringing out the organization of the Universe *by means of Numbers and arrangements of Numbers*?[35] Hence they reject the traditions, and, to begin with, either give little interest to the mention of the 5 Elements *placed at the head* of the *Hong fan*, or even endeavor to assert that it

---

32   *SMT*, IV pp. 219 ff. The *Hong fan*, inserted as a chapter in *Chou king*, was also incorporated by Sseu-ma Ts'ien in his work. Tradition places it as a work of the third or second millennium BC. Modern critics attribute it to the eighth or third century BC. The writing of the *Hong Fan* can hardly be placed below the sixth and fifth centuries BC. It seems to me to date from the earliest beginnings of written literature.

33   P. Wieger, *Histoire des croyances religieuses et des opinions philosophiques en Chine*… p. 57.

34   *SMT*, V, p, 221. I have provisionally retained the translation given by Chavannes. Cf. in this book, chap. IV.

35   *SMT*, IV, p. 219, note 5. Cf. Maspero, *La Chine antique*, p. 440, note 4.

is interpolated.³⁶ But, on the one hand, the place is significant, and, on the other, there is no right to neglect the indications provided by the dialogue which serves as an exordium to the treatise:³⁷ "Ah, it is in a mysterious way that Heaven fixes for men here below the *domains where* they will live in harmony with one another! And I know nothing of the order that governs the regular relations (of beings)!" – "When Kouen obstructed the Great Waters *and caused trouble in the five Elements*; the Sovereign, trembling with anger, did not hand over to him the nine Sections of the *Hong fan*, the regular relations (of beings) were perverted. But Kouen was executed at the Frontiers of the World and Yu came to power. *Heaven, then, gave Yu the 9 Sections of the Hong fan and the regular relations of beings regained their order.*" Is this passage not to be compared with the ancient formulas indicating that civilizing Heroes are entrusted with "the Calendar Numbers of Heaven" which a decadent Virtue can make "*lose their order*"? We have seen that the "Calendar Numbers" do not seem to differ much from the cyclical signs; like the latter, they represent places.

The dialogue which opens the Hong fan *certainly expresses the idea that the arrangement of the Universe implies a distribution of things and men, which can be translated as well by an arrangement into 9 Sections as by a distribution into 5 Elements.*

The 5 elements are assigned the rubric 1. Let us not forget that (1) the simple unit does not differ from (10) the ten, a complete unit. The 5 elements constitute a total. To each of them must³⁸ correspond a numerical value. This is precisely what section I of the *Hong fan* says.

Chavannes translates thus: "(I) Of the five elements, the first *is called*³⁹ water; the second, fire; the third, wood; the fourth, metal; the fifth, earth. (The nature of) water is⁴⁰ to moisten and descend; that of fire, to burn and ascend; that of wood, to be capable of being bent and straightened; that of metal, to be obedient and change form; that of earth, to be sown and reaped." Chavannes translates, in the first element of the sentence, the character *yue*, as "*is called*", but in the second element is translated as "is." *Yue* can indeed mean "is," but when it appears in an enumeration (as is the case here and throughout the *Hong fan*), *yue* is no more than a simple particle. To fully attribute to it a copula value already leads to a distortion of meaning. The text does not say: "(*The nature of*) water is to moisten and descend..."; it says: "(Water) moistens (and) tends downward; (fire) flames (and) tends up-

---

36   NAITO, *On the compilation of the Shoo king* and HONDA, *On the date of compilation of the Yi king*.

37   Dialogue between the founder of the Tcheou dynasty and the brother of the tyrant Cheou-sin, whose decadent virtue brought about the ruin of the Yin dynasty; colloquy corresponding to the inauguration of a new world after the transmission from one family to another of the principles or *protectors* of power.

38   The 5 Elements, as we shall see, are worth respectively 1, 2, 3, 4, 5, i.e., for their total (5, symbols of the center, not to be counted, as we shall see) 1 + 2 + 3 + 4, i.e., a total of precisely 10 (which equals 1).

39   Emphasis mine.

40   *Idem.*

Book II - Chapter III - Numbers

ward..." But the meaning is much more seriously distorted when it lends *yue* in the first sentence – without being able to retain it in the second – the meaning of "is called." One can only fall into this error because of a preconceived idea and if one presupposes that, in the *Hong fan*, numerals are only used as ordinal numbers. But in the *Hong fan* itself, and indeed elsewhere, we have found evidence that the Chinese do not like to distinguish between the cardinal and ordinal functions in numbers.

We will now translate, strictly, word for word: "I: 5 Elements. 1: Water; 2: Fire; 3: Wood; 4: Metal; 5: Earth," understanding that Water comes first and Fire second because 1 and 2 symbolically express their essence and rank. 1, 2, 3, 4 and 5 should be considered as indexes specifying the *value* of the different elements.

And, indeed, if the Chinese, under the influence of different doctrinal concerns, sometimes vary the sequence of the Elements, they never attribute to them numerical values that can be considered different from those assigned to them by the *Hong fan*.

By serving as indexes to the places which place them in an overall scheme, these values alone – even when the *sequence* adopted for the enumeration varies – attest to the true and *primary order* of the Elements.[41] In the *Yue ling*, for example, the Elements are presented in the sequence: Wood, Fire, Earth, Metal, Water.[42] However, the *Yue ling* assimilates them respectively to the numbers 8, 7, 5, 9, 6. Now, the 1 and 6 (= **1** + 5) which the *Hong fan*, on the one hand, and the *Yue ling*, on the other, assign to Water are considered equivalent by their symbolic value, because both are congruent to **5**. The same is true for 2 and 7 (= 2 + 5), for 3 and 8 (= 3 + 5), for 4 and 9 (= 4 + 5). Moreover, if the *Yue ling* assumes an emblematic equivalence between Water, for example, and, in the decimal series, *only* the number 6 (the strong number of the congruent pair 1-6), it also asserts that, in the denary series, it is a *pair* of cyclic numbers to which Water corresponds. Let us note here that, in analyzing the *cyclic pairs* of the denary series, the *Chouo wen* presents the *first* of the two signs as the symbol of an Orientation and the *second* as the symbol of the corresponding Season.[43] The *Hong fan* and the *Yue ling*, which

---

41 Chavannes (*SMT*, IV, p. 219, note 5) states that the order followed by the *Hong fan* is singular. For this reason, he does not hesitate to propose the correction of the text. This is because he began by admitting that "the earliest enumerations" (which he reports to the third century) followed a different order (Introduction, p. CXLIII), the so-called triumphal order. Since he attributes to the *Hong fan* a date earlier than the third century BC, he must find in the enumeration of the *Hong fan* (the earliest, in fact) an error which he will correct to resemble the enumerations first claimed to be older. Chavannes' successors abandon his correction, which they consider unacceptable, because another text confirms the wording of this passage in the *Hong fan*. But they refrain from investigating the possible meaning of the order indicated, limiting themselves to affirming that the numerical interpretations that can be given are anachronistic.

42 This sequence corresponds to the so-called order of production of the Elements.

43 Except the pair *meou ki* (center), the two signs of which are said to be symbols of the "Central Palace." Note that the *Yue ling* defines the Earth by the center and gives, like the *Hong fan*, the 5 (and not the 10) as symbol.

assign to the Elements, the one the first of the numbers of a *congruent pair* and the other the second of these numbers (the strong number), apparently consider the numerical correspondences from different points of view, but which complement each other: both are inspired by a general system of classification whose antiquity and prestige are attested by numerous myths.

Elements	Water	Fire	Wood	Metal	Earth
Hong fang	1	2	3	4	5
Yue ling	6	7	8	9	5

This system consists of a combination of equivalences established between the Seasons, the Directions…, the Colors, the *Flavors*… and the Elements, as well as the Numbers. The *Yue ling* relates number 6 and the salty taste (*hien*) to Winter (= North), which it places under the influence (*tö* = virtue) of Water; number 7 and the bitter taste (*k'ou*) to Summer (= South), which it places under the influence of Fire; number 8 and the sour taste (*siuan*) to Spring (= East), which it places under the influence of Wood; number 9 and the spicy taste (*sin*) in Autumn (= West) which it places under the influence of Metal; number 5 and the sweet taste (*kan*) in the Center which it identifies with Earth; while (designating the cardinal tastes by the same words as the *Yue ling*) the *Hong fan* reads: "(That which) moistens (and) tends downward (Water: 1), produces salty; (that which) flames (and) tends upward (Fire: 2) produces bitter; (that which) bends (and) straightens (Wood: 3) produces sour; (that which) is ductile (and) multifaceted (Metal: 4) produces pungent; (that which) is sown (and) harvested (Earth: 5) produces sweet." The *Yue ling* and the *Hong fan* undoubtedly refer to the same classification system. However, as a treatise on the Calendar, the *Yue ling* is concerned with showing the function of the Numbers in the organization of the year. It considers only the strong numbers (*second* numbers) of the pairs 1-6, 2-7, 3-8, 4-9, because their sum (6 + 7 + 8 + 9) totals 30. 30 (one of the principal divisors of 360) can, by itself, evoke the perimeter of the year; 6, 7, 8, 9 (by showing how the total 30 breaks down) thus deserve to serve as classifiers of the four seasons that make up the year[44] (and which are symbolized by the second numbers of the cyclic pairs). The *Hong fan*, on the other hand, sets out, by evoking a progression of categories, to reveal the constitution of the universe. When, to begin with (section 1), it indicates a division into elements, it is a *spatial device* that it undertakes to describe, and it describes it by marking, as it were, the stages of its construction. It uses only the weak numbers of the congruent pairs (they form the *first* terms; they are the *first* terms of the cyclic pairs that are assigned to the different sites of the Space). These numbers can be used as rubrics for the device sites because, placed at the beginning of the numerical series (1, 2, 3, 4), they are particularly suitable for indicating the *order of assignments* that identify a given site with a given rubric.

---

44 The 5, retained as the symbol of the Center by the *Yue ling*, is reserved for the days (not counted, but perhaps 6 – not the 5 – since the solar year has 366 days) that mark the pivot of the year.

Book II - Chapter III - Numbers 103

Indeed, the enumeration that determines both the domain and the numerical value of the different elements *reproduces the layout of a temple and marks the times of the operation*. Water {= North = 1 (= 1 + 5 = 6)} and Fire {= South = 2 (= 2 + 5 = 7)} oppose each other at the two ends of the branch that is first drawn and traced vertically, starting from the Bottom (= North) {*to which Water tends* (*as expressly stated* by the *Hong fan*)} to the Top (= South) {*to which Fire tends* (*as stated* by the *Hong fan*)}; Wood {East = 3 (= 3 + 5 = 8)} and Metal {= West = 4 (= 4 + 5 = 9)} face each other at the two points of the second branch which cuts perpendicularly to the first and which must be traced horizontally from the Left (= East = Wood) to the Right (= West = Metal);[45] the Earth {= Center = 5 (which equals 10 = 5 + 5)} occupies the central point which the crossroads serves to determine and which defines the place of the Head.[46]

Water is named first because its spatial domain is the site (North) which is the first to be constituted – because rubric 1 governs it – while classifier 6 commands its temporal domain (Winter). Fire, likewise, is called the second because it must occupy its place in the second place of the device where it must occupy the East, (South) whose rubric is 2; 7 constitutes a classifier to the corresponding season (Summer).

Linked to the Elements, the numerical Symbols cannot be imagined without linking them to concrete Spaces and Times. These connections, and the very connection of Times and Spaces, have as their first effect to make irrelevant the distinction of ordinal, cardinal and even of distribution; these functions, in Numbers, remain undifferentiated, to the point that in them the classificatory function prevails. But, in addition, the impossibility of conceiving them outside the concrete Space-Time that forms the warp and woof of a finite Universe, has the consequence of tearing the numerical symbols away from the abstract linear arrangement that the unlimited character of their sequence seems to demand. They are forced to organize themselves in the form of a cycle; rich in geometrical and rhythmical representations, they can, much better than simple cyclical symbols, serve as headings to groups of realities which they identify by indicating their situation and their order, their form and their composition.

II. Numbers, Places, Divinatory Symbols

It is by means of numbers that the logical sectors, the concrete categories that compose the Universe, must be represented. And if we want to represent them in accordance with their essence and with the constitutional order which the *Hong*

---

45 The equivalences are: Bottom: North: Water – Top: South: Fire – Left: East: Wood – Right: West: Metal, are essential data in the Chinese system of classifications and correspondences. The formulas of the *Hong fan*: "Water moistens and tends Downward; Fire flames and tends Upward" clearly prove: 1° that the *Hong fan* refers to this system explicitly; 2° that the enumeration of the Elements implies a spatial device; 3° and finally (since the Elements are characterized by numerical symbols) that the science of numbers is not detached from a geometrical knowledge.

46 *Houang ki*: 5. The two terms of the pair of death corresponding to the Center serve interchangeably as symbols of the Central Palace.

Fan calls "the regular relations of beings," we shall think that we can do so by means of numerical arrangements. By choosing this or that arrangement of these numbers that allows us to represent their interaction, we believe that we have made the universe both intelligible and enjoyable.

Yu the Great possessed all the virtues that allow a hero to fix the world. Thus he founded the Hia dynasty, and Heaven is said to have entrusted him with "the 9 sections of the *Hong fan*".

This does not mean that Heaven gave Yu a nine-point dissertation. In the literary composition which a prince of the fallen house recited to the founder of the *Tcheou*, after the end of the Yi, the supreme knowledge secluded in Yu's *Hong fan* was undoubtedly expressed. But the meditations which this celestial document may have inspired differ from it in the same way, apparently, as the literary glosses which seem to compose this sacred book of the diviners. Sixty-four drawings, the Hexagrams, alone constitute the true text of the *Yi king*; all the rest are mere commentaries, amplifications and legends that help to decipher the divinatory symbols. In these 64 graphic symbols is contained knowledge, a total power. In the same way, no doubt, before it became manifest in the nine points of the dissertation recited to King Wou, such a Sum of Wisdom was already in the nine sections of the *Hong fan* – just as Yu possessed it. *Hong fan* means "great pattern" or "supreme plan." What could the Sections of the Great Plan represent but a grouping of symbols capable of arousing in reality as well as imposing on the mind the dispositions of the categories that evoke the universal order? Arranged around the number 5 (emblem of the sovereign position and center of Space), what could these 9 numbered sections be, if not, simply, the first 9 numerical symbols?

Certainly, what Heaven gave Yu was not the gloss of the text, but its own letter, or rather its number; it was a model to decipher, an *image made of numbers*, the World itself.

While scholars did not bother to criticize the traditions to give ancient history a reasonable and correct appearance, the Chinese identified the *Hong fan* granted to Yu by Heaven with a mythical diagram, called *Lo chou*, in which they tried to see an ordering of numbers.

The traditions related to Yu and the *Hong fan* refer to a set of myths too coherent to be ignored. It is known that Yu the Great, as befits a Founder or Demiurge, was both a master forger and a master surveyor.[47] He traveled and measured the 9 Mountains, the 9 Rivers, the 9 Marshes, laying out the land which was finally put into cultivation, i.e., divided into fields, which were squares, which in turn were *divided into 9 squares*; in short, we are told, Yu *divided the World into 9 Regions.*.

He also had 9 three-feet cauldrons. The 9 Shepherds offered metal as tribute, and in his cauldrons Yu was able to draw the "symbols" of the beings of all countries, for these "symbols" were given to him as tribute by the 9 Regions. The power embodied in these symbols was such that the 9 Cauldrons were worth the World; thanks to them, order and peace reigned throughout the Universe; the various be-

---

[47] Granet, *Danses et légendes de la Chine ancienne*, pp. 482 ff.

Book II - Chapter III - Numbers

ings remained calm in their domains, so that it was possible to travel safely through the 9 Swamps, the 9 Rivers and the 9 Mountains… In this way the "union of the High and the Low" was assured and "the favor of Heaven" was received.[48] To Yu, who possessed with his 9 three-feet cauldrons an *image of the World* and power over the World, Heaven transmitted the 9 Rubrics.

It was a tortoise that brought them to him. Almighty in the World, turtles are an *image of the Universe*. If diviners can know through them the effective indications that advise effective acts, it is because they participate in the longevity of the Universe, and if the Universe gives them *long life*, it is because they take an intimate part in the universal life, living closely wrapped in a habitat conditioned according to the model of the macrocosm; their shells, in fact, are square at the bottom, and round at the top. Turtles represent the World so well that they necessarily appear in myths in which we see a Hero working to consolidate universal order. If some evil Genius, by breaking one of the columns of the World, and leaving it with only three, causes Heaven and Earth to collapse and delivers the Universe to the Flood, a beneficent Genius can restore stability by restoring to the World four columns made from the severed legs of a tortoise,[49] for tortoises must not be allowed to move and swim freely, or else the Earths would move away and the Waters would swallow them up.[50] After Kouen, the evil monster and three-legged turtle, unleashed the Great Waters that threatened to engulf Heaven and Earth,[51] Yu, who was his son, but a perfect Hero in both virtue and body, restored good order. He knew how to find glory in the mythical works connected with the theme of the World saved from the Waters; a tortoise was thus to figure in his story. Yu the Great, in fact, reduced the Waters to his service and disciplined the Rivers. Now, therefore, a dragon-horse or the river itself, a god with the body of a fish or a turtle,[52] had to come out of the Yellow River and present to him the River Tablet (*Ho t'ou*); and a turtle had to come out of the Lo River to present to him the *Lo chou* (Lo River Scripture) which is – according to tradition – the *Hong fan*.

Image of the World, a turtle brought this image to Yu; to Yu, who, himself, by his voice, his size and his pace, could serve as a pattern for all measurements; for all that the numbers are meant to evoke. Like the nine three-feet cauldrons of Yu, the images that came out of the Waters were preserved, so the story goes, in the treasury of the Kings, Sons of Heaven; they were among the tokens and principles of their power; when the Royalty perished, the three-feet cauldrons vanished in the Waters and no one knows what happened then to the *Ho t'ou* and the *Lo chou*… The *Lo chou* and the *Ho t'ou* did not reappear until the Song dinasty, in the 12th century. This occurred under the reign of an emperor who favored geomancy and collected Taoist grimoires; and who also had nine Tripods[53] cast…

---

48   *Ibid.*, p. 489.
49   Cf. Book III, Chapter I.
50   *Lie tseu*, Wieger, *Les Pères du système taoïste*, p. 131.
51   Granet, *Danses et légendes*…, pp. 568, 244.
52   *Ibid.*, notes 1284 and 1285.
53   This is the emperor *Houei-tsong* of the Song (1101-1125).

Scholars have nothing but contempt for the *Lo chou* and the *Ho t'ou* of the Song. However, these works are not without interest; they are simply arrangements of numbers; after long centuries of brilliant civilization, Chinese scholars did not cease to attribute to numerical symbols the function of representing the universe. The most important thing for us is to observe this bias. Its persistence invites us to consider it as a fundamental attitude of the Chinese mind. But, on the other hand, why do we blame "the counterfeiters"? They did not invent anything, they were just scholars; they merely translated graphically ideas that we do not want to trace back to Yu, the mythical hero, but which are nevertheless old enough to merit our interest. See the figure below:

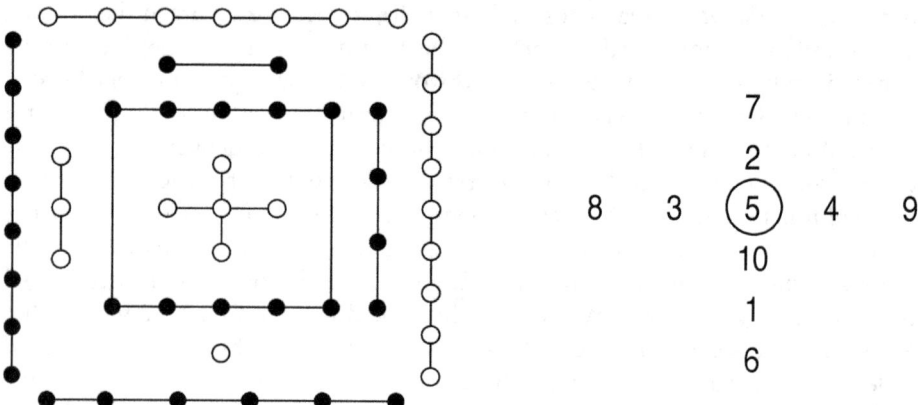

The *Ho t'ou* of the Song shows {by means of white (*yang*) or black (*yin*) circles, depending on whether they are even or odd} the first ten numerals arranged in a criss-cross fashion, with 5 and 10 in the center; as we have seen, this is the arrangement that the *Yue ling* and the first section of the *Hong fan* assume for the numerical symbols of the Elements, the Directions and the Seasons. As for the *Lo chou*, the diagram which purports to restore it is based on data formally attested already in the Han period.[54] This diagram, if not less interesting than the other, is not made to surprise much more. The first 9 numbers are arranged in a magic square (around 5); as might be expected from a World chart offered (through a turtle) to a Hero who divided the (square) Earth into 9 (square) Regions. See the next figure.

Yu, in order to organize the World, surveyed it. Indeed, he went through it. Rulers who are not Founders are content, as we know, to circle the Calendar House. Its circumvallation in the sacred place of *Ming t'ang* is sufficient to order Space and Time and to maintain an exact connection of Seasons and Directions.

Round by its thatched roof and square by its base, the *Ming t'ang* is an image of the World; as perfect as a tortoise can be.

---

54   It will be seen later that they seem to go back at least to the *Hi ts'eu*, a work scarcely less ancient than the *Hong-fan*.

Book II - Chapter III - Numbers

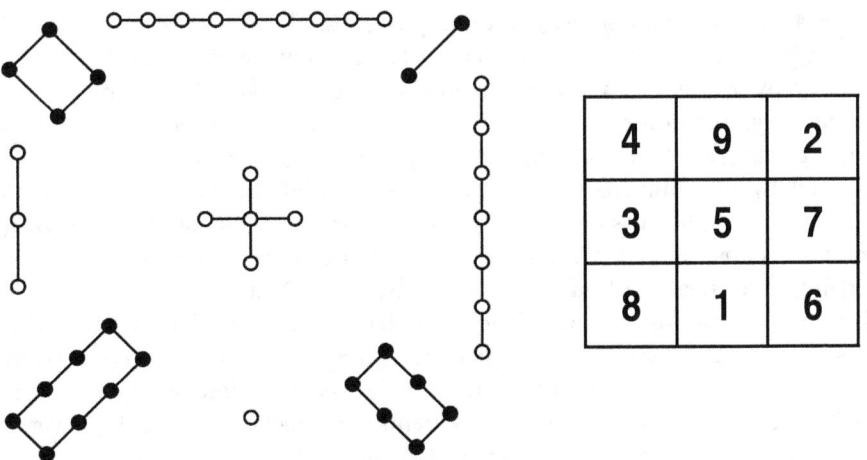

Diviners[55] can conjure from a tortoise shell a complete cycle of signs: 360 kinds of cracks inform them of all circumstances of time and place. They make them appear {using Fire (= High = Heaven)} in the lower {and square (= Earth)} part of the shell. It is the divisions of this lower part of the shell that allow the characterization of the cracks (see next figure). An axial line running from back to front {back is the bottom (= north) and front is the top (= south)} divides the plastron into two halves which are left (= east) and right (= west); this axis is cut by 5 stripes representing the 5 elements; they determine (6 on the left and 6 on the right) 12 sites (which are the sites of the 12 months), 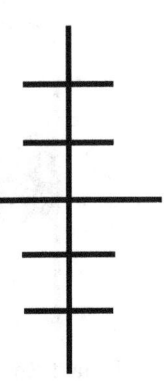 but enclose only 8 domains, which (coupled by two) are arranged forming 4 sectors around the Center marked by the crossing of the middle axis and the central line.[56] Thus, (after having traced (considering **1** axis and **5** transversal trajectories) a crossroads to evoke a distribution by 5), we arrive {even if we operate, it is said, by distinguishing **6** categories (or rather, three pairs of categories, viz: the Up and the Down, the Left and the Right, and – also – the Yang and the Yin)} to distribute the Space – where the 360 signs may appear and be specified – only among 4 (double) domains, which, alone, deserve to bear a name.

Similarly, in the *Ming t'ang*,[57] the Space – where the actual circulation must give rise to the appearance of the complete cycle of days composing a year – is divided into only **5** named domains (and dedicated to the **5** Elements), one of which corresponds only to the Center and pivot of Time, while the other 4 represent the actual Orientation and Seasons. However, also in the *Ming t'ang*, 8 places are arranged to correspond to 12 actual stations suitable for the enactment of the ordinances (*yue ling*) appropriate to the 12 months, 4 of which occupy angular positions and

---

55 *Tcheou li*, Biot, *op. cit.*, II, pp. 75, 70.
56 The middle axis is called the path (*lou* or *tao*) of the 1000 stages (*li*).
57 Granet, *op. cit.* notes on pp. 116-119.

the *other* 4 (*the only ones named*) cardinal positions. This arrangement of sacred space can be expressed in two architectural layouts; both were advocated in the Han period by scholars who claimed to provide emperors with the true blueprints of a *Ming t'ang*. According to some, the Calendar House was to be divided into 9 rooms; according to others, it comprised only 5 buildings or 5 rooms.

Formed by adjoining rooms or independent buildings, the *Ming t'ang* of 5 rooms draws a simple cross inscribed in a square (or in a rectangle); the *Ming t'ang* of 9 rooms occupies this square entirely; but, both including a room situated in the center and, so to speak, without a view, both also have 12 views on the outside; indeed, each of the cardinal rooms of the cross-shaped *Ming t'ang* has three exterior facades (4 x 3 = 12), whereas, in the square *Ming t'ang*, these same rooms have only one facade, the 4 corner rooms, on the other hand, having a double facade {(4 x 1) + (4 x 2) = 12}. Both architectural arrangements are equally suitable if 12 views or 12 cyclic stations are to be arranged around a center.

 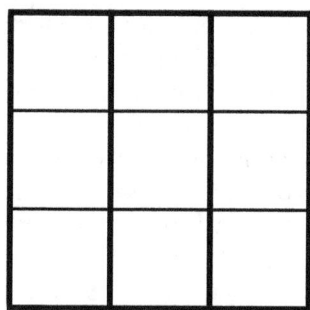

In fact, the *two systems* of construction are only opposed because they are intended to reflect *two different arrangements of numbers*.

One of these arrangements is implicit in the *Yue ling*. This treatise on the calendar indicates the positions to be occupied by the Son of Heaven in the place of the *Ming t'ang* in issuing the monthly ordinances (*yue ling*). For the initial or terminal months of the various seasons, it is sufficient for the ruler to stand to the left or right of one of the four cardinal quarters. On the other hand, it is in these same halls that he must take his place in the months (solstitial or equinoctial) that form the center of the four seasons. It is known that the *Yue ling* assigns to the three months of each season the same number {6 for Winter (North), 8 for Spring (East), 7 for Summer (South), 9 for Autumn (West) and 5 for the Center)}. The 5-room *Ming t'ang* is designed, as can be seen, to evoke the simple cross arrangement of numbers that the Song's *Ho t'ou* was intended to illustrate, and which the *Hong fan* already hinted at.

The square arrangement also has a numerical basis. The *Ming t'ang* tradition of 9 rooms is advocated by the *Ta Tai Li ki*.[58] This work, precisely, assigns to each of the 9 rooms (as the *Hong fan* does to each of the 9 sections) one of the first 9

---

58   *Ta Tai Li ki*, 66.

Book II - Chapter III - Numbers

SUMMER				FIRE			S					
	7				2			7				
								2				
SPRING 8	5	9 AUTUMN	WOOD 3	5	4 METAL	E 8	3	5	4	9	W
	6			1			1					
								6				
WINTER			WATER			N						
Yue ling			Hong Fan			Ho t'ou of the Song						

numbers, and, these numbers, it enunciates in an order (2,9,4; 7,5,3; 6,1,8) which presupposes a magic square arrangement.

4	9	2
3	5	7
8	1	6

This arrangement (which is that of the *Lo chou* of the Song) thus had – at least since the Han period – a ritual value; since then, it seemed to constitute an image of the World to be found on the plane of the *Ming t'ang*; a whole set of traditions inviting, moreover, to think that a Hero could have deciphered it in a tortoise shell.

The traditions relative to the *Ming t'ang* demonstrate it again; the main function of the Numbers is to characterize the places and to express the organization of the Space-Time.

The arrangement of the magic square, whose prestige was imposed on the technicians of the *Ming t'ang*, was no less favored by the theorists of divination. We will look at this fashion and, at the same time, be able to understand the reason for it. Besides dividing the divinatory scale into sectors, by arranging the numbers in a square, we may evoke the Total[59] of the circumstances of time and place which condition the work of the diviners; as well as the work of the Sons of Heaven in the Calendar House.

* * *

The starting point of the fashion for magic squares is to be found in an ancient system of speculations relating to the Divine Symbols and also to the Numbers.

---

[59] *Ta Tai Li ki*, 66, glosses (HTKKSP, 828, p. 11a and HTKK, 705, p. 9b); *Wou li t'ong k'ao*, XXVI, pp. 20 ff.

The essence of this system was recorded, several centuries before the Han, in the *Hi t'seu*. No work, except the *Hong fan*, is closer to the beginnings of the written tradition.

The *Hi t'seu* is part of the *Yi king* cycle. The *Yi king* masters operated with signs provided by yarrow. Yarrow divination, according to the scholars who practiced it, was based on no other knowledge than turtle divination. These two methods of inquiry seemed to be interdependent and destined to complement each other; the *Hi t'seu* itself affirms this, as does the *Hong fan*, and the *Tcheou li*.[60] The myths related to the tortoise suggest that the art of preparing the shell by dividing it into domains is related to the techniques used by *geometric topographers* to divide land. The knowledge of identifying time (and place) with yarrow sticks, on the other hand, seems to be related to a calculating technique. But the ancient Chinese avoided distinguishing between arithmetic and geometry. Numbers and figures provided the sages with symbols, practically interchangeable and equally powerful, that facilitated the identification and manipulation of realities of all kinds.

The word that designates the divinatory tokens also designates the calculating tokens. When drawing spells and making their guesses, the diviners were to hold, between the fourth and fifth fingers of the left hand, one of these sticks representing the Man situated between Yin and Yang.[61] When one was in doubt as to which way to go, he was also to hold one of these tokens in his hand; it then served him as a guide stick.[62] The character representing these sticks is written by adding the key of the bamboo to a graphic group representing, it is said, the tracks which a plough leaves in the ground. If we add to this group of strokes the key representing cultivated fields, of *square* form, we obtain a character of identical pronunciation (*tch'eou*). It means "to cultivate the land, the boundaries of the land, the hereditary domains." This sign is used to designate scholars (astronomers, astrologers, calendar masters) who are hereditarily dedicated to the art of calculation... The genius of numbers, the genius of figures, the genius of government, the genius of divination are merged... It is precisely the word *tch'eou* that is used to designate the 9 sections of the *Hong fan*, the 9 rubrics or the 9 domains of the Great Plan, which tradition identifies with the *Lo chou* that the tortoise brought to Yu, the surveyor.

But it is not under Yu's patronage that the *Hi t'seu* is placed, it is under that of *Fou-hi*. The attribute of *Fou-hi* is the set square, and that of his wife the compass. They are always represented as embracing, for their bodies end in a *knot* of snakes.[63] *Fou-hi* was advocated by the paladins of the *Yi king* as one of the first authors of civilization; he invented the system of *knotted* ropes, as well as divination by *rods* of yarrow, which were the first means of government. He had a miraculous birth; some say that his mother conceived him by the effect of a floating *stick*; others (this is the common version) that he was delivered in a swamp famous for

---

60   *Tcheou li*, Biot, op. cit. t. II, p. 70; *SMT*; IV, pp. 226-227; *Yi king*, L., note 369 and p. 371.
61   *Yi king*, L., p. 365.
62   *Ts'ien Han chou*, 98, p. 7b.
63   *SMT*, I, pp. 3-7.

the dragons that roamed it. He had the appearance of a *Dragon*...[64] Thus, according to the most widespread tradition, it was to him that a *Dragon* brought the *Ho t'ou*, and not to Yu, the three-feet cauldron-maker... But dragons and three-feet cauldrons are not very different. If they are precious, the changing reflections of Dragons[65] can be found in the three-feet cauldrons. And when a Saint deserves to attract Dragons, he begins by taking possession of a three-feet cauldron. The latter, moreover, promises him the arrival of the Dragon only if he is accompanied by *yarrow rods*... The story does not say that *Fou-hi* found or melted 1 or 9 three-feet cauldrons. It is only known that this inventor of the Trigrams divided, long before Yu, the World into 9 Regions.

It is even on the occasion of this feat that the annotators of the Bamboo Annals take the trouble to report a gloss by Tcheng Hiuan in which this famous scholar of the Han period indicates the *order of creation* of the divinatory Trigrams.

Yarrow rod specialists operated by manipulating a set of chopsticks in such a way as to obtain an odd or even result. They translated this result graphically by drawing a continuous line — (odd, *yang*, masculine) or split — — (even, *yin*, feminine). They stopped their operations when they had drawn a figure formed by 6 superimposed lines. By superimposing 6 broken or continuous lines, 64 different Hexagrams can be composed. With 3 lines, only 8 Trigrams can be composed. It is easy to observe that each of the (8^2 =) 64 Hexagrams is formed by two superimposed Trigrams;[66] the 8 Trigrams thus summarize the 64 Hexagrams. These are considered to represent the totality of reality; they provide, so to speak, a concentrated representation of the Universe.

For this picture of the World to be considered perfect, it must include an orientation of the Trigrams.

Mythically associated with the 8 Winds, the 8 Trigrams serve, in fact, to form, arranged in an octagon, a compass rose with eight directions. The *Lo chou* is opposed to the *Ho t'ou*, and we know, both for the *Ming t'ang* and for the Numbers, two competing arrangements; there are also two arrangements of the Trigrams. Both were famous in antiquity. Far from seeming mutually exclusive, they seemed to render complementary services. The *Chouo koua* (which is one of the main treatises of the *Yi king* cycle), refers, depending on the occasion, sometimes to one

---

64 *SMT*, I, pp. 3-7.
65 *SMT*, III, p. 484.
66 I do not hold that the trigrams were drawn before the hexagrams. This is an impossible point to decide. But I do not believe that one could, once the 8^2 hexagrams were formed, not have seen that they were reduced to 8 trigrams. Maspero believes in the anteriority of the hexagrams. He justifies this hypothesis (contrary to Chinese traditions) with the help of reasoning that I am unable to understand and whose starting point is a serious error of observation. Maspero states that, except for the first pair of hexagrams, all the other pairs are formed by inversion, the second hexagram of each pair being the first one inverted. But the pairs 27-28, 29-30 and 61-62, are hardly formed by inversion. They are formed by perfectly symmetrical hexagrams which, if turned around, still have the same shape. Moreover, it would be easy, but a bit long and off-topic, to show that the order followed by the *Yi king* implies the idea that the hexagrams are made of two superimposed trigrams.

Fou-hi Arrangement

Figures and names of the Trigrams in the so-called Fou-hi's arrangement. The line separates the male trigrams (M) {those whose bottom line (turned toward the center) is continuous (*yang*)} from the female trigrams (F) {whose base line is split (*yin*)}.

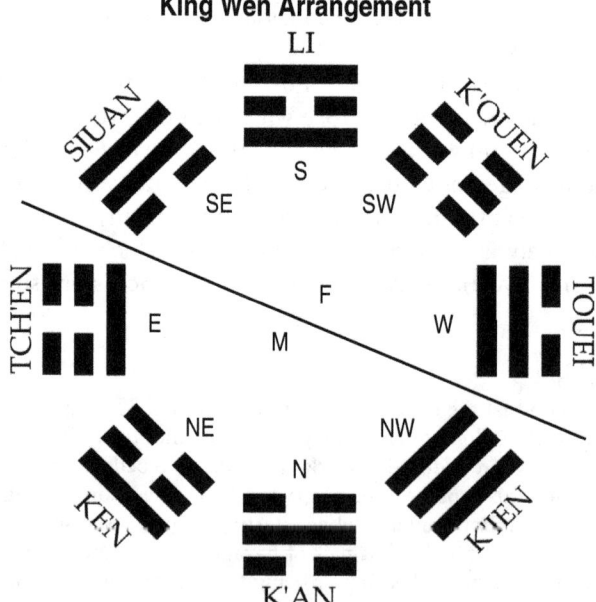

King Wen Arrangement

Figures and names of the Trigrams in the so-called King Wen's arrangement. The line separates the male trigrams (M) (the one formed by 3 continuous lines and the three containing a single continuous line) from the female trigrams (F) {those having an odd number (3 or 1) of dashed lines}.

Book II - Chapter III - Numbers

and sometimes to the other of these arrangements. One of them stands out for the search for graphic symmetry; it is the one that tradition brings close to *Ho t'ou* and attributes to *Fou-hi*, inventor of the Trigrams:

The other is attributed to King Wen, founder of the Tcheou. It is said that the King Wen invented the Hexagrams, and also became famous for the construction of a *Ming t'ang*. The so-called King Wen layout is often linked to the *Lo chou*. Fun fact: although Tcheng Hiuan's gloss is used in connection with the division of the World into 9 Regions which was the work of Fou-hi (the master of *Ho t'ou*), it is King Wen's layout (the builder of the *Ming t'ang*) that this gloss refers to.

According to the traditions collected under the Han by Tcheng Hiuan, it is the Supreme Unity (*T'ai Yi*) that arranges each of the 8 Trigrams in the appropriate place (*kong* = palace, room); each time it has placed four of them, the Supreme Unity returns to rest in the Center. This is the way {*hing*: this is the word which, in the expression *wou hing* (the 5 *hing*), is translated by: Element} that travels. Starting (1) from K'an (N), it passes (2) through K'ouen (SW), then (3) through Ch'en (E), then (4) through Siuan (SE) and from there – after touching the Center (5) (which is its own house) – it arrives (6) at K'ien (NW) from where, passing (7) through Touei (W), then (8) through Ken (NE), it arrives (9) at Li (S), from where it will return to the Center (10 = 5) (See the next figure in the following page).

The order followed is that in which the numbers of a magic square[67] are ordered, beginning with the smallest and ending with the largest; and, indeed, if we substitute the Trigrams for the numerical classifier[68] corresponding to their rank of

---

67 This does not apply to magic squares of the type shown below (of which I have found no trace in ancient Chinese literature).

4	11	3
5	6	7
9	1	8

68 The idea that the Trigrams are, *at the same time*, Directions, and Numbers is not a game of scholars; it inspires even today a method of research widespread throughout the Far East, and for example among the *Man* of Tonkin (cf. BEFEO, VII, p. 109; the author of the remark did not see all the interest in it because he thought it was the disposition of Fou-hi).

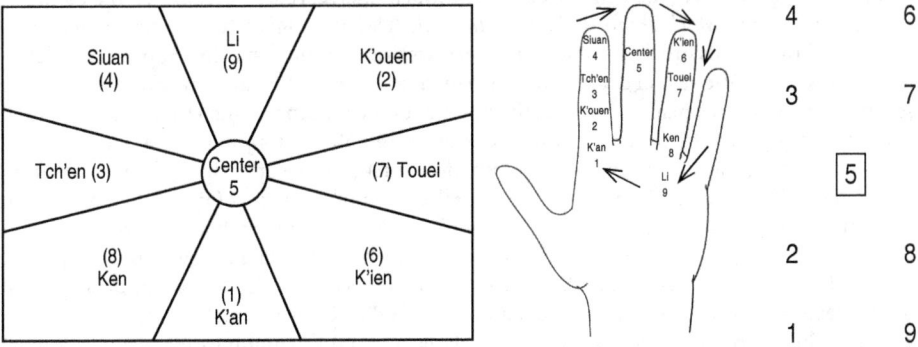

How can we determine, for example, the part of the house in which a pregnant woman should refrain from putting nails, on pain of nailing her fruits? We begin by dividing the house

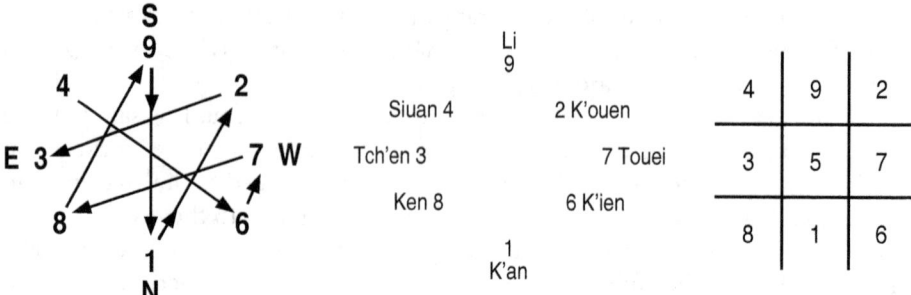

production, we obtain a magic square with center 5; the numbers receive there an orientation identical to that attributed to them when used to qualify the 9 divisions of the *Ming t'ang*.

* * *

Like the Elements (when arranged crosswise), the Trigrams, insofar as they are oriented, are assigned a numerical value; they too have as their symbol the numbers which serve as indexes of their location in Space-Time, and it is through these numbers that their constitutional order is revealed. The same system of postulates is thus at the basis of the two arrangements (numerical square or cross) which provided the ancient Chinese with images of the World considered complementary and not opposed. Already at the time of the *Hong fan*, the constitutional order of the Elements was translated by drawing a numerical cross; the magic square which highlights the constitutional order of the Trigrams must enjoy no less ancient prestige.

This prestige is evident in the traditions collected under the Han[69] by the *Ta Tai Li ki* and by Tcheng Hiuan, but it is the *Hi ts'eu* that enables us to understand the reasons for it.

---

into nine places designated by the central character and the names of the eight trigrams (*oriented according to King Wen's arrangement*). Next, these eight names and the word center are written on the hand; the latter is placed on the second phalanx of the middle finger; on each side (on one side, on the second metacarpal and the three phalanges of the index finger; on the other, on the three phalanges of the ring finger and the fourth metacarpal) are inscribed the names of the eight Trigrams (*which are thus placed in the order assigned to them by Tcheng Hiuan's numbering*). Following this order (direction of the arrows), one counts – starting from a point determined by whether the year of conception is *yin* or *yang* (i.e. occupies an even or odd place in the sexagesimal cycle) – as many seasons as the number of the month in which the conception took place contains units; the trigram at which one stops reveals the forbidden orientation. Let us consider a child conceived in the sixth month of the first (odd) year of the cycle; we start from the center (odd: 5) and, as in the sixth station of the order of the arrows (and of the progression of the numbers), we arrive at K'an, the Trigram of the North, we know that the northern part of the house must be taboo. Let us note that the numbers in the two facing columns add up to 10 (the 5 is in the center); this double-column arrangement has the same value as the arrangement of the magic square, except that, by itself, it does not indicate any orientation.

69   The end of the Earlier (Western) Han dynasty and the beginning of the Later (Eastern) Han dynasty form a period (around the Christian era) when, for political reasons (as for example under the Song), works on the *Yi king* and magic diagrams abounded. These works (labeled

Called by their profession to handle divinatory charts, which are also charts of calculation, the Masters of the *Hi ts'eu* had developed a theory of divination based on a science of numbers. For them, the art of arranging and combining divinatory symbols was confused with the art of numerical combinations.

In a passage referring to the octagonal arrangement of the trigrams, in which they are expressly assimilated to numbers, the *Hi ts'eu* presents them grouped in such a way that they are diametrically opposed, all these oppositions being, apparently, ordered by the formula 3 x 5. Orthodox commentators give only a gloss on this passage which is apparently meaningless.[70] On the other hand, some native interpreters wanted to see in it an allusion to the magic square with 5 as the center, where the pairs of diametrically opposite outer numbers always add up to 10, so that the total of the 3 numbers {including the central one (5)} arranged in the same line is necessarily equal to 15.

The passage is too obscure to be able to affirm this seductive interpretation, but the importance attributed to the number 15 must be retained. This is confirmed by facts that are part of an immemorial tradition.

The diviners who used the *Yi king* to decipher the divinatory symbols used the number 9 to denote the *yang* lines of the various figures and the number 6 to denote the *yin* lines. This is explained by the fact that the relationship between Yin and Yang represents the relationship between Earth and Heaven and, therefore, between the square and the round. This relationship, which is 2 to 3, can be expressed by the numbers 6 and 9. But other diviners, those of the Song, used for their decipherments not the *Yi king*, but the *Kouei tsang*, a manual which was considered older, because it was considered the book of divination in use under the Yin dynasty. For these diviners, the even (*yin*) lines were worth **8**, and the odd (*yang*) **7**. In fact, it seems that in the *Tch'ouen ts'ieou* period both systems of numerical symbols were used simultaneously. As a passage from the *Tso tchouan* shows,[71] opting for one or the other of these systems enabled an astute operator to devise more suitable oracles.

It is necessary to make a double observation; the opposition of Yin and Yang is essentially that of the even (8 or 6) and the odd (7 or 9), and, on the other hand, 8 + 7, like 9 + 6, are equal to 15.

Let us note here that at the origin of the divinatory figures, the *Hi ts'eu* places, after the two elementary symbols (which are said to be constituted by a broken or continuous line), four secondary symbols, to which the whole tradition attributes the designations of Great Yang (or Old Yang), Little Yin (or Young Yin), Little (or

---

wei) constitute a tradition that scholars, indigenous or otherwise, consider impure; it would be uncritical to follow them and date to the Han anything not attested before the Han. Moreover, the *Ta Tai Li ki* belongs to the orthodox tradition, and since *Tcheng Hiuan* corroborates its testimony, there is a presumption in favor of the thesis that the prestige of the magic square predates the Han.

70   *Yi king*, L., p. 369.
71   *Tso tchouan*, C., II, p. 236.

Young) Yang, and Great (or Old) Yin.[72] To each of these symbols corresponds a numerical emblem: Old Yang and Young Yang (odd) are worth respectively 9 and 7, Great Yin and Little Yin (even) are worth 6 and 8.

Now, if the Great Yin (6) corresponds to the North-Winter, whose emblematic Element is Water (6), and if the Young Yin (8) is (normally) assimilated to the East-Spring whose Element is Wood (8), the Young Yang (7) corresponds to the West-Autumn, although Metal, emblem of this quarter of the universe, is worth 9, while 9 is the number of the Old Yang, which commands the South-Summer, whose Element (Fire) is nevertheless worth 7.

The numerical values attributed to the 4 secondary symbols of the *Hi ts'eu* imply an orientation of the numbers different from that which they receive when, connoting the Elements, they are arranged transversely, as the *Hong fan* supposes and as the *Ho t'ou* has represented. The orientation imposed on the numbers of the Great Yang and Little Yang (as well as those of the Great Yin and Little Yin) by the spatial assignments of these symbols is, on the contrary, that of the magic square, where 9 and 4 (congruent numbers) are arranged on the South face and 7 and 2 (congruent numbers) on the West face, 6 (and 1) as well as 8 (and 3) being respectively placed on the North and East faces.

In the figurations, otherwise late, which have been given, the four secondary symbols are represented as formed by two lines.[73] The following are the most common.

Great Yang	Small Yin	Small Yang	Great Yin
═══	═ ═	─ ─	═ ═
9	8	7	6

It is very likely that this representation is due to a work of abstraction derived from a classification of the Trigrams on which the *Chouo koua* insists at length and whose principle proclaims the *Hi ts'eu*.[74] This principle must have been very important for people who, by their profession, were constantly playing with odd and even.

It is based on the observation that the even number is obtained by joining pairs of odd numbers (as well as adding to itself), while the odd number is created by an addition or rather a synthesis (exactly speaking: a hierogamy) of the even and the odd. Also considered as *yin* (even) were Trigrams made of two *yang* lines (even of odd = even) and one *yin* line {even (of odd) + even = even}, and as *yang* Trigrams made of two *yin* lines (even of even = even) to which was added one *yang* line {even (of even) + odd = odd}. The four even Trigrams included a Trigram (made up of three dashed lines) in which the emblem of the *mother* was seen and opposed by

---

72   *Yi king*, L., p. 375.
73   *Ibid.*, pp. 58, 423.
74   *Ibid.*, pp. 388, 422.

three Trigrams, called the three *daughters*, all made up of two male and one female line. Assuming (as seems to be indicated) that each *even* female line is worth **2**, and each odd male line is worth **3**, the last three Trigrams could be expressed as **8** {= (3 + 3) + 2} and the first as 6 (= 2 + 2 + 2). Similarly, with the three *yang* Trigrams, called the three *sons* (made of one *yang* line and two *yin* lines), the value **7** {= (2 + 2) + 3} was appropriate; and the value **9** (= 3 + 3 + 3) with the last Trigram entirely made of *yang*, is qualified as *father*.

We can see that the numbers expressed graphically by the symbols of *father* and *mother* are respectively those of Old Yang and Old Yin, and we can deduce that the numerical symbols attributed to Young Yang and Young Yin depend on the figuration of the Trigrams qualified as *sons* and *daughters*.

The classification of the Trigrams which seems to correspond to these numerical equivalences is that used in the arrangement invented, it is said, by King Wen – famous for his *Ming t'ang*; now the arrangement of the *Ming t'ang* is said to be inspired by the magic square, while the arrangement of King Wen is related to the *Lo chou*, which is figured with the aid of this square.

In this arrangement,[75] the four male trigrams extend from Northwest to East and the four female trigrams from Southeast to West, separated by an E-S-E – W-N-W axis. If we orient the numerical symbols of young and old Yang and old and young Yin according to their traditional equivalence, the odd group (S-W) will be separated from the even group (N-E) by an axis of similar direction. By contrast, in the arrangement known as *Fou-hi*,[76] the yang trigrams {defined, this time, as such by the (male) sex of their bottom line (inner line in the octagon arrangement)} extend from the South to the Northeast, and the yin trigrams (characterized by their broken bottom line) from the North to the Southwest. The axis separating them in this case follows the S-S-W – N-N-E direction.

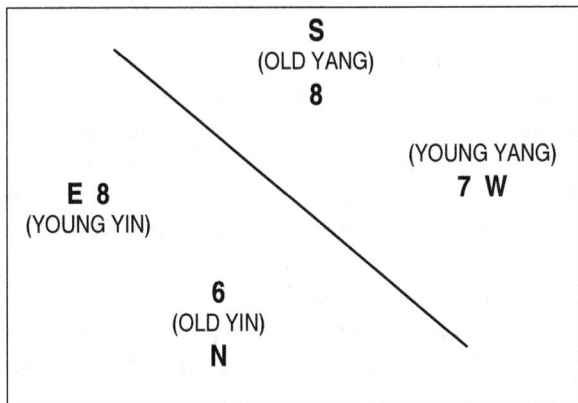

This last distribution perhaps coincides with the arrangement of the numbers when they represent the Elements and form a cross, because, in this case, the pair

---

75   See the figure showing the disposition of King Wen, on p. 112.
76   See the figure showing the disposition of Fou-hi, on p. 112.

7-8 (S-E) is separated from the pair 9-6 (W-N) by an axis whose direction is analogous to that of the line separating the two groups of Trigrams in the arrangement attributed to *Fou-hi*. This diagram is undoubtedly intended to show the balance of Yin and Yang represented by numerical pairs of equivalent value (9 + 6 = 8 + 7 = 15). The same idea is probably illustrated by the arrangement of King Wen.

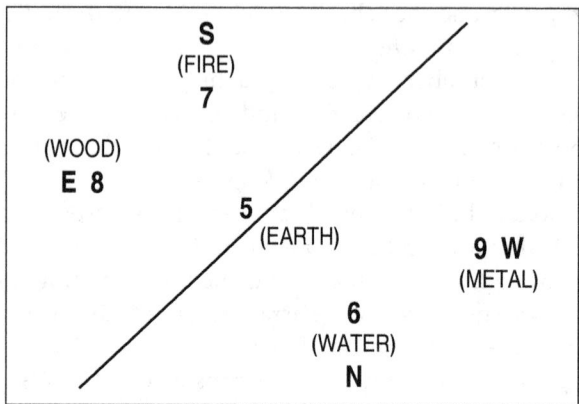

Indeed, if we replace the trigrams (*mother* and *daughters*; *father* and *sons*) by their numerical equivalents, we see that the *yang* and *yin* groups continue to balance {(8 × 3) + 6 = (7 × 3) + 9 = 30}. But, in the arrangement in which only the significant numbers of the 4 secondary symbols of *Hi t'seu* appear, placed at the cardinal points, it is the axis E-S-E – W-N-W, which separates the odd numbers (9-7) from the even ones (6-8). The two pairs thus distinguished have, this time, an unequal value; one is worth 16 and the other 14, that is, 8 × 2 and 7 × 2, which, perhaps, justifies the attribution of the values **8** and **7** to the elementary symbols of Yin and Yang. But, in addition to the proportion **8/7**, this arrangement evokes the proportion **9/6**.

Indeed, a tradition incorporated into the *Po hou t'ong* allows to consider that the central number 5 (= Earth) must be linked to the odd group 9-7. The *Po hou t'ong*[77] states that there are 2 (*even*) *yang* (odd) Elements, namely Water and Wood whose values (6 and 8) are (however) *even*, and 3 (*even*) *yin* (*even*) Elements, namely the 3 Elements (of *even* value however) 5, 7, 9: Earth, Metal, Fire (1). This seemingly paradoxical theory contains a further illustration of a theme I have already mentioned: the Yin and Yang (feminine and masculine) games are based on an inversion of attributes (even and odd) resulting from a hierogamic exchange. The *Po hou t'ong* classification presumably implies an intention to highlight the overall value of the two unequal groups (3 vs. 2) of Elements. Those considered as

---

77   *Po hou t'ong*, 4. The elements are then enumerated in the order, Metal, Wood, Water, Fire (Earth), an order derived from the equivalences established by the *Chouo koua* (*Yi king*, L., pp. 430-432). The Trigrams are listed in an order which presupposes the arrangement of Fou-hi; between K'ien and Metal; Siuan and Wood, K'an and Water, Li and Fire (which presupposes that K'ien and Siuan are opposites; as are K'an and Li; but this is true only in the arrangement of King Wen, proof that the two arrangements imply each other, far from being regarded as contradictory)

yin (given odd symbols and grouped by 3) are worth 21 (= **3** x **7**), while the Elements graded as *yang* (grouped by 2 and given even symbols) are worth 14 (= **2** x **7**); the ratio (*inverted*) between yang (3) and yin (2) is thus shown as 14/21, i.e., 2/3. There is a strong possibility that King Wen's classification of the Trigrams is an illustration of the same theme, since the orientation of the secondary Symbols of which he seems to be linked also opposes 6 and 8 (*total*: **14** = **2** x **7**) to 9 and 7, to which must be added, no doubt, the **5** (emblem of the center) total: **21** = **3** x **7**.

Notably, the relationship (*inverted*) of Yin and Yang is evoked in an analogous way in the magic square which, according to Tcheng Hiuan, testifies to the constitutional order of the Trigrams. We have seen that this order appears precisely in the arrangement attributed to King Wen.

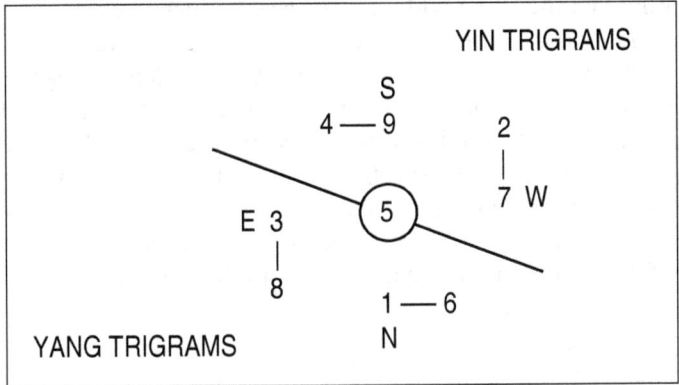

To the Yang Trigrams (N-E) correspond the congruent pairs 3-8 and 1-6, whose total is 18 (= **2** x **9**); to the Yin Trigrams (S-W), the pairs 4-9 and 2-7, which, if the central **5** is added, are worth 27 (= **3** x **9**): this again fixes at 2/3 the (*inverted*) ratio of Yang and Yin represented by the two families of Trigrams.

Now, if the magic square can evoke this relation, we shall see that it is precisely under the aspects in which it is particularly interesting for the *Hi ts'eu*.[78]

* * *

The *Hi ts'eu* contains an important development on numbers. This development is intended to demonstrate that divinatory symbols are capable of evoking the totality of things, what the Chinese call the Ten Thousand Beings or Essences (*wan mou*).

The diviners were able to pinpoint the number, which they said was 11,520. Indeed, the 64 hexagrams comprise 384 lines (= 6 x 64), i.e. 192 even and 192 odd lines. Since the even ones are worth 2/3 of the odd ones, it was admitted that 192 even lines represented 4,608 (= 192 x 24) female essences, while the 192 odd lines represented 6,912 (= 192 x 36) male essences, so that the total of *yang* and *yin* things was 11,520 (= 4,608 + 6,912). 10,000 is a popular grand total. 11,520 is the closest number to 10,000 that is a multiple of both 360 (the theoretical number of days in the year) and 384 {which represents both the total of the emblem lines and

---

78 *Yi king*, L., p. 365.

the total number of days in an embolismal year):[79] 11,520 = 384 x 30 and 360 x 32 or (216 + 144) x 32}.

To a division of the total of things in 5 parts which allows to oppose them according to the relation 3/2 (= 6.912 / 4.608 = 192 x 36 / 192 x 24), according to the observation 60 = 5 x 12 (= 36 + 24), corresponds a division of this total which is the year in 5 parts, each of which is worth **72** (= 6 x 12). We thus arrive at a division of 360 according to the ratio 3/2, opposing 216 (= **3** x 72), emblem of Yang (*even*), to 144 (= 2 x 72), emblem of Yin (*even*).

In addition to the passages in which they express the 3/2 ratio in terms that seem meaningful to them, the authors of the *Hi ts'eu* juxtapose remarks about the first ten numbers inspired by the intention to oppose the even and the odd.

After stating that the first 5 odd numbers are produced by Heaven and the first 5 even numbers by the Earth, they indicate that these ten numbers are arranged in Space in such a way as to form odd-even pairs. These 5 pairs may be – and this is the opinion of the glossators – the pairs constituted by 2 numbers congruent to 5 (1-6, 2-7, 3-8, 4-9, 5-10); we know that these pairs are found, *oriented*, both in the *Ho t'ou* and in the magic square (*Lo chou*). In the *Ho t'ou*, they are arranged in the center and on the branches of a cross. It is sufficient to fold the four ends of the cross at right angles to obtain the magic square arrangement, if we take the precaution of dedicating the cardinal positions to the odd numbers, and reversing the even ones 7-2 and 9-4.

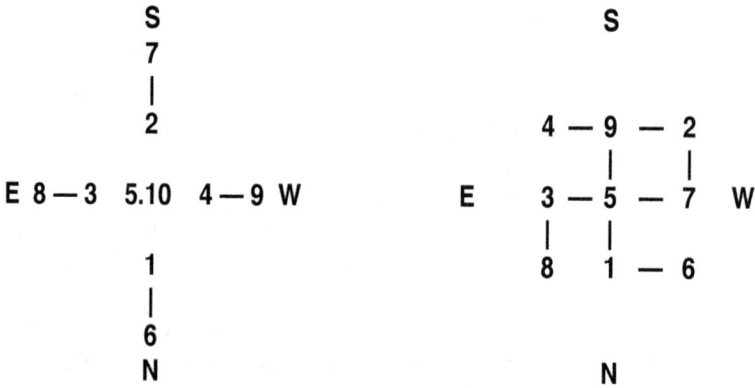

Expressed by authors visibly concerned with the divisions into 5 parts, the idea of arranging 5 pairs of congruent numbers in the sectors of Space can be taken as an allusion to the cross arrangement where the symbols of the 5 Elements are represented with their orientation. But, without refusing to admit this thesis, it should not be forgotten that the traditional interpretation of the *Hi ts'eu* attributes to the

---

79 The least common multiple of 360 and 384 is 11520/2. The lunisolar year (6 months of 29 and 6 months of 30 days) being 354 days, and the Chinese estimating the solar year at 366 days (difference of 12 days), 2 months of 30 days (30 x 2 = 60) were intercalated every five years (12 x 5 = 60); the 3rd and 5th year of a five-year cycle thus counted (354 + 30 =) 384 days. Note the importance of the 5-year cycle, the importance of the 60-day intercalation, and the fact that the ratio of the number of normal years to stroke years is 3 to 2.

Book II - Chapter III - Numbers

Old Yang, symbol of the South, the emblem 9, and to the Young Yang, symbol of the West, the emblem 7. Only in the magic square there are 7-2 in the West and 9-4 in the South.

Now, the *Hi ts'eu*, stresses the possibility of forming 3 odd pairs with the first 10 numbers, but also insists on the total value of these ten numbers which is 55. 55 is worth 5 times 11, *and 5 odd-odd pairs can be formed* (1-10, 2-9, 3-8, 4-7 and 5-6) each having 11 for sum. The *Hi ts'eu* does not fail to point out that the first 5 even numbers are worth 30 (= 5 times **6**) and the first 5 odd numbers 25 (= 5 times **5**). The opposition of the even and the odd, as manifested in the first 10 numbers considered as representative of the whole numerical series, has therefore as its symbol the relation 6/5, which must lend to the number 11 (= 5 + 6) a prestige equal to that of the number 5 {= 3 (Heaven, round) + 2 (= Earth, square)}. The importance attributed to 11 cannot be surprising when one knows the role of privileged classifier that corresponds to **5**, symbol of the Earth (square), as to **6**, symbol of Heaven (round).

Moreover, this value of 11 is affirmed by a remarkable adage quoted by the *Ts'ien Han chou*.

The author of the *History of the early Han*,[80] after qualifying the traditional view that **6** is the Number of Heaven (and its Agents) and **5** the Number of the Earth (as of the Elements), recalls the saying, "Now, 5 and 6 is the central Union (or, also, the Union in its Center (*tchong ho*) of Heaven and Earth." The glossators are content to say that the 5 is at the center of the odd series (1, 3, 5, 7, 9) *created by Heaven*, the 6 at the center of the even series (2, 4, 6, g, 10) *created by Earth*. This note, which brings us back to the numerical speculations of the *Hi ts'eu* in the most precise way, might be surprising, since it explains that the 5 (*even*) belongs to Earth (*yin*), while the 6 (*even*) belongs to Heaven (*yang*). It is only understandable if it is implied that Earth and Heaven, *when united*, exchange their attributes, and one of the intentions of the texts reconciled by the *Ts'ien Han chou* is to state *explicitly* that *this exchange results from a hierogamy*. But the author goes on to state that 11 {the result of the union (*ho*) of the central numbers (*tchong*)} is the number by which the Way (Tao) of Heaven and Earth is constituted in its perfection (*tch'eng*).

This Via, symbolically qualified by 11, runs from 5, placed in the center, i.e., at the crossroads of the odd numbers, to 6, similarly placed at the crossroads of the even numbers, clearly unites by its center (*and rather like a gnomon erected, like a tree, in the center of the Universe*) two superimposed magical squares.[81] (See the next figure in the following page)

In the magic square with center 5, while the even numbers, placed at the corners, mark the end of the square branches of the swastika, the odd numbers occupy the cardinal positions, and 5 is at the center of 1, 3, 7, 9. But, *if we replace each of the numbers in this square by the number which, added to it, gives* 11, we obtain a

---

80 *Ts'ien Han chou*, 21a, p. 9a.
81 I say square, but Heaven is round, and there is reason to suppose that the celestial distance of the numbers must somehow evoke the circle. The octagonal arrangement of the trigrams undoubtedly has the merit of implying a participation of the circle and the square.

	9		7		
3	5	7	8	6	4
	1		10		

new magic square (center 6; total value, in all directions, of the numbers placed on the same line: 18). The odd numbers occupy the four ends of the swastika and, distributed in the cardinal positions, the even numbers frame the 6.

We shall begin by observing that, as the 6 (representing the pair 6-1) passes to the Center, it exchanges its attributes (5-10) with the North, and that, similarly, the West and the South exchange their numerical symbols (2-7 and 4-9). It should be noted that, apart from the passage quoted from *Ts'ien Han chou*, Chinese literature does not seem to contain any allusion to the magic square with 6 in the center. This should lead us to think, not that this square enjoyed no prestige, but, on the contrary, that much of the ancient science of numbers was mysterious; only furtive allusions to this esoteric knowledge can attest to this.

The figure formed by the superposition of squares with 5 and 6 in the center is remarkable because it is made up of 9 odd and 9 even, each of which is worth 11, making a total of 99 (See the figure on the next page).

This was admirably suited to provide a total representation of the Universe, as well as a numerical justification of an essential theory, that of the reciprocal and interlocking action of the celestial Agents and Domains (the 6 *Tsong*) and the terrestrial Agents and Domains (the 5 *Hing*) in the 9 Provinces of Earth and Heaven.

We know, moreover, that the diviners used an instrument whose tracing reminds of this figure. It is mentioned in the *Tcheou li*,[82] and Japanese excavations at Lo lang[83] have uncovered a copy made before the Christian era. This instrument

---

82   *Tcheou li*, Biot, *op. cit.* t. II, p. 108.
83   Yoshito Harada, *Lo Lang*, p. 39 of the English summary; p. 61, of the Japanese text, figure 27 and plate CXII. The fact that the turning irons are made of hard and soft wood suggests that the instrument imitates an ancient fire-making tool. This observation is perhaps not unimportant, since various literary or ritual traditions preserve the memory of an instrument used to obtain fire by friction thanks to a rotating movement. This instrument was perhaps still used in certain cases in feudal times; I must limit myself here to pointing out (reserving a detailed study for another work) the existence of a whole set of mythical data attesting to the link between the theme of fire and the themes of the whirling, the wheel and the pivot, together with the themes of the swing, the pole and the gnomon. The relationship of some of these themes to the notion of Tao and to hierogamic practices is indicated. I will simply add that the invention of the arrangement of the trigrams known as that of King Wen (in relation, as I have just shown, to the magic square, that is, to an arrangement of numbers evoking the swastika), is linked by tradition to a test to which the apprentice chief is subjected. This test, which takes place during the festivities of the long night, leads to the renewal of the year and of the royal virtues, and the festivities end when the torches are lit again. The theme of the lighted torches seems to be linked to a whole set of practices and metaphors related to the idea of hierogamy.

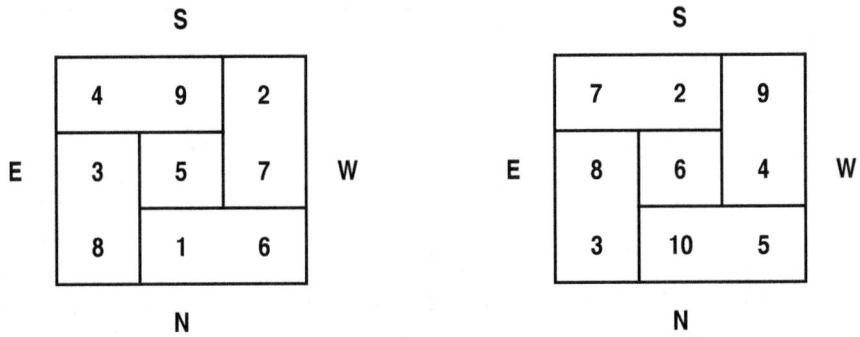

consists of two boards, one of hard wood (*yang*), the other of soft wood (*yin*), one round (Heaven), the other square (Earth); they are made to overlap and pivot independently of each other, for they are pierced in the middle by a small hole intended probably to serve as a notch for a perpendicular rod forming a pivot. On both are inscribed various classificatory symbols: symbols of the months, cyclical signs, constellations and trigrams, the latter placed, *in the arrangement of King Wen*, on the *square (Earth)* tablet. If there is reason, as I believe, to establish a connection between this divinatory utensil and the double magic square, we must conclude that the latter, while evoking the idea of right angles and the *square*, must have suggested the idea of a *circular motion*.

We have already seen that the magic squares, as soon as we deal with joining congruent pairs, reproduce a *swastika-shaped arrangement*; by itself, this suggests the idea of a rotating motion. The *Hi ts'eu* suggests that the two signs inscribed on each branch of the swastika should be read not as a pair of numerical signs, but as a number.

The *Hi ts'eu*,[84] indeed, while insisting on the number 55, attributes a privileged role to 50 (emblem of the Great Expansion). From this fact, we can guess the importance that, for a mind concerned with 5 and 6, and also with 50 and 55 (5 times 11), could present a numerical series formed by numbers that differ from each other by the addition not of 1 unit, but of 11 units and that, starting from 6 {without reaching 105 (= 55 + 50; but 105, which includes 1 and 5, can be assimilated to 6, the starting point of the series)} included – besides 50, the center of the series – 8 numbers that could be opposed by 2 in 2, so that their difference was always 55. This series {6, 17, 28, 39, (50), 61, 72, 83, 94 (105)} was all the more worthy of attention because it was possible to form with it 4 pairs of numbers so that the total of each of them was 100, the numbers in the column of the units following each other in the order in which they appear in the series. The four largest of these numbers are still remarkable because each of them is written with a pair of congruent numbers {61, 72, 83, 94 (and, similarly, 105)}. These are the numbers that can be read from the various branches of the numerical swastikas inscribed in the magic squares (See the next figure in the following page).

---

84 *Yi king*, L., p. 365.

39	94	39	61
28	83	28	72
[50(105)]		[50]	
17	72	17	83
6	61	6	94

The *Hi ts'eu* itself invites this reading. Certain mythical details come, unexpectedly but not surprisingly, to attest to its legitimacy.

The sovereigns who founded the successive dynasties, according as they were animated by the Virtue of Heaven or that of Earth, were alternately high or low, for Heaven extends in height, and Earth in breadth.[85] The Chinese have devotedly guarded the memory of this essential theme. They have even preserved an accurate recollection of the height of the Heroes they most revered.[86] Chouen, who possessed the Virtue of Earth, was stocky and only 6 feet 1 inch (61 inches) tall,[87] while Yao, his predecessor, had a body (or perhaps a scalp) measuring 7 feet 2 inches (72 inches). It may be thought, since the body of a Founder serves as the standard for a dynasty, that these numbers commanded the system of weights and measures which these sovereigns established, while, giving a new calendar to a new era, they reorganized the dimensions of Time. These same numbers – a curious fact, though not unexpected – commanded in any case the divisions of the time of their reign or existence. This time, when dealing with a perfect Sovereign, is 100 years. Therefore, it will suffice to refer to the above table to know that Chouen, who lived 100 years, had 39 years of reign; this Hero of 6 feet 1 inch took power at 61 years of age. As for Yao (72 inches), who reigned for 100 years, he only retained effective authority for 72 years; he lived 28 years as a retired ruler. We do not have precise information on the stature of the founders of the three royal dynasties. About King Wen, founder of the Tcheou, few mythical details have been preserved. However, we know that he gave part of his 100 years of life to his son. King Wen was fat and short; perhaps 50 was a better measure of his height than 100. In the case of Yu the Great, founder of the Hia (whose tall stature has remained famous even though he is credited with the Virtue of the Earth), he lived 100 years, reigned 17 years and, since he ascended the throne at 83, everything seems to indicate that he was 8 feet 3 inches tall. Penetrated by the influence of Heaven, the founder of the Yin, T'ang the Victorious, had even more reason to be very tall. History has not forgotten his height. This, which is not the case with Chouen and Yao, is expressed in whole numbers of feet; T'ang, we are told, was 9 feet tall, that is, 90 inches; therefore, he

---

85 *Tch'ouen ts'ieou fan lou*, 7.
86 Information taken from the *Tchou chou ki nien* and chapter 27 of the *Song chou*.
87 In the Chinese system of measurements, the foot (*tch'e*), is 10 inches (*ts'ouen*) (although the Yin divided it into 9 inches and the Tcheou into 8 inches), and not 12 as in the Anglo-Saxon system (TN).

seems to be 4 inches short, as Chouen and Yu were 61 and 72, and, since the numbers 83 and 50 (or 100) seem to play a role in the life of Yu and King Wen, the only one of the 5 numbers inscribed on the swastika that remains available is 94. But, by a remarkable coincidence, if T'ang is given only 90 inches, he is attributed either long arms – of 4 cubits – or arms with 4 elbows. Now, the word that the mythical iconography, understanding it as "elbow" or "cubit," has taken advantage of to represent, more vividly, the power of T'ang, does not differ sensibly from the word that means "thumb"... It is very likely that, in order to endow the Hero with arms with four cubits or four elbows, four inches were removed from his height.

This set of mythical facts is too coherent not to conclude that the pairs of congruent numbers inscribed in the magic squares read as the numbers 94, 83, 72, 72, 61, 50 (or 105: 5-10 or 10-5). In the two squares, the opposite branches of the swastika form two pairs, one South-North, the other East-West, perfectly balanced since their numerical weights, so to speak, are equivalent, as is appropriate in figures made to suggest the idea of *rotation*. It seems, moreover, that the rotational motion intended to be represented is that of the year. The two figures, in fact, numerically evoke 360.

The square with center 5 has a particular merit; it evokes this number by highlighting the opposition (3/2), so dear to the authors of the *Hi ts'eu*, of 216 and 144. Indeed, 83 + 61 are opposed to 72 + 94, to which should be added 50 represented by **5**, a substitute for the congruent pair 5-10[88] placed in the center of the cross.

The square with center 6 is no less rich in figurative power. The sum of the numbers inscribed in its perimeter, which is equal to 354 (= 2 x 177), expresses the number of days of the lunisolar year, while the 6, placed in the center, allows one to recall the total of 360 (= 354 + 6) and, no doubt also (because 6 is the substitute for the congruent pair 6-1 and 61 x 6 = 366), the total number of days of the solar year

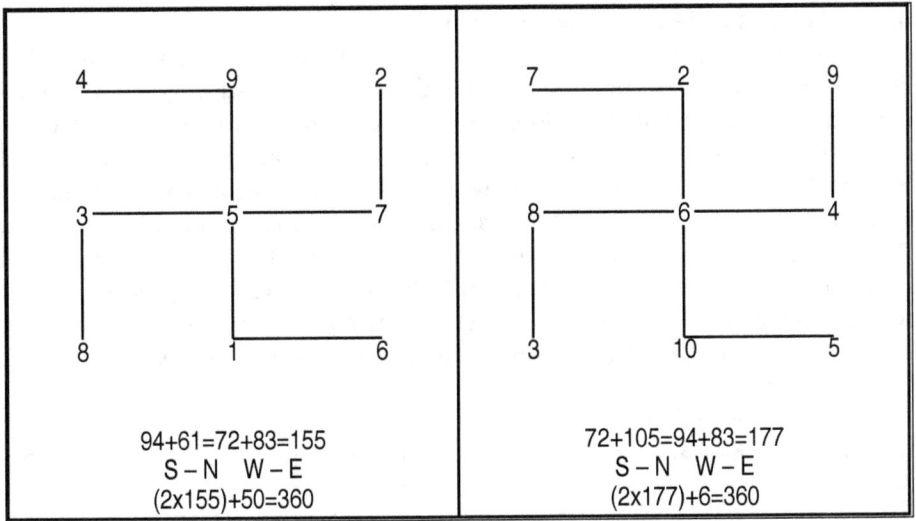

---

88 The 5 (x) and 10 (+) were formerly written with a cross.

(366), which suggests the idea of the necessary intercalations and may indicate their rhythm, the 6 being reminiscent of the 60 (= 12 x 5) days which, in a period of 5 years, must be distributed between the two additional months.

These observations impose the idea that this square (as well as the square with 5 in its center) was known to the Masters of the *Hi ts'eu*, and that these two arrangements (which are in fact interdependent) of the first numbers were regarded by them as numerical translations of the octagonal arrangement of the divinatory symbols. The *Hi ts'eu*, in fact, in connection with these symbols and the handling of the tokens that were used to construct them and also to calculate, expressly alludes to the practice of double quinquennial intercalation.[89]

Rev. Legge indignantly denied any hint of common sense in this passage of the treatise. It is not seen, he said, how by forming even and odd groupings of rods one could determine the number of intercalary days and the rhythm of the intercalations. It is true… It is not by means of cuts on a set of sticks, nor by the construction of magic squares that the laws of the calendar were established. But it was not up to the soothsayers to establish these laws. It was enough for them to make the efficacy of an institution regulating their profession shine.

They had to take into account the social representations of time and space and the interlocking systems of classification. They also had to endow all these conventions with a prestige that would seduce thought and justify action. To this end they used geometric and arithmetical symbols. These, like all symbols, had the power of symbolic evocation. But, more abstract, in a sense, than the others, these symbols also had to inspire a particular kind of confidence; indeed they lend themselves to a multitude of useful games to connect the most diverse classifications together, even when played arbitrarily, they seem to dominate the game. Being used to represent the order of the universe, the image of the world they allowed to construct gave these symbols an air of necessity. It seemed to guarantee the efficacy of the manipulations that it nevertheless facilitated.

By making it clear that the divinatory symbols they were to handle referred to devices in which the Numbers adorned with their own prestige the conventional divisions of Space and the traditional laws of the Calendar, the diviners enhanced their art. This art seemed to be dominated by the ambition to make the world both intelligible and lovable. When they assimilated the octagonal rose of their Trigrams to the magic square and thus made manifest the interactions of Heaven and Earth, Yang and Yin, Round and Square, Even and Odd, the Master diviners could presume to cooperate with the Universal Order in the same way as the Chiefs, when, moving in their square *Ming t'ang*, they strove to set in motion the swastika constituted by the numerical symbols of the East and of the Seasons.

* * *

The above remarks show the value of the traditions collected (or reconstructed) by scholars of the Han or even Song period. The diagrams of *Lo chou* and *Ho t'ou*

---

89   *Yi king, Ibid.*, p. 365 and note p. 368. Legge writes: "But how could such a process be of any value in determining the days necessary to be intercalated in any particular year?"

are certainly reconstructions, but made by well-informed interpreters or those who reasoned correctly. A numerical device is certainly at the basis of the Five Elements theory, which the *Hong fan* expounds, and the Nine Sections of the *Hong fan* are also derived from a numerical device. Both the simple cross and the swastika arrangement of numbers served – as the *Yue ling* shows and as must be assumed in interpreting the *Hi ts'eu* – to provide a Picture of the Universe and its various divisions into Sectors. The myths concerning the arrangement of the world are in consonance with the traditions of the divinatory art; the divisions of the tortoise shell, the oriented grouping of the Trigrams, the plan of the *Ming t'ang* can only be understood if we relate them to the theory of the Nine Provinces or the division of the fields into *nine squares*, and if we recognize that the Numbers, as their essential attribute, have a classificatory function.

This function was not assigned to them late, for simple reasons of mnemonic convenience, and following the development of the scholastic spirit. It has characterized them from their earliest mythical uses and has not ceased to do so. The first speculations about numbers are dominated by the fact that they are considered symbolic rubrics that control the traditional systems of classification. This attitude toward numbers, which appears in both the *Hong fan* and the *Hi ts'eu*, is attested from the earliest beginnings of the scholarly literature.

The uses to which the various techniques have put numbers, far from modifying this fundamental attitude, have reinforced it. Assimilated to locations, and always considered in relation to concrete Times and Spaces, the essential role of Numbers is not that of allowing *additions*, but that of representing and linking various modes of *division*, valid for such and such groupings. Instead of calculating different quantities, they are used to note the *variable organizations* that can be attributed to this or that set. The qualitative differences of these groupings and their absolute total value are of much more interest than their arithmetic value, as we understand it. It is preferred to divide into sectors rather than to think of adding up units.

Hence the importance of numbers, such as 5 or 6, which are assigned to the center and which, considered as privileged expressions of the total, serve above all, when used as divisors, to symbolize *modes of distribution*; on the other hand, large numbers, such as 360, which are easy to divide, appear as *peripheral* expressions of the total. Undoubtedly, these dispositions of the Chinese mind have gained in strength as a result of the Calendar and Music technicians' use of Numbers. As they used them to express – I do not say to measure – relations, sectors or angles, arithmetic, remaining at the service of a geometry adapted to a Space-Time conceived as a concrete medium, has not been transformed into a science of quantity.

III. NUMBERS AND MUSICAL RELATIONS

The Nine Sections of the *Hong fan* were entrusted by Heaven to Yu, whose body deserved to be taken as a standard for all measurements, while his voice could serve as a tuning fork... The tube which gave the initial note was never separated from the divinatory utensil,[90] formed by two tablets, images of Heaven and Earth, superimposed like two magic squares...

It would be difficult to prove that the Chinese theory of musical tubes is directly linked to speculations about magic squares. However, some connections are significant. To illustrate their musical theory, the Chinese had imagined a prestigious arrangement for their pipes, as it emphasized odd and even ratios (2/3 or 4/3) evoking the great unit 360 (= 216 + 144). The prestige of the square arrangement of numbers is due to a similar fact. Because of this prestige, the *Ming t'ang*, like the octagonal rose of the Trigrams, was related to a magic square; in the *Ming t'ang* the rules of each of the 12 months of the year were proclaimed, and it was the 12 months that were represented by the 12 tubes, which, like the months (and by the observation: 12 x 2 = 24 = 8 x 3), were also related to the Eight Winds, of which the Eight Trigrams are the symbols. The year (360) is divided into 12 months (and also into 24 half-months of 15 days) grouped into 4 seasons around a center or pivot; the 8 Trigrams are said to derive from the 4 secondary Symbols assimilated to the 4 Eastern Seasons; in the *Ming t'ang*, although 9 rooms are attributed to it, 4 cardinal rooms have, in addition to the central room, a particular importance, since they are dedicated to the months of the equinoxes and the solstices, so that, the arrangement in *single cross* is found in the arrangement of the *swastika*; for its part the arrangement of the magic square allows to evoke the classification in 5 Elements. The musical theory also juxtaposes a classification of Twelve Tubes, which is used to construct a Twelve Winds Rose, and a classification of Five Notes, which is used to symbolize the Center and the Four Seasons-Directions.

Numerical (and graphic) games serve to link these classifications and pass from one to the other; it is enough to allow these connections and passages so that, by playing these games, one has the impression that one succeeds in revealing the Order of the World and collaborating in it.

Since, thanks to Father Amiot,[91] the Chinese theory of the Twelve Tubes and the Five Notes has been known in the West, it has been brought closer to the musical theories of the Greeks and its scientific character has been emphasized.

But Chavannes observed that the Chinese theorists had not adhered with total respect to the accuracy of the numerical relationships. This observation led him to conclude that the scientific character of the theory had soon left the Chinese indifferent and that, therefore, they had not invented it but had received the principle from the Greeks.[92] Chavannes has defended this hypothesis, contrary to the opinion of most other scholars of the origin of Chinese music, by a philological reasoning which does not seem irreproachable and which has an important defect: it leaves aside all the mythical data of the problem and appeals only to documents from which one hopes to derive historical facts, because they can be dated.

If we go by these documents, it appears that the instruments to which the Chinese applied the theory were sounding bells; with these instruments, mea-

---

90   Both were taken to war in the same chariot: *Tcheou li*, Biot, *op. cit.*, vol. II, p. 108.
91   Volume VI of the *Mémoires concernant l'histoire... des Chinois*.
92   App. 2 of vol. III of *SMT*, pp. 630-645.

surements are infinitely delicate and, consequently, observations on numerical relations are almost impossible;[93] the theory applied was, therefore, a ready-made theory… It is clear that the Chinese had received it from the Greeks. In fact, Chinese traditions place the invention of stringed and wind instruments at the origin of instrumental inventions. In the myth which explains the essential division of the Twelve Tubes into 6 male and 6 female Tubes, a geographical expression is used, it is true, in which Chavannes wished to see the memory of an influence of the countries reached by the Greek civilization.[94] But the division into *yin* and *yang* tubes, especially when it is based (as is the case, as we shall see) on the proportion (3/2 or 3/4) of Heaven and Earth, is linked with the conceptions – mythical or scholarly – of the Universe, which are peculiar to the Chinese, in too perfect a manner for the idea of borrowing to take hold. On the other hand, the myth concerning the Twelve Tubes alludes expressly to sexual dances, and in a significant way; as soon as the twelve bamboo tubes were cut and assembled, they were used to make a *couple* of phoenixes dance (which is no doubt the mythical transposition of a pair of pheasants). Now, throughout the Far East there is a widespread instrument, the *cheng*,[95] the invention of which the Chinese attribute to Niu-koua (*sister* or *wife* of Fou-hi), who also invented marriage. The *cheng*, which is still used today to accompany sexual dances, exists in two forms: there is a male *cheng* and a female *cheng*; in all cases the arrangement of the pipes is made, we are told, to represent the two wings of a bird (phoenix or pheasant). When dancing to the sound of the *cheng*, it is really the phoenix or pheasant pair that dances; it is (for the performers dance while playing the *cheng*) the *cheng* that dances and is danced to.[96] This feature is too archaic, and the prestige of the *cheng* is too great in the Far East, for it to seem legitimate to regard the mythical account of the invention of the 12 male or female pipes as a fable entirely dreamed up by scholars to justify a borrowing.

At the same time (whatever the importance of percussion instruments in Chinese music), Chavannes' remark about the difficulty the Chinese would have had in establishing numerical relationships disappears completely.

On the contrary, the instruments made of bamboo invited these observations. Let us recall here that the Chinese word (*tsie*), which is used metaphorically to express the idea of measurement,[97] has the concrete meaning of "joint, knot of bamboo." The Chinese certainly did not invent the theory on which they based their musical technique by making delicate measurements on bronze bells. On the other hand, they might well have founded the art of Music on the art of Numbers by expressing the length of their various bamboo flutes by their Number of joints; they might also have done so by numerically evaluating the strings (I mean the actual

---

93   SMT, III, p. 640.
94   SMT, III, p. 643.
95   Lu che tch'ouen ts'ieou, 5. The *cheng* is a kind of harmonica. It is said that the same used to have (19 or) 13 pipes. The 13-pipe *cheng* consists of 6 pipes, placed to the right of a central pipe, and 6, placed to the left, arranged to imitate the two wings of a bird.
96   Granet, *Danses et légendes…*, p. 577.
97   Cf. *supra*, in this Book, ch. II.

strings of the royal bows); the two methods will not be thought mutually exclusive if one considers that, according to the Chinese, their earliest and most venerable system of symbolization consisted of *tied* strings.[98]

Moreover, as I hope to show in a moment, the numbers that were first used to express the length of the sound tubes were integers and small numbers. The series they formed was subsequently replaced by several competing series composed of larger but still integer numbers, these substitutions having as their principle certain changes in the system of calculation. Different numbers, used (*successively*, or *concurrently*) to determine the divisions of the units of measurement, also served to multiply the first numerical symbols of the musical pipes. It seems that it was by comparing – and, moreover, interpenetrating – the series obtained by these multiplications that the arithmetical principle of the scale was derived. But, if this was achieved, it was as a result of numerical games controlled by the authority of the total of 360 and the prestige of the opposition of 216 and 144.

Leaving aside any debate on its origin (which is irrelevant to our subject), we refuse to follow Chavannes. We will not say: the Chinese did not discover by their own means the arithmetical principle of their musical theory, for they understood neither its rigor nor its perfection. But we will say: if the Chinese succeeded in basing their musical technique on an arithmetical principle which, moreover, they did not find it necessary to apply rigorously, it is because the reason for their discovery was a game carried out by means of numerical symbols (considered not as abstract signs, but as effective symbols), whose purpose was not to formulate an exact theory that rigorously justified a technique, but to illustrate this technique by linking it to a prestigious Image of the World.

* * *

The theory of the 12 sound tubes seems to be as old as academic literature in China. Sseu-ma Ts'ien[99] devoted an important chapter to it in which the intertwining of the classification by 12 (12 Tubes and 12 Months) and the classification by 8 (8 Winds and 8 Trigrams) is indicated. Many years earlier, Lu Pou-wei[100] had given, in brief and very clear terms, the arithmetical formula on which this theory is based. Moreover, the authority of this formula was recognized when the *Yue ling* was composed.

This treatise on the Calendar already relates the tubes to the months, a relationship which implies for each of them (through the duodenary cycle) a definite *orientation*. There are many references to the sound tubes in ancient literature; some attest that they are imagined to be oriented; the orientations are those of the *Yue ling*.

Among these literary allusions, one is significant. It relates the initial tube called *houang tchong*, the *yellow bell*, to the Yellow Fountains. The archaic myth of the Yellow Fountains, the Land of the Dead – who were buried in the north of the

---

98 *SMT*, I, p. 6. I have already pointed out the importance of the knots in the theory of divination, the relation of which to the speculations on numbers I have shown elsewhere.

99 *SMT*, III, pp. 293 ff.

100 *Lu che tch'ouen ts'ieou*, 5 (third century BC).

cities, with their heads turned northward – places these Fountains at the bottom of the Septentrion. This is indicated in the duodenary cycle by the character *tseu*, meaning "child"; at the same time as the full north, this cyclical sign marks the winter solstice and midnight, propitious times for conceptions. An important set of mythical or ritual themes shows that the Yellow Springs, the Land of the Dead, constituted a reservoir of life.[101] The Chinese thus admitted that, taking refuge in the Yellow Springs, in the shallows (the Bottom is *yin*) of the Septentrion (*yin*), the Yang spent the winter (*yin*) imprisoned and enveloped by the Yin (Water). There it regained all its strength and prepared to emerge by striking the ground with the heel; this image was found[102] in the expression *houang tchong*, which designates the initial tube. The *houang tchong* deserved well – assigned to the eleventh month (month of the winter solstice) – to represent Yang at the lowest level of its potency; the initial tube, which is the longest of all, gives the least acute note; now Yang is acute (*clear*), while Yin is grave (*dark*). The attribution of the tubes to the different months illustrates the continuous growth of Yang from the winter solstice onwards. In the rose of the 12 winds, where the orientation of the months and the tubes is marked, they follow each other from the north in decreasing order.

To obtain this arrangement, implicit in the *Yue ling* as well as in the ancient myths, it is necessary to construct a 12-pointed star. Now, this construction presupposes the knowledge of the arithmetical rule whose formula was given by Lu Pou-wei and which has brought the Chinese theory closer to the Greek.[103] (See the figure in the next page)

Lu Pou-wei and all Chinese authors enunciate this rule by saying that tubes generate (*cheng*) each other, but distinguish between what they call higher generation (*chang cheng*) and lower generation (*hia cheng*), i.e., that in which the tube produced is longer (*chang*: higher) than its producer, and that in which it is less long (*hia*: lower). A lower generation occurs when the length is reduced by removing one third of the length of the previous tube; this is the case, for example, when the initial tube is 81 (= **3** x 27) and the second tube is 54 (= **2** x 27). A higher generation occurs when the length is increased by adding one third to that of the previous tube; this is the case when we go from the second tube which is 54 (= **3** x 18) to the third tube which is 72 (= **4** x 18). The third tube (72) creates by lower generation the fourth (48), this one, by upper generation, the fifth (64) and so on until the seventh tube. This last one, although created in its turn by higher generation, creates, again by higher generation, the eighth tube; from this last one it is, then, the tubes of rank *even* (and no longer those of rank *odd*) that produce by lower generation.

This does not preclude considering all tubes of odd rank as male tubes {= Yang = *Even* = Heaven = Round = **3** (value of the circumference inscribed in a square of

---

101 Granet, *Coutumes matrimoniales de La Chine antique* (*T'oung pao*, 1912).
102 *SMT*, III, p. 304.
103 *SMT*, III, p. 631. The 12-pipe system corresponds to "a progression of 12 just fifths carried to the interval of a single octave and thus successively playing the 12 semitones of an untempered chromatic scale."

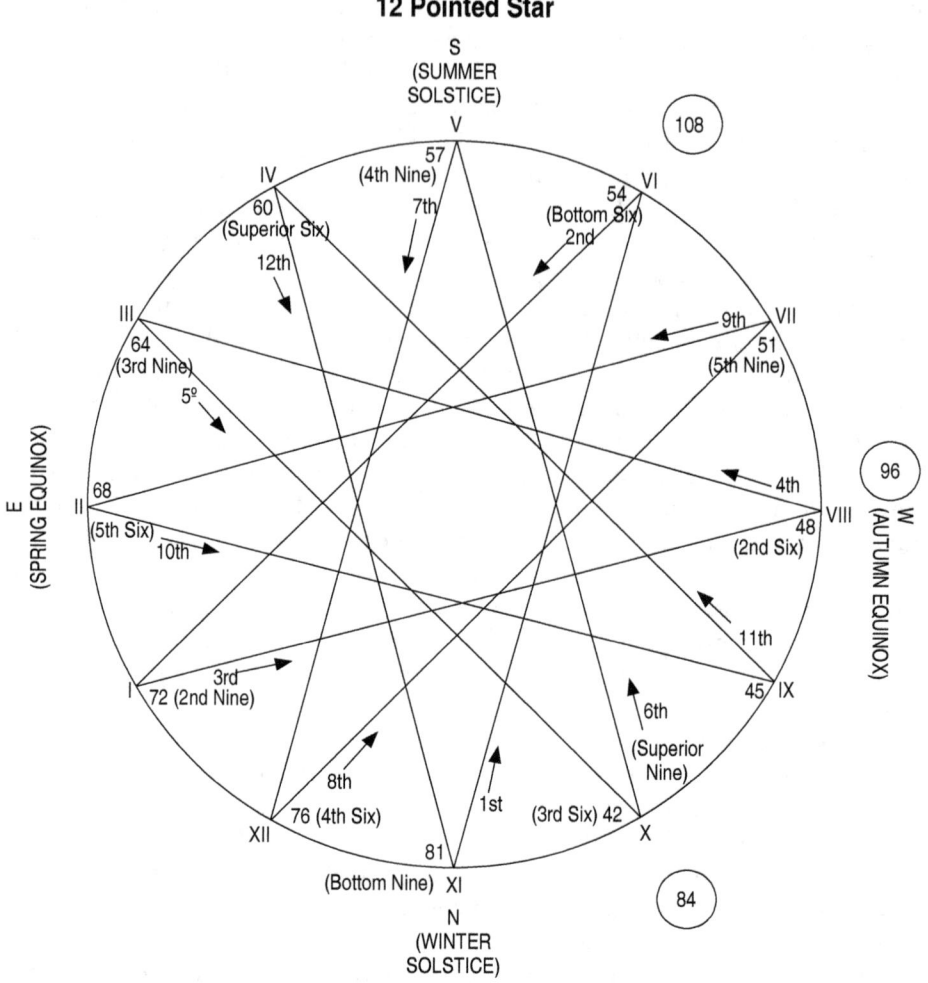

The Roman numerals indicate the months.
The numbers in Arabic numerals indicate the length of the sound tubes.
The signs 1°, 2°, indicate the rank of the tubes in the order of their creation.
The number inside a circle indicates the dimensions that the 2nd, 4th and 6th tubes would have if the note emitted by them were not lowered by an octave.

side 1)} and all tubes of even rank as female tubes {= Yin = *Even* = Earth = Square = **2** (value of the semi-perimeter of the square circumscribing the circumference of value 3)}.[104] The Chinese had good reasons for this decision. If the first three odd tubes are worth 3/2 of the first three even tubes, the last three odd tubes are worth 3/4 of the last three even tubes respectively; 3/2 expresses the ratio between the

---

104 *SMT*, III, p. 632 and p. 637. Lu Pou-wei counts 7 pipes produced by the upper generation against 5 produced by the lower generation; he counts them in order of size and includes among the latter only the 2nd pipe and those whose length is less.

Book II - Chapter III - Numbers 133

circumference (= Heaven) and the semi-perimeter of the square (= Earth) circumscribing it; 3/4 expresses the ratio between the circumference and the perimeter: just as 3/2, and even better, 3/4 can express the ratio of Yang to Yin.

It is possible that the Chinese first attributed to their tubes numerical symbols illustrating the single relation 3/4; it is said, in fact, in a passage of the *Kouan tseu*,[105] that the first five tubes were worth respectively 81, 108 (= 54 x 2), 72, 96 (= 48 x 2), 64, from which we may conclude, it seems, that the sixth was worth 84 (= 42 x 2). The Chinese seem to have divided the dimensions of the first three tubes of the even series by 2, while they avoided changing the dimensions of the last three tubes of this series.

This reform may be a sign of progress in musical technique;[106] but what we care to note is that if the first three *yin* tubes had not been made smaller in length than the last three by halving them, *it would not have been possible to assign to the tubes the orientation which the Yue ling attributes to them in constructing a 12-pointed star, as shows the figure in the previous page.*

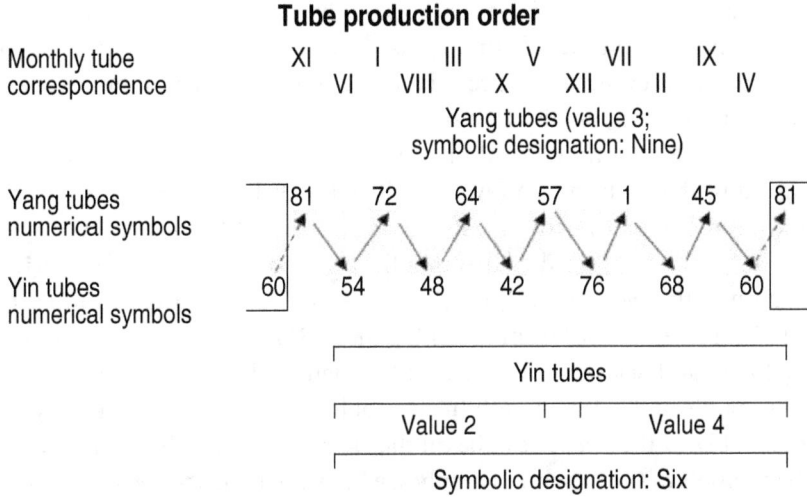

(The numbers give the dimensions of the tubes according to *Houai-nan tseu.*).
Sixty has been added at the beginning of the series and 81 at the end, because, due to its cyclic arrangement, the 12th tube, 60, produces the first, 81).

---

105 *Kouan tseu*, 58.

106 Invention of the 6th and 7th notes with two successive reductions to the octave. Let us note how close the series 108, 96, 84, 72, 64 is to the series 105, 94, 83, 72, 61, (50) (*Interval:* 11) *inscribed on the edges of the magic squares.* The number which, in this last series, comes after 50 is 39. Now (39 + 81) / 2 = 40 *and the* Lu che tch'ouen ts'ieou, *in the passage in which he relates the invention of the twelve tubes, indicates that the initial tube (considered as central) is worth 39.* The glossators, embarrassed, point out that the 39 is to be explained by an *imbrication* (kiao) *with* 81: *that is, I suppose, by the fact that 81 + 39 halved makes the 40 (13th tube, central tube giving, with the difference of an octave, the same note as the* 1st *tube*).

Represented by the integers indicating their traditional dimensions, the 12 tubes occupy in the figure the orientations assigned to the cyclic signs and to the months corresponding to them. They are arranged around the perimeter of a circle starting from the North (11th month; winter solstice; initial tube) in decreasing order of size; their numerical symbols present the image of the continuous growth of Yang (acute). We also see that they occupy the 12 points of a star. *This star is drawn as soon as the symbols of the tubes* (yang *or* yin, yin *or* yang; creators or products) *which*, in the order of production, *are contiguous*.

This graphic construction reveals, on the one hand, the order of production of the tubes and, consequently, the formula that controls their numerical relationships; on the other hand, the *cyclic arrangement* of the tubes as well as the orientations from which their correspondence with the different months results. But, if the symmetrical figure formed by the 12-pointed star can be obtained, it is because two straight lines drawn consecutively (and which, consequently, must join the symbols of the three following tubes in the order of production) always cut an arc of 60°; and also because two distant points on the circumference were first joined by 210° on one side (on the left, in this case, because, in the arrangement adopted by the Chinese, the cyclic signs succeed each other in the order of the succession of times going to the left), and by 150° on the other. The initial tube (81, *yang* series) is assigned to the XIth month (odd month), the 2nd tube (54, *yin* series) should be assigned to the VIth month (even month), the 3rd (72, *yang* series) to the Ist month (odd months), the 4th (48, series *yin*) to the VIIIth month (even month), the 5th (64, series *yang*) to the IIIrd month (odd month), the 6th (42, series *yin*) to the Xth month (even month), the 7th (57, series *yang*) to the Vth month (odd month), (i.e. placed at 180° from the initial tube)(81)…, etc. But, as it was decided to leave the largest section of the circle to the left of the first line drawn, the numerical symbols of the 4th and 6th tubes should, like that of the 2nd (they are the first three tubes of the *yin* series), be on the right side of the circle and meet there with the symbols of the 9th and 11th tubes, which are in turn to the right of the 7th, placed at 180° from the initial tube. Now these three tubes are the last and smallest of the *yang* series. The numerical symbols of the Twelve Tubes would not have succeeded each other in order of decreasing size if the first three tubes of the even series had had dimensions (108, 96, 84) based on the 4/3 ratio between the *yin* and *yang* tubes. To obtain this result, they had to be halved, lowering the note they gave by an octave, while retaining the dimensions according to the 4/3 ratio for the last three even tubes, the symbols of the latter were to be placed in the left half of the circle, interspersed between the symbols of the first three larger *yang* tubes.

The geometrical figure which, in order to *illustrate* the continuous growth of Yang from the winter solstice onwards, justifies the system of correspondences established between the months and the tubes, can only be constructed, as we see, on condition that the tubes are given such dimensions that the first six illustrate

Book II - Chapter III - Numbers

the ratio 3/2 (= 81/54 = 72/48 = 63/42)[107] and the last six the ratio 3/4 (= 57/76 = 51/68 = 45/60). Any allusion to an equivalence between pipes and months according to the *Yue ling* system presupposes this construction and thus implies the prior discovery of the arithmetical rule on which Chinese musical theory is based.

This remark may have historical significance, but its real interest is to show that the Chinese are not mistaken when they assert that their ancient Sages regarded the problems relating to musical theory and the arrangement of the Calendar as related matters. Are we not invited to infer that the discovery of the arithmetical formula of the balance derives from the numerical speculations of the technicians and from that supreme art whose object was to order Space and Time and whose essential problem was to reveal the relations of Odd and Even?

The construction of the 12-pointed rose not only had the advantage of showing the continuous growth of Yang from the Yellow Springs. It also had the merit of justifying, by the alternation of the *yin* and *yang* tubes, the alternation of the *even* and *odd* months to which the 354-day lunar year sometimes attributed 30 days and sometimes 29. The division of the tubes into two equal groups of different types, while permitting new classifications, served in another way to illustrate the laws of the Calendar. The mythical significance of this division can be seen in the various symbolic names used for the tubes. They are called fathers and sons, because they are considered to beget (*cheng*) each other; the opposition of the generations alternating in power may reflect the rhythmic opposition of Yin and Yang. On the other hand, the yin and yang tube symbols alternate on the circumference of the dodecagon, allowing them to be grouped in pairs; two neighboring symbols were said to be *"wife and husband."* Similar metaphorical representations made it possible to put together the 6 male and 6 female tubes of the 12 lines, male or female, that make up the first pair of Hexagrams. This explains another way of naming the sound tubes; it consists in *identifying* them with the solid or split lines of the Hexagrams, evoking again the relations of the Odd and Even. The *yin* tubes were designated by the *Six* and the *yang* tubes by the *Nine*. To better remember the Hexagrams (which were analyzed by numbering the lines from bottom to top), the first tube was called *yang* and the first tube *yin* (like the first male line or the first female line of a Hexagram): *Basic Nine* and *Basic Six*; *the* intermediate tubes: (2nd or 3rd...) *Nine* or *Six* and the last two tubes: *Upper Nine* and *Upper Six*.

A passage from *Sseu-ma Ts'ien*, the importance of which we shall soon point out, guarantees the antiquity of these designations.[108] They are linked to a development of musical technique which must therefore also be considered ancient. As each of the pipes could in turn be taken as the initial pipe and give the first note of the scale, it was possible to constitute 12 scales.[109] These scales, each consisting of five notes, were characterized by the numerical symbols of the pipes which emit-

---

107 The accuracy of this last relation disappears as soon as the 5th tube is given the value 64 {= 48 x (4/3)}.

108 *SMT*, III, p. 316.

109 *Li ki*, C., I, p. 519 "5 notes, 6 male tubes, 12 tubes giving successively the initial note (*kong*)".

*	$\dfrac{60}{80} = \dfrac{3 \times 20}{4 \times 20}$		
	$\dfrac{81}{54} = \dfrac{3 \times 27}{2 \times 27}$	1st relation	
	$\dfrac{54}{72} = \dfrac{3 \times 18}{4 \times 18}$	2nd relation	
	$\dfrac{72}{48} = \dfrac{3 \times 24}{2 \times 24}$	3rd relation	
	$\dfrac{48}{64} = \dfrac{3 \times 16}{4 \times 16}$		
*	$\dfrac{64}{63} = \dfrac{4 \times 16}{3 \times 21}$	4th relation	
	$\dfrac{63}{42} = \dfrac{3 \times 21}{2 \times 21}$	5th relation	
	$\dfrac{42}{56} = \dfrac{3 \times 14}{4 \times 14}$	6th relation	
*	$\dfrac{56}{57} = \dfrac{4 \times 14}{3 \times 19}$		
	$\dfrac{57}{76} = \dfrac{3 \times 19}{4 \times 19}$	7th relation	
*	$\dfrac{76}{75} = \dfrac{4 \times 19}{3 \times 25}$		
	$\dfrac{75}{50} = \dfrac{3 \times 25}{2 \times 25}$	8th relation	
	$\dfrac{50}{51} = \dfrac{2 \times 25}{3 \times 17}$		
*	$\dfrac{51}{68} = \dfrac{3 \times 17}{4 \times 17}$	9th relation	
	$\dfrac{68}{69} = \dfrac{4 \times 17}{3 \times 23}$		
*	$\dfrac{69}{46} = \dfrac{3 \times 23}{2 \times 23}$	10th relation	
	$\dfrac{46}{45} = \dfrac{2 \times 23}{3 \times 15}$		
	$\dfrac{45}{60} = \dfrac{3 \times 15}{4 \times 15}$	11th relation	
	$\dfrac{60}{80} = \dfrac{3 \times 20}{4 \times 20}$	12th relation	

The asterisk indicates the cases in which the number to appear in 2 consecutive relations increases or decreases by one unit.

ted them; but when it was necessary to speak of them, it was sufficient to give the symbolic designation (*Basic Six... 3rd Nine... Upper Nine...*) of the tube taken, in this case, by the initial pipe. With these 12 scales thus constituted, one had, in total, 60 notes relating to the 60 cyclic binomials formed by the combination of the 12 (= 6 x 2) duodenary signs (which – like the 12 tubes – evoke a round arrangement) and the 10 (= 5 x 2) denary signs (which – like the notes of the scale – evoke a transverse arrangement).

This new system of correspondences leads again, by combining the symbols (5 and 6) of Earth and Heaven, to the grand total 360 (= 12 x 5 x 6). Does it not seem, once again, that musical theory owes its development to the numerical speculations of the masters of that supreme art which is the calendar?

* * *

The authors of the theory, in any case, were persons little concerned with the accuracy of numerical relationships in detail and who intended, above all, to emphasize an overall relationship obtained by means of meaningful totals.

The asterisk indicates cases where the number to appear in 2 consecutive relations increases or decreases by one unit.

It is true that Sseu-ma Ts'ien took care to express the lengths of the tubes by fractional numbers more or less in accordance with the theory.[110] This concern for accuracy allowed Chavannes to suppose that the Chinese had at first applied, without negligence, the principle of the construction of the Greek scale. It should be noted: 1° that before writing them down in his History, Sseu-ma Ts'ien, as a member of the Calendar Commission, and *on the occasion of an important reform of the latter*, had to carefully redo all the calculations; 2° that, about the same time, Houai-nan tseu[111] indicated the dimensions of the tubes using only whole numbers. It was these numbers, always reproduced, that really interested the Chinese; to understand their thought, it is from these numbers that we must start.

As it is easy to see, with the 12 numbers (81, 54, 72, 48, 64, 42, 57, 76, 51, 68, 45, 60) of the list transmitted by Houai-nan tseu, it is only possible to establish rela-

---

110 *SMT*, III, p. 314.

111 *Houai-nan tseu*, 3. Houai-nan tseu, like Lu Pou-wei, indicates that the 6th and 7th tubes are produced by higher generation; he gives, however, the distribution by months implying that the 6th is a female tube.

Book II - Chapter III - Numbers

tions conforming to the rule by admitting for these numbers the set of one unit, except in three cases,[112] for 54 which is worth 2/3 of 81 and 3/4 of 72, for 72 which is worth 4/3 of 54 and 3/2 of 48, for 48 which is worth 2/3 of 72 and 3/4 of 64. We must admit that the 5th tube is worth 64, since it is 4/3 of 48, and that it is also worth 63, since it must be 3/2 of 42. Likewise, the 7th tube is both 56 and 57, the 8th 76 and 75, the 9th 50 and 51, the 10th 68 and 69, the 11th 46 and 45. The 12th must therefore be 3/4 of the first (if produced by higher generation).[113] 60, a multiple of 3, can easily be increased by 1/3. For the rule to be respected, the 1st tube must therefore be 80 (= 60 x 4/3), at the same time as 81 (=54 x 3/2); here again the play of a unit is necessary.

In detail, the dimensions attributed to the tubes are, as can be seen, inaccurate.

It is remarkable that for the dimensions of the last tubes 57, 76, 51, 68, 45, 60 have been chosen. If the dimensions 75, 69, 60 had been taken for the *yin* tubes, the total of the three numbers (204) would not have changed. But if, for the *yang* tubes, instead of 57, 51, 45, 56, 50, 46 had been taken, the total of the three numbers would have been 152 instead of 153. The chosen numbers express inaccurately the ratio 3/2, which should exist between the 8th tube (75) and the 9th (51), between the 10th tube (69) and the 11th (45), but express, instead, exactly all the ratios equal to 3/4 (= 57/76 = 51/68 = 45/60); and 3/4 *is also the ratio of the total value of the three yang* tubes (153) to the three yin tubes (204) {153/204 = (3x51)/(4x51)}. The sum of the last 6 tubes is 357; synthesis of the Yin (**4**) and Yang (**3**) {whose ratios the second half of the series of tubes must indicate in the form of 3/4, since the first (57) of its six tubes is worth the 3/4 of the second (76)}, 357 is a multiple of 7; it is, among the multiples of 7, the closest to the grand Total 360 and 354, the total of the days of the lunisolar year.[114] The total of the days of the lunisolar year is 357.

The series of the first 6 tubes begins, on the contrary, with a tube worth 3/2 of the next; it would be convenient if the sum of these 6 numerical symbols were a multiple of 5, synthesis of Yang (**3**) and Yin (**2**); one would expect this multiple of 5 to be 360 and the ratio 3/2 written globally in the form 216/144. If the total of the first *yin* tubes is 144 (= 54 + 48 + 42), that of the *yang* tubes (81 + 72 + 64) is 217, so that the total sum is not 360, but 361. There was no difficulty in obtaining the number 216; for the 1st and 3rd *yang* tubes, one could choose between 80 and 81, 64 and 63; added to 72 (2nd *yang* tube), 80 + 64 (= 144) as well as 81 + 63 (= 144) give 216. But we took 81 and 64. Instead of 80 (= 60 x 4/3), *which would have made the cyclic character of the series of tubes more evident, we chose* 81. Thus, the first ratio (81/54) is strictly equal to 3/2. The adoption of 63 thus seemed necessary for

---

112 One could, at one time, say 4 cases, since 42 is 2/3 of 63 and 3/4 of 56. But 42, taken from 63 and not from 64, is affected by its inexact origin.

113 Chavannes (*SMT*, III, p. 633, n. 1) supposes the existence of a 13th tube whose "length was exactly half of the first". If the first is supposed to give the note *fa*, the twelfth gives the *la sharp*, the thirteenth the *mi sharp* which the Chinese, according to Chavannes, considered equivalent to *fa*.

114 357 appears among the characteristic dimensions of the Universe, which the Chinese claimed to have obtained with the help of the gnomon. It appears next to 360.

the 5th tube, since 63 is exactly 3/2 of the numerical emblem of the 6th (42). However, we have condemned ourselves to make the grand total of 360 and the typical ratio of 216/144 less apparent, since, after having attributed 81 to the 1st tube, we have attributed 64 to the 5th. Just as 81 is exactly 3/2 of 54, 64 is exactly 4/3 of 48 (4th tube). If 81 and 64 were adopted, it is because, thanks to this adoption, the 5 numerical symbols assigned to the first tubes (81, 54, 72, 48, 64) were – *on condition of considering them in isolation and without thinking of their relation to the 6th or 12th* – absolutely in conformity with the principle of the theory.

An examination of the numerical symbols which the Chinese, *thanks to the almost constant use of a unit,* have considered sufficient to express the principle of their musical theory, leads to a threefold observation:

1st The exactness, in detail, of the arithmetical relations does not matter; to almost all the numerical symbols there corresponds a double value, one of which appears only in the list, the other being implied; just as 81 and 63 may be read as meaning again 80 and 64, 361 seems to be well felt as meaning 360. All this suggests that (through implicit mutations of other symbols, and, for example, as a result of a latent equivalence between 60 and 63), 357 may well also mean 360. Above all, it seems that the series of 12 numbers was not established by true arithmetical operations, but by manipulations of symbols inspired by a specific ambition.

2nd The totals 357 and 361 resulting from the sums of the first 6 or the last 6 numbers are, in any case, too close to 360 to have been obtained by chance. The juxtaposition of two sets of symbols, both suggesting the Grand Total, by evoking a division into 5 sections (ratio 3/2) and a division into 7 sections (ratio 3/4), seems to derive from concerns analogous to those that gave rise to the idea of juxtaposing a square with center of 5 and a square with center of 6, recalling two divisions of 360, one into 5 sections of 72, the other into 6 sections of 60. Such concerns attest that the theory of the 12 Tubes is due to the Calendar Masters.

3rd This theory appears as *an artificially superimposed construction on an earlier construction which must be that of the 5-note scale.* Whatever their desire to emphasize 360, the Calendar Masters preferred to keep the first 5 tubes, to which the 5 notes are usually assigned, as numerical symbols implying exact relationships. When they elaborated the theory of the 12 Tubes, thinking of making them the symbols of the 12 months, it was for them to complete a theory of the scale. The five notes of the scale represented the four seasons and the center of the year, and were arranged in the form of a cross. By adapting the image of the crossroads, reminiscent of a *square*, to the image of a dodecagon on whose perimeter the symbols of the tubes and the months were arranged in a circle in a *regular* order, the Calendar Masters attempted to give a more detailed and coherent representation of the universe.

* * *

The Chinese scale consists of 5 notes, called *kong, tche, chang, yu* and *kio*.

According to tradition, King Wen, founder of the Tcheou, invented two new notes. Only the first five notes are considered *pure* and have a name. The names of the 6th and 7th notes, *pien kong* and *pien tche*, show that there was not much difference between them and the 1st and 2nd notes. Moreover, in practice, only the five pure notes count. To define them, we merely say that they correspond to the sounds emitted by the first three pipes. Thus, by giving the dimensions of the 6th and 7th tubes, the 6th and 7th notes were defined. The musical theory of the Chinese has its starting point in the construction of the *first* **5** *tubes*.

Once the dimensions of these tubes and the relationship of the notes to each other are indicated, there is, technically speaking, nothing more to say about the scale. However, if we want to understand the ideas of the Chinese and not rush to speak of possible borrowings from the Greeks, we must bear in mind two facts:

1st At *the same time* that they assign to each of the 5 notes a numerical symbol showing that it is emitted by one of the first 5 tubes, the Chinese assign to it another symbol, which is also a number, and a whole number: *kong*, which has as small and large symbols 5 and 81 (dimension of the 1st tube); *tche*, 7 and 54 (dimension of the 2nd tube); *chang*, 9 and 72 (dimension of the 3rd tube); *yu*, 6 and 48; *kio*, 8 and 64;

2nd 5, 7, 9, 6 and 8 are the symbols of the Center and of the 4 Seasons-Directions (as well as of the 5 Elements). The 5 notes, – as well as the Seasons to which these numerical symbols relate them – apparently form a *cycle*, in the manner of the 12 Tubes which relate to the 12 Months. These data are often neglected, under the pretext that Chinese correspondences (especially when they include numbers) are late and *arbitrary* games, and because no relationship is apparent between the dimensions of the Tubes and the numbers commonly used as symbols for the Notes, the Seasons and the Elements.

Directions	Center	South	West	North	East
Seasons	Central	Summer	Autumn	Winter	Spring
Notes	Kong	Tche	Chang	Yu	Kio
Symbols of tubes and notes	81	54	72	48	64
Seasons-Directions symbols and notes	5	7	9	6	8
Order numbers of the elements	5	2	4	1	3
Pairs of congruent numbers	5 - 10	2 - 7	4 - 9	1 - 6	3 - 8
Elements	Earth	Fire	Metal	Water	Wood

Perhaps a less careless observation would reveal a relationship between the large and small symbols (both expressed by integers), which, for the Chinese, define a note. Let us arrange them, preserving the equivalences, by placing the large symbols in order of size. Apart from 5 (can't 5 represent 10, *the second member of the same congruent pair*?), the small symbols are also arranged in the same order.

81	72	64	54	48
5	9	8	7	6

But by assigning a small symbol to the different notes, was it only intended to indicate the order of magnitude of the tubes that correspond to them? Let us order the two series of symbols taking into account the order of production of the tubes:

81	54	72	48	64
5	7	9	6	8

The last three small symbols are 9, 6 and 8. These numbers, *in the order in which they follow each other*, are sufficient to express the arithmetic rule governing the construction of the scale, such as that of the 12 Tubes (a decrease of 1/3 followed by an increase of 1/3).

9, 6, 8, multiplied by 9 give the dimensions of the 1st, 2nd and 3rd tubes; multiplied by 8, those of the 3rd, 4th and 5th tubes; multiplied by 7, those of the 5th, 6th and 7th tubes. 72 (3rd tube), being a multiple of 9 and 8, assures a perfect union, and the first 5 tubes seem to correspond to rigorously exact dimensions: there are 5 *pure* notes. 64, a multiple of 8, is not a multiple of 9. It must be assimilated to 63 (product of 9 by 7) in order to pass to the series of multiples of 7. From 56-57, the numbers are obtained by multiplying 9, 6, 8, not, as at the beginning, by the whole numbers 9, 8, 7, but by the same numbers increased by 0.5 (9.5, 8.5, 7.5). The 7th tube, produced *by higher generation* (56), produces in turn (57 = 6 x 9.5) by

1st tube {	80	8 x 10		
	81	9 x 9	} Products of 9 by {	9
2nd tube	54	6 x 9		6
3rd tube {	72	8 x 9		8
	72	9 x 8	} Products of 8 by {	9
4st tube	48	6 x 8		6
5st tube {	64	8 x 8		8
	63	9 x 7	} Products of 7 by {	9
6st tube	42	6 x 7		6
7st tube {	56	8 x 7		8
	57	6 x 9,5	} Products of 9.5 by {	6
8st tube {	76	8 x 9,5		8
	76,5	9 x 8,5	} Products of 8.5 by {	9
9st tube	51	6 x 8,5		6
10st tube {	68	8, 8,5		8
	67,5	9 x 7,5	} Products of 7.5 by {	9
11st tube	45	6 x 7,5		6
12st tube {	60	8 x 7,5		8
	60	6 x 10	} Products of 10 by {	6
1st tube	80	8 x 10		8

Book II - Chapter III - Numbers

higher generation the 8th tube (76 = 8 x 9.5). Everything happens as if two 5-note scales (81, 54, 72, 48, 64, and 76, 51, 68, 45, 60) were juxtaposed. The union of the 2nd scale to the 1st, resulting from the assimilation to 81 (1st tube) of 80 {which can, provided there is again a *upper generation*, produce 60 (12th tube) which is derived from 45 by upper generation}, the transition from the 1st scale to the 2nd is ensured *by the addition of the 6th and 7th tubes, corresponding to the 2 additional notes*.

These observations reveal the role of the numbers 9, 6, 8, symbols, as we have seen, of the 3rd, 4th and 5th notes. They show, on the one hand, that the theory of the 12 pipes is linked to the invention, attributed to King Wen of the Tcheou, of the 2 additional notes, one of which (the 6th pipe) has as its emblem the 42nd, and, on the other hand, that one could only imagine a juxtaposition of the 2 scales if the 1st pipe *could be represented* by the 80th as well as by the 81st.

This is the moment to use the observation that, assimilated to the Seasons, the 5 Notes of the scale form a cycle.

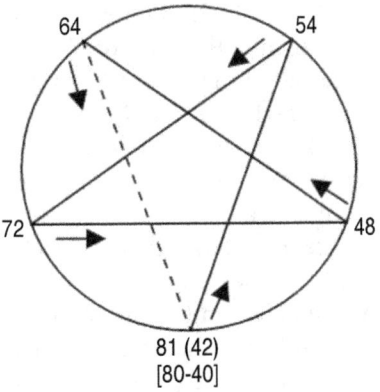

As in the case of the 12 Tubes, a figure can represent this cycle, highlighting the order of production of the notes. Let us arrange their symbols (81, 72, 64, 54, 48) at regular intervals around the perimeter of a circle, starting with 81 (on the left), following the *order of magnitude*. If now, to represent the *order of production*, we join by straight lines 81 to 54, 54 to 72, 72 to 48 and 48 to 64, we will form a 5-pointed star (see the next figure), but the drawing will only be perfect if we join 64 to 81; that is, if, from the 5th tube, we go back to the 1st. Reduced by 1/3, 64, as soon as it assimilates to 63, produces 42. If 42 were half of 81, the notes emitted by the two Tubes – being an octave apart – could assimilate, which would give the right to close the figure. *As the 5 notes form a cycle and the figure must be closed*, it must be admitted (either that, double 42, the numerical symbol of the 1st tube is assigned the value 84,[115] or) that, *representing 80, this 1st tube*, it is considered that from 64-63 one passes, by inferior generation, to a *value of which 40 could be the symbol*.[116]

Although it is difficult to imagine, with the numerical symbols, 81, 72, 64, 54, 48 (chosen to illustrate the rule that can summarize the sequence 9, 6, 8), the construction of the 5-pointed star, necessary for the representation of a cycle, that becomes quite simple if the numbers to arrange on the perimeter of the circle are the same that serve as symbols for the notes (see the next figure), *on the sole condi-*

---

115 Let us observe that, in the system of the 12 tubes, the first one should be evoked by 84 if the emblem of the last one were felt to be equivalent to 63 to complete to 360 the total (357) of the numerical values attributed to the last 6 tubes.

116 Chavannes, to explain the theory of the 12 tubes, supposes a thirteenth which would be exactly half of the first (*SMT*, III, p. 463).

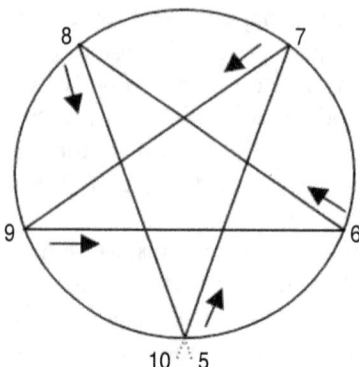

tion of supposing that the 5 represents the congruent pair 10-5.

This leads us to formulate a hypothesis: *the numerical symbols of the notes*, far from being arbitrary, *began to signify real dimensions*. The observation that between 10 and 5, half of 10, there are five intervals, explains the constitution of a *five-note scale*, whose relations are symbolized by the numbers 7, 9, 6, 8 and the pair 10-5 *which gave the idea of the octave*.

For the Chinese, who paid more attention – as we have seen – to the accuracy of global relations than to that of detailed relations, the series 10, 9, 8, 7, 6, 5 had great merit.

It allowed to establish – because 10 + 9 + 8 = 9 x 3 and 7 + 6 + 5 = 9 x 2 – between the set of notes *yang* {10 (1st note), 9 (3rd note), 8 (5th note)} and the set of notes *yin* {7 (2nd note), 6 (4th note), 5 (1st note of the octave)} a ratio equal to 3/2 (which is the ratio of Heaven and Earth), and this ratio was found, typically expressed in the ratio (9/6) of the 2nd note *yang* to the 2nd note *yin*.

The series 10, 9, 8, 7, 6, 5 has another, perhaps greater, merit in Chinese eyes.

It is worth a total of 45, which multiplied by 8 gives 360. Since 5 is half of 10, it was certainly possible to present the image of a cycle by placing the numbers 9, 8, 7, 6 and 10 around the perimeter of a pentagon, evoking 10-5. It was even better to replace these numbers by 72 (= 9 x 8), 64 (= 8 x 8), 56 (= 7 x 8), 11 (= 6 x 8) and 80 (= 10 x 8) mentally associated to 40 (= 5 x 8) which is the half. Thus is evoked the great emblem of the cycle, the 360, and, *with the help of* **5** *numbers, which presuppose a* **6**th, the characteristic division of the 360 into 5 parts, as well as the prestigious ratio of 216 (= 80 + 72 + 64: symbols of the 3 *yang* tubes) to 144 {= 56 + 48 + 40, symbols of the 2 *yin* tubes and of the tube (40 = 80/2) which, unlike an octave, allows to return to the 1st **yang** note}.

The series 80, 56, 72, 48, 64 differs only in its symbolic merits from the series 10, 7, 9, 8, 6 (and 5). It differs from the classical series 81, 54, 72, 48, 64 only in the number 56. It is the prototype of the latter, but derives from the formula 10, 7, 9, 8, 6 (5), the memory of which is preserved in the numerical symbols of the notes.

If we postulate that the numbers of the series 10, 7, 9, 6, 8 (of which the series 80, 56, 72, 48, 64 is only another expression) were suitable to serve as an emblem for the real dimensions of the tubes, our hypothesis does not imply that this numerical translation, which seems incorrect, corresponded to an equally incorrect practice.

Let us suppose, in accordance with Chinese traditions, that the first sound tubes were bamboo tubes. Their dimensions could be represented by a small integer number obtained by counting the articulations (= *tsie*, which also means "measure") of each of the 5 bamboos giving the 5 notes of the primitive scale. It is easy to see that, in order to obtain correct intervals, attributing to the pipes dimensions implying inexact relationships, it was enough for the craftsman to choose, for the

Book II - Chapter III - Numbers 143

1st and 2nd pipes, bamboos whose nodes were, for the 1st, a little further apart, and a little less distant for the 2nd.

Thus a correct practice was legitimized, at first, by means of an inexact theory, but which had, at least, one merit: *it translated the meaning of the octave.*

The flaws in the theory were unimportant – and might not be apparent – as long as, counting by articulations, craftsmen were allowed some leeway in assessing the actual dimensions. But, in order to give the theory greater symbolic perfection, and with the intention of combining *the idea of octave with that of cycle evoking 360*,[117] the Chinese were led to substitute the series 10, 7, 9, 6, 8 (5) for the series 80, 56, 72, 48, 64 (40). This is equivalent to lending 8 divisions[118] to all (practically unequal) intervals between two nodes.

By counting by subdivisions, instead of by joints, the Chinese exposed themselves to substituting a system of *abstract units* for one of *concrete units*.

As soon as they measured their pipes by a system of equal subdivisions, the inaccuracy of the theory had to appear in practice. This is undoubtedly the beginning of the refinement that led to the adoption of the numbers 81 and 54 for the numerical symbols of the first tubes instead of 80 and 56, the numbers 72, 48 and 64 (which conform to the sequence 9, 6, 8) remaining unchanged.

The date of this refinement is yet to be determined, which, by the way, will provide an opportunity to test this hypothesis.

This hypothesis accounts for all the data but, by postulating that the series 81, 54, 72, 48, 64 is later than the two (equivalent) series 10, 7, 9, 6, 8 and 80, 56, 72, 48, 64, it assumes a historical order between the facts.

Any such hypothesis can easily be reversed. Ours does not depart from the facts; it leads to the conclusion, satisfactory enough in itself, that the theory of pipes and scale expounded by the Chinese is an integral part of their musical practice and is strictly related to the system of notions expressing their views of the Universe. But one could not say: the Chinese knew for the first time – by borrowing – formulated in abstract terms or translated (it is possible) by the sequence 9, 6, 8, the arithmetical rule of the scale – invented by the Greeks – they expressed it by the sequence 81, 54, 72, 48, 64, which had (no doubt) the merit, great for them, of evoking approximately 360 and the proportion 216/144; then they noticed the proximity of this sequence with the series 80, 56, 72, 48, 64, entirely formed by multiples of 8; indifferent to the rigor of mathematical facts, they derived from the latter the formula 10, 7, 9, 6, 8, and this allowed them to attribute to the notes numerical symbols, which (it is recognized) are not entirely arbitrary.

If the facts were interpreted in this way, the order that would be established for their history would not be far-fetched. That is true. And it is also true that, in doing so, we would reserve for ourselves the advantage of postulating an origin by way of borrowing; this is the kind of historical fact that a good philologist likes to

---

117 We consider 5 pipes and give names to 5 notes, but the octave (in this case) comprises 6 notes: a wonderful combination of 5 (Earth, square) and 6 (Heaven, round).

118 This is what *Houai-nan tseu* (ch. 3) *seems* to say: *"The notes generate each other with the help of 8; thus man is 8 feet tall."*

establish; by deciding that there is borrowing, one passes on to other specialists the concern of finding the true explanation of the facts. Questions of origin are of no interest to us here. It would be enough for us to agree that the scale theory developed in China under the influence of a worldview, if there were not an important question of fact. Admitting the historical order implied by the hypothesis defended here makes it possible to understand the very essence of the Chinese attitude towards Numbers. It is a question of noting the difficulty the Chinese had in conceiving the idea of *unity* in its arithmetical aspect and of indicating the reasons for this.

We must therefore establish the primacy of the series 10, 7, 9, 6, 8, and we shall do so precisely by showing that the development of musical theory is due to the *competition of various systems of calculation which imposed variable divisions on unity* and which, by retarding the progress of the abstract notion of unity, were opposed to a *quantitative conception of numbers*.

In this connection, we must first show that our view of the passage from the series 10, 7, 9, 6, 8 to the series 80, 56, 72, 48, 64 is not a mere theoretical opinion. Now, it is a fact that the relationship existing between the symbols common to the Notes, the Seasons, the Elements and the dimensions of the 5 Tubes was still felt at the time of Sseu-ma Ts'ien.

The proof is in a sentence inserted by the historian at the conclusion of his chapter on the sound tubes. This sentence is composed of the characters designating the 5 Notes, each associated with a number; the numbers are those which the *Yue ling* gives as symbols for the Notes, but the *Yue ling*'s equivalences are not respected.[119] Thus the commentators, without deciding to correct a venerable text, declare these numbers *inexplicable*. This statement was enough for Chavannes to decide not to look for a meaning to his author's phrase. It is true that he had not understood the two words with which it opens. He translated them (literally) as "Upper Ninth," which has no intelligible meaning. These two words "Upper Nine" designate, as we have seen, a scale; it is the one whose initial note is produced by the last (*Upper*) Yang Tube (*Nine*).

The dimensions of the tubes corresponding to this scale are 45 (11th tube), 60 (12th tube), 81 (1st tube), 54 (2nd tube), 72 (3rd tube). All of them (except 60, but 60, the value of the last tube, must be considered as equivalent to 63, if the total of the last six numerical symbols of the series of tubes is to be equal to 360) are multiples of 9. Dividing them by 9, we would obtain: for 72 (3rd tube), 8 (5th note); for 54 (2nd tube), **6** (4th note); for 81 (1st tube), 9 (3rd note); for 63 (replacing 60, 12th tube), 7 (2nd note); and for 45 (11th tube), **5** (1st note), i.e., *precisely* the symbolic values attributed to the notes by the *Yue ling*.

Sseu-ma Ts'ien wrote this sentence after having collaborated in a reform of the Calendar. This reform led to the attribution of new numerical symbols to the 12 Tubes. The principle was the adoption of a 9-inch gnomon linked to a *division of the inch into 9 sections*, which resulted in the first sound tube, *equal in length to the*

---

119 *SMT*, III, p. 316: The upper ninth is this: "*chang*, 8; *yu*, 7; *kio*, 6; *kong*, 5; *tche*, 9." It is necessary, as we shall see, to correct it as follows: "*kong*, 5; *tche*, 7; *chang*, 9; *yu*, 6; *kio*, 8."

Book II - Chapter III - Numbers 145

gnomon, having a length measured in 81 inch divisions. There is no doubt, in view of this fact, that we are justified in restoring the order of correspondences which has been disturbed by an *unexplainable* error due to a copyist. There is no possibility of misinterpreting Sseu-ma Ts'ien's sentence by translating it thus: "(it is in the scale beginning) *with the* (11th tube, 45) *Upper Nine* (that the initial note) *kong* (has the value of) 5 (which is its symbol because 45/9=5); (that the 2nd note) *tche* (has the value of) 7 (because 60/9, or rather 63/9 = 7); (that the 3rd note) *chang* (has the value of) 9 (because 81/9=9); (that the 4th note) *yu* (has the value of) 6 (because 54/9=6; (that the 5th note) *kio* (has the value of) 8 (because 72/9=8)."

The importance of this passage of Sseu-ma Ts'ien, whose original meaning can be recovered with certainty, is very great. It shows, in the first place – as we have surmised – that the numerical symbols assigned to the notes were not considered arbitrary; they were thought to be related to the numbers fixing the length of the pipes corresponding to a given scale. It also leads to an essential observation: if the relationship between note symbols and pipe dimensions was perceived in Han times, its historian could only point it out by referring, *not to the first scale*, but to the eleventh. This demonstrates the antiquity of the theory of the 12 scales and confirms a fact. From the eleventh scale onwards, it is no longer possible to obtain the 10 for the emblem of the first note; one obtains the 5, and the *Yue ling* also attributes the emblem 5 to the first note. It must therefore be assumed that, already at the time (at the latest in the 3rd century BC) when the *Yue ling* was written, the theory of the 12 scales had been established. But the fact has more important consequences.

The substitution of 10 for 5 at the beginning of the series of 5 symbols did not imply a lack of understanding of its meaning. However, it concealed the main merit of this sequence, which is to give the feeling of the octave. Why, in spite of its advantages, was the formula 10, 7, 9, 6, 8, (5) abandoned? Apparently, it was not possible to relate it as such to any scale, whereas (thanks to the identification of 60 and 63) the eleventh scale offered a resource to bring out the meaning of the symbols of the notes by means of a formula that did not begin with 10 but with 5. It must be concluded that, from the moment when the 5 is presented as the symbol of the initial note, the series formed by the numerical symbols of the dimensions attributed to the first 5 pipes (1st scale) could no longer be reconciled with the traditional sequence indicating the value of the notes.

This is precisely what must happen as soon as the dimensions of the pipes are expressed in obedience to a decision that fixes the sections of the unit at 9.

Sseu-ma Ts'ien (no more, no doubt, than the theorists who inspired the *Yue ling* before him) was not bothered by the difficulty of obtaining 7 by dividing 60 by 9. He could very well, from the classical formula (81, 54, 72, 48, 64) of the tubes corresponding to the *first scale*, have obtained, *without major embarrassment*, the 7 of 54, *if he had divided this number by 8*, and he would have obtained, without major inaccuracy, *with the same divisor*, and still from the classical formula, the series 10 (=81/8), 7 (=54/8), 9 (=72/8), 6 (=48/8) and 8 (=64/8). This is, indeed, what should have happened if, as I said, it was from the *arithmetic* (*original*) formula giving the (*real*) dimensions of the tubes (81, 54, 72, 48, 64) that the (*only symbolic and not original*) formula of the scale was derived (*playing with a divisor that could have been arbitrarily chosen*). But, as we can see, Sseu-ma Ts'ien did not proceed in this way. *Therefore, the divisor 9 was imposed on him.*

Therefore, we can conclude that the formula of the notes was not derived from the form of the pipes *by division*. On the contrary, it is the various formulas for the lengths of the tubes that were derived from the shape of the notes *by multiplication* (and at first without any compromise), the multiplier having been imposed by a system of conventions, 8 being the first multiplier imposed.

The artifice that consisted, in order to find the emblematic formula of the notes, in referring to the eleventh scale – which has only theoretical interest, but little value in practice – was made necessary by the adoption (prior to this artifice) of the index 9. The classical series (81, 54, 72, 48, 64) is not original. It confirms the order of the facts assumed by our hypothesis.

Let us therefore return to this hypothesis. From the primitive rule expressed by the sequence 10, 7, 9, 6, 8, (5), the formula 80, 56, 72, 48, 64 was constructed, preferred for its symbolic virtues and imagined in times or in circles that had adopted the index 8 for the division of the unit.

In other times or in other circles, this index was replaced by the index 9, which the Han put back in honor.[120]

By assigning 9 sections to each of the intervals between two bamboo nodes, it is still possible to represent the octave, but the dimensions of the tubes are then symbolized by the numbers 90, 63, 81, 54, 72, (45) whose total value is greater than 360. To correctly represent 360, 45, half of 90, must be eliminated. In the list thus reduced, 81, 72, 63 appear, whose total value is 216, which is also the total of 80+72+64; as 80, 72 and 64 from which they differ little, 81, 72 and 63 thus deserve to provide the dimensions of the 3 *yang* tubes (1st, 3rd and 5th tubes). There remain, for the *yin* tubes, 90 and 54, whose total is 144. But 90 is too strong for a *yin* tube (which must be 2/3 of a (*yang*) tube), since the strongest of them is 81; 54, on the other hand (it is 2/3 of 81), can measure the first *yin* tube. On the other hand, to represent the octave, it is necessary to be able to indicate 6 lengths of tubes. Therefore, it remains to divide 90 into two unequal parts. In the formula to be constructed, 72 is predisposed to serve as an emblem for the 2nd *yang* tube, since it already has this role in the previous formula, where the 2nd *yin* tube (48) is worth precisely 2/3 of 72. Therefore, we will take 48 as the emblem of the 2nd *yin* tube in the formula we are constructing, and the emblem 42 (= 90-48) will remain for the 3rd *yin* tube, which should yield, in the interval of an octave, the *kong* note emitted by the 1st tube (81).

Now, 42, on the one hand, differs too significantly from 81/2 for a tube of this size not to yield a new note (the sixth) and, on the other hand, 42 is worth 2/3 of

---

120 I write "at other times or in other places" because, in fact, as we shall see, the divisors 9 and 8 were used simultaneously, but for *different units*.

63, as 54 is worth 2/3 of 81 and 48 is worth 2/3 of 72. Hence the idea of making it the symbol of an *independent tube, the sixth*.

At the same time, considering 81, 54 and 72 as the symbols of the 1st, 2nd and 3rd tubes, and 72, 48, 63 as those of the 3rd, 4th and 5th tubes, it was easy to realize that the sequence 9, 6, 8 could be found in both series, *provided one wrote 64 as at the time when the subscript 8 was mandatory*. However, if 63 was written, as index 9 now required, the numerical emblem of the 5th tube appeared as a multiple of 7, as well as 42, which was worth 9/6. Therefore, it was sufficient to multiply 7 by 8 to obtain a number (56) that would become the emblem of a seventh tube.

The substitution of index 8 by index 9 led to:

1° To highlight the sequence 9, 6, 8. This observation made possible the formula of the arithmetical rule that bases the Chinese scale on a progression by fifths and, consequently, made it possible to constitute the theory of the 12 Tubes.

2° To invent – because the sixth tube no longer gives a note that was an octave higher than the initial note – two new notes emitted by tubes of such dimensions as to ensure the union between the 5 primordial tubes and 5 other tubes (75, 51, 68, 45, 60) providing another scale of 5 notes directly connected to the first since the 12th tube (60) is (approximately) 2/3 of the 1st (81). The first of the two invented notes was given the name *pien kong*, still witnessing the feeling of the octave, and the second was given the name *pien tche*, emitted by a pipe whose numerical symbol was 56, *former symbol of the (2nd) pipe*, which emits the note *tche*, at a time when the numerical symbols of the primordial pipes were provided by the formula (80, 56...) constituted by means of multiples of 8.

Now we can summarize the hypothesis. The formula 10, 7, 9, 6, 8, (5) constitutes the first numerical expression of the Chinese scale. This formula, whose arithmetically inexact terms did not hinder practice, is the origin of a correct theory.

The theory became correct as a result of a two-stage progress. The lengths of the tubes, which were estimated concretely *counting the nodes*, were determined by numerical symbols derived from the first formula. These symbols varied as did the *conventional system* of divisions adopted for the unit.

Being thus distinguished from the symbols assigned to the notes, the numerical symbols assigned to the pipes began, however, as simple products of the former. By using the index 8 as a multiplier, the Chinese gave the tubes the lengths indicated by the numbers 80, 56, 72, 48, 64, (40). These numbers had the merit of recalling, with the total of 360, the image of a cycle by linking it to the beginning of the *octave*. Thus, the divisions of the tubes were no longer fixed by a given number indicating concrete divisions, like the bamboo joints, but by a given number of abstract subdivisions. This had a double consequence: technical and practical. In the manufacture of instruments, it was practically difficult not to consider equal the subdivisions whose count indicated the length of the sound tubes; therefore, as instruments made with the numbers chosen for each tube could not give correct notes, musical practice made the Chinese realize the inaccuracy of the original formula. They happily corrected it when they adopted a division for the unit, no longer into 8 but into 9 sections. Once the correction was made, they could begin to perfect the practice by inventing two new notes; and above all, they thought of developing the theory by constructing a series of 12 Tubes that would allow them, once again, to concretely represent their conception of the Universe.

This hypothesis explains all the facts and seems to be in conformity with their historical order.

It is also consistent with Chinese traditions. Under the Yin dynasty, the units were divided into eight sections. The Tcheou adopted the division by 9.[121] It is also said, and this is remarkable, that the invention of the two additional notes is due to King Wen, founder of the Tcheou.

* * *

Chinese traditions are precious; they point out factual connections which, *most of the time*, are not arbitrary. In this case, all the data suggest that the invention of the two additional notes results from the substitution of index 8 for index 9. However, knowing the historical order of events does not allow us to relate these events to precise dates. Chinese traditions faithfully record the connections, but transmit them in the form of myths or legends. It is not to attribute to King Wen (or his contemporaries) a role in the development of music theory that we recall another tradition; the Chinese claim, as we have seen, that a descendant of the last Yin recited to the son of the founder of the Tcheou the true text of the *Hong fan*. If we mention this detail, it is because we must return to the *Hong fan* and its first section. We cannot forget an important fact: the five notes of the scale are related to the five elements.

Recall that the first section of the *Hong fan* lists the elements in a certain order. It assigns each of them a number which is not, as I have shown, a simple order number. The numbers indicated by the *Hong fan* point to the order of the assignments that allow us to identify, by tracing a **temple**, each Element to a place in Space-Time. These numbers are the first terms of a congruent pair whose second term serves, in the *Yue ling*, as emblem of the Seasons-Directions. Water (element 1) is the first named in the *Hong Fan* and is assigned by it to the lower part, which is the north (site 1). As attested by all Chinese mythology, it corresponds to the north (lower) and to winter, to which the *Yue ling* attributes the number 6 (= 1 + 5) as a classifier; it is the same for Fire {Element 2, South-Summer site, classifier 7 (= 2 + 5)} for Wood {Element 3, East-Spring site, classifier 8 (= 3 + 5)}, for Metal {Element 4, West-Autumn site, classifier 9 (= 4 + 5)} and for Earth (Element 5, Center site, classifier 5), because for Center (Earth) the *Yue ling* indicates for classifier 5, not 10, just as for the first note it indicates the value 5 and not 10.

On the other hand, it assigns the note *yu* (6) to the North-Winter (6, Water, Element 1); the note *tche* (7) to the South-Summer (7, Fire, Element 2); the note *kio* (8) to the East-Spring (8, Wood, Element 3); the note *chang* (9) to the West-Au-

---

121 But *no historical conclusion can be drawn from this fact*. The Yin measured with a *sin* of 8 feet, but divided the foot into 9 inches, while the Tcheou, if they measured on mats 9 feet long, divided the foot into 8 inches. The numerical indexes adopted by the dynasties serve to divide units of measurement that are not equal, so that the numbers may differ without the sizes differing (cf. *infra*, in this same chapter, sec. IV).

Book II - Chapter III - Numbers

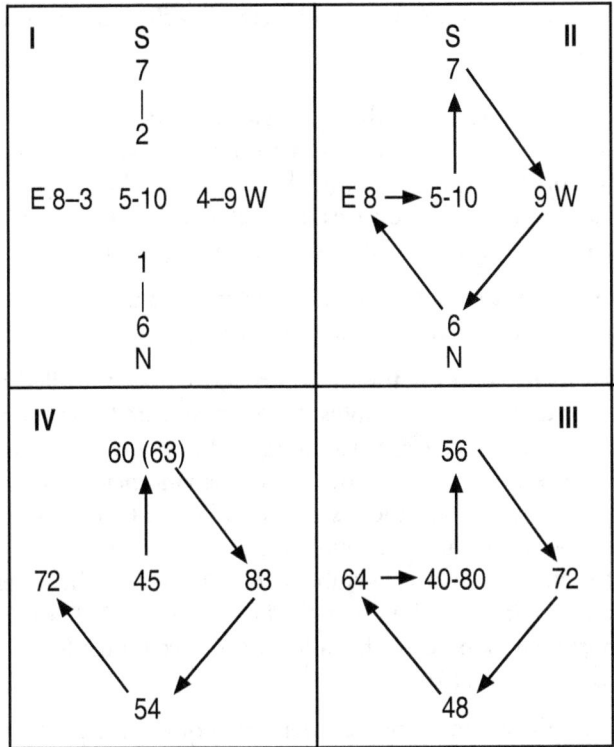

I: Transversal arrangement of the elements (*Ho t'ou*).
II: Oriented arrangement of the note symbols.
III: Dimensions of the tubes (oriented like the corresponding notes) of the 1st scale (dimensions derived by multiplying by 8 the numerical symbols of the notes).
IV: Dimensions of the tubes (oriented in the same way) of the II scale connected by Sseu-ma Ts'ien, through a division by 9, with the numerical symbols of the notes.

tumn (9, Metal, Element, 4). So much the worse for the scholars – so fond of what they call philological methods that they see in them the privileged instrument of archaeological research, and who want, with their aid alone, to discover (by dating texts) not only the order of events, but also the date of the events – so much the worse for them if (after having maintained that the Chinese received their scale in its perfect and mathematical form from the Greeks,[122] or that any interpretation of the *Hong fan* which insists on the importance of numbers in the earliest forms of the theory of the Elements is anachronistic,[123] or that the Elements were first

---

122 *SMT*, III, p. 644.
123 Maspero, *La Chine antique*, p. 440, note 2. Maspero writes: "For the explanation by correspondence with the cardinal points, cf. Granet, *Religion des Chinois*, but the introduction into the discussion of the numerical passages of the *Hi ts'eu* seems to me an anachronism." I have not instituted a discussion (in this passage of the Religion of the Chinese), nor have I used on this occasion the data of the *Hi ts'eu*. In this case it is not necessary.

conceived as triumphant and not as producers of each other,[124]) they are offered the following problem:

Given that:
a. The order of the Elements, when they succeed one another, is not absolutely arbitrary {there is some consistency in the metaphors of the Chinese who say: Water produces the Wood (giving it its sap); Wood produces the Fire (which nourishes); Fire produces the Metal (which liberates from the mineral); Metal produces the Water (since it can liquefy)};

b. The order of the Elements is not at all arbitrary once assimilated to the seasons (they follow one another in a fixed order);

c. The order of the notes is totally controlled {it is controlled by the length of the tubes that emit these notes. If we admit that these tubes have as numerical symbols 10, 7, 9, 6, 8, (5), it follows imperatively that the note *tche*, emitted by the 2nd tube, must occupy the second place, after the note *kong*, emitted by the 1st tube, since (speaking like the Chinese) the 2nd tube is produced by the 1st, and we could equally say, as long as there is no difference between the numerical symbols of the tubes and the notes, that the 1st note produces the 2nd; the same can be said of the 3rd, 4th and 5th notes, and it must be remembered that after the 5th we return to the 1st note (10), which is also the 6th (5)}.

How to explain the assimilation between them of the Elements, the Notes, the Seasons, and their common assimilation to the numerical symbols indicated by the congruent pairs 1-6, 2-7, 3-8, 4-9, 5-10?

How can this be explained if it has been postulated beforehand: that the *numbering* of the Elements in the *Hong fan* is of no interest? That the Chinese equivalences are mere arbitrary games? And that the numerical symbols for the notes are also arbitrary (the latter assumption is required by the hypothesis that the Chinese first received their scale in the arithmetically perfect form of the Greek scale).

Since one of the 5 notes (if we want to orient them) must go to the Center since there are 5 Elements and 5 Space-Time Sites, the first note, 10 (5), could be placed there without difficulty, and it is clear that we could choose for the second an arbitrary place at the intersection. *But once this 2nd note is assigned to the South and Summer, which produces Autumn, the 3rd note, emitted by a tube considered as produced by the 2nd tube, could only be assigned to Autumn and West.* For the same reasons, the 4th and 5th notes could not fail to be assigned, in order, one to the North-Winter, the other to the East-Spring.

The assimilation of the Notes, the Seasons-Directions and the Elements can only be explained by admitting the primacy of the sequence of notes 10, 7, 9, 6, 8, (5). It is from this formula that the Stations received the numerical symbols intended to serve as classifiers of the sites of Space-Time, and it is still from this formula that we derive – together with the theory of the production of Elements

---

124 *SMT, Introduction*, p. CXCI ff.

Book II - Chapter III - Numbers

among themselves – the order of the Elements which commands the arrangement of the **temple**, their arrangement at the intersection and the numbering which the *Hong fan* ascribes to them.[125]

If we can find no other satisfactory answer to the problem posed, we shall have to agree that the sequence 10 7, 9, 6, 8, (5) – which is at the origin of Chinese musical theory – is also at the origin of their "theory" of the Elements, as supposed by the *Hong fan*, and, consequently, that it is prior to the *Hong fan*. There will always remain, it is true, the liberty of supposing that the *Hong fan* is a work of a late period or that the text of its first Section is interpolated or falsified.

But what will be done with the *Yue ling*, rich in so much archaic, perfectly coherent data? Besides, it doesn't matter. We do not care to date any progress in music theory to King Wen, inventor of the two additional notes, or King Wou, his son, auditor of the *Hong fan*. We do not even want to assert that the sequence 10, 7, 9, 6, 8, (5) was authorized before the 5th-4th centuries BC, the time most probably assigned to the writing of the *Hong fan*. We are not interested in dates pushed into a chronology devoid of concrete facts. The fact that the formula 81, 54, 72, 48, 64, is not primitive, but derived from the sequence 10, 7, 9, 6, 8, (5) – the authority of which is attested by a passage in the *Hong fan* – perhaps makes it difficult to suppose that the Chinese received the Greek theory of the omnipresent scale by an indirect effect of Alexander's expeditions. But nothing excludes the possibility of older relations between China and Western countries, where Numbers and the Elements were also speculated upon. This debate is of little importance. What is important for the history of ideas is the historical order of the facts, and the connections that alone can help us to understand them.

The connection established between the order of the Elements and the sequence of the Notes, which boil down to the same numerical formula, is of primary interest to us. It brings an additional probability to our hypothesis. Since the numerical symbols of the Elements testify to the order in which they occur (*cheng*) one after the other, we have a new reason to think that the numbers preserved as symbols to the notes, indicated first the dimensions of the tubes in the order in which they occurred (*cheng*). These numbers became symbols of the notes only as a result of a development of musical theory and technique that the hypothesis is sufficient to explain.

However, here is the main interest of the comparison. It shows that the theory of the Elements, or at least the numerical expression it received, was mandated by the original scale theory. This observation may be valuable. The theory of the Elements, as a result of the assimilation of the Elements to the Seasons-Directions, was one with the supreme Knowledge which consists in ordering the Times and Spaces. The same must have been true of the theory of the balance, and at this point the mention of the *Hong fan* is, in itself, full of significance. The first Section of this treatise, which deals with the Elements, certainly refers to a division of the World into 4 Sectors (square of side 2, subdivided into 4 squares) obtained by the draw-

---

125 Cf. *infra*, in this same Book, ch. IV.

ing of a cross, while the 9 Sections of the *Hong fan* (the great Plan) are related by tradition to a division of the World into 9 Provinces (square of side 3, subdivided into 9 squares) and to an arrangement of the Numbers in a magic square; this division and this arrangement commanded, we are told, the plan of the *Ming t'ang*, the House of the Calendar, where the Chief ensured a just distribution of the places of Space-Time and distributed, at given times, among his followers, the domains of all the districts of the Empire. Perhaps we shall find new connections which will enable us to understand better the attitude of the Chinese towards the Numbers, if we think of confronting their ideas about musical relations and architectural proportions.

IV. Numbers and Architectural Proportions

The ratio between the 1st and the 5th tube, in the formula (80, 56, 72, 48, 64) composed of multiples of 8, is equal to **10/8**. It becomes **9/7** in the formula (81, 54, 72, 48, 63), which results from the adoption of the index 9 as a multiplier. Like musical rules, architectural canons are dominated by the opposition or equivalence of the quotients 9/7 (=81/63) and 10/8 (=80/64), and it is the geometry of builders that reveals the virtues that the Chinese attributed to the correlative pairs 80-64 and 81-63.

* * *

Two elements are fundamental in Chinese constructions. The building itself is less important than the base that supports it and the roof that covers it. Heaven "covers" and the roof represents Heaven; the Earth, which "holds," is represented by the base. A building appears as an image of the Universe, insofar as the proportions given to the profile of the roof and the plane of the terrace evoke, the first the round (odd, **3**, *yang*), the others the square (*fang*, the rectangular, even, **2**, *yin*). These principles govern, in particular, the construction of the *Ming t'ang*. According to tradition, the Calendar House formerly consisted of a square (rectangular) enclosure covered (joined to it by some columns) by a circular thatched roof.

We have only late information on the roof profile. The base of the roof of the *Ming t'ang* was to be measured by the number 144, and its contour by the number 216, the height being represented by 81. As indicated, these dimensions assume that the profile of the thatched roof is an isosceles triangle whose base (2 x 72) represents the Earth (144) and the other two sides (2 x 108 = 216) the curvature of Heaven (3 x 72). This construction is based on a square whose long side is 9 x 9, whose short side is 8 x 9 and whose hypotenuse is 12 x 9. This square (8, 9, 12) is estimated correct, *thanks to the game of one unit*, by virtue of the formula $9^2 + 8^2 = 12^2 (+ 1)$ or $81 + 64 = 144 (+ 1)$.

Let us bear in mind that:

1. The information[126] dates from the Souei dynasty (589-618), i.e., from a time when mathematical knowledge (indigenous or imported) had reached a high level

---

126 *Ta Tai Li ki*, 66, glosses (HTKKSP, 828, p. 11a and HTKK, 705, p. 9b); *Wou li t'ong k'ao*, XXVI, pp. 20 ff.

Book II - Chapter III - Numbers

in China. {But the one-unit set was not intended to hinder carpenters in assembling beams and columns, nor was the obligation to give π the value 3. The essential thing was to use numbers that could evoke the proportion (3/2 or 9/6) of Heaven and Earth;}

Architectural proportions

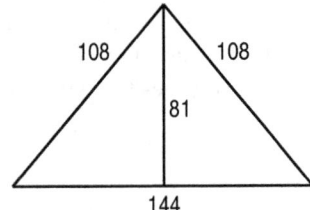 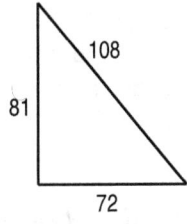 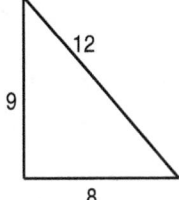

2. The obtaining of the numbers, terrestrial and celestial,

$$144 \{= (8 \times 2) \, 9\} \text{ and } 216 \{= (12 \times 2) \, 9\}$$

of the square 8, 9, 12, supposes the use, as a multiplier, of the index 9. (From the use of this index results, for the scale, the fixation in 9/7 of the relation between the tubes 1° and 5°);

3. The square 8, 9, 12, provides the sequence (9, 6, 8) that governs the construction of the 12 sound tubes. {The 2nd tube (6 x 9) is worth half the hypotenuse (12 x 9); it is known that Kouan tseu, who did not halve it, attributed to it the value 108}.

4. The height (81) has the dimension given to the gnomon, when the index adopted for the sectioning of the unit is 9.

The *Ta Tai Li ki*[127] provides an indication about the plan of the *Ming t'ang* that fits very well with this late information about the roof profile. The ritual area would have comprised 9 (lengths of) mats from east to west and 7 (lengths of) mats from south to north. 9 (the conventional multiplier) measures the length of the mats. The area (square, *fang*) of the *Ming t'ang* thus forms a rectangle (*fang*) of sides 81 and 63. The semi-perimeter is 144, which is an appropriate size since 216 measures the circumference and perimeter of the roof. This is the *Ming t'ang* of the Tcheou; the multiplier adopted is 9, and the ratio of the width (E-W) to the depth (S-N) of the area is **9/7** (expressed as 81/63).

The statements of the *Ta Tai Li ki* are confirmed by a passage from the *K'ao kong Ki*, a precious collection of technical information which today forms the sixth book of the *Tcheou li*.[128] It gives the dimensions of the *Ming t'ang*, measured in 9-foot mats (long), which are 9 x 9 wide and 9 x 7 deep. The passage is especially interesting because it also purports to give information about the Calendar House at the time of the Hia and Yin. The proportion, in both cases, is no longer **9/7** but 5/4 (= **10/8**).

In the case of the Hia, the first royal dynasty, the *K'ao kong ki* expressly states that the ratio is 5/4. The ritual area was 2 x 7 (*p'ou*) deep and a quarter more in

---

127 *Ta Tai Li ki*, 66.
128 *Tcheou li*, Biot, *op. cit.* t. II, pp. 556-561.

length; the multiplier (which is implied) is the *p'ou* or 6-foot step; the area was thus 7 double steps 6 feet deep, or 7 x 12 or 84 feet (= 4 x 21) and 105 feet wide (= 5 x 21). For the second Yin dynasty, only the depth is given, which is 7 *sin*, which, since *the sin measures 8 ft*, gives the number 56. 56 measures the depth of a kind of vestibule adjoining the ritual area of the Hia; the dimensions of this vestibule are 2/3 of the dimensions of the area, i.e., 56 deep and 70 wide. It is therefore assumed[129] that the Yin area measured 70 x 56 (i.e., 5 x 4). *Tcheng Hiuan*, however, the most illustrious of interpreters, for the reason that the Yin are intermediate between the Hia and the Tcheou, states that the breadth was 9 *sin*, i.e. 72 feet; which implies the proportion 9/7 and not 5/4 and gives the half-perimeter

(72 + 56 and not 70 + 56)

a value equal to twice 64 and not twice 63. This hesitation between 70 and 72 is a precious piece of information: it shows that the feeling of opposition or equivalence between the ratios 5/4 (or 10/8) and 9/7 was accompanied by a similar feeling with respect to the numbers 63, 64.

Tcheng Hiuan's opinion of the extent of the Yin area is based on the desire to find some kind of common link or measurement between the ritual areas of the three dynasties. Following *Tcheng Hiuan*, it appears that the sacred rectangle of the Yin (8 x 7 by 8 x 9) contained 8 x 8 small rectangles of 9 by 7 feet, while the *Ming t'ang* of the Tcheou (9 x 7 by 9 x 9 x 9) contained 9 x 9 mats of 9 by 7 feet. Thus the areas of the two areas can be indicated by the squares 64 and 81. In order to compare the sacred area of the Hia with them, it must be possible to measure it with mats; indeed, the *K'ao kong ki* states that it was in mats that areas of this type were to be measured.[130] To make this possible, it is sufficient to modify slightly – as was done in the case of the Yin – the dimension of the width of the area and estimate it not at 105 but at 108. Thus the rectangle (12 x 7 by 12 x 9) will contain 12 x 12, i.e., 144 mats, 9 by 7 feet. Let us observe the measuring procedure; it amounts, so to speak, to treating as squares the rectangles whose two sides appear to have the same numerical symbol (12, 9, or 8).[131] *While the unit area (9 x 7) is a rectangle which is (63), to the unit, a square, (64) the three rectangular areas are measured by squares* (12^2, 9^2, 8^2). These squares are especially remarkable for the fact that the relation they indicate between the three ritual areas derives from the square formula (considered valid for the structure) 8, 9, 12. But, although it seems that he insisted on finding it in the surfaces, Tcheng Hiuan could have underlined the same relationship, without modifying the width of the area of the Yin. It is enough to consider the depths which are equal to 12 x 7 for the Hia, 8 x 7 for the Yin Yin and 9 x 7 for the Tcheou. They show, in themselves, that 12 (or 6), 8 and 9 are valid as symbols of the three royal dynasties. Their ratios are those of three consecutive

---

129 *Ibid.*, vol. II, p. 560, note 1. Biot naively writes: "its length being 7 *sin*, its breadth was about a quarter more, which makes 9 sin (more exactly the length was 56 feet, the breadth 70 feet)."

130 *Ibid.*, vol. II, p. 561.

131 This emblem is, in this case, the dynastic emblem or classifier.

Book II - Chapter III - Numbers

musical tubes – according to the formula 9, 6, 8, which leads, as we know, to fix the ratio of the 1st and 2nd tubes at 9/7 – while 9 x 7 gives the measure of the unity of the ritual surfaces.

* * *

If *the unit of surface* were worth (not 9 x 7) but (5 x 4 or) 10 x 8 (10/8 being the original ratio of the 1st tube to the 2nd), it would be necessary, in order to compare the three ritual surfaces, to modify very slightly the dimensions of the surface of the Tcheou. This would be done with less damage than in the case of the area of the Yin; it would be done without modifying the value of the semi-perimeter, which is particularly sacred in this case: 80/64=5/4 or 10/8 and 80 + 64, since 81 + 63 make 144. Thus modified, the surface of the Tcheou (8 x **8** times 8 x **10**) contains 8 x 8 surface units (8 x 10), and that of the Yin (7 x **8** times 7 x **10**) contains 7 x 7; the surface unit (8 x 10) is indicated by a number (80) equal, within a unit, to a square (9^2) and the surfaces of the two areas (**64** and **49**) are reduced to squares (8^2 and 7^2). It can be seen that, for the Chinese, the importance of the pairs 81-63 and 80-64 lies in the fact that, 81 being the square of 9 and 64 the square of 8, 63 is a multiple of 9, while 80 is a multiple of 8.

The prestige of the division of the square into 9 smaller squares is well known; such were the divisions that the surveyors gave to the smallest domain, the *tsing*; but they grouped the *tsing* by 4, 16, 64… To form the administrative divisions.[132] 9, 8 or 4 were the preferred numbers in surveying technique. If, on the one hand, the plan of the ritual areas is not foreign to this technique, on the other hand, the numbers measuring these areas show the links that existed between the art of the architects and that of the diviners. The 8-sided quadrilaterals, with their **64** divisions, recall the 8 Trigrams, or the 8 Winds, and the **64** Hexagrams. And we shall soon see that the 7-sided quadrilateral, with its **49** divisions, while recalling the 50-1 rods wielded by the diviners, has the primary merit of evoking the only rod they kept in their hands, an "elevated rod" which, like a gnomon, pointed to the "mutations of Yin and Yang." *But first we must observe that, if the ratio of the semi-perimeters of the areas of the Hia* (105 + 84) *and the Yin* (70 + 56) *is equal to* (189/126 =) **3/2** *or* **9/6**, *the ratio of the semi-perimeters of the areas of the Yin* (126) *and the Tcheou* (144) *is equal to* **8/7** {while, on the contrary, the ratio of their areas – when measured with a unit equal to 10 x 8 – that is, evoking the ratio 5/4, becomes approximately equal (64/49) to **9/7** (=63/49)}. We know the prestige of the ratio **9/6** in music, divination and cosmography. We also know that the ratio **8/7** (relation of the Small Yin to the Small Yang) had, (under the Yin and) in the Song country, an equivalent prestige; instead of naming the yang and yin lines of the divinatory symbols *Nine* and *Six*,[133] they were called Seven and Eight. Does the

---

132 *Tcheou li*, Biot, *op. cit.* t. I, p. 227. Let us note here that a tradition says that the *tsing* (square of 9 fields) measured 630 arpendes (old French agrarian measure that had between 20 and 50 areas) (*meou*) under Yin or in the country of the Song (Cf. Maspero, *La Chine antique*, p. 110).

133 And the musical pipes *yang* or *yin*.

ratio 8/7, which has provided one of its expressions for the ratios of odd and even, have, like the ratio **9/6**, a musical or cosmological basis?

The ratio of the half perimeter of the area of the Hia (189) to the half perimeter of its vestibule or the area of the Yin (126) is equal to 3/2 or 9/6. Interestingly, the scale (known as the *Upper Nine*) which allowed Sseu-ma Ts'ien to justify the numerical symbols of the notes, is issued by five tubes of which the first three {45, 63 (= 60), 81} have a total value equal to 189 and the first two (54, 72) a total value equal to 126. It is possible that, in order to show a relationship between the areas of the Yin and Hia (whose proportions are regulated by the ratio 10/8), it was thought to choose dimensions taken from tubes of a certain range. It is also possible that the same procedure was used to show the proportions of the Yin and Tcheou areas (assuming the same proportions).

The first 6 sound tubes are worth 360; 360 = 24 x 15; 15 is worth both **8 + 7** and **9 + 6**; 24 is worth 9 + 8 + 7, and is also worth 10 + 8 + 6. Multiplying 15, i.e., **9** and **6**, by 9, 8 and 7, we obtain the lengths of the first six tubes {81 (=9x9), 72 (=9x8), 63 (=9x7); 54 (=6x9), 48 (=6x8), 42 (=6x7)} which can be arranged in two groups *yang* (9) and *yin* (6), the ratios of two consecutive numbers being equal to (81/54 = 72/48 = 63/42) **9/6**, the overall ratio 216/144, and the 1st tube is worth **9/7** (= 81/63) of the 5th. But multiplying 15, that is **8** and **7**, by 10, 8 and 6, we obtain 6 dimensions {80 (= 8x10), 64 (=8x8), 48 (=8x6); 70 (=7x10), 56 (=7x8), 42 (=7x6)} such that, arranging the numbers in two groups, the overall quotient is equal to **8/7** (= 192/168) as are, in detail, the quotients of the numbers taken by couples

Among the numbers thus obtained, we find 70 and 56, dimensions of the area of the Yin, 80 and 64 dimensions of the area of the Tcheou {reduced to the proportion 10 x 8 without any change in the value of the semi-perimeter (144)}, and moreover, these 6 numbers {80, 56, 70, 48, 64, (42)} differ very little from those indicated by the first formula of the scale {80, 56, 72, 48, 64, (40)}. Only 70 and 40 differ, but 42 should not be considered very different from 40, since it became the symbol of the 6th tube, which was to reproduce, with the difference of an octave, the note emitted by the 1st tube (81 or 80), and, moreover, we have just seen that Tcheng Hiuan did not hesitate to assimilate 72 to 70, in order to establish a relationship between the areas of the Yin and the Tcheou. Now, with the formula 80, 56, 70, 48, 64, (42), not only is the first number (80) worth 5/4 of the fifth (64), but it is also worth 5/3 of the fourth (48) and, in the same way, the third (70) is worth 5/4 of the second (56) and 5/3 of the sixth (42).

It is quite possible that *before deriving from a false square* (8, 9, 12) the sequence (9, 6, 8) which served (by illustrating the relation **9/6** and the proportion **9x7**) to perfect their musical theory, the Chinese thought to justify (approximately) the length of their pipes by relating them to another square which allowed to illustrate the relation **8/7** and the proportion **10 x 8**; this square (3, 4, 5 or 6, 8, 10) is a *fair square*, and is the one that gives the rule of the gnomon.

The prestige of **9/6** and **8/7** as formulas of the relations of the Even and Odd is, perhaps, linked to the fact that 9 and 6, 8 and 7 allow to section the large Total 360 into 6 estimated numbers capable of expressing musical proportions The numeri-

Book II - Chapter III - Numbers 157

cal series obtained by this sectioning are almost identical and, However, they relate to *two different squares*, one of which (8, 9, 12) leads to the adoption of 9 x 7 as the unit of area, while with the other (3, 4, 5) this unit is 10 x 8.

The *K'ao Kong hi* states that the area of the ritual areas is measured by mats (9 x 7), but this does not prevent it from indicating the dimensions of the Yin and Hia areas in *sin* or *p'ou*. Moreover, the *K'ao Kong hi* and the *Tcheou li* indicate, on the other hand, that the standard for architectural dimensions (*tou*) is the *pi sien*.[134]

The *pi sien* is an oval-shaped jade tablet with an average diameter of **9**. It is inscribed in a **10** long and **8** wide rectangle. The perimeter of the rectangle is therefore 36, and the outline of the oval 27. These numbers are significant; they show that the jade pattern and, after it, all quadrilaterals of proportion 10 x 8 or 5 x 4 had the merit of recalling the proportions of the square and the round {36/27 = (4x9)/(3x9) = 4/3}. Areas of 9 x 7 measured in mats have a half-perimeter equal to 144 (= 81 + 63 = 2 x 72 = 16 x 9), provided that the *conventional multiplier* is **9**. Conversely, areas of 10 x 8, derived from *pi sien*, have a semi-perimeter equal to 144 (= 80 + 64 = 18 x 8), provided the multiplier is 8, and in this case the inscribed oval is (27 x 8 =) 216. The ratio 10 x 8 and the square 3, 4, 5 *are linked to the use of the index* **8**, just as the ratio 9 x 7 and the square, 8, 9, 12 *are linked to the use of the index* **9**.

The ratio 216/144 is evoked, as we know, by the arrangement of the first 9 numbers in a magic square. These numbers, which are worth 45, a multiple of 5, can be grouped in such a way as to obtain the quotient 3/2 of the form 27/18 which indicates the ratio between the oval of the *pi sien* and the semi-perimeter of the inscribed rectangle. On the other hand, 45 being a multiple of 9, the first *nine* numbers can be grouped so as to obtain the ratio 5/4 or 25/20; 25 is the sum of the first five odd numbers, 20 that of the first four even numbers. However, the fact that the rectangle in which the *pi sien* is inscribed is worth 36 {= (2x10) + (2x8)}, i.e., 20 + 16, allows us to conclude that this figure illustrates another grouping of numbers. 16 is the sum of the *four* first odd numbers {(1 + 7) + (3 + 5)} and 20 is the sum of the *four* first even numbers {(2 + 8) + (4 + 6)}. The jade standard achieved a perfect synthesis of Odd and Even: a hierogamic synthesis with exchange of attributes since, in the ratio 5 x 4, Odd, 5, evokes the sum (20) of the even numbers, and Even, 4, the sum (16) of the odd ones.

This perfect synthesis also manifests itself in another way; 27 (outline of the oval) plus 36 (perimeter of the rectangle) make 63.

Multiple of 9 and of 7, 63 is a synthesis of 5 and of 4, as well as of 4 and of 3. It can first evoke by itself the ratio (3/4 = 27/36) of the celestial and terrestrial contours, and evokes it even better (27x8)/(36 x 8)=216/(2x144), when we adopt the multiplier 8. Above all, by evoking the quotient 5/4 (=35/28), it can thus recall the proportion 5x4 (*and the square 3, 4, 5*). An inverse virtue belongs to 64; this multiple of 8 contains 4 times 16 and 16 = 9 + 7. 64 can thus recall the ratio 9 x 7 (linked to the multiplier 9 *and the square 8, 9, 12*). It indicates it in a remarkable way, be-

---

134 *Tcheou li*, Biot, *op. cit.*, t. I, p. 490; t. II, p. 524.

cause 64 = 36 + 28. 36 (like 360) is the symbol of the totality of a contour.[135] 28 is the number of lunar mansions. Now the circular canopy which covers the chariot of the Chief and represents Heaven measures 36 by its outline, and 28 arcs unite it to the central column, which unites it to the square body of the chariot (Earth).[136]

* * *

But, if the 28 lunar mansions indicate the interest of the number 7, it remains to understand the meaning of this number and the importance attributed to the proportion **8/7**, *it remains above all to explain the connection of this proportion with the square 3, 4, 5, that is to say, with the gnomon*, to which the central column of the chariot rightly reminds us.

The merits of the square 3, 4, 5 are praised in a famous pamphlet whose title: *Tcheou pei*[137] means: gnomon. The *Tcheou pei* (in which we find the comparison of the sky and the chariot canopy) summarizes the mathematical teachings of a school of cosmographers called the "School of the Celestial Canopy." Its theme is the idea that celestial dimensions can be known through the gnomon and the 3, 4, 5 square. The gnomon is described as a bamboo sign which, pierced at the eighth foot with a 1/10th foot hole, is 8 feet long or (80+1)/10 feet. The author, however, begins by relating the square 3, 4, 5 to the formula 9 x 9 = 81, which is considered the first of the rules.

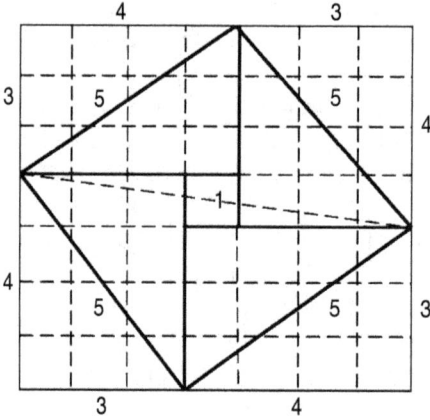

To teach the square 3, 4, 5, the *Tcheou pei* begins by constructing a rectangle of sides 3 and 4, and then draws the diagonal. The text contains nothing else; one does not find in it, as Biot pointed out, any attempt to prove the hypotenuse-square theorem. In the editions of the *Tcheou Pei* that have been preserved, the rule of the square, or rather of the diagonal, is illustrated by three figures. These are three squares of side 7 divided into 49 little squares and enclosing, one, a square of side 5 containing 25 little squares, the other, a square of side 4 (16 little squares) and the last a square of side 3 (9 little squares). No one can claim that these figures

---

135 Terrestrial contour (square of side 9), celestial contour (circumference of diameter 12 or hexagon of side 6), or even terrestrial and celestial trapezoidal contour formed by a half hexagon of side 72 (or 3 x 72, i.e. 216) and a base of value 144 (= 2 x 72).

136 *Tcheou li*, Biot *op. cit.* t. II, p. 477.

137 The translation of the *Tcheou pei*, published in the "Journal asiatique" in 1841, is due to Ed. Biot, whose father, the astronomer J.-B. Biot, added a famous commentary to the translation. The setting of *Tcheou pei* resembles that of king *Houang-ti nei* and *Hong fan*. It features the brother of King Wen, founder of the Tcheou, who interrogates a scholar about the origins of the science of numbers and the measurement of celestial dimensions. The booklet abounds in very obscure technical formulas alternating with esoteric formulas; the latter amount to stating that Heaven is the circle, Earth the square, and that the Circle comes from the Square.

BOOK II - CHAPTER III - NUMBERS   159

existed, in that form, in the original editions. As they are sometimes drawn, they seem to have no other purpose than to illustrate for the eyes the formula $3^2 + 4^2 = 5^2$.

They are, however, intended, although this has been discussed,[138] to propose a geometrical demonstration of this formula. *The insertion of a square* (of side 5) *of value 25 inside a square* (of side 7) *of value* **49** is directly related to a datum found in the text of *Tcheou pei*: *consider hypotenuse 5 as the diagonal of a 3 x 4 rectangle. In a square of side 7, four of these rectangles fit, and their four diagonals form an inscribed square whose area is half that of the four rectangles* {i.e., 4 (34)/2, i.e., 24} *plus 1 little square* that is left in the center by the arrangement of the four *rectangles*. This is the geometric verification of the formula: $3^2 + 4^2 = 5^2$.

Here is the proof of the antiquity of this demonstration, which the figures of the current editions give a glimpse of, even if they surround it with a certain mystery. To insert the three squares 9, 16, 25 *in a square of side 7*, is *to suggest the equivalence of 45 and of* (9 + 16) + 25, or, in other words, *the equivalence of 25 + 25 and of* **49**; this is equivalent to affirming that *the isosceles right triangle of side 5 has a hypotenuse*[139] *which is approximately 7*. Now, as much or more than the right square 3, 4, 5, this approximate square 5, 5, 7 interested the Chinese.

This interested them from antiquity. I have already said that the diviner or the chief – and we shall see that the Chief, the One Man, is identical with the gnomon – took a rod from the batch of fifty divining rods, which he held in his hand while operating. This removal made it possible to divide the lot (49) into two parts, one of which was necessarily even and the other odd. The rod he held in his hand presided over divination with him; this staff of command represented the central square, the Center, the Unity – *the Unity which does not count, but which is worth and makes* the whole –, *the distributor, the pivot of Yin and Yang*.[140]

The idea *that what we call unity is not added to, but merely mutates from Yin to Yang or from Yang to Yin, and thus merges with the Whole or the Total into which*

---

138 A. Rey (*La science orientale*, p. 394) relied on Biot's description of the figures of the *Tcheou pei* to refute an interpretation suggested by Zeuthen and taken up by Milhaud. In fact, these figures, as drawn in the best editions of the *Tcheou pei* (those of the *Sseu pou ts'ong kan*, for example), justify Zeuthen's suggestion.

139 Needless to say, the Chinese ascribe to the hypotenuse of the isosceles right triangle of sides 5 and 5 the value 7. The figure shows that the diagonal does not join the side of the square. Fou-hi is known to be the patron saint of fortune tellers who use 49 wands. The emblem of Fou-hi (cf. *Civilisation chin.*, pp. 19-21) is apparently a square with equal branches. I would like to think that it is the square 5, 5, 7 (or 10, 10, 14). The *Tcheou pei* professes that the round comes out of the square. Now the diameter of the wheels (*Tcheou li*, Biot, *op. cit.*, t. I, p. 471) is 7, and 14 – or 7 x 2 – measures the diameter of the cosmic wheel of which Man, whose size is 7, is the spoke.

140 Fr. Gaubil had already noted that the formula $3^2+4^2+4^2+5^2=(3+4)^2 +1$ is implicit in the rules of divinatory practice laid down by the *Hi ts'eu* (*Lettres édifiantes*, t. IX, p. 435). The two superimposed magic squares (with centers 5 and 6) comprise a total of 18 numbers. They revolve around a pivot (11) which may be worth as number 19; $19^2 = (4 \times 90) + 1 = 360$ (+ 1, central square).

Yin and Yang mutate, is connected with the political theories of the Chinese about the universal – though only ordering – power of the *One Man, who, from the Center of the World, orders all things without interfering with any thing, without adding anything particular to the Total which makes it what it is*. This idea is also related to the tendency we have so often observed *to adjust the whole and determine the proportions by always reserving the play of a unity*. It explains the marked taste of the Chinese *for mathematically imperfect squares, but more effective for them than for others, precisely because they preserve a certain play in their whole, and the part, so to speak, of the operative movement, the real Work*.

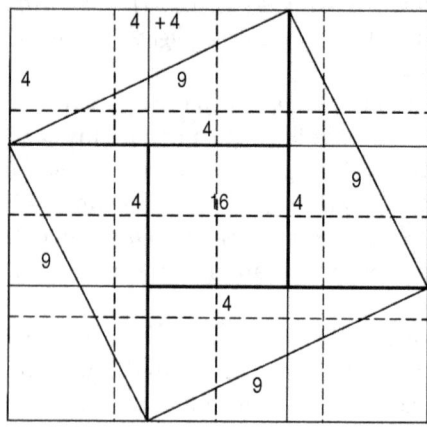

We already know the prestige of the square 8, 9, 12. We can suppose that, like the squares, just or approximate, 3, 4, 5 and 5, 5, 7, it was illustrated by translating geometrically the formula $(a + b)^2 = 4 ab + (a - b)^2 = 2 ab + \{2 ab + (a - b)^2\}$ in a square of side 17 (= 9 + 8), we can inscribe 4 rectangles of 8 x 9, whose diagonals will be worth about 12, since they enclose four half-rectangles of value 72, i.e. 144, plus 1 central square {being 1 the square of 9-8) $(17^2 = 289 = 144 + (144 + 1)\}$.

$$8^2+9^2=12^2(+1)$$

$$9^2(-1)=8^2+4^2$$

A similar construction, *and, moreover, modeled on an essential figure of Chinese geometry or surveying*, was also to serve to show the virtues of 12^2. China, the land of men, has 12 or 9 provinces; being 12 of 3 x 4, it is possible to construct a square of side 12 that can be divided into 9 squares or 12 rectangles. Let us begin with the division into 9 squares, which is that of the *Ming t'ang*, the *Magic Square*, etc. Around the central square, which *perfectly represents the swastika*, are drawn *four rectangles, notable for the fact that their height is twice that of their base*. They are worth 4 x 8, i.e., 2 x 16. By drawing the diagonals, we divide them into triangles, worth 16, like the central square $\{(8 - 4)^2\}$. This construction shows the rule of the triangle area (base x height)/2 with the help of an example according to Chinese taste, since the area of these triangles is expressed by a square (16). *It also leads to drawing* {since the four diagonals enclose four triangles worth 16 and a square also worth **16** (i.e., 16 x 5 = 80)} *an inscribed square that approaches the most*

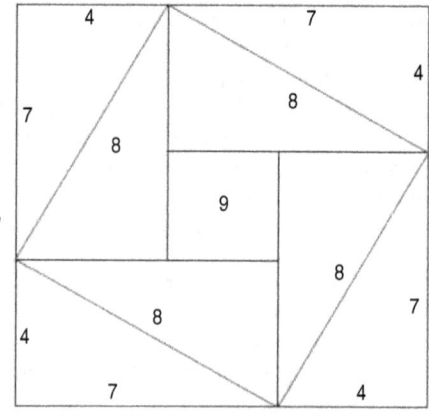

Book II - Chapter III - Numbers

perfect square (9^2), *since it is worth 80*. Hence the formula $8^2 + 4^2 =$ (*with an accuracy of one unit*) 9^2, a valuable formula, since it gives an approximate value of the hypotenuse of a triangle whose base is half the height (approximate square 4, 8, 9).

But here is another approximate square, which is equally useful to establish, since it can help to calculate the elements of the hexagon and, being similar to the square 4, 8, 9, will allow an application of the latter to the hexagon. If 81 (-1) = 64 + 16, 64 (+ 1) = 49 + 16. A square of side (7 + 4 =) 11, divided into 4 rectangles (4 x 7) surrounding a square of value 9 {= $(7-4)^2$} allows us to verify (with an accuracy of one unit) this new square, extremely valuable, since the *hypotenuse is twice the base*, which is the case for triangles formed by the side of a hexagon (hypotenuse), the half side of the hexagon (base), and the height of the trapezoid formed by the half hexagon.

We have now arrived at the reasons for the prestige of the quotient **8/7** and are very close to understanding the connection between this quotient and the square 3, 4, 5, i.e., the quotient 8 x 10 and the gnomon.

* * *

The round derives from the square, as the *Tcheou pei* states, but through the hexagon.

If it is estimated that the circumference is worth 3/4 of the square in which it is inscribed, it is because the side of this square is worth two sides of the hexagon inscribed in the circumference. When the perimeter of the square is 8 and its side 2, the hexagon and the circumference (like it) will be worth 6, the radius and the side of the hexagon will be worth 1, the diameter (2 sides of the hexagon) will be worth 2, and π, therefore, will be estimated to be 3.

From the equivalence established between the circumference and the inscribed hexagon, there remains, as a first testimony, the fact that the wheel has 30 (= **6x5**) spokes. It is said that this is because the wheel is intended to remember the month, i.e., the moon. But the symbol of the moon is, much more than the wheel, the knife, which is curved; the curved knife is the splintered moon, and what splintered the moon is the knife.[141] To test whether the curvature of the knives conformed to the correct rules, they were put together in groups of six and examined whether they formed a

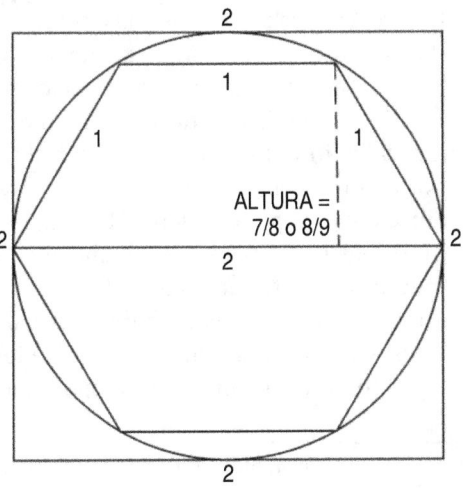

---

141 On the subject of the knife and the splintered moon, see Granet, *Danses et légendes...*, p. 535, and his note 2; p. 533, note 1; pp. 533 and 534.

perfect circle. The knives had to be one foot long.¹⁴² We can see that the hexagon is equal to the circle and that both are equal to 6.

The formula π = 3 is an essential fact of Chinese mathematics and cosmography. It has served and continues to serve as a standard for wheelwrights, who in the past, not only made the wheels, but also the carriage covers.

The Celestial Canopy School accepts that Heaven is a canopy and that it can be measured by means of the square 3, 4, 5; it also accepts that the formula 9 x 9 = 81 is the first rule, while the gnomon is worth 80. With the square of 3, 4, 5, where 5 is the hypotenuse, the gnomon can be given the value 81 (= 3 x 27) or 80 (= 4 x 20), depending on whether the height is 3 or 4. The hypotenuse will then be 135 (= 5 x 27) or 100 (= 5 x 20) and the base 108 (= 4 x 27) or 60 (= 3 x 20). The numbers 108 and 135, 60 and 100, which are in the proportion 4/5 and 3/5, are unusable for those who intend to derive the round from the square, that is, to illustrate the proportions 3/4 or 3/2. The prestige of the gnomon and the claim to derive the round from the square are not, then, related to the construction of a right triangle of sides 3, 4, 5 or of an isosceles triangle of side 5 and height 3 or 4, with base 8 or 6.

On the contrary, one can derive the round from the square¹⁴³ and *justify, in addition, the height of the gnomon*, by constructing a *trapezoid* formed by a half hexagon and a base worth two sides of the hexagon. This can be done (thanks to the one-unit set and the concurrent use of the multipliers 9 and 8) if the ratio between the side of the hexagon and the height of the trapezoid is set to **8/7 or 9/8**. We will prove this and thus succeed in explaining the old fashioned 8/7 as an expression (as valid as 9/6) of the quotients of even and odd. We will also justify our hypothesis about obtaining squares, straight or approximate, from the insertion in a square of four rectangles encompassing a central square, which will be equivalent to proving the antiquity of the demonstration of the hypotenuse theorem.

Let us start from the essential fact; for the school of *Tcheou pei* or of the square 3, 4, 5, Heaven is identical to the canopy of the chariot. The canopy of the chariot is divided into three parts; the central part, which is worth 2 + 2, is flat and is supported in its center by a column; the two edges, which are curved, each measure 4. Since the canopy represents Heaven, its outline, analogous to the celestial outline, must be worth 36 and the diameter (even if the edges of the canopy are curved) must be estimated equal to 12 {= (4 + 2) + (2 + 4)}. The outline of the canopy is thus formed by three lines considered equal to each other (4 + 4 + 4), as are the three sides of a half hexagon, but the angle formed by the edges with the flat part is not equal to 60°; it is much more open; the height of the trapezium formed, with its

---

142 *Tcheou li*, Biot, *op. cit.*, vol. II, p. 492. According to the commentaries, these are writing knives. The knife, a curved weapon, which is nevertheless carried in the right hand – although the right is *yin* and the curved is *yang* – is essentially a *yin* weapon, because it is the emblem of the Moon, while the sword (right) is the emblem of the Sun. (Cf. Granet, *op. cit.*, p. 498, note 2, *in fine*).

143 The compass, female emblem, insignia of Niu-koua, sister of Fou-hi (first magician and bearer of the square) is made (cf. *Civ. Chin.*) of two straight lines or rods crossing each other, forming a cross (simple cross).

Book II - Chapter III - Numbers

base, by the outline of the canopy, is, in fact, fixed at 2. This is an essential datum,[144] to which we shall return.

But let us begin by constructing a trapezium, whose three sides form a half hexagon, the base being worth two sides. Let us assign to each side the value 1, since the 6 sides forming a perfect circle measure each 1 foot. The perimeter of our trapezium breaks down into 5 equal parts, and *for this perimeter to form a total outline*[145] it will suffice to estimate 72. Thereafter, the base will have the significant dimensions of Earth and Yin (144), and the outline of the half hexagon will be equivalent to a semicircular outline, because it will have the dimensions of Yang and Sky.[146]

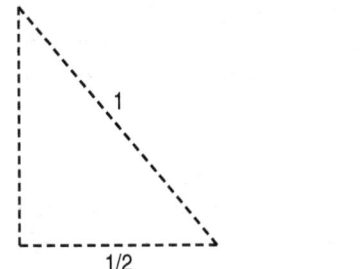
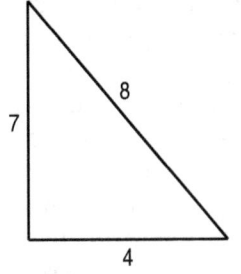
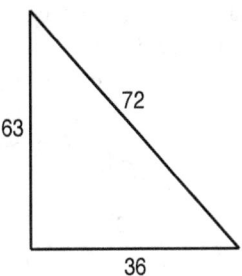

72 is worth 9 x 8. To bring to 72 the value of 1 of each of the 5 sides of the hexagon that form our perimeter, we can proceed by two methods, but always in two steps: multiply, first, by **8** and then by 9 or multiply by **9** and then by 8.

Let's start by multiplying by **8**; the *side of the hexagon* is worth **8**, the half side 4. *If we know the construction mentioned above* (four rectangles of 7 x 4 must form a square of side 11), *we can estimate the height of the trapezoid as 7*.[147] Now multiply by 9; the side will be worth 72, the half side 36, the height 63, and we will have formed on the side of our trapezoid a square 36, 63, 72.

Let us go on to the other method and multiply, to begin with, by **9**. *The side of the hexagon is worth* **9** *and the half side 4.5. If we are familiar with the construction discussed above* (four rectangles of **8** x 4 in a square of side 12), *it will be very tempting to use the (approximate)* square of 4, 8, 9, because if we now multiply the side **9** by 8, we will get, as before, 72, and we will also get 36 (= 4.5 x 8) times half the side {which we must remember (although we are using a square of 4, 8, 9) is, in this case, half of 9, i.e., 4.5}. The height, first expressed as **8**, according to the square used, will be defined after the second multiplication by 64, and we shall have constructed on the side of our trapezium a square of 36, 64, 72, which will differ from the square formed by the previous operations only by the substitution of 63 for 64.

---

144 *Tcheou li*, Biot, *op. cit.*, vol. II, p. 476.

145 *Ta Tai Li ki*, 66, glosses (HTKKSP, 828, p. 11a and HTKK, 705, p. 9b); *Wou li t'ong k'ao*, XXVI, pp. 20 ff.

146 Granet, *Fêtes et chansons anciennes*, p. 79; *Civ. Chin.*, pp. 196, 209 ff.

147 What we here call height corresponds to the real radius of a wheel hollowed out inside in the form of a hexagon. The ratio 7/8 is that which exists between the dimension of a radius and the dimension of the radius of the circumference formed, externally, by the rim.

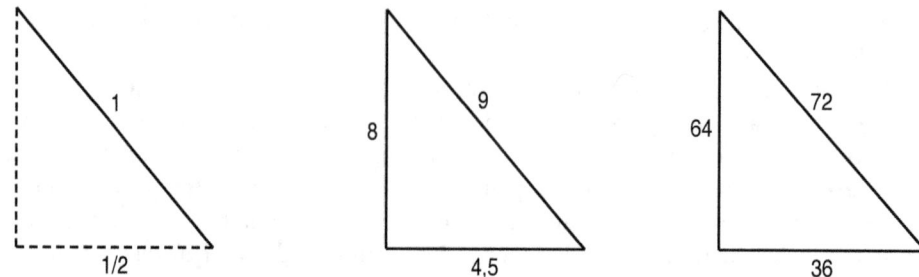

63 is worth 9 x 7 and 64 8 x 8. These heights are perfectly adequate, since it is a question of accommodating, between the body and the canopy of the chariot, a man, and *the height of the man (jen), symbolized by the game character, is estimated – precious hesitation – to be equal to 7 feet or to 8 feet*, that is, in one case, to 63, *if the foot has 9 divisions*, and, in the other, to 64, *if the foot has 8 divisions*.

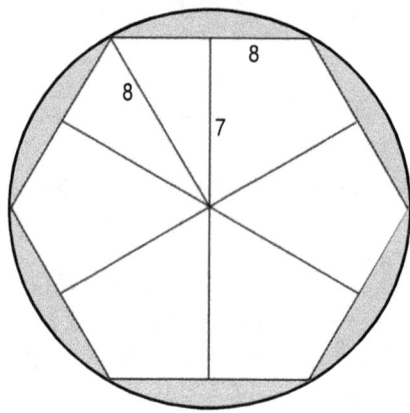

But since, thanks to Tchong-li, the ancient solar hero who became the patron saint of astronomers, communications between Earth and Heaven were cut off, men's heads – not even those of the Chief (unless he climbs the pole) – no longer touch Heaven.

Moreover, a warrior must be able to see when he is enclosed between the box and the curved canopy of his chariot. Therefore, this canopy is raised. When the height of the man is estimated at eight feet, the central column of the chariot is two feet higher.[148] Suppose it is likewise two feet higher when the man (without his height having changed, no doubt, but when the measure of his height has changed, defined by divisions of 63 feet instead of 64) is not taller than 7 feet.

The height of the trapezium (in the first method and 8 being *the first multiplier*) is 7 (cosmic wheel spoke), i.e. 63, since, for the contour of the trapezium to be 360, the second conventional multiplier must be 9. As Heaven must be separated from Earth to break communications, the canopy will be supported by a column which will be (7 + 2) x 9, i.e., 9 x 9 or 81, and such is, in effect, the Number of the *Tcheou pei* (gnomon). But, if the height of man or the actual radius of the cosmic wheel is 8, it will be necessary (9 being the first multiplier) for the second conventional multiplier to be 8 so that the contour of the trapezium is always equal to 360. Therefore, 8 x 8, or 64, gives the height of the man and {(8 + 2) x 8 =} 80 is the height of the central column: it is the size of the gnomon (*Tcheou pei*).

The 81 comes from 63, as the 80 comes from 64. When we divide it into 7 or 8 feet, into 63 or 64 parts, we certainly do not vary the standard height of man. When the height of the gnomon is fixed at 81, or when it is fixed at 80, does the actual

---

148 *Tcheou li*, Biot, *op. cit.*, vol. II, p. 476.

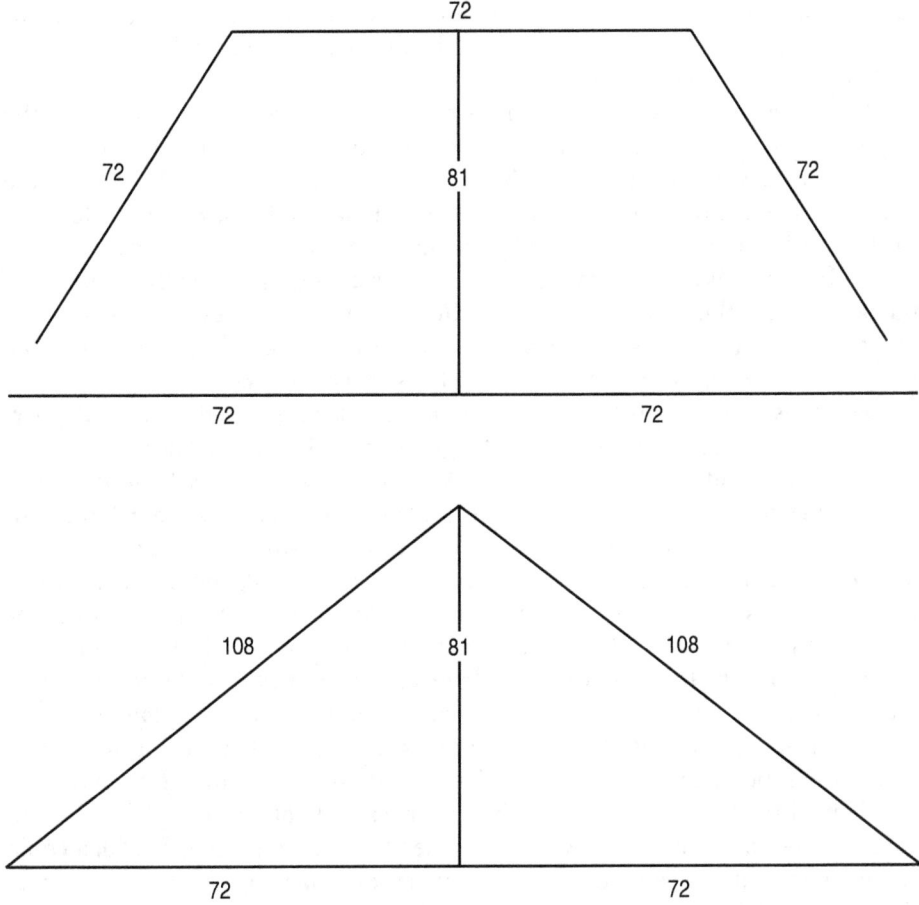

height (the distance to the ground from the hole drilled in the top of the pole) really change? Does 81 only differ from 80 by *one unit that does not count*?

The Chinese have consistently chosen a multiple of 8 to indicate the height of the gnomon... When the chariot workers built the column and the capital to which they attached the canopy, they were careful to leave a very small part of the capital (1/100th of a foot) above the canopy... The number 81 has great merits, especially when it measures a height or a sign erected on a base worth 2 x 72. Do we not know that a square (9, 8, 12) for a height of 81 and a base of 72 (= 12) has a hypotenuse worth 108, i.e. half of 216, a celestial contour, which can be represented, moreover, by three sides of a hexagon?

The height – or gnomon – 81 allows to change the profile of a canopy or roof from trapezoidal to triangular. {The triangular profile is perfectly suited to a circular thatched roof, such as the *Ming t'ang* is said to have had. But tile roofs, which according to the *K'ao kong ki*[149] were less steeply pitched than thatched roofs, re-

---

149 *Idem, Ibid.* in vol. II, p. 571.

sembled (at least in Han times)[150] a half hexagon or carriage roof}. Of triangular or trapezoidal profile, roofs worth 216 must be arranged on rectangles, whose half-perimeter must (therefore) be 144.

When the gnomon is worth 81, it gives the width, while 63, the height of the trapezoid, gives the depth. We have seen that, in this case, the unit of area (the mat) is 9 x 7, the conventional multiplier being 9. The unit is the *pi sien* (10 x 8) and the multiplier 8 when the gnomon, and therefore the width, is 80, while the depth of the buildings and the height of the trapezium is 64. In all cases, the round (216 = 108 x 2 or 72 x **3**) is derived from the square (72 x **2**, the base of the trapezium, half the perimeter of the square.) And when the gnomon is 80, (or even 81 (80 + a unit that does not count), the square 3, 4, 5 is in the ratio 10 x 8, (which is in turn in the ratio 9 x 7 surfaces, since 81 + 63 makes 144 as well as 80 + 64).

By means of the proportion 8 x 10 and of the *pi sien*, we can thus recall the perfect square, 3, 4, 5, the 4 by setting the height of the gnomon at 80 or 80 (+ 1). But, to achieve this and *to illustrate the idea that the round is derived from the square through the hexagon*, that is, to evoke in the form 216/144 the proportion 3/2 or 9/6 of the round with respect to the square, we had to (which, by the way, *allowed us to oppose and assimilate* the proportions 9 x 7 and 10 x 8, and consequently to remember the square 3, 4, 5) to start from the ratio **8/7** (or 9/8) of the radius of the circumference (side of the hexagon) to the real radius of the wheel (height of the trapezoid drawn by the half hexagon). *To obtain this result the Builders* – as well as the Musicians, when they perfected the scale formula – *had to employ simultaneously the conventional multipliers 8 and 9.* This is what our demonstration implies. This is what the tradition states. The Tcheou used 9-foot-long mats for measuring, but divided the foot into 8 inches. The Yin measured with a *sin* of 8 feet, but divided the foot into 9 inches.[151] Moreover, when the gnomon was worth 80, it could still be estimated to be no more than 2/8 the size of a man; to estimate it as equal to the man-standard (8), it was enough (80 = 10 x 8) to divide the foot into 10 inches; such was, it is said,[152] the system of the Hia.[153]

* * *

Whether Man (*jen*) is 7 feet high (square 4, 7, 8) or 8 feet high (square 4, 8, 9), his height varies no more than does the height of the gnomon when it is 81 or 80, that is, when it is given 9 times 9 divisions, or 10 times 8 divisions, or 8 times 10 divisions.

Numbers do not have the function of expressing magnitudes; they serve to adjust the concrete dimensions to the proportions of the universe.

---

150 As shows a terracotta representing a house in the Cernuschi Museum, reproduced in Goldschmidt, *L'art chinois*, p. 71.
151 See Ts'ai Yong's *Tou touan*, in *Han Wei ts'ong chou*.
152 *Ibid.*
153 It was claimed, under the Souei, that the *Ming t'ang* of the Tcheou was square; it was measured, it was said, from north to south with 7 *lengths* of mats, i.e., 7 x 9 = 63, and from east to west with 9 *lengths* of mats, i.e., 9 x 7 = 63.

Book II - Chapter III - Numbers

To perfectly fulfill its mission, a Numerical Symbol must – so to speak – express, or rather, contain two coordinates: one evokes the *permanent structure* of the World, the other a *defined state* of Order or Civilization. The richest Symbols: 3 and 2, 3 and 4, 5 and 4, 10 and 8, 9 and 6, 8 and 7, 64 and 80, 63 and 81, 144 and 216, 108 and 72... are those which bring out the morphology and physiology of the Universe; *their sets are ordered by the grand Total 360* ($= 5 \times 72 = 6 \times 60$).

The structure of the Universe or its morphology is summed up in the double expression of the relations of Yang and Yin, of Odd and Even: **9/6 y 7/8**. We have seen that and this is to pass – through the intermediary of the hexagon – from the square to the circle) we arrive at the relation {7/8 (or 8/9)} of the real radius of the cosmic wheel (the Man-Standard, 7 or 8, the *jen*: height of the trapezium) to the radius of the circumference (side of the hexagon), to pass to the relation (**9/6**) of the celestial Contour (half perimeter of the hexagon) to the terrestrial Base of the hexagon. Through this passage the physiology of the Universe is expressed: the rhythmic alternation of the *straight* and the *curved*, of Yin and Yang. What makes the passage possible is the conjugated use of multipliers which, considered as classifiers of Space-Time, are valid as dynastic Symbols. These Symbols make it possible to represent in different and yet *assimilable* terms {proportions 8 × 10 or 9 × 7, semiperimeters 81 + 63 or 80 + 64 (both equal to 144)} the structure of the Universe characterizing an epoch of civilization. The succession of the different dynastic orders of Civilization {this succession is regulated by a *musical rhythm*, i.e. by the sequence, 9, 6, 8 (6 being the numerical emblem of the Hia, 8 that of the Yin, 9 that of the Tcheou)} does not alter the structure of the World. The permanence of this structure is evidenced by taking care to choose, for the indexes of the divisions of the various units of measurement, *numbers that can be combined in such a way that – only by changing the order of the manipulations – the result*, with the approximation of one unit, *will not be modified*.

Instead of being used to measure, numbers are used to contrast and assimilate. They serve to integrate things into the system formed by the universe. Things cannot be measured. They have their own measurements. They are their measurements. They are like the tool or the craftsman makes them. Their measure is that of the worker, as the measure of the World is that of the Chief, the Standard Man. Chariot-building is the noblest of arts,[154] for the chariot, body and canopy, are Earth and Heaven. The structure of the chariot (canopy and column) illustrates the relationships **9/6** and **8/7**, and what rules in the detail of the proportions (length of the arms, height of the canopy) is the carving of the warrior;[155] but – just as the actual dimensions of the pottery work depend on the actual dimensions of the wheel used by the potter[156] – the artist who builds the chariots determines all the

---

154 *Tcheou li*, Biot, *op. cit.*, vol. II, p. 462.

155 *Ibid.*, vol. II, p. 463. If the height of the man is 8 feet, the height of the box above himself is 4; the height of the canopy (2 x 4) + 2; the stopping stick (which may be leaned against the walls of the box, having 6.6, so that it protrudes by), 4; the fighting stick: 8 x 3, etc.

156 *Ibid.*, vol. II, p. 539. Note the interpreters' remark, "The potter's wheel can determine the square and round shape of objects."

measurements by using *only* the handle of his axe.[157] The greatest triumph of the founder of the imperial unit (Che Houang-ti boasts of this in his inscriptions and, perhaps, boasts of himself)[158] was to get the wheel hubs of all chariots throughout the Empire – all chariots, even before him, were built using the same proportional numbers – to have *effectively* the *same* size.

There is, in the Chinese conception of Numbers, an admirable conciliation of the strictest conformism, or sense of style, of fantasy, and of *most zealous individualism*. This conception makes it possible (apart from its practical uses) to use the Numbers for the sole purpose of revealing the structure of the World and the successive orders of civilization through which the rhythm of universal life is expressed. For those who multiply numerical classifications, for those who avoid adopting a single system of division for all units of measurement, for those who characterize each unit with a special type of division and take care to use complementary modes of division together, Numbers serve to indicate relations and proportions, without preventing either the manipulation of relations or *a certain play of proportions*.

Numbers are but symbols; the Chinese avoid seeing in them the abstract and constricting signs of quantity.

V. Classificatory and Protocolar Functions of Numbers

When Chinese interpreters want to justify the dimensions (10 x 8) of *pi sien*, they point out that all ancient units of measurement are derived from the human body, and then add: the hand, measured from the pulse, is worth 10 (inches) in men and 8 in women. Thus, the pair (8 or 4) governs the dimensions of cloths (which women make), {and even (in principle) of manufactured objects (which are *yin*)}. It also presides over the division of surfaces and especially of volumes:[159] Yin is hollow. As for lengths which are related to the standard size, the gnomon, the Chief, they deserve to be expressed by a *yang* (Odd) number.

The main use of odd and even numbers is to distribute all things into *Yin* and *Yang* categories. This classificatory function is immediately joined by a protocol function. Yang prevails over Yin; Odd is a synthesis of Odd and Even.

We can summarize the Chinese conception of Numbers by recalling a formula of the indigenous etymologists. To explain that a witch can be designated by the graphic symbol (*wou*) which means "witch," but that she deserves, on the other hand, to possess a designation (*hi*) of her own, they say: the witch is *yin*, the sorcer-

---

157 *Ibid.* in vol. II, pp. 574 ff.
158 *Civ chin.*, p. 119.
159 *Tcheou li*, Biot, *op. cit.* t. II, p. 504. The standard of capacity is a kind of bronze bell (which should emit the same sound as the *houang tchong*, the initial pipe), square on the inside (*yin*), round on the outside (*yang*). The inside measures 1 square foot and contains one *fou*, or 64 *cheng*. The bottom of the bell, which is hollow, contains one *teou* (4 *cheng*) and the bell handles measure *cheng*. Four *teou* make one *kiu* (16 *cheng*); four *kiu* (64 *cheng*) make one *fou*.

er is *yin-yang*. The expression *yin-yang* has never ceased to designate the sorcerer, nor has the sorcerer ceased – a privilege deriving from the practice of hierogamy – to be man and woman at the same time, and woman at will. The Odd contains the Even and can produce it. In him and through him *mutates* the odd and the even.

The virtues of *pi sien*, made of 10 (man's hand) and 8 (woman's hand), lie in the fact that its middle diameter is made of 5 and 4, whose synthesis is 9. The 11 {synthesis of 5 and 6 (and also of each of the 5 pairs formed by the first 10 numbers)}, the 7 {synthesis of 3 and 4 (inscribed circumference and half perimeter of the escribed square)}, the 5 {synthesis of 3 and 2 (half circumference and side of the square)} can serve as symbols for *yang* things, which are also *yin-yang*. None of these numbers can do it so well as 9. If 9 is 5 + 4, it is also 3^2, and 3, which is the *first synthesis* of Yang and Yin, is also the *first number*.[160]

Only the One is always the All,[161] and the Two is, in essence, only the Couple. Two is the Couple characterized by the *alternance* (and *communion*, but not *sum*) of Yin and Yang. And the One, the All, is the pivot, which is neither *yin* nor *yang*, but through which the alternation of yin and yang is ordered; it is the central square, *which does not count, but which* (like the cube of which Taoist authors say that, thanks to its emptiness, it can make the wheel turn)[162] *orders the turning* of the swastika drawn by the four rectangles between which the great square, the Whole Space, is divided; it is the Indivisible which cannot be added, because it is not a synthesis of even and odd; it is the Unity which cannot be worth 1 because it is the Whole and, moreover, cannot be distinguished from the Two, because in it all the contrasting aspects are reabsorbed and oppose, but also unite, the Left and the Right, the Upper Part and the Lower Part, the Front and the Back, the Round and the Square, all Yang and all Yin. All the Unity and the Pair, the Whole, if we want to give it a numerical expression, is found in all the Odd numbers and, in the first place, in the 3 (: *One* plus *Two*). 3, as we shall see, is valid as a slightly weakened expression of unanimity.

The series of numbers begins, then, at 3.[163] It is not a continuous series, because the numbers are immediately grouped in two opposite bands. A continuous series could only be used for counting. In practice, the Chinese have been counting well for a long time. But what their sages ask of the Numbers is that the *yin* and *yang* series provide them with classifiers to group beings hierarchically into antithetical categories. They wish, above all, to distinguish by suitable symbols the even and odd groupings, and to indicate, in the first place, the most perfect of these groupings. Hence the importance, attested by their ritual uses, of the double progression

---

160 The *Chouo wen* defines 3 as the way (*tao*) of Heaven and Earth. 3 is a synthesis comparable to 11 (cf. *supra*, in this same chapter, sec. II).

161 *Yi* (One) gives the idea of indivisibility rather than unity. Used adverbially, *yi* means entirely, completely.

162 *Lao tseu*, P. Wieger, *Les Pères du système taoïste*, p. 27.

163 On 3, see Granet, *La Polygynie sororale et le Sororat dans la Chine féodale*, p. 27 and *Id, Danses et légendes....* (Index).

3, 9, 27, 81, and 8, 16, 32, 64. The first merit of this double series is obvious:[164] it opposes, on two occasions, two squares whose sum evokes another square {9 + 16 = 5^2 and 81 + 64 = 12^2 (+ 1)} and invites to construct two squares (both essential, even if one is approximate). Another prestigious reason: 3 + 9 + 27 + 81, as 8 + 16 + 32 + 64 = 120 and together they make 2/3 of 360. When we face these two series, formed by the most perfect and odd pairs, the 120 missing to complete 360 are only missing in appearance. 120 wives and 120 ministers must be at the King's side. The One Man (whose robe is embroidered with 12 insignia, with 12 jade pendants on his ceremonial cap) is worth *alone* the same as the whole group of his vassals and the whole group of his vassals; is worth the same as these two groups which are only his Left and his Right and, as master of the 12 Provinces, is also worth the grand Total 360, in which he does not count for 1, just as the Queen in the group of the 120 wives does not count for 1, because of the hierogamy that reabsorb her into the Lord, she is indistinguishable from the One Man, the Supreme Magician: Couple *Yin-Yang*.

The Odd contains and produces the Even, which is never more than a double projection (right and left, *yin* and *yang*) of the Odd. Neither the Odd nor the Unity *adds* to the Even. They center the Symmetrical and transform it into Odd. Neither Odd nor Unity *add* to Odd: they transform a centered arrangement into a symmetrical one. These *mutations* are only changes of aspect, changes of form, true metamorphoses; they do not seem to imply a quantitative change. Moreover, all pairs are equally valid as expressions of a symmetric arrangement, and all odd ones as expressions of a hierarchical arrangement. So the Odd ones remain valid as expressions of the Whole, that is, of the Unity considered under a more or less complex aspect. One is the Total, and the whole Odd, which is a kind of Total, is One.

Without thinking of an addition, but evoking a different distribution of the whole, an internal change of organization, the Odd *operates* the passage from Even to Odd or from Odd to Even. The passage from Even to Odd is not that from Unlimited to Limited or from Indeterminate to Determinate, it is the passage from Symmetric to Centered, from Non-Hierarchical to Hierarchical. This passage is made without suggesting a properly quantitative representation. The Double (Yin) and the Undivided (Yang), the Square (Symmetrical) and the Round (Centered) produce each other (*cheng cheng*), or rather alternate rhythmically. The geometrical ideal[165] would be an assimilation (after an opposition) of the Straight and the

---

164 The initial tube (which, like the gnomon, is worth 81) is opposed to the capacity pattern (which, as we have seen, is worth 64).

165 The famous diagram of T'ai ki (the Supreme Ruler; on the word *ki*, Ruler, cf. *infra*, ch. IV) is an illustration of this ideal. The figure is intended to show the union of Yin and Yang in producing the 10,000 beings. Yin (dark) and Yang (light) are enclosed in a circle of which each occupies half. The line separating them and winding around a diameter is formed by 2 semicircles, each of which has a diameter equal to half the diameter of the great circle. This line is therefore equal to the half-

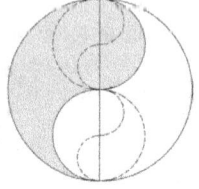

Curved, of the Diameter and the Half-Circle, of 2 and 3, i.e., the prohibition of lending a value to 1.

* * *

The assimilation and opposition of the Even and Odd, the Symmetrical and the Centered, demonstrates sufficiently that the science of Numbers is not distinguished from geometrical knowledge. This knowledge has its origin and its applications in social morphology.

The Chinese see in the Numbers two sets of Symbols capable of characterizing (hierarchizing) the various modes of grouping that fall into the categories of Yin and Yang. Its Sages, rejecting an arithmetical conception of unity, avoid ordering the Numbers in a continuous series formed by successive additions of 1. They do not feel the need to consider the numerical series as unlimited; they prefer to imagine it as a set of finite series capable (the first ten in particular) of representing cycles. Numerical symbols seem to them destined to evoke the device of a finite set, that is to say, to evoke the contour of this set by enunciating the divisions of this contour. The art of numbers is the specialty of the Masters of the Calendar, who are in charge of discovering points of reference in the sky and of dividing the celestial contour into sectors. It matters little to them to divide it into *equal* sectors; on the contrary, an arithmetical conception of unity would prevent them from doing so. Their first duty is to reconcile the classifications and to interweave them in such a way that possibilities of play can be extracted from these interweavings.

Heaven, in addition to its Summit (it is the Central Palace, the Palace of Supreme Unity. *T'ai yi*, counts as 1? doesn't it?), includes 4 quarters, but each of them does not correspond to 90°. The East Palace is at 70° 50' and the West at 75° 40'; the

---

circle. The outline of Yin, like that of Yang, is equal to the outline enclosing them both. If the dividing line were replaced by a line formed by four semicircles of twice the diameter, it would still be worth the same as the semicircle; the same would be true if the operation were continued, and the sinuous line tended to merge with the diameter: 3 would merge with 2. The *T'ai ki* is mentioned by the *Hi ts'eu* (where it appears in connection with the octagonal arrangement of the trigrams) in the paragraph where the *Lo chou* and *Ho tou* are named (*Yi king*, L., p. 373); it is probable that, from the time of Hi ts'eu, the *T'ai ki* has been imagined as the indeterminate form (I cannot say the boundary) toward which the *strong line* (odd, 3 half circumference, 3 sides of the hexagon), i.e., Yang, and the *weak line* (even, 2, diameter, 2 sides of the hexagon), i.e., Yin. A graphic theme similar to that of the *T'ai ki* is found in ancient iconography; it is the motif of the dragon embracing the column {on the theme of ascension and its relation to the idea of *ki* (summit) and tao; cf. *supra*, in this same Book, ch. IV}. The *T'ai ki* diagram appears, like the *Lo chou* and *Ho t'ou* diagrams, only under the Song. Only archaeological finds will be able to tell whether it is older. In any case, the elements of this graphic construction existed since ancient times. The jade jewels, which the Japanese call *magatama* (one of these jewels is, with the Mirror and the Sword, one of the three *protectors* of the imperial family) have a form which does not seem to be different from the half *T'ai ki* (part Yang or part Yin). *Magatamas* have just been found in southern Korea, adorning the necklaces of a man and a woman. Ancient Chinese literature does not mention these hooked jades, but does refer to the crescent moon as a "hooked moon". The moon is associated with jade. The *T'ai ki* diagram was considered an emblem of the phases of the moon during the Song.

North at 101° 10' and the South at 112° 20'.[166] Each quarter is divided into 7 sectors and the whole equator is divided into 28 mansions, which differ greatly in extent and of which two {*Fa* (today *Chen*, the Sword of Orion) and *Chen* (the Sword of Orion, today *Tsouei*} occupy the same region of Heaven. If there are 7 mansions per quarter, it is undoubtedly because the asterism of the Central Palace (Ursa Major), residence of the Supreme Unity, has 7 stars.[167] In a passage of the *Chou king* (which Sseu-ma T'sien has taken care to preserve), it is said: "The Seven Rectors and the Twenty-eight Mansions, the Tubes (= Music) and the Calendar, Heaven uses them to bring into communication (*t'ong*) the influences (*k'i*) of the Five Elements and the Eight Directions (the Eight Winds)?"[168] Moreover, the author (an expert in the field of the Calendar) has devoted an entire chapter of the *Historical Memoirs* to show how, connecting with each other, the classification by 8 (Winds) and the classification by 28 (Mansions) are also linked to the classification by 12 (Tubes and Months).[169] Sseu-ma Sien adds, on the perimeter of Heaven, the 8 winds to the 28 mansions, then divides the whole into 4 quadrants. 28 + 8 make 36, that is, 4 times 9. Sseu-ma Ts'ien thus grants to each of the quadrants 7 mansions plus 2 winds, without feeling hindered by the fact that the 7 mansions of a sector are in no case equal to 90°. Thus, in the detail of the equivalences established between the Months, the cyclic signs, the Winds and the Tubes, there are numerous singularities. The most curious is that the fifth month, which is *the month of the Summer Solstice*, is related to three Mansions depending on the Southeast Wind, while *the South Wind* (and the two Mansions linked to it) correspond to a single site, and the sixth month, the last of the Summer, is linked to the Southwest Wind with which the Autumn and the Western sector begins.[170] None of this worries Sseu-ma Ts'ien,

---

166 L. De Saussure, *Les origines de l'astronomie chinoise*, p. 100. A figure (p. 101) shows the inequality of the 24 mansions. The mean of the equinoctial and solstitial palaces is: 73°15' and 106°50', i.e., approximately 73 and 107 (*ibid*). The ratio is about 108/72 or 9/6. The winter, from the solstice to the cold food feast, lasted (including the 3 days of this feast) 108 days. Kouan tseu (ch. 3), starting from a division of the year into 30 periods of 12 days (15 for summer and spring, 15 for winter and autumn) attributes 96 days to spring and autumn, and only 84 days to summer and winter; in this case the equinoctial sectors are larger than the solstitial sectors. Note that Kuoan tseu opposes spring to summer and autumn to winter according to the ratio 8/7.

167 *SMT*, III, p. 311.

168 *SMT*, III, p. 301. Interpreters say that the Seven Rectors are the Sun, Moon, and Planets; but in another passage of the *Chou king*, where the Seven Rectors are mentioned, it appears that this expression, at least for Sseu-ma Ts'ien, meant the Big Dipper. (Cf. *SMT*; I, p. 58 and note 2). *T'ong*, to bring into communication, evokes the idea of circuit; *k'i* (influence), breath, the idea of rhythm. The phrase of the *Chou king* no doubt wishes to awaken the feeling of a double circular rhythm, earthly (Elements and Winds) and celestial (Mansions and Rectors). Note this ancient mention of the 5 Elements and their connection with the 8 Winds.

169 *SMT*, III, pp. 293 ff.

170 *SMT*, III, pp. 308, 309 and table on page 302. Is the fact that the south wind does not correspond to any of the 12 months to be related to the theoretical existence of a 13th month? This 13th month is assigned to a period after the 7th month, at the end of summer. Dividing 360 by 28 gives approximately 13 (364 = 28 x 13).

Book II - Chapter III - Numbers

one of the Masters of the Knowledge of the Ages. {On the other hand, he is keen to point out that one of the Southern mansions (it is called *e*) has 7 stars; it has 7, he says, because 7 is the Yang Number (and South = Fire)}.[171]

To reconcile and interweave heterogeneous classifications – in the hope that their superposition will facilitate the manipulation of symbols and, consequently, the manipulation of reality – such is the work, such is the ideal of the astronomer. Numbers have, for him, a premium virtue: *they know how to represent the various combinations which, broken down, can be attributed to the elements of a set, and they also allow these combinations to be combined among themselves.* Therefore, after having entrusted to the Numbers the mission of qualifying the compositions, we do not hesitate to ask them, treating them as cyclical signs, to characterize the positions. It is not a function very different from those which they fulfill as symbols of the various cyclic dispositions to which, *as the case may be*, it is appropriate to refer; when a number appears in a place, it is as a symbol of the device imposed, in this particular case, by such or such circumstantial characteristics of Space-Time.[172] Placed at the service of a cosmography and of a geometry whose primary datum is that Time and Space together form a concrete medium, the Numbers serve above all to represent the circumstantial forms of *the Unity or, rather, of the Total*.

It is to 3, the First Number, the Perfect Number (*tch'eng*), that all the great systems of classification are linked: the classifications by 5, as well as by 6, 4 and 7; the classifications by 8, as well as by 9, 10 and 12 (and by 24, 36, 60, 72, etc.).

Notably, it is the myths concerning the Patrons of Astronomy and the Art of Calendars that can bring out an instructive fact: the geometry of the scholars charged with ordering Time and Space is (like the whole system of numerical classifications) modeled on morphology, on the disposition of Chinese society as it begins to order itself by a principle of hierarchy. All Chinese classifications are linked to a square formation – which is a military formation – and to the design, which evokes the idea of roundness and twist, of a simple cross or a swastika.

I have already shown, with regard to the centered arrangement attributed to Time and Space,[173] how the *crossed arrangement* (which makes it possible to divide the Universe into 4 sectors and to place, as the principle of all hierarchy, in the Center, and to give it the emblem 5, the Unity, Total and pivot of the Total) *derives from a confrontation in battle, 3 against 3*, (where we find again, with the image of an axis, the memory of the jousting and of the ancient dualistic organization from which arose the conception of a Couple category, first model of numerical classifications). I have demonstrated this using the myth of *Hi-ho*,[174] who is the Sun, the Mother of Suns, the Solar Pair, but who is also the 3 Hi and the 3 Ho. Yao the Sovereign (who himself had the appearance of a Sun) used this double trinity in such a way as to draw a great cross; sending the cadets of the Hi and the Ho on mission to the four Poles, he kept near him, framing the Center in the manner of a Left and

---

171   SMT, III, p. 308.
172   Cf. *supra*, in this same chapter, sec. I.
173   Cf., in this same Book, chap. I.
174   Granet, *Danses et légendes...*, pp. 252 ff.

a Right, the elder of the Hi and the elder of the Ho, charged with directing the Sun and the Moon, the Yang and the Yin, for the Hi and the Ho, all 6, are astronomers as well as diviners. The Unity, one and double, left, center and right, front, center and back, is projected, as we see, as a double trinity, quartered in a cross, but in such a way that it fixes to the World a Center, either by opposing (the set worth 5) to 1, the Center, the cross that separates 4 sectors, or by opposing (the set worth 7) to 4 (the circumference, i.e. the Square) 3 (the pivot, i.e. the Circle); 4, 5 and 7 (insofar as the Unit decomposes into 6) can express the form and organization of the Universe. A similar theme is found in the myth of Tchong-li. Tchong and Li are also astronomers, and Tchong-li[175] is still the Sun. Like Hi-ho, Tchong-li is one, but he is also half of a Couple, his *right* half, as Tchong-li's brother Wou-houei (and grandfather of six grandchildren who came out of his mother's body, three from the left and three from the right) is said to have possessed only the *left* half of the body.[176] However, only Tchong-li is a fraternal couple: Tchong and Li. One of these brothers ruled Heaven and the other Earth, and indeed, it is from these prudent astronomers that the separation of Earth and Heaven, of Low and High, dates. But it is sometimes said that Tchong and Li are not brothers. Tchong, in any case, is part of a group of 4 brothers – who only count as 3 – two of them, dedicated to the *North* (Yin), are only a couple; the other two, genii of the East and West, frame this double unity; this trio is opposed by the only Li, who, not projecting himself triply, only commands a quarter of the horizon, only a sector of the World, that of the *South*, it is true, of Fire and Yang. Here are the crossroads points and four heroes in charge of the four directions; in the center, next to the Sovereign who must possess the Virtue of Heaven, will be placed a fifth hero, in charge of the Earth (*Heou-t'ou*). The Virtue of Earth belongs to the Minister who is second to the Sovereign and who, being one and threefold, is called "Three Dukes," just as the deans and chiefs of the villages are called "Three Elders." Nothing can show better the virtues which authorize 3, the Odd, to be the master symbol of any device expressing a hierarchical organization.[177] Moreover, we can see that, in the classification by 5, even when it tends to detach itself from the classification by 6, something of the old dualism remains: the central unit retains a *pair* value.

The traces of dualism are still visible when the progress of the Odd and the hierarchical principle lead to the reign of the classifications by 9 and 10. If in Heaven, Hi-ho, Mother of the Suns, has 10 sons, on Earth, a Sovereign like Yao (who has the appearance of the Sun) has himself 9 or 10 sons.[178] Yao had his vassal (or double), the Great Archer, kill 9 Suns who, by preventing his access to power, intended to usurp, in Heaven, the place of the only Sun then qualified to distribute light and shadow. He also had Chouen, his minister and double, kill (or at least banish) the eldest of his sons, of whom only (8 or) 9 were docile. The opposition 1 to 9 is but

---

175 Granet, *op. cit.* pp. 254 ff.
176 *Ibid.*, note 599.
177 *Civ. chin.*, pp. 221 ff.
178 Granet, *Danses et légendes*, p. 253, note 570, note 975 and note 583. The 19 Suns are assigned to each of the 10 days of the deary cycle.

another aspect of the opposition 1 to 3 or 3 to 3. When the Empire and the World are in disorder, 1 and 9 Suns may be seen fighting each other; usually the battle is between the rising Sun going to reign in Heaven and the descending Sun delaying to return to, on Earth, the West;[179] whether the players are counted by 2 or by 10 (1 against 9), the joust marks an opposition of High and Low. But if, at least in one of the fields, the players are 9, it is that the 9 marks, like a plane, the divisions of Space. The classification by 10 (= 9 + 1) comes out of the classification by 9, from which also derives the classification by (9 - 1 =) 8. When a Sovereign does not delegate four astronomers to the Poles, he banishes[180] a square of evil Genii (which, moreover, are also equivalent to a double trio); in this case, as a necessary counterpart, the one Man surrounds himself with a double band of beneficent Genii; he commissions the Eminent Eight to preside over things on Earth (*Heou-t'ou*: this is the title of the Genie of the Center and of the Earth whose emblem is 5), and entrusts to the Eight Excellent Ones the care of spreading the 5 Teachings in the 4 directions. All of them, *at two different levels*: material or moral, earthly or celestial, fulfill their task by delegation of the central authority (5 = Center). However, the mere fact that in each group there are 8, shows that their activity is peripheral. They exercise their activity not only in the four cardinal points, but also in the four angular points, that is, in the domain of the eight Winds and the eight Trigrams; in the eight squares which, placed side by side, form the four rectangles that draw a swastika around a central square, the axis of the World. When the Supreme Unity arranges the octagonal rose of the Trigrams and the 8 numerical symbols around the perimeter of the magic square, it rests, we are told, twice on the center (5 and 10).[181] That is to say (a new trace of primitive dualism) that the Center and the Unity *itself* are double, that a celestial plane is superimposed on the terrestrial plane, a Superior on an Inferior, and that finally the Center, *being a pivot*, unites Heaven and Earth. Thus, the Sovereign needs a double band of 8 auxiliaries to propagate its double central virtue. Sorting by 8 (or 2 x 8) is related, as is sorting by 10, to the division of the square into 9 squares. And the same is true (as I have shown in relation to the *Ming t'ang*, its 8 outer rooms and its 12 views of the horizon) of the classification by 12. The opposition of Earth and Heaven recalls the first dualism, but all these classifications show the progress of the idea of hierarchy. This progress is linked to the success of the Odd. Instead of projecting itself triply only twice, to end at first only in front of a pair of triple units, the Central Unit projects itself triply, forwards, towards the center, backwards;[182] the square is no longer simply delineated, by the tracing of a simple cross; it is totally limited by the branches of the swastika; the Universe no longer has 4 Sectors and 1 Center (classification by 5 Elements): it has 9 provinces, 1 center and 8 directions, winds or trigrams (classification by 8).

---

179 Ibid., pp. 377 and 399.
180 Ibid., pp. 238, 277.
181 Cf. *above*, in this same chapter, sec. II.
182 This triple projection being repeated on two planes, the 9 Provinces of the Earth correspond to the 9 Regions of Heaven.

Hi-ho, patron of soothsayers, master of Yin and Yang, commands the 8 Winds and the 8 Trigrams, just as the Sun and patron of astronomers, commands the play of light and shadow. There is a Hi-ho couple – as there is, among the Trigrams, a K'ien-K'ouen couple, father and mother of the 3 female Trigrams, who are sisters, and 3 male Trigrams, who are brothers –, and there are likewise 3 Hi brothers and 3 Ho brothers. The Hi and the Ho are still considered the Masters of the Sun and the Moon.[183] The Mother of the Suns (of whom there are 10) is not distinguished, mythically, from the Mother of the Moons (of whom there are 12). Both have the same husband. This Sovereign, who was the father of Three Bodies, also begot Eight Heroes who invented Dance and Music.[184] Raven or hare, the Sun and Moon have three legs. The Sun in his day must pass through 16 stations; to preside over the Night, there is, as to assist a Sovereign, a double band of 8 Genii.[185]. The ancient dances pitted the dancers 3 against 3; later, in the dancing choruses, the dancers were pitted 8 against 8.[186] We even know that there was once a confraternity of dancers in which, it is said, they danced for 2 and 3, that is, no doubt, for 8 and 9. The confraternity had, in fact, 81 or 72 members representing either (9 x 9) the 9 Provinces of the World, or (9 x 8) these 9 Provinces again, or) (8 x 9) the 8 Winds and the 8 Trigrams, recalling, in the one case, the Central Unit and the Number of the gnomon (81-80) and in the other the division of the Total (360) into 5 parts.

The origin of the great classifications is to be found in the myths that are usually related to the Sun and to families of Suns, because the numerical classifications were of interest above all to astronomers and, moreover, the Sun is the emblem of the Ruler. These myths are nothing more than a fabulation of jousting and ritual dramas. The geometry of these ballets reflects the structure and arrangement of ancient society. The essential classifications {by 6 and 5 (theory of the Elements), by 8 and 9 (Winds and Provinces)} signal, after the reign of bipartition (Yin and Yang: category of the Couple), the advent of male privilege and Odd privilege. The square formation and the formation by 3 characterize the urban and military organization. The city and the camp had a left district and a right district surrounding the residence of the chief, whose chiefs commanded the left and right legions; the armies were opposed, 3 legions to 3 legions, the royal army had only 6 legions. Cities and camps have 9 or 12 districts.[187] The world has 9 or 12 provinces; the *Ming t'ang* {whether it has 5 halls (simple cross) or 9 halls (swastika)} contains 9 sacred places and casts 12 glances on the horizon; but may not the 3 x 4 square be divided into 9 squares, 8 of which are on the edge; and, divided into 16, has it not,

---

183 Granet, *op. cit*, note 595.

184 *Ibid.*, p. 264. Similarly, the sovereign Tchouan-hiu (*Ibid.*, p. 243, note 4) had 3 sons, according to some, although others say 8 sons. He also had a son who was a three-legged turtle. This last feature is as close to the theme of the dance for 3 (on 1 foot) as it is to that of the 3-foot cauldrons. The three bodied owl (*Ibid.*, p. 523) (which is opposed to the three-legged turtle (*Ibid.*, p. 248)) is the double and 1 antithesis of the three-legged raven (themes of the Sun and the Friend of the Sun, *Ibid.*, pp. 527 ff.).

185 Granet, *Danses et légendes...*, p. 264.

186 *Civ. Chin.*, p. 300.

187 Granet, *Danses et légendes*, pp. 616 ff., note 1667; *Civ. Chin.* p. 229.

Book II - Chapter III - Numbers 177

on its 4 sides, 4 squares, so as to allow 2 x 8 glances on the horizon?[188] The city, the camp, the battle, the jousting of guilds geometrically illustrated the virtues of the numbers 8 and 9, 5 and 6, 10 and 12 intended to serve as multipliers and privileged classifiers, since astronomers could use them (and combine them) so as to divide 360 into (5, 6, 8, 9, 10, 12 or 30, 36, 40, 45, 60, 72…) sectors.[189]

Apart from the Pair category (linked to the idea of confrontation and simple alternation, as well as to the image of a linear axis), all numerical classifications are derived – 6 {simple cross, (6 or) 5 domains, 4 sectors} and 9 {swastika, (10 or) 9 domains, 8 sectors} serving as intermediaries – from 3, the Odd, creator of the Square and emblem of the Curve, synthesis of the Double and the Undivided, *yin-yang* Number, masculine Number, principle of hierarchy, symbol of the Nominal Total, first Number.

* * *

In China, numerical classifications control every detail of thought and life. By combining and interweaving them, a vast system of correspondences has been constructed. The division of things into the various Elements and Trigrams occupies the first place in this system, but other classifications, also numerically based, become entangled, complicating (or even reversing) correspondences and antagonisms. As a result of these entanglements and the infinite use of numerical classifiers, they end up having no more than a kind of mnemonic value; they only help in a purely external and scholastic way to connect the details of realities with the system of the World. This is the case, for example, when the *Hong fan*[190] divides governmental activity into 8 sections (food, goods, sacrifices, public works, instruction, instruction, justice, hospitality, army) or when the *Tcheou li*[191] classifies into numerical categories the powers of the Minister of Heaven (6 ministries, 8 regulations, 8 statutes, 8 principles of emulation, 8 principles of morality, 9 classes of workers, 9 incomes, 9 expenses, 9 tributes, 9 principles of authority…). It is not necessary to insist on the persistent vogue of numerical classifications; but the prestige they continue to exercise shows that, if the Chinese classify by means of numerical indexes, it is because they believe that these indexes are capable of informing them in some way about the nature of things.[192] Numbers began by having a more effective logical role. They were used to adjust things and the measurements

---

188 Cf., in this same chapter, sec. IV.
189 I would like to believe that Biot was not mistaken in stating that the mansions were first 24 and not 28 {the 24 primitive spindles are related to the time division of the day and the 4 additional spindles (8, 14, 21, 28) are related to the tropical year}. On this point, see A. Rey, *La Science orientale*, pp. 377 ff. The question, which is controversial, does not fall within the scope of this paper. I will limit myself to pointing out that the classifier 7 (linked to the idea of axis, to human size and to the size of the cosmic wheel spoke) is used above all to measure ritual time because of the formula $10 = (3 + 4) + 3 = 3 + (4 + 3)$. 7 is not a divisor of 360. When 28 mansions are counted, they must be combined, as soon as the contour of Heaven is to be divided into sectors, with the 8 Winds because $28 + 8 = 36$.
190 *SMT*, IV, p. 219.
191 *Tcheou li*, Biot, *Le Tcheou li, ou les Rites des Tcheou*, t. I, pp. 43 ff.
192 Cf. Book III, chap. II, on the role of numerical indexes in the theory of the microcosm.

of everything to cosmic proportions, to show that everything fits in the Universe. The Universe is a hierarchy of realities. To the classificatory function of Numbers is immediately added a protocol function. Numbers allow the hierarchical classification of all real groupings.

A rule dominates the protocol use of Numbers. This rule can help to understand the Chinese conception of the unit and the numerical series. Ritual techniques sometimes foreground small and sometimes large numbers. While the secondary deities, who are numerous, are entitled to a multiplicity of victims, to Heaven a single bull is sacrificed; Heaven is one and is sacrificed only to him, the One Man, the Sovereign. Quantity, moreover, is of little importance to Heaven and the other deities who are satisfied with the "Virtue" (*tö*) of the victims. But the multitude of common people eat as much as they can (they eat, it is true, only the portions that are not noble). The nobles themselves are not satisfied until the third course. A lord is satisfied with the second course and the king with the first. Yet twenty-six wooden vases full of victuals are placed before the sovereign, only sixteen on the table of a duke, twelve on that of a feudal lord, eight or six for a great officer of first or second rank… I could multiply the examples. Suffice it to say that the principle of these numerical rules was clearly defined by the Chinese. Sometimes "the large number (or size) is a mark of nobility: it is that the heart is turned outward… (sometimes) the small number (or small size) is a mark of nobility: it is that the heart turns inward."[193] That is, the hierarchy is expressed by means of selected numbers, running through the numerical series in one direction or another, with thought dominated alternately by a sense of expansion or concentration, by the idea of the *complete*, which are many, or of the *total*, which is one.

The same principle is found in the constant use of multiples in ritual techniques. The odd series: 3, 9, 27, 81, which seems to be naturally linked to unity, is therefore almost always preferred to the even series: (4), 8, 16, 32, 64. In most cases, it is used to make sensitive a rhythmic back and forth between the simple and the complex, combining at the same time spatial and temporal representations. We know that a king has 120 wives, not including his queen, who is one with him. This female retinue can be divided into four groups, or five if the queen is included. These groups, unequal in *size*, are also unequal in *value*, but in reverse. The king's wives have so much less nobility the larger and, consequently, the more distant from the Lord is the group to which they belong. Thus, there are 81 women of 5th rank, 27 of 4th rank, 9 of 3rd rank, 3 of 2nd rank, though only the queen shares the king's nobility. Viewed in space, these groups, so to speak, fit into each other. A sort of concentric rhythm[194] regulates their life in Time. Divided by 9 into 9 sections, the less noble of the royal women approach the Lord at the beginning and end of the lunations, one of the first nine and one of the last nine nights of the month. The women of fourth and third rank are likewise summoned to the king in sections of nine and twice a month, but for more central nights. To the group of three women of second

---

193 *Li ki*, C., I, p. 550.
194 Cf. Granet, *La polygynie sororale*…, pp. 37 ff. Cf. in this same Book, chap. I.

rank, whom the Lord also admits into his presence on two occasions, belong the 14th and 16th nights, both close to the holy night when the moon, all of her, faces the sun. It is during this one night, but it is during this whole night, that the queen remains, alone, in the presence of the One Man. A comparable use of numbers is found in the famous spring plowing ceremony.[195] The Sovereign plows first, but makes only three furrows. The three dukes of the palace plow after him, each with five furrows. After them come the nine ministers; each of them plows nine furrows; they must open 81 furrows. More numerous in work, they also have a longer task. Their task is secondary; they only repeat, prolong and celebrate the only effective work, the Real Work; the Earth is made fruitful as soon as the one Man has plowed in it. And, in the same way, what do the 120 wives and their multiplied unions count for? It is true that the royal fecundity, diluted, spreads rhythmically, finally reaching, with the 81 last wives, the smallest parts of the Universe; but the whole Universe is fecundated; a unique rhythm is given to universal life as soon as the Royal Couple, inviting the Moon and the Sun to face fixed hours, has united. If the protocol likes to use series of multiples, it is because these, while indicating a certain rhythm, evoke a nature or a disposition of the Total, which remains identical, even when considered under the Complete aspect and in all the detail of its composition. All multiples are basically equivalent, or at least their magnitude matters little, and yet numbers serve to estimate; but it is not the quantity that counts in what they estimate, it is the value, cosmic and social at the same time, of the groupings they label; it is the dignity or the power part of the categories they enable to classify.

It is not important, therefore, in number, the size they have. To hierarchize, to signal, so to speak, a *hierarchical rhythm*, it does not matter whether one goes through the numerical series or a series of multiples in one direction or the other. To be part of a group of 81 women is to be as far away as possible from the master and to receive from him only diluted favors; but to possess 81 women is tantamount to ruling the 9 Provinces and concentrating in oneself total authority. A simple nobleman can feed 9, 18 (= 2 x 9) or 36 (= 4 x 9) persons if he is of 1st, 2nd or 3rd rank; a great prefect can feed 72 (= 9 x 8), a minister 288 (= 9 x 32), a prince 2880 (= 9 x 320).[196] Numbers know how to express dignity, because they indicate the importance of the group they serve. They also know how to express it by indicating a coefficient of power or much prestige, i.e., a *social value*.

This is, for example, the function of the four odd numbers 3, 5, 7, 9. The room where the chief receives and eats forms a raised platform of 3 feet, if he is a simple officer; of 5 feet if he is a great officer, of 7 if he is a lord, of 9 if he is the king.[197] When the king dies, nine cowrie shells[198] must be used to close his mouth; he

---

195 *Li ki*, C., II, p. 335.
196 *Ibid.*, I, p. 326.
197 *Ibid.*, I, p. 547.
198 Cauri is the common name for a group of small and large sea snails, marine gastropod mollusks of the family *Cypraeidae*; these were used as shell currency in China and elsewhere (TN).

is wept continuously for 9 days; weeping continues for 9 months, kicking in series of 9 jumps; finally, after the final burial, the offerings are repeated 9 times.[199] Lords, great officers, officials are only entitled to 7, 5 or 3 offerings, cowries, jumps, months or days of weeping. Their body is more quickly prepared for final burial; it dissolves after less effort. Less time and fewer ritual gestures are needed to help them pass from life to death; vitality is less powerful the lower the dignity. Feudal society is a military society; prestige, rank and dignity are earned through contests and tests. The most important tests are archery; aren't feudatories called "archers"? In archery, one can demonstrate one's skill or loyalty (all is one) and the quality of one's will by shooting one's arrows at the right time (because the competition is done to music) and directly at the target. When one shoots them with force, he demonstrates his vitality, his courage: the power of his genius. Therefore, bows are constructed with the will (*tche liu*) and vitality (*hiue k'i*)[200] of their recipient in mind. To appreciate the dignity that the recipient deserves, it is enough to estimate the strength of his bow. Stronger bows are less bent. That is why it is necessary, in order to form a perfect circle, to take 9 of them, if they are bows that only a king will be able to use; but the circumference will be completed with 7 bows of lords, 5 bows of great officers or 3 bows of officers.[201]

Far from claiming that Numbers are the *abstract* signs of *quantity*, the Chinese use them to *represent the form* or *estimate the value* of some or other groupings which may be presented as groupings of things, but which one always tends to confuse with human groupings. Numbers describe the form or *value* of things, because they indicate the *composition* and *power* of the human grouping to which these things belong. They express, in the first place, the share of power which belongs to the Chief in charge of a human and natural grouping.

The Sages can, therefore, represent by means of the Numbers the protocol order that governs universal life. It is the social rules that allow them to conceive this order. The order of society is feudal. A hierarchical logic will thus inspire the whole system of numerical classifications and the very idea that one has of the Numbers.

* * *

Numbers have a logical function; both classificatory and protocol. They label hierarchical groupings. The numerical labels serve to qualify the value of each grouping as a whole; they make it possible to estimate the content and the tension of the group, its cohesion, its concentration, that is to say, the power of animation signaled by its leader. The scenarios of the ballets or of the danced jousts shed light on the geometrical or cosmological role of numbers; the rules of construction of the arcs used to test the Chiefs explain the function of numbers when they are

---

199 *Ibid*, II, p. 184; II, p. 548; II, p. 141; II, p. 543. Officers and grand officers are buried in the third month; their ancestral temple consists of 3 chapels (they have 3 ancestors to whom they personally worship). The lords have 5 chapels in their temple; they are buried in the 5th month; the king has 7 chapels; he is buried in the 7th month. The weeping continues two months after the final burial (from the rank of great officer): hence the numbers, 3, 5, 7, 9.

200 *Tcheou li*, Biot, *op. cit.*, II, p. 596.

201 *Ibid.*, II, p. 596.

Book II - Chapter III - Numbers 181

used to estimate, not these magnitudes, but the values. In both cases, one observes that the same idea dominates the Chinese conceptions; although the notion of arithmetical unity or of sum remains in the background, the Numbers appear as Symbols representing *the aspects* – more or less noble – *of totality*, of efficacy, of power. These symbols, rather than being quantitatively differentiated from each other, oppose, correspond, evoke or choose each other. All the even numbers are the Even, all the odd numbers are the Odd, and, thanks to the Odd numbers, mutations of the Even and Odd numbers are possible. Numbers can be substituted for each other and, being different in size, can be equivalent;[202] all sets are possible, since the system of division of the units can vary. But mutations, substitutions and equivalences are controlled by a fundamental idea. Starting with 3, the first Number, all numerical symbols are labels of the Many, i.e., approximations of the Whole (*tsin*). 3 is only a synthesis. Only the One, which contains the Two, the Couple, the Community Unity, expresses perfectly the Total, which is the Whole. The Total, Yi, the *All*, is the universal power of animation that belongs to the Chief, to the One Man. The whole Chinese conception of Numbers (as we have seen, the conception of Yin and Yang, and as we shall see, the conception of Tao) comes from social representations, from which it has not claimed to abstract at all. To conclude, we can conclude with an anecdote.

The *Tso tchouan* relates the debates of a council of war:[203] should we attack the enemy? The Chief was seduced by the idea of fighting, but he had to engage the responsibility of his subordinates and follow their advice first. Twelve generals, including himself, attended the council. Opinions were divided. Three leaders refused to go into combat; eight wanted to go into battle. The latter were in the majority and proclaimed it. However, the opinion that gathered 8 votes did not prevail over the one that gathered 3. 3, that is, almost *unanimity*, which is something very different from *majority*. The general-in-chief will not fight. He changes his opinion. The opinion to which he adheres by giving it his *single vote* is then imposed as *unanimous* opinion.[204]

---

202 Cf., in this same Book, the beginning of ch. III.
203 *Tso tchouan*, C., II, p. 59.
204 On the necessity of unanimity in the Councils, see *Civ. Chin.* pp. 326 ff.

Chapter IV
THE TAO

Like the bipartite classification of Yin and Yang, numerical classifications derive their value from a feeling of communal unity or, if you will, of the Total. This feeling is that which a human grouping experiences when it presents itself as an intact and complete force; it arises and is exalted at festivals and assemblies; a high desire for cohesion then prevails over the oppositions, the isolations, the competitions of daily and profane life. The simplest and most permanent of these antagonisms and solidarities has been translated into the conception of Yin and Yang as an antithetical couple, but united by the most perfect of communions. The classifications by 6 and 5, 8 and 9, correspond to a progress of the need for cohesion. They seem to be linked to a more complex organization of society and the idea of a federal union. Whether they suggest the image of a military assembly in a square, or a battle array, or the camp, town or house divisions of male assemblies, it is a feudal organization that they bring to mind. Like feudal groups, the oriented groupings of active realities, of which the Five Elements and the Eight Winds are symbols, do not merely confront and commune with each other; these sectors of the World are organized around a Center upon which they seem to have depended from the beginning. It is because men see in their Chief the author of a harmonious distribution of all activities, human or natural. The Sovereign orders the World and animates it; by the mere fact of holding his Court at the center of the confederation, everything coexists and endures in the Universe. The attribution of total authority to a personage, whom we prefer to call the One Man, is accompanied by the conception of a regulating power. This power is imagined, more or less realistically, under the aspect of a supremely effective principle of order: the Tao.

Of all Chinese notions, the idea of the Tao is not the most obscure, but the one whose history is the most difficult to establish, so great is the uncertainty about the chronology and the value of the documents in this respect. The practice of calling Taoists or followers of the Tao those advocates of a doctrine considered to be very definite may lead one to believe that the notion of Tao belongs to a particular school. But I believe that it should be ascribed to the realm of common thought.

All authors, Taoist and non-Taoist, use the term Tao to point to a set of ideas that remain very similar, even in systems whose orientation is very different. At the heart of all conceptions of the Tao are the notions of Order, Wholeness, Responsibility and Efficiency.[1] Writers considered Taoist are marked by a desire to eliminate from these notions whatever they may contain of social representations. Far from attributing the original conception of the Tao to the authors who are sometimes called the "Fathers of Taoism," I believe that through them it presents itself under the aspect most distant from its primary value. These thinkers use the word Tao to express the effective Order which dominates – an *undefined power* – over the whole of apparent realities, remaining, in turn, rebellious to any determinate realization. However, when they come to illustrate this idea, they often content themselves with evoking the *total art* which enables a Chief – usually Houang-ti[2] who is its patron, but who is also the first Sovereign in Chinese history – to rule the World and the Empire. The Tao, the one principle of all success, is for them the art of ruling.

This art, for the authors of the so-called Confucian school, is also a sovereign art that embraces all knowledge. They see in the Tao the Virtue proper to the upright man (*kiun tseu*); the latter, like the Prince (*kiun*), prides himself on possessing no particular talent.[3]

The Taoists, for their part, oppose the word *tao* to various terms (*chou, fa*) meaning "recipes, methods, rules" and recalling the procedures of specialized technicians.[4] This does not prevent one from possessing, with the help of the total Knowledge implied in the Tao, the Genius which makes it possible to succeed in astronomy or physics, to be an Immortal or to command this or that province of nature.[5] By giving these examples, Tchouang tseu wants to make visible the indefinite possibilities conferred by the Tao. It is remarkable that he borrows them from common mythology. In an ancient hymn in honor of Heu-tsi, the Prince of the

---

1   In 1913, I brought the notion of *tao* closer to that of *mana* (in *Coutumes matrimoniales de La Chine antique*). All my readings since then have confirmed me in the idea that this comparison was correct. Just as the concept of *mana* remains latent in the most archaic societies and only begins to express itself in the most evolved civilizations, the idea of *tao*, latent in China from the time the Yin and Yang symbols were conceived, only emerged when the Chinese adopted a hierarchical organization; it bears the mark of the latter.

2   See, for example, *Tchouang tseu*, in L. Wieger, *Les Pères du système taoïste*, p. 287, *ibid.*, p. 417.

3   This is the main theme of *Tchong yong* (*Li ki*, C., II, pp. 427 ff.; *Civ. Chin.*).

4   *Tchouang tseu*, chapter T'ien hia, Wieger, *op. cit.* pp. 499 ff.

5   *Tchouang tseu*, Wieger, *op. cit.*, p. 255, and *Houai-nan tseu*, II; Granet, *Danses et légendes...*, note 1428.

Harvest, the poet proclaims that this Hero "possessed the Virtue (Tao) of helping (Nature)":[6] he succeeded in making everything he planted grow. Most probably the word *tao*, in mythical and religious language, expressed the idea of an efficacy indeterminate in itself, but which was the principle of all efficacy.

The "Fathers of Taoism" hardly used the word *tao* without relating it to the word *tö*. For them, this term designates Efficiency when it tends to particularize itself. The double expression *tao-tö*[7] has never ceased to convey, in common language, the idea of Virtue, but not in the purely moral sense of this word. *Tao-tö* means "prestige," "princely ascendancy," "effective authority."[8] *Tö*, in the language of myths, is the quality of the most complete, the most real geniuses.[9] It is no doubt the desire to analyze, by opposing them, two notions, in principle not very different, that has led to giving *tö* the value of "specific virtue" and to indicate with this term, in philosophical language, the idea of an Efficacy that is singularized by its realization. While *tö* awakens above all the feeling of particular successes, *tao* expresses the total Order which expresses the totality of achievements.

Tao (or Tao-tö) is Efficiency, but it is characterized by its regulating action, insofar as it merges with a sovereign principle of organization and classification.

* * *

The first meaning of the word tao is "way"; this is also the meaning of the word *hing*, which we have come to translate as "Element."

As with the notions of Yin and Yang, scholars who have endeavored to interpret *hing* and *tao* in European terms are divided into two groups: some do not hesitate to recognize in the Tao and the Elements an acting principle and natural forces;[10] others, without further hesitation, see in the Elements substances and in the Tao also a substance, for they render it the sum of Yin and Yang, which would also be substances.[11]

These divergent statements are often related to views on the chronology of the documents.

For many scholars, the "theory of the five elements" is of recent invention (3rd-2nd centuries BC). If it is alluded to in the *Hong fan*, it is either because this document is itself recent or because it has been interpolated.[12] According to Chavannes, the vogue of the theory can only be traced back to Tseou Yen (4th-3rd centuries BC). We may attribute to Tseou Yen much genius and all sorts of inventions; we

---

6   Che king, C., p. 351; Granet, *Le dépôt de l'enfant sur le sol*, p. 31.

7   Although we include at the end of this book a table showing the equivalences between different types of romanization, given the importance of the term *tao-tö*", we will indicate its equivalences below. Using the Wade-Giles romanization system, *tao-tö* is written *tao-te*, using Pinyin it would be *dao-de*. The name of the book attributed to Lao tseu (*Lao tseu* in Wade-Giles, also *Lao tze*; and *Laozi* in Pinyin) is well known: *Tao-tö-king*, written as *Tao Te Ching* in Wade-Giles and *Daode Jing* in Pinyin. (TN).

8   Civ. Chin. p. 278; Granet, *Fêtes et chansons anciennes*, pp. 79, 197.

9   Civ. Chin., pp. 21, 25.

10   SMT, Introduction, p. CXLIV.

11   Maspero, *La Chine antique*, pp. 483, 440.

12   Ibid., note 684.

know him only from a few lines, added by Sseu-ma Ts'ien to the biography of Mencius.[13] It follows that Tseou Yen had founded a very flourishing school at Ts'i.[14] He is said to have patronized the idea that the Elements succeed one another by *destroying* each other. If this were indeed the primary theory, one might conclude, as Chavannes did, that the Elements "are great natural forces which succeed one another by destroying each other."[15]

An observation by Chavannes goes beyond this hypothesis. He assumed that the theory of the Five Elements (*wou hing*) expounded by Tseou Yen coincided with the theory of the Five Virtues (*wou tö*: five efficiencies), which flourished around the same time.[16] The latter served as a framework for politicians who used mythical or folk traditions to reconstruct ancient Chinese history. They wanted to show that events, both in the historical order and in the natural order, are ordered by a succession of a cyclical kind; every Virtue (*tö*) exhausted must be replaced by another Virtue whose time must reign. The idea, no doubt, was not new – the notion of Tao (or Tao-tö), as we shall see, at least as used by divination theorists, implies the concept of cyclic succession – but only the form in which it is presented. By insisting on the ideas of destruction and triumph, it tended to justify the spirit of conquest which had become very powerful during the period preceding the founding of the imperial unit.[17]

Perhaps we are entitled to declare the theory of the Five Elements recent when we relate it to the theory, thus understood, of the Five Virtues.[18] But it must be added (such is the interest of the comparison) that the Elements, when they characterize a dynastic Virtue, appear as Symbols. To say that they succeed one another by way of triumph is to say that, in order to define its emblematic Virtue, a Dynasty must choose the Element which is opposed, in the quadrangular rose, to the Element adopted by the vanquished Dynasty. It must be concluded, not that the Elements are natural forces, but that they are valid as Symbolic Rubrics.[19]

Did the "theory of the Five Elements really begin with the idea of a succession secured by triumph"?

Indigenous interpreters agree that the "order of triumph" of the Elements derives from their order of production. The latter is reflected in the oriented arrangement attributed to the Elements by the *Hong fan*. The arrangement of the *temple* leads to placing Water (1) in the North, Fire (2) in the South, Wood (3) in the East, Metal (4) in the West, and Earth (5) in the Center. We have seen that this order results from the formula of the scale {10, 7, 9, 6, 8, (5)}. In order to establish an

---

13   SMT, ch. LXXXIV (cf. note 450).
14   SMT, Introduction, p. CXLIV.
15   SMT, Introduction, 1. c.
16   GTS, Introduction, fn. 230.
17   Civ. Chin., pp. 42 ff. On traditional history and its frameworks, see *Ibid*.
18   See above for the relationship drawn between the 5 Virtues theory, the rules of ancestral worship, and the divisions of the family group.
19   The Ts'in, who attributed to themselves the symbol of water, gave honor to black, severity, etc., and adopted, for the division of the unit, the index or classifier 6; 6 feet equaled one step, carriages had 6 horses. Cf. M. Granet, *op. cit.*, p. 49.

Book II - Chapter IV - The tao

equivalence between the numerical symbols of the tubes which follow one another and the stations which also follow one another in a fixed order and can be said to follow one another, it was necessary to attribute to the different sites, starting from a given point on the horizon (the South, for example), and in order, the symbols 7, 9, 6, 8. This imposed order facilitated the union of the Notes and the Seasons-Directions, on the one hand, with the Elements, on the other.

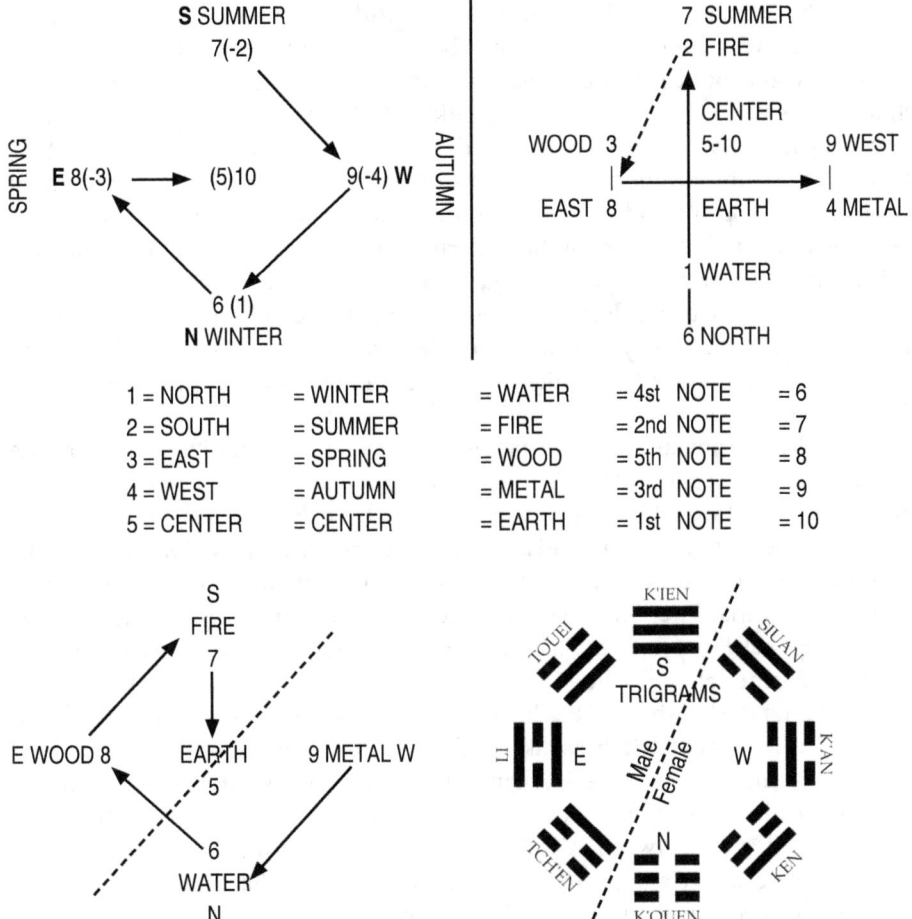

The latter, in fact, are distributed in two pairs (Water-Fire, Wood-Metal), each consisting of antithetical terms, and the attribution of a direction to the two terms of one of these pairs was indicated *in advance*. Fire "tends upward" and upward is the same as southward, while fire may well characterize summer, the warm season. Water "tends downward," and Down is North, while Water may well characterize Winter, which is a season without water; for the Waters then disappear from the Earth and are at the bottom of the North of the World. The center was perfectly adapted to the initial note emitted by this pattern tube and, consequently, to this same note lowered by an octave; the congruent pair 10-5 was thus placed in the center of the cross. Since the second note and the congruent pair 7-2 were assigned to the South, the order of the Stations and Notes required the assignment of the pair 6-1 to the North. If, therefore, we began by assigning the Water Element to the Bottom and to the North-Winter, the order imposed allowed assigning the Fire Element, antithetical, predisposed to be assimilated to the Summer, to the South and to the Top. The 3rd note, 9, and the pair 9-4 must necessarily go to the West, and to the East, the 5th note, 8, and the pair 8-3; the antithetical pair of Elements formed by Metal and Wood must, consequently, be distributed between these two opposite sites. Wood could advantageously be placed in the East and linked to Spring, while it was easy to imagine reasons for linking the Metal Element to Autumn and converting the West symbols[20] of the Notes (7, 9, 6, 8) respectively into the symbols of Fire and South-Summer, Metal and West-Autumn, Water and North-Winter, Wood and East-Spring and 10, (with the congruent number 5) going in the Center, 5 and the four small numbers of the congruent pairs (2, 4, 1, 3) could legitimately indicate the order of the assignments symbolized by the arrangement of the *temple*. The solidarity of the two orders of enumeration of the Elements is not doubtful; the one indicated by the *Hong fan*, which obeys the arrangement of the *temple*, and the one assumed by the *Yue ling*, which is the order known as "the succession of the Elements by production".

We could take advantage of this fact to claim a certain antiquity in favor of "the theory" of the succession of the Elements by production, and this not because the order of enumeration followed by the *Hong fan* (whose date can always be lowered) seems to agree with this theory. It is, on the contrary, an anomaly found in the latter, which assumes the antiquity of the order followed by the *Hong fan*. Although it is easy to say that Fire (Summer) produces Metal (Autumn) which liquefies, the Chinese say that *Fire produces Earth* and Earth produces Metal. These metaphors are not altogether absurd {the minerals are found in the Earth, and the Earth is cultivated after the brushwood has been set on fire and the Wood has been reduced to ashes; it can be said (strictly speaking) that Fire produces it}. But they imply that the order of succession of the Elements is no longer considered strictly equivalent to the order of production of the notes. Instead of being placed, as the latter order would dictate, between Wood (Spring) and Fire (Summer), Earth (Center) is placed between Fire and Metal. This order (Wood, Fire, Earth, Metal, Water) is explained by a rule of the Calendar. It is between Summer and Autumn that the ideal month is inserted,[21] whose conventional duration corresponds to the position held by the head (*pivot* of Time) in the center of the Calendar House. This month

---

20   If the transversal arrangement (*Ho t'ou*) of the numbers, the notes, the Seasons-Directions and the Elements deserves to be considered as an image of the world, it is because it breaks the coherence of the various systems of classification. This image seems effective because it shows that the order of production of the musical symbols reproduces the natural order of the seasons and takes into account an opposition of the elements that also seems natural. It is the numbers that show the coherence, hence its prestige and that of the numerical classifications.

21   Cf. *supra*, in this same Book, ch. I.

without duration is probably not a very recent invention; it implies a division of the year grouping autumn and winter, spring and summer, as if the year were traversed by an N-E – S-W, axis analogous to the axis separating the male and female trigrams in the arrangement of Fou-hi.[22] The usage, however, corresponds to an innovation; the end of summer and the beginning of autumn are, like this month without duration, empty of any kind of religious festivity. By contrast, a season in the *center* (= Earth) of the Calendar House seems much more appropriate for the Chief at the end of Spring (= Wood). It is then the time of a series of feasts, perhaps the most important of the year, and these feasts involve a kind of retreat, for they have been called the "cold food" feasts.[23] They included the ceremony of moving the fireplaces into the open air; the fire, in winter, had been kept indoors in adobe buildings or underground dwellings, and it could well be said, at the inauguration of the Warm Season *the Earth produces Fire*. Moreover, at the moment when the sap rises and nourishes the plants, the Chief, as we shall see, must remain motionless in the *Center* of Space, placing himself between Earth and Heaven. However great the antiquity of the order of production of the Elements, which conforms both to the order of the Seasons and to the rules of Chinese seasonal morphology, we will not claim for it any primacy. The order of triumph is closely associated with it. It results from the cardinal opposition of the elements Fire-Water and Wood-Metal, an opposition illustrated and respected by the cross arrangement that highlights the order of production.

Some Westerners admit, following Chinese interpreters, that the idea of production and that of opposition or triumph are equally ancient. On the other hand, they concede to the *Hong fan* a certain antiquity.[24] But instead of concluding, as the text and arrangement of the *Hong fan* seem to invite, that the Five Elements are the rubrics presiding over a given system of classification, they profess that "there must therefore have been various theories" about them. They thus take sides against Chavannes' idea and, refusing to see in the Elements natural forces, make them "five real substances."[25] The interpreter who uses this expression, however, recognizes the authenticity of two important passages of the *Hong fan*. In one of these, each element is defined by a certain taste; this taste is intended to be the "physical property" of the "real substance" which is the corresponding element; fire, for

---

22   Cf. *supra*, in this same Book, ch. III, sec. II.
23   The Chinese "Lent" begins on the third day of the third month (last month of spring), 105 days, it is said, after the winter solstice. (We have seen that 105 characterizes the North, in the magic square with center 6). The festivals of the low season, the season of the dead which ends when the living return the souls of the dead to their subterranean abodes and prepare to resume the work of secular life, is followed by a period of almost voluntary starvation; it is the time chosen for the various games (swinging, pole vaulting) intended to ensure the success of the harvests.
24   Maspero, p. 440.
25   *Ibid.*, p. 440. Maspero writes: "(The elements) are simply the five real substances which bear these names (Water, Fire, Wood, Metal, Earth), and have the physical properties thereof." I am not sure I understand Maspero and the meaning he gives to the expression "real substance" when, for example, he applies it to Fire.

example, "produces bitterness." The other passage[26] is devoted to the "Five Activities (*wou che*)," which "produce" five kinds of Virtues. The "activities" are thought to correspond to the Elements. Will it be said that these Five Activities, Gesture, Speech, Sight, Hearing, and Will, are (real) substances, and, in what they produce, we shall see "their moral properties"? The Five Flavors appearing in the system of correspondences preserved in the *Yue ling*, and the Five "Activities" of the *Hong fan* are the first evidence of a great system of correspondences established between the macrocosm and the microcosm, of which we shall speak later. Do we not see that the Five Elements are the great Rubrics of a system of correspondences, that there is no need to treat them either as substances or as forces, that they are, above all, the symbols of the Five groupings of emblematic realities distributed in the Five Sectors of the Universe?

In the expression *wou hing*, the word "five" (*wou*) has perhaps more meaning than the word *hing* translated as "Elements".

The *wou hing* are always associated with the *wou fang* and the *wou wei*. The *wou wei* are the five cardinal positions and, in the language of Hi ts'eu, the five positions each marked by a pair of congruent numbers.[27] The *wou fang* are the five directions, or rather the five sectors formed by the Center and the four Orientals, when considered in a square arrangement, for *fang* means 'square'. The *Hong fan* itself evokes, in enumerating the Elements, the image of a crossroads. The Five Elements must therefore be seen as symbols of a general distribution of things in a Space-Time where the *temple* delimits four areas and marks a center.

We know the importance of the classification by 5, which is linked to the classification by 6. The *Hong fan* opposes to the Five Happinesses the Six Calamities, and the Five Elements themselves are sometimes counted as Six. They are mentioned in a chapter of the *Chou king*, of whose authenticity and antiquity there can be no doubt. This chapter contains the text of a harangue said to have been delivered before a battle by the son of Yu the Great,[28] where he accuses the enemy of having despised the Five Elements and the Three Regulators.[29] Glossologists do not agree as to what the Three Regulators were; it seems that the expression belongs to the art of the Calendar and is to be compared with the expression *wou ki*; the latter, in the *Hong fan*,[30] designates the Regulators of the year. It may be that the Three Regulators refer to a ranking by 6, linked to the ranking by 5. The main interest of the harangue in which the Five Elements are mentioned lies in the fact that it was recited in a camp, and that it was addressed to the Six Chiefs and the Six Legions of the royal army; it is by drawing a *temple* that camps and cities are built. When the Elements are counted as Six, the Element Earth may be doubled by substitut-

---

26 This is section II of *Hong fan*; it immediately follows the section on the Five Elements (cf. Book III, chap. II).
27 Cf. *above*, in this same Book, ch. III, sec. II.
28 *SMT*, I, p. 164.
29 We have seen that 3 counts as half of the total of 6.
30 *SMT*, IV, p. 221.

ing Food and Drink, or simply coupled with Cereals;[31] there are, in addition, 5 or 6 Cereals, as there are 5 or 6 Domestic Animals or 6 Domestic Animals and 5 Wild Animals. Significantly, at least when counted as six, the Elements are assimilated to the six *Fou. Fou* means "storehouse."

The idea of a concrete distribution and classification could not be better evoked.

The notions of Yin and Yang also evoke the idea of a concrete distribution and classification. Yin and yang are the symbols of two opposing and alternating groupings characterized by their location in space-time. This conception expressed an organization of society based on a double morphology and on the principle of rotation. Yin and yang can appear both as a pair of alternating forces and as a bipartite group of antagonistic realities; they cannot be described solely as forces or substances. The same must be true of the Elements. Used as sub-rubrics under the domain of Yin and Yang, a pair of master rubrics, they can sometimes resemble, if not forces, at least active principles, and sometimes, if not substances, at least groupings of active realities. Linked both to the Seasons and to the Directions, they alternate or oppose each other, fight or succeed each other peacefully. However, the theorists who have speculated about them have considered them mainly as dynastic symbols or rubrics capable of specifying a certain order of Space-Time. Whether the Elements are Wood, Metal, Fire, Water and Earth is, after all, a secondary fact and a matter of nomenclature or metaphor; the main idea of the conception (I refrain from calling it "theory") is that of a grouping in sectors, not simply facing each other, but united to a center. Are the Elements forces or are they substances? There is no point in taking sides in this scholastic debate. What is essential is to observe the interlocking arrangement of the elements.

This arrangement is fundamental, just as the image of two fields on either side of a kind of sacred axis is fundamental to the conception of Yin and Yang.

What does the design of the *temple* relate to? This is the first question: why did the Chinese call the symbols of the different sectors of the world *hing*? This is the second point of the problem. We must decide whether it is correct to translate *hing*, "way" by "Element." One could, without ignoring the value of the word, because *hing* expresses the ideas of conducting oneself and acting, *wou hing* for "Five Agents." This is the translation that comes to mind when we treat the Elements as natural forces. When we treat them as substances, and allow ourselves to be dominated by the fact that the name given to each of the Elements seems to evoke an aspect of matter (water, wood, etc.), we may retain more validly the translation "Elements"; in this case, it would be well to explain the fortune of a word chosen to express a notion so far removed, at first sight, from its original meaning. For us,

---

31   *Tso tchouan*, C., III, p. 380, and *Ibid.*, I, p. 468. The six storehouses are mentioned together with the 9 cantos; the latter are related to the 5 notes and, consequently, to the 5 Elements. I could multiply the examples of solidarity of the classifications by 5 and 6 (see Granet, *Danses et légendes…*, Index of the words Five and Six). However, I will point out a passage from the *Chouen tien* (SMT, I, pp. 59-61); no text is more venerable. It speaks of a sacrifice to the Six *Tsong* (usually regarded as the Six Dominions or Celestial Agents, the Elements) and, immediately afterward, of a distribution of the Five Badges (to the Five Categories of officials).

who link the notion of Elements to the idea of *thistle*, if we justify our interpretation, we shall have justified, at the same time, the translation of the word *hing* by the term already used to translate στοιχετον.

Tao means: "Way." It is the same set of facts that will give rise to the images from which the Chinese began to designate with two words that arouse the idea of "way" the five cardinal headings and the great principle of order and classification.

* * *

The words *hing* and *tao* evoke the image of a path to follow, a direction to give to conduct. *Tao*, in particular, brings to mind the best and most regular conduct, that of the Sage or Sovereign. These derivative meanings have enabled commentators to give a purely moral interpretation to literary fragments steeped in mythical thought. Some of these fragments, in which poetic forms are found, are still very instructive.

Some fragments of a versified feat whose hero is Yu the Great have come down to us. One of them may help to understand the relationship between the words *hing* and *tao* and the early metaphorical values of these terms.

It is about the work of Yu. Every Dynasty founder has to do the work of a demiurge. However, no one was as qualified as Yu to organize the World. We know that his step was the standard for measuring length and that a tortoise brought him the Nine Tch'eou of the *Hong Fan*, the image of the World. It should be remembered that *tch'eou* suggests the image of traced furrows, which means domain and boundaries of the earth and that the same word can designate divinatory letters. The turtle did not come out of the waters alone to favor Yu the Great. If the Hero managed to overcome the Flood, it was thanks to a Dragon who was able to open a path to the Waters by making drawings on the ground. The word *tao*, "way," is hardly distinguishable from a word with a similar pronunciation, which itself means "to open the way, to put in communication." When a ruler is qualified to rule, such as Yu, Heaven is said to "open the way" (*k'ai Tao*) for him. By this is meant that Heaven authorizes him to re-establish good manners, and a Prince or a Sage is indeed obliged, most of the time while traveling, to build up the World with his Virtue. But in mythical times, when Heaven opened the Way (*Tao*) to him, a Hero had, in a more realistic sense of the word, to build the whole Universe. This is how Yu, going through the Earth of Men, managed to adjust it to its true measure.

We are told that *taking into account the seasons*, he "opened (*k'ai*) the 9 Provinces (of the World), made the *9 Roads* (*tao*) communicate, dammed the 9 Marshes, and leveled the 9 Mountains."[32] In describing the details of these works, the word *tao* is used to express the idea that Yu knew how to make the rivers flow.[33] The same word is found at the beginning of a detailed description of the Rivers and Mountains, arousing both ideas of traversing and putting in order: Yu "*tao* (traversing and putting in order) the 9 Mountains..., *tao* (traversing and putting in order) the 9 Streams."[34] When the Hero had finished arranging the 9 Provinces so

---

32   *SMT*, I, p. 101.
33   *SMT*, I, p. 127.
34   *SMT*, I, pp. 135 (n. 1) and 140.

that the World, in all 4 directions, could be inhabited and cultivated, he found that he had also put the Six *Fou* in perfect order. The Six *Fou* are known to be the Six Storehouses {namely: the Five Elements (*hing*), plus the Cereals}. Yu immediately *distributed the lands* (domains) and the names of the families, and then shouted, *"Let them take (my) Virtue (tö) as their guide! Let them not deviate from my Ways (hing)."*[35]

The formula used by Yu should be regarded as a declaration of advent. It crowns the mythical work in which the Hero's virtue (*tô*) has been expended to trace the Ways (*tao*). No doubt the connection between the word *hing* (if we do not follow the gloss which, as is natural, gives it the moral meaning of "conduct") and *tö* (if we do not give it the moral meaning of "Virtue" and if we remember that it is an equivalent of *tao*) is significant. Perhaps the hypothesis is justified that the word *tao* began by evoking the image of a *real circulation* whose purpose was to delimit, by means of a tracing of paths (*hing*, *tao*), the sets of realities (inheritances, names, symbols, insignia) that were to be distributed among the faithful of the Four Directions and to which the Five Elements were assigned as rubrics.

This hypothesis makes it possible to attribute to the original meaning of the word *tao* its meaning of regulatory power and effective order. It also makes it possible to understand the value of the expressions *Wang Tao* and *T'ien Tao*: the Real or Celestial Order (the *Tao*).

It is by circulating on the Earth that the Sovereign, imitating the march of the Sun, comes to be regarded by Heaven as a Son.[36]

Such is the ritual tradition attested by an ancient poem which attempts to explain the title of Son of Heaven and the principle of the Royal Power.[37] When, in turn, they wish to define the Royal Power, the Calendar Masters declare that the role of the Chief is to institute the Five Elements and the Five (categories of) Officers, to assign to men and deities (*chen*) very distinct tasks.[38] By dividing the functions, by classifying things and beings, the king avoids a mixture of vulgar and divine activities, a disorderly contact between Heaven and Earth.[39] The contact between Earth and Heaven can only be established in a useful and splendid way through the intermediation of the Sovereign, the sole master of public worship. He travels the Empire in the direction of the Sun (*T'ien tao*), to adjust, both the Directions and the Seasons, the Badges of the faithful to the symbolic Virtues of the four quarters of the World; he thus demonstrates that he is able to make a celestial Order (*T'ien Tao*) reign over "the Earth of Men (*T'ien hia*)." He deserves to be called Son of Heaven (*T'ien tseu*), for he has demonstrated that he possesses the

---

35   SMT, I, p. 146.
36   The circular path of the Sun is called the "Celestial Way (Tao)".
37   Che king, C., p. 424.
38   SMT, III, p. 323. I translate here by "gods" the word *chen*, which designates all the sacred powers, the chiefs, as well as the divinities whom alone they could worship.
39   SMT, III, p. 325. This theme is related both to the myths of the separation of Heaven and Earth and to the distinction between religious rites (public and of public interest) and magical rites (private and for private purposes).

Heavenly Way (*T'ien Tao*). He deserves to be called King-Sovereign (*Wang*) when he demonstrates that he possesses the Royal Way (*Wang Tao*); for this he must demonstrate that he is the One Man and the only Way by which Heaven, Man and Earth can communicate.

Between the two subjects of *T'ien Tao* and *Wang Tao*, there is only a difference in appearance. Both are related to the same ritual conception. The development of epic poetry and political literature brought the idea of *T'ien Tao* to the surface, while the idea of *Wang Tao* remained closer to the lyrical expression that ritual events had first received. By compelling the sovereign to go and check the insignia of the feudatories at the four ends of the Empire, to mark the extremities of a gigantic crossroads, epic poetry found the material for a heroic narrative into which many myths, and in particular that of the World Saved from the Waters, could be incorporated. To the accounts of these epic labors were naturally joined descriptions of administrative geography; such is the origin of one of the oldest works of scholarly literature, the famous *Tribute of Yu*, where administrative themes are interwoven with poetic passages.[40] Magnified by poetry, the theme of the imperial trek retained all its prestige for centuries. The founder of the Chinese Empire, Che Houang-ti, and the great Han ruler, Emperor Wou, never ceased to undertake great journeys; both wanted to put the Empire in order by building an immense crossroads from North to South and from East to West.[41] The lyrical theme of the Royal Road itself has persisted for a long time; but, disguised in mystical formulas, it is expressed in the ambition of many potentates to ascend to the heavens. However, it is possible to reconstruct the ritual events that this theme first translated.

The epic legend of the royal walk corresponds to another legend, closer to the ritual truth. The Sovereigns send delegates to the Four Poles or, a more dramatic and at the same time more real theme, they expel Four Evil Genii from the Four Cardinal Mountains, while receiving as guests the vassals of the Four Directions led by their Chiefs called Four Mountains. For this purpose they open the four gates of their city or camp. Thus a reign or a new era is inaugurated.[42] The traditions connected with the *Ming t'ang* are linked to this legend. The *Ming t'ang* is not only the Calendar House where all the periods of Time are inaugurated; it is also the place where the vassals form themselves into a square; as they do at every military gathering, around the square mound on the Ground, each wearing the Badge appropriate to his Direction.[43] Whether one starts from five halls or nine, the plan of the *Ming t'ang* reproduces the plan of the camps and cities, and thus the plan of the World and its Nine Provinces; it matters not whether this plan gives the idea of a simple cross or of a swastika. It is enough for the Sovereign to circulate through the House of the Calendar for this cross to be set in motion and the Sun and the Seasons to follow the celestial Order or Path (*T'ien Tao*). We have seen that there was a time when the Chinese drew, with the aid of numbers, the cross of the odd

---

40   *SMT*, I, pp. 103 ff.
41   *Civ. Chin.*, pp. 119, 140.
42   Granet, *Danses et légendes...*, pp. 238 ff.
43   Cf. *supra*, in this same Book, chap. I

numbers superimposed on the cross of the even numbers, just as a square small board (the Earth) and a round small board (Heaven) were superimposed on an instrument used by diviners and connected by a *pivot*.

Now, to qualify the 11, *hierogamic synthesis of the central numbers 5 and 6, representing Earth and Heaven, this number was said to constitute in its perfection* (tch'eng) *the Way* (Tao) *of Heaven and Earth*.[44]

Is not the Royal Way (*Wang Tao*) the axis that starts from the Center of *Ming t'ang*, the pivot around which, inflated or simple, the cross revolves when the king, imitating the Sun in its path, travels through the House of the Calendar? Or rather, is it not the One Man, master of the celestial and royal Tao, who is this axis and this pivot?

The word "king" (*wang*) is written with a sign composed of three horizontal lines representing, according to etymologists, Heaven, Man and Earth, which are joined in the center by a vertical line, because the role of the king is to unite. The traditions preserved on the graphic symbols are, in this case, no less instructive than the traditions preserved on the numerical symbols. To close the winter, the ancient Chinese held a festival which served to renew the Chief's Virtue or to establish a King of the Year.[45] It included many games and tests, for a Chief must prove his Virtue by triumphing in public games. There was a drinking challenge; after getting drunk, one had to be able to *stand upright*. There were sexual tests; the first chiefs, who seem to have borne the title of "Great Intermediary," were responsible for universal fertility and, from time immemorial, the Chinese have thought that the Sun *is lost* (*T'ien tao*) if the King does not, at the right time, sleep with the Queen. Doubtless there was another test of endurance; the Chief, skidding limply or motionless as a stump, waited and caused the sap to rise.[46] There was, above all, a test on the May pole. This pole stood in the center of the House of Men which was the prototype of the *Ming t'ang* and which was a underground house, for, when one reached the top of the pole, one could suckle from Heaven – that is how one becomes a Son of Heaven – or rather the Heavenly Bell, but the nipples of the "Heavenly Bell" (these are the stalactites) hang from the ceilings of the caves. By winning the test of ascension, the new Son of Heaven deserved, *becoming the link between Heaven and Earth*, to impose his stature on the *gnomon*, his measure on the *pattern tube*; he had identified himself with the Royal Way.

The Chinese have retained some memory of this triumphal ascent; from time immemorial, they have always dreamed that they ascended to Heaven, or even suckled from it, and, moreover, it is said that to accede to the throne is to "ascend to the summit" (*teng ki*).

---

44 Cf. *supra*, in this same book, chap. III, sec. II.

45 I briefly mention here some facts to which I reserve the right to return in another book. See *Civ. Chin.*, pp. 223 ff.

46 The expression *jen tao* (word for word: the way of man) designates the virile act. Tao is not, strictly speaking, a creative power, but it is the emblem of the rhythm of universal life.

Now, the 5th Rubric of the *Hong fan* – it is the central Rubric, and we know that when the tortoise brought it to Yu, the *Hong fan* was a magic square with a center of 5 – has as its emblem the *Houang Ki* or the *Wang Ki*, "the August or Royal Peak."⁴⁷

These terms are usually translated as "the highest (*ki*) (Perfection) of the Sovereign (*Wang* or *Houang*)." However, a venerable gloss, which the Chinese attribute to K'ong Ngan-kouo, interprets this expression as "*the great Way* (Tao) *Central*." Any gloss, I know, is suspect, even when attributed to Kong Ngan-kouo. But, by a stroke of fortune, an apparently ancient poem has been incorporated into the text of the 5th Section of the *Hong Fan*; this poem recalls Yu's remarkable statement quoted above, "*Let there be no deviation from my Ways* (hing)!" and it is impossible not to understand it as a declaration of advent. I translate it word for word:

> Let there be no bending! Let there be no bowing!
> Follow real equity (*Yi*)!
> No special affection!
> Follow the Real Tao!
> No particular hatred!
> Follow the royal path (*lou*)!
> No bowing down! No factiousness!
> The Real Tao, how broad it is!
> Nothing factious! Nothing bending!
> The Real Tao, which is united!
> Nothing that turns backwards! Nothing that bends sideways!
> The Royal Tao is straight!
> Join the one who possesses the Ki!
> Run to the one who possesses the Ki!⁴⁸

It cannot be guaranteed that this is the text of the proclamation that the lucky winner of the royal test pronounced to the faithful from the top of the pole. But it is a fact that he who possesses the Royal *Tao* is also "he who possesses *Ki*" and that *Ki* means *peak* and also *ridge beam*. It is also a fact that the poet sees no difference between *Ki* and *Tao*, nor between the ideas of *Tao, Lou* and *Yi*. Like *hing* (Element) and *tao*, *lou* means "way," but only in the material sense of the word; does not "the actual *tao*," which is described as "broad" or "united," also evoke a material image? As for *Yi*, equity, it is a virtue, but one which may well relate to all these concrete terms; it is the virtue which inspires respect for yours and mine and which must preside over the distribution of *lots*, names or ranks (*ming*) and inheritance (*fen*).⁴⁹ Now, what is the *Houang ki*, emblem of the 5th Section, center of the *Hong fan*?

---

47 Within the sign *houang* is the sign *wang* (image of contact). The terms *houang* and *wang*, which may be translated as "august," belong to political nomenclature (Chinese history knows the Three August and the Three Royal (Dynasties) (cf. M. Granet, *op. cit.*, part I, chap. I)) and to religious nomenclature; the fathers are called august, *houang* or *wang*, when, after their death, they have ascended to the Court of the Heavenly Sovereign.

48 *SMT*, IV, p. 222.

49 Cf. *infra*, Book IV, ch. I, sec. III.

In feudal assemblies, the sovereign collects and then redistributes the 5 Badges. Is not the *Wang ki* or the Royal *Tao* the principle – equitable, when taken in a moral sense – of the distribution of the fiefs and the 5 Badges among the vassals coming from the Four Directions to the Center of the confederation? Let us note here that the "Fathers of Taoism" imagine the Tao under the aspect of a kind of responsible distributor (it is through him that a being is – it is not said: god, table or bowl, but – sword of price or vulgar sword)[50] and that Tchouang tseu sees in the *Tao* "the *Ki* of all things: *Tao, wou tche Ki*."[51] The connection between the two terms is all the more remarkable in that it closes a passage in which the *Tao* is regarded as both the medium and the center of equivalences and contrasts, of attractions and repulsions, of the alternating hierogamy which constitute the *giratory* evolution of the universe. I cannot deny it; for the interpreters (or authors) of the *Hong fan* who thought to quote this old poem, the idea it was intended to express was indeed that of a moral perfection, made of impartiality, of elevation, of uprightness; in short, of the perfection implied by the central position of a Chief situated above all factions, above all particular groupings. But it remains to explain this whole set of metaphors and to say why the words chosen to designate a central and complete Perfection are sometimes *ki*, ridge beam,[52] sometimes *lou*, road, or *tao*, which may be described as "broad" and "united." Why, above all, all these images that seem to evoke the spectacle of a vertical station – the one imposed on drinkers for the drinking challenge – or the sight of a vertical pole?

When the chiefs founded a capital and determined the crossroads through which the tributes of the Four Directions would reach them, they had to observe the play of light and shadow (the Yin and Yang) and plant a gnomon.[53] The political mysticism of the Chinese has always maintained the principle that in the capital of a perfect ruler, at noon in midsummer, the gnomon should cast no shadow,[54] The myths are even more instructive. In the very center of the Universe – where

---

50 *Tchouan tseu*, Wieger, *Les Pères du système taoïste*, p. 257. Note the idea of hierarchy.

51 *Ibid.*, p. 439. At the heart of this conception are the themes of *potlatch* and communal union.

52 Although he does not seem to have thought that such a translation should be justified, Fr. Wieger (*Histoire des croyances religieuses et des opinions philosophiques...*, p. 61) has interpreted the expression: *houang ki* as "pivot": "The king," he says in his interpretation of *Hong fan*, "is the pivot around which everything on earth revolves, as in Heaven everything revolves around the pole, the seat of the Sovereign on high. These expressions show that Fr. Wieger has based his interpretation on ideas common in Han times. The procedure may seem abusive, but if it has led to a correct interpretation, it is because the ideas in use under the Han, as expressed by Sseu-ma Ts'ien, for example, were derived directly from ancient conceptions. Sseu-ma Ts'ien writes (*SMT*, III, p. 342): the Bush {(The Big Dipper) whose 7 stars correspond to the 7 Rectors (see pp. 235, 242, 321)}"is the chariot of the Sovereign; *moves in the Center*; governs the 4 Directions; separates Yin and Yang; determines the 4 Seasons; balances the 5 Elements; evolves the divisions of Time and the degrees (of Heaven and Space); *fixes the various accounts*". Sseu-ma Ts'ien (*Ibid.*, 339) states elsewhere that *T'ai yi* (the Supreme Unity, cf., in this Book, ch. III, sec. II) resides in the Pole Star which is called *Tien ki: the Peak of Heaven*.

53 *Civ. Chin.*, p. 265.

54 *Civ. Chin*, p. 229.

the perfect Capital should be – stands a wonderful Tree; it unites the Nine Fountains with the Nine Heavens, the Snow World with its Top. *It is called the Erect Log* (Kien-mou), *and it is said that at noon nothing standing near it, perfectly erect, can cast a shadow.* Nor does anything there produce an echo.[55] Thanks to a synthesis (which is perfect, because it results from a hierogamy), all contrasts and alternations, all attributes, all insignia are reabsorbed in the central Unity.

The expressions *Houang* (or *Wang*) *Ki* and *Wang Tao* together acquired a moral value, and *Tao*, like *Ki*, entered the language of the sages. All these terms evoke the ideas of Real Perfection and Real Virtue; but *Tao* became the symbol of efficient Order only after having pointed to a complex of very concrete images and feelings. If the *Tao* (way) could assume the meaning of Efficiency, Virtue, Authority, suggesting at the same time the idea of a total Order entirely conforming to the celestial order, it is because the inauguration of a princely power was accompanied by a distribution of the things of this world among the groups submitted to a new Chief who distributed among them the Sectors of the Universe. To proceed with this distribution, the Chief had to undergo an investiture test. Before he went to distribute the Badges by circulating over the earth in the manner of a Sun (*T'ien Tao*), he had, in order to merit the title of Son of Heaven and One Man, to rise, upright and fused with the axis of the World, upon the Way (*Wang Tao*) through which, at sacred moments, Heaven and Earth enter into communion.[56] The *Tao* became the emblem of a sovereign Order after having represented, at first, the pivot – mast or gnomon – around which both shadow and light revolve.

* * *

If I am right, and if *tao* {way, central way, (*gnomon*)} and *hing* {way, element, (στοιχετον)} are jointly explained from the image of a pivot and a circulation, the oldest of the scholarly definitions of Tao will be easily understood. It is the one given by the *Hi ts'eu* and which we have already encountered:[57] "*yi yin yi yang tche wei Tao*: one (aspect) yin, one (aspect) yang, that is the Tao."

Now we know that we should understand: "*all* yin, *all* yang, that is the Tao." The Tao is a Total composed of two aspects which are also total, because they *totally* (*yi*) replace each other. *The Tao is not their sum, but the regulator* (I do not say: the law) *of their alternation*.

The definition of the *Hi ts'eu* invites us to see in the Tao a Totality, so to speak, alternating and cyclical. The same Totality is found in each of the appearances, and all contrasts are imagined on the model of the alternating opposition of light and shadow. Above the categories of Yin and Yang, the Tao plays the role of a supreme category which is, as a whole, the category of Power, Totality and Order. Like Yin and Yang, the Tao is a concrete category; it is not a First Principle. In fact, it pre-

---

55 Granet, *Danses et légendes...*, note 767. The theme of the sun tree or hollow tree is always connected with the idea of a royal residence. Where the King resides the tree of Life grows.

56 The Tao is the 11, the total unity which resolves in itself the Even and the Odd, Heaven and Earth, the 5 and the 6.

57 And explained from a mythical theme which speaks of the K'ong-sang, the Tree of the Hollow Mulberry, Solar and Real Tree, Tree of Life.

BOOK II - CHAPTER IV - THE TAO

sides over the play of all groupings of acting realities, but without being considered either as substance or as force. It plays the role of regulating Power. It does not create beings: it makes them what they are. It regulates the rhythm of things. All reality is defined by its *position* in Time and Space; in all reality is the Tao; and the Tao is the rhythm of Space-Time.

In the conceptions recorded in the *Hi ts'eu*, the knowledge of the Tao merges with the science of occasions and places to which the divinatory art gives the key. By learning to discern the propitious situations in each particular case, this art develops the sense of the organization of the World; it makes known the details and the whole. It is therefore the prerogative of the King, the Prince (*Heou*), the great man (*Ta jen*), the gentleman (*kiun tseu*).[58] Kings, princes, great men, and gentlemen command the lower class (*siao jen*), the little people, because the divinatory science enables them to acquire a Wisdom which is indistinguishable from Holiness; this active Knowledge is the Tao.

Possessing the Tao, one can order Time and Space, one knows, one is governed as soon as one is initiated into the game of divinatory Symbols. These symbols, as we have seen, exhaust reality. The order of the World comprises 11,520 specific situations designated by the word *wou*, which is applied both to things and to their symbols.[59] The 384 lines of the Hexagrams concretely evoke or rather elicit the whole of the apparent realities of which they are the symbolic realization. Each line alone connotes a set of these realities: 24 or 36, depending on whether it is weak or strong, *yin* or *yang*. Thus, each line has the value of a symbolic rubric. However, in itself it is only the simplest symbol of Yin or Yang, of Even or Odd, of split or continuous. But it is defined and singled out by the place it occupies in a given hexagram. It is, then, its situation in the set of symbols that specifies the attributes of each of these concrete categories that are the 192 *yang* lines, the 192 *yin* lines. These attributes are revealed when we examine the place that the line occupies in one of the 64 hexagrams. We proceed to this examination by successively considering the neighboring lines of the same hexagram, or by comparing two homologous lines of two hexagrams. We see then that one symbol is substituted for another, which is expressed by saying: when two lines, one weak and one strong, interchange their places, a substitution (*cheng*) occurs (*pien houa*).[60]

This passage from one symbol to another, which is considered a substitution, is the index, or, more exactly, it is the active sign, the *sign*, of a *mutation* (*yi*) taking place in the actual course of things. "Alternate productions (*cheng cheng*), that is

---

58 The expression *Ta jen* belongs to the mystical language and designates the Hero who knows the secrets of personal power (Cf. *Civ. Chin.*, p. 421). The expression *kiun tseu* belongs to ritual language. It was used successively to designate the knight, then the honored man (cf. *Civ. Chin.*, p. 263), who owes his authority to the science of rites. All these expressions are used for each other, interchangeably, by the treatises forming the *Yi king*. The distinction between mystical and orthodox currents was far from being realized in the 4th-3rd centuries BC.

59 Cf. *supra*, in this same Book, ch. III, sec. II.

60 *Yi king*, L., p. 350.

what mutations are."[61] This formula is intended to imply that each of the appearances we wish to see realized is the product (*cheng*) of the appearance which it itself must produce (*cheng*). The learned idea of mutation is based on representations similar to those we have discussed in connection with the alternation of (animal) forms under the alternating action of the categories Yin and Yang.[62] It is not things that change, it is Space-Time, which imparts to them their rhythm. The word *houa*, which is used to denote the alternations of forms {and which also designates the actual mutations operated by the magicians (*houa jen*)}, appears in the expression *pien houa*, which is used to express the substitution of a divinatory symbol for another divinatory symbol. The term *pien* alone gives the idea of a cyclic transformation. The *Hi ts'eu* uses it to express the alternation of aspects of which a door, made to open and close, may awaken the idea.[63] It is this alternation which, for the diviners, constitutes the Tao.

Thus, in the technical language of divination, the word *Tao* expresses the essential rule which lies at the bottom of all mutations – both real and symbolic – because it presides globally over all mutations. The Tao appears, then, as the Principle of Order that presides over both the production – by way of alternation – of sensible appearances and the manipulation – by way of substitution – of the symbolic rubrics that point to and give rise to realities. It is all together (for between the technical order, the real order, the logical order, it is not necessary to distinguish) the Power of regulation, which is obtained by manipulating the symbols, the effective Knowledge that presides over the substitutions of the symbols, the active Order that is realized, by means of perpetual mutations, in the totality of the Universe. These mutations are always realized, real or symbolically, without real change, without movement, without expenditure. Chinese authors insist on the meaning of the word *yi* (mutation), which evokes the idea of "ease" and excludes that of work. Realities and symbols *mute*, and we *mute* them without expending energy on it.

* * *

Mythic thought, and with it the various techniques used to order the World, is permeated by the belief that realities are generated by symbols. The work of reflection carried out by the theorists of the divinatory art has led, by giving it a systematic twist, to reinforce this disposition of the Chinese mind. Conceiving the Tao as a principle of Order which governs indifferently mental activity and the life of the World, it is uniformly admitted that the changes which may be observed in the course of things are identical with the substitutions of symbols which occur in the course of thought.

Once this axiom is accepted, neither the principle of causality nor the principle of contradiction could be called upon to take the role of guiding principles, not

---

61   Ibid., p. 356. Legge translates: "Production and reproduction is what is called (the process of) change". The literal meaning of the expression "*cheng cheng*" is: (the) product which produces (in turn its producer)."

62   Cf. *supra*, in this same Book, ch. II.

63   Cf. *supra*, in this Book, ch. II.

because Chinese thought indulges in confusion, but, on the contrary, because the idea of Order, the idea of an efficient and total Order, dominates it, reabsorbing in it the notion of causality and the notion of genus. When we start from the ideas of mutation and efficient Virtue, there is no reason to conceive a logic of extension, nor an experimental physics, and we retain the advantage of not being obliged, in imagining parameters, to take away from Time and Space their concrete character.

The idea of mutation removes all philosophical interest from an inventory of nature in which it is proposed to constitute series of facts by distinguishing antecedents and consequents.

Instead of recording a succession of phenomena, the Chinese record alternations of aspects. If two aspects seem to them linked, it is not in the manner of cause and effect, but they seem to them *paired* like the right side and the left side, or, to use a metaphor in use since the time of *Hi ts'eu*, like echo and sound, or, again, shadow and light.[64]

The conviction that the Whole and each of its component totalities have a cyclical character and resolve themselves into alternations dominates thought so well that the idea of succession is always superseded by that of *interdependence*. Therefore, there is no problem with retrograde explanations. Such a lord could not, during his lifetime, obtain hegemony, for we are told that, *after his death*, human victims were sacrificed to him.[65] Political failure and a bad funeral are aspects of the same reality, which is the prince's lack of virtue, or rather, they are *equivalent* signs.

What they are pleased to record are not causes and effects, but manifestations conceived as singular, though grafted on the same root, the order of appearance being of little importance. *Equally expressive, they seem to be substitutable*. A river that dries up, a mountain that collapses, a man that transforms into a woman, etc., announce the imminent end of a dynasty.[66] These are four aspects of the same event, an obsolete order disappears, giving way to a new one. Everything is worthy of mention, either as a precursor or as confirmation of a sign (or series of signs), but there is no reason to look for an efficient cause.

When a relation is established, one never thinks of *measuring* the terms placed in relation. What is considered are not phenomena, and it is not necessary to take into account their order of magnitude. They are only signals for which quantitative assessments of size or frequency are of little importance. The most useful warning signals are the most singular, the faintest, the rarest, the most furtive. A bird destroying its nest[67] provides the clue (physical and moral) to a disorder of Empire whose gravity is extreme, since the feeling of domestic pity is lacking, even in the humblest beasts. Therefore, the milder apparitions deserve to be cataloged, and the stranger ones are more valuable than the more normal ones. The catalog is not intended to reveal sequences, but is drawn up with the intention of revealing solidarities. Instead of considering the course of things as a series of phenomena that

---

64   *Yi king*, L., p. 369.
65   *SMT*; II, p. 42; Granet, *Danses et légendes...*, p. 105.
66   *Civ. Chin.*, pp. 29 and 30.
67   *Ts'ien Han chou*, 27 b^1, pp. 4b ff.

can be measured and then related, the Chinese see in sensible realities only a mass of concrete signs. The task of enumerating them belongs not to physicists, but to chroniclers, History takes the place of Physics, just as it takes the place of Morals.[68]

Far from pretending to isolate facts from the conditions of time and space, the Chinese regard them only as signs which reveal the qualities peculiar to this or that Time and Space. They do not think of recording them by relating them to a uniform and immutable system of reference points. They try not to forget anything that might reveal their *local value*. To record them, they use indications of time, space and measure, which are proper to a specific epoch of the world, to a specific sector or rubric.[69] They multiply the systems of classification, then they multiply the interweaving of these systems. They avoid everything that would be comparable and focus only on what appears to be substitutable. They avoid anything that might lead to measuring in abstract units. Numbers are used less to add equal units than to represent concretely, to describe and situate, and finally to suggest the possibility of mutations justified by the identity or equivalence of numerical symbols. The principle is to identify *by reference to rubrics*, without abstracting or generalizing and rather singularizing, reserving however, thanks to symbolic versatility, ample possibilities of substitution. Concrete solidarities are infinitely more important than abstract relations of cause and effect.

Knowledge consists in constructing collections of evocative singularities. The king's garden or his hunting park must contain all the animal and vegetable curiosities of the universe. Those that no searcher has been able to find are, after all, really there, sculpted or drawn. Collections pretend to be complete, especially as far as monstrosities are concerned, because one does not gather so much to know as to be able to, and the most effective collections are not made up of realities, but of symbols. He who possesses the symbol acts upon reality. The symbol takes the place of reality. It is a question, then, of realities and facts, not of noticing sequences and quantitative variations, but of possessing and having at one's disposal symbolic rubrics and tables of recurrences constituted thinking only of the interdependencies of the symbols.

When one particular appearance seems to *call* another appearance, the Chinese believe that they are in the presence of two coherent signs which evoke each other by a simple effect of *resonance*;[70] both bear witness to the same state, or rather to the same aspect of the universe. When one appearance *mutates* into another, this mutation serves as a signal to which other signs must respond in unison. It indicates the advent of a new *concrete situation*, comprising an indefinite set of coherent manifestations. As to the manner in which this substitution, which is not a change, takes place, it is known that every mutation affects the Total and is, in

---

68 The chapter cited in the previous note contains a large number of clues of the type noted above. Most of the Dynastic Histories contain similar, extremely long chapters, which purport to give the key to many important historical facts.

69 Cf. *above*, in this same Book, ch. I and ch. III, sec. IV. To each dynastic epoch corresponds a system of measures (*Civ. Chin.*, pp. 27, 29, 31, 49) and of denominations.

70 *Tchouang tseu*, Wieger, *Les Pères du système taoïste*, p. 419.

itself, total. There is no need to look for a common measure between two symbols that testify to two concrete aspects of the whole World. The consideration of second causes is of no interest; it has no application. What explains all the detail of appearances is not a detail of causes, it is the Tao.

The Tao is not in itself a first cause. It is only an effective Total, a center of responsibility, or, again, a responsible environment. It is not a creator. Nothing has been created in the World, and the World has not been created. The heroes who most resemble demiurges merely organize the universe.[71] Rulers are responsible for the Order of the World, but they are not its authors. When they have Efficacy, they succeed, in a given area and during a given epoch – determined according to their Authority – in maintaining an Order of civilization to which the Order of things is linked. The Tao is only the sublimation of this Efficiency and of this Order. In order to give a rule to action and to make the world intelligible, it is not necessary to distinguish between forces, substances, causes, and to bother with the problems involved in the ideas of matter, motion, and work. The feeling of the interdependence of symbolic realities and their apparent achievements is sufficient in itself. It invites us to recognize solidarities and responsibilities. It dispenses with the need to conceive of a Cause, but also to seek causes.

These characteristics of their thinking did not prevent the ancient Chinese from displaying great mechanical aptitude; the perfection of their bows and chariots attests to this. But this is how they imagine the progress of an invention. When one of their philosophers wants to explain the invention of the wheel, he says that the idea was supplied by flying seeds spinning in the air.[72] Rejecting mechanical explanations, Chinese thought does not seek to exercise itself in a domain which would be that of motion and quantity. It stubbornly confines itself to a world of symbols which it does not wish to distinguish from the real universe.

To know the Universe, it is enough to enumerate the signs. But, if to each symbol corresponds a singular reality, each symbol possesses an indefinite power of evocation. By a sort of direct effect, it gives rise to a series of substitutable realities and symbols. This *contagious virtue* of symbols differs radically from the participation of ideas. There are no limits to the suitability of different symbols. Consequently, we see no advantage in classifying ideas or things by genus and species. Since no relative sense can be given to the principle of contradiction, it is not used. Instead of classifying concepts, it is a matter of ordering the realities, or rather the symbols, which seem more real because they are considered more efficacious, and

---

71 *Civ. Chin*, pp. 20, 22, 27.

72 *Houai-nan tseu*, p. 17. In the history of Western science, what has most interested the Chinese is not, perhaps, Newton's apple, but the anecdote of the two cat doors that the physicist made. The idea that the smaller cat deserved to have a hole for itself, and that it was smaller, appealed to the Chinese, no doubt because it was pleasurable. It is not said that they did not find it profound. – The old houses opened with a door made to the measure of the head of the family; woe to the father whose son, born on the longest days of the year, was not immediately put to death. This son would grow up unduly and, as soon as his height exceeded the opening of the door, he would kill his father (Granet, *Danses et légendes...*, p. 532).

it is a matter of arranging them, taking into account their efficacy, in a hierarchical order.

The distinction between Identity and Otherness is overcome by the antithesis of the Equivalent and the Opposite. Realities and symbols arise by simple resonance when they are equivalent; they are produced rhythmically when they are opposites. The world and the spirit simultaneously obey a single rule, which seems, in principle, to be sustained by two formulas. These are not *the like produces the like* and *the opposite comes out of the opposite*, but *the equivalent aligns with the equivalent and the opposite responds to the opposite*. These two formulas, which do not imply the idea of genus any more than that of cause, both express the same sentiment; each of the appearances of the Universe or of the steps of thought results, like the Universe itself, from the interdependence of two complementary aspects.

Yin and Yang are not opposed in the form of Being and Non-Being, nor even in the form of two Genders. Far from conceiving of a contradiction between two aspects, it is admitted that *yin* and *yang* complement and perfect (*tch'eng*) each other, both in reality and in thought. In the multiplicity of appearances, some (those which can manifest simultaneously), linked by a simple and distant solidarity, are equivalent (*t'ong*) and contagious without being confused; the others (those which contrast together) are opposites, but are united by a communal interdependence which is manifested by their cyclic succession (*cheng cheng*). The Chinese avoid entrusting to the principle of contradiction the function of ordering mental activity. They attribute this function to the principle of harmony (*ho*: harmonious union) of contrasts. The effective Order which governs thought and action is formed by contrasts, but excludes the possibility of opposites both in absolute and relative sense. It is not necessary to constitute genera and species. The Order is realized by constituting groupings of symbols that have the value of active rubrics. All these rubrics take turns in the work (the different Elements alternate their reigns, as do Yin and Yang); the more detailed classifications only serve to translate a more complex feeling of Order and an analysis (more advanced without ever becoming abstract) of the rhythmic realizations of this Order in a Space and a Time entirely composed of concrete parts.

The Chinese representation of the Universe is neither monistic, nor dualistic, nor even pluralistic. It is based on the idea that the Whole is distributed in hierarchical groupings in which it is found in its totality. These groupings are distinguished only by the power of Efficiency that is proper to them. Linked to hierarchical Space-Time as much as they are singularized, they are differentiated, so to speak, by their content, and even more, by their tension; we see in them more or less complex, more or less diluted, more or less concentrated realizations of the Effective. Knowledge has as its object, in the first place, a plan of development of the Universe that seems to be realized through a hierarchical distribution of concrete rubrics. Just as they refrain from classifying conceptually by genus and species, the Chinese have no taste for syllogism. What would syllogistic deduction be worth for a thought that refuses to deprive Space and Time of their concrete character? How can we affirm that Socrates, being a man, is mortal? In times to come and in other spaces, is it true that men die? On the other hand, one can say: Confucius is dead, therefore I shall die; there is little hope that anyone deserves greater fortune in life than the greatest of the Sages. Chinese logic is a logic of order or, if you will, a logic of efficiency, a logic of hierarchy. The preferred reasoning of the Chinese has been compared to the Sorites paradox,[73] but, with the exception of certain dialecticians,[74] and the first Taoists who tried to derive from the ancient idea of Totality the notion of Infinity or, at least, of the Indefinite,[75] this reasoning does not resolve itself into a chain of conditions; it tends to reveal the circulation of a principle of Order through the various realizations, more or less perfect, and consequently hierarchized, of this Totality that must be found in each of its manifestations.[76] Disregarding inductive or deductive reasoning, the Chinese strive to bring order into thought in the same way as they introduce order into the World, that is to say, into Society. They give their symbols and rubrics a hierarchical arrangement through which the authority of each of them is expressed.

Neither the principle of contradiction nor that of causality has the empire attributed to the governing rules. Chinese thought does not systematically deny them, nor does it feel the need to give them philosophical dignity. The Chinese apply themselves to distinguish as they apply themselves to coordinate. But, instead of isolating by abstraction of types and causes, they seek to establish a hierarchy of Efficiencies or Responsibilities. The techniques of reasoning and experimentation do not seem to them to deserve as much credit as the art of concretely recording signs and enumerating their resonances. They do not pretend to represent reality by conceiving relationships and analyzing mechanisms. They start from complex representations and retain a concrete value for all their symbols, including cardinal rubrics. These symbols and rubrics serve to stimulate meditation and awaken a sense of responsibility and solidarity. In the end, they conceive the World as if it were regulated by a protocol and intend to organize it in a ceremonial way. Their morals, their physics, their logic are only aspects of a Knowledge of how to behave which is Etiquette.

When they meditate on the course of things, they do not seek to determine the general, nor calculate the probable; they strive to identify the furtive and the singular. But in doing so, they seek to grasp the keys to the mutations that affect the totality of appearances, for they are concerned only with detail in order to penetrate the feeling of Order. Since it moves in a world of symbols and attributes all reality to symbols and hierarchies of symbols, Chinese thought is oriented towards a kind of conventional or scholastic rationalism. But, on the other hand, it is animated by a passion for empiricism which has predisposed it to a meticulous observation

---

73   Masson-Oursel, *Etudes de logique comparée*; Id, *La démonstration confucéenne*, and Granet, *Quelques particularités de la langue et de la pensée chinoises*.
74   Cf. *infra*, Book IV, chap I, sec. II.
75   Cf. *infra*, Book IV, chap III, sec. II.
76   The following is a good example of this type of reasoning used by the early Confucians to show that self-knowledge leads to knowledge of the universe.

of the concrete and which has undoubtedly led it to make fruitful observations.[77] Its greatest merit is that it never separated the human from the natural and always conceived the human with the social in mind. If the idea of Law did not develop, and if, consequently, the observation of nature was abandoned to empiricism and the organization of society to the regime of compromise, the idea of Rule, or rather the notion of Models, by allowing the Chinese to retain a flexible and plastic conception of Order, did not expose them to imagine above the human world a world of transcendent realities. Their Wisdom, imbued with a concrete sense of nature, is decidedly humanistic.

---

77 If we were better informed about the pharmacopoeia and chemistry of the Chinese, and especially about their inventions in agriculture and the breeding, creation, and use of plant and animal species, it would certainly seem to us that the empiricism of the Chinese and the pedagogical virtues of the idea of *mutation* are not without value. Too much has been said of the Chinese scholar who, in the mid-19th century, and certainly for nationalistic glory, claimed that the seeds of the Western sciences were to be found in the *Yi king*. This is not to say that one should blindly believe the claims of contemporary scholars that their ancestors foresaw such wonders as today's theories of the curvature of space or electricity.

Book III
THE SYSTEM OF THE WORLD

The joint ideas of Order, Totality and Efficiency dominate the thinking of the Chinese, who did not bother to distinguish realms in Nature. All reality is in itself complete. Everything in the universe is like the universe. Matter and spirit do not appear as two opposite worlds. Man is not given a separate place by attributing to him a soul that would be of another essence than the body. Men are nobler than other beings only to the extent that, having a rank in society, they are worthy of collaborating in the maintenance of the social order, *foundation and model* of the universal order. Only the Chief, the Wise, the Honest, stand out among the multitude of beings. These ideas are consistent with a representation of the World, characterized not by anthropocentrism, but by the predominance of the notion of *social authority*. The arrangement of the universe is the effect of a princely Virtue which the arts and sciences must strive to equip. Protocol order applies to thought as well as to life; the reign of etiquette is universal. Everything is subject to it in the physical order and in the moral order, which they refuse to distinguish by opposing them as a determined order and an order of freedom. The Chinese do not conceive the idea of Law. They propose only Models for things as for men.

Chapter I
THE MACROCOSM

One fact points to the privileged place that the Chinese give to politics. For them, the history of the world does not begin before that of civilization. It does not begin with the story of a creation or with cosmological speculations. It merges, from the beginning, with the biography of the sovereigns. The biographies of ancient Chinese heroes contain quite a few mythical elements. But no cosmogonic theme could enter literature without having been transposed. All legends are intended to relate facts of human history. The same political philosophy inspires them. Beings and things exist and endure thanks to the harmony (*ho*) instituted by the holy authors of national civilization. It is their Wisdom that enables men and beings to shape their essence (*wou*) and to fully realize their destiny (*ming*). Social harmony, which is due to the ascendancy of the Sages, leads, together with the Great Peace (*T'ai p'ing*), to a perfect equilibrium of the macrocosm, and this equilibrium is reflected in the organization of all the microcosms. The predominance given to political concerns[1] is accompanied by a fundamental repulsion to any creationist theory among the Chinese.

* * *

Only a few metaphors, together with some fragments of their legends, provide information about the ancient Chinese idea of the universe. There is little chance that these folkloric data can be linked to a single, definite system of thought. However, they can point to an essential fact: the conception of the physical world is totally controlled by social representations.

The universe is the chief's chariot or house.

---

1 *Civ. Chin.*, pp. 19 ff.

The world is often compared to a chariot[2] covered by a canopy. The canopy is circular and represents Heaven; the Earth is represented by the square box that supports the occupant of the chariot. But it is not just any chariot. When we say "the Earth… is the great chariot," we think of the ceremonial chariot[3] in which the One Man takes his seat, and no doubt we picture the Son of Heaven when, in order to fulfill the first duty of his office, he goes around the Earth of men, following the route of the Sun. In heaven, the Sun travels his career also mounted on a chariot.

The chariot leader stands at the front of the chariot, under the edge of the canopy. The word (*hien*) designating this place is also used to name the place in the reception hall where, when holding court, the Master must stand. When it is said, "The earth bears and heaven covers,"[4] this refers no less to the house than to the chariot. The building where the sovereign receives the feudatories, square at the base, must be covered by a circular roof. It is under the perimeter of this roof that the Son of Heaven stands when he promulgates the monthly ordinances which adjust the times to the spaces.

The roof of the *Ming t'ang* and the canopy of the chariot are attached by columns to its square support. These columns, which are called the Columns of Heaven, are well known to geographers who know their number and location. They are related to the Eight Directions, the Eight Mountains and the Eight Gates which give way to the Rainy Clouds and the Eight Winds.[5] The Eight Pillars, linked through the Eight Winds to the Eight Trigrams, which are arranged in an octagon, connect the perimeter of the earth with the circular perimeter of Heaven.

The architecture of the World was first imagined in a simpler form. There were only four columns and only four cardinal Mountains were known. The "Four Mountains" is the name of the chiefs whom the Sovereign charged with securing peace in the Four Directions and whom he received by opening the Four Gates of his residence.[6] The Mountains have in nature a role analogous to that of the Chiefs in society. They ensure the stability of the universe. From the mythical point of view, there is no difference between the struggle waged by a usurper against the rightful sovereign and the attack on a mountain by an evil genius who is represented as a wind blowing in a storm and blowing down the roofs of houses.[7] The only famous pillar in the world is the pillar of the mountain, which is the only pillar in the world.

The only famous pillar in the world is a mountain, Pou-tcheou, in the northwest of the World; there is the Gate leading to the Dark Residence; through it blows a

---

2 Ancient Chinese chariots were two-wheeled vehicles, with side and front panels, but the passenger would get into the chariot from behind. They were pulled by two or four horses (TN).
3 *Tcheou li*, Biot, *Le Tcheou li ou Les Rites des Tcheou*, p. 488; *Yi king*, L., p. 430.
4 *Li ki*, C., II, p. 475.
5 *Houai-nan tseu*, 3.
6 SMT, I, p. 79; Granet, *Danses et légendes…*, p. 249.
7 Granet, *op. cit.*, pp. 484, 485, 379, 437.

wind which is also called Pou-tcheou.[8] During the battle he fought against the Sovereign Tchouan-hiu, Kong-kong, genie of the Wind, to whom the Dark Residence serves as a retreat, succeeded in shaking the Pou-tcheou. This was followed by a deluge. The world is only in order when it is enclosed, in the manner of a dwelling.[9]

In the past, when Niu-koua began to arrange the Universe, "the Four Poles overturned, the Nine Provinces cracked, Heaven did not cover all, *the Earth did not support the whole circumference (pou-tcheou)*, the Fire burned without ever being quenched, the Waters flooded without ever being appeased, the fierce Beasts devoured the healthy men, the Birds of Prey abducted the weak. Niu-koua, then, melted the five-colored stones to repair the blue Heaven; she cut off the feet of the Tortoise to establish the Four Poles; she slew the Black Dragon to set the country of Ki in order; he heaped up reed ash to stop the licentious Waters. Heaven was repaired, the Four Poles were raised, the licentious Waters dried up, the land of Ki was balanced (*p'ing*), the fierce beasts perished, the healthy men subsisted, the square Earth held on its back, the round Heaven stood embraced," and Union (*ho*) was made between *Yin* and *Yang*.[10]

In the past, too, the Islands of the Blessed floated up and down with the tides; one could not stand still on them. They were only stabilized on the day when, at the behest of a genius of the sea, giant turtles *carried them on their backs*.[11] The Chinese long thought they could give stability to the ground by carving turtles out of stone and making them support a heavy stela. Mountains or pillars, the columns linking Earth and Heaven give solidity to the architecture that is the Universe.

However, since the revolt of Kong Kong, the balance is no longer perfect. This horned monster, throwing himself on mount Pou-tcheou, splintered it with his horn; "he broke the pillar of Heaven and broke the mooring line (*wei*; the Eight Moorings *pa wei*, correspond to the *pa ki*, the Eight Poles, the Eight Directions) of the Earth." Thus the sky tilted to the northwest, so that the Sun, the Moon and the constellations had to move toward the sunset, while on the Earth, which, being tilted in the opposite direction, was incomplete to the southeast, all the waterways took the direction of this corner of space.

The misdeeds of Kong-kong are also told in another way; it is said that it was he, or Tch'e-yeou, a genie of the Wind, another Horned Monster, who unleashed the overflow of the Waters by attacking K'ong-sang.[12] These myths refer to a slightly different representation of the Universe. K'ong-sang, the hollow mulberry, which is opposed to K'ong-t'ong, the hollow paulownia, is, like the latter, both a hollow

---

8   *Houai-nan tseu*, 3.

9   *Lie tseu*, Wieger, *Les Pères du système taoïste*, p. 131; *Houai-nan tseu*, 3, 1 and 6; *SMT*, I, p. 11.

10   *Houai-nan tseu*, 6. To be compared with the famous formula of *Lao tseu* (Wieger, *op. cit.*, p. 46), often mistranslated, which evokes the production of all things by the effect of the hierogamy of Yin and Yang: "The 10,000 beings are carried on the loins of Yin and held in the embrace of Yang." (Cf. *Houai-nan tseu*, 7.)

11   *Lie tseu*, Wieger, *op. cit.*, p. 133.

12   Granet, *op. cit.*, p. 435. This myth serves to explain the mismatch of the world: the Pole Star is not at the zenith of the capital of men.

tree and a mountain: both serve as a shelter for the suns and a dwelling place for the sovereigns.[13] Other trees stood as celestial pillars:[14] to the east, the P'an-mou, an immense peach-tree situated near the Gate of the Genii; [15] to the west, the Jo-tree, on which, as on the hollow Mulberry, but at sunset, the Ten Suns rest;[16] in the center, the *Kien-mou* (the Erect Log), by which the Sovereigns (we do not say, in this case, the Suns) ascend and descend.[17]

The Chinese used to tell that their ancestors had begun by nesting in trees or lodging in caves. Most legends evoke the idea of a columnar construction, but some mythical features show that Heaven is conceived as the vault of a cave. In their dreams of apotheosis, the Sovereigns, when they ascend to the Heavens, come to lick the nipples of the Celestial Bell, i.e., the stalactites hanging from the ceiling of the caves.[18]

Humble at first as the abode of the first chiefs, the World has grown, unlike that land of the Giants which diminished in extent as the size of its inhabitants became smaller.[19] It was still believed in the time of the Han; that like all bodies which breath (*k'i*) fills, Earth and Heaven have gradually increased in volume. The distance between them has increased.[20] They used to be, when spirits and men lived in promiscuity, so close together (Earth offering Heaven her back and Heaven holding her embraced) that one could "go up and down" from one to the other at any time. Tchong-li, "cutting off communication,"[21] put an end to these scandalous beginnings of the universe.

* * *

Tchong-li is a solar hero, promoted, by the grace of history, to the rank of astronomer. The Chinese never seem to have bothered to derive a systematic cosmogony from their myths. Their astronomers, instead, borrowed most of their theories from ancient legends.

As early as the fourth century BC there were many scholars in China who were interested in astrology, and they were engaged in drawing up catalogs of constellations and noting the movements of the stars. It seems that, at least from the 3rd century BC, they presented various descriptions of the World. Their speculations are known to us only from brief literary allusions or from fairly recent summaries.[22] They are closely related to mythical traditions.

---

13 Granet, *op. cit.* p. 436.
14 *Ibid.*, note 740.
15 *Ibid.*, note 740.
16 *Houai-nan tseu*, 4; Granet, *op. cit.*, p. 305; Maspero, *Les légendes mythologiques dans le Chou king*, p. 20.
17 Granet, *op. cit.* p. 379.
18 *Tchou chou ki nien*, 5; *Heou Han chou*, 10; *Song chou*, 27, p. 3. On the subject of the Tree of Life, cf. *supra*, Book II, ch. IV.
19 *Lie tseu*, Wieger, *op. cit.*, p. 133.
20 *Louen heng*, Forke, *Lun-Heng. Selected Essays of the Philosopher Wang Ch'ung*, I, p. 252.
21 SMT, III, p. 324; *Chou king*, L., p. 593.
22 The oldest surviving treatise is the *Tcheou pei*. (Cf. Biot, *Traduction et examen d'un ouvrage chinois intitulé Tcheou pei, JA,* 1841), which dates at most from the early Han, but may

Book III - Chapter I - The Macrocosm

At the time of the Eastern Han dynasty,[23] these speculations were attributed to three distinct schools. One of these, perhaps the most esoteric, was neglected, if not forgotten; its adherents were said to admit that the Sun, Moon, and all the stars float freely in Space, Heaven not being a solid body.[24] According to the other two systems, the stars adhere to Heaven; it is on its resistant surface that they have their courses; they move as they are carried by Heaven in its circular motion.

Earth and Heaven are separated by vast expanses. Scientists had calculated the dimensions of the world with the help, they said, of the gnomon. According to some the measure of the diameter of the solar orbit is 357,000 *li*,[25] although according to others that is the diameter of the celestial sphere, the distance between two opposite points of the terrestrial circumference being 36,000 *li*.[26] 357 and 360 are, as we have seen in connection with musical pipes, prestigious numbers; multiples of 7 or of 5, they may evoke the ratio 3/2 or 3/4 of the circle and the square. The dimensions indicated by scientists are of no more interest than their size. The universe, whose immensity they want to make us feel, still resembles the world created by the mythical imagination.

The adherents of the School of *Houen tien* assign to Heaven the form of a sphere or rather that of an egg.[27] This conception is linked to the mythical theme from which the legend of Pan-kou arose, as well as to various accounts of miraculous births.[28] Several founding heroes were born from an egg, sometimes hatched in a nine-storied tower representing Heaven. Moreover, the word "Heaven covers" is always used in the exact sense of "hatching." Totally enveloped by the celestial shell, the Earth, like an egg yolk, rests on a liquid mass. It floats, rises, falls, approaches or moves away from the zenith and the four cardinal points, while Heaven, turning on itself *like a wheel*, drags the Sun below the terrestrial horizon every evening. The

---

have been reworked under the T'ang. Chapter 11 (*T'ien wen*) of the History of the Tsin contains many quotations from authors of the Han period. Maspero (*L'astronomie chinoise avant les Han*, TP, 1929, pp. 267 ff.) rightly admits, in my opinion, that cosmographical theories go back to the 4th-3rd centuries BC (Cf. de Saussure, *Les origines de l'astronomie chinoise* and Forke, *Die Gedankenwelt des chinesischen Kulturkreises*). Two chapters of Wang Ch'ong's *Louen heng* (Forke, *Lun-Heng. Selected Essays of the philosopher Wang Ch'ung*, pp. 250 ff.; 258 ff.) may give an idea of the controversies held in the Second Han period about the structure of the World.

23   *Tsin chou*, II; TP, 1929, p. 334.
24   TP, 1929, p. 340. Abandoned for a time, this theory (known as *siuan ye*) was reconstituted in the second century BC, according to oral tradition, it is said (TP, 1929, p. 340). A trace of this may be found in a passage from the *Lie tseu* (Wieger, *op. cit.*, p. 79), where the idea that neither Heaven nor the Stars are solid bodies is used to reassure a man tormented by the fear that Heaven will collapse (*peng*: term used for the fall of a mountain and the death of a ruler) and that the earth will collapse.
25   The *li* is a traditional Chinese unit of length that is now standardized at 500 meters, although historically its value ranged considerably between somewhat smaller and larger distances depending on the periods (TN).
26   TP, 1929, pp. 347 and 350.
27   *Tsin chou*, II; TP, 1929, p. 355.
28   *Civ, Chin., aaa, bbb*; Granet, *Danses et légendes…*, p. 449. *Lu che tch'ouen ts'ieou*, 6, § 8. The legend of Pan-kou is older in China than previously held. The world is the body of Pan-kou.

alternation of day and night is explained by this motion of Heaven; the oscillating motions of the Earth explain the alternation and variety of the seasons. Moreover, since the sky is ovoid and the Sun does not leave it in its march, it is evident that this star is nearest to the Earth in the morning and evening and farthest from it at the moment when it reaches the climax of its journey; it therefore appears smallest at full noon, diminishing in apparent dimensions (but not in brightness) with distance.[29]

The other system, undoubtedly older, compares Heaven to a moving canopy (*t'ien kai*) covering the Earth. The latter lies beneath it, without moving, in an inverted bowl position.[30] The Earth's surface does not form a dome parallel to the celestial canopy that covers it. The Earth is shaped like a chessboard, i.e., a truncated quadrangular pyramid.[31] The upper part (the inhabited Earth) is flat and lies just below the crest of the canopy, where the Big Dipper and the constellations of the Central Palace of Heaven dwell. The waters flow down the four sides of the pyramid; they form around the inhabited Earth the Four Seas; in this system, as in the other, water fills the shallows of the world. The aspect given to the Earth by the School of the Celestial Canopy does not differ from the image offered by the square mound surrounded by water on which sacrifices were made on the ground: when the sacrifices were successful, the vapors formed a canopy over the altar.[32] The variety of the seasons is explained, in the *T'ien Kai* system, by the fact that the Sun travels over the celestial canopy taking different routes which move it away from or towards (the center of) the Earth.[33] If night follows day, it is because, dragged by the canopy in its rotation, the Sun moves successively away from the four sides of the Earth, becoming invisible there in its turn as a result of its distance.[34]

Some imagined that the celestial vault tilted northward, so that the Sun at sunset passed below the horizon.[35] This explanation is related to the legend of Kongkong; the sky has tilted northwestward since this monster broke Mount Pou-tcheou. Wang Tch'ong has preserved an important variant of the theory. Heaven *sinks into* the Earth towards the North, so that the Sun, in the whole northern part of its course, must travel underground.[36] This view is reminiscent of the gate which opened outside mount Pou-tcheou and led to the Dark Abode.

The idea that the Sun ceases to illuminate when it enters the shadow realm is found in the theory of eclipses. These (which may begin at the center of the star as well as at its edges) do not differ in kind from certain veils (*po*) which may be seen at any time of the month. The eclipses themselves occur on the first or last day of

---

29   *Louen heng*, Forke, *op. cit.*, I, p. 253; *Lie tseu*, Wieger, *op. cit.*, p. 139.
30   *Yin chou*, II; *Louen heng*, Forke, *op. cit.*, p. 139.
31   *Sin chou*, II; *TP*, 1929, p. 338. Maspero erroneously describes the earth as a dome. The comparison with the inverted bowl only indicates the idea of convexity. The comparison with the chessboard is what gives the shape.
32   *Civ. Chin.*, p. 412; *SMT*, III, p. 483.
33   *Louen heng*, Forke, *op. cit.*, I, p. 259; *TP*, 1929, p. 340.
34   *Louen heng*, Forke, *op. cit.*, I, p. 362.
35   *Ibid.*, I, p. 360.
36   *Ibid.*, I, p. 361.

the lunation; darkness (*houei*) then reigns, so that the Moon loses its brightness during this period. The Sun, which unites (*kiao*) with it, is in its turn influenced by the dark (Yin) principle; in this case it may be eclipsed.[37] The Moon, which in essence depends on the Yin principle, is subject to more frequent eclipses, which may be observed at different times of the lunation. Lieou Hiang[38] wrote, however, (in the first century BC) that the Sun was eclipsed when the Moon came to obscure it, and Wang Tch'ong,[39] who was not unaware of this opinion, affirmed that this was a regular phenomenon. These theses have not prevented the preservation, as dogma, of the ancient idea that eclipses are caused by the erratic conduct of the sovereigns and their wives.[40]

Chinese cosmographers took advantage of the advances in astronomy in the period of the Warring Kingdoms.[41] These advances were due to astrologers who spied out celestial events on behalf of ambitious princes. The connection of these events with the facts of human history was the beginning of all observation. Although scientists have been compelled to attribute vast proportions to the universe, they have not ceased to conceive the world according to the model created by the mythical imagination. Their knowledge increases in detail without the temptation to seek explanations of a purely physical nature. Those who refuse to admit that, towards the North, the Earth and the celestial vault are intertwined, do not wield any consideration derived from the ideas of resistance movement, impenetrability… They see no difficulty in accepting (better still, they use it in discussion) the myth of the union of Heaven and Earth.[42] Scholars have hardly changed the Chinese representation of the universe. Architects and poets have enriched it much more than they have.

* * *

In the period of the Warring Kingdoms (5th to 3rd centuries BC), feudal potentates played to see who had the largest mansions, the tallest turrets, and the deepest cellars. Their courts were filled not only with astrologers, but also with magicians and poets, engineers and balladeers,[43] purveyors of legends and curiosities. Thanks to all these contributions, the vision of the World was enlarged, the Universe populated, while the palaces were exalted and enlarged and the court, the parks, the ponds and the gardens were filled with wonders. While the Nine Plains of Heaven (*kieou ye*) corresponded to the Nine Provinces of China, Earth

---

37   TP, 1929, p. 292. *Louen heng*, Forke, *op. cit.*, I, pp. 269-270. Darkness (*houei*) is the equivalent of Yin (dark). Cf. *supra*, Book II, chap II.
38   TP, 1929, pp. 291 and 293.
39   *Louen heng*, Forke, *op. cit*, I, p. 271.
40   *Che king*, C., pp. 235 ff. and the notes where Couvreur reports the views of Tchou Hi.
41   On this progress: TP, 1929, pp. 267 ff.
42   *Louen heng*, Forke, *op. cit.*, I, p. 261.
43   The role of balladeers, dancers, musicians, illusionists, and exhibitors of curiosities, who were the bearers of a wealth of legends, arts, and knowledge, cannot be overestimated. Many Chinese legends, related, for example, by King Chan hai, present features that reveal foreign origins, sometimes very distant and, perhaps, also very ancient.

and Heaven, increasing in depth, were staggered in Nine Steps.⁴⁴ At the bottom were the Nine Fountains, at the top the Nine Heavens. And, indeed, by staggering up to nine their holds and terraces, the Tyrants intended to reach the subterranean Springs as well as the High regions where in the clouds the celestial Fire is hidden. From the depths of the world to its supreme summit (*Houang ki*), the palace seemed to merge with the axis of the universe.

Even when it assumes magnificent forms, the imprint of its humble beginnings is found in the universe. In the center of the poorest houses, a sump had to be placed under an opening left at the top of the roof.⁴⁵ Water entered the earth through this pit and, through the hole in the roof, the smoke from the chimney joined the clouds of fire in the sky. Similarly, in the depths of the world there is a vast cesspool, while in the highest heavens there is a slit from which lightning escapes.⁴⁶ The cesspool is guarded by an anthropophagous monster, Ya-yu. Yi the Archer shot murderous arrows at him, thus earning the right to become the genie of the center of the house and the Master of Fate (*Sseu-ming*).⁴⁷ The underworld of the waters is, in effect, the land of the dead. Libations arrive there when they are poured on the earthen floor of the houses. The "Yellow Springs" were at first imagined to be very close to human residences. As soon as the earth was dug a little and the water discovered, the world of the dead was opened.⁴⁸ The spirits escaped as soon as, especially in winter, the parched ground cracked; back to earth, they could be heard moaning.

The Yellow Springs, in the enlarged World, were relegated to the bottom of the Septentrion; the dead ceased to be buried in the houses, and the cemeteries were placed to the north of the cities. It is a little to the west of the due north (in the east corresponding to the beginning of the winter season) that the abyss is dug (the impluvium of the houses is sometimes placed to the northwest)⁴⁹ through which the Waters coming from the Four Directions disappear into the interior of the Earth.⁵⁰ A monster sometimes called the Lord of the Earth (*T'ou-po*) inhabits these regions, where he guards a door by turning nine times about himself.⁵¹ He is often considered a vassal of Kong-kong; he is a nine-headed serpent; the nine heads devour the Nine Mountains, and the monster spreads the infection by vomiting swamps.⁵² Above the abyss are the Nine Gates of Heaven, guarded by wolves and a nine-headed being capable of uprooting trees by nine thousand. Those who would pass through these gates, seized and suspended upside down, are hurled into the

---

44   *Tch'ou tseu, Tien wen.*
45   *Li ki,* C., I, p. 372; Granet, *Danses et légendes*..., note 753; *Tchouang tseu,* Wieger, *op. cit.,* p. 363. *Li ki,* C., II, p. 478.
46   Granet, *op. cit.,* p. 545.
47   *Ibid.,* p. 379.
48   Id., *La vie et la mort*..., p. 17.
49   *Li ki,* C., p. 478.
50   Granet, *La vie et la mort*..., p. 13.
51   *Tch'ou tseu, Chao houen.*
52   Granet, *Danses et légendes*..., 486.

abyss.⁵³ Few are the Heroes who can prevail against the Guardian of the Gate of the heavenly Sovereign. But the saints, properly trained in mystical practices, enter the World Above. They enter it through the cleft opened high in the heavens without being driven back by the rays that shoot forth.⁵⁴

More frequently visited, the interior of Heaven is a little better known than that of Earth. The Celestial Sovereign (*Chang-ti*) has his court there.⁵⁵ There he has palaces, arsenals, and harems. Their names are found on earth; they are those which the chiefs give to the buildings of their capital.⁵⁶ Those who are admitted into the presence of the Celestial Sovereign are delighted by wonderful music.⁵⁷ Gifts are exchanged with him. When a group of beautiful women is offered to him, he gives thanks by conferring ownership of a divine hymn.⁵⁸ One may be invited by him to a bear hunt,⁵⁹ for he has parks as well as fish ponds, and one may shoot with a bow in Heaven as in this world. Do we not see Hi-ho, the Mother of Suns, riding in her chariot, chasing the Heavenly Dog (*T'ien-lang*)⁶⁰ with her arrow? The jousts of the denizens of Heaven (they have preserved their coats of arms much better than the humans) seem to be animal fights. Three-legged crows, the Suns disappear when there is a joust of Ki-lin (unicorn) or when Ki-lin wants to devour them.⁶¹ Similarly, Tchang-ngo, the Moon, is a toad that another toad devours and makes eclipse, while the death of King-yu (the Whale?) makes the Comets appear and the howling of the Tiger unleashes the Spring Wind.⁶²

It is not in Heaven, however, but in the remote regions of Space that the deities have their lairs and often take part in jousts. There the gods are attacked by heroes whose mission is to reduce them appropriately. The Lord of the Winds (*Fong-po*) remains bound in the Green Mound, while the Lord of the River (*Ho-po*) hides in the chasm of Yang-yu.⁶³ Wounded, one in the left eye and the other in the knee, they were tamed by the Archer who killed Ya-yu in his cloaca and sacrificed, on the branches of his mulberry-tree, nine undisciplined Suns.⁶⁴ Thus, in obedience to a wise Sovereign, he evacuated from the inhabited world all that could harm men. In a well-ordered world, only the lost corners which the canopy of heaven does not cover⁶⁵ are the places where beings of a monstrous or divine nature are allowed to subsist vaguely.

---

53 *Tch'ou tseu, Tchao houen.*
54 *Tch'ou tseu, Yuan yeou.*
55 SMT, III, pp. 339 ff.
56 *Civ. chin.*, p. 51.
57 SMT, V, p. 26.
58 Granet, *Danses et légendes...*, p. 582.
59 SMT, V, p. 27.
60 *Tch'ou tseu, Tong kiun.*
61 *Houai-nan tseu*, 3.
62 Ibid.
63 Granet, *op. cit.* p. 379.
64 Granet, *Danses et légendes*, pp. 512, 469.
65 *Ta Tai Li ki*, 5.

In the northeast corner of the world, in the country of Fou-lao, a people of brutes live miserably, feeding on raw vegetables, fruits, and roots, and know no sleep; they move restlessly over a scorched ground which is constantly illuminated by the Sun and Moon.[66] Once, in these lands, there floated in the sea a kind of ox, with a green body and only one leg. His name was K'ouei. When it went in and out of the water, producing wind and rain, it made the sound of thunder. Houang-ti came to take its skin and had the idea of beating it with a bone taken from the Thunder Beast. Thanks to this drum, he inspired the whole Empire with respectful awe.[67] Wiser still than Houang-ti, and displaying the civilizing genius that characterizes true sovereigns, Yao took K'ouei to his court to make him a dancing master; he directed, beating on sounding stones, the ballets danced by the Hundred Animals, finally domesticated.[68]

To the southeast is the Ta-ho, the abyss, immense and bottomless, where the Milky Way, the River of Heaven,[69] pours with all the terrestrial rivers. The Mother of the Suns and the Mother of the Moons find in these regions the water that each day serves to wash their children, like newborn babies, before showing themselves in Heaven.[70]

In the southwest corner is the land of Kou-mang, where Yin and Yang do not join breath and where heat and cold, night and day, do not alternate. The Sun and the Moon do not shine there. The poor people who live there, without food or clothing, in continual somnolence, awake only once in fifty days.[71] The sun and the moon do not shine there.

Worse still is the northwest corner. This is the land of the Nine Darknesses which the Dragon of Flames illuminates. A thousand *li* high, it rises red and staring. If he opens his eyes, it is day. If he closes them, it is night. If he blows, it is winter; if he breathes, it is summer. He neither drinks, nor eats, nor breathes; wind and rain stop in his throat. When he breathes comes the Wind.[72] The Flame Dragon rises at night on the banks of the Red River, where also lives Niu-pa, the Drought, daughter of Houang-ti, whom he helped to defeat Ch'e-yeou, the great rebel, after which she was banished to the horrible land of the Shifting Sands.[73] Nearby is the abyss where Thunder is swallowed up by the whirlwind.[74] This is the sinister region of thirst, stalked by gigantic ants and red wasps, larger than pumpkins, whose sting immediately dries up everything.[75]

---

66 *Lie tseu*, Wieger, *op. cit.*, p. 111.
67 Granet, *op. cit.*, p. 509.
68 *Lu che tch'ouen ts'ieou*, 5, § 5; Granet, *op. cit.*
69 *Lie tseu*, Wieger, *op. cit.*, p. 131 and *Tchouang tseu*, *Ibid.*, p. 303.
70 Granet, *op. cit.*, p. 437; *Chan hai king*, 15.
71 *Lie tseu*, Wieger, *op. cit.*, p. 111.
72 *Chan hai king*, 8 and 17; *Houai-nan tseu*, and Granet, *op. cit.*, p. 523.
73 *Chan hai king*, 17; Granet, *op. cit.*, pp. 315 ff.
74 *Tch'ou tseu, Tchao houen.*.
75 *Chan hai king*, 2; Granet, *op. cit.* pp. 386 ff; *Tch'ou tseu, Tchao houen.*

Book III - Chapter I - The Macrocosm

But the northwest is also the mysterious country where the K'ouen-louen rises, a superb replica of the heavens and of princely palaces.[76] There are hanging gardens with trees that yield pearls or produce jade, nine wells from which springs an elixir, and innumerable gates. The Pou-tcheou wind enters through one of them, but another is indistinguishable, at least in name, from the main gate of the palaces of Heaven. And, indeed, those who succeed in ascending the successive steps of K'ouen-louen rise to immortality; we are told that they ascend to Heaven.[77] The Supreme Sovereign is said to reside in K'ouen-louen. However, the only deity who receives visitors there is the Mother-Queen of the West, Si-wang-mou. She is a kind of leopard-tailed ogress, who has the jaw of a tiger and delights in howling like them. She spreads the plague far and wide. She lives in the depths of a cave and is disheveled like a witch.[78] From this goddess of Death the herb of long life can be obtained,[79] and she sometimes offers banquets on the top of a jade tower.[80]

Similar and equally disparate legends have served to illustrate another cosmological theme; all strange peoples have been situated on the edge of the square of the earth. When Sseu-ma Ts'ien combines the 8 Winds and the 28 Mansions, he is not concerned with the dimensions of the spindles, but to each of the 4 sides of the horizon he makes 9 sites correspond. Houai-nan tseu imagines the distribution of the strange peoples around the square perimeter of the Earth; he places 6 in the East and 10 in the West, 13 in the South and 7 in the North; all the logical needs of the philosopher are satisfied inasmuch as he too has obtained the total of 36.[81]

* * *

Both philosophers and poets have transmitted these legends to us; they used them in their arguments much more than the theories of scientists. The poets who sing of the epic journeys of the Sages or the mystical romps of the Heroes know much of the Beyond, and so do the jugglers or shamans who come from afar to the courts of tyrants. However, the information of the balladeers and the discoveries of the poets only added picturesqueness to the Chinese representations of the world that the scholars, with their great number, contributed to endow with majesty. Always conceived in the image and likeness of a princely dwelling, whether a humble dungeon or a gigantic palace, the architecture of the Universe is still governed by the old rules of indigenous classification systems. Only the hunting park has been enriched and enlarged. It is a remarkable fact that if the Chinese have welcomed, as profitable curiosities, legends or techniques, jugglery or ideas tainted with exoticism or novelty, they have not admitted them into their home. It is still more remarkable that they have not lodged outside History, in the vague and distant time which seems to be the proper one for myths, legends, new or old, in which gods and monsters appear. All Time belongs to men and to History. The Universe only

---

76 *Houai-nan tseu*, 4.
77 *Ibid.*
78 *Chan hai king*, 2 and 16.
79 *Houai-nan tseu*, 6; Granet, *op. cit.*, p. 376.
80 *Mou T'ten tseu tchouan*, 3.
81 *Houai-nan tseu*, 4.

really exists from the moment when the Wise Men instituted the National Civilization. This civilization reigns in the totality of the Nine Provinces. Circumscribing the Space arranged by the Saints, the Four Barbarian Seas extend, an inorganic space, Beyond Space, to which legitimately corresponds a Beyond Time. These imprecise margins of the real world are suitable for monsters and gods as well as for barbarians. The Land of Men belongs to the Chinese, to their ancestors, to their chiefs. They divided the fields into squares and built the *temple*, which gives a correct orientation to the Nine Quarters of their city, of their camp, of the ritual area where they were to officiate. From these sacred uses derive the classifications that allow to order the real universe and to construct its true representation. The fields that were ploughed, the camp where the Chief took refuge, the sacred house where he lived, provided the image of the Nine Provinces of the World, which were initially very small, situated between the frontiers where the divine beasts and the barbarians roam, the hunt of the Chief.[82] Such is the terrain where the warriors achieved their conquests, and the geographers and poets their explorations. The enlarged universe has preserved the architecture, crude or splendid, of the cave, the hut, or the dungeon, which the Founders of ancient China inhabited. Their descendants only accepted to welcome in the park reserved for their hunts, their parties, their games, all that was brought to them – exotic or new ideas or gods – the astrologers, the poets and the balladeers.

---

82   *Civ. Chin.*, pp. 246 ff.

Chapter II
THE MICROCOSM

The sages of China have always hated the tumblers. These, when they stand on their hands, run the risk of upsetting the World. Men have square feet that must rest on the earth. They are guilty if they fail to point their heads upward; the head is round in the image of the sky.[1] The conformation of the human being reproduces the architecture of the world, and both agree with the social structure. Society, man, the world are the object of a global knowledge. Valid for the macrocosm and for all the microcosms that fit into it, this knowledge is constituted by the sole use of analogy.

* * *

Nothing illustrates the Chinese conception of the microcosm better than the ideas, customs and myths concerning the left and the right.

In China, the antithesis of Right and Left is not an absolute opposition,[2] Yin and Yang are not opposed in themselves, like Non-Being and Being or Pure and Impure. The Chinese have not the religious ardor that condemns the division of things into Evil and Good. We honor the Right, we hate the Left, we call everything that belongs to Evil sinister; we blame the Left-handed and we are Right-handed. The Chinese are right-handed like us; however, they honor the left, and some of their greatest heroes, such as Yu the Great and T'ang the Victorious, are left-handed, and others right-handed. They might even be said to be Geniuses of the Right

---

[1] *Tsin chou*, 23, in *Houai-nan tseu*, 7. A chief who possesses the Virtue of Earth in particular has particularly square (*fang*) feet; by this is meant that these feet form a perfect square (*fang*) (*Tch'ouen ts'ieou fan lou*, 7; *Civ. Chin.*).

[2] R. Hertz, in his brilliant article on *La prééminence de la main droite*, merely pointed out the difficulty which the Chinese case presents for this problem.

or Geniuses of the Left; Masters of Rain or of Drought, devoted entirely to Yin or Yang, are pronounced sick with hemiplegia, if not reduced to the right or left half of the body.³ An earthly genius or a heavenly genius must animate the founders of two successive dynasties. But the hero, no more than the dynasty he founds, is better or worse, depending on whether, left-handed or right-handed, he is possessed by the Virtue of Heaven or by the Virtue of Earth. These virtues are complementary. They must take turns at work. Moreover, they permeate successively the most perfect Sages. These, as first ministers, exercise active functions. They deploy their talents in the details of things on Earth. Once they have become sovereigns, they are occupied only with concern for Heaven; they live only to concentrate in themselves the Efficiency (*tao*) superior to all efficiency of detail (*tö*).⁴ Left and Heaven prevail in some way over Right and Earth, just as Yang prevails over Yin, Tao over Tö, Royal work over ministerial tasks. The opposition, however, is reduced to a difference of rank or a distinction of employment.

In the sign representing the Right (hand + mouth), etymologists know how to read a precept: the right hand is for eating.⁵ Therefore, the right hand is suitable for things of the Earth. The element "hand" is found in the sign adopted for the left, united, this time, to another graphic element representing the set square. The set square is the symbol of all the arts, and especially of those religious and magical. It is the insignia of Fou-hi, the first ruler, the first soothsayer. Fou-hi is the husband or brother of Niu-koua, whose insignia is the compass. This primordial couple invented marriage; also to say "good manners" is said "compass and set square."⁶ The engravers⁷ represent Fou-hi and Niu-koua entwined at the lower part of the body. Niu-koua, who occupies the right, is shown holding the compass in his right hand.⁸ Fou-hi, on the left, holds the set square in his left hand. The set square, which produces the Square, emblem of the Earth, can only be the insignia of the Male after a hierogamic exchange of attributes; but since the square (as the *Tcheou pei* teaches) produces the Round (which contains),⁹ the square immediately deserves to be the symbol of the sorcerer who is *yin-yang*,¹⁰ and especially of Fou-hi, who is learned in the things of Heaven as well as in those of the Earth.¹¹ Therefore, Fou-hi may carry the set square in his left hand, which (with the set square) evokes the Royal Work, the primary hierogamy, the magic-religious activity. The Chinese do not strongly oppose religion to magic, nor the pure to the impure. The sacred and the profane do not by themselves form two well-defined genres. The right can devote

---

3   Granet, *op. cit.* pp. 455, 467, 551; cf. *supra*, Book II, ch. IV; *Tch'ouen ts'ieou fan lou*, 7.
4   *Civ. Chin.*, p. 232.
5   The index finger is "the finger of eating" (and not of "showing," showing is dangerous, forbidden).
6   Granet, *Danses et légendes*..., p. 498.
7   *Civ. Chin.*, pp. 19-21.
8   The compass traces the circles; the graphic element, said to represent the mouth in the sign of the Right, was (in archaic writing) a circle.
9   Inscribed circle, cf. *supra*, Book II, ch. II and ch. III.
10 Cf. *supra*, Book II, ch. III, sec. IV.
11 *Yi king*, L., p. 382.

itself to secular works and earthly activities without becoming antagonistic to the left. Chinese thought is not interested in opposites, but in contrasts, alternations, correlatives and hierogamic exchanges of attributes.

The infinite variety of Times and Spaces multiplies these exchanges, these contrasts, as well as the concrete conditions of correlations and alternations. Etiquette must take into account all these complications, which is why it sometimes honors the left and sometimes the right. The Chinese are right-handed, necessarily, for from infancy they are taught to use the right hand, at least for eating.[12] But all boys are also taught that they must bow by hiding the right hand under the left; girls, on the contrary, must place the left under the right. This is the rule which, in normal times, serves to distinguish the sexes: the right is *yin*, the left is *yang*. In times of mourning, Yin and Right prevail; men themselves salute by hiding the Left and presenting the Right.[13] A second prescription shows that the Left, being *yang*, corresponds to happiness or pomp; to uncover the right shoulder is to declare oneself defeated and prepare for punishment; on the contrary, the left shoulder is uncovered when attending a joyous ceremony.[14] However, the word "left" is used to describe "forbidden ways" and seems, in this case, equivalent to "sinister." However pompous the left may be, it is always with a shake of the right hand that one swears and makes friends.[15] The handshake may be completed by an exchange of blood drawn from the arm, apparently from the right arm.[16] On the other hand, when the oath is asserted by smelling the blood of a victim, the blood is taken near the ear (to take it, the left shoulder must be uncovered), and must be drawn from the left ear, for it is the left ear that is cut off before the sacrifice to prisoners of war held by a strap with the left hand.[17] Thus, while the right hand prevails over the left, the left ear is better than the right.

The choice between right and left, although it may seem justified on practical grounds, is inspired by theoretical principles of classification. Horses or sheep, dogs or prisoners of war are offered with the rope that binds them. For the former, which are said to be harmless, the rope is held in the right hand.[18] More dangerous than a horse, the dog can bite; its leash is held in the left hand; the right hand, left free, can control the animal.[19] But is it really because it is still dangerous that the leash of a prisoner whose left ear is cut off is also held in the left hand?[20] In the same way, one holds with the left hand the bow offered to an archer whose place in

---

12 *Li ki*, C., I, p. 673. "As soon as a child was able to take his own food, he was taught to use his right hand."
13 *Li ki*, C., pp. 143 ,675; II, 150; *Yi li*, C., p. 75.
14 *Li ki*, C., I, pp. 153, 160, 246; Granet, *Danses...*, pp. 99, 135.
15 *Civ. Chin.*, p. 353; *Tso tchouan*, C., III, p. 319.
16 *Civ. Chin.*, p. 318; *Houai nan tseu*, 11; *Lie tseu*, in Wieger, *op. cit.*, p. 147.
17 Granet, *Danses et légendes*, pp. 138, 167.
18 *Li ki*, C., I, p. 44.
19 *Ibid.*, C., I, p. 44; II, p. 17.
20 *Ibid.*, C., II, p. 17.

the chariot is on the left.[21] In general, it is given by the left and taken by the right.[22] The gifts must be placed on the left of the prince, where an officer is in charge of delivering them. This intermediary stands on the right of his lord when the latter gives orders and these must be passed on.[23] This rule (considered very important because it refers to the distinction between the "historians on the right" in charge of recording facts and the "historians on the left" in charge of recording words)[24] is formulated alongside a more picturesque, but no less imperative, principle on how to serve fresh fish.[25] If you are serving fish, turn the tail towards the guest; in winter, put the belly to the right; put it to the left in summer. *The Summer, the Left and the Front* (i.e., the side of the breast) *are yang*; the fish, as served in the Summer, seems to be correctly arranged in space; *all that is yang* coincides: the Front, the Left, the Summer. It does not seem to be the same in Winter: the back and back are *yin* and the back is then on the left (*yang*). This is because you eat with the right hand, you start the meal with the right and it is polite to start with the good pieces. If the front, although it is *yang*, is turned to the right (*yin*), it is because the belly is *yin*; it is part of the front but it is the bottom. Now, *winter corresponds to the North and the North is also the Bottom*. When winter reigns, it is the Bottom and Yin that dominate; in fish the belly is the fattest and most succulent part. The belly, therefore, in winter, deserves to occupy the right side as it is the place of choice for food. Of course, if dry fish is given to eat, everything changes: first of all, it must be presented with the head turned towards the guest…

Table service, the ritual of giving or swearing, sad or joyful ceremonies, etiquette orders all this, seeking to choose the best, in the detail of the cases, between the right or the left. But it is in politics that we must look for the origin of the principles of etiquette and the primary attributions of left and right. Politics (and logic with it) is dominated by a feudal conception of subordination. Every vassal is a lord in his own house, and yet remains a vassal. In each domain, everything is dated according to the reigning years of the local lord; however, for the divisions of the year, the prescriptions of the royal calendar are followed. Similarly, when choosing between right and left, local circumstances are taken into account, but it is always stated that reference is made to the organizational plan of the universe. The plan found in the macrocosm and microcosm, cosmography, legislation, physiology, has its beginning in the order of feudal assemblies, civil or military pomps. All the conflicts of left and right, all the protocol of precedence are linked to the feudal distinction of superior and inferior. Only this distinction must (because the category of sex dominates the social organization) be combined with the distinction of male and female, of Yang and Yin. The Chief receives the vassals standing on his platform, facing south, who, facing north, bow to the ground at the foot of the platform. The Chief, occupying the Top, is so placed as to receive the influence (*k'i*) of

---

21   *Ibid.*, C., II, p. 18.
22   *Yi li*, C., p. 67.
23   *Li ki*, C., II, p. 17.
24   Granet, *op. cit.*, 70, note 2; *Li ki*, C., I, p. 678.
25   *Li ki*, C., II, p. 21.

Book III - Chapter I - The Microcosm

Heaven, Yang and South. *Thus the South is the Superior, like Heaven, and the North is the Inferior, like Earth.*[26] The Superior, i.e., the Ruler, extends his *chest* toward the South and toward Yang; the Front, like the South, is Yang. He turns his back to Yin and North, which are the Back, at the same time that they are the Bottom and the Earth. So Earth and Yin hold upon their backs, while Yang and Heaven clutch upon their breasts.[27] The Chief, since he turns to the South, confuses his left with the East, his right with the West; *therefore West is Right and East is Left.* The Chief is a rising and victorious Sun. He is also an archer. Each chariot is occupied by a trio of warriors; the driver's place is in the center, the spearman's is on the right; how can one hold the reins properly if not from the center of the chariot? How (unless one is left-handed) can one usefully wield the spear if one is not situated on the right? Therefore, the archer is on the left. The left is the place of the leader. *The left is the honorable side, and also the East.* The Left, the East and the Levant are *yang*, like the Chief, the South and the Sky; the Right, the West and the Sunset are *yin* like the Earth and the North, like the Chief's Wife, the Queen or the Widow. The palace of the crown prince is in the East (spring) and to the left, the residence of the widow is in the West (autumn) and to the right. *Right is* yin *and belongs to women*, to the right belong autumn, crops and food. *The Left is* yang, *belongs to men*, to the Left belong manly activity, religious activity and higher forms of action. As the Yang, the left hand is placed above, and its palm covers the back of the *lower* hand, which is *yin*, the right, which wields the spear and kills, is the hand of the soldier and not that of the Chief; for, while the soldier must give death and punish (*yin*), the Chief, says Tcheng Hiuan,[28] seeks only, by victory, to preserve life and reward merit (*yang*). Holding his bow, *his left arm uncovered, in his left hand*, the Archer, wherever he goes, stands *on the left*: the side of the rising and victorious Sun."[29] The army carries with it the banner of the lord; which always, whatever its course, is oriented, like the lord, towards the South: the red banner of the South precedes it.[30] The Yang and the East are constantly on its left; the Army is only the camp or the city that moves, never losing its orientation. The left legion, commanded by the chief of the left district of the city, is always on the left and always in the East, as the East district is, for the Lord, on the left.[31] The armies have three legions; the Sovereign has three prime ministers who are called "the Three Dukes." They stand before him facing the North, but in them is seen a threefold emanation of his Virtue. As if they were, in the manner of the One Man, facing South, the left, for them, is East. The duke on the left rules, then, in the East of the Empire.[32]

---

26   Hence the arrangement of Chinese diagrams in which the South is always above.
27   Cf. *supra*, in this same Book, ch. I. Heaven is a breast. Therefore it has udders (cf. *supra*, Book II, ch. IV, and also this same Book, ch. I). The earth is a back; therefore, when sacrificing to the earth, a hill is chosen in the form of a rump (*Civ. Chin.*, p. 412).
28   *Li ki*, C., II, p. 19.
29   *Yi li*, C., pp. 123, 125, 144. In archery jousts, defeated archers should keep their bows unstrained and cover their left shoulder.
30   M. Granet, *op. cit.*, p. 291; *Li ki*, C., I, p. 55.
31   M. Granet, *op. cit.*, pp. 229, 271.
32   Granet, *Danses et légendes*, note 1089; *Li ki*, C., I, p. 89. Cf. *Tso tchouan*, C., III, p. 598.

The regions of the world report to the Chief. Everywhere the East is the left, for the East is to his left. But the Chief, the superior (*changh*) is the one above. It is only for the Superior – for Heaven and its emanation, the Chief; for the Chief and its emanations, the Three Dukes – that the left is the honorable side. For the inferiors, for the Bottom, for the Earth, the honorable side is always the East, no longer the left. At the foot of the chief's platform, the vassals turn to the North and line up from East to West; the noblest is on the right. The vassals, however, are chiefs in their houses. In their own houses they stand at the top and face south. The master of the house has his place above the eastern steps of the reception-room, on the left; on the right and above the western steps is the place of the lady of the house; the left is always *yang*, the right is always *yin*.[33] Men and women, however, go out of their houses. On public roads, the center of the road belongs to the cars. Men should walk on the right, that is, on the West, leaving, for reasons of modesty, women to walk alone on the left sidewalk and the East.[34] Such is the rule, and the *Tcheng Hiuan* states that men occupy, with the right, the more honorable side; they are, in fact, vassals, who, wherever they go, remain, by essence, turned to the North. Everything changes when they return to their homes and everything changes again when they go to bed. When one goes to bed, the proper orientation of the Bottom and of the Earth imposes itself. The wife spreads her mat in the corner where the seeds harvested in autumn and stored in the west are kept; she borrows their fertility and gives them hers. The wife's mat is right against the west wall. The husband leaves the eastern side to spend the night; his mat, however, is placed to the east of the wife's mat. When they lie down to sleep, the husband and wife cannot place their heads in a southerly direction, for that is how the dead are arranged in the Lower World; only the dead are not afraid to turn their feet towards the North, where their homes are. The woman, therefore, remains in the West, but during the night she occupies the left and the man the right. All these inversions are dictated by the feudal structure of society, by the subordination of women to men, by the subordination of the vassal to the lord. They do not prevent the left from being fundamentally *yang*, nor the right from being fundamentally *yin*. A doctor cannot be wrong if he wants to know the sex of a child before birth. It will be a boy if the embryo is placed on the left, a girl if it is on the right.[35] The distinction of Superior and Inferior.

The distinction of Superior and Inferior, which has mainly a political value, leads to giving, according to the occasion, preeminence to the left or to the right. Cosmography, physiology, and history prove the correctness of the principle which determines their attributions. The first duty of the Chief is to move through the *Ming t'ang* or the Empire in imitation of the Sun. Starting from the North, he must move eastward so that Spring succeeds Winter. It does so, placing itself first facing

---

33   In times of mourning everything changes: the chief mourner is in the West; the women are placed in the East (*Yi li*, C., p. 498).

34   *Li ki*, C., I, p. 319; *Houai-nan tseu*, 11. The carriages of a funeral convoy also occupy the left and east of the road (*Yi li*, C., p. 513).

35   *Heou Han chou*, 121b, p. 4a.

Book III - Chapter I - The Microcosm

South (and Center) by moving facing the Center, i.e., *advancing Left*. The leftward march, *according* (*chouen*) to the order of the cyclic characters, is the real march, that of the Sun and Yang. This is the proper direction for things above. Chinese cosmography admits that Heaven is levorotatory, the Earth dextrorotatory.[36] The march to the right, *the opposite direction* (*yi*), is imposed for funeral ceremonies which relate to the world below.[37] This march, in which the preeminence of the Right is evident, is imposed on Yin as on Earth. Physiology proves this. One of the great principles of this science is that the numbers 7 or 8 order the female or male life;[38] men end their sexual life at 64 years, women at 49; boys set their teeth at 8 months; they change teeth at 8 years; they become pubescent at 16 years; girls, who reach puberty at the age of 14, lose their first teeth at 7 months and 7 years; the 7, emblem of the Young Yang, presides over the development of women who are *yin*; the 8, emblem of the Young Yin, over the development of men, who are *yang*. Where does this virtue come from? The 8 corresponds to spring (*yang*, left) and to the sign *yin* of the duodenary series; the 7 to autumn (*yin*, right) and to the sign

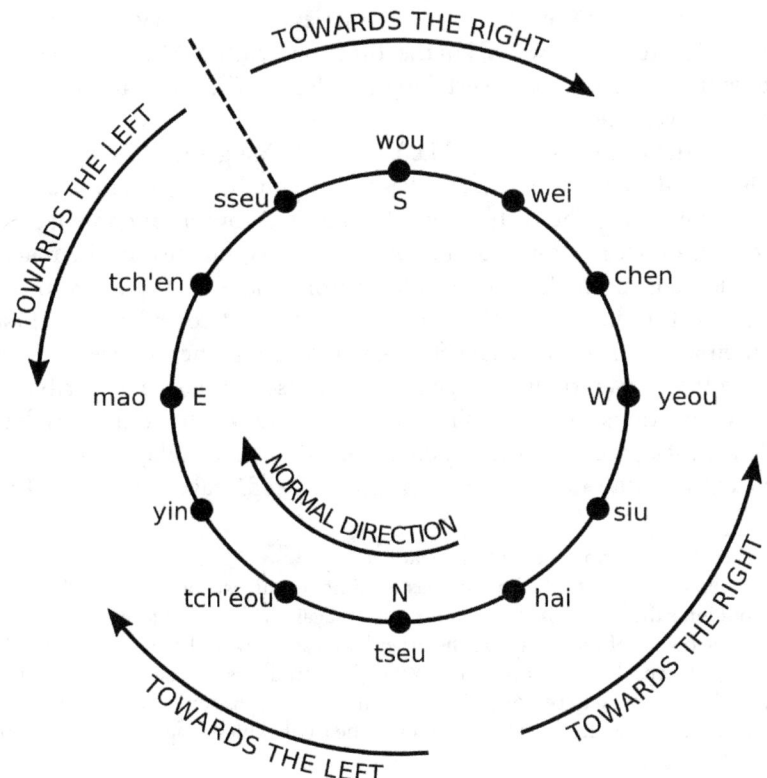

---

36 *Louen heng*, in Forke, *Lun-Heng…*, vol. I, p. 265. *Tch'ouen ts'ieou fan lou*, 12.
37 *Li ki*, C., I, p. 146.
38 Granet, *La vie et la mort…*, p. 3.

chen; the sign *sseu* marks the place of conception; pregnancy lasts 10 months. Now, 10 cyclic seasons[39] are traversed going from *sseu* to *yin*, if the march is to the left, in the direction of the Sun and Yang (male).

Also 10 stations are counted, but on condition of following the opposite direction, to go from *sseu* to *chen*; the movement is dextrorotatory. It is the proper one for a female embryo; *carried on the right side, this embryo makes its turn by advancing to the right*. Similarly, starting from the North, to meet at *sseu*, the place of conception, the man and the woman (men marry at 30, women at 20) must travel, the first 30 stations, the other 20 stations, if they advance, the first to the left, the second to the right. The march to the left, proper to the things of the High and Yang, also characterizes the heroes animated by the genius of Heaven. Those animated by the genius of Earth and Yin are destined to walk to the right. History contains convincing evidence of this. To walk to the left is to walk with the left foot forward, without the right foot overtaking the left.[40] Thus walked T'ang the Victorious, who only touched the Earth with tiny feet, so much did the Virtue of Heaven possess him. He also came out through the breast (*yang*) of the maternal body. Yu the Great, who came out of her back (*yin*), possessed, with very large feet, the Virtue of Earth. Therefore, he walked in the direction befitting Yin, with the right foot forward, without the left foot overtaking the right.[41] The chest and forepart, with the right foot, were the same.

The chest and front, the East and Left, belong to Yang, the Masculine, the Higher and Heaven; the back and rear, the West and Right, belong to Yin, the Feminine, the Lower, the Earth. The distinction of High and Low, a fundamental political metaphor, introduces a double asymmetry in society, but also in the macrocosm and the microcosm. The left imposes itself from above, the right from below. A myth explains this antithesis. The doctors who relate it consider it the first principle of their art.[42] Since the misdeeds of Kong-kong and the rupture, in the North-West of the World, of mount Pou-tcheou have caused Heaven and Earth to incline in opposite directions, Heaven, collapsed towards the West, is only completely full on the left (East), precisely where it collapsed. The Earth collapses leaving a great void. The entire East is dominated by the influence of Heaven and Yang. The West,

---

39   The Chinese term for counting included.

40   When one walks to the left and has to climb a staircase, one starts with the left foot, the right foot joins the left on the first step, and starts again with the left foot: this is what a guest should do. The owner of the house, on the other hand, starts with the right foot, even if he has to climb the east steps, i.e. those on the left. When he introduces his guest, he should walk eastward across the courtyard to the right. It is when he leads the visitor back that both may use, in the East and in the West, the walk to the left or to the right, which is appropriate to these places in space (*Li ki*, C., I, p. 19)

41   *Tch'ouen ts'icou fan lou*, 7; Granet, *Danses et légendes*, p. 549. The passage of Yu, which has remained famous, has always been used by sorcerers for their magical feats; the opposite direction (*yi*) is suitable for magic. In chapter 8 of *Po hou t'ong*, the connection between the step, the advance to the left or to the right, determined by a celestial or terrestrial genie, and the principle that Heaven is levorotatory, Earth dextrorotatory, is clearly evident.

42   *Houang nei king*, p. 2.

Book III - Chapter I - The Microcosm   229

on the other hand, is dominated by Yin, because the Earth remains alone, while Heaven is absent. This architectural arrangement can be found in the microcosm. For the human body, in the West (I refer to the right), Heaven (I refer to Yang) is lacking and Earth (I refer to Yin) abounds. Yin, in the lower part of the body, which is close to the Earth, is the one that reigns; therefore, the Chinese are and must be dexterous with regard to the hands and especially the feet. On the other hand, as regards the eyes and ears (located in the upper part of the body), they are and must be left-handed; in the East (I mean the left) Yin is deficient like Earth, but Yang abounds, like Heaven. Hence it is proper to cut off the left ear of enemies or pluck out their left eye.[43] Hence, to eat the things of the Earth one must use the right hand, which is the one that acts, but kills and hides,[44] while the left is the honorable side by which every man (in normal times) must advance and present himself, the left hand being the one that presents itself in saluting.[45]

* * *

The sky performs its circular motion in four seasons. Thus, we have 4 limbs, each composed of 3 parts. 3 months form a season, 12 months form the year, or 360 (days), which is the number of joints of our body. We have eyes and ears in the heights. Doesn't Heaven have the Sun and the Moon? Wind and rain frolic in the universe; Breath (*k'i*) and Blood frolic in us. All this is taught by a philosopher, one of the best informed: Houai-nan tseu.[46] He also knows many other things, for example, that Heaven, having nine floors, has nine gates. There are also nine openings in our body, for we are better equipped than birds, which, being born from an egg, have one opening less; but their eight openings correspond to the eight kinds of musical instruments; thanks to the phoenix music was invented. And Houai-nan tseu[47] also knows that we possess five viscera, for there are five elements. Ten months of gestation are necessary to form the body with the 5 Viscera and the Apertures that govern: the lungs and the (2) eyes, the kidneys and the (2) nostrils, the liver and the (2) ears, the gall bladder and the mouth… which makes, if we count, 7 Apertures and 4 Viscera only. The art of reconciling the classifications is difficult, but the benefit is great when we manage to intertwine them: the common order of the macrocosm and the microcosm appears.

The theory of the 5 viscera and that of the 9 (or 7) orifices show that the conformation of Man is modeled on that of the Universe. These theories were even used, when the 5 Elements and the 5 Planets were identified, to imagine a doctrine (comparable to medical astrology), some parts of which may be ancient, since, since time immemorial, the 7 Openings seem to be related to the 7 celestial Rulers or the 7 Stars of the Big Dipper. These two theories, in any case, are linked to ancient mythological classifications. We cannot but refer to the latter when we want

---

43 Granet, *op. cit.*, pp. 378, 137 ff.
44 *Lao tseu*, in Wieger, *Les Pères du système taoïste*, pp. 39 and 40.
45 The vassals, for whom the right hand is the honorable side, are considered "the feet and hands" of the Prince.
46 *Houai-nan tseu*, 7.
47 *Ibid.*, 3.

to present a coherent picture of reality. Thought, whether scholarly or technical, far from trying to free itself from mythology, borrows from it its symbolic material and its method. The role of the scholar is to derive a scholasticism from myths. The sum of knowledge is constituted by increasing, by analogy, the repertoire of correlations. As at the time when the couplets of the *Che king* were invented, the great principle of correspondences and interactions (*t'ong*) is the solidarity that unites the natural with the human, the physical with the moral.

The *Hong fan* assumes this principle. It illustrates it by establishing – thanks to the order followed for the enumeration – the correspondence of the Five Elements and their products, the Five Human Activities (*che*) and their results, the Five Celestial Signs (*tcheng*) and the indications they provide by marking the repercussion in Heaven of the good or bad behavior of men and of the morals that the government makes flourish among them.

Order numbers	1	2	3	4	5
Elements	Water	Fire	Wood	Metal	Earth
	Salt	Bitter	Sour	Acre	Sweet
Human Activity	Gesture	Speech	Sight	Hearing	Will
	Gravity	Order	Wisdom	Harmony	Holiness
Heavenly Signs	Gravity	Order	Wisdom	Harmony	Holiness
	Rain	Yang	Heat	Cold	Wind

These signs (as shown in the table above) translate into material symbols the "virtues" resulting from the Symmetrical Activities. There is, as can be seen, a strict correspondence between the celestial Signs and the human Activities that occupy the same rank in the enumeration. The correspondence cannot be less strict between these Activities or Signs and the symmetrical Elements. At this point, moreover, the parallels in detail are instructive, since Yang approaches Fire (= South-Summer) and Water (= North-Winter) to Rain, which seems here to evoke Yin (= Darkness, cloudy weather).[48]. Although the nomenclature subsequently changed and there are, in detail, quite a few divergences, the *Hong fan* system has not failed to inspire the tables of correspondences to which both ritualists and philosophers refer. The list of equivalences is never given in full, because the points of view differ and, for example, the table below, coming from the *Yue ling* hardly covers the scope of things and ritual acts.

---

48 I do not understand why Maspero, *La Chine antique*, (p. 442) has omitted, like P. Wieger (*Histoire des croyances*..., p.62), to point out the importance of the Five Heavenly Signs. Not pointing them out leads to ignoring what the *Hong fan* is: a quick image of the Chinese classification system. Why, instead (because of the translation given by Chavannes who translated *yang* as "illuminating sun"), is the mention (significant because of the opposition with rain) made here of Yang concealed?

Book III - Chapter I - The Microcosm

Items	Wood	Fire	Earth	Metal	Water
Directions	East	South	Center	West	North
Colors	Green	Red	Yellow	White	Black
Flavors	Sour	Bitter	Sweet	Acre	Salty
Smells	Rancid	Burned	Scented	Raw meat smell	Rotten smell
Plant foods	Wheat	Bean	White millet	Oil grains	Yellow millet
Domestic animals	Ram	Chicken	Ox	Dog	Pork
Lares or parts of the house	Inner door	Home	Impluvium	Big door	Hall (or well)
Geniuses of the East	Keou-Mang	Tchou-jong	Heou-T'ou	Jou-Cheou	Hiuan-ming
Sovereigns	T'ai-hao (Fou-hi)	Yen-Ti (Chen-nong)	Houang-ti	Chao-hao	Tchouan-hiu
Musical notes	Kio	Tche	Kong	Chang	Yu
Numbers	8	7	5	9	6
Binomials of cyclical denarian signs	kia-yi	pint-ting	meou-kiki ke	keng-sin	jen-kouei
Animal Classes	With scales	With feathers	With bare skin	With hair	With shell
Viscera	Spleen	Lungs	Heart	Liver	Kidneys

But Houai-nan tseu[49] teaches, on the one hand, that Wind, Rain, Cold and Heat were equated with the action of taking and giving, joy and anger; and on the other hand, that Thunder corresponds to Spleen and Kidneys to Rain. Gestures and emotions are thus related, through the Elements and the Viscera, to cosmic phenomena or, better said, to the "celestial signs".

Directions	East	South	Center	West	North
Wood	Fire	Earth	Metal	Water	Water
Wind	Breath (k'i)		Clouds	Rain	Thunder
Liver	Lungs	Heart	Bile	Kidneys	Spleen

Furthermore, Sseu-ma T'sien tells us that, through the Five Notes, the Five Fundamental Virtues were connected with the Five Viscera.[50] Like the *Hong Fan*, Sseu-ma Ts'ien assigns Sanctity to the Center. Now, the order of the Elements followed by the *Hong Fan* derives, as we have seen, from the order of production of

---

49 *Houai-nan tseu*, 7. Note that here there are 6 viscera.
50 *SMT*, III, p. 290.

the Notes. Therefore, the connection between the Notes, the Elements and the Virtues may be considered ancient. Their common link with the viscera must be no less ancient; ritual technique, as the *Yue ling* attests, required that at each station, the emblem of which was a certain note, a certain viscera should be given preeminence in the sacrifices.[51] "The note *kio* (= East-Spring = Wood) moves the liver and brings man into harmony with perfect Goodness. Nothing can so well point out the emblematic interplay and the profound solidarity that unites the physical and the moral under the dominion of the cosmic rhythm as this sentence of Sseu-ma Ts'ien.

Directions	East	South	Center	West	North
Numbers	8	7	5	9	6
Notes	Kio	Tche	Kong	Yu	Chang
Viscera	Liver	Heart	Spleen	Lungs	Kidneys
Virtues	Kindness	Ritual Spirit	Holiness	Equity	Wisdom

Pan Kou, in his *Po hou t'ong*,[52] develops similar ideas. One distinction complicates them; it is that of Superior and Inferior, that of Heaven and Earth. It is not lacking in the *Hong fan*, where the Five Heavenly Signs are opposed to the Five Elements.

Directions	East	South	Center	West	North
Symbols	Stars	Sun	Earth	Mansions	Moon
Seasons	Spring	Summer		Autumn	Winter
K'i	Wind	Yang		Yin	Cold
Elements	Wood	Fire	Earth	Metal	Water
Body Elements	Bone	Breath	Muscles	Fingernails	Blood
Passions (tö)	Joy	Pleasure		Sorrow	Anger

An excellent physician delivered a beautiful speech to comfort a dying man, which is recorded in the *Tso tchouan*,[53] in which he contrasted the Five Flavors, Colors and Notes with the Six Influences (*k'i*): Yin, Yang, Wind, Rain, Darkness and Light. This list differs little from the list of the Five Signs: Yang, Wind, Rain, Cold and Hot. A passage in the *Kouan tseu*[54] brings the Passions closer to the Influences by giving correspondences with the Seasons-Directions, the Elements, but without explaining the Influences (*k'i*) of the Center. In all these cases, the celestial

---

51 The connection of the cardinal virtues with the seasons-directions is, moreover, implied in several myths; goodness (*jen*), for example, is the characteristic virtue of the Orientals.
52 *Po hou t'ong*, 8.
53 *Tso tchouan*, C., III, pp. 30-39, (cf. note 674).
54 *Kouan tseu*, 14. The correspondences established by Kouan tseu differ from those of the *Po hou t'ong* and the *Houang-ti nei king*. Note the opposition of Breath (*k'i*), which is related to Fire, and Blood, which is related to Water, and the fact that the passions are described as *tö*, a word whose meaning (virtue) is reminiscent of influence (*k'i*).

Book III - Chapter I - The Microcosm 233

is opposed to the earthly. This opposition is found in the *Li yun*[55] (where the *Six* or Seven Passions are opposed to the Six or Five Duties) indicated by the numbers 5 and 6, which are those of Heaven and Earth. The same is true in the *Po hou t'ong*, where Pan Kou (in contrast to Houai-nan tseu) counts 5 (and not 6) Viscera, but opposes them to the 6 storehouses {*Fou*: the 6 Fou, as we have seen, are the 5 Elements plus the Grains (which duplicate the Element Earth)}. The 6 storehouses of the body {small and large bowels, stomach, intestines, bladder and gall bladder (distinguished from the liver, which is considered (here) as a viscera)} are linked to the 6 *Ho*, that is to say, to the 6 Directions when we enumerate them by dividing the Center into an Upper and a Lower. This is how Pan Kou manages to oppose, like the Stores to the Viscera, the 6 Passions (Anger and Joy, Pain and Pleasure, Love and Hate) to the 5 Cardinal Virtues. A similar distinction plays an important role in the *Houang-ti nei king*, the breviary of ancient Chinese medicine. As in the *Po hou t'ong*,[56] there is much talk of correspondences between the microcosm and the macrocosm. The picture that can be drawn from the second chapter is, in detail, often contradictory to other passages of the treatise; it is not to the detriment of the medical art to increase, at the cost of some contradictions, the symbolic parallels from which the principles of treatment and the elements of diagnosis are

---

55   *Li ki*, C., I, pp. 516, 519 ff. Perhaps the 6 *K'i* (Influences) should be regarded as the products of the 6 Tsong, of the 6 Heavenly Domains which the *Chou king* (SMT, I, pp. 59-61) puts in relation to the 5 Badges. There is disagreement about the list of the 6 Tsong, but Rain and Wind or Water and Drought are always included among them. A passage from the *Tsi fa* (*Li ki*, C., II, p. 259) seems to authorize comparing the sacrifice made to the 6 Tsong with the sacrifices made to: 1° the Four Seasons; 2° the Heat and the Cold; 3° the Sun and the Moon (Yang and Yin); 4° the Stars and the Rain (the Count of the Wind and the Lord of the Rain reside in two stars)… a) Now, the text of the *Hong fan* on the 5 celestial signs contains a double difficulty; contrary to most of the other epigraphs, the signs are not numbered; however, the second part of the text considers 5 signs and begins with the word "five"; b) the first part of the text contains 6 times the word *yue* (cfr. *supra*, Book II, ch. III, sec. I), which seems to indicate a list with 6 numbers; the sixth *yue* precedes the word *che*, where Chavannes saw a demonstrative and which he linked to the following sentence. But this word means "station," and we see that the *Tsi fa* indicates a sacrifice to the Seasons, most interpreters admitting, on the other hand, that the Seasons figure among the 6 Tsong. It seems that the editors of the *Hong fan* hesitated between 5 and 6.

56   I simplify the tables taken from Pan Kou and the *Houang-ti nei king*, suppressing odors, colors, etc. (according to the equivalences of the *Yue ling*). Pan Kou gives three different distributions for the openings (I, II, III), which I isolate. I also isolate (A, B) the correspondences of the Passions and the Orientals, of the Passions and the Stores, which Pan Kou gives separately. (653b) *Yi king*, L, p. 429; Granet, *Danses et légendes*…, (note 1187). The distribution is according to Wen Wang's orientation:

```
                    S
                   Head
         Mouth            Buttocks
    E   Eyes                Ears    W
         Feet             Hands
                   Belly
                    S
```

drawn. This image does not differ much from that which can be drawn from the eighth chapter of Pan Kou. Both distinguish between the Virtues and the Passions. Both show the importance attributed to the orifices of the human body. Just as the theory of the Five Virtues is related to that of the Five Viscera, the theory of the Apertures is related to the theory of the Passions. Such are the foundations of the knowledge of the Microcosm.

	East-Spring	South-Summer	Center	West-Autumn	North-Winter
	Liver	Heart	Spleen	Lungs	Kidneys
	Goodness	Ritual Spirit	Good Faith	Equity	Wisdom
I	Eyes	Ears	Mouth	Nose	
II	Eyes	Tongue	Ears		
III	Eyes	Tongue	Mouth	Nose	Ears
A	Anger	Hate	(High) Pleasure	Joy	Love
A	East	South	Center	West	North
B	Bile	Small Intestine	Stomach	Large Intestine	Bladder
B	Liver	Heart	Spleen	Lungs	Kidneys

In order to inventory Man, both physically and morally, a great effort of ingenuity had to be made; it was necessary to reconcile the classifications or, rather, to demonstrate that, in the human world as in the natural world, order and life result from the interweaving of the numerical classifications proper to Earth or Heaven.

East-Spring	South-Summer	Center	West-Fall	North-Winter
Wood	Fire	Earth	Metal	Water
Sour	Bitter	Sweet	Acre	Salty
Liver	Heart	Spleen	Lungs	Kidneys
Muscles	Blood	Flesh	Hair	Bones
Eyes	Tongue	Mouth	Nose	Ears
Calling	Laughing	Singing	Wailing	Groaning
Grasping	Shaking	Burping	Coughing	Trembling
Anger	Joy	Will	Sadness	Fear
Kindness	Ritual Spirit	Good Faith	Equity	Wisdom

The theory of the openings seems no less ancient than that of the viscera. It also inspires various ritual practices. Mythology takes it into account. We can believe that the authors of the *Hong fang* took it into account as well. The human Activities that these scholars list are (apart from the Will or the Thought, to which a central place corresponds): Sight and Hearing, Gesture and Speech. In this conception appears a desire for symmetry. It also appears in the division of the human body into eight parts (assimilated to the Eight Trigrams) professed by the masters of divination: the Eyes were assigned to the East, the Ears to the West.[^653b] The *Hong fang* likewise places the Ear in the West and the Sight in the East. When the orifices are distributed, the Kidneys are assigned to the North and Water, and, behind them, the Ears. The Eyes are always in the East, and the Tongue in the South. Sight and Speech also occupy the East and South in the *Hong fan*, which assigns Gestures to the North. North is the direction of the Kidneys; these, as we shall see, preside over dance and gesticulation.

If the theory of the orifices is ancient, divergences in its application prevailed from the beginning, since divergent classifications had to be reconciled from the start. The *Po hou t'ong* is a notable example.

East	South	Center		West	North
		High	Low		
Anger	Hatred	Pleasure	Grief	Joy	Love
Rain	Yin	Light	Darkness	Wind	Yang

He bases his system of distribution on the authority of an adage taken from the *Li yun*: "The Six Passions are that by which the Five Natural Qualities (*wou sing*) are realized."[57] However, this adage is no longer found in the *Li yun*, because it has been edited since it was incorporated into the *Li ki*.[58] On the other hand, we find the indication that there are Ten Duties and *Seven* Passions, viz: *joy, anger, sadness, fear, love, hatred* and *desire*. The glossators do not mention a *different* text preserved by Pan Kou, but one of them recalls the *Tso tchouan* passage on the *Six Heavenly Influences* (*k'i*), and then adds that, on Earth, they correspond to the Six Passions: joy, anger, sadness, pleasure, love, and hatred. These are the Six Passions of the *Po hou t'ong*, which are not cited, preferring to indicate the equivalence with the Six K'i. And it is concluded, "Desire is pleasure… fear is the seventh passion."[59]

There are 6 celestial Influences. – There are 6 or 7 Passions. – There are 7 or 9 Orifices. – And if there are 6 Stores, there are only 5 Viscera. – It is difficult to name the orifices without saying: the 7 orifices. They are the 7 orifices of the face: the two eyes, the two ears, the two nostrils and the mouth. The two lower orifices, which are *yin*, are rarely mentioned. If we consider the 9, it seems easy, in principle, to distribute them among the 5 viscera. The eyes, ears, nostrils, *yin* orifices, which go in pairs, count as four and the mouth makes 5. The lower orifices are easily assigned to the Kidneys, a double viscera, and, likewise, the nostrils to the Lungs. The Eyes, without too much difficulty, will go with the Liver, to which the Bile may

---

57   *Po hou t'ong*, 8.
58   *Li ki*, C., II, p. 516. The Ten Duties are: brotherly affection and filial love; kindness of the elder brother and submissiveness of the younger; justice of the husband and obedience of the wife; beneficence of the elder and docility of the younger; kindness of the prince and fidelity of the vassal. These 10 duties refer to 5 relationships.
59   Kong Ying-ta's gloss on the T'ang. The equivalences with the Directions indicated in the table are those of Pan Kou.

serve as an annex viscera. This leaves the Spleen and Heart, the Ears and Mouth. To confer the Mouth to the Spleen, a single and central viscera, is very appropriate; Good Faith will follow the Mouth to the Center. Therefore, to the Heart will correspond the Ears.[60] But is it proper to assign it thus? The Heart is a *yang* viscera, a simple viscera. It has a right to be lodged in the Front (*yang*), in the Chest (*yang*), in the very Top (*yang*) of the body, like a Prince (*yang*).[61] Is it not – like the Heroes of Yang and *Left* that taper to the Earth – large at the Top (*yang*), slender at the Bottom (*yin*)?[62] The Ears (replacing the lower orifices), will suit (they are cut off for prisoners of war whose virile strength is to be weakened) the Kidneys lodged in the Belly (*yin*), below (*yin*), (as subjects that are "the feet and hands of the lord" and well placed to animate the feet to dance.[63] As the lower orifices are no longer taken into account,[64] there remain only three pairs of orifices besides the Mouth, and there are five Viscera to fill. But is it not usual to *double* what is *central* and the Mouth does not contain the Tongue? The Eyes remain with the Liver, the Nostrils with the Lungs, the Mouth with the Spleen, the Tongue, the orifice of salivation, will be assigned to the Heart.[65] To continue counting 7 Apertures, the Eyes, the Nostrils or the Ears always counting respectively two, it will suffice to count by one the Mouth and the Tongue.

Once the classifications have been reconciled and nested by 9, 8, 7, 6, 5, it only remains to justify the equivalences. For the learned, this is a game from which the healer will take advantage. The Heart is red; it is the color of Fire; it is the color of joy; Thunder is the sound of fire and is the laughter of Heaven;[66] the Heart presides over Laughter, Restlessness and Joy. Lamentations and sadness depend, like coughs, on the lungs. They are white, the color of autumn, the West, the Tiger, the Sunset, the Great White (Venus) and Mourning. The West is the region of the Mountains and the Gorges where the Wind rushes and from where the Rain comes. The Nose, orifice of the lungs, rises high up in the face; deep cavities pierce it; it is through it that the mucus comes out; it is thanks to it that one breathes.[67] The Eyes are the orifices of the Liver, which is green and corresponds to Spring, Wood and Wind. The wind sweeps away the dark clouds, makes the raindrops luminous.[68] These are the words of the poets. As for the physiologists, they explain that Wood, when it comes out of the Fire, projects light, and that it causes buds to appear and sap to

---

60 See the table of the *Po hou t'ong*, I. The heart and the prince belong to the left.
61 *Po hou t'ong*, 8. The *Houang-ti nei king* wants the back to be *yang*. (Yin and Yang, when united, are not reduced to the single position occupied by Heaven and Earth.) Therefore, it assigns (ch. I) the heart to the back.
62 *Po hou t'ong*, 8. cf. *supra* in this same chapter.
63 *Lie tseu*, in Wieger, *op. cit.* p. 145.
64 See the table of the *Po hou t'ong* (III), and the table of the *Houang-ti nei king*.
65 *Po hou t'ong*, 8; *Houang-ti nei king*, 2 and 14; a third solution {table of the *Po hou t'ong* (II)} would be to give the Ears to the Spleen.
66 *Houang-ti nei king*, 2 and 8; *Po hou t'ong*, 8; *Chen yi king*, I.
67 *Po hou t'ong*, 8.
68 *Tch'ou tseu*, 9.

flow every spring.⁶⁹ Does not the light come from the East? Has not the East, like the spring, a beneficent influence? The lungs are the viscera of goodness…

Physiology and psychology are completed once the theory of the apertures and that of the viscera have been combined. But they do not serve to know only the Microcosm, but lead to a total knowledge of Heaven and Earth; the viscera, the virtues, the elements, the apertures, the passions and the celestial influences correspond. He who knows Man knows the World and the structure of the Universe, as well as its history. It is not necessary to create, with great difficulty, special sciences; knowledge is one. The geographer knows nothing of the mountains inasmuch as he has recognized in them the bones of the earth; they give to the world, as the skeleton does to the body, solidity and stability.⁷⁰ The physiologist knows at once that the blood circulates; he knows exactly the role of the vessels through which the bodily humors pass; it is enough for him to have made an observation: the universe is traversed by rivers that carry water.⁷¹ Hair and trees, vegetation and fluff are of the same order; politicians know this very well, as do all fair weather people; they can combine the means of action; when the vegetation of a mountain is cut down, or when a chief makes the sacrifice of his hair, the rains, those fertile humors, cease to flow.⁷²

Happy are the historians and psychologists! Must they draw a portrait of Kao-yao, give his genealogy or that of Confucius, and characterize the spirit of the Master? Their quest soon comes to an end. Kao-yao was Minister of Justice and Chouen charged him with criminal investigations; the viscera of good faith is the spleen; the mouth depends on the spleen; Kao-yao had a very large mouth and opened it wide… as do horses or birds; Kao-yao is none other than Ta-yé, son of Niu-sieou, who conceived by swallowing an egg and whose descendants (who resemble birds) know how to breed horses.⁷³ Confucius was descended from Yin who reigned by virtue of Water; he had a depression at the top of his skull (his surname means "hollow," his personal name "hollow mound") similar to that of hills that hold a body of water at their summit; water corresponds to the kidneys and to the color black; Confucius' complexion was very black (a sign of depth) and his mind was characterized by sapience, for sapience depends on the kidneys.⁷⁴

More fortunate still are the philosophers and physicians. To them belongs the wonderful mastery of mythological classifications. What admirable material for people whose job it is to argue! It offers an infinity of subjects for diagnosis or judgment, the secrets of therapy or moral guidance. One can find in it, with the ability to reason about the macrocosm and the microcosm, all the recipes for good living or for living well and, at the very least, the means to force one to accept that, such being the course of events, all is for the best. A prince of Tsin is ill; a sage and

---

69   *Po hou t'ong*, 8.
70   *Louen heng*, in Forke, *Lun Heng…*, 1.
71   *Ibid.*, II, p. 250.
72   Granet, *Danses et légendes…*, pp. 285, 484.
73   *Ibid*, pp. 373, 374. *Po hou t'ong*, 7 and 8.
74   Granet, *op. cit.*, pp. 432 ff; *Po hou t'ong*, 7; *Louen heng*, in Forke, *op. cit.*, I, p. 304.

a physician are called in; both conclude that there is nothing to be done, and the answer is: "That is very true," because the two experts have disserted eruditely. The sage, with much historical or astronomical information, explained the action of the spirits and the physician, with a series of apothegms, spoke of the evil spell: "The 6 influences (*k'i*) of Heaven become the 5 Flavors below (on Earth), manifest themselves in the 5 Colors and have as indexes the 5 Notes. Excess generates the 6 Diseases. The 6 Influences (*k'i*) are Yin and Yang, wind and rain, darkness and light. (Properly) distributed, they form the 4 Seasons; (put) in order, they form the 5 divisions (of 72 days each) of the year. As soon as they are excessive, there is calamity. Excess of Yin causes cold; excess of Yang, fevers; excess of Wind, diseases of the limbs; excess of Rain, diseases of the stomach; excess of Darkness, mental disorders; excess of Light, ailments of the heart. Woman is the thing of Yang and of moments of darkness (the companion of the night). If used in excess, there is internal fever and evil mental disorders (*kou*)... The *Kou* (malefic) is related to excesses and mental disorders. This word is written with the signs 'vase' and 'vermin'; the winged (being) coming out of the grain (*kou*) (placed in a vase) is the *kou* (malefic).[75] The *Yi (king)* of the Tcheou says: 'The girl disturbs the boy's mind; the wind overturns the hill', is (the hexagram) *Kou*.[76] All these things correspond (*t'ong*)!" "What an excellent physician!" exclaims one as soon as he finishes this discourse, and is pleased to pay handsomely for the consultation.[77]

* * *

There is nothing more reasonable for a patient than to go to a consultation with a loquacious physician and a wise man versed in history. Physiology and hygiene or morals merge with physics, or rather with history, that is, with the art of the calendar; anatomy and psychology or logic merge with cosmography, geography or politics; and the essence of politics is that art, later called geomancy (*fong chouei*), by which the Chinese intended to order the world by applying to it their system of classifications, that is, the rules of their social morphology. Geomancy and the calendar, morphology and physiology common to the macrocosm and microcosm, this is the total knowledge and the only rule. This knowledge and this rule dictate and teach all the behavior of men and things. Every being would be rebellious and disorderly if he contravened the slightest prescriptions of etiquette. Etiquette is the only law. Through it the order of the universe is realized. It must order every gesture, every attitude of beings, great and small.

---

75   This procedure for "feeding the evil spell" is still used in southern China, at least among the barbarians. "Grain" and "evil spell" read: *kou*.
76   Hexagram 18 (*Yi king*, L., p. 95) formed by the trigram Ken (Mountain) superimposed on the trigram Siuan (Wind). See *Ibid*. p. 290.
77   *Tso tchouan*, C., III, pp. 30 to 39. (Cf. *Ibid*., p. 380).

Chapter III
Etiquette

Instead of applying themselves to measure effects and causes, the Chinese naively enumerate correspondences. The order of the universe is indistinguishable from the order of civilization. How can one think of establishing necessary and immutable sequences? To make an inventory of traditional conventions requires a more subtle art and has a completely different interest. To know, then, is power. Sovereigns, when they are wise, secrete civilization. They maintain it, they propagate it by extending a coherent system of attitudes to the whole hierarchy of beings. They do not think of the limitation of laws, since the prestige of traditional norms is sufficient. Men only need models and things are like them. They dare not see the physical world as the realm of necessity, just as they do not claim freedom for the moral realm. The macrocosm and the microcosm are equally content to maintain venerable habits. The universe is but a system of behaviors, and the behaviors of spirit are indistinct from those of matter. There is no distinction between matter and spirit. The notion of soul, the idea of an entirely spiritual essence that would oppose the body as a collection of material bodies, is completely alien to Chinese thought.

* * *

Lie tseu develops at length the thesis that the most real actions are those without contact and without loss of energy.[1] To act is to influence. The idea that one acts by mere influence is not specifically Taoist. An anecdote from the *Tso tchouan*[2] demonstrates this. A good coachman is able to drive a cart fully loaded with parts about to break. Change the coachman and just load the cart with a little wood; the

---

1   *Lie tseu*, in Wieger, *Les Pères du système taoïste*, pp. 139-150.
2   *Tso tchouan*, C., III, p. 611.

parts break at once; they no longer have any cohesion; they are no longer influenced by the ascendancy of a master driver. Matter and spirit (or rather what we call spirit) do not form separate realms. Such is the common idea in China; it is, for Lie tseu,[3] one of the main ideas of his system. Thus, with all the earnestness that a philosopher can preserve when arguing, he complacently relates a comic scene which was enacted with puppets in the time of King Mou of the Tcheou. The puppeteer who showed them had made them of leather and painted and varnished wood. These figures bent as well as men and even sang well and danced beautifully. The reason was that their entrails were full of wooden viscera and they lacked no orifices. If their kidneys were removed, they could no longer dance. If their livers were removed, they could no longer see. Equipped with their Five Viscera and all their Orifices, they experienced all the Passions. King Mou was incensed; the puppets winked impudently at his favorites. These artifacts of magical-philosophical demonstration were worth what men are worth; they looked just like him. When Chaos, having shown signs of civility, deserved to be received among men, two friends (these were the genii of the Ray) spent a whole week, opening a breach for him every day, to give him the human face he deserved.[4] On the seventh day of the operation, Chaos died, says Tchouang tseu. This means that every initiation or birth resembles a death. True death, on the contrary, is accompanied by the closing of all the orifices of the body. The eyes and mouth of the deceased are closed. From ancient times, no doubt, all orifices were sealed with jade; this practice is similar to the custom of drawing the Seven Stars of the Big Dipper on the coffins.[5] The following is an example. It is convenient to enclose in the corpse the funerary infection and the very principle of death. It is also necessary to enclose in the criminal the principle of his crime and of his malfunctioning; it is out of precaution, rather than out of cruelty, that the orifices of his body are sealed.[6] In the wise and pure, all the orifices open and function freely, the seven orifices of the face and the seven orifices of the heart corresponding to them. The quality of life is obtained and preserved only if the first are wide open; holiness is obtained as soon as the others are unblocked or close to being so.[7] The power of life reaches its maximum when nothing impedes the endosmosis of the Microcosm and the Macrocosm. Hence the importance of the openings.

This importance, recognized by the whole tradition, is explained by the prestige which the magic of secretions, excretions and respirations has always enjoyed in China. The precautions required by etiquette and which seem to be part of the

---

3 *Lie tseu*, in Wieger, *op. cit.*, p. 145. The wandering player was received by King Mou near K'ouen-louen, i.e., in Central Asia or in the region (on the fringe of civilization) which is the domain of the gods and magicians. The wandering player is an expert in the art of mutations (*houa*); he is a *houa-jen* (the sign *houa* is written with the image of a standing man and that of a lying man).

4 Granet, *op. cit.*, p. 544; *Tchouang tseu*, in Wieger, *op. cit.* p. 269.

5 *Civ. Chin.*, pp. 303, 360. The Big Dipper is the emblem of the heart, which also has seven openings: *Po hou t'ong*, 8; *Houang-ti nei king*, 14.

6 *SMT*, II, p. 410; *Civ. Chin.*, p. 55.

7 *SMT*, I, p. 206; *Lie tseu*, in Wieger *op. cit.*, pp. 119, 123; Granet, *op. cit.*, p. 225.

Book III - Chapter III - Etiquette 241

care of cleanliness are imposed by the concern not to let a superior suffer or an enemy benefit from the exhalations, losses or degradations of what constitutes the power of life. It is up to the relatives, to the children[8] to collect and carefully hide the spittle and snot of the parents; it is up to them to collect the last breath, to close the eyes, the mouth, to pile clothes over all the orifices, not to let anything of the paternal substance be lost, to bury on the floor of the house the nails, the hair of the deceased and the water that was used to wash the corpse.[9] One can act on another (and on all one's own) as soon as one possesses a part or a residue of his substance. By stealing from him a selected portion, one can also annex to oneself what the other possesses of life, the power of his sight or hearing if one seizes the eyes or ears, life at its very source if one steals the first blood of virgins or the embryo just formed. These practices, still punished by the codes of the most recent dynasties, are not new. It was not out of cruelty or tyrant dilettantism that Cheou-sin, the last of the Yin, disemboweled pregnant women and ate the flesh of his enemies.[10] Every ruler, every magician needs to regain power, substance, life, for he must expend all his vitality for the benefit of all. The magician wears out his power when he animates the puppets or makes the pieces fight on the chessboard;[11] the coachman also wears out his power when he gives cohesion to the reins. But how much more the Chief! He gets, by a direct effect of influence (we might also say, in more modern words: by a spirit-to-spirit effect), that the horses of his chariot go straight ahead when he thinks straight, that the arrows of his subjects hit as soon as he thinks straight. It is enough that the magician strikes his enemy with his spittle or blows upon his shadow for the wretch to perish riddled with ulcers;[12] in his spittle or in his breath, the magician has concentrated the essence of his magical virtues. But the Royal Work requires the concentration of a truly total power of animation. The single breath of the Chief passes through all his warriors; he, beating the drum, communicates to the whole battle the rhythm of his own ardor.[13] A decree has the force of execution as soon as the prince has said "yes"; it is efficacious, in itself, instantly, and it matters not that in practice it is executed; in this "yes" is condensed all the animating virtue which the practice of etiquette keeps intact in the prince. If there is an etiquette of dress, of hairstyle, of laughter, of lamentation and of coitus; if the inferior, out of respect, must sometimes dress and sometimes not. Whether the chief sometimes shaves his hair to offer it to the gods, sometimes dresses, girded like a woman, and sometimes dances with his hair loose like a witch; whether yawning, sneezing, spitting, blowing one's nose, coughing and belching are to be avoided; whether one should neither laugh nor cry inconsiderately, but in times of

---

8   *Li ki*, C., I, pp. 622 ff.
9   Yi li, C., p. 450; Granet, *Danses et légendes...*, note 345; *Civ. Chin.*, p. 360.
10 J.-J.-M. de Groot, *The Religious System of China*, IV, p. 398. *Ta Ts'ing lu li*, 36. One eats mainly the liver, seat of courage (the liver commands the muscles, the eyes, the anger). One dishonors the enemy if he refuses to eat his liver: it is to treat him as a coward.
11 *SMT*, III, p. 479.
12 Granet, *op. cit.*, (fn. 760).
13 *Civ. Chin.*, p. 301.

mourning should lament aloud; whether friends are made by laughing or smiling; whether the father should laugh when he gives the right to life to his little son; whether the child should laugh as soon as he receives a name from his father and cry to deserve this name; whether it is dangerous for a woman to let out a laugh or to hold it back; whether she should hide her smile by veiling her mouth with her sleeves and whether she should never steal a sigh from a man; whether it is necessary to give herself or to keep herself; whether the Head of the family should be the only one to whom the care of the child can be entrusted; if the Head, who must sometimes wear himself out completely, takes more precautions than any other to remain hermetic and mute, it is because the body, through all its orifices, lets penetrate and lets escape; it knows how to retain, project and even capture, the substance that is power, the power that is substance, that which makes being and that which makes being.

All authors, not only Taoists, agree on the principle that activities, passions and sensations wear out the being and diminish its substance and power. All admit that the orifices of the body are the organs of the senses, that the Passions and Activities (or Virtues) depend on the *Stores* (*fou*) or the Viscera which are given the name of *Granaries* (*tsang*), and that Viscera, Stores and Openings correspond to each other. While the Chinese confuse the ideas of *substance* and *power* in the idea of Self, they give, as we can see, extreme importance to food. The worth of an individual is seen in the number of vassals he can feed,[14] and what constitutes his authority is the manner in which he feeds himself; it is the lot of food allotted to him. Respectability, richness of table, abundance of life, quality of efficiency, are related, indistinct things. It could be said (to use our language) that only the nobles have souls; only they have ancestors who deserve to be fed. The nobles, the chiefs, the gods are rich in substance and power; they are providers of food. What they possess in abundance, they flaunt in giving and despise for themselves. All food is theirs; they take only the essence (*tsing*) or virtue (*tö*).[15] They are content to smell or taste. The life in them is at once strengthened and spiritualized. In fact, the formal dosage of food is accompanied by table etiquette.[16] He who eats according to etiquette refines and augments, gives body and ennobles, comforts, completes and condenses in himself a vitality of subtler essence and richer content. The King alone has "the precious nourishment," says the *Hong fan*; he is the center, the pivot of the World.[17] The physicians combine the flavors for him[18] and his prime minister – the best minister is the one who can cook[19] – nourishes the Royal Virtue (*Wang Tao*)[20] in the person of the Sovereign; he arranges the tribute in such a way that nothing is lacking to conform the soul of the master, viz: To sustain an Au-

---

14 Cf. *supra*, Book II, chap. III, sec. V.
15 Granet, *op. cit.* note 52; p. 88, note 2.
16 *Civ. Chin.*, pp. 283, 330, 334.
17 SMT, IV, p. 225.
18 *Tcheou li*, Biot, *op. cit.*, I, p. 94.
19 Granet, *Danses et légendes...*, pp. 419, 420.
20 *Ibid.*, p. 41.

BOOK III - CHAPTER III - ETIQUETTE

thority which, worthy of the Universe, is the most complete possible and the most unique, the least material and the least perishable; such, in short, that the focus of undiminished radiation may be seen in it. To preserve this principle of influence intact, it is enough to collect, at the right time and place, the essence of all that is life in the universe. The prime minister sends for his master watercress from the swamp of Yun-mong, *yun* beans from Mount Yang-houa, and, from the depths of K'ouen-louen, the four-leaved marsilea.[21] He teaches the physicians how the flavors (*tiao ho*) should "combine and unite."[22] The sauces, according to the season, will be based on vinegar, wine, ginger or salt, but always linked to honey, because the sweetness corresponds to the Earth, which is in the Center.[23] Wheat will be eaten in spring with mutton and a vinegar sauce, because mutton has a rancid smell, and acid, which goes with rancid, is suitable for spring, which "slackens" and during which it is necessary to "gather."[24] Moreover, the East is the place of the Muscles which depend on the Liver, which the Acid, "produced" by Wood, "produces" in turn (so decrees the breviary of medicine).[25] By combining the meats of the 5 (or 6) Domestic Animals, the 5 (or 6) Vegetable Foods, the 5 Smells and the 5 Flavors, the 5 Viscera[26] will be repaired according to a rhythm conforming to the Order of the World, and the experts can verify their good condition by inspecting the 9 Openings and by examining, with the help of the 5 Sounds and the 5 Colors, the 5 Exhalations (*k'i*).[27] It would be an ominous sign and a proof of a derangement of the Microcosm and Macrocosm if, in winter, when the Son of Heaven should put on black ornaments, he should not have a black complexion, that is, the color of the kidneys, for the influence (*k'i*) of the kidneys should predominate (as the winter food of the savory seasons, millet and pork). For the same reasons, in winter the voice should emit the note *yu*. "Man is the heart of Heaven and Earth, the ruler of the 5 Elements; when, nourished by the 5 Flavors, he distinguishes the 5 Notes and puts on the 5 Colors, then he has life!"[28] The nobles "eat their fief";[29] the One Man, season by season, eats the Universe. He stores up, in due time, in the 5 Barns of his body, the essence of the most exquisite things that universal life produces. He gathers life in its utmost freshness from the 5 Eastern seasons. He nourishes his being with the first fruits. "The grains they contain have life," says the *Che king*.[30] Life is drawn, most powerfully, from fresh living food,[31] when it is drawn from it in its freshness, which is so pure, that, to the impure, it is then a deadly poison. The entrails of a wicked prince, as soon as he eats new wheat, become rottenness and

---

21 *Lu che tch'ouen ts'ieou*, 14, § 2 (Ferns similar to four-leaf clovers – Translator Note).
22 *Houai-nan tseu*, 20.
23 *Tcheou li*, in Biot, *op. cit.*, I, p. 94, and note on p. 96.
24 Ibid., I, p. 94. See tables.
25 *Houang-ti nei king*, 2.
26 *Yue ling* and *Tcheou li*, in Biot, *op. cit.*, I, p. 93.
27 *Tcheou li*, in Biot, *op. cit.*, I, p. 96.
28 *Li ki*, I, p. 520.
29 Granet, *op. cit.*, note 180.
30 *Che king*, C., p. 441.
31 "Cheng," "living," is said of fresh food.

dung;[32] those of the wise man remain clean, and purity increases in him with life when he sacralizes himself by tasting, in the likeness of the gods, the virtue (*tö*) of the seasonal offerings. If life is in food, in food there is also a principle of death and corruption. Every meal is a test, and still more every drink, for drink is an extract, an extract of life or an extract of death, which executes the guilty and comforts the good.[33] It is therefore at the time of renewal that etiquette imposes upon the Chief the decisive test of drink. He must show himself capable of ensuring the continuity of the crops, the perpetuity of life. He will deserve to remain the Chief, he will be acclaimed to the cry of "Ten thousand years,"[34] if the success of the test proves that, for him, life is not poisonous. If he drinks as much as he should and stands erect,[35] it is because he is pure and that, through the renewal of his vitality, he coincides with the Macrocosm.

Only the Chiefs seem to have a "soul." Joy and sacred festivals maintain their power, rejuvenate their substance, and attune their lives to the rhythm of the universe. The Chinese do not believe that the soul gives life to the body; rather they believe, one might say, that the soul only appears after an enrichment of bodily life. But it is better to avoid the word "soul," to which nothing corresponds in Chinese if the meaning of solely spiritual essence is to be given. The words *kouei* and *chen*, which are translated as "demons" or "apparitions" and "spirits" or "gods," refer to tangible manifestations. Talking stones, killing boars, fighting dragons,[36] the *kouei* or *chen* always appear in material form. The ancestors themselves only drink and eat because cult ceremonies allow them to reincarnate in the body of one of their descendants. To deserve the name *chen*, one must have a recognized place in the feudal hierarchy; one must be honored with a noble title, as are the Duke of Thunder and the Earl of Wind. On the contrary, a lord may, because he is the head of a cult, be called *chen*.[37] The word is appropriate to any person invested with religious authority. We speak of *kouei* when an unexpected, disturbing, and illicit event occurs. Sages do not believe that stones speak, that dragons joust and fight, that the dead return to slay their enemies.[38] The latter case is the one that seems to occur most frequently; the sages calm the emotion of the public by authorizing a sacrifice; any being who eats is appeased. Appointed regularly, each of the *chen* receives a ceremonial portion of food and life; like the nobles who eat on the Chief's platform, they live in the court of the Sovereign above, whence they can smell the smoke of the sacrifices. All those who do not receive a seasonal tribute of offerings, the irregular spirits who do not appear on the lists of protocol, the ancestors at the

---

32   *Tso tchouan*, C., II, p. 85.
33   No poison should have dominion over the pure. Hence the idea that the container can neutralize the effect of the contents. This idea seems to be at the origin of the first attempts of Chinese alchemy (*SMT*, III, p. 465), which first proposed to make a long-lasting dish, the container of which destroys the harmfulness of the contents.
34   "Year" means "harvest."
35   See *supra*, Book II, ch. IV.
36   *Tso tchouan*, C., III, p. 153; I, pp. 143, 533; Granet, *Danses...*, p. 558.
37   Granet, *op. cit.*, p. 344.
38   *Tso tchouan*, C., II, pp. 153, 302, 141.

BOOK III - CHAPTER III - ETIQUETTE 245

end of their career whose *name* (*ming*) has been assumed by the living, the vulgar dead who have never *deserved to have a name* (*ming*), all these (which the word *kouei* can designate) are only occasionally fed. These are beings whose place is in the world below and who must no longer leave the Yellow Springs. However, they escape if, unfortunately, the ground cracks.[39] To return them to the underground, appeased, it will suffice to moisten the ground by making a libation penetrate it; this libation, as in sacrifices to the Earth, will be made with the blood that flows from the raw flesh. Only the *chen* are entitled to the *exhalations* (*k'i*) that escape from cooked meats. Fed differently and unequally, neither *chen* nor *kouei* have the full vitality (*cheng*) that characterizes men, amply endowed with Blood (*hiue*) and Breath (*k'i*). The masters of divination admit that the end and the beginning, death and life depend on the play of Yin and Yang, on the combinations of Darkness (*yeou*) and Light (*ming*), on the jousting and the union of Heaven and Earth. "It is *Tsing* (Essence) and *K'i* (Breath) that constitute the Beings (*wou* = the 10,000 beings; Man has no special place); it is the *voyages of Houen* that are (the principle) of the alternations (of state of beings), and it is thus that we can distinguish the essential aspects of (what is) *kouei* or *chen*[40]." When asked about *kouei* and *chen*, Confucius, or so it is said, replied: "Breath (*K'i*) is the full perfection (*cheng*) of (what is) *chen*; *Po* is the full perfection of (what is) *kouei*."[41] The Chinese, in fact, oppose Blood and Breath, *Houen* and *Po*. The formula attributed to Confucius shows that *Houen* is not distinguishable from Breath. *Po* is indistinguishable from Blood. A famous definition (attributed to Tseu-tch'an of Cheng (534 BC), and doubtless expressing very ancient conceptions), made *Po* the beginning of embryonic life, *Houen* appearing only after birth,[42] i.e. – the rites show this – when the father, laughing and making the child laugh, has communicated his breath to it *giving it a name* (*ming*). Death takes place when the *Houen* goes on a journey and, as soon as it is noticed that the Breath is gone, the *Houen* is called to return (by shouting the *ming*) and an attempt is made to catch him on top of the roof, before he goes up to join the luminous Heaven. As for the *Po* (the newborn child takes life from the earth), it returns (*kouei*) to the earth and then becomes *kouei*. The body must decay and disintegrate in the Lower, in the Darkness (Yin), and all odors are emanations (*tsing* = the Essences which the *Hi ts'eu* opposes to the *k'i*, to the Breaths) which come from the buried bodies; thus Confucius is said to have expressed himself, and he added that the *K'i* rises to the Upper to shine there. If we are forced to translate the words *houen* and *po*, we should say that *Houen* is the soul-breath and *Po* the soul-blood; but apart from the impropriety of the word "soul," the use of the singular certainly gives rise to misunderstanding. *Houen* is the *K'i* (i.e., the Breath), and it is the *K'i*, the Influences, the Exhalations, and the *Po* is the Blood, but it is the *Ts-*

---

39   This happens: during winter, the *yin* season, the season of the dead; in times of drought; when a waning dynasty disturbs the order of the world; the groaning of the *kouei* (the sages say: the people) is then heard.
40   *Yi li* (*Hi ts'eu*), L., pp. 353-354.
41   *Li ki* (*Tsi yi*), C., II, p. 289.
42   *Tso tchouan*, C., III, p. 142.

ing, the Essence, and the *Tsing*, the Emanations. Indeed, in the *k'i* and *tsing*, which constitute beings (beings of all kinds), as in the Blood and Breath which constitute the living, we must see complex pairs. They are couples because the antithesis of Yin and Yang dominates thought; they are complex couples because below the category of Couple there are other numerical categories, classifications by 5 and 6, by 7, by 8 and 9… The theory of "visceral souls"[43] is not attested before the Christian era, but the connection of the Passions – called *tsing* as well as the Emanations[44] – with the Viscera is an ancient fact, as is the correspondence established between the Passions and Emanations and the *K'i*, Influences or Exhalations from Heaven, Exhalations from the viscera and orifices of the body. The *Kouei* and *Chen* are not incorporeal souls. *Houen* and *Po* are not two souls, one material, the other spiritual; we must see in them the initials of two sets of life principles, some of which belong to the Blood and all the humors of the body, others to the Breath and all the exhalations of the organism. Some are *yang*, because the father provides the breath and the name, others *yin*, because the mother provides the blood and the nourishment. The latter come from the Earth, which supports and nourishes; the former from Heaven, which embraces and warms[45] and to which the hot smoke of the offerings ascends, while the ground, which is moistened by libations, is fattened by the products of the decomposition of the bodies. The earth will return them in the form of food, for life alternates with death, and everything returns to life as everything returns (*kouei*) to death, a cyclical order and quinary rhythm presiding over the reincarnations as well as the return of the seasons.

* * *

Rejecting any spiritualistic postulates, Chinese psychology is a psychology of behavior that is adapted to a moral attitude.

Missionaries today readily recognize that no vestige of the idea of an original fall or fault is to be found in China.[46] But their predecessors were so concerned to decide whether, in the Chinese conception, human nature was fundamentally good or bad, that they imposed on Sinologists the translation of the word "nature" from the term "*sing*". *Sing* is written with the key of "heart" (suggesting a purely moral meaning) added to the sign for "life." It is this last graphic symbol that gives the pronunciation of the whole. It is the significant element. *Sing* is used to describe the lot in life that characterizes an individual. It is also used when one wants to speak of the *personality* or, rather, of the set of gifts that constitute – both physically and morally, indistinct domains – the *individuality* and *value* of a being. It is therefore often difficult to maintain the translation "nature" or even "character" (in the moral sense of the word) for *sing*. The difficulty becomes apparent when one has to translate a sentence that is not intended to define – the Chinese never define – but

---

43   J. J. M. de Groot, *The religious system of China*, vol. II, pp. 46, 47.

44   Between these two words, *tsing* (passions or emanations, essences) and *ts'ing* (clarified part of a liquid), there is only a superficial difference in spelling.

45   *Li ki*, C., II, p. 84. Heaven is compared to the Father. It "covers" the earth and "covers" all beings.

46   P. L. Wieger, *Histoire des croyances…*, p. 714.

Book III - Chapter III - Etiquette 247

to convey what *sing* is. "Man is *composed* of material elements and an intelligent soul," writes Fr. Couvreur;[47] Chavannes[48] writes: "Man has, by birth, blood and breath, a heart and an intelligence." These two translators intend to reproduce the same sentence, the meaning of which is as follows: "He is a *sing* {an individuality, an ensemble of vital gifts (mainly) constituted by} blood, breath, will (the heart), sapience." The use of the word "heart," which designates (the seat of) the will (*tche*) because it is the name of the central viscera, and of the word *k'i*, symbol of Breath, but also of ardor, temperament, energy, sufficiently shows that there is no intention to oppose the faculties of the spirit to the principles of bodily life. Heart and wisdom refer, rather than to the spiritual life, to the functions of expenditure more or less distinguished from the functions of recuperation; will and wisdom employ and utilize the vital force, which is nourished (among other elements) by blood and breath. This phrase taken from the *Yo ki* deserves to be confronted with the aphorism of the *Hi ts'eu* quoted above: "Beings (*wou*) are made of *tsing* (and) *k'i*," that is, of Exhalations and Emanations coming from Heaven where the Breath (*k'i*) reigns, and from the Earth which produces the nourishing Essences (*tsing*). Physicians see in *tsing* (and *k'i*) what is inhaled or exhaled; they call *tsing-k'i* the fertile fluids of the human body.[49] As for the word *wou* (being, symbol), it refers to all beings which we call animate and inanimate, for all that is symbolized is. As soon as there is a "symbol," there is a "being." It is also admitted that everything, and for example, both Earth and Heaven, has a *sing*,[50] i.e., a being and a mode of being. Each individuality is a complex and corresponds to a certain combination of elements. The components (*tche*) are never conceived as solely spiritual or solely corporeal. *Mei tche* is used for good qualities, *tche k'i* for mood or character, *ts'ai tche* for natural talents; *ts'ai li* is called the strength to stand upright and procreate, and *Tien tche* are called the procreative faculties or, equally, a celestial nature, and *tche* (elements) can mean "nature" or "appearance" when it is a piece of stone or metal. Every "nature" (*sing*) is thus the product of a certain dosage and of a more or less harmonious combination (*ho*) – like the broths with which the Chiefs feed[51] – of elements belonging to Water, Fire, Wood, Metal, Earth, and belonging to Yin or Yang. It is the proportions of the dosage that characterize the intimate "nature" (*tchong*, inner, equivalent to *sin*, heart) of a being; this "nature" is the result of an imbrication (*kiao*) of the Exhalations (*k'i*) of Yin or Yang that are qualified as weak or strong (in the manner of the lines of the Hexagrams),[52] or also of *ts'ing* and *chouo* (in the manner of the sounds); *chouo* evokes the heavy, the thick, the mixed, the dark, the low; *ts'ing* (= *tsing*, essences, emanations), the faint, the clear,

---

47   *Li ki*, C., II, p. 71.
48   *SMT*, III, p. 261.
49   *Houang-ti nei king*, 1; Granet, *Fêtes et chansons*…, pp. 7 ff.
50   *Li ki*, C., II, p. 52; *Tso tchouan*, C., III, p. 380.
51   M. Granet, *Civ. chin.*, p. 282.
52   *Li ki*, C., II, p. 73.

the limpid, the sharp, the light.[53] It is, then, to an opposition of the subtle and the gross and not to an opposition of spirit and matter that the distinctions which are drawn, I do not say between substances, but between the states or, rather, the *rhythmic* aspects assumed by the elements whose combination produces being and personality, refer. Thus the *sing*, the way of being, corresponds to a certain aptitude of being, to a kind of life belonging to a certain temperament. A man who as a child sucked greedily and drank too much milk because of the *k'i* (Breath) with which he was endowed, will never have a balanced constitution (*sing*); he will live like a sick man and die early.[54] Another who is sick because his will (*tche*) imposes too great an expense on him, given his *k'i* (his ability to recover breath), will be able to recover; he will get well if he finds a physician to help him change his heart (*sing*: heart, and will: *tche*, are indistinguishable) with the heart of another patient whose *k'i* in relation to *tche* is overabundant; but, as soon as the operation succeeds, both of them, having changed their feelings (*sin* = heart), will also have to change their wives, children, home, and social situation.[55] As we see, there are good, bad and improvable "natures"…

Vitality, constitution and destiny differ among men. Man (like other beings) is made of the *sing* of Heaven and Earth; he draws from Earth his blood, his fertile and nourishing humors, like sap; he draws from Heaven his warm and subtle breath; he draws from both the *rhythm* – pulse-beat and breath – which sustains or rather constitutes life in him. But it is Heaven (honored as a father, endowed with authority, praised for its permanence and unity) that distributes the lots, the ranks, the duration of life, the destinies; the word *ming* ("*ming*" means to order and is often confused with another "*ming*" meaning "to give a name") signifies all this. The breath, which comes from Heaven, varies chiefly in its power; the blood, which is nourished by the Earth, varies chiefly in its composition. To Heaven is attached *personality*, to Earth *individuality*, which depends on the infinite variety of Spaces. The unity of Heaven, however, is quite relative; it diversifies according to the seasons; Time has continuity only in the sacred moments in which it is inaugurated; moments rich in duration are opposed by periods in which duration is exhausted. When a new and enduring order of civilization reigns, the ruler can deal out fiefdoms for a long time and Heaven can deal out much longevity; men live to old age and, moreover, everything lasts when a wise ruler establishes in the world an order which deserves to be permanent. The value of personality diminishes when Empire and Heaven lose their unity; in times of decadence, the variety of Spaces pollutes Time; the duration of life is shortened; monsters appear; individuality develops abusively and impairs personality; more accurately, temperaments become singular and vital power immediately diminishes. This is not to say that

---

53 See *supra*, Book II, ch. II. The opposition of *chouo* and *ts'ing* (dregs and clarified liquid) leads (by an image taken from the manufacture of beverages) to the antithesis of Low and High (heavy and light), of Yin and Yang (dark and light).

54 *Lie tseu*, in Wieger, *Les Pères du système taoïste*, p. 147.

55 *Ibid.*, p. 141. The physician operates only after having anesthetized the two patients by numbing them, for three days, with wine mixed with poison.

Book III - Chapter III - Etiquette

the Chinese hate monsters or utterly despise specialists. There are, as we have seen, occasions and places where the Chief himself must be only right-handed or left-handed. The wise man uses all weathers. He knows how to take advantage of the ardor of the Southerners, in whom the *k'i* prevails to such an extent that they can only eat raw vegetables.[56] He knows how to use the hunchbacks (numerous in the West) whose backs resemble a sack {for autumn (= the West) is the harvest season}; they will carry, leaning forward, the sounding stones, while, leaning backward, beings with concave backs will strike the bronze bells.[57] Moreover, most Heroes, like bows tense or slack, bend forward or backward.[58] Ideally, however, the Chief should be straight as a gnomon. The sage uses all ages. He knows how to use, as witches, to control the weather, old women whose menstruation has caused them to lose a good part of their blood; almost reduced to breathing, bent backwards, they stretch their nostrils towards Heaven, so that, fearing to obstruct with water an orifice made to suck in the Breath, Heaven forbids itself to make rain fall.[59] The sage also knows how to make use of the consumptives whose sputum exhausts the blood, and admits that sorcerers (and even chiefs) train themselves to obtain, by emaciation, an overabundance of *k'i*. He tolerates, but watches – for they are dangerous, although may occasionally be used – excessive individualities indicating some deficiency or hypertrophy. He sends experts to look for emanations that may betray the incipient power of a rival genius.[60] He employs historians to catalog physical deformities in which the art of physiognomists knows how to see signs of fortune or proofs of talent.[61] He also relies on ethnographers and geographers to inform him of complexions that depend on the structure of the soil or the type of life. "Complexions (*ts'ai*) vary according to Heaven and Earth, Cold and Hot, Wet and Dry. In the broad plains and in the long valleys, the construction is different.[62]" The morals also differ. The tribes of the four directions of the Empire "have songs, modes of being, which vary," because "the five flavors combine in different ways," and the diversity of food makes men weak or strong (like the lines of the Hexagrams), heavy or light (like the sounds and parts of a drink), slow or lively; some are carnivorous, others frugivorous, and if the latter are light and stupid, the others are brave and bold... The wise man allows to exist on the margins of the world those ways of living and being that do not conform to the label. He does not disdain individuals with an eccentric genius, if he can keep them at bay or tame them. For himself and his family, he seeks the balanced constitution that accompanies a wealthy destiny. When he expects a child, he imposes on his wife strict seclusion and constant supervision; this is called "educating the embryo."[63] If it is

---

56 *Li ki*, C., I, p. 295.
57 *Kouo yu*, 10.
58 *Louen heng*, in Forke, *op. cit.*, 1, p. 304.
59 Granet, *Danses et légendes...*, p. 315; *Houang ti nei king*, 1.
60 *SMT*, III, p. 331; *Civ. Chin.*, p. 54.
61 *Louen heng*, in Forke, *op. cit.*, I, pp. 304 ff.
62 *Li ki*, C., I, p. 295.
63 *Ibid.*, I, pp. 295, 296; *Ta tai Li ki*, 80.

a child of the king that is to be born, customs are followed under the invocation of T'ai Sseu, the blameless wife of King Wen. (T'ai Sseu, during her pregnancy, never allowed herself, even in private, any indulgence; she never stood on one leg, nor sat crookedly on her mat; she avoided any loud laughter and, even in anger, refrained from imprecation.) Three months before the birth, the music master came, with a tuning fork, to stand guard on the left of the door; the grand butler (prime minister and head of the kitchen) stood on the right, with a dipper in his hand. When the queen asked for music, if it was not a suitable tune, the music master would tangle the strings of his guitar and play ignorant; when she asked for food, if it was not a suitable dish, the grand butler would bend his ladle and say that he dare not serve it to the crown prince. Thus, when he would have been born and before receiving the name (*ming*) which would define his destiny, they would begin by determining, with the aid of the tuning fork, which of the five notes would make him cry and (by a process unknown to us) which of the five tastes would suit him, so they could be sure that the breaths and nourishing juices, the potency and substance, the lot of life and his constitution, all in him will be of the best quality.[64]

We shall see, when speaking about Taoists, and the practices of the *long life*, that Holiness is acquired by undergoing rhythmic gymnastics and by training what we call the nutritive, sexual and respiratory functions… This beatific rhythm is sometimes used by heterodox followers of the Tao to obtain, with magical gifts, certain special talents. All true sages admit, without distinction of schools, that the first duty of every being is to seek a complete development of his temperament. Some mystics claim to be free from the limits that traditions impose on human destiny. But in the case of all others, it is the traditional rules of the art of living that enable each person to make the most of his lot in life and his constitution. To take care of *ming* and *sing* is to protect personality and individuality as a whole, that is, to defend – within the limits allowed by protocol and the hierarchical organization of society – a properly measured and qualified set of power. To the extent that there is a Chinese psychology and metaphysics, its function is to glorify etiquette.

* * *

The music teacher is entitled to the left side, the place of honor, and the cook faces him on the right.[65] The Chinese hardly distinguish substance from power; all their notions are dominated by ideas of social rhythm and authority. Hence the importance they attach to Rites and Music; they contrast them as the two complementary aspects of Etiquette. Rites establish the necessary distinctions between men and all that depends on them. Music compels all beings to live in good harmony.

> "The Rites," said (apparently) Tseu-tch'an[66], "are the delimitations (proper) of Heaven, the equitable distributions (*yi*) (proper) of Earth, the conduct that suits men. Heaven and Earth have their own boundaries and men take

---

64   *Sin chou*, 10; *Ta tai Li ki*, 48.
65   The right hand is the eating hand, cf. *supra* in this same Book, ch. II.
66   *Tso chuan*, C., III, p. 379. On Tseu-ch'an, cf. *infra*, Book IV, ch. I, sec. IV.

Book III - Chapter III - Etiquette

them as models (*tsö*); they are based on the brightness (stars) of Heaven; they are based on the constitution (*sing*) of Earth. When the 6 *k'i* (Influences, Exhalations) are produced and the 5 Elements are brought into activity, the Exhalations form the 5 Flavors, are manifested by the 5 Colors and symbolized by the 5 Notes. If there is an excess (in their use), confusion and problems arise. Men then lose their own constitution (*sing*). The Rites serve to preserve it. There are 6 Domestic Animals, 5 Wild Animals, 3 Sacrificial Animals which serve for the presentation of the 5 Flavors; there are 9 Symbols, 6 Ornaments, 5 Drawings to present the 5 Colors; there are 9 Songs, 8 (Musical Instruments corresponding to the 8) Winds, 7 Sounds, 6 *yang* Tubes (and 6 *yin* Tubes) to present the 5 Notes; there are (the relations of) lord (to) vassal, (of) superior (to) inferior, by which the equal distributions (*yi*) (proper to) the Earth are modeled; there are (the relations of) husband (to) wife, (of) outer (and of) inner which serve to delimit[67] the two (kinds of) beings (*wou*: essences, symbolic realities); there are (the relations of) father (to) son, (of) elder brother (to) younger brother, (of) aunt (to) younger aunt, (of) son-in-law (to) father-in-law, (of) allies by marriage, (of) brothers-in-law, which serve to symbolize the brightnesses of Heaven (the relations of the stars); there are the acts of government, the labors of the people, which serve to obey the 4 Seasons; there are the punishments, the penalties, which inspire people to respect the prohibitions and which correspond (*lei*) to the destructions of Thunder and Lightning; there is gentleness, affection, benevolence, concord, which serve to imitate the productive force of Heaven and its nourishing action.[68] Men have (the 6 Passions, viz.) Love, Hate, Joy, Anger, Grief, and Pleasure, which are born of the 6 *k'i* (Heavenly Influences, Exhalations). Therefore they (the Sages) have taken, after study, to regulate the expediencies and correspondences to regulate the 6 *Tche* (Wills, Impulses). Sadness causes moaning and groaning; pleasure, singing and dancing; joy produces benevolence; anger, fighting and quarreling. Pleasure is born of love; anger of hatred. Therefore (the Sages), after study, have put into use and, in good faith, have ordained, Rewards and Punishments {word for word: (distributions of) Happiness (and of) Misfortune}, Burdens and Punishments. Life is a thing loved; death, a thing hated; a thing loved gives pleasure; a thing hated gives pain. When Pain and Pleasure are well used, there can be harmony {between (the constitution of) man} and the constitution of Heaven and Earth; and this is what makes (life) last long."

Rites are the foundation of (social and cosmic) Order: through them an *equal distribution* (yi) *of the portions* (fen) *of social authority is achieved.*

---

67   Here the same word (delimit) is used as was used before in connection with Heaven. The two Beings (the two emblematic rubrics) are Yin and Yang, feminine and masculine.
68   Is this nourishing action that of Heaven or Earth?

> "Heaven and earth are the principles of life... What distinguishes (beings) is that those who are noble serve nobly (while) the vile serve in vile tasks; it is fitting that the great should be great, and the vile vile."[69]
>
> "Music is what unites people (*t'ong*); Rites are what differentiate (*yi*). From union results mutual affection; from differences mutual respect... To enable the passions (*tsing*) to come into harmony, to give manners beautiful appearances, such are the functions of Music and the Rites."[70]

As soon as music is set in motion,

> "social relations are well observed; the eyes and ears see and hear well; *a harmonious equilibrium is established between blood and breath*; morals are civilized; the land of men is peaceful."[71]
>
> "From Music results *the harmonious union of Heaven and Earth*, and from the Rites the right ordering of Heaven and Earth; when there is union and harmony, all beings (*wou*) obey the civilizing action (of the Son of Heaven); when there is right ordering, all beings retain their distinct place (allotted to them). Music derives its (civilizing) performance from Heaven; the Rites borrow from Earth their regulating (capacity). (If) too much regulation were demanded, the spirit of anarchy would develop; (if) too much efficiency were demanded, the spirit of domination would develop... The essence (*tsing*) of Music is to see to it that relations (between beings) do not create disorder, which, through contentment and joy, contentment and love, invites action. To maintain without deviations a just and right balance,[72] this is the constitution (*tche*: constituent elements) of the Rites which, through gravity and self-respect, through respect for others and docility, they help to regulate."[73]
>
> "When the Music is perfect, there is no more rebellion; when the Rites are perfect, there is no more fighting."[74]
>
> "The guitar is 81 inches long; the longest string plays the note *kong* (81); it is placed in the center: it is the Prince. (The string of the note) *chang* (72) extends to the right; the others are placed, one in relation to the other, according to the order of their dimensions, without any error; therefore, the vassals and the prince are in their places."[75]
>
> "*Kong* (81, center) is the prince; *chang* (72, west, right), the vassals; *kio* (64, east), the people; *tche* (54, south), the affairs of state; *yu* (48, north), the resources (of the people, designated here by the word *wou*: the ten thou-

---

69 *Ta Tai Li ki*, 42.
70 *Li ki*, C., II, p 55; *SMT*, III, p. 245.
71 *Li ki*, C., II, p. 78.
72 Word for word: "Center, straight, without deviation". Cf. *supra*, Book II, ch. IV.
73 *Li ki*, C., II, p. 60; *SMT*, III, p. 249.
74 *Li ki*, C., II, p. 57.
75 *SMT*, III, p. 291. It will be observed that the right (west) is the place assigned to vassals. Chang must therefore be assigned to the West (right).

sand beings).⁷⁶ When, in the 5 Notes, there is no disturbance, everything is harmoniously modulated. If (it is of the note) *kong* (that comes the) disturbance, (the modulations are) harsh: (it is because) the prince is arrogant. If (it is of the note) *chang* (that comes the) trouble, (the modulations give the image of) inclination: (it means that) the trades are badly fulfilled. If (it is of the note) *kio* (that comes the) trouble, (the modulations are) grievous: (it is that) the people become rebellious. If (it is from the note) *tche* (that comes the) trouble, (the modulations are) plaintive: (it is that) the affairs of state are overwhelming. If (it is from the note) *yu* (that comes the) trouble, (the modulations give the image of a) precipice: (it is that) the people lack resources. If the trouble comes from all the notes encroaching on each other, (it is that) the state will perish incessantly!"

"Notes and music stir the blood and its channels, set the vital spirits in motion (*tsing chen*, this expression can mean fertile humors) and give harmony and uprightness to the heart."⁷⁷

"If one deviates for a moment from the Rites, there is only cruelty and arrogance on the outside; if one deviates for a moment from Music, there is only licentiousness and perversion on the inside. Music enables the wise (*kiun tseu*) to increase (among men the feeling of) equal (*yi*) distribution."⁷⁸

These quotations are self-explanatory. The Rites and Music are responsible for inculcating in the Chinese a respect for protocol distinctions and for the traditional harmony resulting from a hierarchical distribution of lots. The Rites and the Music, moreover, communicate to them, as a supreme consolation, the feeling that obeying the Etiquette allows individuals to rhythmically integrate each of their gestures in the great rhythmic system of behaviors that constitutes the Universe. Thus the endosmosis of microcosm and macrocosm becomes possible; from this endosmosis arise, with life, individuality and personality. Etiquette thus receives the combined value of hygiene and morality: morality is distinguished neither from the physiological nor from the physical.

The formal expression of feelings, precisely because it is done with the help of agreed symbols and obligatory gestures, has the virtue of disciplining the passions. Chinese mourning rites clearly demonstrate this.⁷⁹ Grief, in mourning for example,⁸⁰ must be expressed at specific times, according to a rhythm that the protocol defines taking into account the social value of the deceased. It is expressed through meticulously regulated gestures, dress, lifestyle and quarantine. The very

---

76 *Li ki*, C., II, p. 48. If we compare these data with those provided by the above text taken from Sseu-ma Ts'ien, we see that the central chord is equivalent to the initial tube (81); the others are thus equivalent to the length of the 4 following tubes. *Chang* (72) is to the *right*, i.e., in the West; it follows that *kio* (64) is to the *left*, i.e., in the East. All this is in accordance with the indications of *Yue ling* and the ritual of left and right (cf. *supra*, Book III, ch. II).

77 SMT, III, p. 290.

78 Granet, *Le langage de la douleur d'après le rituel funéraire de la Chine classique*.

79 SMT, III, p. 291.

80 Grief and mourning are said with the same word.

manner of weeping – howling without ceasing, or without ceasing to wail, or lowering the voice after a triple modulation, or, finally, simply adopting a plaintive tone – was something imposed, controlled. Nothing was left to the inspiration of the moment; every personal impulse, every fantasy, was severely censored and disqualified, whether one did little or much. A man who had lost his mother wept like a child:

> "Let him mourn (*ngai*), then let him grieve (*ngai*)," said Confucius. "But it would be difficult to imitate, and the principle of the Rites is that they must be obeyed; therefore, it must be possible to conform to them. For lamentations and leaping, there must be a measure."[81]

All the gestures of mourning are intended to evacuate the contagious impurity of death; all the gestures of grief tend to evacuate an impression of horror or fear: all are intended to render grief harmless. Two disciples of Confucius once saw a grieving man jumping up and down like a child lamenting a lost object. One of them said that he did not like the use of jumping. He preferred less exuberant grief. The other said:

> "There are rites to moderate the passions; there are also rites to excite them from without. *To give free rein to one's passions is to imitate the conduct* (tao) *of the barbarians.* The conduct prescribed by the Rites differs from this. When a man is happy, his appearance is cheerful; he is cheerful and sings; he sings and swaggers; he swaggers and dances. He dances and pain comes to him. In the clutches of pain he sighs; he sighs and beats his breast; he beats his breast and jumps. To fix a measure and rules, that is the object of the Rites. A dead man inspires us with horror (textually: hatred). He is incapable of everything: we distance ourselves from him. The Rites prescribe to wrap him in a shroud, in clothes… so that we cease to be horrified…"[82]
> "When a son mourns and leaps and moves his limbs, he calms his heart and lets his breath fall (*k'i*)."[83]

Ceremonial leaping enables him to re-establish a certain rhythmic regularity in his breathing and heartbeat.

The great virtue of Rites (and of Music) lies in the regular rhythm they impose on gesticulation and vital functions. When the manners of the being are governed by Etiquette, the being is ennobled and deserves to endure. If he makes this symbolism his own, the individual incorporates the national civilization in him. Then he can be received among men. He has acquired a personality.

* * *

Man owes everything to civilization; he owes it his balance, his health, the quality of his being. The Chinese never consider man isolated from society; they never isolate society from Nature. They do not think of placing a world of purely spiri-

---

81 *Li ki*, C., I, p. 161.
82 *Ibid.*, C., I, p. 217.
83 *Ibid.*, C., II, p. 553.

Book III - Chapter III - Etiquette   255

tual essences above vulgar realities; nor do they think, in order to magnify human dignity, of attributing to man a soul distinct from his body. Nature forms a single kingdom. A single order presides over universal life: it is the order imposed by civilization.

This order arises from custom. In the society that men and things form in common, everything is distributed in hierarchical categories. Each category has its own status. The regime is in no case that of physical necessity, nor that of moral obligation. The order which men agree to revere is not that of law; neither do they think that laws can be imposed on things; they only accept rules or rather *patterns*. Knowledge of these rules and patterns forms knowledge and gives power. To determine relationships and hierarchies, to establish, by categories, taking into account occasions and ranks, models of behavior and systems of correction, that is Knowledge. Power is to distribute ranks, places, qualifications; it is to endow all beings with their way of being and their aptitude to be. Principle of the regulating power that belongs to the Chief, of the organizing talents possessed by the erudite, of the exemplary authority possessed by the wise, Etiquette inspires the whole of the disciplines of life or of the knowledge to act that constitutes the universal Order.

What remains to occupy the activity of the founders of Sects or Schools?

As for ideas, the passion for orthodoxy will prevail in all. Ideas only serve to justify practices by linking them to the system of common notions. No wise man will discuss the concrete character of Space and Time, nor will he see in Numbers the symbols of quantity. The play of numbers, the interweaving of numerical classifications, the jousting of Yin and Yang will provide all with symbols sufficient to make the behavior of Nature and man appear to have a *regular rhythm* and an *intelligible order*. This is enough for a metaphysics which refuses to distinguish between matter and spirit, which prefers the idea of *model* to that of *law*, which is only interested in hierarchies, conveniences and ways of being. No progress in what we call knowledge can move it or enrich it.

Only a few great minds in the Taoist camp will think of (taking advantage of the findings of explorers and astronomers, but using the legendary or the theoretical as easily as the confirmed) using the idea that the world is immense to illustrate the theme of the indefinite power conferred by Holiness. Even then, the idea only serves to justify, for the sake of polemic, a system of practices, a corporate attitude. The rival teachings do not first seek to distinguish themselves by an original doctrine; it is enough for them to procure a *recipe*. As soon as it is no longer a question of ideas, but of practices, the passion for the singular asserts itself and, with it, the spirit of a sect. Every company presents its knowledge as a kind of secret of exploitation. But each discipline also claims to be the only one capable of equipping the Universe and those who govern it, Civilization and those who produce it. The specialists propose a certain method that corresponds to the best way of being, a way of governing that constitutes the only way of governing; the more specific secrets are always given as panaceas, so that the sectarian teachings end up acquiring a doctrinal scope. They come to defend, along with a set of prescriptions, a system of attitudes which seems to proceed from a more or less defined conception. In the Taoist camp, they begin by procuring prescriptions for a long life; they end by presenting a partially new and, at certain points, very audacious conception of Holiness and Efficiency. In the corporation of the Legists, they begin by advocating prescriptions for regulation; they end with a revolutionary and potentially fruitful idea of Law and Principled Power. Thus, out of various business and technical concerns arose a set of philosophical problems on which, for some time, Chinese thought was exercised.

The number of these problems has remained small. The interest they aroused did not last. They hardly touch anything but morality, or rather, politics. They always raise again, in more or less new terms and always for practical purposes, the great question of the relationship between the Microcosm and the Macrocosm, between the Individual and Civilization. As the proposed solutions attest, all the activity of thought that these problems have provoked has been determined by a social crisis in which the feudal system and the traditional conception of etiquette could have collapsed. However, the feudal order was basically kept alive. The philosophical upheaval that makes the period of the Warring Kingdoms so interesting led to the triumph of scholasticism. An archaizing conformism reinforced the prestige of etiquette and of the whole old system of classifications, behaviors and manners.

Book IV
SECTS AND SCHOOLS

It was during the lesser known period of Chinese history that philosophical thought achieved its greatest success. These centuries (V to III BC), described by native historians as a time of anarchy,[1] must be considered as one of the great moments of Chinese history.[2] China was trying to free itself from the feudal regime; under this regime, Chinese civilization had been formed and spread widely; it remained to make China a Nation and to create a State there. To prepare the Empire, vast kingdoms were created and collided during the 5th, 4th and 3rd centuries BC. The country developed, became populated, knew great wars, there was a great mixing of populations and classes, there were violent oppositions between nobles and upstarts, rich and poor, everything was called into question: destinies, ranks, inheritances, traditions, customs; there was no hesitation in borrowing, even from the barbarians, techniques, ideas, symbols, ways of being;[3] everything changed and everything innovated. Despots were on the lookout for all kinds of knowledge. They welcomed, wherever they came from, the defenders of techniques, the inventors of stratagems, the givers of advice, the possessors of recipes. Guilds, sects and schools abounded.

Some were hosted, subsidized and patronized by princes; others were free, sometimes fixed, sometimes wandering; some had a vast clientele; others were reduced to a master surrounded by a few apprentices; sometimes the teaching was exclusively technical; sometimes they dominated the liberal arts; sometimes the master taught specialties that may seem quite diverse: such as rhetoric, ballistics,

---

1 *Civ. Chin.*, p. 42.
2 *Civ. Chin.*, pp. 90 ff., 101 ff.
3 *Civ. Chin.*, pp. 104, 310.

and beneficence.⁴ What constituted the unity of the group, whether it resembled a sect or a corporation, was a particular way of life and above all of dress. One belonged to the School of Tseou, other one claimed to be under the patronage of Confucius as soon as one wore a round cap and square shoes; it was to show oneself to be an expert in the things of Heaven (round) as well as in those of Earth (square), an expert capable of bringing harmony to both the Macrocosm and the Microcosm, for one was still careful to adorn one's belt with amulets giving all the notes of the scale.⁵ If one was attached to Mö tseu, one had to be content with clogs and coarse cloths, as the *Tchouang tseu states*.⁶ Did a disciple, in turn, act as a teacher? He would immediately adopt a rallying signal. Yin Wen tseu, a follower of Mö tseu, and then head of the school, chose the "cap of Mount Houa" as a head-dress.⁷ Did he belong to one of the sects advocating a return to nature? One was reduced to eating only acorns and chestnuts; the uniform was then the skin of a beast, which, moreover, did not prevent one from practicing the arts, for a wise man, dressed in deerskin, amused himself by playing the lute.⁸

Joining a sect or a School does not seem to have differed from joining a clientele. The patron one chose did not communicate his prescriptions unless one came, with all his own, to place oneself under his recommendation. After seven days of purifying fasting, the recipient was invited to the Master's table; such at least is the procedure described in a passage of the *Lie tseu*.⁹ The apprentice went to live near the master. He took the title of *men jen*, which designates the clients, those who gather near the door (*men*) of the Master to receive the daily teaching. The bond of vassalage thus created was reflected in the obligation to wear mourning; this duty was imposed on both the master and the apprentice.¹⁰ The latter did not immediately become acquainted with the Master. Lie tseu remained for a long time without receiving a single glance from his master. At the end of five years he was given a smile and at the end of seven years he was given a mat.¹¹ At the end of the apprenticeship, the disciple was discharged and given a snack. Sometimes the chief would take advantage of the occasion to try to retain his client by letting him know that he had not revealed the last word of his talent.¹² Of course, tuition was paid for (the amount of school fees varied from case to case). It does not seem to have been distributed to all with equal liberality. Confucius, for example, in the chanting lesson, did not have it repeated "if it went well," but then took the trouble to "accompany himself."¹³

---

4   Taught, *it is said*, by Mö tseu.
5   *Tchouang tseu*, in Wieger, *Les Pères du système taoïste*, p. 383.
6   *Ibid.*, p. 501.
7   *Ibid.*, p. 503. Mount Houa is a sacred mountain, rich in hermits.
8   *Ibid.*, 373; *Lie tseu*, in *Ibid.*, p. 75.
9   *Lie tseu*, in Wieger, *op. cit.*, p. 149.
10 *Li ki*, C., I, p. 146.
11 *Lie tseu*, in Wieger, *op. cit.*, p. 85.
12 *Ibid.*, p. 143.
13 *Louen yu*, L., p. 69.

"He explained nothing to anyone who did not show a great desire to learn; when he had shown one aspect of a subject, if they did not respond (testifying that they had glimpsed) the other aspects, he would not repeat his lesson."[14]

He gave the impression (or so it is claimed) that behind his detailed teachings was a principle of wisdom sufficient to penetrate everything.[15] His disciples believed him:

"The Master's teachings on the Liberal Arts can be learned! But the Master's words on the Heavenly Way (*T'ien tao*) as well as on the complexions (*sing*) and the lots (*ming*) cannot be learned!"[16]

However, of the 3,000 apprentices, there were only 72 (72 exactly: this is the typical number of brotherhoods) who fully understood Confucius' lessons. One of them was fond of saying:

"When I had exhausted all my capacities, there was still something that was very high, and when I wanted to reach it, I could not find my way."[17]

This statement is all the more significant because it was made by a follower of the School that is considered to have given the most positive and down-to-earth teaching. To apprentices excited by the hope that one day "the one principle which makes all things understandable" would one day be revealed to them,[18] knowledge was dispensed in the somewhat meager and advantageous-looking manner that characterizes esoteric teachings.

It would be quite useless to try to trace in detail the history of ideas in this fruitful but almost unknown period. When Che Houang-ti founded the imperial unity, he wanted to destroy the memory of the feudal epoch. He had the "Discourses of the Hundred Schools" burned.[19] Of most of the famous masters nothing remains but their names or apocryphal works. The few works that have been preserved – authentic only in part – contain almost never a dogmatic statement, nor a historical account, nor an essay on the history of schools and especially of ideas. Many thinkers are known only by the statements of their opponents. Did they quote them exactly? Did they interpret them in good faith? Polemics are inspired by prestige concerns; the feeling of the proper value of ideas appears little; teachers seek less to show doctrinal originality than to shine the efficacy of the panacea they advocate. Confucius expressed himself in half-words and Tchouang tseu in allegories.[20] They taught a Wisdom rather than a Doctrine; they claimed to have venerable patrons, who lent them complete wisdom, total knowledge. From its

---

14 *SMT*, V, p. 405.
15 *SMT*, V, p. 407.
16 *SMT*, V, p. 412,
17 *SMT*, V, p. 413.
18 *SMT*, V, p. 367.
19 *Civ. Chin.*, p. 50.
20 *Tchouang tseu*, in Wieger, *op. cit.* p. 449.

beginnings, every School must claim to be ignorant of nothing. Teachers travel and gather together to compete for talent; disciples move from one school to another, gathering all the skills.[21] The spirit of sectarian appropriation has already done its work when the teachings appear presented in their original purity. The authentic works that we possess date from the last stages of a period abounding in polemics; if there were original doctrines, we only grasp them once they have been contaminated; something that has been admitted.[22] To pretend to reconstruct the history of the "Doctrines," one would have to have a strange confidence in oneself and in the documents. It is already very ambitious to try to distinguish the main currents of Chinese thought during the period of the Warring Kingdoms. Without departing significantly from the classifications proposed in China, but starting from the prescriptions advocated rather than the theories defended, I will distinguish three currents. I will try to describe the new contributions, first technical and then theoretical, of the thinkers who defended the true prescriptions of government, public good and sanctity – the order followed is determined by a historical fact difficult to dispute. It was the efforts of the governments of the potentates (some of whom played the role of enlightened despots) to build the state on a renewed social order that gave rise to the corporate competition and sectarian polemics that marked the 5th, 4th and 3rd centuries BC. Many fruitful ideas were then brilliantly defended, although none of them succeeded in profoundly changing the mentality of the Chinese.

---

21   *Lie tseu*, in Wieger, *op. cit.*, p. 95.
22   (Leang K'i-tch'ao) Liang Chi-Chao, *History of Chinese political thought*, p. 37. Thus Leang K'i-tch'ao only pretends to define the doctrines of the main schools by studying them in their final aspect just before the foundation of the Empire.

Chapter I
The Prescriptions of Government

While feudal customs reigned undisputed, it was etiquette that gave the princely "yes" its efficacy and the virtue of making decisions unanimous in the court of vassals, after advice and reprimands. Owners, not of a narrow hereditary domain, but of vast territories conquered from Nature or from the barbarians, the potentates ceased to take care of business by summoning the vassals to the council, but relied instead on a secret council and called whoever they wished. Then began the ruin of the feudal system. The customary statutes and traditional etiquette lost their prestige when the princes exercised their authority in a new way. New foundations had to be found for the authority of the prince.

Surprisingly, the schools of Wisdom that claimed to be traditional developed in the towns of the manors that remained small and weak, such as the State of Lou; in contrast, the capital of the great States, such as Ts'i, was where the supporters of a new order lived or came to learn. The Confucius School (or of Tseou, a city of Lou) was under the patronage of the founder of the manor of Lou, Tcheou-kong, brother of King Wen. Cheou-kong, in his fief, had applied himself to the reign of etiquette.[1] Lu Chang, founder of the house of Ts'i, is said to have permitted the inhabitants of his dominions to act according to his customs.[2] Lu Chang had been the adviser of King Wen; it was with him that this founder of the dynasty "secretly planned the means of practicing Virtue by overthrowing the rule of the Yin." This enterprise required great military might and very skillful plans. Hence all who, in later generations, have spoken of the war and the secret power of the Tcheou have

---

1 Granet, *Danses et légendes…*, p. 407.
2 *SMT*, IV, p. 40.

venerated Lu Chang as the instigator of their plans.[3] In Ts'i lived Kouan Tchong, patron of economists and Legists;[4] Yen Tseu, enemy of Confucius, political realist, fertile in stratagems;[5] Tseou Yen, inventor (so it is said) of the theory of succession by violence and of the triumph of the Elements and of the Dynasties, a theory which, moreover, goes back to Lu Chang.[6] In Ts'i also lived, stayed or passed Yin Wen tseu, the Master of the School of Names; Chen Tao, the jurist; T'ien P'ien "with the divine mouth"; Song Kien, of the Mö tseu School; Chouen-yu K'ouen, the jester; Mencius, who claimed to be the continuator of Confucius; perhaps also Tchouang tseu, the great Taoist;[7] and Siun tseu himself, to whom orthodoxy refers. If the Tsi Gate School at Lin-tso, the capital of Ts'i, of which King Siuan (342-322 BC) was the great patron, welcomed scholars by the "hundreds," the princes of Ts'in, Ch'ou and Wei succeeded in attracting to their court a large number of these peddlers of wisdom.

However, the despots, who worked to supplant the later Tcheou kings,[8] sought above all to attract to their court politicians skilled in devising plans and making them succeed.

I. The Art Of Success

Politicians are the great heroes of history in the era of the Warring Kingdoms. In earlier times, the *Tso tchouan*, the *Kouo Yu* and the *Chou king* show private advisors on the scene. But the exploits of the latter almost alone fill the Discourses of the Combatant Kingdoms.[9] These characters, who willingly offer their services to all the states, come from all walks of life. Among them are jesters[10] and professional musicians, such as the master K'ouang, who was powerful under Duke P'ing (557-532 BC) of Tsin.[11] There are also historians and astrologers such as Mo of Ts'ai, consulted by Chao Kien-tseu (512 BC),[12] and Po, who (in 773 BC) informed the first prince of Cheng on the art of choosing a territory where his house could prosper.[13] There are even merchants, such as Fan Li, who was minister to Keou-tsien, king of Yue (496-465 BC); Sseu-ma Ts'ien has devoted a romantic biography to this adventurer.[14] Moreover, almost all these personages, especially diplomats and military men, were the heroes of some Gesta, such as Wou K'i, general of Wei[15] or Sou

---

3   *SMT*, IV, p. 36.
4   *Civ. Chin.*, p. 103.
5   *Civ. Chin.*, p. 324.
6   Cf. *supra*, Book II, ch. IV; *SMT*, IV, p. 37 (gloss).
7   *SMT*, V, pp. 258-260.
8   *SMT*, II, p. 171.
9   *SMT*, V, 1, p. 3.
10   *Tso tchouan*, III, p. 755; *SMT*, ch. 126.
11   *SMT*, III, p. 289.
12   *SMT*, IV, p. 125; *Tso Chuan*, Ch., III, p. 452.
13   *SMT*, IV, p. 450; *Kouo yu*, p. 16.
14   *SMT*, IV, p. 439.
15   *SMT*, V, p. 148 and ch. 63.

Book IV - Chapter I - The Prescriptions of Government

Ts'in, the deserter, who went from Ts'in to Chao.[16] To many of them are attributed various works, such as the pamphlet in which Li K'ouei (or Li K'o – it is not known whether it is one or two characters) taught a prince of Wei (424-385 BC) the means to triumph.[17] The most interesting of *these forgeries* is the *Kouan tseu*, attributed to Kouan Tchong, a semi-legendary sage of the 7th century BC, and which may have been written around the 4th-3rd century BC.[18] In fact, only folkloric traits remain of all the heroes, real or imaginary, of these dark times. However, Han Fei tseu has preserved some aphorisms attributed to one of the masters of Politics, Chen Pou-hai, who was a minister of a Han prince (358-353 BC).[19] They are very valuable in helping to understand the partly new ideas of the politicians. Two words sum them up (almost untranslatable): *chou*, recipes, methods, artifices, and *che*, conditions, situations, circumstances, forces, influences.[20]

Our word "chance" is, perhaps, the least erroneous word to translate the word "*che*." The various situations and conditions of time and place contain opportunities whose influence and force we must be in a position to grasp in order to risk destiny with the maximum of possibilities. The importance of this idea is explained by the concrete character universally attributed to Space and Time and by the nature of the political problem then at hand. The despots lived in a state of revolutionary expectation. They were all preparing to usurp the rank of Sons of Heaven, that is, to impose a new order on civilization. Now, to change the slightest thing is to change everything; and to grasp the slightest sign of change is to seize the opportunity for total change. After having taken (for he was risking his throne) infinite pains to get his relatives to accept his decision, a king of Tchao who wished to adopt the costume of the Huns concludes by saying: one must "seek advantage" everywhere; "the merit one has in conforming to custom is not enough to raise a man above the century."[21] The potentates kept specialists of all kinds as political advisers; they employed them all to watch for favorable signs. It would have been an unpardonable fault to mistake the opportunity, a crime to miss it, a crime not

---

16 J. Escarra and R. Germain, Études asiatiques (published on the occasion of the XXVth anniversary of the École française d'Extrême-Orient, 1925) II, pp. 141 ff.

17 Wieger, *Histoire des croyances…*, p. 236; Maspero, *La Chine antique*, p. 520.

18 P. Pelliot, *Meou tseu, ou les Doutes levés*, p. 585. The work we have, perhaps reworked under the Han, is still rich in archaic data.

19 The work attributed to him has been lost since the Han period, Maspero, *La Chine antique*, p. 521.

20 J.J.L. Duyvendack, *The Book of Lord Shang*, pp. 96 ff. Leang K'i-tch'ao has rightly insisted on the importance of the ideas pointed out by these two terms which his translator (the latter, rather than a translation, has given an interpretative summary) thought he could translate into English by the words: "Favouritism" and "Despotism" (Cf. Leang K'i-tch'ao, *History of Chinese political Thought*, p. 116 and J. Escarra and R. Germain, *La conception de la loi et les théories des légistes à la veille des Ts'in*, pp. 28 ff.) It is certainly an abuse to speak, as Leang K'i-tch'ao did, of a "School of *chou*" and a "School of *che*", especially when one wants to conclude that *chou* and *chi* note absolutely opposite ideas and yet professed by the same men (Escarra and Germain, *op. cit.*, p. 32).

21 SMT, V, p. 84.

to "solicit" (*kieou*) it at the right moment.²² To reproach politicians with fatalism, as Han Fei tseu did and as was repeated after him, is to make a purely misleading criticism.²³ They have no idea that to govern is to let oneself be carried along by the course of things. Their art, on the contrary, consists in *using Fate by tempting it*. On this point they followed the common opinion. The Chinese admit, for example, that a dream is a real force. It must therefore give place to reality; it does not, however, interfere with the course of things until it is treated as a reality; until then its efficacy remains null; one whose dream is an omen of death, and who, at first prudently disregards it, continues to live for three years, but dies on the very day when, believing that he has exhausted the time, he has his dream interpreted and finally makes it come true.²⁴ Just as to change symbols is revolutionary, so to capture signs is to interfere. Princes who employ Politicians to point out the chances of chance, as soon as they solicit luck, risk increasing as well as diminishing their Fate. Any use of circumstances implies a wager on Fate where the gambler is also the wager. The idea was not new, but politicians, by cultivating the desire to constantly tempt fate, weakened the prestige enjoyed by customary rules and the idea of status. Without the slightest notion of determinism, and simply because they diminished the dominance of custom, they made the Chinese mind, for a time, less resistant to the idea of laws (valid under such and such conditions).

The circumstantial elements of success vary in the extreme. However diverse the prescriptions of etiquette may be, they are always aimed at maintaining the status quo. A prince, avid for growth, needs always to have new means of success. The role of professional politicians is to provide him with a suitable recipe for success (*chou*) for every lucky chance (*che*). The great Patron of Politicians is Wang Hiu, "the Master of the Valley of Demons," a probably legendary figure; nothing is known of him except that he was considered the inventor of the system of alliances and barrier leagues by which the diplomacy of the Warring Kingdoms is explained (apparently as an afterthought).²⁵ The only principle of politicians seems to be the interest of the moment combined with disregard for traditions and sworn faith; the past is not binding as circumstances change everything. All that political folklore can teach us is that the Chinese were masters in the art of weakening a rival by giving him an ill-timed opportunity to create a favorable opportunity for themselves.²⁶ Possibly this art was expressed in formulas. Keou-tsien, king of Yue, after having used the politician Wen Tchong, allowed him to commit suicide; he gave him a sword and said:

> "You taught me the Seven Recipes (*chou*) to fight Wou; three were enough for me to triumph over Wou; four Recipes remain in your possession; go try them, I beg of you, with the king, my predecessor."²⁷

---

22   Granet, *Danses et légendes...*, notes on pp. 85, 85, 88, 91.
23   Escarra and Germain, *op. cit*, p. 34.
24   *Tso tchouan*, C., II, p. 158.
25   Wieger, *Histoire des croyances...*, p. 236; M. Granet, *Civ. chin.*, pp. 110, 44.
26   *Civ. chin*, 38, 39; Granet, *op. cit.* note 178.
27   *SMT*, IV, p. 432.

The glossators enumerate these Seven (or Nine) Recipes; they are (in appearance) only vulgar tricks (e.g., the rival is induced to weaken by luxurious expenditures or by a taste for women), but it is all in the art, entirely personal, which implements them; the precaution taken by Keou-tsien shows this very well. Political recipes are no different from all other recipes, tricks of the trade that cannot be taught, pure operative knowledge. A sorcerer makes his son learn his formulas; the latter knows how to recite them very exactly, but they produce no effect.[28] A wheelwright, at seventy years of age, still makes his wheels alone; he has not been able to transmit his art to his children.[29] In the same way, the art of making successful political plans corresponds to a vocation; every recipe is, in essence, secret (*yin*) and private (*sseu*). On this point, again, there is nothing original in the principles of political art; however, they have also led to a new conception: namely, the distinction between custom (or Law) and governmental art. Only the Prince – indeed, the Privy Council – should know the *che* and the *chou*, the situations from which power can arise, the know-how that makes power emerge from situations. Han Fei tseu will no doubt reproach Chen Pou-hai for having neglected the Law and the regulations in favor of the Prescriptions, but he will recognize that, while the Laws – published and permanent – are necessary for good administration, princely authority and governmental efficiency have their principle in the power that the Prescriptions – kept secret – derive from circumstantial conditions.[30]

II. The Art of Persuasion

To the innovative impulse given to Chinese ideas by the politicians was added, in the fourth and third centuries BC, that attempted by the dialecticians and logicians. Mr. Forke has called attention to writers whom he has described as Sophists, suggesting a very legitimate connection with Greece.[31] The Chinese tend to confuse in a single School, which is called the School of Names (*ming kia*), the logicians whose concerns seem to have been very diverse. Some were led to Logic by Rhetoric or Eristics; others by political and moral, if not juridical, concerns. The latter are the representatives of an ancient indigenous logic. There is no way to prove it, but I would venture to believe that the former represent a tradition of foreign origin which, moreover, has failed to acclimatize in China.

---

28   *Lie tseu*, in Wieger, *Les Pères du système taoïste*, p. 197. These incantation formulas are designated by the word "Numbers" and are qualified as *chou* (Recipes).

29   *Tchouang tseu*, Wieger, *op. cit.* p. 317: "The mouth cannot say (what the art consists of). There is a number!" That is to say, an operative formula that can only be appropriated by intuition and thanks to a previous vocation. Note that the idea of Number evokes not the determinate or the mechanical, but Art, but the Effective.

30   *Han Fei tseu*, 43 and 40; Escarra and Germain, *op. cit*, pp. 28 and 30.

31   Forke, *The Chinese Sophists, JRAS, Études asiatiques*, pp. 1 ff. The study of the Sophists was brilliantly taken up in China by Hou Shih (*The development of logical method in ancient China*, pp. 111 ff.). See also Suzuki, *A brief history of early Chinese philosophy*, pp. 57 ff. and *TP*, 1927, pp. 1 ff.

The most sectarian and militant of the ancient schools is that of Mö tseu. It has been compared to an order of chivalry that had assumed the mission of helping the downtrodden; it might even be better compared to a congregation of preaching brothers. Its members set out to restore wisdom to princes who had been led astray by ambition. They chose as their adversaries the pernicious advisors skilled in enlisting support. Hence the importance attributed to the teaching of rhetoric; all the members of the School kept models of homilies whose writing was attributed to the Master. From at least the middle of the fourth century, some of them formed separate congregations {the *Pie-mö*: (disciples) separate from Mö (tseu)} which devoted themselves to Eristics. It is unlikely that they invented the thing and were the first to deserve the name of disputants (*Pien-tchö*). Historical folklore shows us, long before the 4th century BC, disputants speaking in private councils.

To leave one's adversary *bewildered* by buffoonery is one of the significant themes of the literature[32] of these centuries of disputation, and even more significant is the use of apologies and blatant allegories.[33] All this seems to stem from a touted wisdom whose international inspiration is still felt. The Chinese sophists had only a small number of paradoxes. All that remains of them are a few lists. As for their opponents, all that has been preserved is a list of scholastic exercises intended to prepare disciples not to remain silent in the face of a professional contender. The latter uses the paradoxes of which he has the secret to force attention, reduce to silence and, finally, slip an opinion. King K'ang of Song forbade anyone to talk about anything in front of him except bravery and power grabs: "I have knowledge (*tao*) on these subjects," a sophist told him. He proposes, and the king accepts, to talk about the power grabs that sometimes succeed and sometimes fail. In this way, he leads the king to consent to talk to him about what can make things succeed. The sophist soon takes up that what can succeed is etiquette and love of peace. Here he is, ranting about forbidden subjects... He retires triumphantly without waiting for the king to find something to retort.[34] Will war or peace prevail in Wei's counsels? A sophist is introduced:

---

32   For example, in a book such as the *Yen tseu tch'ouen ts'ieou*, written around the fourth and third centuries BC and attributed to Yen tseu (late sixth century, early fifth century BC), whose tradition makes him a dwarf and adviser to a prince of Ts'i, a lover of dwarves and jesters (Maspero, *La Chine antique*, note 980; Granet, *Danses et légendes...*, pp. 171 ff.).

33   That is (*SMT*, IV, p. 387) a diplomatic attempt before the battle; the aim is to persuade the enemy general not to fight, not to do anything excessive. The envoy is counting on an apology. Several servants have only one cup of wine for themselves; instead of sharing it, they play with it: the first one to pull out a snake will drink it. The fastest one takes the cup, but boasts, "I still have time to add my feet." The cup is taken away: "A snake has no feet; now that you have made feet for it, it is no longer a snake." Compare the paradoxes (which seem to imply a distinction between essence and accident) dear to Mö tseu's disciples such as: "A cart is made of wood; riding in a cart is not riding in wood", or "A fighting cock is not a cock", or "To kill a thief is not to kill a man". This last theme was used by Mencius (L 231) to avoid a direct and dangerous answer in one of his rhetorical exercises at the court of King Siuan of Ts'i.

34   *Lie tseu*, in Wieger, *Les Pères du système taoïste*, p. 103.

Book IV - Chapter I - The Prescriptions of Government

"Do you know what a slug is?"

"Yes," said the king.

"On the left horn of the slug is the kingdom of the Agitators; on the right horn, that of the Brutes. All the time they are fighting for their territories and fighting each other. The corpses number in the thousands. A fortnight after a defeat, they return to battle."

"Fools!" says the king.

"May your highness please find some foundation for them. Do you not think that on the four sides, and on the Upper as well as on the Lower, there are no limits?"[35]

"There are none."

"Don't you know how to frolic at ease (*yeou sin*) in that which has no limits? Doesn't it seem irrelevant to you then whether or not there are realms that limit each other?"

"Certainly."

"Among these bounded realms is (your state of) Wei. In Wei is Leang (your capital). His Highness is in Leang. How does it differ from the King of the Brutes?"

"There is no difference," said the king.

And the sophist retreated in triumph, leaving the prince stunned and as if lost.[36]

The sophists whom these accounts portray favorably were apparently part of the entourage of Houei tseu (or Houei Che), a native of Wei, where he lived and served (it is said) as minister to King Houei (370-319 BC). Was Houei tseu, the most famous of Chinese dialecticians, a friend of peace, like the sophists who surrounded him? Induction is probable. should it lead us to link Houei tseu with the school of Mö tseu? can we go further and affirm that the whole dialectic of Houei tseu tended to give a metaphysical foundation to the doctrine of universal love attributed to Mö tseu? The basis of this metaphysics is said to be "the theory, of Taoist origin, of the essential identity of things and beings."[37] In fact, Houei tseu is only known for the Taoist slander against him.[38] He was accused of possessing only false knowledge (*tao*) and of speaking without concern for reality. There is an excess in

---

35   Space is one and indivisible like the body of the slug.

36   *Tchouang tseu*, L., H, p. 118; Wieger, *op. cit.* p. 433. Compare the following anecdote from *SMT*, V, p. 155. The crown prince of Wei goes to fight. A man asks to be received by him. He says that he has a recipe which, in a hundred fights, gives a hundred times victory. Presented, he says something like this (I summarize it): if you are victorious and annex a territory, you will never be more than the king of Wei; if you are defeated, you will lose Wei; "such is my recipe for a hundred victories in a hundred battles." In other words, there is no point in fighting to enlarge a territory. In this paradox, which retains its popular form here, we may find, as in the others, a theory of the indefinite character of space.

37   Maspero, *La Chine antique*, p. 532.

38   What remains of *Houei tseu* is contained in chapter 33 of *Tchouang tseu* (L., II, pp. 229-232), to which are added some anecdotes (Wieger, *op. cit.*, pp. 215, 221, 249, 347, 349, 351, 419, 431, 445, 451, and 507-509).

the account that Houei tseu "had studied the science of his time, astronomy, astrology, the science of Yin and Yang, the Numbers, etc.,"[39] on the sole pretext that Tchouang tseu mocked him because, without hesitation or reflection, he spoke of all things, indefinitely, one day someone amused himself by asking him why the sky was not falling, why there was wind, rain, thunder… As much as one would like to inform readers, it is worth telling them first of all that all that remains of Houei tseu is a small number of ironic anecdotes and a list of his main paradoxical themes.

One of them (V) has given translators a lot of difficulty:[40]

> "The distinction (*yi*) between what approaches (*t'ong*) more (*ta*) and what approaches (*t'ong*) less (*siao*) is the minimum (*siao*) of approach (*t'ong*) and distinction (*yi*); (what) in all beings is entirely proximate (*t'ong*) and entirely distinct (*yi*) (corresponds) to the maximum (*ta*) of approach (*t'ong*) and distinction (*yi*)."

This convoluted aphorism is but a pungent way of formulating the distinction (glossators see nothing else) between correlative and independent aspects. The correlative aspects (life and death, happiness and unhappiness, cold and heat, day and night, rest and movement…) are linked and complementary (minimum of distinction), but are perceived successively (minimum of approach). Independent aspects (such as white and solid) are united (for example, in a stone) in the same object (maximum of approximation), although they are totally separable (maximum of distinction).

> "To unite (*ho*: to join in the manner of two halves, in fact inseparable) the close and distinguishable (*t'ong yi*: the complementary aspects), to separate (*li*: to divide as adherent but distinguishable parts) the white and the solid (the independent aspects)."

such is the work of the sophist.[41]

---

39   Maspero, *La Chine antique*, p. 531.

40   Legge (*Tchouang tseu*, II, p. 229) translates: "(When it is said that) things very much alike are different from things a little alike, this is what is called making little of agreements and differences; (when it is said that) all things are completely different, this is what is called making much of agreements and differences." Wieger, *op. cit.* p. 507: "The difference between a great likeness and a small one is the little likeness-difference; when beings are altogether alike and different, it is the great likeness-difference." Maspero, (*op. cit.*, p. 533): "(To say that) what has many points of identity is different from what has few points of identity is what is called Small Identity and Dissimilarity; (to say that) all things are entirely identical (with each other) and entirely different (from each other) is what is called Great Identity and Dissimilarity." Maspero adds, "Under these conditions, all distinction was illusory, and thus was founded Mö tseu's principle of universal love without distinction: 'Love all things equally, the world is one.'" The phrase in quotation marks is the translation of Houei tseu's tenth paradox, which I understand as follows: "If affection extends to the details of beings, the Universe (literally: Heaven and Earth) is (already) one body."

41   *Tchouang tseu*, L., I, p. 387.

BOOK IV - CHAPTER I - THE PRESCRIPTIONS OF GOVERNMENT 269

Dialecticians argue about even and odd, about like and unlike (*t'ong yi*), about white and solid,[42] but what they pride themselves on is making clear, "like a house on a background of sky, the separation (*li*) of solid and white."[43] The rule of the categories Yin and Yang, combined with the ritual prestige of an indefinite system of correspondences, tends to prevent the Chinese from reducing everything to contrasts. To separate white from metal or black from water leads to the ruin of etiquette, to free thought from it, to permit the reclassification of things which must entail a reorganization of the social order. Hence the success of the sophists in the court of the enlightened despots. Whether they had made the discovery themselves or had the merit of understanding the value of imported ideas, the dialecticians knew how to give their discourses a new appeal. They learned to abstract and to play with abstract notions.

Reacting in the extreme against the Chinese tendency not to escape from the concrete and to reason without opposing contradictions, they made abstractions and used the principle of contradiction by giving it an absolute value. This abstract realism led them to imagine a host of paradoxes involving a strictly formal analysis of the ideas of magnitude, quantity, time, space, motion, continuity, unity and multiplicity… But, while Houei tseu's Fifth Paradox indicates the beginning of all paradoxes inspired by an abstract notion of quality, paradoxes that pretend to exhaust physical realities are expressed without any attempt at systematization.

> "(I) Extreme greatness (and such that leaves) nothing outside (of itself) is the whole (*yi*: unity, total) greatest; extreme smallness (and such that retains) nothing within (itself), is the whole (*yi*) smallest. – (II) (That which) has no thickness and cannot be added (*tsi*: to accumulate) is a thousand stadia high. – (III) The sky is not higher than the earth; a mountain is as flat as a swamp. – (IV) The Sun, when it reaches its noon, reaches its sunset, and when a being reaches its birth, it reaches its death… – (VI) The South extends without limit and yet it has limits. – (VII) Today I go to Yue and yet I arrived there yesterday. – (VIII) Chained rings can be separated. – (IX) I know the center of the World: it is north of Yen (extreme north) and south of Yue (extreme south). – (X) If the affection extends to the details of beings, the Universe (word for word: Heaven and Earth) is (but) a single body."[44]

"Houei tseu wrote enough to carry five chariots, but his knowledge was misleading and his words were meaningless." This is the judgment of Tchouang tseu, who saw very well the principle common to all these paradoxes, namely, the ap-

---

42 *Ibid.*, II, p. 220.
43 *Ibid.*, I, p. 317. The word *li* has the meaning of separating, distinguishing, cutting; in the language of the *Yi king*, it is said of things attached; it indicates separations made over what is attached by association (*ping*). I do not understand how it was possible to translate it as "to make a synthesis of…" (Maspero, *op. cit.*, p. 536) and to write (*T.P.*, 1927, p. 63): "This operation (of the mind) is, to use the Kantian expression which exactly translates the word *li*, a synthesis."
44 *Tchouang tseu*, L., II, p. 229. Tchouang tseu discusses the principle of all these paradoxes. Cf. *ibid.*, I, pp. 181 ff, pp. 187 ff.

plication of an exhausting division to all concrete things. He amused himself by showing Houei tseu, the abstract, forced to admit, in concrete terms, the ineffectiveness of his principle:

> "The king of Wei," says Houei tseu, who has just told Chiang tseu of his misadventure, "had given me the seeds of a large gourd. I sowed them and they grew into fruits so large that they could hold fifty bushels. I made (by cutting them in half) basins for my toilet. They were so heavy I couldn't lift them. I split them (again) to make drinking vessels. The (pieces of) dry bark were still too big and, moreover, unstable, they did not hold the liquid; they were just useless and big objects. As they were of no use to me, I cut them into pieces."[45]

The Chinese were not very favorable to the abstract realism of Houei tseu and his followers or rivals. The best known is Kong-souen Long, who also lived in Wei towards the end of the 4th century BC His main disciple, according to Lie tseu, was Prince Meou of Chong-chan.[46] Kong-souen Long excelled in:

> "disguising human desires and transforming intentions. He was always able to triumph in discussion, but without being able to convince deeply."[47] He was always able to convince profoundly."[^826

He seems to have abused the distinction of independent aspects, employing it in demonstrations by absurdity on the occasion of paradoxical subjects: "a white dog is black," "a white horse is not a horse," because a black dog and a white dog are both dogs, a white dog is a black dog; and, if white, a horse can only be considered a horse if it is accepted to confuse it with a black horse or a bay horse, so that no white, black or bay horse is a horse. These dialectical games were intended to prohibit any qualification by equating all qualifications and, after having used it too rigorously, to deny the principle of contradiction in favor of an absolute relativism. They astonished, but tired, their contemporaries. Only a few initiates, like the Prince of Tchong-chan, were willing to recognize their profound meaning. "A white horse is not a horse (indicates) the distinction (*li*) between object (or rather the symbol of an object: *hing*) and qualification." "He who has (desires) does

---

45 *Tchouang tseu*, L., I, p. 172.
46 *Lie tseu*, in Wieger, *op. cit.* p. 127. Tchouang tseu (*Ibid.*, p. 419) makes him a rival of Mö tseu, Yang tseu, the followers of Confucius, and Houei tseu himself. He compares these five teachings to the five notes of an out-of-tune lute. In chapter 33 of the *Tchouang tseu*, it is said that Kong-suen Long and other sophists were merely surpassing the paradoxes of Houei Tzu, the one great inventor. I see no basis for the opinion (Maspero, *La Chine antique*, p. 535) that Kong-souen Long was the inventor of the theme of "indefinite divisibility," which is essential to Houei tseu. Kong-souen Long, who has been identified with Tseu-che, a disciple of Confucius, and who may have been a traveling sophist, is known from a small pamphlet which has come down to us in rather poor condition. It has been partially translated (Tucci, *Storia della filosofia cinese antica*, p. 44 ff.); the interpretation given in Fr. Wieger's *Histoire des croyances religieuses*.... (pp. 218 ff.) is misleading.
47 *Tchouang tseu*, L., II, p. 231 (Wieger, *Tchouang tseu*, p. 509).

Book IV - Chapter I - The Prescriptions of Government 271

not have (a) heart (seat of desire), means: (only) the absence of desires allows the unification of the heart."[48] "He who has (fingers) does not get (touch), means: one would not have to have fingers to get (touch) at all." "(The subject:) a hair supports thirty thousand pounds (serves to illustrate the idea of) *che* (force, conditions of influence),"[49] and "(The subject:) a shadow cannot move (or 'the shadow of a flying bird cannot move'), (the idea of) change (*kai*: change and not movement)."[50]

The prince of Tchong-chan also admired the paradox of the arrow, but did not comment on it. However, this is (from several points of view) the most interesting paradox of Kong-souen Long, and the one with the least uncertain interpretation. There are two picturesque variants. The theme of the arrow follows that of the motionless shadow and is stated thus:

> "Whatever the speed of the arrowhead and the arrow (*tsou che*),[51] there is time (for them not to move and not to stay in place."[52]

This is how Kong-suen Long illustrated this riddle. He once said to Kong Ch'ouan:

> "A master archer has the power to make the point of a second arrow touch the tail of the arrow shot before; shot in a row and meeting each other, all his arrows follow each other, the points and tails touching each other without interruption, so that, from the first to the last, they continually unite the target with the bowstring and seem to be one."

Kong Ch'uan was dumbfounded…

> "There is no reason to be surprised," said Kong-souen Long. "An apprentice of P'eng-mong (patron of archers), whose name was Hong-ch'ao, was one day angry with his wife and wanted to frighten her; he took the crow's bow,

---

48 This theme is closer to Taoism than to the doctrine of Mö tseu.
49 Another Taoist theme: influence without contact (cf. Book III, chap. III).
50 *Lie tseu*, in Wieger, *Les Pères du système taoïste*, p. 128.
51 One could translate "arrow with point" (but not arrowhead); it is probably not gratuitous that the formula begins with this expression inviting one to distinguish the head and body of the arrow, an important distinction for the explanation by the chain of arrows. (Compare with the chain of rings, which can be divided).
52 This paradox has been translated and glossed without regard to the concrete illustrations that come from Kong-souen Long himself. – Legge translates (*Tchouang tseu*, L., p. 230): "As fast as the *point of the arrow* is, there is a *moment* when it neither flies nor is at rest." – Wieger, (*op. cit.*) "an arrow that hits the target no longer advances and does not stop". – Maspero (who reproaches Hou Che for "making the paradox unintelligible" by understanding: "the arrow has moments of both motion and rest" translates himself "the rapid motion of an arrow is (the succession of) moments in which it is neither stationary nor at rest" (*La Chine antique*, p. 537). I have not been able to understand the sense of the discussion instituted in note 2 on this page, nor to know on what Chinese data one can rely to interpret the paradox in writing "in motion; if one takes as a unit the space traversed by the arrow from the bow to the target, it stops if one takes as a unit the space occupied by the arrow and considers not the whole path but each of these units separately."

the Hi-wei arrow, and aimed at her eyes; the arrow grazed the pupils without the eyes blinking, and fell to the ground without raising dust."[53]

Launched with power and mastery, the arrow, pure speed, moves, and stops, speed abolished, never producing any effect. Between the absolute of speed and the nothingness of speed *which follow each other*, the *difference* is total, but it is null – for when it finishes its course without even falling, moving, or *making it move*, the arrow is still in flight – and it is motionless when it passes so fast that, just as if it were neither passing nor moving, it does not make anything move either. Moreover, perfect immobility and extreme mobility are absolutely fused: the string of arrows that goes from the bow to the target is both mobile and immobile, immobile since, while everything moves, nothing has moved, the tail remains on the string while the tip reaches the goal, mobile since everything moves, nothing moves, the tip is at the end of its travel while the tail receives all its velocity from the string.

The interest of this paradoxical subject lies in the fact that it deals not only with the indefinite divisibility of time and space, but, as a whole, with the notion of effective force (*che*) and change (*kai*). As such, it should be compared to certain themes dear to the Taoists. The mightiest sword – the one that kills everything without blood staining it – can cut an enemy three times from neck to waist without the slightest effort, but the passing of the sword has parted nothing; the severed body remains intact.[54] The paradox of the arrow is also related to an important mythical theme; the master archer's string of arrows is the equivalent of the royal arrow that establishes contact between the King and Heaven; a continuous contact, like that of the string and the goal, but not a one-way contact; the arrow leaves the shooter and returns to him and there is circuit and immobility (just as there is communion but no contact).[55] At the bottom of the paradoxes inspired by the idea that everything is change, but that change (and, consequently, movement) is impossible, there appears a *magical realism* to which the *abstract realism* of the dialecticians is directly linked.

Only the Taoists seem to have drawn some fruit from the analyses which their dialectical verve inspired in the Sophists. They used, in a thousand ways, the formula:

> "A ruler a foot long which is halved every day, (even) after ten thousand generations, will not be exhausted."[56]

Undoubtedly, the taste of many Chinese writers, and in particular Wang Ch'ong, for sorites comes from the dialecticians. However, the Taoists themselves have nothing but contempt for the sophists. They reproach them for their arrogance, accuse them of jealousy, and reproach them for having lived without friends, on

---

53 *Lie tseu*, in Wieger, *op. cit.*, p. 127.
54 *Ibid.*, p. 149.
55 On this subject, see, tentatively, M. Granet, *Civ. Chin.*, pp. 223 ff.
56 *Tchouang tseu*, Wieger, *op. cit.* p. 509.

the fringes of any school, satisfied as soon as they found an opportunity to speak, thinking, uninterested in ideas or things, only in having the last word, happy if their interlocutors remained "with their mouths open, their tongues glued to the roof of their mouths."[57] At most, they conceded to Houei tseu a talent for music and the charm of eloquence.[58] Perhaps it is true that the Sophists were primarily concerned with dazzling and surprising the audience. On the contrary, the later disciples of Mö tseu seem to have wanted to create and formulate an art of persuasion.[59]

It is very difficult to say whether, as has been argued, these rhetoricians clearly conceived the principle of causality and the principle of contradiction; the aphorisms in which these principles are found seem, read in the Chinese text, extremely vague.[60] If it were admitted that they were conceived and formulated with a certain rigor, how can one explain that they could have passed unnoticed and have not had the slightest fortune? Similarly, if it were true that the logicians already had the idea of opposing deduction (*hiao*) and induction (*t'ouei*), it would be very curious if they had limited themselves to arguing with the help of examples, to developing with the help of analogies. It was already a good idea to realize that practical rules were needed to learn – not to proceed by formal reasoning, but – to argue in good faith when illustrated by examples (*hiao*) and expanded using analogy (*t'ouei*); this is, no doubt, the meaning of the technical terms that brought induction and deduction to mind.[61] Mr. Forke does not seem to have been mistaken in stating that Mö tseu's disciples wanted to do practical work.

They should not be seen as theorists of reasoning; they were interested only in the art of conducting a discussion victoriously.[62] They were concerned only with oratorical prescriptions. However, it would not be fair to ignore the difficulty of their efforts or to fail to point out their theoretical importance. Chinese does not mark tense, number, or gender; this made it possible to formulate certain paradoxes nicely, but it made the analysis of concepts difficult. Chinese does not distinguish between verb, noun, adjective, and adverb… Under these conditions, it is wonderful that the idea of analyzing the relations of terms brought together by discourse was conceived, and it is not surprising that the analysis was not carried

---

57 *Ibid.*, p. 347; *Lie tseu, Ibid.*, p. 127.
58 *Tchouang tseu*, Wieger, *op. cit.* p. 221.
59 A trace of his efforts has been preserved in sections 40-45 of *Mö tseu*, translated by Forke (*Mo Ti, des Socialethikers und seiner Schüler philosophische Werke*); the text is in such a poor state that it is almost impossible to derive anything precise from it. Several contemporary Chinese authors, Messrs. Chiang Ping-lin, Hou Che and Leang K'i-tch'ao, have endeavored to extract from it the elements of a formal logic. Their investigations, very meritorious, were perhaps vitiated by too narrow a knowledge of Stuart Mill; this is what Maspero reproached them for (*Notes sur la logique de Mö tseu et de son école*, T.P., 1927, p. 10). In fact, innumerable difficulties arise as soon as one attempts to specify the value of the terms used in a technical sense by the authors of these treatises.
60 Maspero, *La Chine antique*, p. 540.
61 T.P., 1927, pp. 11, 26, 32.
62 Forke, *Mo Ti*…, p. 85.

much further.[63] The discussions of white and solid, horse and white, qualification (*ming*) and object (*che*) or its symbol (*hing*), are surprising in their unexpected character and their revolutionary merit. They tended to ruin a venerable system of classifications and correspondences. The dialecticians were undermining Etiquette at its core. So they caused a fuss and were not very successful. But they did not prevail over the proponents of the old indigenous logic.

III. The Art of Qualifying

The Chinese like to argue and are skilled at it, but they do not care much about the form of reasoning. However, they attach great importance to the art of qualifying (*ming*). They therefore group together, in what they call the School of Names (*ming kia*), all those whom they consider to be not mere disputants (*pien-tchö*), but logicians. The object of logic is correct designations or qualifications.

Tradition regards Confucius as the inventor of traditional logic. It is based on a passage from *Louen yu*:

> Tseu-leu said (to Confucius):
> "The lord of Wei proposes to entrust the government to you. What do you consider to be the first thing to do?"
> "The main thing is to make the designations (*tcheng ming*) correct," replied the Master, and added:
> "If the designations are not correct, the words cannot be correct; if the words are not correct, the affairs (of state) do not succeed; if these affairs do not succeed, neither rites nor music flourish; if rites and music do not flourish, punishments and penalties cannot be just; if they are not just, people do not know how to act. Therefore, the Sage (*kiun tseu*), when he awards designations, always makes sure that the words can conform to them and, when he uses them in speaking, he also makes sure that they are realized in action. Let the Sage, in his words, not commit any frivolity. that is enough!"[64]

This anecdote is intended to provide information about the relations between Confucius and the house of Wei. Taken as such, it is worth no more or less than all the information given by the *Louen yu* about the Master. There is no reason to claim that Confucius did or did not know the theory of correct designations. But Confucius does not matter here. What is important to note is that the theory is first and foremost a moral and political doctrine. Good order depends entirely on the

---

63 Cf. *supra*, Book II, ch. III, sec. III and Granet, *Quelques particularités de la langue et de la pensée chinoises*, p. 124. On the use of true and false analogies in non-academic discussions, see Granet, *Fêtes et chansons...*, p. 64. Note again the kinship of paradoxes like "an orphan calf never had a mother" (when it had its mother, it was not an orphan calf) that resemble peasant jokes and pure jokes like that of the man with the well (Granet, *Danses et légendes...*, note 1387; a man who wanted to dig a well found a capable craftsman, dug his well, and said, "I have dug a well! I had found a man." It was understood (anteriority was not expressed: "I dug a well! I found a man in it!").

64 *Louen yu*, L., p. 127; *SMT*, V, p. 378.

Book IV - Chapter I - The Prescriptions of Government

correctness of language. Whether invented or not, the anecdote has the merit of illustrating this principle. It also has the merit of revealing its basis.

It is not gratuitous that the anecdote involves the Prince of Wei. Duke Ling (534-493 BC), with whom Confucius was associated, was an indulgent husband and an unnatural father. His wife, Princess Nan-tseu, was incestuous. His eldest son was a rebel; he fled from Wei after plotting to kill Nan-tseu.[65] Confucius' words allude to these disorders.

> "Nan-tseu having hated the heir son, the son and the father exchanged (*yi*) their names (*ming*)."[66]

Thus expresses Sseu-ma Ts'ien, who says elsewhere:

> "Confucius said: 'The essential thing is to make the designations correct.' In Wei the places (*kiu*) did not match (with the designations)."[67]

Confucian doctrine asserts that there is no order in the state unless everything conforms to order in the princely family. In Wei, Nan-tseu, the wife, did not behave like a wife, nor the husband like a husband, nor the father like a father, nor the son like a son. This is expressed by saying either that no one was in his place (*kiu*), or that father and son had exchanged their designations (*yi ming*), since the relations of situation were reversed, it was as if the designations themselves had been reversed.

A passage from the *Yi king* illustrates similar ideas. The thirty-seventh hexagram includes, in the *upper part*, the trigram which is the emblem of the elder daughter; in the *lower part*, the one symbolizing the younger daughter.[68] The two "daughters," as we see, occupy places in relation to their ranks. Thus, this hexagram, which bears the name *kia jen* (the family), evokes a family where order reigns. The first gloss reveals this teaching: the prince extends his good influence to his whole family and is strict to prevent his wives and children from misbehaving.[69] The second gloss[70] adds:

> "The wife correctly occupies (*tcheng*) her place (*wei*: her rank) in the gynaecium and, likewise, the husband correctly occupies his place outside the gynaecium. When the husband and wife are correctly situated (in their respective places), there is a completely equal (*yi*) distribution (of all things) of Heaven and Earth... (Let a) father (merit the name of) father, a son (the

---

65 *Civ. Chin.*, p. 399; *Tso chouan*, C., III, p. 586; *SMT*, IV, p. 205. Nan-tseu slept with his own brother.

66 *SMT*; ch. CXXX and *SMT*, V, p. 379.

67 *SMT*, III, p. 208.

68 Here the original text lacks clarity. The lower trigram represents the middle daughter, not the youngest one, although she is certainly younger (TN).

69 *Yi king*, L., p. 136. A song from *Che king* (Granet, *Fêtes et chansons...*, p. 10, verse 12 and its note) is interpreted as an illustration of the theme: a good wife knows how to put a proper order in the family (*kia jen*).

70 *Yi king*, L., p. 242. First appendix to *Yi king*.

name of) son, an elder brother (the name of) elder brother, a youth (the name of) youth, a husband (the name of) husband, a wife (the name of) wife! The order (tao) of the family will be right (*tcheng*). (Make) the family right (*cheng*) and the land of men (will enjoy) stable order!

From this passage the equivalence of the expressions: *tcheng wei* (right places, positions) and *tcheng ming* (right designations, appellations).

Two common law adages make the meaning of this equivalence clear: "Appeals (*ming*) are the great ordering principle of human relations." "When (in the family) appellations (*ming*) are manifest, the rules of the separation of the sexes are respected."[71] These adages are used to justify a rule of sexual morality whose importance is extreme in the organization of the family: brothers-in-law and sisters-in-law cannot mourn for each other, and there can be no conversation between them; they could not, since they belong to the same generation, and the elder sister-in-law, for example, could not be called "mother," nor could they call each other anything but "wife" and "husband," which would be no less serious than establishing marital relations between them. Denominations dictate morality because denominations give rise to reality; it is necessary, then, that they correspond exactly to the distinctions of sex and generations, of attributions and ranks, which form the basis of the domestic order. There would be promiscuity if a sister-in-law were called "wife." There is incest if father and son "exchange designations." When a father strips a son of his bride, he ceases to be a father and descends to the rank of his own sons. The reverse happened when a son married his stepmother.[72] Chinese ethnographers violently express their contempt for the barbarians of the North or South, where fathers and sons (*tseu*: sons or daughters) live together or go to the toilet together. Moralists fulminate against what they call modern dances, where not only men and women, but even fathers and sons (or daughters) mix, i.e., the different sexes and opposite generations lose their proper status. These feelings are violent because they are relatively new. They are the fruit of a transformation of the domestic organization and of the substitution of the promiscuity proper to the large family by the discipline of the patriarchal family.[73] We can see that, historical or not, the anecdote in which Confucius is shown expressing the rule of correct designations on the occasion of the domestic disorders of the princely household of Wei, has the merit of expressing very precisely the original value of this rule.[74] Besides a rule of thought, it is a rule of action.

This rule has always retained the imperative character of a moral precept. It is usually formulated (more or less as in the *Yi king*) in the manner of a *brief commandment*, repeating twice, in order to give it its full force, a word which is already worth by itself. When one shouts: "Prince, (to be) prince! vassal, (to be) vassal!

---

71 *Li ki*, C., p. 780 and *Yi li*, Steele, *I Li, or the Book of Etiquette and Ceremonial*, II, p. 29.
72 *Civ. Chin.*, pp. 368, 369.
73 *Civ. Chin.*, p. 443.
74 Another anecdote (*Louen yu*, L., p. 120; *SMT*, V, p. 305) has Confucius uttering in similar circumstances the formula "prince, prince! vassal, vassal!" which illustrates the doctrine of correct designations.

Book IV - Chapter I - The Prescriptions of Government

father, (to be) father! son, (to be) son!...," it is clear that words are used to animate realities. We have seen, with respect to language, that to designate (*ming*) things is to give them the individuality (*ming*) that makes them be. We have also seen that civilization came into being when the first Sages gave all beings their correct designations.[75] At the origin of the theory of designations – as at the origin of dialectical paradoxes – lies a kind of magical realism.

While the dialecticians enjoyed abstracting and disrupting received ideas, the logicians tried to preserve the concrete and traditional value of symbols. At least in its beginnings, the theory of correct naming is far from being a mere theory of "correct preaching," as Chinese critics (when speaking in English) claim. If it had only sought to avoid verbal confusion and incorrect qualifications, it is difficult to see how, by distributing names alone, one could have hoped to introduce order among men and, moreover, in Nature.

The doctrine of correct names is a doctrine of order.

Its success is explained by the prestige enjoyed by Etiquette. Chinese traditions certainly do not distort the facts when they link this doctrine to the techniques of Ceremonial; this leads, in fact, quite legitimately, to admit that it was professed by Confucius. "In the past, names (*ming*) and ranks (*wei*) were diverse, so that rites (*li*, ritual honors) were calculated (*chou*)[76] differently (according to ranks and names). Confucius said,"The main thing is to make the names correct..."[77]

As long as feudal order and Etiquette reign, correctness in speech and, from it, logical correctness, are inseparable from correctness in dress and, consequently, from moral correctness. The axiom that the behavior of the universe depends on the conduct of princes is not disputed. There is no order in things and in thoughts if the ruler, for whom speech is an act more than for any other, does not qualify (*ming*) anything lightly and does not invest (*ming*) anyone without observing protocol. Every gentleman (*kiun tseu*) or every sage (*kiun tseu*) should, like a prince (*kiun*), strive to match his dress to his status, that is, to the rank (*wei*) and name (*ming*) with which he is invested (*ming*). *Ming* (personal name) is used to designate the individual and his share of honor, his lot in life (*ming*) and his inheritance (*fen*), the whole of his belongings, the totality of his attributes. It is a ritual principle that no one should go outside his attributions (*cheou fen*). "When the Etiquette extends to all, the attributions (*fen*) (of all beings) remain fixed (*ting*)."[78]

The feudal order has a second principle. Princes and vassals live under the control of history.[79] It is the official writers of the annals who, using traditional rules, name and *qualify* their actions. They *honor* and *depose* them by the mere virtue of

---

75 *Li ki*, C., II, p. 269. Cf. *supra*, Book I, ch. I, sec. II.
76 Cf. *supra*, Book II, Ch. I, sec. V.
77 *Ts'ien Han chou*, 30, p. 15. Note the connection between *ming* and *wei*, already suggested by the first appendix of the *Yi king*. The *Han chou* classifies, in the School of Names, Yin Wen tseu together with Houei tseu and Kong-souen Long.
78 *Li ki*, C., I, p. 515.
79 *Civ. Chin.*, p. 288.

the terms they use to designate and judge them and their actions.[80] Historical writing is valid as judgment; it confirms or modifies, for eternity, the statutes.

A remarkable passage in the *Tchouang tseu*[81] links to the notion of *Tao-tö* (Primary Efficiency) those of *jen* and *yi*,[82] which order the conduct of the gentleman (*kiun tseu*). From them derive respect for attributions (*fen cheou*), (the concordance of) realities and (names) (*hing ming*), the (correct) distribution of offices, the (exact) discrimination of men and their deeds, the (correct) distribution of *approvals and disapprovals* (*che fei*; word for word: yes and no), *rewards and punishments*.

> "When it is clear (the principle) of rewards and punishments, the most stupid know what is expected of them, the noble and the vile maintain their ranks (*wei*), the good and the bad do their best, for there has been no lack of *fen* (distribution) of talents taking into account the *ming* (names, dignities), so that the superior are served, the inferior fed, (the whole) of beings governed and (each) personality cultivated (*sieou chen*)... and this is what is called the Great Peace, the perfection of the government."[83]

Tchouang tseu (before turning to his critique) here expounds the ideas that bring the School of Names closer to the School of Laws by linking them to the theories attributed to Confucius on the efficacy of *jen* and *yi*.

Another passage in the *Tchouang tseu*[84] insists, significantly, on the latter point. It speaks of bookish teaching in honor of the Confucian School and states that the *Tch'ouen ts'ieou* was used to explain *ming* and *fen*, i.e., to learn to grade and distribute, to apportion and judge. This is the idea which the Chinese have formed and preserved of the *Tch'ouen ts'ieou*;[85] they do not see in this work a mere chronicle of Lou's country; they admit that Confucius took over the writing of the official chroniclers. The Master was careful, weighing his words "even more carefully than when judging judgments, to lower what ought to be lowered." He seems to have obtained the approval of Tseu-hia, a difficult judge. He declared, however, that, if he was praised or blamed in future times, it would be because of the *Tch'ouen ts'ieou*.[86] Interpreted in the light of what the *Tchouang tseu* reports, these traditions are instructive. Not for nothing was Confucius called a king without a kingdom; he had arrogated to himself the right to distribute honors and qualities (*ming*). Since in China there were not only vassals who spoke in the name of their lords, but sages

---

80   Granet, *Danses et légendes...*, p. 64.
81   *Tchouang tseu*, L., pp. 336-337.
82   On these terms, cf. in this Book, ch. II, sec. I.
83   This passage is to be compared, even in form, with a famous passage from the *Tai hio*. In this passage, Tchouang tseu goes on to criticize the doctrine of names (which he relates to the doctrine of punishments and rewards of the School of Law); he grants names and laws only an efficacy of detail, a merely technical efficacy. "To speak of realities and names, of punishments and chastisements, is to show that one knows the instruments of government and not the principle (*tao*) of government... it is to be only a dialectician."
84   *Tchouang tseu*, L., II, p. 216.
85   Woo Kang, *Les trois théories politiques du Tch'ouen ts'ieou*, 1, pp. 77 ff.
86   *SMT*, V, p. 422.

or writers who judged in their name, the subject of the correctness of language took on a new meaning. It was an axiom, reigning Etiquette, that, distributed by the grace of the Prince, the lots of honors and appurtenances allotted, by name, to individuals, were rightly assigned. A problem will arise: what right has a mere individual to judge another individual? What are the prescriptions that enable the common man to qualify himself correctly?

The problem of individual judgments and the relationship between I (*wo*) and Thou (*tseu*), combined with that of This (*ts'eu*) and That (*pei*), preoccupied the dialecticians. Tchouang tseu, seeing the fish frolic, exclaimed:

> "This is the pleasure of fish!"
> "You are not a fish," said Houei tseu; "how do you know what a fish considers pleasurable?"
> "You are not me," replied Tchouang tseu; "how do you know that I don't know what makes a fish pleasurable?"
> "I am not you, and certainly I cannot know you, but certainly you are not a fish, and all this concurs to prove that you cannot know what gives a fish pleasure."[87]

The Sophists professed total subjectivism; they aimed at ruining received ideas. The followers of Mö tseu had an ideal of uniformity and social peace.

> "What a being is, what is known about him, what is made known about him, may differ,"[88]

they conceded, but postulated that denominations (*ming*) should be eliminated from discussion (*pien*). So long as there is no confusion in their application, i.e., so long as the language is not deliberately incorrect, the qualifications (*ming*) correspond to the object (*che*). If there are no confusions for which the Self or the This is responsible, the qualifications really belong to the This.[89]

This, at least, seems to have been the opinion of Yin Wen tseu. This sage came to base the value of judgments on opinion, whose decisions are valid provided that society is stable enough to make possible the correct use of language.[90] Yin Wen tseu seems to have been considered a follower of Mö tseu. The Taoists, however, spoke of him with some indulgence:

> "To free oneself from customs, to despise ornaments, not to neglect individuals, not to be obstinate against the multitude, to desire the tranquility of the Empire so that men may live their lot in life (*ming*) to the end, to be satisfied as soon as others and oneself have enough to live on... this was the rule he followed... Yin Wen tseu... In his dealings with others, whatever

---

87 *Tchouang tseu*, L., I, p. 392.
88 *Mö tseu*, 41.
89 Masson-Oursel and Kia Kien-tchou, *Yin Wen-tseu*, p. 570. It is curious to note that the *Mö tseu* (41) uses the expression: *correct denomination* in connection with the distinction between This and That.
90 *Ibid.*, p. 585.

the disputes, he showed amenity; he bore insults without feeling outraged; he sought, in the midst of quarrels, to help, to avoid aggression, to prevent battles. He went through the Empire, rebuking the great, indoctrinating the small; no one in the world would welcome him; he never flinched and persevered."[91]

Was Yin Wen tseu, like Mö tseu, a preacher of peace? Was he an eclectic, influenced by both Taoism and the Legists? It is very difficult to say. We know nothing about him, except that he probably lived in the late 4th century BC and (perhaps) remained in Ts'i at the time of King Siuan (343-324 BC). His work, which has been lost several times and reconstructed with the help of quotations (mostly around the 11th century AD), has come down to us in the form of an incoherent pamphlet. It is far from certain that all the elements are authentic; there are serious contradictions; the style shows no unity and there is no way of determining, for the most important terms, whether they are always used with the same technical value. In particular, we run the risk of betraying the author if, mistaking him for a pure logician, we translate the expressions *fen* and *ming fen*[92] as "specificity" or "specificity of names." From the text as a whole, as it has come down to us, it appears that the dominant feeling of the writer is a horror of confusion and indistinction, for these are sources of dispute.

A first remedy for confusion is logical or rather linguistic; one must define the meanings and distinguish the This from the That.[93] But it is also necessary to distinguish between judgments which attribute to objects properties (*fen*) of indefinite application and which must have a foundation in the That, and judgments, wholly dependent on the Self, which involve preferences and aversions.[94] To obtain social peace, to a *discipline of language* which permits correct naming (*ming*) and guarantees the objectivity of predictions must be added a discipline of morals which guarantees, with fair estimates, a distribution of honors (*ming*) and of destinies (*fen*) which has the virtue of preventing any usurpation.[95]

Honorific and pejorative (*ming*) appellations (*ming*) must be effectively distributed between the good and the bad; appreciative judgments constitute an art whose object is precisely to avoid quarrels and disputes.[96] There is, then, a policy of names (*ming*) which uses them as rewards or punishments to establish conditions (*fen*), so that the merchant, the artisan, the husbandman, or the nobleman cannot abandon his state; "*their name limits them*," and "the inferiors cannot exercise their ambition," each being content with his place, good or bad.[97] Yin Wen tseu calls for the condemnation to death of sophists whose knowledge does not prevent

---

91 *Tchouang tseu*, L., II, p. 221.
92 Masson-Oursel (*op. cit.*) has made a very careful translation of this pamphlet, but in which the various technical uses of the words are not sufficiently distinguished.
93 Masson-Oursel, *op. cit.* p. 570.
94 *Ibid.*, pp. 570-571.
95 *Ibid.*, p. 577.
96 *Ibid.*, p. 570.
97 *Ibid.*, pp. 572, 576, 579.

them from being vile (for eloquence serves to corrupt, flatter, and deceive), and of all those who "are heroes among vile men" capable (by their personal talents and their "dangerous knowledge"), "of embellishing injustice and disturbing the multitude."[98] Indeed, "names (which) rightly distribute (assign) ranks" can serve (misused) to foster ambition and usurpation; the power to qualify and honor with names must therefore remain a princely prerogative,[99] but with two reservations. The prince is bound to be beneficent, and if he must, by keeping conditions (*fen*) fixed (*ting*), prevent "those who are clever and strong" from being arrogant, he must also avoid not making proper use of the talents due (*fen*) to individuals.[100] On the other hand, the prince, while he must strive to remain the sole source of liberality, has no right to play favorites and to act after his own heart.[101] He must therefore avoid ruling by using men. He must rule only by means of *names* (i.e., by impartially distributing ranks, honors, attributions) and *laws* (i.e., by subjecting "beings of every condition" to "uniform" decisions).[102]

Yin Wen tseu's originality seems to be summed up in the effort he made to distinguish estimates from mere ratings. However, even for him, defining or rating, estimating or classifying are interrelated arts. Their practice is possible only if society is sufficiently stable for opinions to be uniform. The ideal of the logician is therefore social stability and the conciliation of conflicts under the rule of law. It is no longer the label that gives authority to judgment; it cannot be the individual; it must be the agreement of individuals; this depends on the impartiality of the Prince. *Logical authority belongs to the Prince as the source of all peace and stability*. The art of qualifying is confused with the art of legislating. It is undoubtedly that Yin Wen tseu, *as a logician*, has been classed among the advocates of the School of the Legists. For the latter, as for him, designations (*ming*), such as attributions, ranks and inheritances, do not depend on customary statutes; these can endow them neither with stability nor universality, nor even with flexibility and efficacy: but all this can come from the authority of the Prince, author of the law and sovereign evaluator of circumstantial (*che*) data.

This is the doctrine that almost triumphed with Che Houang-ti. The great emperor standardized writing, published an official dictionary, and wrote on his steles, "I have put order in the multitude of beings and have tested acts and realities: each thing has the name that suits it."[103]

---

98 Ibid., pp. 574, 590, 588, 589.
99 Ibid., pp. 585, 586.
100 Ibid., pp. 597, 577, 576.
101 Ibid., p. 595.
102 Ibid., pp. 586, 587.
103 SMT, II, p. 188. It has been said that the expression *tcheng ming* (to make the designations correct) meant first: to correct the characters of the script (SMT, V, note 439). The script only became uniform under Che Houang-ti, and it was during the time of the Warring Kingdoms that the Κοινη from which Chinese emerged was probably formed. The explanation of *tcheng ming* as "correctness of writing characters" is certainly an afterthought. The correct use of vowel or graphic designations was not primarily intended to achieve the universal diffusion of a system of symbolism. It was simply a matter of borrowing from etiquette, before borrowing it

IV. The Art of Legislating

Under the heading: *School of Law (fa kia)*, are grouped the writers who were chiefly concerned with administration and whose ideal was to be the Prince's men.[104] They are distinguished from the Politicians. The latter were chiefly concerned with the success of diplomatic combinations. The Legists, on the other hand, were interested in the prescriptions from which States could draw their internal strength. The organization of territory and army, economy and finance, social prosperity and discipline were their favorite subjects. While the Sophists, enemies of the whole system of traditions, seem to have been the best auxiliaries of the politicians or diplomats, the administrators or Legists relied on the logicians (*ming kia*), dominated by the idea of a stable order. The former thought to take advantage of the convulsions of the feudal world to push their masters towards hegemony; the latter, in their eagerness to justify brand new administrative practices, were driven to imagine a new idea: that of the sovereignty of the Prince and of the Law. They had to administer territories that had sometimes been conquered by diplomacy and war, sometimes wrested from the barbarians, or recovered from nature itself thanks to princely initiatives. In this case, they were not bound by tradition, nor by customary statutes. The conqueror's orders were the law. The administrators wanted these orders to be the law in their lord's ancient domain and any custom or statute to be of no value before the will of the prince.[105] It is possible that their ideas took a more theoretical turn after having served as topics for scholarly debates from Tsi to Lin-tsö. They were not formed in the idleness of these discussions of verbiage,[106] but directly in administrative work. The organic link between them is a sentiment that proclaims their origin and their technical value. What justified the rule of etiquette was the efficiency lent to it. What makes it possible to declare the law as sovereign is the *effective realization* (*kong yong*) of administrative practice when it is based on the laws.

There is no way to indicate the historical progress of ideas in the field of the Legists. We know quite well the life of the last of them, Fei of Han, called Han tseu or Han Fei tseu. It is said that he belonged to the princely house of Han and may have been a pupil of Siun tseu. He served the Han princes and later the princes of Ts'in. The future Che Houang-ti admired him and then imprisoned him with permission to commit suicide, for it is said that the minister Li Sseu, who had been his fellow-student, slandered him out of jealousy.[107] Han Fei tseu died about 233 BC, leaving a work in 53 chapters. Indeed the *Han Fei tseu* preserves 53 chapters, but several, after being lost, have been reconstructed; criticism has not yet suc-

---

from the law, the authority to make a judgment. The order imposed on the multitude of beings is an administrative order.

104 The *Ts'ien Han chou* (30, p. 15a) relates the Law School to the Administrators (*li kouan*) and the Doctrines of the Politicians (30, p. 16b) to the Diplomats.

105 *Civ. Chin.*, pp. 424, 104.

106 See, conversely, *Chine antique*, by Maspero, p. 516, and (less categorically) *The book of Lord Shang*, by Duyvendack, p. 72.

107 *SMT*, ch. 63.

ceeded in separating the false parts from the remaining ones; in the text, badly set down and sometimes incomprehensible, interpolations abound.[108] Another work, the *Chang tseu*, or *Chang kiun chou* (Book of the Lord of Chang) is a collection, made at an unknown date (perhaps between the third and sixth centuries AD), of pieces, some of which perhaps date back to the third century BC.[109] It is supposed to be the work of Wei-yang (or Yang of Wei), minister to Duke Hiao (361-336 BC) of Ts'in. He is credited with the revolutionary decrees[110] which abrogated the feudal system in Ts'in; appointed lord of Chang[111] after a military success, he was deposed on the death of his lord; he had erred in compelling the crown prince to respect the laws.[112] The oldest patron of the Legists, Kouan tseu, is known only from legends[113]. Nothing authentic is preserved of several works, written doubtless, like the *Kouan tseu*, about the third century BC, and placed, also, under the name of ancient heroes of the Law, such as Teng Si, minister of Tcheng, who was (some say) executed[114] by his rival Tseu-tchan, another Legist, whom the Tso tchouan frequently introduces.[115] Tseu-tch'an, whose death, it is said, caused the people of Tcheng and Confucius himself to mourn, and whom history praises for his love of his neighbor and his beneficence, had fallen into disgrace at first because he attempted to fight against private associations.[116] To the crime of attempting to increase the strength of the State, the Legists added another villainy. These indiscreet servants of the Prince demanded that work should be done and that the granaries should be full, in order to provide for the needs of the armies and times of famine. Undoubtedly, they demanded much from the peasants. However, when their compatriots claim that the "people (*min*)" hated them, it must be remembered that this word (*min*) means "the great families" and designates, not the plebs (*chou jen*), but those who were considered the peers of the lord. At the time of the Warring Kingdoms, some Chinese countries had a regime similar to that of the Tyrannies. The Prince fights against nobility and feudal customs. He tries to increase the revenue and military power of the state by giving land to the peasants. These two principles of tyrannical administration are linked to the theory of "efficiency" and the practice of publishing laws. The latter served as a starting point for the reflections of the

---

108 Part of the work was translated into Russian by Ivanov in 1912 (Publ. of the Faculty of Oriental Languages of the St. Petersburg Academy).

109 Chang's Book of the Lord has been translated in full, with great care, by Duyvendack (*op. cit.*), who has taken pains (pp. 141 ff.) to distinguish stylistically the pieces of different periods.

110

111 *SMT*, III, p. 316.

112 *Civ. Chin.* pp. 43, 222; *SMT*, II, pp. 62 ff. Duyvendack's book contains a translation of the biography of Wei-yang written by Sseu-ma Ts'ien, pp. 8 ff.

113 Granet, *Danses et légendes...*, (index).

114 *Yi king*, L., p. 350.

115 See *supra*, Book II, ch. II and M. Granet, *Civ. Chin.*, p. 106. On the disastrous fate of the Legists in the time of Emperor Wou of the Han, see *Ibid*.

116 *Civ. Chin.* p. 43. History has never forgiven the Legists for this crime, any more than it has failed to disgrace Mö tseu's attacks on the spirit of patronage.

administrators and the former was the basis for the doctrine of the Legists on the sovereignty of the Prince and the Law.

In the absence of historical facts that could provide information on the evolution of the ideas marked by the *Han Fei tseu*, the *Tso tchouan* relates two anecdotes which their symmetry makes worthy of interest. After having distributed land to several nobles in order to reconcile a party among them, Tseu tch'an, minister of Tcheng, instituted a new hierarchy, distinguishing each rank by a garb; he then proceeded to a distribution of land and established among the neighbors a bond of military fellowship (*wou*). Some of the great ones helped him; the others were "knocked down." After some riots and even some satirical songs, everything calmed down. Five years later, Tseu-ch'an fixed land taxes; he was called a scorpion; he demanded too much for the state. Two years later (535 BC), he cast cauldrons to inscribe penal laws (*hing pi*); a sage immediately threatened him with celestial fires, and indeed, a fire broke out in Tcheng. The sage recalled that ancient rulers were content to institute punishments (*hing*) and chastisements, to strike terror into the hearts of the wicked; they did not enact penal laws (*hing pi*) for fear of developing the litigious spirit (*tcheng sin*).

> "When people know that there is a (criminal) law (*pi*), the *greats are no longer sacrosanct* (*ki*) for them. The litigious spirit is aroused and the written text (*chou*) is appealed to in the hope that the arguments may succeed… Of what use will their laws (*pi*) be? When people know what to base their litigious spirit on, they will mock the Rites. They will rely on written texts; they will develop their litigious spirit on any trifle. Troubles and lawsuits will multiply and grow; gifts to win judges will proliferate!"[117]

In 512 BC (?), in Tsin, after a military success, criminal laws (*hing*) were engraved on iron cauldrons. These cauldrons were to be regarded as the common property of all, since everyone had to contribute his share of iron. One sage expressed his disapproval. It was Confucius himself who is said to have said:

> "People will cling to these cauldrons! *Will they continue to honor the nobles?*"

Confucius is said to have added that the people would continue to respect the nobles if the rules of etiquette (*tou*) and models of conduct (*fa*) prescribed by the ancient princes were preserved in Tsin, but not if the criminal laws enacted in the past (620 BC ?) during a military parade in which ranks and offices had been revised were put into effect.[118]

These anecdotes, whatever their historical value, reveal two important facts. 1° In China (as in other countries, at the same time and for similar reasons), the aristocracy was divided into two parts: some nobles were concerned to save feudal privileges, others favored the advent of tyrannies. 2° One of the foundations of the prestige of feudal chiefs and nobles lay in their discretionary authority in matters

---

117 *Tso tchouan*, C., II, pp. 549, 660 ("we must first satisfy the great"), pp. 661-662; *Ibid.*, II, pp. 87-88, 116 ff.

118 *Ibid.*, C., III, p. 456; *Ibid.*, I, pp. 385 and 469.

Book IV - Chapter I - The Prescriptions of Government 285

of dispute that arose between their vassals. Their glory consisted not so much in judging according to ritual customs, the secrets of which they alone knew, as in making sure that no dispute arose in the courts. Punishments (*hing*) were instituted not to be enforced, but to frighten; role models (*fa*) were intended to edify, but not to compel. Prescriptions (*hing* or *fa*) were valued only for their symbolic efficacy (*siang*); moralists said (and still say)[119] that they had the virtue of preventing by improving evil inclinations. This meant that any conflict was resolved by a conciliatory procedure. The chief conciliated and reconciled or, better still, the fear of the chief (not to speak of the price of the peace procedure carried out with the help of ritual gifts, *li*) invited the complainants to settle their disputes among themselves.[120] Penal provisions did not have to be applied; since no crime was manifested, there were no crimes. And all this was a demonstration of the commanding virtue of the chief.[121] Only in one case did the spirit of discipline and command prevail: when the feudal militias were assembled. On the occasion of wars and triumphs, the chiefs got rid of the fractious ones.[122] It is significant that all the admonitions in which we see the ancient codes are said to have been issued during military parades.[123]

When the regime of tyrannies was established, the potentates despised and feared the feudal militia, which was dangerous to them and had no strength against the enemy. They invented the system of the armed nation, always under arms. If they gave land to the peasants, it was by virtue of the principle: he who has the land must serve it. Thus, the distribution of land was accompanied by the establishment of a system of military comradeship (*wou*) among the peasants. Camp discipline must then be imposed throughout social life. The warnings promulgated on the occasion of military parades provide for Tsin – as the *Tso tchouan* states – the basis for the new laws, conceived, from then on, not as exhortations, but as prescriptions intended to be effective. To inscribe a law in a cauldron is to warn the guilty that he will be boiled;[124] it is to say that the law will be enforced. It is also to publish the law, thus limiting the discretionary power of the Chief and admitting, moreover, that the Virtue of the Chief is not sufficient to prevent the crime. It means, then, to renounce basing authority on the prestige that nourishes the label. It means basing

---

119 Escarra and Germain, *La conception de la loi...*, pp. 10 ff.
120 Granet, *op. cit*, p. 394.
121 The principle did not change when the imperial dynasties promulgated codes; it continued to be accepted that the best magistrate was the one before whom the fewest cases were brought.
122 Civ. Chin., p. 309.
123 *Ibid.*, p. 247; Escarra and Germain, *op. cit.* pp. 6 ff. By virtue of an aristocratic prejudice, Leang K'i-Tch'ao does not distinguish between the plebs and the barbarians, who are the only ones subject, according to him, to punishment. In reality, these punishments are reserved for indecent vassals.
124 Death in the cauldron is the characteristic punishment of the ministers of war (*Civ. Chin.*, p. 303). It was, under the emperors, the punishment of all bad administrators (*Ibid.*, p. 135.) Che Houang-ti boasts of having plunged into it all rebellious feudatories (*SMT*, II, p. 198).

it on the power conferred by military command. When Wei-yang had Ts'in adopt the principle of publicity of laws, he waited to promulgate his code until he had achieved decisive success in arms. He then built the Ki pillars. On these triumphal monuments the new laws were exhibited.[125]

Up to the moment when the Legists, by creating a state justice, wrested from the nobles not only their privileges, but also the prestige conferred on them by their role as arbiters, the words *hing* (criminal laws) and *fa* (law) had the meaning of "models," or "molds," operative prescriptions, or, if you will, half-moral, half-technical precepts. These terms do not imply either the idea of obligation or that of coercion.[126]

The Legists tried to introduce into the idea of *fa* (law) the notion of imperative force. For them, the magistrate is not a conciliator who is concerned only with peace. He must apply the law to his constituents; he must publish it; he is obliged to declare the law. It is the publication of the law that gives it its binding character. The early codes, engraved on cauldrons, still retain some of the dynastic *protection*. Everything changes when laws are engraved on bamboo tablets, an innovation attributed to Teng Si of Tcheng (500 BC ?).[127] Han Fei tseu writes:

> "Laws should be compiled and displayed in tablet form; the tablets should be displayed in good order in (all) administrative offices; they should be made public among the people."
> "There is a law when decrees and orders have been published in (all) administrative offices and when punishments and penalties seem *inevitable* to all minds. Respectful observance of the laws is rewarded and their violation is punished."[128]

The importance of these two definitions is increased by the fact that they occur in passages in which the author contrasts *fa* and *chou*, two terms which at first meant interchangeably "prescriptions, ways of doing things." *fa* takes on an imperative meaning and signifies *law* insofar as it applies to rules made public, while *chou* retains its value of *recipe* because (*chou* or) *recipes* must remain secret. Han Fei tseu considers that laws (*fa*) must inexorably regulate administrative practice. Ministerial tasks are summed up in the strict application of legal provisions. Administrators are only instruments of the law; they cannot modify it. Citizens are only subjects of the law; they are bound to discipline without fault. The published law reigns through the compulsory cooperation of all. Any infraction must be denounced, any compliant action pointed out. No one may conceal either the just or the unjust act. No one may evade punishment or reward for himself or oth-

---

125 *SMT*, II, p. 65. The construction of these pillars coincided with the relocation of the capital (inauguration of a new era) and an overhaul of the entire administrative system.

126 See, in Escarra and Germain, *op. cit.* (preface, VIII and IX), a remarkable example given by M. Padoux of the fact that, even today, the law has the authority of a council and not sovereign force.

127 *Tso tchouan*, C. III, p. 550.

128 *Han Fei tseu*, 38 and 43.

ers. Neither initiative nor interpretation can be tolerated. Wrong was the minister of Tch'ou who condemned as a bad son a man who had denounced the theft of a sheep committed by his father. And still more culpable was Confucius in praising a recidivist for desertion, on the pretext that he had an aged father to care for.[129] There is no conflict of duties; as the law is public, all are bound to uphold it, on pain of ruining the principle of order. Dangerous would be administrators or subjects too educated and disposed to argue outside the written law.

> "In the land of a wise Prince there are no books: *only the Law is taught; there are no sentences of ancient kings*: only the officials (who speak the Law) have authority."[130]

No discussion is possible, since legal provisions (*ming*) define the meaning of words (*ming*: vocable or spelling). Order reigns.

It is a correct order, because it is totally anonymous and impartial: "When superiors and inferiors do not interfere, the names are correct," said Yin Wen tseu,[131] and in the ranks there is no confusion. The Prince – like the feudal ruler, but by very different means – is a creator of hierarchy. Only it is a *military* hierarchy born of his power of command. It is the result of fully automatic sanctions. The government has "two fists," the *Hing* and the *Tö*, the power to apply negative (*hing*) and positive (*tö*) sanctions. It is not the administrators who, per se, nor the lord who, in private, promote or degrade, it is the Law. The Prince cannot intervene in administrative matters in which only the published law governs. Conversely, no subject, no minister can intervene in the affairs of the Prince.[132] The high direction of the State is his alone. On him alone depends the Policy; to him alone privately belong the Prescriptions (*chou*) which, thanks to the *k'iuan* {diplomatic combinations which extract from every occasion the weight (*k'iuan*) which inclines fate to its own side} make it possible to attain the *che* (circumstantial conditions of success). "Laws (*fa*) are the rule of administrators. The prescriptions (*chou*) are the reins held by the Master."[133] The Legists strongly distinguish from Law the Art of government.[134] The prescriptions, non-transferable by definition, make up the personal power of the Prince; they constitute his intimate efficacy, his proper value – great if the Prince is a Saint.

It is in their conception of the Art of government that the profound influence which the Taoists have exercised on the Legists, through the politicians, is revealed.[135] This influence is more external, if not only formal, as regards their conception of law. For the ritualists, princely power, based on custom, results from

---

129 Ibid., 49.
130 Ibid., 49.
131 Masson-Oursel and Kia Kien-tchou, *op cit.*, p. 580.
132 Ibid., p. 580.
133 Han Fei tseu, 44.
134 Ibid., 43: "Chen Pou-hai speaks of prescriptions (*chou*); but Wei-yang makes laws (*fa*)" cf. Masson-Oursel and Kia Kien-tchou, *op. cit.*, p. 569: "Prescriptions are what the Prince uses in private; inferiors are not to be informed about that."
135 Cf. *supra*, in this Book, ch. I, sec. II.

a Prestige which is not private but patrimonial. All authority, for the Taoists, is constituted by the power, strictly personal, provided by Sanctity. The Legists admit that part of the princely authority derives from personal talents, but they hasten to strictly limit the use of these virtues. In fact, they demand from the Prince not talents but impartiality. Han Fei tseu certainly compares this impartiality to that of the Tao, and seems to argue as a Taoist. However, there is a gulf between the subjective and secret impartiality of the Saint and the impartiality demanded of the Prince; all objective and based on a military idea of discipline, it is confused with the inexorability of published law.

The Legists arrived at the ideas of Prince and Sovereign Law because they sought to define a discipline suitable for great States. At the same time that they were thinking about the administration of men, they had to think about the administration of things. Economic facts and the observation of these facts were the basis of their conception. The rapid growth of China's population posed, since his time, a problem that has never ceased to be tragic: that of subsistence.

> "In ancient times,[136] men did not cultivate; the fruits of the trees were enough to feed them. Women did not weave; animal skins were enough to clothe them. There was no need to work, but there was enough to live on. Men were few and resources abundant; the people had no litigious spirit. There was no need to reinforce rewards or redouble punishments; the people governed themselves. Today, five children are not much to a man; a grandfather can count in his lifetime twenty-five grandchildren. Men are numerous and resources are scarce; one must work hard to survive in poverty. Therefore, the people are litigious. Even by multiplying rewards and increasing punishments, there is no escape from disorder."
>
> "If there is disorder in the state, there is famine, and the population is scattered, without resources… There are sufficient resources, and the population is maintained, when the laws are put into practice."[137]

For the Legists, law consists in an impartial distribution of punishments and rewards that increases production and, consequently, makes less formidable the distribution, not of wealth, but of the most necessary goods. It is a matter of preventing peasants from selling their daughters and, in the end, becoming vagabonds; the State is then threatened by private associations which may make the fortune of some adventurer. Now, in economic matters, two facts are obvious: one cannot count on exceptional chances (and wait, by abandoning the plow, for a hare to hitch itself to the branches where a hare used to hitch itself),[138] nor can one disregard changing conditions (and use, for example, a pitcher to water the field, after

---

136 *Han Fei tseu*, 49.
137 *Yin Wen tseu*, in Masson-Oursel and Kia Kien-tchou, *op. cit.* p. 31.
138 *Han Fei tseu*, 49.

BOOK IV - CHAPTER I - THE PRESCRIPTIONS OF GOVERNMENT

the hand pump had been invented to draw water).[139] Yield (*kong yong*)[140] is the first fact to be considered in the administration of things. Performance must also be taken as a basis when it comes to the management of people.

Several consequences follow from this. It is absurd to imitate the ancients. The antiquity of a process speaks against it: different times, different laws. It is absurd to rely on the Virtue of the Wise. There are few wise men and daily solutions are needed. To save a drowning man in central China, one does not send for the best swimmer in Yue (the far south). Instead of happily waiting for luck or a savior, you have to face current and normal conditions, *calculate the probable and foresee the possible*. If you want to go far and fast, don't wait for a coachman like Wang Leang, who can make his horses travel a thousand stadium in a day. Calculate your stages by taking into account the average skill of the coachmen, the average quality of the carriages, and organize the relays accordingly. An administrator is not interested in the exceptional and does not rely on fortune but on calculations (*chou*: numbers). He does not waste his time looking for talented people to help him, it is enough for him to apply the laws thought out for the average case.[141]

> "In actions and in words, the rule is performance (*tchong yong*). If, after sharpening an arrow, you shoot it at random, it may pierce the finest bag; no one will say that you are a master archer; this (shooting) is not (the effect of) a *constant rule*. If a master archer shoots at ten paces over a five-inch target, it is not certain that he will hit the target: it is a constant rule."[142]

Instruments such as the ruler and compass, the weight, and the balance are also used in practice. Merchants weigh with scales and estimate in inches; they do not rely on personal judgment. Likewise, if a safe return is desired, recourse must be had to laws,[143] not to men.

> "The Great Peace... is not due to the government of the Holy One, but to that of holy laws."[144]

The Legists strongly opposed the Prince to the Sage and the Law (*fa*) to the Rites (*li*); they tried to make prevail a completely objective conception of the lawful. What is licit is that which contributes effectively to social peace by assuring a good average yield of the productive activity of men.

* * *

Che Houang-ti, when he founded the Empire, thought of establishing the rule of law. The regime did not last. The Chinese hated it, reproaching the Legists for

---

139 I choose this example because Tchouang tseu used it to condemn perfected recipes (Wieger, *Les Pères du système taoïste*, p. 301). This is an essential point on which the Legists and Taoists oppose each other.
140 It is, in my opinion, a serious error to translate this expression as "efficacy." (See Maspero, *La Chine antique*, p. 527). It is a question of positive efficiency.
141 *Han Fei tseu*, 40.
142 *Ibid.*, 41.
143 *Ibid.*, 27.
144 *Yin Wen tseu*, in Masson-Oursel and Kia Kien-Tchou, *op. cit*, p. 592.

their harshness and cruelty. The Legists were guilty, in fact, of believing in the unique virtue of discipline. They started from a rather limited psychology and a military spirit. Men love life and hate death, said Tseu-ch'an.[145] This is the principle of the system of automatic punishments and of the militarized hierarchy which serves to enlist the whole population.[146] This conception is crude and rigid, but at least they had the courage to want to apply it in a country whose great scourges were banditry, the respect accorded to every gang leader, the attraction of vagrancy and the mediocre performance of work.[147] The Legists fought both against the spirit of improvisation and against that of old customs. They wanted to discard the idea of the Sage, whose virtue can do everything and who is taken for a savior as soon as he presents himself modestly as a disciple of the Ancients. They wanted to limit governmental arbitrariness. They condemned legislative incoherence[148] and advocated codification. They defended the principle that laws are effective only under two conditions: if the Prince ensures that his interest coincides with the totality of particular interests,[149] and if, condemning the regime of princely benevolence, he takes care to adapt the norms to concrete circumstances. They combined an ideal of discipline with a feeling for the evolution of social customs and conditions. They preferred impartial judgments, objective evaluations and concrete arguments. These positive spirits, enamored of scientific rigor, achieved only fleeting success. The Sophists failed to get the Chinese to accept the idea that there were contradictory terms. Similarly, the Legists did not succeed in accrediting the notion of constant rule or the conception of sovereign Law.

---

145 Cf. Book III, Ch. III.
146 *Civ. Chin.*, p. 116.
147 Wei-yang is said to have imagined a system of traffic permits to curb vagrancy.
148 *Han Fei tseu*, 49.
149 *Yin Wen tseu*, in Masson-Oursel and Kia Kien-Tchou, *op. cit.*, p. 593.

Chapter II
THE PRESCRIPTIONS OF THE PUBLIC GOOD

Politicians and Legists are either prestigious adventurers or, like Wei-yang and Han Fei tseu, sons of great families; rather than heads of schools, they are patrons whose names add authority to a doctrine. Neither Confucius nor Mö tseu played a political role. They belonged to that part of the nobility that the regime of tyrannies condemned to ruin. The council of the faithful was replaced by the secret council. It was not the members of the local nobility who were favored by the potentates. Idle, impoverished, far from the court, the lesser nobles often served as servants, stewards or squires, and formed the clientele of a more powerful noble. Sometimes they lived pitifully on their lands, and some were "hidden sages." Sometimes, when one of them had acquired a certain renown, he gathered a clientele of apprentices who pushed the Master towards glory, hoping to share his fortune if he managed to inspire confidence in some Prince; such was undoubtedly the hope of the disciples of Confucius. But sometimes, too, this clientele was more like a brotherhood; such was the case with the followers of Mö tseu. In the eyes of his followers, Mö tseu and Confucius appeared as "princes without dominions, chiefs without vassals."[1] The epithet "King without a kingdom" was officially attributed to Confucius when, with the Han, Confucian orthodoxy triumphed. Mö tseu, from then on, would be considered a heretic; his sect, however, was at first the most active and brilliant. Recruited from the same circles, the two colleges had similar tendencies. While the grandees and their favorites sought prescriptions that could increase the power of the state and the efficiency of the administration, the followers of Mö tseu and Confucius were concerned solely with the public good. In this environment of hapless nobles, a conservative turn soon

---

1   *Lie tseu*, in Wieger, *op. cit.*, p. 103.

distorted the doctrines. This in no way proves that the Masters themselves lacked genius and daring. Confucius and Mö tseu appear as innovators betrayed by their followers. Mö tseu attempted to create a doctrine of social duty by denouncing the evils of the client spirit. Confucius seems to have had the even bolder idea of basing the whole discipline of morality on a refined sense of humanism.

I. Confucius and the Humanistic Spirit

Confucius has often been compared to Socrates. His fame, though less immediate, was no less lasting. His prestige among his followers was equally great. But if there is, perhaps, some analogy in the spirit of the teachings imparted by these two sages, in terms of their performance no comparison is possible. The Chinese have recognized in Confucius a "Teacher for ten thousand generations," only after having made him the pattern of a conformist morality. They see in him the most perfect example of national wisdom; no one gives him credit for original thought. There is no faithful testimony about Confucius. This is not sufficient reason to concede to orthodoxy that the Master was only the greatest of orthodox scholars. But it is a very fortunate attempt to try to say what he was.

We know nothing for certain about Confucius' life, except that he taught in the early fifth century BC in a city of Chan-tong, perhaps in the state capital of Lou. He was buried a little to the north of this city, and it is around his tomb that a village named K'ong li[2] was formed, where his relics were kept: his cap, his guitar, his chariot... The most faithful of his disciples remained there. Tradition says that he was born in 551 BC and died in 479 BC; these dates do not agree very well with those assigned to his descendants, and to his grandson Tseu-sseu in particular; but there is no reason to prefer one over the other; they are all part of the uncertainty of Chinese chronology for this ancient period. Confucius[3] belonged to the K'ong family; settled in Lou for three generations, they were natives of Song, related to the princely family of that country, and connected through them with the kings of the Yin dynasty; there is no reason to regard this genealogy as purely fictitious; it is confirmed by several passages in the *Tso tchouan*, but no genealogy, especially for that troublesome period, can inspire great confidence.[4] It is said that Confucius was born in Tseou, a town in the country of Lou, of which his father was governor; to have been orphaned at a very early age, to have lived in poverty, to have exercised some humble employments, to have appeared at court, to have had to travel, and to have returned to his own country to end his days surrounded by many disciples; there is no reason to reject these biographical data in substance, but neither is there reason to accept them in detail. The *Tch'ouen ts'ieou*, the chronicle of the State of Lou, makes no mention of Confucius at any time, which does not prove that the latter never held official functions. The adventures attributed to the Master, though full of contradictions, repetitions, and impossibilities, are not in

---

2   The "Confucian village." *SMT*, V, pp. 436 ff, p. 435.
3   Latinization of K'ong Fou-tseu (*fou-tseu*, master, is an honorific title).
4   Granet, *Danses et légendes...*, pp. 431 ff. Cf. *Ibid*, p. 556.

Book IV - Chapter II - The Prescriptions of the Public Good

themselves implausible. It is claimed that Confucius taught the liberal arts and professed a wisdom based on several works which (more or less subsequently reworked) became the Chinese Classics: the *Che king* (Book of Odes), the *Chou king* (Book of History), the *Yi king* (Book of Divination or Mutations), the Rituals (from which emerged the *Yi li* and *Li ki*), the *Tch'ouen ts'ieou* (Chronicle of Lou – said to have been reworked by the Master himself), and a work on music (now lost). It seems certain that, in the teaching given by the disciples, the commentary on these works occupied an important place from the beginning,[5] combined with practical exercises in good ritual conduct; nothing allows us to affirm that the Master's teaching was so bookish, or that it was much less so. It is no longer believed that Confucius wrote any works. There is no evidence, however, that tradition is wrong in supposing that he introduced into the *Tch'ouen ts'ieou*, by a slight reworking of the style, a certain number of judgments on works and persons;[6] if he did make revisions, their importance and theoretical significance are impossible to determine. The aphorisms of Confucius, collected at the end of the 5th century BC, form the *Louen yu*. This work was lost and then reconstituted under the Han, half a millennium after the Sage's death. There is reason not to suspect its value.[7] It should be noted, however, that the Master's words are given from the beginning with an implicit interpretation; this is suggested by the indication of the circumstances which prompted these teachings; the *Louen yu* is thus supported by a biographical framework;[8] however, it was not written before polemics among hagiographers had obscured the memories left by Confucius. Other traditions, incorporated in several chapters of the *Li ki*, give a better idea of the polemic from which they arise. They are no less instructive and no more reliable. The discontinuous aspect of the collection of aphorisms forming the *Louen yu* has imposed the idea that Confucius' thought was by no means systematic. Thus, the theories expressed in the *Tchong yong* and the *Tai hio*, two short treatises now included in the *Li ki*, are not attributed to him but to *Tseu-sseu*, his grandson. In fact, there is no way to distinguish Confucius' personal teaching from that of the first generations of his disciples.

Since Confucius was considered the patron of orthodoxy (*jou kiao*), history strove to portray him as the most orthodox of scholars (*jou*). The biography written by Sseu-ma Ts'ien[9] is affected by this bias; the concern to erase the vivid colors imposed by hagiography is hardly mitigated by the desire, quite natural for a historian, to appear broadly informed. But if it was less anachronistic, the image of the Sage in the fifth and fourth centuries BC was no less conventional. Confucius had a history only after he had earned the right to leave a legend. Once we admit

---

5   *Tchouang tseu*, in Wieger, *op. cit.* p. 499.
6   Woo Kang, *Les trois théories politiques du Tch'ouen ts'ieou*, pp. 173 ff.
7   *SMT*, V, p. 442.
8   See, for a contrary opinion, Maspero, *La Chine antique*, p. 456, note, and p. 461, note. See supra, in this Book, ch. I.
9   *SMT*, V, pp. 281 ff. Significantly, Sseu-ma Ts'ien ranked the biography of Confucius among the monographs of the manors.

that we know nothing of the Master's life, we could certainly, by selecting the most exquisite hagiographic features, satisfy the piety of those who ask to see, if only in a scholarly portrait, the highest souls of the past come to life. You will excuse me if I do not speak of the scenery of Chan-tong, of the mystic temperament of its inhabitants,[10] of the stories that ran among them about the Duke of Tcheou, who revisited Confucius in his dreams,[11] or about Yi Yin, whose soul still haunted the outskirts of T'ai chan, and if I do not mention that sacred mountain whose stern lines, dark cliffs and evergreen cedars the Master could admire as a boy, and whose memory filled him in his last moments. Then he had a moment of anguish, thinking of his unfinished work, and cried out:

> "Behold, the T'ai chan collapses… the master beam is marred… and the sage is gone like a withered flower."[12]

It will suffice to note that Confucius possessed the classical virtues of the saints of his generation. He was very tall, only a little less than Yu the Great.[13] He was very strong; he could single-handedly lift the bar that closed the gate of a city.[14] He had the keenest senses and could use them without the least fatigue; from the top of a mountain he could distinguish objects several leagues away, that the best of his disciples could only vaguely see, but with so much effort that his hair instantly turned white. Extreme physical power accompanied a kind of omniscience[15] in the Saint. Confucius could, at a glance, enumerate prehistoric objects, identify gigantic bones, tell the true names of the most mysterious beasts and the strangest concretions.[16] Although he was questioned by all, he would not reply by saying, "I know"; but would say, "I have been told that…" "After the disappearance of King Wen, was not his perfection deposited in this man?" he would say naively,[17] for he believed that he had received from Heaven, with a mission to accomplish, all the gifts necessary to carry it out.

He also inspired absolute confidence in his followers. One of them, in a moment of danger, passed for dead; he said, when he reappeared, "O Master, as long as you live how shall I die?"[18] The powerful hope of something great that could not be delayed inspired in all a faith that sometimes exalted, but also sometimes fell to denial:

> "We are neither rhinoceroses nor tigers to be in these deserted regions,"

---

10   Sectarian movements have always been frequent in Chan-tong.
11   *Louen yu*, Legge, p. 60. "How much, alas, I despair! Long ago, alas, the Duke of Tcheou appeared to me in a dream."
12   On Yi Yin and Confucius, see Granet, *Danses et légendes…*, pp. 431 ff. *SMT*, V, p. 424.
13   *SMT*, V, pp. 338, 298. Yen tseu, his enemy, is a dwarf.
14   *Lie tseu*, in Wieger, *op. cit.*, p. 189.
15   *SMT*, V, pp. 341, 312, 310.
16   Granet, *op. cit.* p. 552.
17   *SMT*, V, p. 333.
18   *SMT*, V, p. 332.

said the Sage once when his troop was in danger and he felt the irritation in all hearts.

"Is it my wisdom that fails?"
"We are not wise enough,"

replied one disciple, and another said:

"Your wisdom is too high!"

But Confucius said:

"A good husbandman can sow; it is not certain that he can reap…"
"Your wisdom, O Master, is too high," said his favorite disciple. "So no one admits it. However, Master, don't slacken… If we did not practice wisdom, shame would fall on us; if we practice it fully and no one uses us, shame falls on the masters."
"Oh, son of the Yen family," replied Confucius with a smile "if you had many riches, I would be your steward."[19]

This is how the Master held courage. He even knew how to take the blame when his conduct scandalized his own people. Once he had the idea of entering the service of a bandit who promised success, and courted a princess who lived badly; Tseu-lou, the most upright of his pupils, became angry:

"He who calls me to him, how could he do so without reason?," said the Master calmly, or else:
"If I have done wrong, it is Heaven that has forced me to do it! Heaven has compelled me to do it!"[20]

Among this restless people, proud of their independence but eager to serve, one of the great disputes was which was better: to withdraw from the world with reproachful indifference, to cry out in disgust and hurl invectives, or to serve and endure compromises and outrages while remaining pure. Confucius condemned neither ascetic haughtiness, nor stoic humility, nor even strident prophethood.

"I differ from all these people," he said; "nothing suits me and everything suits me."

He had the naive faith that refuses no opportunity and that difficulties exalt:

"We cannot live with the beasts nor make them our company. If we do not accept to live among men, with whom shall we keep company? Surely, if the empire were well ordered, would there be need for me to change it?"[21]
"If a lord employed me, in a year I would have done something; in three years I would have succeeded… Suppose there were a king (worthy of the

---

19 *SMT*, V, p. 367.
20 *SMT*, V, pp. 317 and 324.
21 *Ibid.*, L., p. 198.

name of king); it would take only one generation for the *jen* (i.e., an order worthy of men) to be established."²²

The anecdotes of the *Louen yu* give a good understanding of the spirit and life of the School. They impose the feeling that the Master had a faith in human virtues which placed him above his disciples. Some of these accounts seem to indicate the reasons for his rise; perhaps they reveal something of his personality; they are not, as one might think, those preferred by orthodoxy. The Sage had movements of sensitivity that his own considered contrary to protocol. True grief wrung more tears from him than were necessary.²³ He did not consider himself bound by ritual forms. To fulfill an oath extorted by violence was, for his contemporaries, a means of improving one's reputation; for him, an extorted oath should not be fulfilled.²⁴ He did not hesitate to affirm that for the pure all things are pure:

> "Is it not said, 'That which is hard may be rubbed without wearing away?' Is it not said, 'That which is white, put in dye, does not become black?' Am I a gourd that must remain hung up without being eaten?"²⁵

The Master's doctrine seems to have been a doctrine of action. He taught an active morality, and was less interested in the letter of the principles than in the moral action which he intended to exercise. It is as a director of conscience that he seems to have attained his prestige. He did not hesitate, depending on the man and the circumstances, to give instructions that turned out to be contradictory. To some he told them to think first of putting the precepts into practice, but to Tseu-lou, the bold, he advised them to do nothing without consulting his father and elder brother. "The laggards, I push; the fiery, I restrain."²⁶ He did not speak to formulate unqualified precepts, thus exposing himself to be denied the credit of firm doctrine. He preferred to draw from each occasion the lesson from which one of his followers might profit:

> "Here is a man you can talk to; if you don't talk to him, you lose a man. Here is a man you must not speak to; if you speak to him: you waste your words. Wise is he who loses not a man nor a word."²⁷

But for him the true teaching was not that which is conveyed by words.

> "I prefer not to speak," he said.
> "If you do not speak to us," said Tseu-kong, "what will we, your disciples, have to teach?"
> "Does Heaven speak? The four seasons follow their course, all beings receive life, and yet does Heaven speak?"²⁸

---

22   *Ibid.*, p. 131.
23   *Ibid.*, p. 104; and *Li ki*, C., I, pp. 141-142.
24   *SMT*, V, p. 345.
25   *Louen yu*, L., p. 185.
26   *Ibid.*, p. 108.
27   *Ibid.*, p. 161.
28   *Ibid.*, p. 190.

Book IV - Chapter II - The Prescriptions of the Public Good

The influence of the sage, like that of Heaven, is silent, profound, life-giving. Like the behavior of beings subject to the regulating action of Heaven, the behavior of men is subject to the ascendancy of the order which is expressed in the conduct of the sages. Thus, many traits have been preserved which show the strict control that Confucius exercised over his every gesture and his constant concern to take into account situations and circumstances.[29] He had a refined and personal way of practicing etiquette.[30] He recognized the educated man (*wen*: civilized) by a certain elegant delicacy of manners and bearing. He held that, to deserve this title, one had to be active, eager to learn, never ashamed to question (even) an inferior.[31] "If I have (only) two men with me, I am sure to have a Master,"[32] he would say, for his great concern was to mark that life in common (and better still, no doubt, life in a School) is, with the control it entails of the smallest details of conduct, the principle of perfection which makes the human individual a complete man (*tch'en jen*).

To love any virtue "without loving learning" leads only to the enlargement of a defect.[33] "Men differ less in their natural constitution (*sing*) than in the culture (*si*) they give themselves. Only the wisest of the wise and the worst of the fools do not change."[34] When such a clear statement has been read, and when, moreover, the whole *Louen yu* shows the emulation that reigned in the School and the passion with which the Master excited it, it is difficult to understand that interpreters have said of Confucius: "The thought of individual improvement does not even occur to him."[35] The whole thought of the Sage, and in particular his politics, is summed up in the assimilation he establishes between the Master and the Prince. The latter deserves the name of Prince (*kiun*) and the former the appellation of *kiun tseu*, if both possess the Tao or the Tö (or the Tao-tö), that is, the efficacy which enables "those who are (already) good to be promoted and those who are (not yet) talented to be instructed, so that all may be *enthusiastic in striving* (*k'iuan*)."[36]

This obligation to strive and the duty to encourage it refer above all to the moral life. The most important thing for a government is to make trust, good understand-

---

29   *Louen yu* (all of chapter X), L., pp. 91 ff.
30   Granet, *Le langage de la douleur*, p. 115.
31   *Louen yu*, L., p. 42.
32   *Ibid.*, p. 66.
33   *Ibid.*, p. 186.
34   *Ibid.*, p. 182.
35   Maspero, *La Chine antique*, p. 462. Maspero added (p. 464): "Study is not everything, one must know how to impose moral perfection on oneself" and, three pages later (p. 467): "The perfection of each individual appears only incidentally", and finally (p. 479), Confucius "sought the foundation of morality, outside the conscience, in the Rites, and that of social relations, on the contrary, inside the conscience, in Altruism". I am afraid I have not understood these formulas nor what Maspero means when he states that "the individual, as such, remains completely foreign to his research" (to Confucius' research). I suspect, however, that Maspero is using the term "individual as such" to refer to mere private individuals as opposed to the Prince (cf. *supra*, in this Book, ch. I, sec. IV).
36   *Louen yu*, L., p. 16. The expression *kiun tseu* means the nobleman who has the soul of a prince (*kiun*), the gentleman who is an honest man.

ing, and probity (*sin*) prevail. Abundance of resources and military strength are only secondary.³⁷ Like the Prince, worthy gentlemen (*kiun tseu*) are not interested in material benefits; they do not seek advantage (*li*).³⁸ This word has a very broad meaning. Confucius condemns not only the pursuit of interest, but any vulgar competitive spirit (*k'o*). The honest man seeks only to surpass (*k'o*) himself,³⁹ "The noble (*che*: the learned) tends his will toward the Tao and should not be ashamed of being ill-clad or ill-fed." "The gentleman (*kiun tseu*, or the good man, *chan jen*) thinks only of the *Tao*; the lowly people (*siao jen*) think only of goods (word for word: of the earth)."⁴⁰ "Have we learned in the morning what the *Tao* is and die in the afternoon? It is perfect!" In this proud maxim is summed up a morality of effort, of the aristocratic spirit, the originality of which is marked by the new nuance given to the words *tao* and *tö*.

Tao-tö, princely efficiency, is no longer conceived by Confucius as a kind of patrimonial quality. He certainly retains the idea that this efficiency only reaches its fullness in the Chief. Only he alone can free himself completely from all base concerns. Confucius is also convinced that only a gentleman can claim *Tao* and *Tö*, because the life he leads removes him "from the earth," that is, from vulgar tasks and concerns; he can polish himself by practicing etiquette.⁴¹ The fact remains, however, that the acquisition of *Tao* and *Tö* is a matter of personal effort. It requires constant application, ceaseless effort at all times. Not even the time of the meal is to be avoided.⁴² At most, one can hope to obtain it as the crowning achievement of a life entirely directed to this ideal end.

> "If they ask you about me," said Confucius, "why do you not answer, 'He is a man whose constant effort makes him forget to eat and who finds in it a joy that makes him forget his sorrows: he does not realize that old age is coming'?"

However, he did not flatter himself that he had attained sainthood (*cheng*) and deserved the name *jen*:

> "Of me it can only be said that I persevered without tiring and taught others without discouragement."⁴³

This unceasing effort deserves a prayer. When the Master was near death, the disciples wanted to offer sacrifices:

> "My prayer is already made," said Confucius.⁴⁴

---

37   Ibid., p. 118.
38   Ibid., p. 33.
39   Ibid., p. 114.
40   Ibid., p. 33.
41   A disciple encouraged a lord to give Confucius a vast estate: "He will not benefit personally," "what he seeks is the Tao proper to *kiun tseu*." (SMT, V, p. 387).
42   Louen yu, L., p. 30.
43   Ibid., p. 70.
44   Ibidem.

Book IV - Chapter II - The Prescriptions of the Public Good

In Confucian thought, *Tao-tö* tends to be confused with an ideal of perfection obtained through the practice of purely human virtues; these are *jen* and *yi*, virtues that can only be cultivated in contact with other men and in polite society.

The relation established by Confucius between *jen*, *yi* and *Tao-tö* has been very objectively emphasized by the Taoist Tchouang tseu.[45] Moreover, on this point, the *Louen yu* contains the clearest indications: "Tö is not for one who lives alone; one must have neighbors."[46] Nothing is more important than the choice of friends and the maintenance of friendly relations (*yeou*).[47] Excessive familiarity, too lively friction, and indiscreet advice should be avoided. Above all, one should only associate with people who are capable of cultivating *jen* and *yi* in common. All men's faults come from the group (*tang*) of which they are a part. There is no progress outside the control of a group of friends, but beware of the partisan (*tang*) spirit!

Only "the gentleman has vision of equity (*yi*); people of little means have vision only of advantage (*li*)."[48] To cultivate *yi* is to try to acquire a *fully equitable* notion of you and me, not just yours and mine. It is not just a matter of not doing material wrongs and of having regard only for rights, status, and property; all this is already the duty of mere villains. For honest people, it is also about being obliged to make only fair, impartial, and *reversible* (*chou*) judgments about others. Of this reversibility (*chou*), the *Louen yu* has, on three occasions, given a beautiful definition: "What you do not wish (to be done to you), do not do to others."[49] This heightened sense of reciprocity, constituted by scruples regarding oneself and others, has a twofold aspect: respect for others (*king*) and respect for oneself (*kong*).[50] From the constant concern for equitable reciprocity and the sense of respectability refined by the elegant practice of Etiquette (*1i*), arises, when indulgent and affectionate dispositions are added, the supreme virtue, *jen*, that is, an active feeling of human dignity.[51]

Perpetually questioned about *jen*, Confucius gave the most diverse definitions. These definitions were always concrete or rather practical and were inspired by the desire to take into account, in the moral direction, the dispositions of each disciple. If these definitions are diverse, it is because it was a virtue complete in itself, which no term could exhaust, except the word itself that designated it. Without this virtue, which is definite and complete, and which is acquired by living in a society of carefully selected friends, no one knows how to love or hate, how to practice loyalty, how to free himself from the apprehension of death or all anxiety, how to make himself respected, loved and obeyed, how to show himself enduring, firm, simple and modest, how to avoid violence, how to overcome himself, how to possess true

---

45 See the passage from *Tchouang tseu* quoted *above*, in this Book, ch. i, sec. iii.
46 *Louen yu*, L., p. 36.
47 *Ibid.*, pp. 126, 26, 31, 134, 164. The word rank is applied to schools and sects.
48 *Ibid.*, pp. 34 and 144.
49 *Ibid.*, pp. 164, 41, 115.
50 *Ibid.*, p. 42.
51 *Ibid.*, p. 135.

eloquence or true courage.⁵² The first conditions of *jen* may be indicated: they are self-respect, magnanimity, good faith, diligence and benevolence. But Confucius preferred to confess that he could not express what *jen* really is.⁵³ However, he once said that the honest man should love others and that if the wise (*tche*) know (*tche*) men, he who possesses *jen* or, rather, he who is *jen* should love men (*jen*).⁵⁴

Father Wieger stated that Confucius "demanded, what?... charity, devotion... oh, none of that. He demanded *neutrality of mind and coldness of heart*."⁵⁵ Thus, after exclaiming, "Do not translate *jen* by charity," he proposed the word altruism. This is killing two birds with one stone – and an anachronism is of little consequence – but it is surprising that, without having the same excuses for committing the sin of anachronism as Fr. Wieger (if any) and other interpreters⁵⁶ have allowed themselves to be seduced by a translation which neglects all the definitions of *Louen yu* and conceals two essential characteristics of *jen*: respect for others and respect for oneself. The Confucian conception of *jen* or the realized man, and who alone deserves the name of man, is inspired by a feeling of humanism which may be unpleasant, but which one has no right to conceal. The whole *Louen yu* (as well as the *Tchong yong* and the *Tai hio*) shows that the main idea of Confucius and his early disciples (of Confucius, or of his early disciples? I cannot tell) was to reject all speculation about the universe and to make man the proper object of knowledge. For them, the principle of this knowledge, the only interesting and effective one, was life in society, the work of knowledge, of control, of improvement pursued in common, the humanistic culture, thanks to which man is built in dignity.

Cultivation (*sieou ki* or *sieou chen*) is not considered a mere duty of personal morality. It is thanks to life in society that human dignity is established; it is society that benefits from the culture attained by the wise:

> "The honest man (*kiun tseu*)," said Confucius, "cultivates his person and (consequently) knows how to respect (others)!"
> "Is that all?" asks Tseu-lou.
> "He cultivates his person and (consequently) gives peace of mind to others!"
> "Is that all?"
> "He cultivates his person and gives peace of mind to all the people⁵⁷! Without having to intervene (*wou wei*), ruling the Empire, this is what Chouen

---

52   Ibid., pp. 30, 114, 115, 116; 126, 140.
53   Ibid., p. 184, 39.
54   Ibid., p. 183. (This love of others is the effect produced in the gentleman by the study of the Tao), p. 124. The word *jen*, pronounced as the word man, is written with the sign man plus the sign two.
55   Wieger, *Les Pères du système taoïste*, p. 133. This is not my emphasis. Wieger writes on p. 135 (after reserving the word charity) this judgment on the disciples of Confucius: "To love to monopolize minds, that is their love of men." This formula is inspired by a spirit of denigration which is, to say the least, imprudent.
56   Maspero, *La Chine antique*, p. 464.
57   *Louen yu*, L., p. 156.

did and how? He had self-respect (*kong ki*); he turned to look to the South: that was enough."⁵⁸

The *Tai hio*⁵⁹ expands on this theme.

> "The ancient (Kings) who wished to make the *Tö* (Efficiency) shine in the Empire, began by ruling their domain well; wishing to rule their domain well, they began by putting their family in order; wishing to put their family in order, they began by cultivating themselves; wishing to cultivate themselves, they began by making their will (their heart) conform to the rules (*tcheng*); wishing to make their will conform to the rules, they began by making their feelings sincere (*tch'eng*); wishing to make their feelings sincere, they began by bringing their wisdom (*tche*) to the highest degree. To bring one's wisdom to the highest degree is to scrutinize beings. When they had examined beings, their wisdom was brought to the highest degree; when their wisdom was brought to the highest degree, their feelings were sincere; when their feelings were sincere, their will was in accordance with the rules; when their will was in accordance with the rules, they themselves were cultivated; when they themselves were cultivated, their family was in order; when their family was in order, their domain was well governed; when their domain was well governed, the Empire enjoyed the Great Peace. From the Son of Heaven to the common people, everyone should have as a principle: cultivate his person (*sieou chen*)."

This reasoning, although it has been compared to the sorites, does not rely on a chain of conditions; it seeks to make sensible the unity of a principle of order (the *Tao-tö*), uniting, in the manner of a reversible stream, hierarchical but closely interdependent groupings ranging from the Individual to the Universe.⁶⁰

Likewise, the author of the *Tchong yong*,⁶¹ who seems to give equal value to the expressions *sieou chen*⁶² (to cultivate one's own person) and *sieou Tao* (to cultivate, to practice the Tao),⁶³ writes:

> "The wise man (*kiun tseu*) cannot but cultivate himself (*sieou chen*); as soon as he thinks of cultivating himself, he cannot but serve his kinsmen; as soon as he thinks of serving his kinsmen, he cannot but know men; as soon as he thinks of knowing men, he cannot but know Heaven."⁶⁴

---

58   Ibid., p. 159. The expression *wou wei* is generally given as specifically Taoist.
59   This treatise (*Li ki*, C., II, pp. 614 ff.) sometimes attributed to Tseu sseu, grandson of the Master, sometimes to Tseng tseu (one of the disciples), consists of a very short text and long commentaries.
60   See Granet, *Le langage de la douleur*, pp. 178 ff.
61   Treatise attributed to Tseu-sseu (*Li ki*, C., II, pp. 427 ff.).
62   *Li ki*, C., II, p. 427.
63   Ibid.
64   Ibid., II, p. 450. Cf. p. 452. "When one knows how to cultivate oneself (*sieou chen*), one knows how to govern men; when one knows how to govern men, one knows how to govern the Empire or a State" "The Tao is not far from man" (p. 436). "One cultivates oneself with the help

To know men and to cultivate oneself is to know oneself, but *not by mere introspection* or with a view to mere knowledge. What the wise man sets out to know, with a view to regulating conduct, is the behavior of individuals, which he refrains from considering as autonomous realities. The individual never detaches himself *abstractly* from the hierarchical groups among which he passes his life and where he acquires, together with his personality, all that constitutes the dignity of man. It is not an abstract science of man that Confucius and his followers tried to found; it is an art of life that embraces psychology, morality and politics. This art is born of experience, of the observations suggested to those who know how to reflect on life in relation to others, to which is added the knowledge bequeathed by the ancients.

This art or knowledge is called humanism. It is inspired by a positive spirit. It takes into account only observable, lived and concrete data. Confucius said, "I do not want to look into mystery, to work wonders, to pass to posterity as a man with recipes (*chou*)."[65] He refused to speak of spirits: "You know nothing of life, what (can you) know of death?"[66] "He rarely spoke of Ventura, Fate, *jen*"[67] and only in connection with particular cases. "He refrained from speaking of marvelous things, of feats of strength, of troubles, of sacred things,"[68] not out of agnosticism, not even out of ritual prudence; he was only interested in the everyday, the neighborly, the positive. Perhaps he wanted to disassociate his compatriots from the old classificatory knowledge, in which politics and physics were obscurely amalgamated. He hoped, no doubt, to distance them from scholastic or mystical speculation. It seems that only an art of living arising from friendly contacts between educated men seemed beneficial and valid. He identified human culture with the public good.

II. Mö Tseu and Social Duty

We know nothing of the life of Mö Ti (or Mö tseu). He was born in the country of Lou (or Song), perhaps made a trip to Tch'ou, probably settled in Lou and died in the early 4th century BC. Like Confucius, Mö tseu was a nobleman without wealth. He founded a prosperous school, which in the 4th and 3rd centuries BC had far more glory than the Confucian school. No school is more like a sect. Towards the end of the 4th century BC, it split into several cliques that retained a certain unity. This unity was at first stricter; the sect was subject to the authority of a Grand Master (*K'iu-tseu*), considered a saint.[69] It is not known what disciplinary or doctrinal authority can be attributed to him, but it seems that the sect had an organization and recognized a hierarchy. Up to the time when a separate clique

---

of the Tao; one cultivates the Tao (*sieou Tao*) with the help of *jen*. What is *jen*? It is man (*jen*)" (p. 449). "It is with man that man regulates himself." (p. 436).

    65   *Li ki*, C., II, p. 434.
    66   *Louen yu*, L., p. 104.
    67   Ibid., p. 80.
    68   Ibid., p. 65.
    69   *Tchouang tseu*, L., II, p. 221.

Book IV - Chapter II - The Prescriptions of the Public Good   303

(*Pie-mö*) devoted itself mainly to logic,[70] the repetition of the Master's discourses was the chief duty of the faithful. These appear, as they are described to us, as preaching brethren going everywhere to spread the good word. They sought to impress by showing extreme poverty in their dress. The patron they had adopted was not a ceremonial hero, like the Duke of Tcheou, who inspired Confucius. He was Yu the Great, who went all over the Empire to build rivers and mountains,[71] carrying the sacks himself, wielding the shovel himself, wearing himself out for the common good, to the point of having no hair left on his calves, relying on the wind to wash himself and the rain to comb his hair. Anyone who did not swear to live in Yu's way (*tao*) was not admitted to the sect.[72] It was especially important to be able to preach. Therefore, followers were taught rhetoric. They were given model sermons which, it is said, the Master had written. Extracts, divisions, definitions, refutations, conclusions, repetitions, oratorical movements, nothing was missing, not even poignant titles: "On frugality," "Against violence," "The will of heaven," "Against shows," "Against strong minds," "Against the learned"… These sermons have come down to us, for the most part, in three substantially different drafts.[73] Do the differences date from the time when they were put in writing?[74] Are they due to a bad transmission? It is difficult to decide.[75] In the case of Mö tseu and his disciples, the doctrinal basis, which is rather meager, is of less interest than the sectarian faith perceived in them.

On the spirit of the sect, the *Tchouang tseu* has preserved a judgment which agrees very well with what can be gleaned from the preserved documents.

> "To oppose the taste for luxury, to avoid waste, not to seek splendor in figures and protocol measures, to submit to strict rules, to prepare oneself for the difficulties of life, such were the principles… of Mö tseu… He wrote 'Against shows'… 'On frugality.' (According to him) the living should not sing, nor the dead be mourned. (He advised) extending (to all) impartial affection (*fan ngai*), (impartially considering) benefits (of all kinds) (*kien li*) and opposing disputes (*fei teou*). He condemned anger. He loved study, but he did not want distinctions for scholars…"[76]

---

70 See *supra*, in this Book, ch. I, sec. II, and *Tchouang tseu*, L., II, p. 220.
71 According to tradition, Mö tseu was a skilled technician (see *Lie tseu*, in Wieger, *Les Pères du système taoïste*, pp. 145 and 189). The last sections of Mö tseu (52-71) concern the art of sieges and ballistics.
72 *Tchouang tseu*, L., II, p. 220.
73 It is these eleven sermons (books 2 to 9 of the present editions) which form the oldest part of the Mö tseu. The whole book has been translated by Forke (*Mö Ti, des Socialethikers und seiner Schüler philosophische Werke*). Many passages are badly damaged and incomprehensible. A study of the sources of the *Mö tseu* remains to be made.
74 Forke, *op. cit.*, p. 22.
75 Those who admit the homogeneity of style of the *Mö tseu* admit it only with embarrassing restrictions (Maspero, *La Chine antique*, p. 472, note).
76 *Tchouang tseu*, L., p. 219.

"As the *Tchouang tseu* points out, this sad fanaticism and this ideal of mortification (*tseu hou*) had little chance of success in China. Yet for nearly two centuries the sect was successful, which can only be explained by the crisis that Chinese civilization was undergoing at the time.[77] The fashion of Mö tseu was short-lived; the sect disappeared when Che Houang-ti founded the Empire. Unlike Confucianism, it did not flourish again under the Han. Long considered an enemy of culture, a proponent of mediocre utilitarianism, Mö tseu has recently come back into vogue. Some want to see in him a forerunner of socialism and others a beautiful soul who believed in God..."[78]

Mö tseu was a pessimistic conservative. It is easy to define his attitude, but it is difficult to identify his ideas. This preacher was more interested in convincing than in demonstrating; there is something demagogic in his way of arguing. Was the same vulgarity to be found in his thinking? When he spoke of the public good, he never appealed to anything but self-interest. Did he reduce everything to interest? Confucius (or his disciples) conceived life as a perpetual effort of cultivation, made possible by friendship and openness, pursued in intimacy, worth a prayer, but a selfless prayer. Mö tseu seems to admit, without any restriction, the principle of authority; it is the established chiefs and gods who determine what is lawful and unlawful, and, since they are the ones who apply the sanctions, one has only to submit to their will if one does not want to expose oneself to punishment.

The main point of the doctrine is a view of the origin of government. It stresses the primacy it gives not to the social character (*jen*) of men, but to their strictly individual sense of yours and mine (*yi*). Men could only emerge from anarchy (*louan*) by agreeing to submit to the decisions of a ruler in all matters:

> "In the beginning there was no government, no penalties. Each man had a different idea from yours and mine (*yi*); one man had one; two men had two; ten men, ten; as many men, as many different opinions (*yi*). Each man accepted only his own idea of yours and mine and refused to accept that of others, so that there was (only) mutual hostility (*fei*: denial) among men. In families there was hatred, discord, division and disunity between parents and children, old and young; (parents) could not live together in harmony. In the Empire, all men hated each other like water and fire, (hated) each other like poison. What energy they had left, they could not use to help each other. They lived in anarchy, like beasts. Then they realized that the anarchy came from the absence of leaders. They chose the wisest to be the Son of Heaven. The Son of Heaven, fearing that he alone would not have enough

---

77 Tchouang tseu (in Wieger, *Les Pères du système taoïste*, p. 491) speaks of a family divided between the followers of Mö tseu and Confucius. Another passage (*Ibid.*, p. 473) shows the same prestige of the two sages.

78 Wieger, *Histoire des croyances religieuses...*, p. 209. "He was," says Fr. Wieger, "the only Chinese writer who can be said to have believed in God, the only apostle of charity and gentleman of the law that China has produced. He preached, in magnificent pages, the necessity of returning to the faith of the ancients." In this reckless dithyramb, there is, to say the least, a certain frivolity.

energy, chose the wisest to be his ministers… The ministers, fearing that they did not have enough energy, divided the Empire into lordships, and chose the wisest to be their leaders… (And so on down to the heads of the villages)."[79]

After this initial contract, there is nothing left but to passively submit to the opinion of the chiefs.

> "If one does not know whether (a thing) is lawful or not, he must go to the chief; if the chief says yes, they all say yes; if he says no, they all say no… The village chief is the best (*jen*) in the village… The district chief is able to unify all the ideas (of the people) of the district into his and mine… He is the best in the district.. The Son of Heaven is able to unify in the whole Empire the idea of yours and mine… When the Son of Heaven says yes, they all say yes; when he says no, they all say no."[80]

Mö tseu's thinking is much more brutal than that of the Legists. The ideal of uniformity (*t'ong*) which he professes admits of no extenuating circumstances. There is anarchy if uniformity is not total and constant. For the Legists it is enough that the Prince should dictate the law. For Mö tseu, he must dictate opinion. This is the meaning he gives to the word *yi*, while the word *jen* designates the best, the holy, i.e., the Chief.[81]

This sectarian admiration of despotism is related to a religious conception in which some discern a high piety. Mö tseu lashes out against the strong-minded, whom he calls fatalists. They undermine traditional morality; filial piety, brotherly love, loyalty, prudence. They ruin good opinion (*yi*), the authority of the holy kings (*cheng*), the wise, the best (*jen*), by holding that happiness and misfortune are a matter of chance.[82] Happiness and misfortune are, in reality, the rewards and punishments bestowed by Heaven. There are no more brilliant passages in Mö tse's sermon than those in which he deplores the decline of ancestral faith. If crime is increasing, it is because people no longer believe {as in the old days, when "there were holy kings and (when) the Empire had not lost its good opinion (*yi*)"} in the intervention of spirits (*kouei chen*) who come "to reward the wise and punish the wicked."[83] At Ts'i, many people saw the author of a false oath gored by the ram that was to be sacrificed; when King Siuan was struck down with arrows by the spectre of his victim, many were the witnesses; and, moreover, how can these miracles be doubted, they were recorded in the official Annals…[84] But it is above all the Sovereign above, it is above all Heaven that we should fear. Fear of relatives, of neighbors, of chiefs, from whom one can escape, is only a mediocre barrier against

---

79 *Mö tseu*, 11.
80 *Ibid.*, 11.
81 The ideal of the sect is theocracy: the great teacher considered holy was appointed by his predecessor (Liang Chi-Chao, *History of political thought*, p. 110).
82 Or rather the use of opportunities, cf. *supra*, in this Book, ch. I, sec. I.
83 *Mö tseu*, 29.
84 *Ibid.*, 31.

anarchy. There is no escape from spirits and even less from Heaven. There are no forests, no defiles, no shelters from which to escape their wrath, for their light sees all.[85]

Heaven is more especially concerned with rewarding and punishing the Sons of Heaven. To curb the criminal tendencies of the people, Mö tseu appeals above all to popular beliefs about the vengeful power of the spirits; to curb the vices of tyrants, he evokes, following the poets of the royal court, the idea of a justiciary Heaven, of the Sovereign from on high, the dynastic patron. He also speaks of the Will of Heaven (*T'ien tche*) in terms very similar to those he uses to demand total submission to the decisions of the sovereign:

> "The Will of Heaven is to me as the square and compass to the wheelwright or the carpenter. If it says: this is right, it is right; if says: this is not right, it is not right."

Confucius conceived of moral teaching as a friendly and nuanced stimulus to personal reflection. Mö tseu teaches submission to Heavenly Will and uses a kind of catechism to indoctrinate:

> "How do we know that Heaven loves all men?"
> "Because it enlightens them all uniformly."
> "How do we know that it enlightens them all uniformly?"
> "Because it has them all uniformly (for the faithful)."
> "How do we know that it has them all uniformly (for the faithful)?"
> "Because they all feed it uniformly."
> "How do we know that they all feed it uniformly?"
> "Among all the rice-eaters, there is not one who does not raise oxen, sheep, dogs and pigs, who does not prepare rice and rice wine to offer to the Sovereign above and to the Spirits."[86]

It is difficult to decide whether Mö tseu added to the utilitarian conception of religion expressed in his sermons the sentiments of piety which it is fashionable to attribute to it. In any case, there is a long way between this piety and the Confucian "positivism" which forbids any self-interested prayer.

To see in Mö tseu a successor of Confucius, to attribute to him "a deeper thought than that of his predecessor," and to define his originality by a lesser "devotion to the ancients,"[87] is, I think, to appreciate his "doctrine" not without prejudice and superficially. It is true that Mö tseu makes great use of the terms *jen* and *yi*; he makes use of their prestige, but he gives them a very different value from that assigned to them by Confucius. For Confucius, the public good is based on the personal effort of cultivation that makes the individual a complete man as soon as he acquires a nuanced sense of you and me. For Mö tseu, the distinction between you and me is the beginning of all social plagues. It is not the individual that con-

---

85   *Ibid.*, 26.
86   *Ibid.*, 26.
87   Pelliot, *Meou tseu ou les Doutes levés*, p. 479.

cerns him, but the public good, which he does not distinguish from the good morals of yesteryear. He had known only the regime of tyrannies, of which Confucius saw only the first beginnings. While the Legists tried to oppose the interest of the State and the sovereign law to the good will of the despot, Mö tseu demanded total submission to the established authorities, for there could be no good morals if the coercive power of the chief was limited. But the ruler himself must obey morality, and the role of the sages is to remind him of this. Hence the need for preaching and its purpose: to achieve the public good by making princes, threatened by divine wrath, adhere to good morals and impose them on their subjects.

Here comes what is usually called the doctrine of universal love. It is presented as a pure moral doctrine. What dominates, however, is only the idea of social order, or more precisely the horror of misery. The expression *kien ngai* (which translates as "universal love") is opposed to *pie ngai*, which designates partial affection, that which is limited to the immediate environment: *kien ngai* is *the impartial affection* which is not distorted by the *clan spirit*, which is not transformed by the *clan spirit* into egoism, or rather, into an *odious passion of rivalry*. A characteristic fact (and already well pointed out by *Tchouang tseu*),[88] is that Mö tseu always unites *kien ngai* with *kien li*, *pie ngai* with *tseu li*. *Tseu li* is the will to reserve all benefits for oneself or for the close group; *kien li*, on the contrary, is not to be partial in the attribution of the advantages and goods of this world. Mö tseu professes that everything – and everyone – suffers insofar as there is profit spirit (*tseu li*) and clan spirit (*pie ngai*).

Well-understood interest merges with public interest to counsel a distribution of benefits and affections that is not inspired by narrow sentiments, but by a sense of impartiality (*kien li*, *kien ngai*). "He who loves (*ngai*) others will be loved in turn; he who benefits others will benefit in turn." "To a prince who only knows how to cherish (*ngai*) his own domain, and has no affection for the domains of others, nothing prevents him from using the full power of his domain to attack the domains of others. A head of a household who knows only how to take care of himself… nothing prevents him…. to take possession of (what belongs to) others," hence the usurpations, the banditry, the robberies. But if "all men had mutual affection for one another, the strong would no longer prey on the weak, those who are numerous would not violate those who are less numerous, the rich would not bully the poor, the intelligent would not deceive the simple…"[89] Impartiality in affection does not harm personal affections; on the contrary, it adds to them a kind of guarantee. A prince, a father who cherishes only his own patrimony, his own family, why should he not love only himself? But if a son cherishes his father, should he not wish to secure for him the benefit of the affection and impartiality of others?

Mö tseu gives as the foundation of the social order not the refined sense of reciprocity (*chou*) which Confucius makes arise from friendly contacts between educated men, but the ancient feudal and peasant duty of mutual aid. On this point,

---

88   Cf. *supra*, in this Book, ch. II, sec.II, the quotation from *Tchouang tseu*. Liang Chi-Chao (*op. cit.*, pp. 98 ff.) has rightly insisted on this fact.

89   *Mö tseu*, 14 and 15.

he refers again to the wisdom recorded in the poems of the *Che king*: "If you would give me a peach, I would owe you a plum!" "Every word brings an answer, every benefit demands payment!"[90] Thus he admits that nothing is easier to practice than this mutual aid, at least if, as in the old days, the rulers set a good example. For the spirit of mutual aid and impartial understanding to produce its full effect, it must reign universally, imposing itself upon all, and in the first place upon the leaders themselves.

A double duty is thus imposed on all, and in the first place on the great ones; labor and economy. Mö tse's thought, like that of the Legists, is dominated by the fear of seeing man lacking in resources; only, instead of encouraging production with a view to increasing the strength of the State, he condemns hoarding, and even more so luxury, the development of taxation and the increase of military power. It asserts forcefully that war is only brigandage without real profit. It prevents the two belligerents from producing useful goods; it ruins the victor himself; to enlist soldiers is to leave the fields without laborers, the girls without husbands; and yet, to perpetuate itself, society needs food and children. By depriving people of even the necessities of life, taxes ruin the taste for work. Moreover, the luxury which taxes allow to be maintained in the courts of tyrants is not only an unproductive expense, but an encouragement to idleness. Hard-working temperance should be the common rule. It is wrong to squander; a garment is sufficient if it protects the body; it is a sin to add embroidery. All the work of artisans should be regulated to be useful, controlled to avoid waste of time. It is wrong to be idle; sumptuous expenses of mourning should be forbidden, as well as too long mourning; three months are enough for mourning. Why should widows be forbidden to remarry before three years? It is a mistake to recreate oneself; rituals and feasts, games and shows only serve to diminish the surplus necessary for the practice of mutual help. Every man should use all his strength with the common good in mind. He must first seek to be self-sufficient. "If he has strength left over, he must use it to relieve others. If he has anything left over, he should share it with others."[91]

Mö tseu's preaching, very crude in its expression and its appearance, seems, most of the time, to appeal only to self-interest; it has a harsher and more powerful flavor than a simple doctrine of love for one's neighbor. The misfortunes of the times, the spectacle of material misery, led this conservative to draw from the old idea of mutual aid two new, revolutionary ideas, the failure of which proclaims its audacity, if not its merit. Possessed by a sense of the public good, he attacked both the spirit of anarchy and that of the clan. He compromised the idea of social duty that inspires his morality by linking it to a conservative utopia and to the apology of mortification, of work without rest, of the most frugal discipline. His compatriots have reproached him for his lack of humanity, his disregard for the deepest individual feelings, his apparent contempt for the Confucian ideal of educated life and personal culture. Some have well understood that Mö tseu's preaching tended

---

90 *Ibid.*, 1; *Che king*, C., p. 381.
91 *Mö tseu*, 11.

to institute a despotism based on sectarian organization.[92] In general, they are content to blame him for subordinating family duties to social duty. All felt, but none said expressly, that Mö tseu's doctrine had failed not only because it clashed with an ideal of individualism, but above all because it denounced the clan spirit and saw in it a principle of anarchy.

---

92   Liang Chi-Chao, *op. cit.*, p.110.

Chapter III
The Prescriptions of Sanctity

An insidious adversary once asked Mö tseu why he took the trouble to run after men:

"A pretty girl stays at home and is careful not to go out; men are always looking for her. Will she come to us? If so, no one would pay any attention to her."

"We live," replied Mö tseu, "in a corrupt century. There are many who are looking for beautiful girls. A pretty girl doesn't need to leave her house to be sought after. But in these times those who seek goodness are few. If there are no men who will take the trouble to go and exhort them, the people will pay no attention."[1]

The proselytizing and rhetorical powers of Mö tseu are in contrast to the self-indulgent and reserved life of the sages of Taoism. Carefree, they live in solitude or, in the midst of men, they take refuge in ecstasy. They are not concerned with recruiting followers. If they make converts, it is by the effect of silent teaching. They seek holiness so disinterestedly that they have no idea of benefiting others or themselves in any way.[2] They are ascetics, but they hate mortification. They are believers, but care nothing for gods, dogmas, morals, or opinions. They are mystics, but never were prayers or effusions more cold or impersonal than theirs. They are – at least they do not doubt it –, the only true friends of man, but they do not care for good works. They know, they say, the true way to lead the people; yet they hurl their harshest sarcasm if they hear of social duty. They have provided China with

---

1 *Mö tseu*, 48.
2 *Tchouang tseu*, in Wieger, *Les Pères du système taoïste*, p. 423.

formidable sectarian leaders, shrewd politicians, its subtlest dialecticians, its most profound philosophers, its best writer. Yet they value only modesty, abstention, self-denial. No one is a saint, they insinuate, if he leaves a trace.[3]

We know nothing about the early history of Taoism, nothing about the lives of the major Taoist writers, very little about the history of the works attributed to them.

The only surviving ancient works are the *Lie tseu*, the *Tchouang tseu* and the *Lao tseu* or *Tao tö king* (Book of *Tao-tö king*). The latter was once known as the work of Houang-ti (the first of the five mythical rulers) and Lao Tan (or Lao tseu). It is a famous and frequently quoted book since the end of the 4th century BC. It is possible that it has been reworked (ancient quotations do not always exactly match the current text), but it is unlikely to be the work of a forger in the 2nd century BC. This view, supported by H. Giles, has only one fact in its favor: the book has no sequence and little unity. For purely mystical reasons, it has been divided into 81 or 72 chapters. In fact, only verse divisions are observed; it is composed of a succession of apothegms mixed with versified passages, assembled no doubt (more or less in their present order) from the beginning of the 4th century BC or the end of the 5th century BC. It must be admitted that this book, translated and retranslated, is properly untranslatable.[4] Apparently, the short sentences of which it is composed were intended to serve as subjects for meditation. It would be useless to attempt to attribute to them a single meaning, or even a particular meaning. The formulas were valuable for the manifold suggestions they contained. They had one or more esoteric meanings, today indistinguishable; the glosses that pretend to explain them are frankly mediocre and external.

The *Lao tseu* seems to be a kind of breviary intended for the initiated. The *Lie tseu* and the less hermetic *Tchouang tseu* are works of polemical tendency; both are composed mainly of symbolic narratives, apologies, and discussions.[5]

However, the *Tchouang tseu* is the work of a very personal writer. It is possible that this work may have been expanded in some passages and even chapters, due to disciples imbued with the Master's thought and trained to imitate his style. Under the Han, it contained 52 chapters; today it contains 33. It is not known if 19 chapters have been lost or if the divisions of the work have been modified. Composed toward the end of the 4th century BC, perhaps expanded in detail and no doubt augmented in its later chapters (especially the last one) during the 3rd century BC, the *Tchouang tseu* is, on the whole, a reliable and relatively easy-to-interpret document. However, Tchouang tseu had too much genius for his work to be considered a neutral statement of prevailing doctrines.

It is not certain that the *Lie tseu* can help not to confuse Taoism with Tchouang tseu's thought. The *Lie tseu* is a compilation made, perhaps, in imitation of the *Tchouang tseu*. Was it due to followers belonging to the same clique? By disciples of a

---

3 *Lao tseu*, in Wieger, *op. cit.*, p. 37, and *Tchouang tseu*, *ibid.*, p. 233, *ibid.*, p. 487.

4 One of these translations, that of Stanislas Julien, (1842) deserves mention; perfectly conscientious, it does not betray the text, but neither does it enable one to understand it.

5 *Tchouang tseu*, L., II, p. 227.

Book IV - Chapter III - The Prescriptions of Sanctity 313

rival teaching? I do not think we can define it. This work, which lacks unity, may have been expanded with interpolations up to about the Christian era, if it was not completely recomposed. Under the Han, the *Lie tseu* comprised eight sections, just as it does today. One of the present sections (the seventh, entirely devoted to Yang tseu)[6] gives an account of the theories of a very independent thinker. The book is replete with valuable accounts that provide information about favorable ideas and practices in Taoist circles. Unfortunately, it is impossible to determine whether the period to which they refer is the third, second centuries BC, or the early Han dynasty.

Lie tseu is the hero of some anecdotes of the *Tchouang tseu*. Is he a legendary master, a real character? There is no way to answer this question. Was there a character named Lao Tan? A hagiographic anecdote, famous from the time of Tchouang tseu, relates that Lao tseu was visited by Confucius, his younger brother, whom he is said to have mortified.[7] After having been an archivist at the court of the Tcheou, Lao Tan or Lao tseu is said to have retired to the south of Chan-tong. He is said to have left China for a mysterious journey to the West.[8] It is added that on this occasion he met Kouan Yin tseu, another famous teacher, of whom nothing is preserved.[9] There are many teachers or patrons of ancient Taoism who are named in the *Tchouang tseu* or the *Lie tseu*; in neither case is there any way of knowing whether they were anything more than a name. Only Tchouang tseu[10] seems to be a real person; however, nothing is known of his life except his name (Tchouang tseu) and that he may have been born and lived in Wei towards the end of the fourth century BC. It is not impossible that he made a trip to Tch'ou and another to Ts'i, where he would have met the masters of the Lin-tsö Academy. In any case, he was admirably informed of all the ideas in vogue. Few Chinese were more curious and open-minded. No one was more free and objective in his judgments. In this, at least, he was a perfect Taoist; no trace of his life remains, except a book that shines with genius and fantasy.

Tchouang tseu lived in northern China, as did Lao Tan (if he existed). The simplistic and gratuitous hypothesis that opposes Taoism to Confucianism as two philosophies, the former born in the south of China and the latter in the north, does not deserve to be discussed. It has long been held that Taoism, before becoming "a mixture of gross superstitions," began as a "pure doctrine" ("that of Tchouang tseu and Lao tseu"), a "philosophy" of "rare elevation."[11] However, the "neo-Taoists" use expressions to designate its "superstitious practices" found in the works of "ancient

---

6 Cf. *infra*, in this chapter, sec. II.
7 *Tchouang tseu*, in Wieger, *op. cit.*, p. 313.
8 *Lie tseu*, in Wieger, *op. cit.*, p. 107.
9 *Tchouang tseu*, in Wieger, *op. cit.*, p. 357.
10 SMT, ch. 63. Legge (*Texts of Taoism*) has given a conscientious, but external and formal, translation of *Tchouang tseu* (and of *Lao tseu*). Father Wieger has published a sort of paraphrase of the *Lao tseu*, the *Lie tseu* and the *Tchouang* tseu which is not very faithful in detail, but which gives a fairly vivid, if tendentious, idea of these works.
11 SMT, Introduction, p. XVIII.

Taoism." Are we to consider, in order to save the hypothesis, that these expressions, which were originally mere metaphors, were "subsequently taken literally?"[12] Or must we abandon the idea that between what is called *neo-Taoism* and what is considered a doctrinal system invented by the "Fathers" of *ancient Taoism* there is not the same gulf that separates "superstition" from "philosophy"? One must choose between these opposing views.

It is easily recognized that the thought of the first Taoist authors cannot be explained without taking into account the practice of ecstasy,[13] common in the environments in which they lived. This is to admit implicitly that Taoism has as its starting point, not pure speculation, but religious customs.[14] It would be curious if ecstasy were, as people seem to think, the only practice that marked the doctrine. Would we want to attribute to it alone, with an eminent religious value, a philosophical dignity that would risk discrediting any comparison with practices considered less pure or less elegant? The ecstasy described by the early Taoist thinkers when they speak of their mystical frolics does not differ at all from the trances and magical walks through which Chinese sorcerers, heirs of an ancient shamanism, increased their sanctity, increased their vital power and refined their substance. These were also the objectives of a whole series of practices known as the practices of long life. Ecstasy is only one of them. If we separate it from the whole, do we think that we can better see its true scope? And that we will discover its precise interest if we limit ourselves to comparing Chinese mysticism with Christian or Muslim mysticism? All the "Fathers" of Taoism make numerous allusions to the art of long life. For example, reading Siun Tseu[15] shows that the Taoists were not the only ones to recognize its value. It is a discipline that could be called national. It is still honored today, even among the humblest, and is linked to China's most ancient religious past. The rites of long life are linked to the festivals of the *long night*.[16] It is not possible to consider them in detail here. What is important is to indicate their spirit. They constitute an asceticism tending to an ideal of a natural, free, full and joyful life.

The attachment of the Taoists to this discipline explains their opposition to Confucius, their contempt for Mö tseu, and their greater success with the humble and the great than with the middle class of officials. To the praise, however moderate, of ritual restraint, to the brutal apology of mortification, to any morality of etiquette, honor, sacrifice or social duty, the Taoists responded with a mystical plea for pure freedom, which, for them, is confounded with full power and sanctity.

---

12 Wieger, *op. cit.* notes 105 and 118.
13 Maspero, *La Chine antique*, p. 493.
14 Granet, *La religion des Chinois*, p. 142; *Id.*, Remarques sur le Taoisme ancien, *As. maj.*, 1925, p. 146 ff. I reserve for another work a detailed examination of the religious and aesthetic usages out of which Taoist mysticism arose; in the following pages, I can only indicate some of the conclusions to which this examination has led me.
15 *Siun tseu*, section 2.
16 On these festivals, see, tentatively, *Civ. Chin.*, pp. 223 ff.

BOOK IV - CHAPTER III - THE PRESCRIPTIONS OF SANCTITY

I. THE ART OF LONG LIFE

Holiness, for the *neo-taoists*, is essentially the art of not dying. Already in Christian times it was imagined that perfect success in this art was sanctioned by a true apotheosis. It was said that the prince of Houai-nan was able to ascend to heaven followed by his entire household and even by his animals[17] (for holiness is not reserved for men). Emperor Wou (140-87 BC) would have willingly abandoned his whole family and the Empire itself, if a Dragon had been willing to ravish and take him to Heaven as happened to Houang-ti, the supreme patron of Taoism.[18] Emperor Wou tried to enter into communication with the genii; he sent missions to K'ouen-louen and to the East Sea to discover the way to Paradise. The same had been done by Che Houang-ti, who, from the end of the 3rd century BC, accepted to live, hidden from everyone, in the back of his palace, to attract the genies to him and to find the drug that prevents death. He wished to "last as long as Heaven and Earth," to "enter water without getting wet and fire without burning."[19] The myths concerning the herb of life seem very old,[20] as do the stories about the Islands or Mountains of the Blessed. The "Fathers" of Taoism knew many paradises, and also professed that neither water nor fire, nor evil beasts, could do anything against the saints.

Tchouang tseu considers narrow-minded those who treat such beliefs as fables and refuse to believe, for example, in the wonders of the Kou-che islands.

> "There live genies (*chen jen*) whose flesh and skin are fresh and white as ice and snow. They have the exquisite elegance of virgins. They abstain from eating cereals. They breathe in the wind and drink the dew. They are carried by the air and the clouds, dragged by flying dragons. They frolic outside the Four Seas (beyond Space). Their power (*chen*) has become concrete (*ying*: like water when it forms ice cubes), so that it can preserve beings from plague and give prosperous crops and years... Nothing can do anything (against the Holy One)! A flood rising to the heavens would not succeed in drowning him, nor would a drought that liquefies metals and stones, that toasts the plains and mountains, burn him![21]
>
> "The Supreme Man (*tche jen*) has such power (*chen*) that he cannot be heated by setting fire to an immense bush, nor can he be cooled by freezing the greatest rivers; the most violent thunders will ruin the mountains, hurricanes will unleash the seas without being able to astonish him, but he, who is carried by the air and the clouds, and who takes for steeds the Sun and the Moon, frolics beyond Space (outside the Four Seas)! And death and life

---

17   *Louen heng*, in Forke, *Lun-Heng...*, I, p. 335. Lieou Ngan (Houai-nan wang), prince of the imperial family, was forced to commit suicide in 122.
18   *Civ. Chin.*, pp. 57, 419 ff.
19   *Civ. Chin.*, pp. 51, 418.
20   Granet, *Danses et légendes...*, pp. 314, 344, 376.
21   *Tchouang tseu*, L., I, p. 171. Cf. *Lie tseu*, in Wieger, *op. cit.*, p. 83.

make no difference to him. And what does it matter to him what may harm or be of use."²²

"I know," says Lao tseu, "that he who is skilled in guarding his life (*che cheng*), will not meet rhinoceroses or tigers in his travels, and in battle will not have to put away the weapons from him. A rhinoceros would find in him no place to stick his horn, nor a tiger to sink his claws into, nor a weapon to make his edge penetrate him! And why? *There is no place in him for death!*"²³

Pure power, free power, *a Saint is only Life*. It is life that frolics, power that plays. Let us begin, however, by noting that he possesses the magical powers which later emperors sought to obtain, and which in ancient times were compulsory for chiefs and shamans.

To expose oneself to the elements in the bush, to be unmoved by lightning and hurricanes, to emerge victorious from various trials of water and fire, these are the feats which were required of the early magicians, just as they were required, when taken as leaders, to be able to drive out pestilence and make crops grow.²⁴ The apotheosis which crowns these labors is in itself a supreme feat. Long before the time when emperors dreamed of completing their career in heaven, their humble predecessors annually underwent the test of ascension and knew the art of ascending to the heavens.²⁵ Tchouang tseu invents no metaphor, but evokes ancient beliefs when he tells us that, "world-weary," "after a thousand years of life," "supreme men (*tche jen*) rise to the rank of geniuses (*sien*) and, riding on a white cloud, reach the abode of the Sovereign on high."²⁶ King Mou, like other heroes of antiquity,²⁷ was taken to the heavens. An account in the *Lie tseu* shows that he owed this favor to the power of a magician (*houa jen*) who took him, clinging to his sleeve, to cavort (*yeou*) with him, leading him first to the Palace of the Magi (*houa jen*). Then she led him to the "City of Purity," where, in a paradisiacal landscape – with gold, silver, pearls and jade – the Sovereign (from Above) offers fairy-tale spectacles. Finally, beyond the Sun and the Moon, he led him to a world of pure dazzlement.²⁸

These "long walks" (*yuan yeou*), these "spiritual romps" (*chen yeou*) were the specialty of the witches and sorcerers whom the potentates, and later the emperors, kept at their court.²⁹ The official poets sang of their exploits in a language that did not differ much from that of the Taoist philosophers.³⁰ Che Houang-ti and Emperor Wou liked to be referred to by terms (*tchen, ta jen*), implying that they possessed the ascendancy due to the practice of the magical arts and association

---

22   *Tchouang tseu*, L., I, p. 192.
23   *Lao tseu*, L., p. 93.
24   Granet, *op. cit.*, pp. 280 ff, 199 ff, 466 ff.
25   Cf. *supra*, Book II, Ch. IV.
26   *Tchouang tseu*, L., I, p. 314.
27   Granet, *op. cit.*, p. 562.
28   *Lie tseu*, in Wieger, *op. cit.*, p. 107.
29   *Civ. chin.*, p. 422.
30   Cf. *supra*, LIbro I, ch. II, and *infra*, in this chapter, sec. II.

with the genii.[31] Taoist thinkers claim for themselves or their teachers similar privileges and titles, which they share with the inhabitants of those paradises which can only be reached by running or walking with the mind (*chen hing, chen yeou*).[32] *Ta jen* (Great Men), *Tche jen* (Supreme Men), *Tchen jen* (True Men), *Cheng jen* (Holy Men), *Chen jen* (Men-geniuses)…, such are these titles. They are reminiscent of the positions or ranks of a college of shamans. Some masters are called *Tö jen* (Men of *Tö*), while the Tao is called Master (*Che*) or Celestial Master (*T'ien che*) and the disciple greets the Master who confers an initiation with the name of *T'ien* (Heaven).[33] The mystical theories of the "Fathers" of Taoism were elaborated in an environment in which (as tests of initiation to various degrees of sanctity) they were confronted with sorcerers, soothsayers and thaumaturges: all masters of the esoteric arts.[34]

Of all these secret arts, Taoism has never ceased to be the inspirer or the refuge, for all of them (including alchemy),[35] have as their main object to increase the power of life which gives Authority and constitutes Holiness.

These arts, by their very object, form a whole. There is none of them that one does not know how to use with a view to a "long life." To the practices, however, which aim essentially to give, with a surplus of vital power, the ascendancy that confers authority (these are the practices that explain the aristocratic successes of Taoism) are opposed, in a certain way, the practices that aim above all to obtain that there be in the Saint "no place for death." These are the practices that have ensured the fortune of Taoism among the humble, and are in fact inspired less by an asceticism for aristocratic purposes than by a peasant understanding of the art of living.

They constitute a kind of *sanctifying hygiene*, known, in antiquity, as *yang cheng*, the art of nourishing (or augmenting) life. Various techniques (dietary, sexual, respiratory, gymnastic) are based on this art. Subject of a more or less esoteric teaching, these disciplines may have been enriched over the centuries with more or less refined and more or less secret recipes, but it would be a great mistake to consider them as recent disciplines or consisting only of "superstitious practices." The masters of Taoism appreciated their value, and there is hardly any that cannot be related to ancient rites or myths. I must confine myself here (it would be too long and beyond the scope of my subject to demonstrate) that one great principle dominates these various techniques. In order to increase or simply preserve its vitality, every being must adopt a *regimen which conforms to the rhythm of universal life*.

---

31   *Civ. Chin.*, pp. 418, 420.
32   "Neither defiles nor mountains stop its steps; it is a race of the spirit"; "neither chariots nor boats could carry it, it is a spiritual romp" *Lie tseu*, in Wieger, *op. cit.*, p. 82).
33   *Tchouang tseu*, L., I., pp. 168, 324, 332, 299, 303; II, 97.
34   An anecdote common to the *Tchouang tseu* (L., I, pp. 262 ff.) and the *Lie tseu* (in Wieger, *op. cit.*, p. 95) may give an idea of these jousts: the vanquished loses prestige and disciples, just as the defeated chief loses his rights to chieftainship in the shamanic jousts (Granet, *op. cit.*, p. 282: fight between Chouen and his brother).
35   Cf. *supra*, Book II, ch. III.

All these techniques are the result of a systematization of the seasonal rules of rustic life, whose main law was the alternation between periods of joyful activity and periods of starvation, restriction and obligations. From this follows, in particular, the idea that fasting is only valid as a preparation for the popular feast. Deprivations, far from being inspired by the desire to macerate the body, tend only to purge it of everything that can be poisonous, evil, seed of death. It is not a question of mortifying oneself, but of invigorating oneself; not of weakening oneself, but of training and acquiring (so to speak) an athletic form. The idea of play dominates all this asceticism, whose ideal is the free flow and unlimited states of the golden age or of childhood.[36]

> "To preserve vitality (*wei cheng*)," says Lao tseu,[37] "one must be like the newborn baby; its bones are tender, its muscles are supple, and yet it squeezes hard! He knows nothing yet of sexual union, and yet his penis is erect!"[38]
> "All day long he cries out, and yet his throat does not become hoarse! All day long he gazes, and yet his eyes do not blink!"

The child is only life:

> "No venomous beast bites him! No ferocious animal seizes him! No ravenous bird carries him away!"

Subjected equally (for birth is an initiation and initiation a birth) to the test of exposure in the bush, the hero and the newborn are equally invulnerable. Life is constituted or renewed through close contact with Nature.

In the paradises, the geniuses live mingled with the beasts.[39] The saints (unlike the Confucian sages who do not accept to be reduced to the society of rhinoceroses and tigers) seek and know how to obtain the familiarity of animals.[40] They profess that all beings having blood and breath cannot differ much in sentiment and intelligence.[41] Far from thinking of humanizing animals, still less of domesticating them, they teach them the art of avoiding the harmful effects of domestication imposed by life in society. Domestic animals die prematurely.[42] So do men, who are forbidden by social conventions to spontaneously obey the rhythm of universal life. These conventions impose a continuous, self-interested and exhausting activity. The example of hibernating animals shows that it is necessary, on the contrary, to alternate periods of slow life with periods of free frolic. The Saint submits himself to retirement and fasting only to achieve, through ecstasy, to escape to "long walks." The invigorating games, taught by Nature, prepare this liberation. One trains for the paradisiacal life by imitating the frolics of animals. To sanctify

---

36 *Lie tseu*, in Wieger, *op. cit.*, p. 137.
37 *Lao tseu*, L., p. 99. Compare *Tchouang tseu*, L, II, p. 80.
38 The text here presents two lessons; I follow the one adopted by Legge.
39 *Lie tseu*, in Wieger, *op. cit.*, p. 101; *Tchouang tseu*, *ibid.*, p. 275.
40 Cf. *supra*, in this Book, ch. II, sec. I and in the *Lie tseu* (*ibid.*, p. 93).
41 *Lie tseu*, in Wieger, *op. cit.*, p. 101.
42 *Tchouang tseu*, in Wieger, *op. cit.*, p. 273.

oneself, one must first become stupid, that is, learn from children, animals and plants, the simple and joyful art of living only for the sake of life.

When dancing, sorcerers enter into a trance and let themselves be carried away by ecstasy. The saints who have penetrated the highest secrets and deserve the title of "Heaven" do not cease, even when teaching, to "jump like sparrows, while beating their buttocks."[43] To nourish life and "obtain the Tao," in the manner of P'eng-tsou, who managed to last more than seven hundred years, one must perform flexibility exercises (*tao yin*) or, better still, dance and frolic in the manner of animals.[44] Tchouang tseu and Houai-nan Tzu mention some of the themes of this naturalistic asceticism. It is recommended to imitate the dance of birds when they stretch their wings, or that of bears when they wiggle stretching their necks towards the sky. With the help of these gymnastics, birds practice flying and bears become perfect climbers. There is also much to learn from owls and tigers, who are experts at bending their necks to look backwards, and from monkeys who know how to hang upside down[45]... The first benefit of these games is that they provide the indispensable lightness for those who wish to practice ecstatic levitation.

They also serve to *refine the substance* (*lien tsing*). They are, in fact, a *breathing discipline*. They allow to ventilate the whole body, including the extremities. If the breath (*k'i*), says Tchouang tseu, accumulates in the heart, illness follows; or loss of memory, if it remains in the lower parts of the body; or anger, if it remains in the upper parts. He who wishes to avoid passions and dizziness must learn to breathe not only through the throat, but with the whole body, starting from the heels.[46] Only this deep and silent breathing refines and enriches the substance. Moreover, breathing is necessary, both during *hibernation* and during *ecstasy*.[47] By breathing with the neck relaxed or tense, one succeeds, so to speak, in reducing the Breath and purifying its vital power. The supreme aim is to establish a kind of *inner* circulation of the vital principles, so that the individual can remain perfectly *still* and undergo the test of immersion without harm. One becomes *impermeable*, autonomous, invulnerable as soon as one possesses the art of feeding and breathing, in a closed circuit, as an *embryo*.[48]

The newborn child owes to this art, which it has not yet forgotten, not only the secret of being able to wander without becoming tired or fatigued, but also the flexibility of its bones and muscles. We have seen that Lao tseu considered perfect the virile power of the young child, who suffers no loss of vital energy.[49] This theme is linked to a whole sexual asceticism which, since before the Han, had given rise

---

43 *Tchouang tseu*, L, I, pp. 300 ff.
44 Ibid., I, p. 245; I, 265.
45 *Houai-nan tseu*, 7; *SMT*, ch. 105.
46 *Tchouang tseu*, L. II, p. 19 and I, p. 238.
47 Ibid., I, p. 176.
48 The expression "breathing in the manner of an embryo" does not seem to appear before the Han, but the *Lao tseu* (L., pp. 53; 95, 100) contains very precise allusions to this practice.
49 *Lao tseu*, L., p. 53.

to numerous publications under the patronage of various Taoist heroes.[50] Various methods were taught, all aimed at increasing longevity and based not on an ideal of chastity but on an ideal of power. Moreover, folklore tells us of a kind of sexual ordeal imposed on the Saint. Surrounded by many virgins or lying on one of them, he was not to "change color."

To refine the vital breath, as well as the virile energy, one must first respect – as do animals and plants, whose sap circulates only during the summer season – the rhythm that governs the life of the Universe and makes Yin and Yang alternate and perfect each other. Breathing gymnastics is only beneficial in the morning. Relaxation exercises only have a positive effect in spring. The young shoots are then very flexible. Spring is the season of rustic dances that encourage *the ascent of sap and aid renewal*; the gentle bending of budding stems mimic under the fertile breath of heaven. Only these gymnastic dances and frolics can preserve the original suppleness. When this disappears, death triumphs in humans who *stiffen*, as in plants who *lignify*. What is hard and resistant wears out and perishes. Only that which knows how to bend itself remains invulnerable and alive.[51]

Similar ideas inspire a dietary system that does not prescribe constant fasting or even sobriety. It forbids feeding on cereals, as the common man does,[52] but invites one to savor the juice of things. It advises to drink the fruitful dew. It does not forbid alcoholic beverages, since it considers them extracts of life. An adult will no more injure himself than a new-born child by falling (even if from the top of a chariot and even on hard ground) if the fall takes place when he is drunk; this is because, thanks to drunkenness, his vital power (*chen*) is intact (*ts'iuan*).[53] Drunkenness brings us nearer to holiness, for, like dancing, it prepares us for ecstasy.

Only ecstasy can keep the power of life (*chen ts'iuan*) perfectly intact. Holiness, i.e., full life, is attained as soon as, taking refuge in Heaven (*ts'ang yu T'ien*), the Saint succeeds in maintaining himself in a state of ecstatic intoxication or, rather, of permanent apotheosis.[54] Having reached the point where he is nothing but pure, imponderable, invulnerable, and totally autonomous power, the Saint moves freely through the elements, none of which can harm him. It passes through solid bodies with impunity. *All matter is porous to him*. The emptiness he has created in himself, thanks to ecstasy, *extends in his favor to the whole universe*.[55]

The mystic masters affirm that this state of *magical grace* is *the state of nature*, that of the newborn calf. The most beautiful feats are the work of those who have remained in the simplest.[56] However, from reading Lie tseu or Tchouang tseu it is clear that this perfect simplicity is the result of systematic training. To become a master in the art of levitation or in the art of ecstasy, long practice is necessary, as

---

50 *Ts'ien Han chou*, 30, p. 338b; *Tchouang tseu*, in Wieger, *op. cit.*, pp. 360 and 357.
51 *Lao tseu*, L., p. 118, 120.
52 *Tchouang tseu*, L., II, p. 171.
53 *Ibid.*, II, p. 14; *Lie tseu*, in Wieger, *op. cit.*, p. 87.
54 *Tchouang tseu*, in Wieger, *op. cit.*, pp. 251, 259, 289, 265, 325.
55 *Ibid.*, p. 357.
56 *Ibid.*, p. 391; Lie tseu, *Ibid.*, pp. 85, 89.

Book IV - Chapter III - The Prescriptions of Sanctity

well as successive initiations. Lie tseu (who took it upon himself to entrust himself to the best masters) never managed to remain in a trance state for more than fifteen days. However, it took him nine years of apprenticeship to obtain the recipe (*chou*) that allowed him to "ride the wind." When he had regained the original simplicity,

> "his heart (will) crystallized (*ying*), while his body dissolved and his bones and flesh liquefied. He no longer felt that his body was supported or that his feet were supported by anything. He went with the wind eastward and westward like a leaf or a *withered stubble*, unable to see whether it was the wind that was dragging him or he himself that was dragging the wind."[57]

It is worth remembering the expression "withered stubble, empty gale," which is used in connection with aerial excursions, for in representing the saint in ecstasy, it is never said that his heart is like extinguished ash and his body like dead wood. What has become of the youthful suppleness which the practices of long life are intended to preserve? Dead wood evokes cataleptic rigidity. All that in the individual is the principle of death has been, so to speak, evacuated in the bodily sheath (*hing*), which has become a corpse, while the flexibility, intact, has been concretized, with all life, in what mystical language calls the double (*ngeou*: the half, the partner) and common language the breath-soul (*houen*).[58] Being is then nothing but a breath that mingles with the life-giving breath of the Universe and, free, plays in the wind.

Thus the sanctified ascetic can, without fear of any obstacle, without any collision, without anything tiring or wearing him out, frolic (*yeou*), riding on light, in the immensity of the void: the Breath of the Universe is at once void and light, heat and life.[59] In connection with these ideas there is a popular metaphor that mystics use when they say that death has no power over them.

> "It was said that the Sovereign (above) hangs (the bundle) and then unties it… The bundle burns, the flame is passed on…"[60]

As the principle of flexibility and vital heat, the Breath, which ecstasy serves both to refine and concentrate and to release, escapes from what is now only death and "extinguished ash," to unite with pure life and light.

Thus what we cannot call soul[61] is externalized and separated from the perishable, for it is not a spiritual entity: it is – heat, fluidity, luminous emptiness – only the universal, subtle and concrete principle of life. Beginning with free frolics and invigorating games, through which the being refines itself by bending to the rhythm of the Universe, the asceticism of the long life ends in an illumination from

---

57 *Tchouang tseu*, in Wieger, *op. cit.*, p. 211; *Lie tseu*, Ibid., p. 85.
58 Ibid., pp. 159, 215. The newborn child, like the saint in ecstasy, has a body and a heart comparable to dead wood and extinguished ash: therefore it is all flexibility (*Ibid.*, p. 407).
59 *Tchouang tseu*, in Wieger, *op. cit.*, pp. 259, 305, 325, 331, 287, 289, 223.
60 *Tchouang tseu*, L., pp. 201, 202.
61 Maspero (*La Chine antique*, p. 494), was not afraid to translate the word *k'i* (breath) as soul.

which the Saint obtains, with all the gifts of the Magician, an unlimited power of life.

II. The Mystique of Autonomy

In addition to a whole series of prescriptions for life and holiness, taught no doubt by rival masters, which are very diverse, though drawing from the same source, there is the doctrine of the "School of the Tao." This expression, established by usage, is not a happy one. The idea of *Tao* is not proper to the masters of Taoism, and they, rather than professing a doctrine, have confined themselves to advocating a Wisdom. This wisdom is of mystical tendency, which does not imply that it is at all favorable to personalism and spiritualism. It would be a greater betrayal than any of the other favorable teachings in ancient China if, in expounding it, one were to indulge in the use of the word "God" or the word "Soul." The "Taoism" of Lao Tseu and Tchouang Tseu is a kind of *naturalistic quietism*.

Vomiting your intelligence[62] is, in principle, the only rule of Wisdom. All dogma is harmful. There are no good works. Only silence and stillness (*tsing*) are effective.

> "I will tell you what the Supreme Tao (*tche Tao*) is! Withdrawal, withdrawal, darkness, darkness; this is the culmination of the Supreme Tao! Twilight, twilight, silence, silence. Look at nothing, hear nothing! Keep your vital power (*pao chen*) embraced, remain in stillness. Your body (will not lose) its (native) correctness! Keep your tranquility (*tsing*), keep your essence (*ts'ing*). You will enjoy a long life! Let your eyes have nothing to see, your ears nothing to hear, your heart nothing to know. Your vital power will preserve your body, your body will enjoy a long life! Watch your inner self, turn away from the outer world, to know many things is harmful…"[63]

The quietism of the Taoist sages is expressly connected, as we see, to the ancient ideal of long life. These sages, however, seem to have been reformers, as was Confucius, but in a different setting. They, too, wanted to base wisdom on man's knowledge. But Confucius seems to have set out to free psychology from an ancient magico-religious knowledge, while extolling the educational virtue of etiquette. The "Fathers of Taoism," on the other hand, are much more concerned to distinguish psychological knowledge from the science of behavior governed by social conventions than they are concerned to separate it from speculations about the Universe. They tend to see (current) society not as the natural environment of human life, but as a spurious system of constraints. It is not the company of elders, the conversation of honest people, mutual control, it is not friendship or observation that can give information about human nature. *Solitary meditation is the only way to knowledge and power (tao)*:

> "To know others is only science; *to know oneself is understanding*."[64]

---

62   *Tchouang tseu*, in Wieger, *op. cit.*, p. 289.
63   *Ibid.*, p. 287.
64   *Lao tseu*, L., p. 75.

Civilization degrades nature; everything is conventional as far as observation is concerned. Dialectic has only a negative interest; it demonstrates the arbitrariness of all knowledge that is not due to meditation alone. The latter is sufficient for the saint. Beyond the artificial, it makes him apprehend reality and life at the same time. He has only to withdraw into himself: "forgetting in stillness (*tsouo wang*)" all that is conventional knowledge, he purifies his heart (*sin tchai*) of all the false desires and temptations that society has invented. Thus he re-establishes in himself the perfect simplicity (*p'ouo*), which is the native state of all being and of the whole universe. To find the natural man and Nature within oneself, one need only return to being oneself and

> "keep in peace the essence of life that is one's own (*ngan ki sing*)."
> "Do not go through your door; you will know the whole empire. Do not look out of the window; the *heavenly Tao* will appear to you."[65]

Meditation is not exhausted in knowledge. It purifies and saves. But salvation is but a return to nature, and it is not from what we call matter that the apprentice saint seeks to free himself. Only the *century* (*che*), not the world, deserves the name of quagmire. What is impure and the seed of death is the artificial, the acquired; all that by which civilization has deformed and distorted nature. Every invention, every supposed improvement, is no better than an annoying growth. It is rather a noxious tumor.[66] Nature must not be violated, especially under the pretext of rectifying it. What is curved must remain curved. Do not try to shorten the legs of the crane or lengthen those of the duck. If it were artificial, any long-lived technique would be pernicious, and any tendency to improvement would be reprehensible if inspired by moral prejudice. The worst thing would be to try to unite by *jen* and *yi*, by these bonds, these nets, these glues, these false varnishes which are the rites, the laws, the etiquette, of beings who can only subsist on condition of remaining themselves. One "loses one's nature (*sing*)" if one becomes attached to customs; one "destroys oneself" if one becomes attached to other beings.[67] The "I (*tseu*)" must not allow itself to be contaminated by the "other (*pei*)." On the contrary, it is advisable to "take refuge in your own *tö* (specific essence) (*tsang yu ki tö*),"[68] for this is "taking refuge in the Heavenly (*tsang yu T'ien*)," i.e., in Nature.

The opposition of *T'ien* and *jen* (which is not the human, but the social, the civilized) is at the heart of the doctrine of Lao Tseu and Tchouang Tseu. It differs entirely from an opposition between the divine and the human.[69] Meditation, and even ecstasy, do not claim to give access to a transcendent wisdom. They reveal to man what he is, what he can continue to be, if civilization (*jen*) does not erase in him the tao, the tö, the T'ien, that is, his own essence (*sing*), pure of all contamination. Thus, the true Man (*T'chen jen*) is he who, shunning his fellows, *has no com-*

---

65   Ibid., L., p. 89.
66   *Tchouang tseu*, ch. VIII, ch. IX.
67   *Tchouang tseu*, L., I, p. 373.
68   Ibid., I, p. 274.
69   See, conversely, Maspero, *La Chine antique*, p. 495.

panions: "He who does not gather with other men (*ki jen*) is equal to Heaven." It may also be said of him that he "frolics in truth," that "the gate of Heaven opens for him," that "he is a Son of Heaven," that "he is equal to the Sovereign (above)."[70] These are mythical formulas, which should not mislead; Taoist meditation does not seek solace in the hereafter. It is strictly solitary. *Its ideal is autonomy*. Only the wicked are alone, the followers of Confucius would willingly say.[71] Its opponents make absolute autonomy the condition of salvation and of life itself. It is *for himself alone*, that the Saint must live.

Salvation and holiness are achieved insofar as the self (*tseu*), freed from all commitment to others, is nothing but pure life and spontaneity (*tseu jan*). Reduced to himself, the individual is equal to the Universe, for the spontaneity of which he now makes his only law is the only law of *Ten* or *Tao*. He who knows how to remain autonomous possesses the *T'ien tao*, the Way, the celestial Virtue.

Indeed, it is *tseu jan*, spontaneity, or rather, it is a total power of spontaneous realization which is the characteristic of Heaven as well as of the Tao. *T'ien* (the Heavenly, which is opposed to *jen*, Civilization) evokes an idea which the word "nature" can convey, and in so far as it seems correct to translate φυσις by nature, it is still this term which will best express the Taoist notion of Tao.[72]

Starting from the common idea that the Tao points to the universal power of realization of which the regulative power of the Ruler is, in the human order, the highest expression, the Taoist Masters lent to this notion a more intellectual, if not more abstract, value. In the notion of Tao was summed up the religious and at the same time familiar feeling of close sympathy and complete solidarity that unites nature and man. For schools concerned with political or moral action, the natural order, conceived according to the model of the social order, seems to emanate from the chief, the responsible guardian of statutes and customs. But the thought of the Taoist masters is less directly influenced by politics than by the magical arts. The idea that man does not form a kingdom in nature is accompanied by a very strong feeling for the *unity of the world*, and this is even more powerful in their thought than in that of all other Chinese sages. The diviners characterized all *mutations* (*yi*), real or symbolic, as *easy* (*yi*); they occur, they said, without expenditure of energy. The magicians presented the most miraculous feats of strength as *direct effects* of an inexhaustible operative genius. It is from these conceptions, combined with the (half-popular, half-wise) belief that Heaven, invariable, impartial, remains immutably in itself, while governing the four seasons, that the essential thesis of Taoism is derived: the Tao (like Heaven, i.e., Nature) is imagined as the immanent *principle* of universal *spontaneity*.

It is thus initially characterized by a kind of total indifference and absence of differentiation. It is "*empty* (*hiu*)," empty of *preformations* as well as prejudices; it does not prevent any free initiative; no individuation confronts it, which is the Unnamable (the Total incapable of retaining any specification). The Tao (Heaven, Na-

---

70 *Tchouang tseu*, in Wieger, *op. cit.*, pp. 325, 261, 233, 333, and L., p. 367, note 2.
71 Cf. *supra* in this Book, ch. II, sec. I.
72 Legge, *Texts of Taoism*, Introd, pp. 12 ff.

ture) is not *binding*, but unbinding, but impartial; it *animates the game* and *places itself outside the game*. Its only rule is *wou wei, non-intervention*. It is certainly thought to act, or rather to be active, but in the sense that it *irradiates tirelessly a kind of continuous emptiness*. As the overarching principle of all coexistence, it forms a *neutral medium* which therefore favors the indefinite ebb and flow of spontaneous interactions.

Some Taoists (as is evident from the *Lie tseu*) make little distinction between the interactive environment of the Tao and the world of magical actions. When they insist on the *continuity* (*kiun*) of the Universe and contrast it with simple *contiguity*,[73] they are thinking above all (in what we would call mind-to-mind actions) of magic tricks, tricks of operation, the games of illusionists. It is thanks to the cosmic continuum, it is thanks to the Tao – indeed, it is thanks to its very efficacy (*tao*) – that a fisherman (whose line is made of a single strand of silk) pulls huge fish out of a deep abyss and that a guitarist (by simply plucking one of his strings) gets, if he pleases, crops to ripen from the first days of spring, or in midsummer, snow to fall and rivers to freeze. Similar powers are acquired, the *Lie tseu* expressly says, by those who know the secrets of illusory jugglery (*houan*), by those who know the science of *transformations* (*tsao houa*).[74]

It is often said that the *Lie tseu* is a work of Taoism that has already decayed, but it is a fact that actions without contact or expenditure of labor are one of Tchouang tseu's favorite themes. More surprisingly, he uses the words *tsao houa* to describe the Tao. Some interpreters do not hesitate, in this case, to translate *tsao houa* by the *Creator*, precisely on the occasion of a passage in which Tchouang tseu shows the Tao *mutating* a left arm into a cock and a right arm into a crossbow.[75] Nothing is more alien to Taoist thinkers than the creationist or personalist tendency. They do not separate the ideas of spontaneity (*tseu jan*) and non-intervention (*wou wei*), impersonality and autonomy. Precisely because they see in the Tao only the immanent and neutral principle of all spontaneous realization, they have tended, especially Tchouang tseu, to make it the principle of the *natural development* of things and, consequently, of their *true explanation*.

Their effort has been characterized by saying that they wanted to free themselves from the animistic conceptions which dominated the Chinese mind at the time.[76] It would be more accurate not to speak of animism, but of magic. By intellectualizing, so to speak, the idea of the Tao and insisting on the notions of impersonality and impartiality, the Taoist Masters tried to interpret as a principle of rational explanation what had hitherto been conceived only as the concrete and total principle of Order or the effective means of magical actions. However, it did not

---

73 Fr. Wieger (*op. cit.*, p. 139) was the first to propose the translation of *kiun* by continuity (sometimes he says: "mystical continuity" (*Ibid.*, p. 142)), but without pointing out the magical character of this notion.
74 *Lie tseu*, in Wieger, *op. cit.*, p. 109.
75 Maspero, *La Chine antique*, p. 502.
76 This is the thesis held by Hou Che in a pamphlet entitled *Houai-non wang chou* (Shanghai, 1931).

occur to them to link to the idea of the natural development of things a technique of experimentation. However powerful the naturalistic inspiration that animated them, they remained, like their adversaries, under the influence of *humanistic* concerns. They thought only of defending a certain way of understanding life. Their idea of the Tao or of the nature of things is explained by their taste for meditation {which they combined (at least in the case of Tchouang tseu) with a great interest in dialectics} at least as much as by their knowledge of magic or physics.

The notion of continuity is linked, in the *Lie tseu*, to the thesis that Space and Time are not limited.[77] When he wants to hint at what the Tao may be, Tchouang tseu also insists on this thesis. He illustrates it abundantly by means of allegories or mythical anecdotes, on the one hand, and, on the other, by means of an argumentation nourished by themes taken from the Sophists.[78] Like the latter, Tchouang tseu professes a rigorous relativism, but far from any abstract realism.

For him, the world resolves itself into a flux of concrete, occasional, singular appearances, among which there are no common measures, except external, human, artificial ones. All sensations have as much or as little reality as others. All judgment is only a value judgment, always an arbitrary estimate. In my dream, I am a butterfly; I wake up and I am Tchouang tseu. Who am I? Tchouang tseu dreaming that he is a butterfly! A butterfly imagining that he is Tchouang tseu?[79] These two successive appreciations testify to a transformation (*wou houa*) of which it cannot be said whether it is real or imaginary. Similarly, it is not possible to draw a definite distinction not only between neighboring terms, but also between This and That, existence and nonexistence, life and death, the beautiful and the ugly, the useful and the harmful, well-being and discomfort. In fact, they are not *really opposite terms*, they are simply *contrasted judgments*, totally subjective, merely momentary. Lying in the mud is only unhealthy for such and such a person at such and such a time.[80] Moisture, heat, exist only for those who are hot or feel wet and *only at the time* when they feel it. The Whole and each being are in perpetual change. Here I am another when I think I am the same as before.

> "Man's life between Heaven and Earth is like a white horse that jumps a ditch and suddenly disappears."[81]

To be born or to die is certainly a total and instantaneous change (*kai*); it is no different from the complete changes of which life is composed at every moment. The individual, like the world, is manifold, and the world does not remain the same;[82] however, the universe is one, and so is every being. *Complete changes are only mutations.*

---

77 *Lie tseu*, chapter V.
78 *Tchouang tseu*, ch. I, ch. II, ch. XVII.
79 *Tchouang tseu*, in Wieger, *op. cit.*, p. 227. comp. *ibid.*, p. 225.
80 *Tchouang tseu*, Legge, I, p. 191.
81 *Ibid.*, II, p. 65.
82 *Ibid.*, I, p. 277; *Lie tseu*, in Wieger, *op. cit.*, p. 79.

Book IV - Chapter III - The Prescriptions of Sanctity

Therefore, there are no errors, not even possibilities of errors. Therefore, all the paradoxes of the Sophists can be held to be true. The Self and the Other, the This and the That being only different *situations*, it is legitimate to say that a centenarian is not old, nor a stillborn young, that a hair is worth a mountain, and that between such and such a mite and the Universe there is no difference, neither in nobility, nor in power, nor by age, nor by greatness.[83] On the other hand, there are only occasional, impermanent, multiple, singular, concrete truths, or – what amounts to the same thing – there is only one truth, *abstract, total, indefinite*, which is the Tao: the *medium* – indifferent and neutral, impassible, indeterminate, supremely autonomous – of the set of transitory truths, of contrasted appearances, of spontaneous mutations.

The dialectic honored by the sophists allows Tchouang tseu to present the Tao as the medium where the synthesis of all antagonisms is produced. When, ceasing to "remain confined between the Six Poles of the Universe and to be dazzled" by the play of light and shadow, one decides *to ride in the chariot of the Sun*,[84] one enjoys, from this neutral and sovereign observatory, a point of view that is neither neither that of the This nor that of the That, but one in which the This and the That can only be united. It is the point of viewpoint of the Center of the ring, where the vanity of (seemingly) *diametric oppositions* becomes evident. For the one who stands at the center of the ring, "there is nothing that cannot be *equalized (tö ki ngeou)*," all contrasts being reabsorbed into the total Order that governs them, for this is the *pivot of the Tao*.[85]

Seen from the indifferent principle of all autonomous realizations, and no longer with the passionate preferences of the small over the great or the great over the small, *the minuscule and the majuscule merge, for they are equally immense*. "The supremely tenuous" (as the dialecticians say) is that which has no sensible appearance (*wou hing*); the supremely great is that which cannot be circumscribed. In this aphorism, which evokes concrete sensations and operations, but is inspired by an abstract realism, Tchouang tseu substitutes a formula for that which affirms his thesis that only the operations of the mind count, and that there is neither small nor great, but only the *immense*. Thus he characterizes that which has no sensible appearance by the impossibility of *dividing it by calculation*; that which cannot be circumscribed, by the impossibility of *suppressing it numerically*.[86] Tchouang tseu's relativism is of idealist inspiration.

With him appears the *idea of infinity* in Chinese philosophy, destined, moreover, to mediocre fortune. The infinitely large, the infinitely small, is not what, materially, would be indivisible, or what, technically, could not be circumscribed; it is what, still and always, remains to be imagined as soon as the mind has begun to imagine. Unless one is a frog confined in a well, a mushroom born for a single morning, how can one not feel that Space and Time (and, with them, any being or

---

83   *Tchouang tseu*, L., I, p. 182.
84   Ibid., II, p. 96.
85   Ibid., I, p. 183 (see p. 321 for an analysis of the idea of *Houang ti*).
86   Ibid., I, p. 378.

situation in Space-Time) are unlimited? However great the extent or duration may be represented, there will always appear an insufficiency of grandeur, once one has ventured to think of a beyond.[87] Think, for example, of the P'eng, that immense bird, which needs only six months of flight to soar in the air to a height of ninety thousand stadia. Where could it (where could you) stop its flight? This allegory or similar mythical themes are sufficient to impose the idea of infinity.[88] In fact, it corresponds to a need of the mind. And this need is satisfied by the notion of Tao.

Totally indeterminate and *absolutely autonomous*, the Tao is found in all things. All things contain spontaneity, indeterminacy and those indefinite possibilities of mutation which belong to all being, for every symbol contains them.

> Where is the Tao?
> There is nothing where it is not!
> Give an example, it will be better.
> It is in this ant!
> Could you give a more humble example?
> It's in this grass!
> Even lower?
> It's in this fragment!
> Is this the lowest?
> It's in this excrement!

But it is no use asking about the Tao the way experts,[89] in the markets, value a pig by pushing their foot into the fat as long as they can. "Ask not for examples, there is nothing where the Tao is not." The Tao deserves to be called "the Supreme," "the Universal," "the Total," that is, "the All-One (*Yi*)."[90] Immanent in all things (it should not be said: animate or inanimate, but: the most vulgar as well as the noblest),[91] it points to a principle of indeterminacy from which proceeds, for each of them, with absolute singularity, a complete independence. It would not suffice to say that every being, like every thought, is free, fleeting, unlimited, or that it partakes of an *infinity of power and freedom*; to this infinity, there is nothing that is not equal to itself, and *to be worth the All, it is enough* – for every being – to be and to become; *it is enough to be oneself*, with all its possibilities.

Dialectic and mythic imagination show that this *immanent infinity* is a necessity of thought. Ecstasy, which makes it possible to feel it in its pure splendor, shows that it is the only reality, the total reality.

> "O my Master! O my Master! Thou givest to all things and dost not intervene for equity (*yi*)! Thou art generous to the generations of all times and dost not intervene for friendship (*jen*)! Thou art older than the most ancient

---

87 Ibid., I, pp. 164 ff; 374 ff.
88 Ibid., II, p. p. 164.
89 That is, the Sophists when they argue by evoking a progressive sequence of actual divisions.
90 *Tchouang tseu*, L., II, p. 166.
91 Taoists do not refuse to admit a certain hierarchy.

BOOK IV - CHAPTER III - THE PRESCRIPTIONS OF SANCTITY

ages and art not old! Thou coverest and supports (as) Heaven and (the) Earth! Thou chisel and sculpt all appearances and thou are not a craftsman. It is in you that I frolic (*yeou*) {or else (it is another clause); it is to you that we give the name of *Heavenly Joy*!}."

This is the (*stereotyped*) prayer with which Taoist ecstasy ends.[92] This ecstasy is attained by a training which purges the being of all artificial contradictions, superimposed on his nature by contact with others and social conventions. One retains, in old age, the freshness of a child, when one rejects from oneself first "the world of men," then "all reality" (external) and, finally, the very idea of "existence." One then obtains, in a diffused light[93] which is that of the dawn (*tchao tche*), the vision of a "solitary independence," so that, "past and present annihilating themselves," one "enters into that which is neither living nor dying."[94] Thus it is that:

"By dropping body and limbs, banishing hearing and vision, separating oneself from all bodily appearances and eliminating all knowledge, one unites with that which *pervades everywhere* (*ta t'ong*)[95] and gives *continuity* to the Universe (*T'ien kiun*)."[96]

Thanks to the "purification of the heart" and "emptiness (*hiu*)," one "adheres to the Tao (*tao tsi*)."[97]

After having "embraced Unity (*pao yi*)" and since "the ten thousand beings are but one"[98] and since he himself has been able to "preserve unity in himself,"[99] the Saint, having no longer "an 'I', no private activity, no proper name (*wou ming*)"[100] merges, indeterminate and free, into the principle, unnamable (*wou ming*) and total, which – being only the axis, the crest (*ki*), the pivot, the *empty* center of the wheel hub[101] – has neither activity nor existence of its own, but outside of which there is no reality, no freedom, no truth, for it is the *Unbroken Efficiency* from which, with all arts, all efficiencies proceed, the *One Knowledge* which, like a *diffused light* (it is called the celestial – that is, natural – Light *T'ien kouang*),[102] illuminates everything, uniformly, giving each thing its true appearance.[103]

The originality of the Taoist masters, or at least of Tchouang tseu, lies in the fact that they were able to justify a *technique of Sanctity*, dominated by an ideal of

---

92 *Tchouang tseu*, L., I, p. 256. Compare with *Ibid*., p. 352.
93 The word *tche* means "to penetrate" and "to spread everywhere uniformly."
94 *Tchouang tseu*, L, I, p. 245. *Ibid*., II, p. 145, and *Lie tseu*, in Wieger, *op. cit.* p. 121.
95 *Tchouang tseu*, L., I, p. 257.
96 *Ibid*., II, p. 83.
97 *Ibid*., I, p. 209.
98 *Ibid*., I, p. 224.
99 *Ibid*., I, p. 229.
100 *Ibid*., I, p. 169.
101 *Ibid*., L., II, pp. 129 ff.; *Lao tseu*, L., I, p. 54.
102 *Tchouang tseu*, L., II, p. 83.
103 *Ibid*., I, pp. 243 and 311.

autonomy, combining it with a theory of *knowledge*,[104] very much in keeping with the postulates of their *naturalistic quietism*.

In this theory, the share of the mystical tendency is no greater than that of the intellectualistic tendency. Regarded as the immanent and neutral principle of all free developments, the Tao (although, in the exaltation of ecstatic vision, it is described as mysterious and ineffable) is, first of all, conceived as a principle of rational explanation. Moreover, its indeterminacy and impartiality (reflected in the impersonal coldness of mystical effusions and prayers, always stereotyped in their form) exclude any tendency to personalism, while any tendency to spiritualism is excluded by the idea of the continuity of the universe.

The Tao, which can be said to be both Nature and Reason (or, if you will, φύσις and λόγος), is a principle of universal intelligibility. The formula "vomit your intelligence" does not express contempt for the activity of the mind, but, simply, contempt for discursive science, for the games of dialectics, for any kind of abstract realism.

The Taoist masters have no difficulty in using (nor, it seems, any effort to perfect) the system of classifications that their contemporaries use to order thought. They admit that the vulgar are dominated by 6 Appetites (those of honors and riches, those of distinctions and prestige, those of fame and Fortune), 6 Impediments (those imposed by posture and behavior, sensuality and reasoning, temperament and reflection), 6 (Feelings that hinder) the Tö (hatred and desire, joy and anger, grief and pleasure), 6 (Attitudes that hinder) the Tao (those of avoiding or anticipating, taking or giving, acquiring knowledge or exercising talents). These 24 dispositions must be suppressed in order to obtain righteousness and tranquility, enlightenment and emptiness.[105] It is also necessary, on pain of "losing the essence that is proper to us (*sing*)," to avoid the five perversions[106] that result from the civilized use of the senses: painting, music, perfumes, cooking, and the predilections of the heart corrupt sight, hearing, smell, taste, and judgment.[107] In itself, the natural use of the senses can be pernicious, if no attempt is made to defend the original simplicity (*p'ouo*) of being against the multiplicity of appearances. Vision, hearing, smell, taste, and knowledge only deserve the name *tche* (all-pervading, all-extending) if no particular object *stops* them.

---

104 This is no doubt what Hou Che wanted to express (*The development of logical method in ancient China*, pp. 142 ff.) when he presented Tchouang tseu as a theoretician of logic, a thesis rejected as paradoxical by Maspero (*La Chine antique*, p. 492, note), who concedes little originality to the Taoist masters in terms of "their doctrinal theories" and sees, in "the practice of the mystical life, their great discovery (Maspero, *Le saint et la vie mystique chez Lao-tseu et Tchouang tseu*, 7 and 9).

105 *Tchouang tseu*, L., II, pp. 87, 89.

106 The 5 perversions come from the 5 Colors (which disturb the two eyes), the 5 Notes (which disturb the two ears), the 5 Smells (which disturb the two nostrils), the 5 Tastes (which disturb the mouth) – altogether seven orifices and four senses – and the likes and dislikes which disturb the heart (which also has seven orifices).

107 *Tchouang tseu*, L., I, p. 328. (1128) *Ibid.*, p. 268, and *Lao tseu*, L., p. 55.

Book IV - Chapter III - The Prescriptions of Sanctity

For perception to be pure, it must be diffuse and refer to the total and not to the details of things. It must also be all-encompassing, and supplied not by one of the senses, but by the whole being. It must be the result of a union (*ho*) of that which, in the individual as in the universe, constitutes the power of life {the *k'i* (breath)[108]}. The true sage "hears with his eyes and sees with his ears." Not that he has found the secret of paracoustic hearing or paroptic vision. He readily admits that it is not possible to switch the functions of the various organs. He only knows to unite his body with his heart, his heart with his *k'i* (breath), his *k'i* with his *chen* (vital power) and the whole with the *wou* (i.e., not with "nothing," but with the *undetermined Whole*...) If therefore:

> "A sound is produced, whether far away, beyond the Eight Steps of the Universe, or near, between the eyelashes and the eyebrows, he cannot fail to be informed of it, without knowing, however, whether it is through his ears or through his four limbs that the perception is made or whether it is through his heart, his belly, or his five viscera that it is informed; that is all."[109]

The only valid perception seems to be the spontaneous and global one, resulting from a free communal fusion. The wise man refrains from using his eyes to see, his ears to hear; he refuses to make separate use of his senses for fear that the orifices which are his organs will become obstructed; he "uses his eyes only as he uses his ears and uses his nose as he would use his mouth"; only thus does he "establish communication between the external and the internal" innocently.[110]

Any partial sensation is exhausting and corrupting. To collide with the multiplicity of things in one part and then in another of his being would exhaust the individual. A saint, whose first duty is to take care of his vitality, fears these shocks, especially when, as a good Taoist, he is penetrated by the idea that, where multiplicity appears, there is no end to foresee. He is careful not to want to know in detail:

> "Living has limits and there are no limits to knowledge! It is a danger for that which is limited to pursue that which is not limited!"([111]

In ancient China no one is unaware that every image is the result of a contact, this clash can occur in the waking state as well as in sleep.[112] The saint does not allow himself to dream or to think, or to tire his muscles,[113] for he fears attrition and, even more, contagion. As soon as there occurs, not the corroborative union with the indeterminate Whole, but the undue proximity of the Other and the Ego, there is the shock, that is, the wear and tear, and the harmful contact, or, rather, the contamination.

---

108   *Ibid.*, II, p. 139.
109   *Lie tseu*, in Wieger, *op. cit.*, pp. 117-119.
110   *Ibid.*, p. 121.
111   *Tchouang tseu*, L., I, p. 198; *Lao tseu*, L., p. 90.
112   *Lie tseu*, in Wieger, *op. cit.*, p. 109.
113   *Tchouang tseu*, L., I, p. 366.

To avoid these evil contacts and doubly sacrilegious invasions that wound the autonomy of the Other as well as that of the Self,[114] the Taoist masters should, it seems, limit themselves to ecstatic union with the Tao, profess the most rigorous of mystical subjectivisms. They escape this subjectivism thanks to their thesis on the continuity of the universe. This thesis also allows them to free themselves from the abstract realism of the dialecticians.

To the sophist Houei tseu, who was walking with him on the bridge of a stream and who reproached him that, not being a fish, he pretended to recognize what was the pleasure of fish, Tchouang tseu replied:

> "You asked me: 'How do you know what the pleasure of fish is?' Since you have asked me this question, it is because, first, you knew that I knew. And I know it because I am on the bridge of the stream."[115]

The possibility of communication between the Self and the Other is a fact. If, even for him, it were not a constant fact, the dialectician would be absurd, since – and precisely on this fact – he questions the Other. But if the fact – which authorizes the dialectic while revealing the ineffectiveness of reasoning in the abstract where it is confined – is constant, it is the proof that there is a concrete continuity between all parts of the Universe.

For Taoist masters, communication from human individual to human individual is only possible because communication between individuals of all kinds is first possible. Excluding all spiritualistic bias, it is not a matter of soul-to-soul communication, nor of the transmission of ideas by means of artificial symbolism, such as human language. If the Self can know the Other, it is through the Unity of the world. It is thanks to the "natural continuity (*T'ien kiun*)" that "the true (*jan*) and the false (*pou jan*) are distinguished (*tseu*)," spontaneously manifest (*tseu jan*).[116]

The unity of the world was brilliant, and knowledge of things was easy in times when civilization had not perverted men by deforming and isolating them.

> *In the past they lived in brotherhood with the animals and were one family with the ten thousand beings.*

There was no concern for the "science of details," but all beings got along and understood each other, for the magpies themselves "let look into their nests."[117] Therefore the sages said that, as far as understanding was concerned, there was little difference between all living beings. Hence they communicated freely with "quadrupeds, birds, insects, genii, and demons of all kinds." And, indeed, "human behavior" was not yet opposed to that of other beings.[118] But today, most people find themselves enclosed and circumscribed by artificial barriers, arbitrary distinctions imposed by culture and etiquette. They have lost their native simplicity.

---

114 *Ibid.*, I, p. 274.
115 *Ibid.*, I, p. 392. Cf. *supra*, in this Book, ch. I, sec. III.
116 *Ibid.*, II, p. 143 (in Wieger, *op. cit.*, p. 449).
117 *Ibid.*, II, p. 278.
118 *Lie tseu*, in Wieger, *op. cit., p. 101, ibid*, p. 91.

They can no longer understand the only thing that can be understood: the natural behavior (*sing*) of beings.

Only some barbarians still listen to the language of animals, and some breeders to their nature; they themselves have retained a simple nature. It is from them that we must ask the secret of true knowledge: "Keeping always the same disposition," they do not cease to be natural, so that with them "tigers believe themselves to be in the midst of mountains and forests," in the midst of nature. An impartial and free sympathy[119] unites the Self and the Other in these cases. *This true understanding is the beginning of true knowledge.* To the one who loves them and, out of pure friendship, comes to greet them every morning, the seagulls give themselves familiarly. Between them and their friend, the game is disinterested and, consequently, the *intimate communication*. But if one day man approaches them with the desire to seize them, the seagulls perceive this secret intention and flee at once.[120] No one can understand unless he respects, while preserving his own nature, the free nature of others.

Knowledge results from a spontaneous agreement of two autonomies, of two benevolent indifferences. Water is thus the symbol of wisdom; it offers the image of tranquility, welcome and disinterestedness. Indifferent, "supple, unwearying," seeking neither to act nor to know, "water has no pretensions"; it accepts all forms, all places; it "descends to the depths that all despise"; it is "the great confluence of all things,"[121] which does not prevent it, since all impurity only passes through it (for to the pure everything is pure), from offering itself as a limpid mass; it only becomes turbid when agitated, but its agitations do not last, for they do not proceed from it. By itself, water is inert, hospitable and peaceful. *Therefore, things freely entrust their true image to it.*

> "Men do not look at themselves in running water like a mirror, but at still water; *only still water can stop them all.*"[122]
>
> "When water is still, its clarity (*ming*, meaning to understand) illuminates even the hairs of the beard and eyebrows. It has such perfect balance (*p'ing*: peace) that the rule of leveling has been derived from it. *When the water remains calm (tsing), it illuminates (ming: to comprehend, illuminate) all things.*"[123]
>
> "The Supreme Man uses his heart as a mirror. He does not take hold of or anticipate anything. He responds to everything and *holds nothing back*. He can overcome everything *without harming anything*" because "if he is the receptacle of all that Nature (*T'ien*) gives him, he does not consider himself its possessor."[124]

---

119 *Ibidem.*
120 *Lie tseu,* in Wieger, *op. cit.* p. 93.
121 *Lao tseu,* L., pp. 54, 104. 120 (in Wieger, *op. cit.,* pp. 24, 61, 53).
122 *Tchouang tseu,* L., I, p. 225 (in Wieger, *op. cit.,* p. 243).
123 *Ibid.,* L., I, p. 330 (in Wieger, *op. cit.,* p. 309).
124 *Ibid.,* L. I, 266 (in Wieger, *op. cit.,* p. 267).

> *"For the one who abides in himself without limiting himself to it,"* said Kouan Yin tseu, *"things manifest themselves by themselves and as they are, for their behavior is that of water, their stillness that of the mirror, their response that of the echo."*[125]

Only tranquility provides true knowledge of *nature*. Always disinterested, the Saint, without making any effort, nor spoiling anything within or without himself, reflects, immutable and pure, for the indefinitely moving images that constitute the Universe are not traces that penetrate and persist. It knows all nature in its integrity. It knows it without concern for details, but concretely. It has precise perceptions, but they are valid only in the moment. All abstraction, all generalization and even all reasoning by analogy (*a fortiori*, induction or deduction) are forbidden to him. All science is impossible, especially history; nothing can remain of what has been, except a trace. A trace is something dead and signifies nothing.[126] Only the fleeting reflection is an exact, complete and innocent image. There is no true knowledge outside of the Instant and the Total.

There is also only a total Efficiency and singular Recipes.

Any supposed technique can only be deceptive and only apt for beginners.[127] Every recipe is non-transferable,[128] every knowledge is incommunicable, at least dialectically. It is thanks to stillness that we perceive natural behavior. They are also behaviors that can only be taught, and this can only be achieved by the only effective attitude: that of disinterested and peaceful concentration.

A good boss does not bother to explain the details of the job. He conducts himself in such a way that the principle of all efficiency becomes evident to the disciple. He who knows how to do things knows neither why nor how he does them; he only knows that he succeeds, and that one always succeeds when, with one's whole being, one thinks only of success. To shoot down cicadas in full flight, it is enough to see only the cicada in question in the whole universe; you cannot fail, even if you are puny, hunchbacked or crooked.[129] Would you like to be a master archer? Don't worry about technical standards. Spend two years lying under your wife's loom, and force yourself, when the shuttle brushes your eyes, not to blink. Then, for three years, occupy yourself only with raising a louse on a silk thread, which you will contemplate, facing the light. When the louse seems to you bigger than a wheel, when, it is bigger than a mountain and hides the sun from you, when you see its heart, then take a bow and shoot boldly; you will hit the louse right in the heart, without even touching the silk thread.[130] The good blacksmith forges with-

---

125 *Ibid.*, L. II, p. 226 and *Lie tseu*, in Wieger, *op. cit.*, p. 129.
126 *Ibid.*, I, p. 361 (in Wieger, *op. cit.*, p. 329). The books are "the detritus of the ancients" (*Ibid.*, I, p. 344, (in Wieger, *op. cit.*, p. 317).
127 *Ibid.*, Wieger, *op. cit.*, pp. 273, 279, 301.
128 *Ibid.*, p. 317.
129 *Ibid.*, p. 359.
130 *Lie tseu*, in Wieger, *op. cit.* p. 145.

out thinking about it, nor getting tired; the good butcher cuts without thinking about it, nor wearing out his knife; both cut or forge spontaneously.[131]

> "To teach without words, to be useful without any intervention, few succeed," and yet "the supreme word is to say nothing (to others), the supreme act is not to intervene (*wou wei*)."[132]
>
> "Don't speak! Express yourself without speaking! There are those who have spoken all their lives without saying anything. There are those who have not spoken all their lives and have not remained silent."[133]
>
> "He who speaks does not know," "he who knows does not speak."[134]

Wisdom and Power can only communicate through *silent teaching*, which alone respects the nature of things and the autonomy of beings.

The Holy One knows and lives only for himself, but he teaches all and sanctifies all. He teaches and sanctifies by the direct effect of his efficacy. Totally introverted, he abstains from any particular word or action. It intervenes in nothing (*wou wei*),[135] it limits itself, like the Tao, to radiating an emptiness conducive to the spontaneous development of all beings.

This *beatifying emptiness* is, so to speak, the atmosphere of Paradise. They are myths about the Golden Age or the Lands of the Blessed, which serve to illustrate Taoist morality and politics. There is a country far to the northwest where:

> *"There is* no leader; *(everything is done)* spontaneously and that's all. There is no love of life and no hatred of death. So no premature deaths! There is no affection for oneself, no distance from others. So there is neither love nor hate! Neither clouds nor mist arrest the sight; neither thunder nor lightning disturbs the hearing; neither the beautiful nor the ugly corrupt the hearts; neither mountains nor valleys hinder the steps..."[136]

In the old days,

> "when men behaved naturally..., and there were no roads and no boatmen... everyone stayed at home without knowing what he was doing there or went for a walk without knowing where he was going. People yawned and laughed. They would slap each other on the belly and laugh a lot. And these were their only talents!"[137]

---

131 *Tchouang tseu*, in Wieger, *op. cit.*, pp. 399, 229.
132 *Lao tseu*, L., p. 87; *Lie tseu*, in Wieger, *op. cit.*, p. 187.
133 *Tchouang tseu*, L., II, p. 143.
134 *Lao tseu*, L., p. 100.
135 *Ibid.*, p. 90.
136 *Lie tseu*, in Wieger, *op. cit.*, p. 82.
137 *Tchouang tseu*, L., I, 278-280. This image, intended to glorify the simple joys of the ages without rites or restrictions, has been used to accuse Taoists of sharing with other Chinese sages a "cynical contempt for the people" (Maspero, *La Chine antique*, p. 557). *Lao tseu* (Legge, p. 49) advises, it is true, to fill the belly and weaken the will, but he advises it to all and says "the saint works in favor of his belly (which he can satisfy) and not of his eyes (which are insatiable)" (Legge, p. 55).

In this happy time, men could remain in a state of innocence. They lived, in fact, without coming into contact with their neighbors, without forging artificial desires. They remained autonomous.

> "Satisfied with their manners, peaceful in their homes…, they died of old age without having entered into any intercourse" even with those "whose dog they heard barking and whose cock crowed."[138]

Some inhabitants of the Far South still retain this spirit of independence and simplicity.

> "Innocent and rustic, they keep selfishness and desire to a minimum. They give, but ask for nothing in return (*pao*)."[139]

These are the principles of true morality:

> "Be simple, be natural! Reduce selfishness and desire to a minimum!"

Lao tseu commands and adds:

> "The wise man keeps the pledge of the contract, but never claims what is his due."[140]

Any society, any morality based on the respect of an authoritarian hierarchy, on the forced execution of contracts, on coercion, is pernicious and degrading.

Unrestricted autonomy, spontaneous harmony, this is the only principle in politics, the only rule in morality. Rites and rewards, laws and punishments, and (worse still) social service and devotion to the public good, these abominable theses of Mö tseu, of the Legists, of the disciples of Confucius, the morality of sacrifice, of discipline, of honor, are the sources of the worst disasters and of anarchy.[141] Built to exploit some passion, this false morality unleashes all passions. From them springs the taste for intrigue, the litigious spirit, and the passion to dominate. He who, in order to profit by them, contrives to arouse artificial desires, and yet sets out to restrain desires, will not be able to achieve his aim. To have good soldiers, do you glorify contempt for death? Will you make your men obey you by threatening to punish them with death? You will create bandits whom you will not frighten. It is laws that make criminals, regulations that provoke anarchy. He who follows nature wants to remain free and, to remain free, avoids all desire. That is how one remains innocent and harmless… But there can only be misery, crime, disorder, as soon as one begins, by deforming human nature, to oppress the individual.[142]

However, far from professing absolute individualism, the Taoist masters repudiate the theories of Yang tseu. Tchoang tseu, who frequently attacks Yang tseu,

---

138 *Tchouang tseu*, L., I, p. 288. (Comp. *Lao tseu*, L., p. 122.)
139 *Ibid.*, II, p. 30.
140 *Lao tseu*, L., pp. 52 and 121.
141 *Tchouang tseu*, ch. X, ch. XI.
142 *Ibid.*, ch. XV, ch. XXIX, and Wieger, *op. cit.* p. 405; *Lao tseu*, L., p. 117.

reproaches him (as well as Mötzu) for being one of those enemies of nature who willfully cage man like a bird of prey.[143]

If these attacks are violent, it is because Yang tseu's individualism has no counterpart and, moreover, is linked (like Mö tseu's sectarianism) to a pessimistic tendency. Yang tseu[144] despises the life that Taoists sanctify.

> "One hundred years of life is a maximum! Half the time is spent as a child carried in arms and the other half as an old man wandering. The other half is divided between sleep and the waking state, the latter occupied by illness, pain, sorrow, grief, disappearances, losses, fears and worries. In the ten years or so that may be left, there is perhaps not a moment that does not have its worries!"[145]
>
> "A hundred years of life is too much to endure! Worse would be the trouble taken to make life last!"[146]

Yang tseu condemns long-life practices (*kieou cheng*), highly prized by Taoists. He blames suicide without energy, though. One can go, he says, to the end of one's existence, when one is convinced that the end is near.[147]

This weariness, which excludes even despair, is clearly opposed to Taoist ataraxia. It starts from the feeling that man is nothing and can do nothing, that nothing does nothing to nothing, that absolute isolation is the lot of all beings. All happiness is vain, all glory vain, all punishment indifferent. Praised or hated, all end up rotting, insensible to glory or guilt.[148] Is it more painful to spend one's life in prison, bound hand and foot, or, to avoid punishment, to deprive oneself of everything?[149] No one can do better than to obey cheerfully his instincts and circumstances... The shepherd cannot pretend to lead the flock; the animals go where they will, and the shepherd follows them. The wisest man would not be able to impose his will on a single sheep.[150]

There are no leaders of men. There are no valid morals, no effective politics. Those who present themselves as heroes and pretend to sacrifice themselves usefully for the public good are impostors. One of the great themes of the Mö tseu sect was the beautiful story of Yu the Great, who consumed all the hair of his legs and

---

143 *Tchouang tseu*, in Wieger, op. cit., p. 307. Yang tseu is also mentioned together with Mö tseu, pp. 269 and 279.

144 Nothing is known of Yang tseu, except that he lived before Tchouang tseu and Mencius, who opposed him. Nothing has remained of his work, if he wrote at all. Many anecdotes in which Yang tseu comes on the scene form Chapter VII of the present *Lie tseu*. It is a gratuitous assumption to claim that this pamphlet contains Lie tseu's analysis of Yang tseu's theories (Liang Chi-chao, *History of Chinese political Thought*, p. 87), or that it is "a fragment of the works" of Yang tseu (Maspero, *La Chine antique*, p. 509).

145 *Lie tseu*, in Wieger, op. cit. p. 165.
146 Ibid., p. 173.
147 Ibid.
148 Ibid., p. 165.
149 Ibid., pp. 165, 175 and 177.
150 Ibid., p. 177.

all the nails of his hands for the benefit of the Empire.¹⁵¹ Therefore, someone in the School asked Yang tseu if he would give a hair of his body to help the World. He got only this answer:

> "The world certainly cannot be helped with a hair!"
> "But," insisted the other, "supposing it could be helped, would you do it?"
> Yang tseu disdained to answer him.¹⁵² He therefore deserved to be quoted.

For this, he deserved to be cited (in all Chinese literature) as the type of the egoist. In fact, as an uncompromising individualist, he simply refused to admit that, even in the realm of magical actions (or political myths), no being could do anything that was efficient over other beings.

Taoist masters escape Yang tseu's integral individualism, but not only, as in the case of subjectivism, because of their thesis on the unity of the universe. They are not at all pessimistic. Although they shun human pride, they have a strong sense of the equal dignity of all things. All, darkly, and the Saint, in glorious illumination, participate in the indefinite efficacy of the Tao. This is the moment to recall all that the conception of the Tao owes to the notion of *magical efficacy* – to repeat that the Saint is the heir of the shamans – to repeat, finally, that all social authority seemed to depend on the possession of magical-religious powers. Neither the idea of pious works nor that of the public good played the slightest role in Taoist politics. Tchouang tseu mocks mutual aid as conceived by Mö tseu. He ends by saying that when bandits are killed, men are not killed.¹⁵³ These sophisms only serve to justify a cruel despotism. And, moreover, one is only saved individually. Do you admire the fish who, when drought empties the streams, think they can save themselves by crowding into the holes? "Instead of sticking together to keep moist", would they not do better to reach the deep waters one at a time? A better resource than "dripping on each other"!¹⁵⁴ And certainly it is no wiser than to entrust one's fate to a prince who thinks he governs by worrying about rites, precedents, and asking advice; all this has as much effect as a mantis pretending to stop a chariot.¹⁵⁵ No political expedient is valid, but there is a Policy, and there is only one. Only *he who saves himself can save others*. Just by saving himself, he saves the world.

Having placed himself "in the center of the ring," he "*let everything be fulfilled*,"¹⁵⁶ and devotes himself to the supreme Work, which is to refrain from all intervention (*wou wei*):

---

151 Cf. *supra*, in this Book, ch. II, sec. II. It is known that Yu, in order to reduce the overflowing waters, consecrated himself to the Yellow River. Devotion is made by throwing nails and hair to the god (he who gives the part gives the whole) (Granet, *Danses et légendes*..., p. 467).
152 *Lie tseu*, in Wieger, *op. cit.*, p. 173.
153 *Tchouang tseu*, in Wieger, *op. cit.*, p. 327.
154 *Ibid.*, pp. 253 and 327.
155 *Ibid.*, p. 301.
156 *Tchouang tseu*, Legge, II, p. 117. Cf. *supra*, in this same section.

"His knowledge extends to the whole world without his thinking anything on his own; his talent extends limitlessly to the inland seas without his doing anything on his own."[157]

"He feeds the Empire. He has no desire, and the Empire has enough for itself. *He intervenes in nothing, and the ten thousand beings are spontaneously transformed.* He has the tranquility of bottomless water, and the Hundred Families remain in peace."[158]

Identical to Holiness, Efficiency is the exact opposite of profane utility.

Only unproductive trees with hollow trunks, discarded by carpenters who could not get anything out of them, grow, prosper, become venerable and end up being promoted to *gods of the soil and earth*.[159] They have done nothing to obtain this honor, and they do not care. It is not their official sainthood that protects them. Their longevity (*their true sainthood*) is due solely to their utter worthlessness. Men who can be called "geniuses" (*chen jen*)[160] must be equally useless in the profane sense. A sage, even if he flees into the wilderness, is joined there by apprentices. Soon a village forms around him which owes its prosperity to him. Now the villagers want to make him their *god of the soil and earth*. The disciples rejoice. The sage is saddened... He knows that one can only have real action if one is unsuccessful.[161]

To be able to do, in addition to knowing, one must be surrounded by indifference and absorbed in it.[162] The hermit, demoted to the rank of minister, can certainly take refuge in ecstasy. However, by letting his power show, he has betrayed sanctity.[163] He would have done better to commit suicide.[164] Absolute independence, unfailing autonomy are the conditions of Efficacy.[165] To be truly useful to the world, it is important to forget the world and think only of subsisting peacefully.

Houang-ti once wanted to obtain

> "the recipe for mastering the essence of the world in a way that helps the harvest to come in and feed the people, and for Yin and Yang to obey you in a way that comforts the living... If you ruled the world in this way (said a true sage) the clouds, even before they gather, would rain! The plants would lose their leaves before they turned yellow. And the light of the Sun and Moon would soon be extinguished."

---

157 *Ibid.*, I, p. 324.
158 *Ibid.*, I, p. 308.
159 A "god of soil and earth" is a tutelary deity of a locality in the Chinese folk religion, Taoism. One can also ask for his protection to travel safely and peacefully. There are as many as there are territorial communities, some of them ruling uninhabited places such as farming areas or cemeteries (TN).
160 *Ibid.*, I, pp. 217 to 220.
161 *Ibid.*, II, pp. 74 ff.
162 *Tchouang tseu*, in Wieger, *op. cit.*, p. 425.
163 *Ibid.*, p. 423. Cf. *Lie tseu*, in Wieger, *op. cit.*, pp. 97, 125.
164 *Ibid.*, p. 463.
165 *Tchouang tseu*, ch. XXVIII.

After staying in retreat for three months, Houang-ti merely asked questions about the art of "*regulating* oneself to last and subsist."

"That," said his master, "is the real question."[166]

Autonomy, withdrawn life, non-intervention are the principles of Efficiency, Majesty and Autocracy.

Identified with the Tao through the practice of solitary meditation, the Saint possesses "the science of transformations (*tsao houa*); he could make thunder in midwinter, produce ice in summer," but he does not deign to use his power.[167] A disinterested magician, he lets the world go its way. He allows it to subsist by remaining himself undisturbed. He does not wish to wear it out, nor to wear himself out. He limits himself, for the benefit of all things, but without charity or pride, to concentrate in himself an intact Majesty. This sovereign Majesty is not spent for the benefit of anything, precisely because it is indispensable for the existence of all things. It is indistinguishable from pure Power and from "integral Knowledge (*yi tche*)."[168] Master of the Universe, but condemned to remain master of himself, the Holy One

> "could choose the day of his apotheosis. Then there would be no man who would not wish to follow him! But how would he consent to take care of beings?"[169]

The Saint, an *unknown autocrat*, does his work without anyone noticing, and this work is done without any interest in the one from whom it emanates. His Holiness is sufficient for itself and sufficient in itself. He is, and everything retains its own essence. He lasts and nature subsists.

The political ideal of the Taoist masters seems to have been a regime of small peasant communities. In an isolated village, a saint (revered as a god of the soil and earth) can, in the most modest way, exercise his undefined powers. Tchouang tseu asserts that all goes well in the Empire when local traditions, which he calls village maxims, are given free rein.[170] However, by professing that the Saint is equal to the Universe, that all efficacy is total in itself, and that the principle of Holiness or Efficacy is to be found in absolute autonomy, the Taoists prepared the autocratic thesis which the founder of the Chinese Empire claimed for himself. Eager to frequent the geniuses, but invisible to his subjects, Che Houang-ti pretended to animate the Empire by his Majesty alone.[171] This did not prevent him from commanding or punishing. The Legists had seized on the idea of non-intervention (*wou wei*) to give a theoretical foundation to the conception of law as impartial and

---

166 *Tchouang tseu*, L., I, pp. 297 ff.
167 *Lie tseu*, in Wieger, *op. cit.*, p. 109.
168 *Tchouang tseu*, L., I, p. 226.
169 *Ibid.*
170 *Tchouang tseu*, L., II, pp. 126 ff.
171 *Civ. Chin.*

Book IV - Chapter III - The Prescriptions of Sanctity

sovereign.[172] Taoists abhor punishment, coercion, and regulation. At most, they value the flexible rules that arise naturally from practice and are written down in the maxims of the people.[173] And yet Tchouang tseu himself, that determined enemy of all intervention, delighted in imagining some somewhat brutal measures. He kindly advised that the ears of musicians be stopped up, the eyes of painters be put out, the fingers of artisans be broken, and, above all, that the mouths of all doctrinaires, his enemies, be sealed.[174] To suppress all creators of artifice was not, in his opinion, to intervene. If the saints of Taoism had consented to exercise their efficacy in restoring the golden age, the return to nature might have been made with some harshness...

Hidden under the philosophical elegance of the most ancient masters, the most ancient Taoism hides a religious mentality, a sectarian spirit. Witness to this is the adage invoked by Tchouang Tseu: "Suppress the sages! Expel the scholars! And the Empire will be well regulated."[175] In fact, like other mystical doctrines – and all the more so since it defines Holiness by Autonomy – Taoism, even more perhaps than it has favored autocracy, has encouraged sectarian movements. The ancient masters showed no respect for the established powers. For them it was an axiom that a prince was indistinguishable from a brigand.[176] And it was also, as a direct consequence of their mysticism, a fundamental truth that every *individual*, however ignoble, however deformed, however mutilated after condemnation, is – in so far as he has communed with the Tao – *a Son of Heaven*.[177] Once this principle was established, it was as difficult for Taoism to provide the creed of an organized Church as it was to inspire, without alteration, a constitutional doctrine. Hostile to any constituted authority, Taoism inspired numerous sectarian movements without ever producing an organized religion. Moreover, Taoist wisdom is a quietism, but a naturalistic quietism. It was dominated by a spirit too exclusively humanistic to have developed a taste for a science of nature. On the other hand, and in spite of the *affected* contempt of the ancient masters for all that is merely technical, it was destined to maintain and increase the prestige of all knowledge inspired by *magic*.

* * *

The vogue of Taoism and its value as a source of artistic inspiration[178] is attested as early as the end of the 4th century BC by the poems attributed to K'iu-yuan. The *Yuan yeou* (The Far Journey) is a tale of amorous ecstasy under the guidance of a

---

172 Cf. *supra*, in this same Book, ch. I, sec. IV.
173 The opposition of *Tchouang tseu* and Siun Tzu (cf. *infra*, in this same Book, ch. IV, sec. II) is only formal.
174 *Tchouang tseu*, L., I, pp. 286, 287.
175 *Ibid.*, I, p. 207.
176 *Tchouang tseu*, chapter X.
177 *Tchouang tseu*, L., II, p. 82.
178 The ancient influence of Taoism on the plastic arts seems certain, so far as can be judged from the documents. These are scarce and, for the most part, difficult to locate historically, so that Chinese archeology (which is ceasing to be purely bookish) still depends (and the damage is greater in this case than for any other discipline) on literature, or rather on literary amplification.

"Genius" and a "True Man" who lead the poet to the "City of Purity." It speaks of the Tao in terms found in the *Lao tseu* and the *Tchouang tseu*. K'iu-yuan, a court poet, served as a model during the Han period for Sseu-ma Siang-jou, another court poet,[179] who also liked to sing ecstatic walks. It is clear that, in the milieu of the potentates, Taoist-inspired poetry was used to magnify the ceremonies in which it was attempted, opening wide for the Master "the Gate of Heaven," exalting his Majesty by a kind of half-poetic, half-magical apotheosis.

The *Houai-nan tseu* attests even better to the success of Taoism in aristocratic circles. There is nothing in this composite work to suggest that, since Tchouang tseu, Taoist metaphysics has been enriched or renewed. The *Houai-nan tseu*[180] is a kind of encyclopedia in which a wide range of knowledge is included. It shows that Taoism, remarkable from the beginning for its indifference to all dogma and its ease of acceptance, is decidedly oriented toward the syncretism which, at least in China, marks all orthodoxies.

This propensity for orthodoxy and syncretism can perhaps be explained by a greater recruitment of followers. It seems that Taoism benefited, even more than the Confucian School, from the ruin of the Mö tseu School (which was completed at the founding of the Empire). Apparently, this is the reason for the strengthening of the sectarian spirit that led to the Taoist revivals around the Christian era. As little known as these revivals are, there is a religiosity, even an ascetic tendency, which contrasts with the spirit of the ancient Taoists.

However, the latter did not lack the will of propaganda to the point that one does not find, in Tchouang tseu itself, surprising concessions to the religious traditionalism claimed by Mö tseu. For example, this passage: "Whosoever does evil in the daylight, men find opportunity to punish him! Whosoever does evil in the dark, spirits find occasion to punish him! (Let every action) be known to men or known to spirits, that is what should inspire conduct, even when one is alone!"[181]

Sounds like Mö tseu. If it is Tchouang tseu who speaks in this way, it is because he does not disdain to bring back to Taoism all those whom his adversary's religiosity might attract. In any case, it seems that belief in retribution was not entirely foreign to ancient Taoist wisdom. It was not introduced into Taoism only through the influence of Buddhism. Chinese Buddhism owes more ideas to Taoism than it brought to it,[182] but, from the time Buddhism was introduced into China, the syncretistic tendency of Taoism was powerful enough to enable it to take up many ideas that were partly new to it.

---

179   *Civ. Chin.*

180   The name given to a collection of opuscules published under the patronage of Lieou Ngan, a prince of the Han family, who was king of Houai-nan from 164 to 123 BC. He was a patron of the arts and a bibliophile. He is credited with having, if not rewritten, at least marked with his style the rather varied, but always Taoist-inspired, treatises that form the *Houai-nan tseu*.

181   *Tchouang tseu*, L., II, p. 83.

182   The debts of Chinese Buddhism to Taoism are well indicated by Pelliot (*Meou tseu ou les Doutes levés*). Comp. Hackmann, *Chinesische Philosophie*, p. 229.

Chapter IV
Confucian Orthodoxy

The attacks of his adversaries prove it: if not in his lifetime, at least by the end of the fifth century BC, the name of Confucius was famous throughout the Chinese Confederacy. According to tradition, the Master had many disciples. It is said that seventy-two had fully understood the teachings of the Sage. Undoubtedly, they did much to spread the glory of their patron. It is less certain that they were faithful to the spirit of his wisdom.

Some of Confucius' disciples entered the service of the princes who ruled in northeastern China, mainly Lou, Ts'i and Wei. Their careers are not well known and do not seem to have been very brilliant. They may have acted as state advisors and may have had disciples. However, it was in a village formed around the Master's tomb that the Confucian tradition was perpetuated. In the late 5th century BC, those who claimed to be Confucians were shown grouped in several schools claiming the patronage of Tseu-kong, Tseu-yeou, Tseu-hia, Tseng tseu and Tseu-sseu.

The latter was a descendant of the Sage. He is credited with writing the *Tchouang yong* and the *Tai Hio*, and it is generally considered that a Taoist influence is noticeable in these two works. They attempt to raise the prestige of the philosophical doctrines attributed to Lao tseu to a fairly high level. It must also be admitted that a syncretic tendency reigned in the Confucian School almost from its foundation.

It is also assumed that the first generations of disciples, and perhaps Confucius himself at the end of his life, were interested in the *Yi king*.[1] In all the treatises that now compose this work, one can hardly find more than moral and political con-

---

[1] *SMT*, V, p. 400.

cerns, the same ones that predominated in the Confucian group. The fact that this group was interested in divination and in commenting on natural signs or testimonies is sufficient proof that, far from being accentuated, the humanistic tendency characteristic of the Confucian reform was weakening.

On the other hand, the passion for teaching by commentary indicates the weakening of the taste for pragmatic forms of teaching to which Confucius apparently owed his prestige. The Master had tried to establish the value of positive psychology by getting his disciples to think together about everyday incidents. His successors taught *commenting* on the verses of the *Che king*, as well as the formulas of the *Tch'ouen ts'ieou*, the aphorisms cherished by soothsayers and the adages of the masters of ceremonies. From the end of the 5th century BC onward, they could be accused of sticking only to bookish knowledge and of giving value only to ritual appearances.[2]

As humanistic inspiration diminished, so did the attachment to archaic decorum. Instead of observing humane behavior and trying to perfect a sense of human dignity, the Master's infidel heirs tried to subordinate all knowledge to the study of ritual traditions. Moreover, they seem to have succeeded in bringing to the surface a notion destined for a great future: that of sincerity (*tsch'eng*). The honest man must in all things obey the rites with scrupulousness and meticulousness. He deserves to be called sincere if, at all times, both for his smallest gestures and for his most important actions, he "exhausts his heart"[3] in the fulfillment of ritual prescriptions.

A morality of intention thus underlies conformism. In Taoist terminology, the term "heart" evokes the former life. Its use by ritualists claiming Confucian patronage indicates an important advance in the syncretistic trend that favored the victory of Confucian orthodoxy. It was through his theory of ennobling intention (*leang sin*)[4] that Mencius gave new impetus to the Confucian School.

I. Mencius: Government by Charity

Mencius (Meng tseu, late 4th century BC)[5] seems to have been the first talented writer who expressly regarded Confucian doctrine as the orthodox doctrine.

He was born, like Confucius, in the manor of Lou (or thereabouts). He was apparently descended from the princely family of Lou. He was educated by his mother, a prudent woman who is praised for the care she took to protect her son from evil influences. He may have attended the Tseu-sseu School and then tried to recruit some disciples. When he was about forty years old, he went to Ts'i. He

---

2   *SMT*, V, pp. 307, 438.
3   *Li ki*, C., II, pp. 319, 320.
4   Mencius, L., pp. 283, 284. The expressions *leang neng* and *leang tche* are similar to the expression *leang sin*: noble talent and knowledge.
5   Legge (t. II of *Chinese Classics*) has given a good translation of Mencius' works. Sseuma T'sien devoted a brief biographical note to Mencius (ch. LXXIV). According to tradition, Mencius lived between 372 and 288 B.C.; dates disputed and impossible to pin down.

Book IV - Chapter VI - Confucian Orthodoxy 345

was for some time among the "scholars" protected by King Siuan (342-324 BC). He was not successful enough to remain there and left to seek the favor of various potentates, the princes of Song, T'eng and Wei. He eventually returned to Ts'i, where King Min may have employed him as an advisor. Disgraced, he returned to his native country. He remained there until his death, surrounded by a few disciples, of whom only one, Yo-tcheng K'o, had fame.

Mencius does not seem to have enjoyed great credit among his contemporaries. His fame did not come until the Han dynasty applied itself to justifying imperial institutions by favoring orthodoxy. It was then that the theory of government by benevolence outlined by Mencius was recognized as the basis of official policy.

Mencius' work, which is quite brief, seems to have been handed down without much deterioration. It is easy to read. A brilliant writer, Mencius is more of a polemicist than a thinker. He likes to put himself on the stage and argue with great people.[6] He presented himself as a man who had set out to publish the principles of Confucius in order to prevent "the words of Yang tseu and Mö tseu (filling) the World."[7] He defended Confucian wisdom by defining it as an *intermediate wisdom*, equally far removed from two pernicious utopias. Mencius is a politician, and argues as a rhetorician; the opponents he attacks head-on are not the ones he most desires to reach. His real opponents are the Legists. He opposes the government of the Laws to the *government of the Sages*.

The adepts of the Tao and even those of Mö tseu could have no sympathy for a doctrine that denied the value of wisdom. Mencius addresses them in order to win them over. He attacks only what may be extreme in his own tendencies. He tries to divert them from pure individualism (which he presents them, in Yang tseu, as crude egoism), or from fanaticism and sectarian devotion to the Public Good (accusing Mö tseu of denying the value of domestic sentiments). Thus, he writes (caring little about being fair):

> "Yang tseu starts from (everyone) by himself. He would not have plucked out a single hair for the benefit of the Empire. Mö tseu, (is) the affection that does not distinguish, if it had to be crushed (from) the neck (to) the heel for the benefit of the Empire, it would have done so."
>
> "Those who leave Mö tseu go to Yang tseu, those who leave Yang tseu go to Mö tseu. They would have to go to the literati (*jou*: the followers of Confucius)![8] They should only be welcomed. Those who argue with the disciples of Yang and Mö are like those who, chasing a pig when it is already in the stall, continue to call and chase it."[9]

Mencius, instead of critically analyzing the theories, prefers to appeal to sentiment. He shames a disciple of Mö tseu for the stinginess of burying parents with

---

6   For example, King Houei of Wei (died ca. 323 B.C.), and the crown prince of T'eng.
7   Mencius, L., p. 158 (§ 9).
8   Mencius, L., p. 340 (§ 1).
9   *Ibid*, p. 367 (§ 2).

parsimony. Is it not through them that affection begins? Here the man returns at once to *good ideas*.[10]

To win over his opponents, Mencius takes much from them. His orthodoxy is based on syncretism.

The Legists expect nothing from the good will of men and everything from coercion alone. Mencius counterattacks by borrowing from the Taoists[11] their optimism. He asserts that "the great man (the *ta jen*) is the one who has not lost his *heart* as a newborn."[12] Only, when he speaks thus, he is not thinking of the native simplicity which all civilization distorts.[13] He means: only the great man (i.e., who works not with his muscles, but with his heart, who lives nobly),[14] can, unlike the "little people" (*siao jen*), because he escapes all self-interested activity, freely develop natural feelings of benevolence and compassion. The morality of Mencius is a *moral* (aristocratic) *of the heart*.

There is no one who, without even thinking of reward or praise, would not want to save a child who has fallen into a well.[15] All men have "a compassionate heart." This is the "principle" of *jen* (of human friendship), while the principle of equity (*yi*), ritual sense (*li*), and discernment (*tche*) is found in the heart's sensitivity to shame, modesty, acquiescence, or contradiction.[16] These principles, which are common to all humans and which make it possible to say that the essence of man is good (*chan*),[17] are only developed in a noble and distinguished way (*leang*), constituting the four fundamental qualities, if we cultivate them. In the gross state, "they do not even allow one to serve one's parents." Nourished, and transformed into *jen, yi, li* and *tche*, they "enable the whole world to be preserved from all evil."[18]

Men, according as they nourish in themselves what is great and noble or what is small and vile, are great Men or small persons.[19] Only in great Men do qualities become excellent (*leang*). *Excellence of heart depends on education and education on the status of life*.

> "In good years, common people are mostly honest; in bad years, most become violent. It is not that Heaven has bestowed upon them a different constitution, but that (in the latter case) the conditions of life have been sufficient to *degrade the heart*."[20]

---

10   *Ibid.*, at p. 135 (§ 1).
11   Remarkable fact: Mencius avoids fighting and even naming the Taoists, whom he could not fail to know; he may even have met Tchouang tseu in Ts'i.
12   Mencius, L., p. 198.
13   See, for a contrary interpretation, Pelliot, *Meou tseu ou les Doutes levés*, p. 561.
14   Mencius, L., p. 125 (§ 6).
15   *Ibid.*, p. 78 (§ 3). Similarly, Mencius admits that (despite the taboo that separates them) a brother-in-law may reach out to his sister-in-law if she is about to drown. The intention, the heart, prevails over ritual forms.
16   *Ibid.*, p. 79 (§ 4-7). These principles are as essential to man as his four limbs.
17   *Ibid.*, pp. 110 ff.
18   *Ibid.*, p. 80 (§7).
19   *Ibid.*, pp. 292, 293 (§2).
20   *Ibid.*, p. 280 (§ 1).

Certainly, in no human heart are friendly and equitable dispositions (*jen* and *yi*) absent.

"For men to lose the excellence of the heart, they must be like trees under the axe."

But it is also necessary, for trees to grow, that day after night and night after day, rain and dew should moisten them. Without proper nourishment, nothing grows.[21] Excellence of heart (*leang sin*) is not innate, in the exact sense of the word. It results from the cultivation of a seed of goodness, like a seed of barley that benefits from good soil, from a happy year.[22] The honest man, the *kiun tseu*, the *cultivated man*, is the only one who can lead the noble life that makes a noble nature flourish. All his actions are inspired by the intention of ennobling his heart.[23] He is the only one who can lead the noble life that makes a noble nature flourish.

Mencius does not merely direct the tendency to naturalistic optimism so profound in his compatriots toward an ideal of humanistic culture.[24] After having attracted the Taoists to Confucius, he continues to work to attract the disciples of Mö tseu to the Sage.

The latter attached great importance to the material conditions of life; it was in this respect that they came dangerously close to the worst enemies of the Scholar-officials, the Legists. Like the Legists – and this is their main originality, in the Confucian School – Mencius was interested in economics. However, he was interested in it with moral concerns, like Mö tseu, and, like the latter, to defend a conservative utopia. He advised the princes to restore the *tsing* system,[25] to abolish individual property and taxation, to distribute land periodically and to demand only serfdom[26] or tithes, to abolish customs, and to impose, not taxes on goods, but a simple tax on market stalls.[27] He was hostile to the regime of the *tsing* system,[28] but he was not a conservative.

Mencius was hostile to the regime of tyrannies and to all the innovations which served the Legists to introduce into China the idea of Law and the idea of the State. He conceived of no other government than that in which the adviser is not a technician but a learned man.

---

21   Ibid., pp. 283-284 (§ 3).
22   Ibid., p. 280 (§ 2).
23   My interpretation is similar to that given by Liang Chi-Chao, (History of Political Thought, 54) and is opposed to the thesis (Maspero, *La Chine antique*, p. 552) which states that Mencius, like the Taoists (…) admits "the dualistic character of the human mind". Mencius merely contrasts noble culture with plebeian coarseness.
24   Taoist inspiration is manifested in the formula "Man, in essence, tends to the good, as water descends". Legge, p. 271.
25   *Civ. Chin.*
26   In the original French, the word translated as "servitude" is "*corvée*", meaning free and compulsory work rendered by the vassals to their lord (TN).
27   Mencius, L., pp. 75-76 (§ 1 ff.).
28   Mencius, L., pp. 75-76 (§ 1 ff.).

Only the great man can right what is wrong in the Prince's heart.[29] Thus, before any economic measure, Mencius demands that the sovereign "honor the wise and employ the skillful,"[30] i.e., scholars inspired by Confucian teaching on *jen* and *yi*. And, likewise, when he defends the system of common tenure and collective labor in the field reserved for the Prince, he immediately adds that the first duty of the lord is the maintenance of the schools. Schools have the sole task of teaching the (five kinds of) relations between men (those of lord to vassal, father to son, elder to younger, husband to wife, friend to companion). This teaching should be sufficient to reign "mutual affection"[31] among the little ones and to "strengthen the country." It tends to curb the wandering spirit of the little ones, always ready to enlist in sects or associations of thieves. This is the worst disaster, the one to be feared in bad years, when people (despite their good nature) become "violent".

> "This is the way of conduct (*tao*) of the common people. When they have secure livelihoods, they have secure hearts. But without secure livelihoods, there are no secure hearts. When hearts cease to be secure, there are no ramblings and debaucheries to which the people do not yield. They engage in crime. But if, then, they are persecuted and punished, one is catching the people in the net."[32]

Here he duly criticizes the punitive mood of the Legists. And here he also affirms the benefits of Confucian teaching:

> "To have no sure means of existence, and to keep a sure heart, is what only nobles (*che*, equivalent to *jou*, literate) are capable of doing."[33]

The prince, well advised, who practices *jen* and does not let the Legists catch the people in the net, must provide the latter with sustenance and instruction. The principle of government must be benevolence, its object the *ennoblement of the hearts* of the little people, while the function of moral culture is to strengthen in every man the intention of ennobling himself.

This is the means by which, while attempting to turn his contemporaries away from the sectarian demagogy of Mö tseu and to ruin the influence of the technicians of government by laws, Mencius endeavors to induce "enlightened despots (*ming kiun, ming tchou*)"[34] to patronize orthodox teachings.

---

29 Mencius, L., p. 186. Thus it is advised "the prince practices *jen* and there is no one who does not practice *jen*. He practices *yi* and there is no one who does not practice it. The prince is correct and everything is correct. As soon as (the adviser) has made the prince correct, the country is established.

30 Mencius, L., p. 75 (§ 1).

31 Mencius, L., p. 118 (§ 6-10).

32 Mencius, L., p. 115 (§ 3). See (*Civ. Chin.*) how the Wou emperor's lawmakers used the laws to "ensnare the people" and enslave them.

33 Mencius, L., p. 23 (§ 20).

34 Mencius, who avoided speaking of the Lawgivers, borrows from them this significant designation of the ruler {L., p. 23 (§ 21-22)}: "An enlightened prince fixes the means of existence

Mencius' ideas are less original than intelligent. Perhaps it is for this and for their lack of precision (conducive to commentary) that they have gained fame. In fact, what made Mencius famous was not his rhetorical thesis, but his attitude.

He was the first champion of orthodoxy. He was also the first polemicist who knew how to present an aristocratic morality in democratic colors, and the first who knew how to use sophistry to shut the mouths of tyrants by sounding old principles.[35] He proclaimed that those who work with the mind (*sin*, the heart) must be maintained by those who work with the muscles, whom they must govern.[36] He was the first of the scholars. And he defined the type.

Always ready to give courageous rebukes, but never asking for an discussion, never taking the first step, and always demanding to be invited as he should be, willingly accepting an office, but refusing mere gifts, proud, disinterested, concerned with honor and independence, the scholar must, by his whole attitude, inspire in all the people the feeling that no one, not even a prince, is superior to the Sage.

II. Siun tseu: Government by Ritual

Siun tseu, like Mencius, is not what we would call a brilliant writer. He is, however, an original and profound thinker. He, too, was influenced by several factors, although he did not try to cunningly reconcile them, but was able to extract from them a perfectly coherent system. He defended and consolidated in Confucianism the sense of the social and the positive spirit.

Siun K'ouang (or Siun tseu, sometimes called Siun-king: Siun the minister, because he received an honorary title at the court of Ts'i) was descended from a powerful family related to the lords of Tsin. His life is not well known. If one were to use the historical data contained in the brief biography dedicated to him by Sseu-ma Ts'ien,[37] one could attribute to him an existence of almost one hundred and fifty years. He seems to have died at a very advanced age, about 328-325 BC. He was born in the country of Chao and visited most of the great courts, those of Ts'i, Ts'in and Ch'ou. Towards the end of his life he directed a flourishing School, devoted mainly to the teaching of ritual technique. Current editions of his work contain 32 sections, of which only 27 (some say 4) are considered authentic.[38] Many of his developments are of technical interest only, and some of them smack of scholastic

---

for his people, so that each has enough to subsist and support his parents, wives, and children… otherwise how can we ask the people to cultivate rites and equity, *li-yi*?"

35   Mencius, L., p. 231 (§6). Cf. *ibid*, p. 359. A prince cannot transmit his power: he presents a successor to Heaven and then to the people; Heaven and then the people accept. The people are the noblest, then come the altars of the earth and of the harvest; and, lastly, the prince.

36   Mencius L., p. 125 (§ 6) quotes this adage during an oratorical tournament against Hiu-hing, a physiocratic economist.

37   *SMT*, ch. LXXIV.

38   Maspero. *La Chine antique*, p. 565, note. (Cf. Bubs, *The works of Hsüntze*).

amplification. But Siun tseu was able to condense the essence of his theses into a few short and vigorous passages.[39]

Siun tseu's originality consists in the very reflective and inquiring effort, which led him to constitute a morality of perfection; this morality of positive spirit and liberal tendency is entirely commanded by a humanistic rationalism.

Siun tseu owes much to the Legists and Taoists, whose authoritarian empiricism and mystical aestheticism he tried to overcome. He owes even more to the wisdom traditions of his nation. The deep taste for measure, rule and intelligibility that animates all his countrymen gave him the impetus. He was, however, the first to place Reason (*Li*) at the center of philosophical interest. He sees Reason as both a product of human social activity – for the Confucian spirit inspires him even more than the spirit of the Legists – and a principle of objectivity, for he uses the theses of Tchouang tseu, but without agreeing to recognize in *Li* that germ of universal indeterminacy which, for the Taoists, constitutes the essence of the Tao.

Like the Taoists and the Legists, Siun tseu starts from the opposition of the natural and the social. Unlike Mencius, he makes no concessions to Taoism on the fundamental point; he refuses to identify goodness and nature. He refuses to do so, not out of pessimism, but, on the contrary, because he has a very high idea of civilization, a very high idea of the rank that society has allowed man to attain in nature.

> "The Elements (Water and Fire) have *k'i* (*breath*) without having Life; plants have Life without having Knowledge (*tche*); animals have Knowledge, but not (the sense of) Equity (*yi*); men have Breath, Life, Knowledge and, in addition, Equity (the sense of yours and mine). That is why they are the noblest thing in the world. The strength of men is not equal to that of buffaloes, nor their speed to that of horses; yet buffaloes and horses are at their service. Why? *It is because men know how to form a society (neng kiun) and the other beasts do not. And why do men know how to form a society? It is because they know how to make a distribution (neng fen). But how can these distributions (fen) be made?* Thanks to equity! When equity presides over distributions, there is good agreement. From good agreement arises unity, and from unity arises abundance of force. This abundance of strength gives power, and power enables (men) to *master* (*all*) *things*. Thus they have mansions where they dwell; obeying the order of the seasons, they rule the ten thousand beings and impartially do good (*kien li*)[40] to everyone. All this they achieve through Equality of Distribution (*fen yi*). Men cannot live without forming a society. But if they were to form a society without making distributions, there would be strife, anarchy, separation, and conse-

---

39   Two sections, certainly authentic, have been translated, the 22nd (on correct designations) into French, by Duyvendack (*TP*, 1924), the 23rd (on the bad nature of man), into English, by Legge, in the Prolegomena to his translation of Mencius. On the doctrine of Siun tseu, Duyvendack has published (Études de philosophie chinoise, *Revue philosophique*, 1930) an excellent analysis.

40   Compare this thesis with that of Mö tseu, *supra*, in this same Book, ch. II, sec. II.

quently weakness. Now, reduced to this weakness, men would not have any control over things."[41]

Thus society is the principle of the eminent dignity of men, being the condition of all social life (not exactly the division of labor), but the distribution of attributions (*fen*), i.e., of ranks as well as of jobs, of goods as well as of dignities. This primary condition of social life determines the object of society, which is not, as some Legists would have us believe, the simple control of things or the power of human groups. This object is the constitution of a properly moral activity. For there to be a society, and not an anarchic gathering, men must acquire the wisdom that makes them accept the distinction between yours and mine. They must practice Yi (Equity). Although they would not do so, left to their own nature, they decide to do so under the influence of that set of conventions which are the Rites (*Li*).

The power of societies and the moral value of human beings have a common foundation, not natural, but added to nature; civilization, an invention of the Wise, a human invention, born of the needs of social life. The good is not in nature; it is society that produces it.

This is the meaning of Siun Tseu's famous thesis: "Human nature is evil; what is good in it is artificial" (*wei*). It must be understood, not that this nature is *fundamentally* evil, but that the good is a contribution, an improvement.[42]

The evil of which Siun tseu speaks is not a metaphysical vice, nor the opposite of a hypostatized Good. It is only selfishness, the tendency not to yield, the appetite that wants to monopolize, the desire that opposes the self to the other and turns into violence as soon as its satisfaction is taken away.[43] Nor is it a material evil. Society would not suppress it if it aimed merely to control things in order to increase the possibilities of satisfaction. It is a psychological vice from which civilization, by artifice, derives some benefit, for it teaches – not to repress (Siun Tzu is not, like Mö Tzu or Lao tseu, a sad sectarian or a mystic) – but to discipline and educate the appetites. Far from being an enemy of the arts, Siun tseu believes in their virtue. True to the Confucian tradition, he saw music and dance as more than mere entertainment. He saw in them a kind of training for good understanding. Dances and songs (provided they are not irritating and dissolute, like the melodies of Cheng's country) maintain human harmony.[44] Feasts, insofar as they are ritualized, appease the appetite for merriment and the passion for play.[45] But for the more brutal appetites constant discipline is needed. The supreme art that provides this is etiquette.

---

41 Siun tseu, section 9; Liang Chi-Chao, *History of Chinese Political Thought*, p. 63.
42 Siun tseu, section 23 (Legge, *Chinese Classics*, II, p. 82 of the Prolegomena).
43 *Ibidem*.
44 It is not impossible that Siun tseu, without saying so too explicitly, attributed a kind of cathartic value to the dancing and singing festivals. He did not believe in the reality of the Sovereign above, nor in the reality of the gods, nor even of the spirits, but he approved of the ceremonies performed in their honor, the sacrifices to Heaven, the sacrifices to the Ground; these ceremonies, by the very fact of being regulated, serve to purge the hearts of men of fears or hopes that might disturb them.
45 Siun tseu, chapter 14.

Only rites (*li*) can bring forth and prosper the spirit of equity (*yi*). It is through doing good that *well-being* is created.

All men have desires and *share* the same desires: to eat, to warm themselves, to rest. *All men are, in essence (sing), the same thing: this is evil.*[46]

Rites are the artifice from which good arises. Rites, in fact, enable men to accept a *conventional distribution of labors and resources.*

This distribution, which *specializes appetites* and *doses them, has a first merit*: without it, there would be no way of satisfying needs.

> "What is the origin of rites? Men are born with desires. These desires cannot be fulfilled, and it is not possible for them not to seek to do so. If they seek to do so without *rules* and *measures* of distribution and sharing, it is impossible to prevent disputes. Disputes lead to anarchy, and anarchy to exhaustion (of goods). The ancient kings hated anarchy. That is why they instituted the Rites and Equity (*li yi*), to proceed with distributions (*fen*), in order to satisfy men's desires and give (to each) what he sought. *They made sure that desires were not limited by things, nor things exhausted by desires, but that there was (on the contrary) a symmetrical development on both sides.*"[47]

This passage, which is followed by an exposition of several *rules of protocol*, is of twofold interest. It demonstrates that, for Siun tseu, the *distribution of activities* underpinning the social order consists less in the distribution of labor than in the distribution of jobs and honors. Along with the specification of desires, the protocol dosage of appetites, firstly, opposes the exhaustion of things by men and, secondly, contributes, first by *singularizing* and then *hierarchizing* individuals, to a development of personalities which, finally, brings to the surface the feeling of human dignity.

On the other hand (and this is its main interest), this passage reveals the primordial virtue of a *distribution of jobs*. If anything good follows from it, leading to a better life, the principle of progress lies in the absolutely *conventional* character of the distribution. From a mass of men equally mediocre in themselves, because of the vulgarity of their appetites which are identical in principle, society draws, by decree, a hierarchy of ennobled personalities, in unequal proportions, by the employment with which they are invested. It is, then, the simple social *conventions* which, *in themselves*, create the *best* in man, *realizing* this best in each of them by the mere fact that the rites oblige him to act well, that is, to conform his conduct to his work and to the rank and dignity it confers on him.

Siun tseu has thus demonstrated his thesis. The good in man does not belong to his nature; it does not belong to the essence common to all humans (*sing*). The good comes from an improvement imposed by society, the only one capable of drawing *moral individualities out of raw man.*

Siun tseu believes in the perfectibility of the individual, just as he believes in the material progress made possible by social life. However, only moral perfection

---

46 Section 4, Liang Chi-Chao, *op. cit.*, p. 64.
47 Section 19, see *SMT*, II, p. 212.

and individual training in good behavior and good thinking really count for him. But every individual can only be trained in goodness by penetrating *li* and *yi*; by learning to respect the hierarchy of fortunes, dignities and talents. *The principle of government is fused with the principle of education*; one governs by means of rites, for it is by means of rites that one is educated. Every man improves by the mere fact of knowing the benefits of the *conventional distribution* to all imposed by society. To this end, he must submit to the *rules of etiquette* derived from this fundamental convention. *Individual cultivation is thus conditioned on the acceptance of moral and social conformity.*

Thus Siun tseu is often accused of having introduced into the Confucian tradition a conservative spirit from which, thanks to the theory of *jen*, Confucius escaped.[48] For the Master, human dignity is acquired through moral reflection practiced freely in a group of friends. Siun tseu seems to have a less liberal conception of culture. Mencius names four essential virtues: *jen, yi, li* and *tche*.[49] Siun tseu, omitting (apparently) *jen* and *tche*, the friendly dispositions and moral discernment, retains only *yi* and *li*. But does he conceive of *li-yi*, of which he makes the principle of all good, as an internal principle, after the manner of Mencius? He is reproached for speaking of it in the same tone in which the Legists, desirous of using only objective rules (*fa*: law), speak of the set square or the compass.[50] Siun tseu writes, in fact:

"It is necessary to take as a rule what no one can falsify."[51]

And he adopts for the Rites the definition which the Legists give of the Laws.

"In the chalk line is the perfection of the law… in the set square or the compass is the perfection of the square and the round. In the Rites is the perfection of human conduct."[52]

Siun tseu believes in the need for *objective rules*.

However, he does not make good out of simple coercion. He does not have a strictly authoritarian, rigid, mechanical conception of moral or even social good. "A piece of wood that is bent must be softened and straightened so that it becomes straight"; similarly, human nature that is not good "must submit to the action of Masters and Rules or Models (*fa*)."[53] "The most convenient way to cultivate oneself is to enter into a *friendly relationship* with a Master. *Fulfilling the Rites is next*."[54] The

---

48 Liang Chi-Chao, *op. cit.*, pp. 66 ff.
49 Cf. *supra*, in this same chapter, sec. I.
50 Liang Chi-Chao, *op. cit.*, p. 70. Siun tseu was a friend of Li Sseu, who was to become Che Houang-ti's chief adviser, and is said to have been Han Fei tseu's teacher. There is nothing in his work to suggest that he thought of increasing the power of the state, or that he was a supporter of the authoritarian manner of the Legists.
51 Section 23.
52 Section 21. *SMT*, III, p. 227.
53 Section 23.
54 Section 1. Compare with Section 23: "Human nature, being evil, needs teachers and models."

Master plays the role of the artist; the Rites, that of the set square or the chalk line. But where do the Rites come from? Siun tseu seldom forgets to recall[55] that it was the *Ancient Kings* or *Sages* who, proceeding to the conventional distribution of the works, instituted the *li yi*. The rules necessary for *moral education (as for government)* are objective without being *external to mankind*. They are imperatives, but they do not exert a coercive or mechanical action. Civilization, which conditions individual improvements, is based on a collective effort of improvement, material and moral. It is civilization which, by providing objective rules (*li-yi*), presides, through the Master, over the progress of the good in each man, and, consequently, over the formation in each individual of *moral discernment* and Reason (*li*).

The true has no other origin than the good. It escapes the vulgar, the little people (*siao jen*), because "what they hear with their ears comes out of their mouths." Only the saint has the inner calm that allows him "to fix in the heart, to extend in the four limbs (to assimilate into the whole being)"[56] the teachings that will make him a teacher and model.

The only essential teaching is that of good behavior.[57] Indeed, "he who (only) remains within the limits of the rites is capable of good thinking and reflection." And, conversely, "only he who is capable of reflection and firmness... is a saint."[58] In other words: only moral perfection leads to true knowledge.[59] Moral perfection is a fruit of civilization; likewise, knowledge would be impossible for men who had remained frustrated and simple. If men can attain reality, it is because they have been civilized by the Ancient Kings, by the Sages.[60] The latter have given to each reality (*che*) a designation (*ming*); this designation is correct (*tcheng*), because, by the mere fact that it results from a commonly respected *distribution* of different names for different beings, it prevents, in *social practice*, any error, that is to say, any discussion.[61]

Siun tseu, when he takes up the ancient doctrine of correct designations, is careful to eliminate anything it may contain of magical realism. What constitutes the property of names is not an efficacy that allows them to summon and arouse reality. They only serve to designate, but they designate with profit. The attribution of names is the result of a completely arbitrary convention which, precisely because it is a social convention, imposes itself on everyone and allows us to agree.

Names have precisely the same merits as rites. They constitute a valid symbology for individuals as a rule. An objective rule, but not an external one. People reason correctly (just as they act correctly), learn to think correctly (just as they learn to do correctly), come out of stupidity (just as they come out of uniformity, i.e. evil)

---

55 Cf. *above*, in this same section.
56 Section 1.
57 Siun tseu personally taught the rites and had a certain contempt for the teaching of poetry (*Che king*) and especially for that of history.
58 Section 19.
59 Duyvendack, Études de philosophie chinoise, p. 387.
60 The opposition with the Taoists is absolute.
61 Section 22. *TP*, 1924, pp. 234 ff.

by conforming to conventional symbolism formed by verbal signs and ritual gestures.

Rites and language serve in the first place, when properly practiced, to suppress arguments and disorder, disputes and anarchy. Practiced with gentleness (and under the guidance of a Master whose teaching penetrates "into the four limbs," into the deepest part of the being), they *introduce into the mind the calm which they also bring to society*. From this calm arises true knowledge: it is the sign that the mind is totally "open" to Reason.

To define this inner calm, Siun tseu resorts to Taoist metaphors,[62] and compares the human heart "to a pool of water." When nothing stirs it, the muddy sludge remains at the bottom. The surface, clear and bright (*ts'ing ming*), makes the smallest eyelash appear" to those who look at it.[63] "Perfect clarity and purity" are necessary for the heart to obtain a completely correct representation of realities. All this may be expressed by saying that the heart must, in order to eliminate error, "be kept *empty*, unified, in *stillness of state*." The remarks following these metaphors show that Siun tseu (with a completely different and even more resolute orientation than Tchouang tseu, whose analyses undoubtedly helped him) is a pure intellectual.

What he means by emptiness of heart is not an ecstatic emptiness, but a state of impartiality. Error comes from *incomplete judgments*[64] made by the mind (*sin*: heart) when a passion "clouds and obstructs" it completely. This is the principle of Siun tseu's criticism of the doctrines of his opponents, for example, when he reproaches Mö tseu, Houei tseu and Tchouang tseu, who were "obsessed" by the consideration of the useful, the expressed or the natural, for having forgotten culture or realities, or civilization. Siun tseu refuses to distinguish between ideas and feelings and between the good and the true. Judgment must refer to the totality of the object. It has no value if it is not the result of an *effort of synthesis* of the mind. Unlike the Taoist masters, Siun tseu does not ask the mind to passively reflect the flow of moving appearances. What he calls knowing is something very different from mere perception of the instantaneous. When he speaks of the unification of the heart, he is thinking of a *synthetic operation* that completes a review, carried out, not to be incomplete and partial, with the most minute attention. The buzzing of a fly can, according to him, disturb judgment. The activity of the mind, as he conceives it, is nothing like wandering meditation or ecstatic flight. It must consist of thoughtful, tenacious and serious meditation. Its aim is to "unblock" the mind by putting in order the partial passions that "shut the door to the Supreme Judge (*Ta Li*)".

---

62   This led Maspero to attribute to Siun tseu a mysticism which clashes with the whole of his doctrine, so coherent (cf. Duyvendack, *op. cit.*, pp. 385 ff.); Maspero confuses the synthetic effort of the mind with the state of trance in which the mind is transported out of itself (in *La Chine antique*, p. 572). There is no expression in Siun tseu (or in Tchouang tseu, which is more intellectual than mystical) to justify this gloss.

63   Section 21 (from which all the following quotations are also taken).

64   Siun tseu insists on the illusions of the senses due to the passions: "One mistakes a rock for a tiger ready to pounce if, at night, one allows oneself to be dominated by fear".

This is what Siun tseu calls Reason. The expression is significant. The word *Li*, used long before Siun tseu to designate any principle of order, is opposed to the word *tao*.⁶⁵ Tao evokes the idea of sovereign Power, Li that of the *administration of justice*, at the same time as that of work well finished and carried out taking into account the adjustment of the parts to the whole. Siun tseu refuses to confuse truth with instantaneous and personal intuition. He believes that there are rules for judging and that the handling of these rules is acquired through education. The individual possesses them after having trained himself to make correct, and then distinguished, use of the *conventional symbolism* (rites and language) *conventional* that has put order into thought as well as morals.

However, the teaching of rites constitutes the essential part of the training that leads individuals to conceive of the good and to practice the true.

Reason (*Li*: Siun tseu writes respectfully: *Ta Li*), the supreme Judge, allows the Sage, when he incorporates it, to know the World and to govern it. He who succeeds in "opening" his mind and making it fully possessed, brings "perfect clarity and purity."

> "Of the ten thousand beings, there is not one who does not appear to him and whose rank he cannot estimate without error.⁶⁶ Sitting in his house, the World appears to him,⁶⁷ and while he remains in the present, he can estimate the more distant past. He penetrates the ten thousand beings and knows their essence. He examines order and disorder and understands their principle. He draws the warp and woof of the universe and *distributes to the ten thousand beings their functions*."

Such is the power of the great Man animated by Reason.

Truth and good reign in the world if the Sage governs it, that is, if the world is governed by the rites, by the *li-yi* in which *Civilization* and *Reason* express themselves together.

III. Tong Chong-Chou: Rule by History

Siun tseu's influence was considerable. It gave a new impetus to the study of rites. This fashion may account for the fact that (despite the early Han's disdain for etiquette for nearly half a century) the ritual literature that flourished in the third century BC left abundant memories. Once the fashion was restored, it was easy to assemble the elements of which two of the classics, the *Yi li* and the *Li hi*, are formed.⁶⁸ The reading and commentary of these Rituals became the basis of the

---

65   Siun tse (same section) frequently uses the word *Tao* in the sense of human reason. "The *Tao* is the honest man's way of acting. The *Tao* is practical reason; the *Li*, pure reason and practical reason.

66   Appropriately, Siun tseu's logic is a logic of hierarchy.

67   Cf. Lao tseu's formula, *supra*, in this same Book, ch. III, sec. II. Siun tseu, who expressly claims to be Confucian and orthodox, works for syncretism.

68   The *Yi li* is a manual for masters of ceremonies, the *Li ki* a composite collection in which ritual matters occupy the largest place.

teaching intended to train upright individuals and officials. Moreover, from then on, people became accustomed to read history by first examining the actions of ancient personages to decide whether or not they conformed to etiquette.

This collusion of archaeology and ritualism was not at all in keeping with Siun tseu's ideas. A positive and critical spirit, certainly traditionalist but not reactionary, Siun tseu, like a good intellectual, distrusted archaic tastes and even history. He opposed Mencius, for whom the rule of the Sage was to resemble that of Yao and Chouen. What, said Siun tseu, could be known of these ancient heroes?[69] But, once consolidated in power, the Han tried to justify the institutions of imperial administration by means of precedents. It was recalled that Confucius had written the *Tch'ouen ts'ieou*, weighing each of its terms so that it contained a judgment, i.e., a *ritual teaching*. Two schools of commentators on this ancient chronicle, the Kong-yang School and the Kou-leang School, were much admired. The disputes of their adherents sometimes took the form of jousting in the Council of State.[70]

There then appeared the theory of government by history, which was to give a new orientation to orthodox doctrine. Tong Chong-chou was one of the great advocates of this theory.

Tong Chong-chou[71] was a scholar who thought he would succeed in administration. He held only secondary positions and ended his retired days writing. Three important speeches and a collection of essays (most of which are considered authentic) have survived;[72] but the main part of his work consisted of commentaries intended to illustrate one of the interpretations of *Tch'ouen ts'ieou*, that of Kong-yang.

Tong Chong-chou, more than a thinker, is a representative figure. He was hostile to the Legists and a supporter of government by benevolence. He admitted that human nature needs to be perfected, that music can help, and rites even more, and that, consequently, the first duty of government is to instruct the people. This duty is all the more urgent the more agitated the times are. To check the popular tendency to quarrel and disorder, it is necessary to restore good manners.

This can be done by propagating Confucian doctrine and spreading the six arts, i.e.[73] the teachings of the six canonical books: *Che king* (Book of Odes); *Chou king* (Book of History); *Li king* (Book of Rites: the *Yi li*?), *Yo king* (Book of Music, now lost); *Yi king* (Book of Mutations) and *Tch'ouen ts'ieou* (The Annals). But it is also

---

69   Section 5.
70   *SMT*, Introd., p. CLI.
71   He was born about 175 and died about 105 BC. He was appointed "scholar of vast erudition" in the reign of Emperor King (156-141 BC), and under Emperor Wou held provincial offices; he had to resign because, while speaking of prodigies, he allowed himself, according to his enemies, to criticize the Han government. He composed three famous speeches in response to a questionnaire from Emperor Wou (*Ts'ien Han chou*, ch. 56). His works, consisting of several articles, form today the *Tch'ouen ts'ieou fan lou*. Cf. Franke, *Das Confuzianische Dogma und die chinesische Staatsreligion*, Woo Kang, *Les trois théories politiques du Tch'ouen ts'ieou* and Hackmann, *Chinesische Philosophie*, pp. 205 ff.
72   Woo Kang, *op. cit.*, p. 51.
73   *Ibid.*, p. 73.

necessary to exterminate heterodox doctrines and to institute a corps of official interpreters of the classics.[74]

Tong Chong-chou, as can be seen, was decidedly orthodox. He asked (and his advice was followed by the Han) that the officials charged with teaching by example good ideas and good conduct should be chosen from among the learned. He demanded of them a noble selflessness. Officials should neither seek wealth nor, above all, hoard it; they should not "keep their goods in chests, as the little people do," but circulate wealth. This was the duty of nobles in feudal times. The duties of rulers are different from those of ordinary people, Tong Chong-chou said. He deserves to be ranked among the group of men who, under the Han, worked to create a kind of official class that lived by propagating an orthodox doctrine. Neither Confucius, no doubt, nor Siun tseu would have wanted to confuse wisdom with bookish teaching and caste morality.

Siun Tseu and Confucius were moralists with a positive spirit and a strictly humanistic tendency. Tong Chong-chou represents a political tendency. Therefore, this scholar was primarily concerned with constructing a *myth* that would facilitate the governmental task and, moreover, the reign of the orthodox caste in administration.

The starting point of this myth is the old idea, on which Mencius insisted, that the Prince exercises his power under the control of Heaven and the people. This formula was once understood to mean that political initiative is limited by a set of traditional rules endowed with a kind of religious prestige. But, on the one hand, the Legists have shown that the maintenance of customary statutes deprives social activity of the effective output that a large State needs, and, on the other hand, in a large State, the voice of the people, which is that of Heaven, hardly reaches the Prince. The partisans of orthodoxy are resigned, no doubt (as they should be), to let the State legislate to satisfy its new needs. On the other hand, they claim for the officials – who must be literate, the new nobility, the custodian of the old traditions – the privilege of controlling governmental practice by giving the Prince the voice of ancient wisdom.

Here again, a corporate practice is at the origin of a theory. It is the ancient practice of rebuke, the sacred duty of the vassal.[75] Government by history was the theory, which purported to grant to the "learned and erudite" an eminent power: the privilege of a kind of censorship.

The decisions of the Prince and his councilors would be justified and condemned by using precedents, that is, by interpreting the facts of history. The latter and their decrees would be judged by Heaven and the people, as soon as a scholar, having presented a *historical fact*, had interpreted it by showing what was, in the past, in a *stated situation analogous* to the present one, the judgment of the people and Heaven. This theory has had a serious consequence. It has prevented any prog-

---

74 In 136, Emperor Wou created the office of "scholars with extensive knowledge of the Five Canonical Books." In 124, fifty disciples joined this College of scholars, destined to become high officials.

75 *Civ Chin.*, pp. 326 ff, 425 ff.

ress of the historical spirit in China. It has led to the conception of history as an *ordering of the past* considered effective *for the organization of the present.*

The most curious parts of Tong Chong-chou's work are those in which he asserts the principle that each change of dynasty corresponds to a reclassification of the old dynasties.[76] The doctrine of the Three Kingdoms and the Four Modalities are related to this principle. The Four Modalities correspond to four types of institutions which must succeed one another as the Seasons succeed one another. In the same way, the Black Kingdom is succeeded by the White Kingdom; then comes the Red Kingdom; then the Black Kingdom appears again, each of which carries a particular formula of civilization. All this scholastic history allows us to reconstruct the past with astonishing precision. Tong Chong-chou does not hesitate, by virtue of a sort of inverse determinism, to present as the true portrait of a real personage the characteristic traits, according to the Kingdom or the Modality brought out, which theory imposes on a dynastic Founder.[77]

This fabulous construction, which must not waste or spoil historical folklore, is linked, by means of a gloss, to an insignificant fact. When a secondary character of the *Tch'ouen ts'ieou* is designated by a certain title, one sees in this title (which is supposed to have been given with intention) an indication of the principles of etiquette which were really appropriate in the period of the *Tch'ouen ts'ieou*, which enables one to restore to its true correctness the whole history of ancient China, justifying, as an essential benefit, a rule such as one would like to see applied at the present day.[78] In defining each Kingdom or each Modality, we have traced the plan of government necessary at such and such a time in history.

The theory of government by history is summed up in the idea that history and government depend upon the art of the Calendar.

Thanks to this idea, orthodoxy has been enriched with a very prosperous set of doctrines and techniques, not without a fatal blow to the humanism of Confucius or Siun tseu.

Siun tseu despised divination as well as history. He repudiated speculation about the past, the gods, fate, the unknowable. He condemned the search for signs. As for Confucius, it is said that he always refrained from speaking of supernatural beings and prodigies. But it is the task of the Chroniclers to record prodigies and signs; the *Tch'ouen ts'ieou* (written, it was said, by Confucius) mentions them repeatedly. Following this observation, the Kong-yang school, led by Tong Chong-chou, claimed that history enables us to know the rules of conduct of Heaven.

The first merit of history (that of the chroniclers) is that it reveals the connections between human events and signs, celestial or otherwise (eclipses,

---

76 *Tch'ouen ts'ieou fan lou*, 7; Woo Kang, *op. cit.*, pp. 111 ff.
77 Cf. *supra*, Book II, ch. III, par. II.
78 The gloss which serves as a starting point (*Kong-yang tchouan*, 11th year of Duke Houan) indicates that to confuse the three titles of count, viscount, and baron into one class is to adopt the celestial principle of government, for heaven has three luminaries and the classes of nobility are then reduced to three. If there were five (five elements), then the principle of government would be derived from the earth.

earthquakes, floods, epidemics, famines and monstrosities of all kinds…). Tong Chong-chou, according to the chronicle, while serving as a great counselor in the principality of Kiang-tou, was engaged in explaining, based on the *Tch'ouen ts'ieou*, disasters, prodigies, and the action of Yin and Yang.[79] This, it seems, gave him the opportunity to criticize the acts of the imperial government, and thus nobly fulfill his profession as a scholar (substituting, by virtue of his erudition, his voice for that of the people or that of Heaven). By offering his advice in this way, he did not succeed at the time, but he achieved great glory. At the end of the last century (in 1893), a Chinese reformer admired in Tong Chong-chou the greatest of Confucius' disciples. His doctrine seemed to him capable of leading China on the path of progress.[80]

It is true that Tong Chong-chou contributed mightily to the success of orthodoxy. He brought together the followers of the Yin and Yang Schools, of the Five Elements; all the technicians who speculated on Nature. These scholars threw all folklore into the framework of the old system of classifications and produced a scholasticism. To this scholasticism, scarcely freed from magic, was allied orthodoxy, unfaithful to the humanistic and positive thought of Confucius.

* * *

The solidity of the alliance is confirmed in the time of the Eastern Han dynasty, with works such as the *Po hou t'ong*, written by Pan Kou.[81] The work of Wang Tch'ong (the *Louen heng*), dating from about the same time, also shows the effects of official teaching.[82] Wang Tch'ong was born poor, remained poor, had a very mediocre career, escaped from the slavery of honors, and wrote freely. He was always caustic, sometimes violent, and liked to revise all the ideas of his century. He was a strong spirit. He did not believe in gods, spirits, monsters or miracles. Confucian heroes hardly held sway with him, let alone Taoist saints. He had no respect for history. He was not afraid to talk about legends and forged texts. He distrusted books. And yet there is something bookish in his skepticism. He, who seemed to possess the most attractive qualities of fantasy and vivacity, offered little more than pedantic observations. He commented bitterly, but only commented… He did not go outside the texts and teachings… He wore out his fantasy by glossing over glosses…

Commentators abounded in China from the time the Empire was founded and Orthodoxy began its reign. But it was not until many centuries later that an original thinker reappeared. Buddhism only acclimatized in China by becoming Chi-

---

79 *SMT*, ch. CXXI, and *Ts'ien Han chou*, 27a, p. 5. ff.

80 This is the reformer K'ang Yeou-wei (1858-1927), who was the teacher of Leang K'i-tch'ao (cf. Woo Kang, *The Three Political Theories of Tch'ouen*, p. 164).

81 The *Po hou t'ong* records the work of an imperial commission. The influence of Tong Chong-chou is evident.

82 On Wang Ch'ong (born 27 AD, died ca. 100), one may consult the study which Forke has placed at the head of his translation of the *Louen heng* (*Selected Essays of the Philosopher Wang Ch'ung*). Perhaps Forke shows excessive benevolence when he compares Wang Ch'ong to Lucian and Voltaire.

nese; its most powerful product, the mystical doctrine of the *tch'an* sect, is a form of Taoism thinly disguised as foreign symbolism. Manichaeism may have exerted a more active influence, if indeed from it originated the dualistic tendency of Tchou Hi's rationalism, which is new to China. It is to Tchou Hi (1130-1200), in fact, and to the Song period that we must come to see philosophical activity flourish again. This revival seems to draw its sap from an ancient foundation; the philosophy of the Song is linked – no doubt more faithfully than is usually taught – to the earliest speculations of Chinese thought. This thought is now trying to renew itself. Contact with the West has served as an impetus. However, when it comes to acclimatizing in their own country truly new notions, since they arise from a scientific movement entirely new to the West itself, it is still by ingeniously commenting on the works of their ancient sages that the more modernist Chinese think they will succeed.[83]

It would be a mistake to be surprised at this fidelity to the ancients and the apparent lethargy of philosophical thought. Meditation is, for the Chinese, a game whose subject matters little, but it is the most serious game in the world. Their thought is playing, thrown on a subject of meditation, at a time when they may seem to be engaged only in glossing over. The sayings of the *Yi king*, which in translation seem hopelessly flat and vulgar, have never ceased to be – as for some Westerners the verses of the Bible – a stimulus to the most inquiring and free thought. In China, in fact, thought is not directed to knowledge, but to culture. It is accepted that everything that can be studied helps to develop the personality. This perfecting of the whole being through study, conceived as a play of the whole being, gives a feeling, which is sufficient in itself, of freedom and growth. The ancient sages felt this deeply and expressed it very well. That is why their works were sufficient for their compatriots for many centuries.

To note the triumph of orthodoxy and a long hiatus in philosophical production is not to note a numbness of thought. Discarding all discursive science and concerned only with culture, the Chinese were able to limit themselves to meditation, once their Sages taught them to feel that thought is a source of liberation.

---

83 This is the inspiration for the work of Hu Shih (see *The Development of Logical Method in Ancient China*) and also, but less explicitly, that of Liang Chi-Chao (see *History of Chinese Political Thought*).

Conclusion

The Chinese ask their Sages for subjects conducive to free meditation, not ideas, much less dogmas. It does not matter whether they classify the Master who awakens in them the play of the intellect as Taoist or Confucian; it does not matter whether the practices that prepare them for the liberation of their spirit are aimed at creating the impression of unconditioned autonomy or at creating the feeling of the sovereign dignity of man. Neither the actual purpose of the training, nor the spirit of the methods themselves differ. It is always a matter of training the whole being. Whether holiness or wisdom is sought, whether it is accomplished by sanctifying games or ennobling rites, this training is always inspired by a desire for liberation, and it is always done in a spirit of freedom. In Taoism and Confucianism, even when they degenerate into orthodoxies, even when sectarian or caste interests seem to push toward doctrinal rigorism, the spirit of conciliation does not cease to dominate, and eclecticism remains the norm. The ideal, in both fields, is a complete wisdom. If the proposed wisdom resembles more – among Confucians – a Stoic wisdom (but more or less devoid of religiosity) or, rather – among Taoists – an Epicurean wisdom (but little concerned with science), the common ideal is complete self-knowledge, or rather self-mastery. This self-mastery, and the knowledge it brings of both the self and the world (for the universe is one), is achieved through the release of appetites and desires. The result is an exalted sense of power. As soon as he feels master of himself, both the Confucian sage and the Taoist saint think that they have acquired a self-sufficient mastery that extends to the whole universe. It is based on the practice of wholehearted rituals or games to which the whole being is surrendered. Whether one borrows the ritual models of society or the themes of games from nature is a secondary matter, as is insisting, in polemic, on the excellence of the conventional or the natural. In the training that purifies or ennobles, what is important is the intimate and total effort to escape from the servitude of the appetites. Whether they are considered artificial or natural, whether one thinks of returning to nature or rising above it, whether one sanctifies or glorifies civilization, whether one seeks to attain a Taoist naturism or a Confucian humanism, only the free effort towards pure power counts. It is from *deeply serious* play, from pure play, that a sovereign liberation, conferring holiness or wisdom, is expected. It cannot be the result of external imposition, even if merely dogmatic.

The Chinese have conquered the entire Far East with their customs, their arts, their writing and their Wisdom. Throughout the Far East, even today, no people, whether it appears to be fallen or boasts of being a new power, would dare to deny Chinese civilization. This civilization, whatever luster experimental science may have lent to the West, retains its prestige; it remains intact, even though China has lost the superiority which, up to the Renaissance, it had over the countries of Europe in many technical aspects. However great China's technical superiority over the entire Far East may have been in the past, it is not this superiority or even the power of imperial China that accounts for Chinese prestige. This enduring prestige has other foundations. What the inhabitants of the Far East are determined to preserve, having borrowed it from Chinese civilization, is *a certain understanding of life*: it is a Wisdom. The moral authority of China begins to establish itself at the moment when, unified in the form of an Empire, it is able to make its influence reign far and wide. It was at this time that the Chinese seemed to resolve to adopt an archaic conformism as a standard of morality, and that (since philosophical production stops as soon as two complementary orthodoxies are constituted) they also seemed to resolve to entrust themselves solely to the wisdom of the Ancestors. Chinese civilization seems to have reached maturity at that point. When we attempt to describe the system of conduct, the conceptions and symbols which seem to define this civilization, perhaps, at the moment when it shows itself ready to dominate for many centuries an immense mass of men, we are obliged to say in what consists the *moral authority* which has been recognized. We will not do this without stressing how presumptuous it would be to attempt to define the spirit of Chinese morality. The rule that imposes the history of realities before the history of ideas and the latter before the history of literature is more imperative in the Chinese case than in any other. Now, if we approach the things of China with a realistic spirit and a little critical imagination, we must recognize that all that China seems bent on showing about herself is only literature… Undoubtedly, for both the nation and the individual, orthodoxy serves, along with conformity, to shelter a deep life… All that constitutes the living background of Chinese civilization – technical life, folklore – remains hidden under a layer of literary amplifications… Those who might be disturbed by these flattering comments on ancient remarks, in which we find self-serving falsifications, would no doubt indulge in a malicious witticism if they allowed themselves to be deceived by comparing these glosses of official wit with advertisements which conceal nothing but trade secrets… Every civilization needs a certain unconsciousness and is entitled to a sort of modesty... But the fact is that nothing allows, except trespassing, to penetrate the real life of China... For the indiscreet, the chances of a good reception are nil, and the chances of getting it right and seeing clearly are slim (a greater misfortune). If, in conclusion, we must try to indicate the most notable features of Chinese civilization, the least imprudent formula will be the one that presents a negative aspect. Precisely because of this aspect, what I am going to propose, not so much to define as to situate the most massive and long-lived of the known civilizations, will perhaps be of some interest, at least for Westerners. Insisting on the fact that the Chinese do not willingly submit to any coercion, however dogmatic, *I will limit myself to characterizing the spirit of Chinese morality with the formula*: neither God nor Law.

It has often been said that the Chinese have no religion, and it is sometimes taught that their mythology is as much as non-existent. The truth is that in China *religion* is – no more than *law* – a *distinct function* of social activity. When dealing with Chinese civilization, without wishing to force the facts into frameworks which, for one civilization or another, may seem valid, one should not reserve a chapter for religion. The feeling of the sacred plays a great role in Chinese life, but the objects of veneration are not (strictly speaking) gods. A scholarly creation of political mythology, the Sovereign Above has only a literary existence. This dynastic patron, sung by royal court poets, must never have enjoyed great credence among the "little people," as the failure of Mö tseu's theocratic propaganda seems to demonstrate. Confucians or Taoists attach no importance to it. For them, the only sacred beings are the saints or sages. For the people, they are the Magicians, the Inventors, the Chiefs. Chinese mythology is a heroic mythology. If historians have been able, without much difficulty, to present the heroes of ancient legends as simply great men, it is because they never possessed the majesty that isolates the gods. The story of this well-endowed schoolmaster, of whom the peasants wanted to make their god of the earth, is significant; one cannot conceive of gods alien to men, having an essence distinct from their own. The universe is one. The Chinese have no tendency to spiritualism. There is hardly any trace of incoherent animism in popular beliefs. They believe in ghosts, spirits of the dead, avenging demons and all sorts of goblins; they may sometimes inspire terror, but a few exorcisms remove them, and they immediately become the subject of good stories. Among all the wise men the incredulity is total, much more laughing than aggressive. The bonhomie of the anecdotes they tell shows that they come from a peasant background.[1] The mind does not concern itself with the gods; the clientele of each of them is restricted, their existence is local, momentary: the feast is over, the god is over. There

---

1 See, for example, in Siun tseu (section 21), the story of the boy who, walking under the moon, was frightened of his shadow and, looking up to see it no more, saw his own hair, which he then took for a giant spirit: "He fled, came home breathless and died, the poor fellow!" Or again (same section) about people cooking a pig and beating the drum to exorcise the disease: "Here is a worn drum and a lost pig, but no cure!"

is no organized clergy;[2] the gods have no support; *they have no transcendence*. Too involved in the concrete, too singular, *they also lack personality*. And in no sage, in fact, is there any tendency to personalism or spiritualism. Whatever magical realism may remain in academic thought is easily converted into agnosticism or positivism. When, if only to avoid arousing them, care is taken not to speak of miracles or extraordinary beings, the very idea that they might occur is soon banished from the mind. The Chinese adopt an attitude of quiet familiarity toward the sacred (if they do not attempt to eliminate it from their thinking). Hence the feeling of their immanence, a deep, but furtive, but impermanent feeling. This *occasional immanence of the sacred* certainly favors a certain mysticism, just as it facilitates a certain *artistic* (or *political*) use of superstitious folklore. Confucius is visited from time to time by a familiar genius, Taoists enter, from time to time, into the intimacy of the Tao; but the Tao is not conceived as a transcendent reality; Confucius' familiar genius is only a historical figure; he represents an impersonal tradition of Wisdom, whereas the Tao is only the impersonal principle of all holiness. Confucians never allow anything individual to slip into a prayer formula; Taoists in ecstasy merely repeat stereotyped oratory. Except for Mö tseu (if it must be admitted that this preacher believed in his rhetoric), there is no Chinese sage in antiquity who really thought of founding the rule of morality on divine sanctions. Banished to a space and time without reality, removed from men without being elevated, neutralized by worship without a clergy working to aggrandize them, the divinities, always occasionally – sometimes too familiar and most often inactive – do not offer a sufficiently moving representation of the sacred for us to be tempted to make them the principle of morality or wisdom. Chinese wisdom is an *independent* and wholly human wisdom. It owes nothing to the idea of God.

The Chinese have no preference for abstract symbols. They see Time and Space only as a set of occasions and places. It is interdependencies and solidarities that constitute the order of the universe. It is not thought that man can form a kingdom in Nature or that spirit is distinct from matter. No one opposes the human and the natural, nor thinks of opposing them, as well as the free and the determined. When Taoists advocate a return to nature, they attack civilization as contrary both to the true human order and to the blissful society as yet undistorted by false prejudices; their individualism is not such as radically to oppose the natural to the social. When Confucians extol the benefits of friendly contacts or the division of roles, their sense of the betterment of life in society does not lead them to radically oppose the social to the natural either. Between the Taoist ideal of sanctity and the Confucian ideal of ennoblement, the difference is insignificant, as I have already said. It is that which separates games from rites, and neither side would agree to deny the kinship between games and rites, for they intend to lend to games the efficacy of rites, and have no intention of depriving rites of their value as games; rites require sincerity, games require rules, or at least models. The Taoists insist

---

2   See, on the contrary, Schindler, *Das Priestertum im alten China* and, following the latter, Maspero, *La Chine antique*, pp. 187 ff.

on the value of *autonomy*, the Confucians on the value of *hierarchy*; but the ideal – the Golden Age, the Kingdom of Wisdom – which they aim at is always an ideal of good understanding; good understanding between men, good understanding with nature. This understanding of things and persons is a flexible regime of interdependencies or solidarities that can never be based on *unconditional prescriptions*: on Laws. The prestige of the concrete, the sentiment of the occasional are too powerful, the human order and the natural order seem too closely interdependent for the principle of any order to be praised as of a mandatory or necessary nature. Neither in nature nor in thought do we find true opposites, but only opposites of aspects arising from simple differences of situation. Thus the naturalistic asceticism of the Taoists contains neither contraindications nor formal indications; nor does Confucian etiquette contain imperative prescriptions or strict taboos. *As everything depends on congruence, everything is a matter of expediency.* Law, the abstract, the unconditional are excluded – the universe is one – from both society and nature. Hence the tenacious hatred aroused by the Legists and also by the Dialecticians. Hence the contempt for everything that presupposes uniformity, for everything that would permit, induction, deduction, any form of reasoning or constrictive calculation, for everything that would tend to introduce into the government of thought, of things, of men, something mechanical or quantitative. All notions, even that of Number, even that of Fate, must be preserved with something concrete and indeterminate which reserves a possibility of *play*. In the idea of rule, one hardly wants to see anything but the idea of *model*. The Chinese notion of Order excludes, in all its aspects, the idea of Law.

People like to talk about the gregarious instinct of the Chinese, and they also like to attribute to them an anarchic temperament. In fact, their associative spirit and individualism are qualities of the country. Their idea of order derives from a healthy and rustic sense of goodwill. The failure of the Legists and the combined success of the Taoists and Confucians prove this; this sentiment, which is wounded by administrative intrusions, egalitarian limitations, and abstract codifications or regulations,[3] is based (in varying proportions, no doubt, according to the individual, but, in general, more or less equal) on a sort of passion for autonomy and on a no less acute need for companionship and friendship. The State, the Dogma and the Laws can do nothing in favor of Order. Order is conceived under the aspect of a Peace which the abstract forms of obedience cannot establish, nor can the abstract forms of reasoning impose. For this peace to grow everywhere, a taste for conciliation is necessary, which requires a keen sense of actual conveniences, of spontaneous solidarities, of free hierarchies. Chinese logic is not a rigid logic of subordination, but a flexible logic of hierarchy: they wanted to preserve in the idea of Order, all that the images and emotions from which it originated had of concrete. Whether one takes the Tao as a symbol and sees in the Tao the principle of all autonomy and harmony, or whether one takes the Li as a symbol and sees in the Li the principle of all hierarchy or equitable distribution, the idea of Order preserves

---

3   Both in the matter of measures and in the matter of money.

in itself – very refined, certainly, and yet very close to its rustic background – the feeling that to understand and to agree is to achieve peace in oneself and in one's environment. All Chinese wisdom springs from this feeling. However mystical or positive, however naturalistic or humanistic its inspiration, in all schools one finds the idea that *the principle of universal understanding merges with the principle of universal intelligibility*, expressed in symbols which remain concrete and are all the more effective. All knowledge, all power, comes from Li or Tao. Every ruler must be a saint or a sage. All authority is based on Reason.

Bibliography

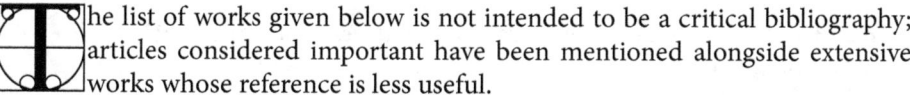

The list of works given below is not intended to be a critical bibliography; articles considered important have been mentioned alongside extensive works whose reference is less useful.

Periodicals

As. Maj: Asia Major
BEFEO: Bulletin de l'École française d'Extrême-Orient
ChR: China Review
JA: Journal Asiatique
JPOS: Journal of the Peking Oriental Society
JRAS: Journal of the Royal Asiatic Society
MAO: Mémoires concernant l'Asie orientale
MSOS: Meetings of the Seminars for Oriental Languages
NChR: New China Review
OZ: Ostaslatische Zeitschrift
OS: Ostasiatische Studien
Sh: Shinagaku
TP: T'oung pao
VS: Variétés sinologiques

Books and Miscellaneous Works

ANDERSSON (J. G.), *An early Chinese culture*, Peking, 1923.
- *Preliminary report on archaeological research in Kansu*, Peking, 1925.
ARDENNE DE TIZAC (H. D'), *L'art chinois classique*, Paris, 1926.
ARNE, *Painted stone age pottery from the Province of Honan*, China, Peking, 1925.
ASHTON (L.), *An introduction to the study of Chinese sculpture*, London, 1924.
AUROUSSEAU (L.), *La première conquête chinoise des pays annamites*, BEFEO, 1923.
BIOT (E.), *Le Tcheou li ou les Rites des Tcheou*, Paris, 1851.
- *Recherches sur les moeurs des anciens Chinois d'après le Che king* (JA, 1843).
BLACK, *The human skeleton remains from Sha kuo t'un*, Peking, 1925.
- *A note on physical characters of the prehistoric Kansu race*, Peking, 1925.
BŒRSCHAN (E.), *Chinesische Architektur*, Berlin, 1926.
BRETSCHNEIDER, *Botanicon Sinicum* (Publication of the Chinese Branch of the R.A.S., XXV).
BUSHELL (S. W.), *Chinese Art*, London, 1914.
CHALFANT, *Early Chinese writing*, Chicago, 1906.
CHAVANNES (Ed.), *Les mémoires historiques de Se-ma Ts'ien*, 5 v., Paris, 1895-1905.
- *La sculpture sur pierre au temps des deux dynasties Han*, Paris, 1893.
- *Le T'ai chan*, Paris, 1910.
- *Mission archéologique dans la Chine septentrionale*, Paris, 1913.
- *Le jet des Dragons* (MAO, III), Paris, 1919.
- *Confucio* (Revue de Paris, 1903).
- *La divination par l'écaille de tortue dans la haute antiquité chinoise d'après un livre de M. Lo Tchen-yu* (JA, 1911).
- *Trois généraux chinois de la dynastie Han* (TP, 1906).
- *Les documents chinois découverts par Aurel Stein dans les sables du Turkestan*, Oxford, 1913.
- *De l'expression des vœux dans l'art populaire chinois*, Paris, 1922.
CONRADY, *China*, Berlin, 1902.
CORDIER (H.), *Histoire générale de la Chine et de ses relations avec les pays étrangers*, Paris, 1920.
DEMIÉVILLE (P.), C. R. TCHANG HONG-TCHAO, Che ya, *Lapidarium sinicum* (BEFEO, 1924).
- *La méthode d'architecture de LI MING-TCHONG des Song* (BEFEO, 1925).
- HOU-CHE, *Tch'ang che tsi* (BEFEO, 1924).
DUBS (H. H.), *The works of Hsüntze*, London, 1927.
DUYVENDACK (J. I. L.), *The book of Lord Shang*, London, 1928.
- *Études de philosophie chinoise* (Rev. philos., 1930).
DVORAK (R.), *China's Religionen*, Munster, 1903.
EDKINS, *The evolution of chinese language* (JPOS, 1887).
ERKES, *Das Weltbild des Huai-nan-tze* (OZ, 1917).

- *Das älteste Dokument z. chines. u. Kunstgeschichte: T'ien-wen; die "Himmelsfragen" des K'üh Yuan*, Leipzig, 1928.
ESCARRA and GERMAIN, *La conception de la loi et les théories des légistes à la veille des Ts'in*, Peking, 1925. Études asiatiques, published on the occasion of the XXV anniversary of the École française d'Extrême-Orient, Paris, 1925.
FORKE (A.), *Lun-Heng. Selected Essays of the philosopher Wang Ch'ung*, (MSOS, 1911).
- *Mo Ti, des Socialethikers und seiner Schüler philosophische Werke* (MSOS, 1923).
- *The world conception of the Chinese*, London, 1925.
- *Yang Chu, the Epicurian in his relation to Lieh-tse the Pantheist* (JPOS, III).
- *Geschlchte der altern chinesischen Philosophie*, Hamburg, 1927.
- *Der Ursprung der Chinesen.*
FRANKE (A.), *Das Confuzianische Dogma und die chinesische Staats religion*, 1920.
FUIITA, *The River Huang in the Reign of Yu* (Sh., 1921).
GABELENTZ (von der), *Beitrage z. chines. Grammatik (Abhandl. d. Sachsischen Gesells. f. Wissens, 1888).*
- *Confucius und seine Lehre*, Leipzig, 1888.
GIESLER, *La tablette Tsong du Tcheou li* (Rev. Arch., 1915).
GILES (H. A.), *History of chinese literature*, London, 1901.
- *Chuang Tsu, mystic moralist and social reformer*, London, 1889.
- *Lao Tzu and the Tao tê king* (Adversaria sinica, III).
- *The remains of Lao Tzu* (ChR, 1886-1889).
- *Religion of ancient China*, London, 1905.
- *Confucianism and its rivals*, London, 1915.
GRANET (M.), *Fêtes et chansons anciennes de la Chine*, Paris, 1919.
- *La Polygynie sororale et le Sororat dans la Chine féodale*, Paris, 1920.
- *La religion des Chinois*, Paris, 1922.
- *Danses et légendes de la Chine ancienne*, Paris, 1926.
- *Coutumes matrimoniales de la Chine antique* (TP, 1912).
- *Quelques Particularités de l'alangue et de la pensée chinoises* (Rev.philos., 1920).
- *La vie et la mort, croyances et doctrines de l'antiquité chinoise* (Ann. of the Éc. des Hautes Études, 1920).
- *Le dépôt de l'enfant sur le sol* (Rev. arch., 1922).
- *Le langage de la douleur d'après le rituel funéraire de la Chine classique* (Rev. de Psychologie, 1922).
GROUSSET (R.), *Histoire de l'Asie*, Paris, 1922.
GROTT (J.-J.-M. DE), *The religions system of China*, Leiden, 1892-1921.
- *The religion of the Chinese*, New York, 1910.
- *Universismus*, Berlin, 1918.
- *Sectarianism and religious persecution in China*, Amsterdam, 1903.
- *Chinesische Urkundenz. Gesch. Asiens*, 1921.
GRUBE, *Geschichte der chinesischen Literatur*, Leipzig, 1902.
- *Die Religion der alten Chinesen*, Tübingen, 1908.
- *Religion und Cultus der Chinesen*, Leipzig, 1908.

HACKMANN (H.), *Chinesische philosophie*, Munich, 1927.
HALOUN (G.), *Contribution to the history of the clan settlement in ancient China* (As. Maj., 1924).
– *Seit wann kannten die Chinesen die Tocharer* (As. Maj., 1926).
HAUER, *Die chinesische Dichtung*, Berlin, 1909.
HAVRET and CHAMBEAU, *Notes concernant la chronologie chinoise* (VS, 1920).
HIRTH, *The ancient history of China to the end of the Chou Dynasty*, New York, 1909.
– *Chinese metallic mirrors*, New York, 1906.
HONDA, *On the date of compilation of the Yi king* (Sh., 1921).
HOPKINS, *Chinese writings in the Chou Dynasty on the light of recent discoveries* (JRAS, 1911).
– *Metamorphic stylisation and the sabotage of signification, a study in ancient and modern Chinese writing* (JRAS, 1925).
HU SHIH, *The development of logical method in ancient China*, Shanghai, 1922.
IMBAULT-HUART, *La légende des premiers papes taoïstes* (JA, 1884).
KARLGREN (B.), *Studies on Chinese phonology*, Leiden and Estocolmo, 1913.
– *Sound and symbol in China*, London, 1923.
– *Analytic Dictionary*, Paris, 1923.
– *On the authenticity and nature of the Tso chuan*, Göteborg, 1926.
– *Philology and ancient China*, Oslo, 1926.
– *Le protochinois, langue flexionnelle* (JA, 1920).
LALOY (L.), *La musique chinoise*, Paris.
LAUFER (B.), *Jade, a study in chinese archaeology and religion*, Chicago, 1912.
– *Chinese Pottery of the Han Dynasty*, Leyde, 1909.
– *Ethnographische Sagen der Chinesen* (in Festschrif. f. Kuhn).
(LEANG K'I-TCH'AO), LIANG CHI-CHAO, *History of Chinese political thought* (tr. by L. T. Chen), London, 1930.
MAILLA (Fr. DE), *Histoire générale de la Chine, traduite du Tong-kien-kang-mou*, Paris, 1777-1789.
MARTIN, *Diplomacy in ancient China* (JPOS, 1889).
MASPERO (H.), *La Chine antique*, Paris, 1927.
– *Les origines de la civilisation chinoise* (Ann. de géographie, 1926).
– *Les légendes mythologiques dans le Chou king* (JA, 1924).
– *Notes sur la logique de Mö tseu* (TP, 1927).
– *Le mot ming* (JA, 1927).
– *Le saint et la vie mystique chez Lao-tseu et Tchouang-tseu* (Bulletin of the *Assoc. franç. des amis de l'Orient*, 1922).
– *Le songe et l'ambassade de l'empereur Ming* (BEFEO, 1910).
MASSON-OURSEL (P.), *La philosophie comparée*, Paris, 1923.
– *Études de logique comparée* (Rev. philos., 1917).
– *La démonstration confucéenne* (Rev. d'hist. des relig., 1916).
MASSON-OURSEL y KIA KIEN-TCHOU, *Yin Wen-tseu* (TP, 1914).
MAYERS, *Chinese reader's manual*.

Mémoires concernant les Chinois, par les missionnaires de Pékin, Paris, 1776-1814.
MESTRE (L.), *Quelques résultats d'une comparaison entre les caractères chinois modernes et les siao-ichouan*, Paris, 1925.
NAITO, *On the compilation of the Shoo king* (Sh., 1923).
PARKER, *Kwan-tze* (NChR, 1921).
– *Hwai-n an-tze* (NChR, 1919).
PELLIOT (P.), *Le Chou king en caractères anciens et le Chang chou che wen* (MAO), Paris, 1919.
– *Jades archaïques de la collection*, C. T. Loo. Paris, 1921.
– *Notes sur les anciens itinéraires chinois dans l'Orient romain* (JA, 1921).
– *Meou tseu ou les Doutes levés* (TP, 1918-19).
PLATH, *Fremde barbarische Stämme in alten China*, Munich, 1874.
PRZYLUSKI, *Le sino-tibétain* (en *Langues du monde*, Paris, 1924).
RICHTHOFEN, *China*, Berlin, 1877-1912.
ROSTHORN, *Geschichte China*, Stuttgart, 1923.
SAUSSURE (L. DE), *Les Origines de l'astronomie chinoise*, Paris, 1930.
SCHINDLER (B.), *On the travel, wayside, and wing offerings in ancient China* (As. Maj., I).
– *The development of Chinese conception of Supreme Beings* (As. Maj., 1923).
– *Das Priestertum im alten China*, Leipzig, 1919.
SCHMITT (E.), *Die Grundlagen der chinesischen Che*, 1927.
Steele (J.), *I Li, or the Book of Etiquette and Ceremonial*, London, 1917.
Suzuki, *A brief history of early Chinese philosophy*, London, 1914.
TCHANG FOND, *Recherches sur les os du Ho-nan et quelques caractères de l'écriture ancienne*, Paris, 1925.
TCHANG (Fr. M.), *Synchronismes chinois* (VS, 1905).
TERRIEN DE LACOUPERIE, *Western Origin of chinese civilization*, London, 1894.
– *Languages of China before the Chinese*, London, 1887.
TSCHEPE (le P.), *Histoire du royaume de Wou* (VS, 1896).
– *Histoire du royaume de Tch'ou* (VS, 1903).
– *Histoire du royaume de Ts'in* (VS, 1909).
– *Histoire du royaume de Tsin* (VS, 1910).
– *Histoire des trois royaumes de Han, Wei et Tchao* (VS, 1910).
TUCCI (G.), *Storia della filosofi cinese antica*, Bolonia, 1922.
UMEHARA, *Deux grandes découvertes archéologiques en Corée* (Rev. des Arts asiatiques, 1926).
VISSER (M. W. DE), *The Dragon in China and Japan*, Amsterdam, 1913.
VORETZCH (E: A.), *Altchinesische Bronzen*, Berlin, 1924.
WALEY (A.), *The Temple and other Poems*, London, 1923.
WEDEMAYER, *Schauplätze and Vorgänge der alten chinesischen Geschichte* (As. Maj., Prel. V).
WERNER (E. T. C.), *Myths and legends of China*, London, 1924.
Wieger (P. L.), *Histoire des croyances religieuses et des opinions philosophiques en Chine, depuis l'origine jusqu'à nos jours*, Hien-hien, 1917.

– *Les Pères du système taoïste*, Hien-hien, 1913.
– *La Chine à travers les âges*, Hien-hien, 1920.
– *Textes historiques*, Ho-kien-fou, 1902.
– *Caractères* (*Rudiments*, V, 12), Ho-kien-fou, 1903.
WILHELM (R.), *Dchuang dsi, das wahre Buch vom südlischen Blütenland*, Jena, 1920.
– *Lia dsi, das wahre Buch vmt quellenden Urgrurnd*, Jena, 1921.
– *Lu Puch-wei, Frühling und Herbst*, Jena, 1927.
WOO KANG, *Les trois théories politiques du Tch'ouen ts'ieou*, Paris, 1932.
WYLIE, *Notes on Chinese literature*, Shanghai, 1902.
YUAN (Chaucer), *La philosophie politique de Mencius*, Paris, 1927.
ZACH (E. VON), *Lexicographische Beiträge*, Peking, 1902.
ZOTTOLI (Fr.), *Cursus litteraturae sinicae*, Shanghai, 1879-1882.

Concordance Tables

Concordance of the transliterations of the *Ecole Française D'extreme-orient* (EFEO), *Wade-Giles* and *Hanyu PinYin*
Transliteration or romanization means representing the signs of one writing system by the signs of another.

This work uses the EFEO romanization system, which is the system of the *École française d'Extrême-Orient*, which was the most widely used romanization system for Chinese languages in the French linguistic area until the middle of the 20th century, before it was gradually replaced by *Hanyu PinYin*. In the rest of the West, since the 19th century, the most widely used romanization method was *Wade-Giles*. That method was created by two British scholars, Sir Thomas Wade and Herbert Allen Giles. *Hanyu Pinyin* – usually known as *Pinyin* – is a new system of romanization of Chinese characters, developed by Chinese scholars and accepted as a standard worldwide since the late 20th century.

It is important to note that the romanization cannot uniquely identify the Chinese characters whose pronunciation it represents, because there are many Chinese characters that share the same pronunciation.

The following tables show different romanizations of Chinese proper names and texts cited in this work.

The first table shows different names and titles (composed of several characters), the second table shows all the graphemes of the different romanization systems.

EFEO	Wade-Giles	PinYin	Chinese
Chan hai king	Shan-hai ching	Shanhaijing	山海經
Che king	Shih ching	Shi Ying	詩經
Chou King	Shu ching	Shu Jing	書經
Chouo wen	Shuo-wen chieh-tz	Shuowen Jiezi	說文解字
Fong chouei	Feng shui	Feng shui	
Fou-hi	Fu-hsi	Fuxi	伏羲
Han Fei tseu	Han Fei Tzu	Hanfeizi	韩非子
Hi ts'eu	Hsi tz'u	Xi ci	
Ho tiao	He tiao	He diao	
Houai-nan tseu	Huai-nan tzu	Huainanzi	淮南子
Houang-ti	Huang Ti	Huang Di	黄帝
Kou wen	Ku wen	Guwen	古文
Kouan tseu	Kuan tzu	Guan Zi	
Kouang ya	Kuang Ya	Guangya	廣雅
Kouei tsang	Kuei tsang	Gui Zang	
Lao tseu	Lao Tzu	Lao Zi	老子
Li ki	Li Chi	Li Ji	禮經
Lie tseu	Lieh-tzu	Liezi	列子
Louen yu	Lun yu	Lunyu	論語
Lu che tch'ouen ts'ieou	Lü-shih Ch'un-ch'iu	Lüshi Chunqiu	呂氏春秋
Ming t'ang	Ming tang	Ming dang	
Mö tseu	Mo Tzu	Mozi	墨子
NI koua	Nu wa	Nuwa	女媧
Sseu-ma Ts'ien	Ssu-ma Ch'ien	Sima Qian	司馬遷
T'ai chan	T'ai shan	Tai shan	
T'ien kan	Tien kan	Tiangan	天干

Concordance Tables

EFEO	Wade-Giles	PinYin	Chinese
Tao Tö king	Tao Te Ching	Daode Jing	道德經
Tcheou li	Chou Li	Zhou Li	周禮
Tchouang tseu	Chuang Tzu	Zhuangzi	莊子
Tch'ouen ts'ieou	Ch'un-ch'iu	Chunqiu	春秋
Tch'ouen ts'ieou	Lü-shih Ch'un-ch'iu	Lushi Chunqiu	呂氏春秋
Ti tche	Ti-chih	Dizhi	地支
Ts'ien Han chou	Ch'ien Han Shu	Qian Han shu	
Ts'in Che Houang-ti	Ch'in Shih-huang	Qin Shi Huang	秦始皇
Tso tchouan	Tso chuan	Zuo Zhuan	左傳
Wou wei	Wu wei	Wu Wei	無為
Yi king	I Ching	Yi Jing	易經
Yi li	I li	Yi li	儀禮
Yi ts'ing yi tchouo	I ch'ing I cho	Yi qing yi zhuo	
Yue Ling	Yüeh ling	Yue ling	

Trigrams of the *Yi king*

EFEO	Wade-Giles	PinYin	Chinese
K'an	K'an	Kan	坎
K'ien	Ch'ien	Qian	乾
K'ouen	K'un	Kun	坤
Ken	Ken	Gen	艮
Li	Li	Li	離
Siuan	Sun	Xun	巽
Tch'en	Chen	Zhen	震
Touei	Tui	Dui	兌

EFEO	Wade-Giles	Pinyin	EFEO	Wade-Giles	Pinyin
a	a	a	kiang, tsiang	chiang	jiang
ngai	ai	ai	k'iang, ts'iang	ch'iang	qiang
ngan	an	an	kiao, tsiao	chiao	jiao
ngang	ang	ang	k'iao, ts'iao	ch'iao	qiao
ngao	ao	ao	kiai, kie, tsie	chieh	jie
tcha	cha	zha	k'iai, k'ie, ts'ie	ch'ieh	qie
tch'a	ch'a	cha	kien, tsien	chien	jian
tchai	chai	zhai	k'ien, ts'ien	ch'ien	qian
tch'ai	ch'ai	chai	tche	chih	zhi
tchan	chan	zhan	tch'e	ch'ih	chi
tch'an	ch'an	chan	kin, tsin	chin	jin
tchang	chang	zhang	k'in, ts'in	ch'in	qin
tch'ang	ch'ang	chang	king, tsing	ching	jing
tchao	chao	zhao	k'ing, ts'ing	ch'ing	qing
tch'ao	ch'ao	chao	kieou, tsieou	chiu	jiu
tchö	che	zhe	k'ieou, ts'ieou	ch'iu	qiu
tch'ö	ch'e	che	kiong	chiung	jiong
tchei	chei	zhei	k'iong	ch'iung	qiong
tchen	chen	zhen	tcho, tchouo	cho	zhuo
tch'en	ch'en	chen	tch'ouo	ch'o	chuo
tcheng	cheng	zheng	tcheou	chou	zhou
tch'eng	ch'eng	cheng	tch'eou	ch'ou	chou
ki, tsi	chi	ji	tchou	chu	zhu
k'i, ts'i	ch'i	qi	tch'ou	ch'u	chu
kia	chia	jia	kiu, tsiu	chü	ju
k'ia	ch'ia	qia	k'iu, ts'iu	ch'ü	qu

Concordance Tables 379

EFEO	Wade-Giles	Pinyin	EFEO	Wade-Giles	Pinyin
tchoua	chua	zhua	fang	fang	fang
tchouai	chuai	zhuai	fei	fei	fei
tch'ouai	ch'uai	chuai	fen	fen	fen
tchouan	chuan	zhuan	fong	feng	feng
tch'ouan	ch'uan	chuan	fo	fo	fo
kiuan, tsiuan	chüan	juan	feou	fou	fou
k'iuan, ts'iuan	ch'üan	quan	fou	fu	fu
tchouang	chuang	zhuang	ha	ha	ha
tch'ouang	ch'uang	chuang	hai	hai	hai
kio, kiue, tsio, tsiue	chüeh	jue	han	han	han
k'io, k'iue, ts'io, ts'iue	ch'üeh	que	hang	hang	hang
tchouei	chui	zhui	hao	hao	hao
tch'ouei	ch'ui	chui	ho, hö	he	he
tchouen	chun	zhun	hei	hei	hei
tch'ouen	ch'un	chun	hen	hen	hen
kiun, tsiun	chün	jun	heng	heng	heng
k'iun, ts'iun	ch'ün	qun	heou	hou	hou
tchong	chung	zhong	hi, si	hsi	xi
tch'ong	ch'ung	chong	hia	hsia	xia
ngo	e	e	hiang, siang	hsiang	xiang
ei	ei	ei	hiao, siao	hsiao	xiao
ngen	en	en	hiai, hie, sie	hsieh	xie
ngeng	eng	eng	hien, sian	hsien	xian
eul	erh	er	hin, sin	hsin	xin
fa	fa	fa	hing, sing	hsing	xing
fan	fan	fan	hieou, sieou	hsiu	xiu

EFEO	Wade-Giles	Pinyin
hiong	hsiung	xiong
hiu, siu	hsü	xu
hiuan, siuan	hsüan	xuan
hiue, siue	hsüeh	xue
hiun, siun	hsün	xun
hou	hu	hu
houa	hua	hua
houai	huai	huai
houan	huan	huan
houang	huang	huang
houei	hui	hui
houen	hun	hun
hong	hung	hong
houo	huo	huo
yi	i	yi
jan	jan	ran
jang	jang	rang
jao	jao	rao
jö	je	re
jen	jen	ren
jeng	jeng	reng
je	jih	ri
jo	jo	ruo
jeou	jou	rou
jou	ju	ru
joua	jua	rua
jouan	juan	ruan
jouei	jui	rui
jouen	jun	run
jong	jung	rong
ka	ka	ga
k'a	k'a	ka
kai	kai	gai
k'ai	k'ai	kai
kan	kan	gan
k'an	k'an	kan
kang	kang	gang
k'ang	k'ang	kang
kao	kao	gao
k'ao	k'ao	kao
ko, kö	ke	ge
k'o, k'ö	k'ê	ke
kei	kei	gei
ken	ken	gen
k'en	k'en	ken
keng	keng	geng
k'eng	k'eng	keng
keou	kou	gou
k'eou	k'ou	kou
kou	ku	gu
k'ou	k'u	ku
koua	kua	gua

EFEO	Wade-Giles	Pinyin
k'oua	k'ua	kua
kouai	kuai	guai
k'ouai	k'uai	kuai
kouan	kuan	guan
k'ouan	k'uan	kuan
kouang	kuang	guang
k'ouang	k'uang	kuang
kouei	kuei	gui
k'ouei	k'uei	kui
kouen	kun	gun
k'ouen	k'un	kun
kong	kung	gong
k'ong	k'ung	kong
kouo	kuo	guo
k'ouo	k'uo	kuo
la	la	la
lai	lai	lai
lan	lan	lan
lang	lang	lang
lao	lao	lao
lö	le	le
lei	lei	lei
leng	leng	leng
li	li	li
lia	lia	lia
leang	liang	liang

EFEO	Wade-Giles	Pinyin
leao	liao	liao
lie	lieh	lie
lien	lien	lian
lin	lin	lin
ling	ling	ling
liu	liu	liu
leou	lou	lou
lou	lu	lu
liu	lü	lü
louan	luan	luan
liue, lio	lüeh	lüe
louen	lun	lun
long	lung	long
lo, loue	luo	luo
ma	ma	ma
mai	mai	mai
man	man	man
mang	mang	mang
mao	mao	mao
mö	me	me
mei	mei	mei
men	men	men
mong	meng	meng
mi	mi	mi
miao	miao	miao
mie	mieh	mie

EFEO	Wade-Giles	Pinyin
mien	mien	mian
min	min	min
ming	ming	ming
mieou	miu	miu
moio, mo	mo	mo
meou	mou	mou
mou	mu	mu
na	na	na
nai	nai	nai
nan	nan	nan
nang	nang	nang
nao	nao	nao
ne	ne	ne
nei	nei	nei
nen	nen	nen
neng	neng	neng
ni	ni	ni
niang	niang	niang
niao	niao	niao
nie	nieh	nie
nien	nien	nian
nin	nin	nin
ning	ning	ning
nieou	niu	niu
no	no	nuo
neou	nou	nou

EFEO	Wade-Giles	Pinyin
nou	nu	nu
niu	nü	nü
nouan	nuan	nuan
nio	nüeh	nüe
nong	nung	nong
ngo	o	o
ngeou	ou	ou
pa	pa	ba
p'a	p'a	pa
pai	pai	bai
p'ai	p'ai	pai
pan	pan	ban
p'an	p'an	pan
pang	pang	bang
p'ang	p'ang	pang
pao	pao	bao
p'ao	p'ao	pao
pei	pei	bei
p'ei	p'ei	pei
pen	pen	ben
p'en	p'en	pen
peng	peng	beng
p'eng	p'eng	peng
pi	pi	bi
p'i	p'i	pi
piao	piao	biao

EFEO	Wade-Giles	Pinyin
p'iao	p'iao	piao
pie	pieh	bie
p'ie	p'ieh	pie
pien	pien	bian
p'ien	p'ien	pian
pin	pin	bin
p'in	p'in	pin
ping	ping	bing
p'ing	p'ing	ping
po	po	bo
p'o	p'o	po
p'eou	p'ou	pou
pou	pu	bu
p'ou	p'u	pu
sa	sa	sa
sai	sai	sai
san	san	san
sang	sang	sang
sao	sao	sao
sö	se	se
sen	sen	sen
seng	seng	seng
cha	sha	sha
chai	shai	shai
chan	shan	shan
chang	shang	shang
chao	shao	shao
chö	she	she
chei	shei	shei
chen	shen	shen
cheng	sheng	sheng
che	shih	shi
cheou	shou	shou
chou	shu	shu
choua	shua	shua
chouai	shuai	shuai
chouan	shuan	shuan
chouang	shuang	shuang
chouei	shui	shui
chouen	shun	shun
chouo, cho	shuo	shuo
so	so	suo
seou	sou	sou
sseu	ssu	si
sou	su	su
souan	suan	suan
souei	sui	sui
souen	sun	sun
song	sung	song
ta	ta	da
t'a	t'a	ta
tai	tai	dai

EFEO	Wade-Giles	Pinyin
t'ai	t'ai	tai
tan	tan	dan
t'an	t'an	tan
tang	tang	dang
t'ang	t'ang	tang
tao	tao	dao
t'ao	t'ao	tao
tö	te	de
t'ö	t'e	te
tei	tei	dei
t'ei	t'ei	tei
ten	ten	den
teng	teng	deng
t'eng	t'eng	teng
ti	ti	di
t'i	t'i	ti
tiao	tiao	diao
t'iao	t'iao	tiao
tie	tieh	die
t'ie	t'ieh	tie
tien	tien	dian
t'ien	t'ien	tian
ting	ting	ding
t'ing	t'ing	ting
tieou	tiu	diu
to	to	duo

EFEO	Wade-Giles	Pinyin
t'o	t'o	tuo
teou	tou	dou
t'eou	t'ou	tou
tsa	tsa	za
ts'a	ts'a	ca
tsai	tsai	zai
ts'ai	ts'ai	cai
tsan	tsan	zan
ts'an	ts'an	can
tsang	tsang	zang
ts'ang	ts'ang	cang
tsao	tsao	zao
ts'ao	ts'ao	cao
tsö	tse	ze
ts'ö	ts'e	ce
tsei	tsei	zei
tsen	tsen	zen
ts'en	ts'en	cen
tseng	tseng	zeng
ts'eng	ts'eng	ceng
tso	tso	zuo
ts'o	ts'o	cuo
tseou	tsou	zou
ts'eou	ts'ou	cou
tsou	tsu	zu
ts'ou	ts'u	cu

EFEO	Wade-Giles	Pinyin	EFEO	Wade-Giles	Pinyin
tsouan	tsuan	zuan	wai	wai	wai
ts'ouan	ts'uan	cuan	wan	wan	wan
tsouei	tsui	zui	wang	wang	wang
ts'ouei	ts'ui	cui	wei	wei	wei
tsouen	tsun	zun	wen	wen	wen
ts'ouen	ts'un	cun	wong	weng	weng
tsong	tsung	zong	wo	wo	wo
ts'ung	ts'ung	cong	wou	wu	wu
tou	tu	du	ya	ya	ya
t'ou	t'u	tu	yen	yan	yan
touan	tuan	duan	yang	yang	yang
t'ouan	t'uan	tuan	yao	yao	yao
touei	tui	dui	ye	yeh	ye
t'ouei	t'ui	tui	yin	yin	yin
touen	tun	dun	ying	ying	ying
t'ouen	t'un	tun	yeou	yu	you
tong	tung	dong	yu	yü	yu
t'ong	t'ung	tong	yuan	yüan	yuan
tseu	tzu	zi	yue	yüeh	yue
ts'eu	tz'u	ci	yun	yün	yun
wa	wa	wa	yong	yung	yong

www.ingramcontent.com/pod-product-compliance
Lightning Source LLC
Chambersburg PA
CBHW050508240426
43673CB00004B/155